W9-DIM-481

Of Philosophers and Kings

Political Philosophy in Shakespeare's
Macbeth and *King Lear*

LEON HAROLD CRAIG

Of Philosophers and Kings

Political Philosophy in Shakespeare's *Macbeth* and *King Lear*

UNIVERSITY OF TORONTO PRESS
Toronto Buffalo London

Toronto Buffalo London
Printed in Canada

ISBN 0-8020-3571-X

Printed on acid-free paper

National Library of Canada Cataloguing in Publication Data

Craig, Leon H., 1941–
Of philosophers and kings : political philosophy in Shakespeare's Macbeth and King Lear

Includes bibliographical references and index.
ISBN 0-8020-3571-X

1. Shakespeare, William, 1564–1616. Macbeth. 2. Shakespeare, William, 1564–1616. King Lear. 3. Shakespeare, William, 1564–1616 – Knowledge – Political science. 4. Politics in literature. I. Title.

PR3017.C72 2001 822.3′3 C2001-901399-X

University of Toronto Press acknowledges the financial assistance to its publishing program of the Canada Council for the Arts and the Ontario Arts Council.

This book has been published with the help of a grant from the Humanities and Social Sciences Federation of Canada, using funds provided by the Social Sciences and Humanities Research Council of Canada.

University of Toronto Press acknowledges the financial support for its publishing activities of the Government of Canada through the Book Publishing Industry Development Program (BPIDP).

For Tobin and Jessica

Contents

ACKNOWLEDGMENTS ix

NOTICE TO THE READER xi

1. The Political Philosopher as Dramatic Poet: Preliminary Remarks on the Study of Shakespeare 3

2. Living in a Hard Time: Politics and Philosophy in *Macbeth* 25

Machiavelli Visits Scotland 30

The Metaphysics of Macbeth 51

The Natural Workings of Good and Evil 76

Infections in the Casing Air 100

3. The Discovery of Nature: Politics and Philosophy in *King Lear* 112

The Perils of Political Improvisation 113

The Problem of Nature 133

A King Becomes Philosophical 168

A Philosopher Becomes a King 189

4. "Sweet Philosophy": Further Illustrations of Shakespeare's Portrayal of Philosophy in Relation to Political Life 192

Elementary Matters in *Othello* 194

The True Test of a Wise Poet: *The Winter's Tale* 214

High-Minded Negligence in *Measure for Measure* 230

Final Remarks on Shakespeare as Philosopher-Poet 251

NOTES 269

BIBLIOGRAPHY 391

INDEX OF NAMES 401

Acknowledgments

This book is the result of some two decades of studying and teaching Shakespeare. And since much of my understanding of his plays germinated in seminars with graduate students whose fellowship has been the great blessing of my academic life, I wish here to acknowledge publicly my indebtedness to them: Judith Adam, Liz Bacchus *née* Alexander, Bill Bewick, Kent Cochrane, Sue Collins, Wasseem El-Rayes, Patrick Kernahan, Lorna Knott *née* Dawson, Stuart Munro, Murray Krantz, Steve Lange, David Livingstone, Patrick Malcolmson, David Martin, Lise Mills, Keith Morgan, Laura Morgan *née* Moskuwich, Andy Muwais, Allison Smith *née* Greckol, Bryan Smith, Stacy Sylvester, Kevin Thomas, Mark Unchulenko, David Verbitsky, Dennis Westergaard, Rod Williams, and Darcy Wudel. With respect to the book itself, however, I owe a very special thanks to four individuals. Professors John Baxter of Dalhousie University and Paul A. Cantor of the University of Virginia each subjected the entire manuscript to a careful, thoughtful critique, suggesting numerous ways that it could be improved (several quite substantial). The book is *much* the better for their generous efforts. My colleague Professor Heidi D. Studer graciously proof-read the resulting text, and was most helpful in compiling the index. But my greatest debt is to the late Christopher Drummond, Professor Emeritus of English – congenial colleague, scrupulous critic, and dear friend, from whom I learned so much and now sorely miss. He read and assessed (and challenged) this work at every stage of its composition save the last, for he died suddenly while the pages were being set. I can now only hope he would not have been too dissatisfied with the final version. I am also grateful to the editorial staff of the University of Toronto Press, who have been unfailingly helpful and indulgent.

Lastly, I have, as always, my wife Judith to thank, helpmeet good and true for over thirty years.

Notice to the Reader

The following monograph resembles Rousseau's *Second Discourse* in one respect: the primary text is augmented by a prodigious quantity of endnotes that collectively amount to half as much material as the text they amplify. They serve a variety of purposes (address scholarly literature, explore tangential issues, provide additional argument and evidence, point to connections with other important works, and so on). To my mind, they all contribute one way or another to the strength and value of the book. But as Rousseau said of his, "These notes sometimes stray so wide of the subject that they are not good to read together with the text. I have therefore relegated them to the end of the Discourse, in which I tried my best to follow the straightest path." I will not go so far as to say that mine are simply 'not good' to read in conjunction with the portion of the text to which they refer, but given their number (and often their length), they are bound to distract a reader from the main line of argument, making it at times difficult to follow. And so I invite the reader to ignore them, at least initially. If then one finds the primary text sufficiently interesting, one may derive further profit from consulting the notes.

Of Philosophers and Kings

CHAPTER ONE

The Political Philosopher as Dramatic Poet: Preliminary Remarks on the Study of Shakespeare

To preface commentaries on some of the most famous dramas in English literature with advice on how to read them is apt to seem both needless and presumptuous. It is unlikely that anyone interested in lengthy and detailed interpretations of particular plays would feel the want of such instruction. Besides, there already exist countless essays, chapters, and entire volumes devoted to providing it, including several good ones. Still less should a reader of this book need persuading of either the artistic merit or the cultural significance of Shakespeare's literary legacy. No author has been more lavishly praised by other authors of high distinction themselves, nor is more beloved by the intelligent reading public. Translated into every language of consequence, often by men of considerable poetic talents themselves, Shakespeare has long had a devoted following among French, Spanish, Italian, German, and Scandinavian, as well as English-speaking readers. And if his popularity in Russia were not evidence enough, the enthusiasm with which he has been embraced by the Japanese attests to his extraordinary cross-cultural appeal.[1] His trans-historical allure has been similarly proven: nearly four centuries after they were written, his plays continue to be performed at a rate greater than those of any dozen other playwrights combined. Indeed, special theatres have been constructed for their performance at locations all around the world, from Texas to Tokyo, Perth to Berlin. As one appreciative scholar notes, "He is the only classical author who remains popular," and as such "is practically our only link with the classic and the past."[2] Nor is Shakespeare's influence confined to literature. He has shaped whole nations' conceptions of history. He is the single greatest contributor to the English language. He dominates the standard collections of English quotations (the King James Bible runs a distant second, Milton a far-distant third). And although he wrote but three dozen plays, they have inspired over two hundred operas,[3] along with dozens upon dozens of ballets, overtures, symphonic poems, and suites. Suffice it to say, Shakespeare's poetic greatness is conceded by all but a churlish few, at least among those who read him in his native English.

However, the premise of this book: that Shakespeare is as great a philosopher as he is a poet – that, indeed, his greatness as a poet derives even more from his power as a thinker than from his genius for linguistic expression, and that his continuing appeal and influence is a reflection of his possessing great *wisdom* – would not be so widely conceded today as in an earlier time. To some extent, the reasons for this militate more or less equally against all past masters of philosophical literature. I have in mind, first of all, the doctrinaire belief in the 'fact-value' distinction which so pervades contemporary thinking about what is right, noble, good, beautiful, and decent. This implausible dogma, derived from a since-discredited misconception of modern science, declares, in effect, that there neither is nor can be any genuine *knowledge* about these vital human concerns, that they necessarily entail 'value judgments' which are incorrigibly subjective.[4] By implication, anyone who has failed to recognize and abide by this basic distinction (a category that would include the most eminent philosophers that have ever lived), must have a profoundly mistaken view of things, hence can hardly be presumed wise. For subscribers to this creed, there can be no reason to accord Shakespeare's portrayals of what is just, virtuous, honourable, noble, admirable, magnanimous, or good (contrasting with the wrong, vicious, shameful, base, contemptible, mean, or evil) more respect than the views of an ignorant savage or a talk-show host.

Second, there are the various current 'isms' that assure us on one ground or another that it is impossible to be wise – period – because there is no objective knowledge to be had, not merely about 'values,' but about *anything*. Or at least none apart from that provided by the favoured 'ism,' each of which claims to demonstrate rationally that rationality is invariably nothing more than rationalization, and that the truth is, 'truth is relative' (to one's time, place, culture, sex, class, paradigm, language game, whatever). Despite such doctrines being but so many universalizations of the old Cretan paradox ("All Cretans are liars," said Kleinias the Cretan), adherence to some sort of relativism has come to be widely regarded as a touchstone of intellectual sophistication. For such sophisticates, anyone who does not appreciate the relativity of all human 'knowing,' or that the very idea of Reality is nothing but a 'social construct,' anyone who thinks that truth is 'absolute' – much less that he knows some such truth – is naïve (to put it kindly), and perhaps liable to fanaticism, or tainted with authoritarian aspirations. It would be hard to imagine an age more thoroughly infatuated with relativism than is ours. One theory purporting to justify it is no sooner laid to rest than, like a phoenix, some new version rises again from the ashes. One can scarce help wondering what it is about *our* historical circumstances that accounts for this. And why do the apostles of relativism proselytize for it with such fervour, as if they knew it to be the simple truth?[5]

These, then, are features of the current intellectual scene that operate with equal prejudice against all previous thinkers, and compromise one's ability to take any of them seriously as communicators of hard-won wisdom. Beyond these, however, are special obstacles to treating Shakespeare as a worthy teacher about human affairs, and they derive from what we fancy we know about his life. Here, however, scepticism is quite in order.[6] For certain assumptions and conjectures about what sort of man Shakespeare was, what he did, and why he wrote, have come to be accepted as established facts. Any major library can be counted upon to possess whole shelves of volumes purporting to be 'The Life of Shakespeare.' Whereas, the truth of the matter seems to be, we *know* almost nothing *for sure* about the author of these plays; most of what we believe about him is (at best) plausible speculation.[7] As W.H. Auden put it, "Shakespeare is in the singularly fortunate position of being, to all intents and purposes, anonymous."[8] The Cambridge historian Sir Hugh R. Trevor-Roper, a recognized authority on the relevant period of English history, notes that "of all the immortal geniuses of literature, none is personally so elusive as William Shakespeare":

> It is exasperating and almost incredible that he should be so. After all, he lived in the full daylight of the English Renaissance, in the well-documented reigns of Queen Elizabeth and King James I ... Since his death, and particularly in the last century, he has been subjected to the greatest battery of organized research that has ever been directed upon a single person. Armies of scholars, formidably equipped, have examined all the documents that could possibly contain at least a mention of Shakespeare's name. One hundredth of this labor applied to one of his insignificant contemporaries would be sufficient to produce a substantial biography. And yet the greatest of all Englishmen, after this tremendous inquisition, still remains so close to a mystery that even his identity can still be doubted.
>
> During his lifetime nobody claimed to know him. Not a single tribute was paid to him at his death. As far as the records go, he was uneducated, had no literary friends, possessed at his death no books, and could not write. It is true, six of his signatures have been found, all spelt differently; but they are so ill-formed that some graphologists suppose the hand to have been guided. Except for these signatures, no syllable of writing by Shakespeare has been identified. Seven years after his death, when his works were collected and published, and other poets claimed to have known him, a portrait of him was painted. The unskillful artist has painted the blank face of a country oaf.[9]

Since the received accounts of Shakespeare's life, when subjected to rigorous historical scrutiny, turn out to be scarcely more reliable than the tales of Robin Hood, a scrupulous agnosticism regarding Shakespeare the man would seem the only prudent disposition. One cannot presume, that is, to interpret the plays in light of assumptions about their author (or the circumstances under which they were written) unless these can be derived from the plays themselves. In my view, we had best agree with Dickens that "the life of Shakespeare is a fine mystery."[10]

The point bears emphasizing, for time and again one encounters scholarly efforts that have been prejudiced, if not fatally compromised, by commonly accepted but unjustifiable assumptions.[11] Ignoring the countless instances of dramatic details being explained as attempts to curry favour with the high and mighty, there are two main ways that these assumptions tend to discredit Shakespeare as a suitable teacher about matters of permanent importance. First, there is a tendency to depreciate his actually being *knowledgeable* about much of what he wrote: of the behaviour and attitudes of royalty and nobility and all those who wield power; of military and diplomatic strategy; of the major religious and philosophical alternatives; of foreign lands, alien races, and ancient times; of arts and sciences, as well as the esoteric traditions of alchemy, astrology, and numerology. How *could* he have been knowledgeable about such things (the argument would run), given his petty bourgeois antecedents, his (at best) provincial and quite limited schooling, his subsequent engagement in a low-class occupation, and his own preoccupation with financial gain? Although employing almost supernatural poetic gifts to persuade – indeed, mesmerize – his audiences, he can only be regarded as an especially skilled imitator of the superficial appearances of whatever he portrays. As such, he is capable of deceiving those who are themselves ignorant about the reality of these matters, and who do not think to question his credentials. If assessed by adequate intellectual criteria, however, Shakespeare must be likened to a television scriptwriter who can create a convincing appearance of medical practitioners without being truly knowledgeable in medicine himself. We all realize it would be foolish to study such television shows in order to become a doctor. Nor is that their purpose; they are meant to entertain, and their apparent medical 'realism' is intended merely to lend credibility to the drama. So, we are to believe, it must be with Shakespeare. He tells a rousing good story (invariably borrowed) in captivating if somewhat rustic language, and no more can be credibly expected of him.[12]

The second interpretive prejudice is partially derived from the first, namely, the view that Shakespeare did not take his plays all that seriously himself, and (consequently) did not lavish upon them the kind of literary craftsmanship as would warrant comparable care in interpretation.[13] They were written primarily, if not solely, to serve the needs of a theatre company in which he acted, one of several competing for the entertainment dollar of the day, and were a means whereby he earned a bit of extra money on the side.[14] Given, then, the author's own cavalier attitude towards his plays (the story goes), we should not presume them to be all that carefully written. No one would expect works that are dashed off primarily for commercial purposes, rather as are television screenplays today, to be free of inconsistencies, improbabilities, puzzling lacunae, and outright contradictions – especially if the existing text is the result of successive revisions that the author never troubled to harmonize. Hence, interpretive efforts premised on each play's making perfect sense, on its having neither loose ends nor inconsequential details, are doomed to frustration and irrelevancy. With there being such ready grounds for disregarding any and every feature one might otherwise find perplexing, textual enigmas cannot be treated as if they were soluble mysteries whereby one might better understand the play, much less the world it so fallibly mirrors.[15]

One can advance any number of considerations that challenge the plausibility of these common scholarly assumptions. But they can be convincingly rebutted only by interpretations that provide proof of what sceptics claim is not there – interpretations that make manifest the depth and breadth of Shakespeare's understanding by showing the intellectual as well as the dramatic coherence of his plays. Standing between the reader and any possibility of such interpretations, however, are several more narrowly literary questions concerning proper 'Shakespearean hermeneutics.' As critical assessment of his plays has become increasingly an academic specialty, it has become proportionally subject as well to changing trends in scholarship. Shakespeare specialists are doubtless familiar with the various evolutionary strands that have interwoven to produce the present skein. Even so, since I hope this book will be of interest to a readership beyond that of specialists, I beg them to bear with my briefly discussing a few points relevant to the emergence of a view that, if accepted, significantly impairs one's capacity to appreciate Shakespeare's philosophical merit.

For the likes of Samuel Johnson, and in a somewhat different sense for the Romantics, Shakespeare is *the* poet of Nature, of human nature especially but necessarily also of the whole natural order in which we find ourselves.[16] He could not be this, of course, except insofar as one credited him with some understanding of that which he portrays. Hence, the task of interpreting Shakespeare would necessarily be akin to that of interpreting the world he is judged to have faithfully reflected, a task for which there are no a priori restrictions or rules beyond those inherent in rational inquiry per se. From that catholic perspective, however, the interpretive focus has tended to become more narrow.[17] Picking up this story at the close of the nineteenth century, the dominant critical approach was one that conceived the analysis of the plays primarily in terms of understanding thoroughly the inner make-up of each character, and especially of how 'character' determined the fates of the main protagonists.[18] Properly pursued, this undertaking is still quite broad in scope, and is centred on what is naturally of greatest interest to most people: themselves and their fellows. Moreover, if one presumes there to be universal truths of human psychology, and that they are manifested in virtually all social milieux (thus are potentially accessible to any intelligent, perceptive, thoughtful observer, whatever his own social standing), one need not balk at attributing to Shakespeare some genuine wisdom of this kind.

'Character analysis,' however, was not long acknowledged as the key to Shakespeare's kingdom before it was challenged as an impoverishing abstraction. Not that legitimate grounds of complaint were lacking; for in emphasizing what is but a single constituent of a play, one is apt to neglect other constituents that contribute to its total effect.[19] In particular, there was a polyphony of claims that distinctly poetic means had been given too short shrift. Some critics stressed that it was as important – perhaps even more important – to see the plays as collages of symbols (that do much of their work subconsciously) as it was to view them as realistic ensembles of characters.[20] Similarly, that one must attend more to the distinctly melodic qualities of Shakespeare's language if one is to understand how and why his plays affect us in the ways they do. Various breeds of historicists also weighed in, insisting that Shakespeare's creations be viewed in the context of his times: of the dramatic conventions of his own age, and of the medieval Morality Play tradition that preceded it; of the social and intellectual assumptions of his audience (or more narrowly, of the social class to which he himself purportedly belonged); of contemporary political events that the plays may be presumed to address, and so on.[21]

Especially important, however, was a new insistence that what we now may study as literature was originally written as a play to be performed, and that we must be ever conscious of the requirements of stagecraft and of what makes for dramatic effectiveness, if the interpretations we generate are to have legitimacy.[22] But from this seemingly reasonable caution came some unreasonable restraints on what sorts of interpretive sallies are acceptable. The sheer fact that something is a play, and as such must be intelligible to a viewing audience, cannot be made to imply that it is *only* a play, nor that it could not possibly be intended to communicate something to a careful reader that goes well beyond what is accessible to even its most astute and attentive viewer. Shakespeare, evidently well acquainted with the literature of antiquity that so powerfully stimulated the Elizabethan age,[23] was perforce aware that it is possible to create works of lasting, transhistorical importance – that a person of sufficient genius might write something that could still be read with profit and enjoyment two thousand years later. Moreover, he knew that *dramas* could be counted among these finest works of literature, and studied as such. Any number of scholars argue that Shakespeare was heavily indebted to Seneca, for example. But neither I nor anyone else knows whether he ever saw an actual performance of a Senecan play. If indebted he was, it is more probable that it was as a student of Seneca's texts. Given, then, the possibility that he meant his own plays also to bear studying as literature, it cannot be a sufficient principle of their interpretation to allow apparent inconsistencies (or any other puzzling features) to be disregarded, provided only that one judges they would not likely be noticed by a live audience, nor compromise a play's dramatic effectiveness if they were. The very details that are apt to be overlooked at the pace one views them in performance, but not by a careful reader taking his own sweet time to compare and reflect upon each and every thing said and done, may supply clues to a play's deeper meaning, and convey insights never intended for mere theatre-goers.[24]

Nor should we agree to disallow any and all speculation about characters and their situations that cannot be supported, more or less directly, by what someone in the play is seen to say or do. Those who argue for such a restriction may do so on the grounds already alluded to (that as a matter of principle, a play must be fully and immediately intelligible to its viewing audience), but sometimes also as part of their rejecting the idea that the plays can be treated as reflections of natural reality. After all, how *could* they be that, a literal-minded reader or viewer may ask, filled as they are with people speaking blank verse? We are admonished to remember that the characters are *not* real persons with real histories, whose lives carry on out of our sight – and about whom it would be possible (in principle) to have definite knowledge. Whereas, speculation concerning 'how many children had Lady Macbeth' is illegitimate precisely because the answer is utterly indeterminate; the character has no existence independent of the text (to cite a question that I shall argue bears importantly on one of the plays to be examined later, but that serves only as a satiric title for an influential essay contending all such questions are out of order).[25] On this view, a play must be recognized for the profoundly artificial thing it is, something to which we passionately respond in consequence of its entire array of actions, ideas, associations, and symbols (among which are to be included its characters), as these collectively express "the system of values that gives emotional coherence to the play."[26] A Shakespeare play is not to be confused with a depiction of perceptual reality; it makes "a statement not of philosophy but of ordered emotion."[27] It is "a dramatic poem [whose] end is to communicate a rich and controlled experience by means of words."[28] If we are to be receptive to the experience its author actually intended, we must let his words establish the limits on that experience and be ever wary of adding anything that is ours but not also his.

One may agree with this prescription as it pertains to the effect of witnessing the theatrical presentation of a play. But insofar as that is the covert assumption underlying such claims – that Shakespeare's 'dramatic poems' are (literally) *defined* by their theatrical purpose, and must be analysed exclusively in the terms set by that purpose – one truncates the range of Shakespeare's possible intentions, especially those having more to do with reason than emotion. In effect, it a priori precludes recognizing any deeper philosophical purpose to his plays. Moreover, in restricting the scope of what it is legitimate to think *about* in contemplating them, the potential benefit to be derived from doing is so greatly diminished. Even with respect to the theatrical experience, one cannot strictly abide by what is being insisted upon: that we attribute nothing to the characters beyond what the text itself directly supplies. Yet surely the poet's capacity to stimulate *our* imaginations to fill in and thereby 'flesh out' *his* characters and their actions is a measure of his genius. One constituent of Shakespeare's greatness is the *economy* with which he does just that – in how few appearances, with how few lines he establishes the profile of (say) Lady Macbeth, which we then conjure into a 'reality' of such awesome proportions. Refusing to use our imaginations to endow the characters with an existence beyond the field of our perception (something we routinely do with respect to people we meet in everyday life) would render the plots incoherent. When the fourth act of *Othello* opens with Iago asking, "Will you think so?" – and Othello replies, "Think so, Iago?" – are we to suppose they just materialized out of the thin air into which they had evaporated when last we saw them, and begin speaking in utter abstractions? Obviously not. We rightly surmise that we have encountered them in the middle of a conversation which had a beginning we did not see, and about which we naturally will (and should) speculate based on what follows and what has gone before.

Everyone does this to *some* extent – *must* do it on pain of reducing the plays to little more than disjointed babble – and the only real question can be, how *much* is legitimate? Our distinguished critic gently ridicules those who would "conjecture upon Hamlet's whereabouts at the time of his father's death."[29] However, it *is* an issue worth wondering about, moving one to speculate as to the various possibilities, assessing how each might bear on the play – and even to imitate Shakespeare in concretely imagining alternative scenarios, thereby experiencing, thus better understanding, the task of dramatic creation. To be sure, one may not in the end be able to resolve the matter to one's own satisfaction, but such indeterminacy is of minor importance for the *philosophical* purpose of a play. It has done its primary philosophical work whenever it stimulates a curious reader to think carefully and rigorously about an issue worthy of a serious person's time. But here is the important interpretive point: unless one raises these sorts of questions, and thus focuses attention on them, one is not apt to scrutinze the text especially alert for evidence whereby they can be answered, evidence that may be there but otherwise go unnoticed, unobtrusive evidence the author has supplied to reward a reader who can recognize the pertinent questions, namely, those that point to a play's deeper meaning. In my experience, when through a conjunction of deduction and imagination one has hit upon the valid explanation for some puzzling feature of a play, a fresh reading of it will produce a confirming echo (albeit often in the least suspected of places).

I shall conclude my case for a more liberal critical approach by pointing to a set of questions that many scholars, concurring with the interpretive restriction I here argue against, would almost surely disallow, but which I contend is vital to any adequate interpretation of the other play this book is mainly about: *King Lear*. When in the midst of the storm the old King and his meagre retinue of Kent and the Fool have sought shelter in the hovel occupied by Edgar (disguised as Poor Tom), a conversation ensues between the latter, who is feigning madness, and the former, who seems to be going mad. To onlookers both within and without the play, neither Lear's nor Edgar's contributions make much sense. Subsequently Gloucester arrives and urges the King to come to where better shelter has been prepared:

> *Lear:* First let me talk with this philosopher.
> What is the cause of thunder?
> *Kent:* Good my Lord, take his offer; go into th'house.
> *Lear:* I'll talk a word with this same learned Theban.
> What is your study?
> *Edgar:* How to prevent the fiend, and to kill vermin.
> *Lear:* Let me ask you one word in private.
> *Kent:* Importune him once more to go, my Lord;
> His wits begin t'unsettle.
> *Glouc:* Canst thou blame him? ...
>
> (3.4.151–9)

Philosopher? Theban? What does Lear wish to ask this "philosopher," this "learned Theban," and why "in private"? As I shall later endeavour to show, one *must* ask these questions. Moreover, they *are* answerable, and together their answers provide an essential key to a fuller understanding of the play.[30]

As doubtless is evident from the foregoing, I have old-fashioned views about literature: about what one seeks from it and what the point is of discussing it. Accordingly, I have tried to write an old-fashioned book, one intended to engage the opinions of a select group of scholars, many from an earlier generation, who for all of their interpretive differences nonetheless share a general disposition towards Shakespeare which I find more profitable than that which has recently gained ascendancy.[31] To the extent my effort is successful, I hope it might help restore confidence in that disposition, as well as contribute to reviving interest in a body of scholarship of which I regard myself a beneficiary.

Insofar as one reads for sheer enjoyment, critical discussion is of interest only as it enhances that enjoyment. And it may well be able to do so without referring to anything beyond the piece under consideration. But to the extent that one expects great literature, as a requisite of true greatness, to increase in some way one's understanding of the larger reality – including the reality of language and its uses – critical assessment of literature necessarily entails reference to the world it purports to be about. This is to say, the study of literature cannot be an autonomous enterprise. Any author worthy of serious consideration is first of all a student of his subject matter, and hence of other such students, and bids us be so as well. He bids us, that is, turn from his work to the relevant portion of the world, and to other accounts of that portion, confirming or denying his view of things by what we ourselves see. In practice, of course, this dialectical process of reflective comparing can be repeated indefinitely, refining one's understanding of both the world and the work in question. It is inherently, inescapably a *philosophical* activity.

As my use of this term implies, I also have old-fashioned views about philosophy – or to speak more precisely, about political philosophy. Because these untimely ideas are not apt to be familiar to readers schooled only in modern conceptions, but are nonetheless essential to my contention that Shakespeare ranks high among the true philosophers, it will be convenient to expand on two points here at the outset. The first concerns the primary meaning of the term 'philosophy.' I subscribe to the original view: that philosophy is an *activity*, the activity of *thinking* for the primary if not sole purpose of *understanding*; or better still, a way of life in which this activity is the dominant organizing principle. That is, philosophy, or 'love of wisdom,' is *not* a set of doctrines, teachings, writings, policies, or whatever might be the concrete *result* of this philosophizing – although that is how one most commonly hears the word used today, for example, 'the philosophy of Aristotle,' meaning the view of the world made manifest in all those treatises that bear his name. But this is a secondary, derivative meaning of the term. Moreover, in my view, all the truly great philosophers, whenever they write, have as an aim – often it is their principal aim, it seems to me – the promotion of philosophy in this primary sense of the word. That is, they seek to induce, or seduce, their readers, at least so far as a reader is by nature suited for it, to engage in this distinctly human (and thus humanizing) activity of thinking, thereby experiencing philosophy first-hand. And what most effectively promotes philosophical activity is questions, not answers.

A second point concerns the qualifying term, 'political.' The ordinary understanding of 'political philosophy' would be something to the effect that it is 'philosophizing' (whatever that is) about 'politics' (whatever *that* is). But it could also mean – and this, in my view, is both a broader and deeper conception – philosophizing (about anything) in a 'politic' way, in a prudent or 'polite' way, with due regard for the possible political *consequences* of one's philosophizing, either for oneself or others. One can get some immediate sense of what I have in mind by trying to imagine how carefully, how prudently, how discretely, one would write about almost anything in Iran these days. Here we might recall how many of the great works of our philosophical tradition were written under conditions closer to those of contemporary Iran than to those of contemporary liberal democracies. Indeed, the founder of political philosophy was put to death, ostensibly for religious crimes (for not believing in the gods the rest of the city allegedly believed in, and for corrupting the youth likewise).[32] Therefore, in publishing the artefacts of one's philosophizing about politics, special care may be called for – and seems to have been bestowed, I should add, by all the major political philosophers of our tradition, among whom I count Shakespeare. To repeat, in calling him a 'political philosopher,' I mean to suggest that he is both a politic writer, and one whose primary aims include the promotion of philosophical activity.[33]

His means towards this end are multifarious. But underlying every technique whereby he stimulates his reader to philosophize is the recognition that it is questions that awaken and enliven us, whereas answers tend to sedate us, allowing us to doze, to sleepwalk through life. Accordingly, Shakespeare is never overtly didactic, much less dogmatic. He never in his plays speaks in his own name, other than in his choice of titles, so it is impossible to quote him, and to that extent impossible to be dogmatic *about* him – much as it is impossible to quote Plato: when we say we are doing so, we are, of course, actually quoting one or another of his characters, and how that character's views stand to the author's is necessarily a matter of conjecture. Shakespeare's own views are presumably reflected in the *whole* of what he wrote, and as such are not reducible without loss or distortion to any of the parts, and reflected, first and foremost, in the fact that he chose to write at all; second, in that he chose to write (mainly) *plays*. Each of these plays requires interpretation as a whole unto itself. Each having a beginning and an end, we can presume that it is meant to be independently intelligible, whatever further light one play may throw on another. An adequate interpretation coherently synthesizes all that is said and done (and sometimes even what is *not* said and *not* done) by every character, however seemingly minor, who figures in that play.

On the basis of my admittedly uneven, incomplete, and hence ongoing study of the canon, I would hypothesize that each of Shakespeare's great dramatic creations takes up an important question (or constellation of questions) and allows us to see why such questions are important: how each typically involves a complex of considerations, bearing on various legitimate concerns, and therefore admits of several plausible points of view. Shakespeare's plays invite us – indeed, *compel* us, if we wish to understand them – to see things from the perspectives of different kinds of people differently situated. This need not mean that all such views are equally valid, of course, nor that there is always some way to reconcile them, nor that there is no simply best or true view. Ideally, one should be seeking to reconstitute *Shakespeare's* view: that transcendent, synoptic perspective whence the various characters' partial perspectives were created. The fact remains, however, one does not fully comprehend an important question if one has not seen why it remains controversial (thus, a question), or why it is important (its centrality to either the practice or the understanding of human life). The plays may supply some answers, but only through the conscious collaborative efforts of the reader who, having been awakened to the important questions they address, has proceeded to address them seriously himself.

Moreover, I would further hypothesize that Shakespeare's plays typically present one or more puzzles that, when recognized as such, point to the play's deeper issues, and whose resolution is the key to an adequate interpretation. But it bears emphasizing that this recognition of puzzles generally requires some thoughtful effort, for they do not often come as clearly earmarked as is the most famous one in *Macbeth*: the mysterious Third Murderer (about which I shall have more to say in the next chapter). Sometimes the puzzle, or mystery, is baldly announced, but then discreetly allowed to fade into the backround, as in the case of *The Merchant of Venice*, which begins with the merchant Antonio lamenting:

> In sooth I know not why I am so sad,
> It wearies me, you say it wearies you;
> But how I caught it, found it, or came by it,
> What stuff 'tis made of, whereof it is born,
> I am to learn:
> And such a want-wit sadness makes of me,
> That I have much ado to know myself.

Explaining the sadness of Antonio – and the play, after all, takes its name from him, apparently – involves subterranean explorations that result in one's seeing the 'Christian versus Jew' theme in a radically different light.[34] Or consider the intriguing hint inconspicuously woven into the dialogue of *Measure for Measure*. Duke Vincentio is explaining to Friar Thomas why he is putting Angelo in charge of purging corrupt Vienna while he, though supposedly absent, will observe things disguised as a fellow friar. Then he adds, "Moe reasons for this action / At our more leisure shall I render you" (1.3.48–9). As we are not privy to their subsequent leisurely conversation, we are left to ponder on our own the riddle of these additional reasons. Similarly, when Richard of Gloucester, scheming to become King, reveals in soliloquy his plan to "marry Warwick's youngest daughter," he mysteriously adds, "The which will I, not all so much for love / As for another secret close intent, / By marrying her which I must reach unto" (*King Richard III* 1.1.157–9; see also 1.2.234). What this "secret" reason is, we are never told; that is, we are left to figure it out for ourselves (for we must assume there to be some purpose to his alluding to it in our presence, given that Shakespeare was free to make his characters speak whatever words he pleased). The more one thinks about the 'accidental' encounter between the mysterious intelligence-bearing Roman 'Nicanor' and the Volcian Adrian in act 4, scene 3 of *Coriolanus* – their sole appearance in that play – the curiouser it seems (*Rom:* "I know you *well*, sir, and you know me: your name I *think* is Adrian." *Vol:* "It is so, sir: truly I have forgot you." *Rom*: "I am a Roman"). Is this 'Nicanor,' initially unrecognized by the very man sent to contact him, who he says he is? And what might be the "most strange things" he has to tell (4.3.40–1)? Sometimes the puzzles lurk in the seemingly most inconsequential of details, as in *Julius Caesar*. To mention but a few: What is the significance of Caesar's informing us (along with Antony) that his left ear is deaf? Or of Caius Ligarius's *not* being present at the assassination as promised? How does the rhetorician Artemidorus know precisely who is conspiring Caesar's death? What explains Brutus's telling Metellus he has heard nothing about Portia (4.3.180–4), whereas we saw in the preceding private conversation with Cassius that he had (146–56)?[35] In other cases, the basic puzzle can be in the very title, for example, *The Tempest*. Is the fact that the opening scene of the play features a great storm whereby Prospero instigates the unlikely rendezvous of characters truly an adequate explanation – or is there another 'tempest' we are invited to discern and understand? Sometimes a puzzle seems peripheral to the main action, but is actually pivotal: how did the "trusty Welshmen" (but only they) – the Welsh army in which "the king reposeth all his confidence" – come mistakenly to believe their king is dead, and thus melt away, effectively dooming Richard's chances of suppressing Bolingbroke's revolt (*King Richard II* 2.4.5–7, 15–17)? Other times the puzzle lies at the very heart of the plot, so obvious it can be overlooked: why *is* Othello so peculiarly vulnerable to Iago's poisonous insinuations? Or, to mention another equally vital but less conspicuous curiosity: what is the significance of Othello's alleging two distinct origins for the notorious handkerchief he gave Desdemona (*Othello* 3.4.53–4; 5.2.217–18)?

Lest the point be lost, this lowly business of *figuring out the plot*, which is after all the very basis of the play, from which any adequate analysis must always take its departure and to which it must always return – this task of seeing the consistent reality operating beneath an often confusing but more familiar appearance (which succeeds in captivating almost everyone), seeing what is *really* going on and why – is itself a philosophical activity, requiring us to exercise the same set of powers, and in the same order of importance, as when one sets out to understand political life and its broader natural environment.[36] With this in mind, one may surmise there to be a principle of philosophical pedagogy behind Shakespeare's many allusions to the world itself being but a stage, and its people but so many players.

Speaking of people, whatever else Shakespeare has to teach us, he is obviously a master psychologist in the original, literal sense of the term: one who possesses a *logos* ('rational account') of the *psychē* ('soul'), or *psychai*, rather – and who, moreover, supplies the material whereby a sufficiently thoughtful reader may begin to become one, too. Shakespeare's plays portray human nature in its full significant diversity, loving and striving, learning and changing, dreaming and dying in archtypical political circumstances from ancient to modern times. In contrast to (say) Plato's dialogues, in Shakespeare's plays we confront the entire gamut of human types, from the high and rare to the most lowly and ordinary, allowing us to observe the various ways they interact and how they perceive each other and their environing world. For all the criticism that has been directed towards the 'character analysis' approach, the fact remains that understanding a given play depends fundamentally on 'psychoanalysing' each character (again, meaning this term in its philosophically open, rather than in any modern, quasi-technical sense). This, in turn, requires one to observe, remember, deduce, and evaluate an heterogeneous array of evidence, collected from a diversity of sources, and synthesize it into a single coherent entity that 'makes sense.'

This is not to say that Shakespeare never presents divided, confused, or discordant people – quite the contrary: he often does. After all, that is what the world mainly consists of. But the reasons for the various inner contradictions, disharmonies, ambivalences, and vacillations people exhibit or suffer are there to be discovered in the dramatic evidence rightly interpreted. Just as in everyday life, understanding a given character requires that one attend what he says, not only about himself but about others; compare what he says with what he does; compare what he intends with what actually results; integrate all this with what others say about him, and how they treat him; assess his aspirations, his judgment, his motivations, his morals, the circumstances that have shaped him, the changes he undergoes – and through it all, not forget to 'read thyself,' reflecting on why one *feels* a certain way about a given character, liking this one, loathing that, admiring another, pitying a fourth, and why one's feelings and assessments *alter* (as they invariably do) with increasing familiarity and deeper understanding. All such analysing of souls – done rigorously and thoroughly – counts as philosophizing in the primary sense of the word. For only through understanding individuals from across the entire spectrum of human types, discerning the respects in which we are the same as well as what differentiates and 'individualizes' us, can anyone progress towards the thing most needful for political philosophy: a clear and accurate idea of human nature. This is something which can only be intellected, not seen, since at no time does any single individual we might observe – whether on the stage of Shakespeare or the stage of life – manifest the *totality* of human nature, and only *human* nature. The intelligible reality of the nature in which we each and all participate is refracted in its various perceptible instantiations, and it is with them that one must begin.

A play, however, is more than the sum of its human parts, its characters. As noted before, the *plot* is primary: the characters are understood only insofar as they are seen to 'fit' the plot. However, in order to comprehend fully the action, the story that unifies the drama, one has to analyse not merely the structure of the characters' various relationships, but also the material and cultural setting in which they pursue their ends. In Shakespeare's plays, just as in everyday life, this larger structural setting is always some *complex* of nature, artifice, convention, and chance – and the challenge of understanding it, and how it bears on what people say and do, is the same as that faced in trying to understand the basics of any political situation: what is due to what. Nor is the answer to this question ever as obvious as so often it seems to people who do not think enough about such matters. What at first blush appear but arbitrary conventions (such as various shows of courtesy) or irrational prejudices (against bastards, say) may have their roots buried deep in the necessities of political life, and those roots can be exposed only through sustained thought. To understand a given political situation, or a particular strategic policy, or set of political institutions, or political life in general, one must grasp its inner rationale, and this is accessible only through thought, through thinking one's way 'into' it, and then exploring it from the inside, as it were. To attempt this, be it with respect to political actuality, or one of the political scenarios Shakespeare so cunningly crafted, is (once again) to engage in what is essentially a philosophical activity.

Thus, there are a number of ways that reading Shakespeare involves philosophizing in the primary meaning of the word. But one special advantage he provides someone drawn to political philosophy is the opportunity to train *prudential judgment*, using the terms in their old-fashioned sense of recognizing the general in the particular and of applying the general to the particular. As such, studying his plays is a partial corrective for the main liability inherent in the artificial way most people today make their initial acquaintance with philosophy. That is, philosophy arises *naturally* out of the concrete experience of puzzlement or 'perplexity' (the famous *aporia* of the Platonic dialogues). For anyone the least bit thoughtful, this experience is fairly common in confronting the world. In a practical sense, puzzlement is more fundamental than curiosity, the simple desire to see and experience and know for oneself. Were the world straightforwardly intelligible, curiosity alone would not give rise to any special effort to understand it. Rather, it is the discovery of so much that is 'problematic' that compels one to raise the kinds of questions, and consider the kinds of answers, that have come to distinguish our philosophical tradition. One may think of philosophizing, then, as nothing more nor less than the rigorous, persistent, thus usually systematic employment of one's natural powers to resolve one's puzzlement, and thereby satisfy one's curiosity, proceeding a step at a time, one question naturally leading to another (often more general) question, and so on for as long as one's interest continues.

However, this is not how philosophy is typically thought of or encountered today. Instead, we associate it mainly with university courses and textbooks, with their prepackaged surveys and expositions in which the certified 'classics' are authoritatively identified, historically ordered, standard taxonomies of problems and approaches provided, famous doctrines adumbrated along with standard objections to them, the most important questions already specified as such (along with the major alternative interpretations of famous responses to these questions), everything conveniently labelled and rationally organized. To be sure, there are obvious advantages to this arrangement, which is why something like it has existed for well over two thousand years. Doubtless it allows those of us less gifted than Plato and Aristotle, Descartes or Bacon, Hobbes, Rousseau, Nietzsche, and suchlike to ascend the ladder of questions much higher, much faster than ever we could were we dependent solely on our own resources, even aided and abetted by dialogue with like-minded friends. But precisely because we have thereby been artificially catapulted to a level of thinking quite remote from that of everyday life – because we have not ourselves ascended step by careful step, with full awareness of the concrete connections between everyday particulars and the most general problems we are taught to think of as philosophical – we have to learn to see those connections retrospectively, as it were.

The ability to do so, to 'make the connection' between the general and the particular, is (as I noted) the business of prudential judgment, and the practical value of whatever wisdom one might acquire from one's philosophizing will be no more than one's prudential judgment can provide. This points to the peculiar weakness of our cloistered or 'hothouse' way of cultivating philosophy. Nor is there much that can be done to remedy this problem – prudence *is* learnable, but strictly speaking it is not *teachable*, for it is learned only through personal experience. However, the intelligent reading of well-wrought texts can itself supply a kind of experience similar to that gainable in everyday life, and through which may be trained one's powers of observation, of memory, of recognition, of imagination, of analysis and synthesis – indeed, all the same powers of reason one needs to make sense of the world, and to act accordingly. Plato's dialogues do this exceedingly well, for these conversations always take place in a concrete setting among particular individuals, and seeing how these concrete particularities both reflect, and reflect upon, the general issues discussed is essential to their adequate interpretation. It is my contention, however, that the author who most beguilingly unites the general with the particular, thereby best provides that surrogate experience whereby one may train one's prudential judgment along with one's other rational faculties, is Shakespeare.

To understand the still broader educative capacity of Shakespeare's plays, however, it is necessary to distinguish analytically two different kinds of knowing, blended though these so often are in practice.[37] One might be called 'intellectual' (or 'conceptual,' 'propositional,' or 'cognitive') knowing, being almost exclusively confined to the soul's rational part; involving, that is, only reasoning and memory, though sometimes imagination as well. The other, 'experiential' knowing, affects the whole soul, and thus typically the body too insofar as our passions, appetites, and repulsions become physically manifest; there are sights from which we feel so impelled to 'look away' that we actually turn our heads, others that arouse us to intervene. With respect to certain topics – celestial mechanics, for example, or metallurgy, or paleontology – intellectual knowing is the only kind there is. One may have a passionate enthusiasm for such knowledge, but strictly speaking, the passion is no part of the knowing. Whereas in other matters, only the latter kind, experiential, would count as knowing in any significant sense; for example, about the various pleasures and pains, desires and hates, about fervent hoping and desperate fearing – unless one has actually *felt* such things, one's understanding of them and their effects is bound to be shallow at best, partial and abstract, 'bloodless.' The understanding of fine music for one who gains no enjoyment from hearing it is scarcely better than that of someone who is deaf; and consequently the devotion of people who dedicate their lives to music is not really understood, either. The musically insensitive person hears the sounds, and may even be able to provide a mathematical analysis of their harmony; he sees a broad array of evidence of other people's appreciation; he has no doubt that music is real, nor of its great importance to some people. But the 'why' of it remains opaque. Thus it is with love for people who have never passionately loved, or with grief for people who have never deeply grieved. Thus it is with philosophy.

Regarding many matters of importance to human life, true understanding involves rational apprehension (often requiring careful and extensive observation, as well as rigorous analysis and sound synthetic judgment – a great deal of thought), but also felt experience. In cases where we have some or even much of the former but little or none of the latter, we both do and yet do not understand the phenomena. The fortunate person who has never had occasion to grieve over a loved one lost knows that it must be a profoundly wounding experience – the evidence that this is so is unmistakeable, as are the various consequences to which it may lead, including illness, revenge, apostasy, insanity, bitter cynicism, or renewed faith. Still, this knowing lacks a depth of understanding that only the experience of actually *feeling* grief can provide; thus, similarly lacking is any real understanding of grief's power to produce these and other effects. Here, then, great dramatic art may educate by supplying surrogate experience. Having first been made acquainted with a character for whom one feels increasing affection and admiration, but who then untimely dies, allows one to feel something of the loss, and so acquire that much insight into grief. Analogously, a dramatic genius may teach us what it feels like to be left abandoned by those one trusts, or be despised out of blind prejudice, or to be the victim of gross injustice, or to be torn between burning ambition and sacred duty; but also to feel the peculiar exhilaration of one's innocence being vindicated, or of triumphing against all odds, or perhaps even the all-consuming rapture of young love. What one learns from such dramatic experience, this substantial deepening and intensifying of what one already formally knew, cannot be expressed in ordinary prose without its seeming trite. Hence, the problem one confronts when recommending a given piece of literature for what it has to 'teach.' As another scholar put it, "It often happens that when critics speak of what we may *learn* from a work of art the lesson in question sounds all too familiar, while the critic sounds more like a tired but dutiful museum guide than like a man who has been startled into new knowledge."[38]

I do not mean to suggest, however, that Shakespeare's educational effects are confined to this experential side of knowing, simply ratifying while deepening and enhancing the significance of that which we already intellectually know. Much less is he merely providing "homely truth a wonderful, a beautiful investiture."[39] He also, through effective appeals to our reason, informs us of things we may not already know, explains things we may not adequately understand, exposes mistaken assumptions, demonstrates uncomfortable truths. Sometimes this instruction comes directly from the mouths of his characters. Cold reflection on the confrontations between Angelo and Escalus, and between Angelo and Isabella, concerning the practicalities of law enforcement, especially in the given Viennese situation, confirms that Angelo is dead right (*Measure for Measure* 2.1.1–31; 2.2.28–41, 71–106). A reader who heretofore may have rather thoughtlessly favoured a position akin to Escalus's or Isabella's, but being now obliged to confront Angelo, has the opportunity to learn some hard truth about political life. And that Shakespeare has this truth be so trenchantly articulated by an unsavoury martinet conveys a lesson in itself. Other times, no one in the play (fully) explicates the lesson, but the plot demonstrates it – for example, that disastrous consequences may flow from an overtrusting nature, or from misplaced or excessive compassion, or from a moral fastidiousness inappropriate to the rough work at hand. In Shakespeare's ten plays portraying English history, he teaches the what and the who, the when and the where, as well as the how and the why. These plays provide the most convenient illustration of the two kinds of knowing, intellectual and experiential, being conveyed simultaneously, and thus to greatest effect – one great *political* effect being, to make Englishmen: to inform their minds with a view of who they are, while shaping their souls accordingly.[40] Exposed to the charisma of Shakespeare's King Henry V, Agincourt acquires a depth of significance that no plain historical recounting, however detailed, could possibly provide.

The studies that follow are intended to demonstrate what can be gained from reading Shakespeare 'philosophically' – that is, as a dramatic poet who is first of all himself a philosopher (and thus has a clear rational understanding of everything he is doing, and why), and whose foremost aims include the promotion of philosophical activity among his readers to whatever extent they are suited for it.[41] But since there are at least another dozen plays that might serve equally well for such a demonstration, this purpose does not in itself account for the particular two chosen for intensive examination here. To explain the special significance of *Macbeth* and *King Lear*, more needs to be said, both about them and about what seems to be a general concern of Shakespeare. To begin with the latter. Shakespeare displays a subtle – yet once noticed, striking – preoccupation with the relationship between politics and philosophy, and all that this relationship entails (which turns out to be a good deal: virtually everything all over again, in fact). Speaking more precisely, one may detect a persistent fascination with the idea of a philosophical ruler, a 'philosopher-king.' It is at least curious how often problems posed by the various facets of that idea turn up in his plays. Some portray apparent failures of philosophical rulers (e.g., *Measure for Measure*, *The Tempest*, and perhaps *As You Like It*; and in a tangential way, the character Hamlet also seems implicated in their kind of deficiency); these contrast dramatically with plays that show us successful kings (*Henry V* would be the most famous example) or other rulers of great accomplishment (especially the two Caesars). Of course, the successful kings contrast as well with rulers who fail through no fault of philosophy (e.g., Richard II, King John), and their cases, too, are used by Shakespeare to illumine further the relationship between knowledge and power.

Also relevant to this theme are those plays in which the characters of greatest intelligence, and with the most insight into human nature, happen to be the most villainous (men such as Richard of Gloucester and Iago) – again, a Platonic thesis: those with the greatest capacity for good are necessarily those who are also capable of the greatest evil (cf. *Republic* 491e, 495b, 518e-519b). Wondering what it is that determines which way great potential will turn, one may probe the pertinent plays in search of some understanding of why these master villains went bad.

The two plays selected for detailed exposition here were chosen for the special light they cast on this most comprehensive of problems: that of the relationship, traditionally seen as one of tension, between politics and philosophy.[42] As my chapters on each endeavour to make clear, both *Macbeth* and *King Lear* show age-old philosophical questions arising naturally out of political ones.[43] They show, that is, how the pursuit of an adequate understanding of certain practical issues, transient yet recurring, necessarily leads to considerations that far transcend the particular circumstances in which these practical problems arise – for distinctly *political* circumstances are, virtually by definition, always 'particular,' always more or less parochial, restricted, impermanent, thus ever subject to change. However, some issues arising therein point beyond the fluid, shifting urgencies of political practice to a consideration of the larger, unchanging natural environment in which all political life proceeds, and to the natures of its constituent parts. *Macbeth* shows not only how invaluable can be a philosopher's understanding of politics; it also lets us see how several of the most challenging metaphysical and cosmological questions bear directly on people's lives, how the answers they accept affect all that they think and do, and why self-contradictory views necessarily manifest themselves in irrational plans and practices. *King Lear* portrays philosophy itself arising out of man's confrontation with Nature; it shows, that is, how a particular man, once lord of all he surveyed and accustomed to obedience throughout his long adulthood, came at last to an adequate understanding of Nature, including an appreciation of both the value and the limits of mankind's efforts to accommodate itself therein.

The above observations are enough to suggest that these two plays, although about very different kinds of kings, may have a special relationship with each other. That such is indeed the case is signalled, moreover, by their sharing peculiarities of language and incidental details. Begin with one of the most arresting of the many memorable phrases unique to Shakespeare: "aroynt thee, witch." It occurs in only two places: *Macbeth* (1.3.6) and *King Lear* (3.4.121). These are also the only two plays in which someone speaks of being "tied to a [or the] stake" (*Macbeth* 5.7.1; *King Lear* 3.7.53). Each play presents an instance of what could be (and has been) argued is the most shocking piece of violence presented on the

Shakespearean stage: the murder of Macduff's son in *Macbeth* and the gouging of Gloucester's eyes in *King Lear*. In both plays, the extreme violence of Nature is contrapuntal to this appalling violence of men, with each play featuring storms said to be of unprecedented force (*Macbeth* 2.3.53–62; 2.4.1–9; *King Lear* 3.1.8–11; 3.2.45–9). Both emphasize the healing power of sleep (*Macbeth* 2.2.35–9; 3.4.140; *King Lear* 4.4.12–15; 4.7.12–16). Both eponyms refer to the world as but a stage, and those who people it as fools (*Macbeth* 5.5.22–6; *King Lear* 4.6.181). Both present an image of apocalyptic ruin in strikingly similar terms: Macbeth insisting the witches answer, "though the treasure of Nature's germaines tumble all together, even till destruction sicken" (4.1.58–60); Lear exhorting the storming powers, "Crack Nature's moulds, all germaines spill at once that makes ingrateful man" (3.2.8–9) – the only two mentions of 'germaines' (i.e., germens, germs) in the canon. Clothing has a pervasive symbolic and metaphorical importance in both plays (see *Macbeth* 1.3.108–9, 145–6; 1.7.33–6; 2.3.124–5, 131; 5.2.15–22; and *King Lear* 2.4.265–8; 3.4.99–107; 4.7.21–2, 67). Both plays involve the eponyms becoming temporarily deranged. Then there is the curious fact that in both a vacant stool is taken by these deranged protagonists to be the site of an absent person: Macbeth believes the chair reserved for him to be occupied by the murdered Banquo (prompting his wife to rebuke, "O proper stuff! / This is the very painting of your fear ... When all's done, / You look but on a stool" 3.4.59–67); Lear, conducting a mock trial of his ungrateful daughters, commands: "Arraign her first; 'tis Goneril" (which elicits from the Fool, "Cry you mercy, I took you for a joint-stool" 3.6.51).[44] Both plays feature a noticeable abundance of references to various species of life, and include taxonomies of dogs (*Macbeth* 3.1.92–100; *King Lear* 3.6.63–71). With but a couple of exceptions, the use of 'milk' as a disparaging term for softness in men is peculiar to these two plays: Lady Macbeth laments her Lord's being "too full o'th'milk of human kindness" (1.5.17); Goneril chastises her husband for his "milky gentleness" (1.4.340; see also 4.2.50). Each play ends with the victor vowing to settle accounts with both friends and foes: Malcolm in *Macbeth* (5.9.25–35), Albany in *King Lear* (5.3.301–3). Both involve gross violations of the guest–host relationship: Macbeth murdering his guest (1.7.14–16), Cornwall and Regan assaulting and expelling their host (3.7.30–41). In both, that most basic of philosophical questions – 'What are you?' – focuses attention on the central issue of each play, being asked of the witches in *Macbeth* (1.3.47) and of the multi-personae Edgar in *King Lear* (5.3.118).

All of this may be no more than a coincidental effect of *Macbeth* being written immediately after *King Lear* (such being the common scholarly view: that *Lear* was written around 1605, *Macbeth* within the next year). Thus, these and other parallels of speech and dramatic feature may indicate nothing more than an accidental closeness in the circumstances in which both were composed. In that case, of course, they have no larger significance. On the other hand, these two plays about quasi-legendary kings from the opposite ends of pre-Norman Britain may have been composed one after the other precisely because their author conceived their respective themes as having a deeper relationship, and so hints at that deeper relationship by various similarities of dramatic details, such as those I have above catalogued. Only in light of an adequate analysis of the two plays themselves might one determine Shakespeare's intention in this regard.

Accordingly, in the two chapters that follow, each of these plays is treated independently. In the course of presenting my interpretations, however, I have made a special effort to indicate (mainly by means of the notes) Shakespeare's affinity with the preceding philosophical tradition, and with Plato's writings in particular. My final chapter offers briefer treatments of certain other plays (*Othello*, *The Winter's Tale*, and *Measure for Measure*), focusing especially on aspects that bear directly on the theme that titles this book. I conclude the chapter with an analysis of Plato's critique of poetry as presented in his *Republic*, and of how the dramatic art of Shakespeare transcends that critique.

CHAPTER TWO

Living in a Hard Time: Politics and Philosophy in *Macbeth*

And the angel which I saw
stand upon the sea and upon the earth
lifted up his hand to heaven,
And sware by him that liveth for ever and ever,
who created heaven, and the things that therein are,
and the earth, and the things that therein are,
and the sea, and the things which are therein,
that there should be time no longer:

Revelation 10:5–6

For time sweeps everything before it and can bring
with it good as well as evil and evil as well as good.

Machiavelli, *The Prince*

Macbeth, on first acquaintance, might seem to offer little scope for philosophical inquiry, other than perhaps in the psychology of the criminal mind. It is a fast-paced action story that begins and ends in war, with brutal assassinations and other atrocities central features of its plot – hardly more, that is, than a tapestry of violent and especially bloody deeds most graphically described: the whole torso of an enemy sliced open ("unseam'd from the nave to the chops");[1] a body left in a ditch "with twenty trenched gashes on his head," each a killing blow (how they must have hacked and whacked upon it); a particularly messy murder in the night ("who would have thought the old man to have so much blood in him?");

heads lopped off for public display. And as if these reports were not sufficiently gruesome, images equally hideous to imagine express the characters of those who use them: a nursing mother plucking the nipple from her baby's "boneless gums" and dashing its brains out on the stone floor; men bathing in other men's "reeking wounds"; a mind assaulted by stinging scorpions. One episode of barbarous cruelty allegedly surpasses even a hardened survivor's will to describe it: a castle surprised, its mistress, children, and servants slaughtered in a manner so savage as might cause their master's death merely to hear of it. As for the principal characters of this drama, their rude, coarse scheme of life is matched by such a primitive mentality that they seem to exist more in the realm of fantasy than fact. Occult practices abound, and superstition is so pervasive that to enter their world requires a wholesale suspension of our rational disbelief in the supernatural. Starkly presented without apology for its magical happenings and imaginary beings, the play (one may thus be tempted to conclude) can be treated only as a grim fairy tale, doubtless conveying a moral, but otherwise offering little besides the typical psychic gratifications people seek from exciting theatre.

This appearance could scarcely be more misleading as to the play's real qualities. For in truth, *Macbeth* may be Shakespeare's most metaphysically ambitious – and politically instructive – dramatic creation. As perhaps goes without saying, a play can be profoundly philosophical without any of its characters being so, though doubtless the inclusion of someone who displays at least some perplexity or reflectivity about the how and why of things is among a dramatist's more natural ways to stimulate thought.[2] In fact, the main protagonists in this play are not the ignorant, credulous, superstitious rustics many commentators tend to treat them as being.[3] When the three Weyward Sisters[4] disappear as suddenly as they first appeared upon that blasted heath, Banquo shows a quite sufficient awareness of our susceptibility to delusion, wondering aloud to Macbeth, "Were such things here, as we do speak about, / Or have we eaten on the insane root, / That takes the reason prisoner?" (1.3.83–5). And when Macbeth first sees but cannot grasp that "air-drawn dagger" marshalling him the way he was already going, he immediately questions its reality: "or art thou but / A dagger of the mind, a false creation" – and as such, something to be explained naturally (in this case, "Proceeding from the heat-oppressed brain"). Moreover, that seems to be what he concludes: "There's no such thing. / It is the bloody business which informs / Thus to mine eyes" (2.1.36–49). Similarly, Lady Macbeth offers her lord a wholly natural explanation of whatever gory vision is apparently unnerving him at their great banquet: "This is the very painting of your fear" (3.4.60).

In calling attention to these explicit attempts to explain in more ordinary ways certain bizarre, possibly supernatural occurrences, I do not here mean to suggest that these accounts are adequate, nor that we are obliged to treat everything seemingly magical or fantastic as amenable to a naturalistic explanation. But it is important that we credit the characters with sufficient intelligence and common sense to permit whatever they say being worthy of our own serious consideration, not dismissing it as merely so much evidence of their benighted condition. Moreover, if we care to try, we can readily discern a broad spectrum of human credulousness in the play (rather like that we encounter in our own lives) – indicative in each case, presumably, of intellectual inclinations and powers as well as of education and culture. At one extreme, the Old Man, who apparently trusts everything he hears or thinks he sees, and who is predisposed to ascribe transcendent significance to any occurrence the least bit unusual. At the other end, perhaps, the Thane of Rosse with whom he discusses the past "sore night" (2.4.1–20); there are grounds for suspecting that *his* perspective on life is one of strictest positivism.

Macbeth, in particular, has a surprising depth and complexity of mind. He is much more than the furiously valiant, callous, thoughtless butcher one might presume from either our first report of him, that of the bleeding Captain fresh from the battlefield, or our last, that of Malcolm gazing upon his severed head. It would be an exaggeration, but useful, to suggest that in the interim Macbeth shows himself to be also the very opposite of this: fearful, morally sensitive, and above all pensive, ruminative – indeed, compulsively so. His torment is a consequence of his inability to follow his dear wife's advice and "consider it not so deeply" (2.2.29). Reason doubtless approves her "Things without all remedy / Should be without regard" (3.2.11–12). But Macbeth's restless, obsessive thinking has carried him well beyond that fatalistic, almost brutish acceptance (and forgetfulness) said to characterize the timeless existence of the peasant or the savage, while leaving him still far short of a truly philosophical acceptance of his reality. With a mind toiling between the intellectual lowlands where the great herds graze, and the cold, lonely peaks favoured by goats and sages; and with a poet's imagination that is at once his grace and his curse, he is more – much more – than just another erring barbarian.

As regards Macbeth's practical life, he expresses a genuine respect for the familiar dogmas and conventions that he knows are meant to restrain the very desires that so powerfully tempt him, those all-too-human yearnings for wealth, honour, position, and power. In the privacy of his thought, he acknowledges what are the duties of a kinsman, a subject, a host, and he accepts them as such. He is aware that Duncan's "meek" and "clear" manner of bearing "his great office" will make what Macbeth is contemplating – the murder of this pious king – a "horrid deed," one deeply damnable, and sure to be widely condemned and lamented. He does not (as would an Iago, say, or Richard of Gloucester) hold such views in contempt – quite the contrary: with a scrupulous self-honesty that is far from common, he admits that he has nothing with which to challenge their authority but his own "vaulting ambition." This admission is the more remarkable in that one can readily construct a strong case for Macbeth's having a *right* to the crown: of royal blood himself, Duncan's cousin (1.4.58); the most powerful warrior in a semi-barbaric domain (for "humane statute" has pretty clearly *not* "purg'd the gentle weal"); Scotland needing a strong man as ruler; Duncan ignoring that need in order selfishly to favour his callow son – were Macbeth the least bit given to shading the truth, he could easily rationalize taking matters into his own hands.[5] Instead, his conscience is pained at the thought of doing so. All this, along with his conceding that it would be but "even-handed justice" were his proposed treatment of Duncan to be subsequently visited on him (1.7.10–27), argues for a measure of natural nobility, if not necessarily for any great power of intellect.

Conventional as many of his thoughts and sentiments might be regarded, however, there is none the less a 'theoretical' impulse in Macbeth.[6] As for his manner of expression, it is more than just vigorous and manly; it manifests a poet's gift for thinking in terms of memorable images – indeed, on occasion images and similes and metaphors fairly tumble from what must be an uncommonly fertile, vivacious imagination (e.g., 2.2.35–9; 3.1.54–69; 4.1.52–60).[7] Several of his speeches suggest that he is drawn with unusual persistence to some of the most perplexing and disconcerting questions and puzzles that naturally arise in the human experience, and that he is distinguished by the intensity with which he yearns for the permanent, the absolute, the meaningful, for clarity and order and intelligibility.[8] Macbeth expects things to add up, make sense, behave consistently, and he does not easily shrug it off when they do not. He acknowledges what ought to rule his and every man's soul, even as he alludes to why it too often fails to do so ("my violent love / Outrun the pauser, reason" 2.3.108–9). He understands as well as anyone how and why 'equivocal' evaluations are sometimes appropriate ("So foul and fair a day I have not seen" – the first words he speaks). But he is troubled by what appear to be outright contradictions ("This supernatural soliciting cannot be ill; cannot be good: – if ill, why ...? If good, why ...?"). Moreover, in this play where every third or fourth speech seems laden with fateful irony, Shakespeare has given Macbeth several lines that might be seen as signalling a kind of proto-philosophical nature – such as his exhorting Banquo, "*Think* upon what hath chanc'd" (1.3.154); or when writing to his wife of his meeting with the witches, that he "stood rapt in the *wonder* of it" and that he "burn'd in desire to *question* them further" (1.5.3–6); Or his ruefully observing, "There's nothing serious in mortality; / All is but toys" (2.3.91–2). Even his being subject to fits and raptures (of the mere eight times Shakespeare ever uses 'rapt,' three are in conjunction with Macbeth), and his seeing visions and hearing voices, might be interpreted as indicative of a poetical–philosophical temper.[9] Behind the malicious taunting in which it figures, Macbeth's taxonomy of dogs and men shows not only refinement in observation and judgment, but what is more important: an awareness that this very concern for finer, more accurate 'divisions' sets him above the common ruck. As he notes, the vast majority of people mostly speak and thus think in coarse categorizations that ignore subtle but crucial differences; whereas "the valu'd file *distinguishes*" in accordance with those special powers or "gifts" distributed by Nature, establishing thereby the natural rank order of things (3.1.91–102).[10] When, in an attempt to rationalize his precipitous killing of the dead King's grooms, he asks rhetorically, "Who can be wise, amaz'd, temperate and furious, / Loyal and neutral, in a moment" (2.3.106–7), he might be said to have epitomized unwittingly the recurring predicament of a political philosopher. Finally, one must consider whether Macbeth's tyrannical inclination may not itself evince a nature that could be satisfied, if at all, only by philosophy.[11]

It is not, therefore, as inappropriate as doubtless it first seems that this bold, bloody, brooding Macbeth should be the eponym of what is arguably Shakespeare's most philosophically ambitious play, one in which its basic political questions are addressed in the context of the embracing metaphysical ones, thereby showing concretely how a dogged pursuit of the former sort necessarily leads to the latter. For this purpose, the very primitiveness of the time and place – that both politically and intellectually Duncan's Scotland is only semi-civilized – works exceedingly well. People's propensity to believe in immaterial beings, extraordinary powers, and magical happenings (or their susceptibility to superstitious delusions, if one prefers) itself poses a more worthy philosophical question than we moderns, weaned on scientism, are apt to appreciate. Or constellation of questions, rather: for nothing less than an adequate account of Nature and Reality, of knowledge and the human soul, will suffice to answer them. Notice how readily so-called supernatural phenomena can be made to show the multifarious connections between the important issues of everyday life (the natural focus of political philosophy) and those entailed in trying to understand the environing world as a whole (culminating in the challenges of metaphysics, or 'first philosophy'). For example, few things matter more to man's practical affairs than the weather. Are there, as the most diverse peoples have believed, spirits that can cause the clouds to rain, that command the winds, stir up the oceans, obscure the sun, all according to their pleasure? If not, why not? If so, how so? Or is there any way that anyone or anything "*can* look into the seeds of time" and foretell the future? Perhaps there *is*, if all is determined, preordained, predestined, fated. There could be signs, intelligible to whoever adequately understands the scheme of things. After all, astronomers make precise predictions as a matter of course, and even meteorologists enjoy some predictive success. The positions of the heavenly bodies influence human beings at least as much as does the weather: we order our entire lives with respect to the natural rhythm of day succeeding night (cf. 2.1.49–50; 2.4.5–10; 3.2.50–3).

As the latter question might itself suggest, however, in *Macbeth* Shakespeare has embedded consideration of the 'supernatural,' represented primarily by the power of prophecy, in a still more comprehensive metaphysical problem, one that serves even more effectively to show how the issues of political life point beyond themselves to those of first philosophy. And that is the problem of Time: the nature of time itself, and the significance of the uniquely human awareness of time, of living with a memory of the past and a curiosity about the future – sometimes hopeful, other times anxious, but always cognizant of one's mortality, that abstract premonition of one's eventual death. Sufficiently thought about, the play shows how and why the normal human posture towards time is strangely ambivalent, or 'equivocal,' and necessarily bound up with questions of fate and free will. However, it would be best to approach these matters in the natural way, from the ground up, as it were. So, let us begin with the political story.

MACHIAVELLI VISITS SCOTLAND

A challenging story it is, one that obliges us to exercise the same array of rational powers – of observation, memory, imagination, and deduction, of analysis and synthesis – as is required to understand the equally challenging world of immediate experience. For *Macbeth* incorporates several overt mysteries that we cannot help but wonder about and attempt to solve by a careful sifting of the clues. The most prominent of these, of course, concerns the identity of the Third Murderer involved in the ambush of Banquo and his son: the other two murderers are as puzzled about him as we are meant to be (and like any good mystery writer, Shakespeare has strewn a fair number of false leads). But also, there is the mysterious messenger who calls to warn Lady Macduff just prior to the arrival of Macbeth's assassins. Who is this person who is not known to her, but who knows about Macbeth's murderous designs upon her and her entire household; and why does he not identify himself? Equally curious is Rosse's abrupt volte-face upon his arrival at the English court where Macduff is soliciting the exiled Malcolm – Rosse first placidly assuring an anxious Macduff that his wife and children are safe and well ("they were well at peace, when I did leave 'em" 4.3.179), then a moment later informing him that they have all been "savagely slaughter'd" (like Duncan, "*sent* to peace": after life's fitful fever, now they too sleep well). These are but the more obvious puzzles that challenge the reader to turn detective, and so consider carefully every line of the text, noticing the least nuances of speech or deed, attending to every detail, however seemingly inconsequential – in short, to *think* about the possible implications of everything that happens, about all that is said and done, and what might have been said or done, but was not.[12] That is, to understand *Macbeth*, to understand it as its author understood it, one must practise the activity that, carried to perfection, has traditionally been known as philosophizing.

Approached in such a spirit, the first conclusion to emerge is that the play is designed to illustrate the political teachings we associate most readily with Machiavelli's *The Prince*. And what could be more appropriate for this purpose than the story of a man who would make himself king 'by his own arms and virtue,' and who moreover seems eminently suited to succeed? As is obvious to anyone familiar with both play and treatise, they similarly exploit the natural human fascination with danger, violence, crime, and power (a proven witch's brew for profitable storytelling throughout the ages). Both manifest a comparable 'realism' with respect to what most people regard as all-important – certainly not justice, or virtue, or happiness even – but matters of life and death. Shakespeare's chosen protagonist, however, ultimately fails to retain the princedom he has seized, being supplanted by another, apparently far less promising aspirant. The challenge is to understand *why*: to see what *really* explains Macbeth's failure. That it is the outcome decency would prefer is not an explanation. In addition to the test posed by this central problem, the natures and actions of all the characters in *Macbeth* provide concrete opportunities for analysis in terms of the tough-minded, cold-hearted political principles Machiavelli contends determine success or failure in this world.

Thus, one can reflect on the weakness of gentle Duncan, not a new prince whose situation necessarily involves great dangers, but rather an established prince whose legitimacy is widely recognized, and who should therefore be able to maintain himself without undue difficulty;[13] gracious Duncan, who is loved, but – unfortunately for him and all of Scotland – not feared;[14] who does not lead his own armies, and so is utterly dependent on the great warrior captains who do;[15] honest Duncan, who to the very end is duped by appearances, lamenting upon confirmation of Cawdor's treachery, "There's no art / To find the mind's construction in the face: / He was a gentleman on whom I built / An absolute trust" (1.4.11–14) – as next he does on Macbeth, it would seem;[16] and 'artless' in judging men though he confesses himself to be, he nonetheless condemns Cawdor on the word of a man he does not recognize and may not even know (note 1.2.46); pious Duncan, who publicly shows himself, not "fierce and spirited," but "effeminate and pusillanimous," crying with joyful relief upon greeting the victorious chiefs that have saved his kingdom (1.4.33–5) – this in marked contrast to Macduff, who expressly declines to "play the woman with [his] eyes"[17] (4.3.230); generous Duncan, who acknowledges that his indebtedness to Macbeth surpasses his ability to recompense: "More is thy due than more than all can pay" – yet who then promptly announces his intention to bestow the greatest award of all, the royal succession, on his son Malcolm, an inexperienced youth who, far from contributing to the day's victories, only escaped capture through the efforts of such "good and hardy" soldiers as the bleeding Captain (1.4.15–21, 35–9; cf. 1.2.3–5, 5.3.3).[18] In short, "this Duncan hath borne his faculties so meek, hath been so clear in his great office," that Scotland is wracked with rebellion from within and threatened with conquest from without.[19]

However, there are things to be said in Duncan's favour as well. He apparently enjoys the affection and loyalty of a majority of the warrior elite (cf. 1.7.16–25), and not least of all, of Macduff (2.3.62–72). And while Duncan could hardly be called cruel, we see he is not invariably merciful. He readily applauds the bloody labours of Macbeth ("O valiant cousin! worthy gentleman!"); and confronted with Cawdor's first rebellion, he ensures there will not be another. Moreover, subsequent developments could be said to justify his passing over Macbeth in favour of Malcolm. Duncan may know his cousin well enough to have grounds for suspecting that Macbeth, though of surpassing excellence as a soldier, is not apt to make a temperate, prudent, and just king. In particular, Duncan may have some inkling of Macbeth's moral weakness. For resolute as he is in war, Macbeth shows himself far from *morally* resolute, given to wavering between 'I dare not' and 'I would' (like some poor cat i'th'adage). Whereas Malcolm proves a sound choice; his later behaviour provides an illuminating contrast with that of his father, perhaps because he learned from Duncan's mistakes.

To be fair, Duncan *is* confronting a tough political problem: that of ensuring a peaceful succession. If we credit him with some awareness that Macbeth poses the principal difficulty – ambitious to be king himself, yet temperamentally unsuited for it; unsurpassed as a military commander, hence invaluable as a loyal subordinate, but by virtue thereof capable of seizing power should he have a mind to[20] – we can begin to see Duncan's reasoning. To delay the announcement of his choice for successor might help keep Macbeth loyal, hoping to be that choice. But Duncan, an old man (5.1.37), could die at any time, thereby exposing the realm to the paramount evil of civil war were a legitimate successor not already named (and preferably well established as such in people's minds). So he cannot risk indefinite delay. Moreover, now would seem an opportune moment: in the full flush of victory, with local dissident barons firmly quashed and a foreign invasion repulsed at great loss to the invaders (which should discourage like attempts for the immediate future), there is a plenitude of honours as well as material rewards to be distributed (1.4.39–42). Thus, Duncan hopes to mollify Macbeth with lesser goods: the status and wealth attached to the just-vacated Thaneship of Cawdor; an effusive public declamation of royal gratitude, meant to elicit in return – as it does – a fresh public confirmation of Macbeth's loyalty to the throne (this *prior*, we should notice, to the naming of Malcolm Prince of Cumberland, and as such the royal heir-designate); the honour of a royal visit to Macbeth's estate at Inverness, offering the prospect of more cordial personal relationships developing ("And bind us further to you"; 43); finally, the presentation of "great largess," including a rich gift for Macbeth's wife (2.1.14–15). By such means, Duncan hopes to "plant" Macbeth, promising he will "labour to make [him] full of growing" (1.4.28–30). And there is evidence that Duncan's plan might have succeeded, at least temporarily, for Macbeth informs his wife:

> We will proceed no further in this business:
> He hath honour'd me of late; and I have bought
> Golden opinions from all sorts of people,
> Which would be worn now in their newest gloss,
> Not cast aside so soon.
>
> (1.7.31–5)

But Duncan's calculations have failed to reckon adequately with Lady Macbeth. She is not the sort of woman to be put off with baubles and flattery.

Events prove, however, that neither is she quite as tough as she thinks she is – nor, consequently, tough enough for the enterprise she undertakes: engineering Macbeth's ascendance to Prince of the realm. When first we meet her, she seems formidable indeed, contrasting herself with her husband, whom she privately criticizes for being too pious, honest, timid, and scrupulous – altogether "too full of the milk of human kindness" (this of a man who disembowels opponents with a single stroke and makes trophies of their heads). In her "Thou wouldst be great; / Art not without ambition, but without / The illness should attend it" (1.5.18–20), one recognizes a view unmistakeably akin to Machiavelli's "It is necessary to a prince, if he wants to maintain himself, to learn to be able to be not good, and to use this and not use it according to necessity."[21] Lady Macbeth means to be her lord's teacher, confident that she can through well-chosen words instil in him the requisite spiritedness, as well as exorcise any inner compunctions that might prevent him from "catching the *nearest* way" ("Hie thee hither," she prays, "That I may pour my spirits in thine ear, / And chastise with the valour of my tongue / All that impedes thee from the golden round"; 25–8). We are subsequently treated to a display of her potent speech, wherein is revealed the nature of the power she wields over Macbeth: not merely to permit or deny access to her female charms, but to validate or nullify his very manliness[22] (1.7.35–54; cf. 2.2.63–4; 3.4.57–74).

Initially, however, she professes an intention to carry out Duncan's removal herself, having like a sorceress called down those "spirits that tend on mortal thoughts" to "unsex" her for this very purpose (while nonetheless preferring "thick Night" so to obscure things "that [her] keen knife see not the wound it makes" 1.5.40–52). Thus she first broaches the project to Macbeth: "you shall put this night's great business into *my* dispatch"; his sole responsibility will be to maintain an innocent appearance ("Only look up clear; ... Leave all the rest to me" 67–73). When next she speaks of this same "great business," it has become a joint enterprise: "What cannot *you and I* perform upon th'unguarded Duncan?" (1.7.70–1). And when the deed is finally to be executed, her role has somehow shrunk to that of drugging the grooms and laying out their daggers – although apparently she still had the opportunity to complete the job herself, privately musing, "Had he not resembled my father as he slept, I had done't" (2.2.11–13). Some reason, given the defeminized killer she aspired to become but apparently could not, even with the help of strong drink. Perhaps the Machiavellian ideal is more difficult to realize than it might first seem. In any event, from the moment she learns of Macbeth's precipitous murder of the grooms, she begins to lose her grip on events, and finally on herself as well (whether her fainting then is genuine, or feigned as a distraction, it is a symbolic premonition of her fatal weakness). Macbeth is increasingly led by the inner logic of his crimes, less and less by her. As she feels her isolation growing, and her power diminishing accordingly, she complains of his keeping so much alone, deserting her live companionship for that of "sorriest fancies" (3.2.8–12). With the atrocious violence of Macbeth's reign continuing to escalate, and he no longer consulting her on matters of gravest moment,[23] she comes quite apart, recognizing that what she set in motion is out of her control, wreaking effects she never envisaged ("The Thane of Fife had a wife: where is she now?").[24] In sum, the psychic career of Lady Macbeth is the inverse of her lord's. At the outset, she is resolute and single-minded, whereas he vacillates, his soul divided. But in the course of the play, they exchange conditions, and she discovers too late that she is not really made of the right wrong stuff.

As for Macbeth himself, he provides a casebook illustration of how *not* to succeed in establishing oneself as a new prince. He assassinates Duncan, but fails to extinguish the rest of the line at the same time (and especially Malcolm, the formally recognized heir-apparent).[25] That is, Macbeth does not thoroughly and dispassionately reason out all of the injuries he must do to secure power – which would include killing not only Malcolm and Donalbain, but almost surely Banquo and perhaps Fleance as well – and then do them all at once, so that "being tasted less, they offend less" (whereas benefits ought to be done little by little so that they may be tasted better and longer, something every successful politician knows).[26] Moreover, Macbeth had the perfect opportunity for doing what was necessary, since he had them all housed together under his own roof, and thus at his mercy; as his dear wife puts it, "time and place ... have made themselves" (1.7.51–3). But he is troubled by his conscience (a dangerous stupidity, Machiavelli teaches), and thus that much more inclined to wishful thinking. He realizes that if it is to be done at all, and done completely, "then 'twere well it were done *quickly*." He is daunted, however, by the scale of what might be required. If only the assassination of Duncan alone "Could trammel up the consequence, and catch / With [its] surcease success; that but this blow" – a single ignoble act – "Might be the be-all and the *end*-all" (1–6). So, instead of engaging in cruelties "well-used" (by which Machiavelli means those done at once for the necessity of securing oneself, and which are afterward not continued, but are converted to the greatest possible utility of one's subjects), Macbeth temporizes, and thereby unwittingly commits himself to a course of actions that exemplifies "cruelty *badly* used."[27] The injuries he inflicts increase over time, with the result that his subjects grow increasingly desperate, and he becomes profoundly hated – one thing above all that a prince must avoid, according to Machiavelli.[28] In short, Macbeth becomes a tyrant. This word is not mentioned until the play is more than two-thirds over (3.6.22), but thereafter it is used more often than in any other of Shakespeare's plays, necessarily raising the question of what in essence tyranny truly is. It is a term conspicuously absent from *The Prince*. According to Machiavelli's discussion of Agathocles (his prime example of one who has 'Attained a Principality through Crimes,' and who would certainly qualify as a tyrant in most people's eyes, willing as he was to "kill [his] citizens, betray [his] friends, ... without faith, without mercy, without religion," a man of "savage cruelty and inhumanity," having commited "infinite crimes"), such 'tyranny' need not preclude political success.[29] So, why is Macbeth's bid to establish himself securely as sovereign prince such an abject failure?

The short answer has already been given: he went about it all wrong. But that simply raises the further question, why did he do so, given that he eventually shows himself fully capable of imitating the various crimes of Agathocles? To this, too, part of the answer has already been given: his initial lack of moral, or rather, immoral resolution; that is, his unwillingness, or inability, to commit himself whole-heartedly to doing *whatever* needed to be done to achieve success – well expressed by the person who knew him best:

– Yet I do fear thy nature:
It is too full o'th'milk of human kindness,
To catch the nearest way. Thou wouldst be great;

Art not without ambition, but without
The illness should attend it: what thou wouldst highly,
That wouldst thou holily; wouldst not play false,
And yet wouldst wrongly win; thou'dst have, great Glamis,
That which cries, 'Thus thou must do,' if thou have it;
And that which rather thou dost fear to do,
Than wishest should be undone.

(1.5.16–25)[30]

Eventually, having "in blood stepp'd in so far, that ... returning were as tedious as go o'er" (3.4.135–7), Macbeth acquires the resolution to wade on, come what come may. By then, however, it is too late; the political damage done cannot be undone. It was a matter of timing. Failing to lay to rest his moral reservations (or whatever) straight from the outset, he should have abstained from any attempt to become prince. That he did not see this himself points to his second serious limitation.

Macbeth seems singularly incapable of sound practical reasoning. For all his higher ponderings, there is scant evidence of his making solid connections between his theoretical reflections and his everyday affairs. In the first place, he evidently has not bestowed on political life the thoughtful attention it deserves, not having recognized what Machiavelli saw so clearly: that for all practical purposes, politics can be treated as a realm distinct unto itself, presenting problems every bit as perplexing as those posed by the heavens, and operating largely according to principles neither derivative from things higher nor reducible to things lower. Accordingly, Macbeth lacks prudential judgment. Lacking that perspicacity to discern the general principles at work in particular situations, and consequently unable to apply them himself, he has only a most ordinary capacity to respond rationally to concrete practical difficulties. That is, to think a problem through, evaluate alternative solutions, consider various contingencies that might arise, anticipate the responses of other interested parties, plan for each possible eventuality, and see clearly how it is to be finally resolved.[31] Every time Macbeth attempts to plot some action, he bungles it; he evidently needs what Machiavelli offers Lorenzo, namely, himself as political adviser.[32] Macbeth's only adviser, however, is Lady Macbeth, and she is no Machiavelli.

Simply consider the plan she and he concoct for killing Duncan without the blame falling on them: do it when he is asleep, besmear his drugged chamberlains with blood so that they will be blamed, and appear to grieve deeply when the murder is discovered. And should anyone doubt their version, just brazen it out (1.7.62–80). No thought given to credible motivation on the chamberlains' part, nor to why anyone truly guilty would remain at the murder site "Steep'd in the colours of their trade, their daggers / Unmannerly breech'd with gore" (and conveniently lying upon their pillows, no less; 2.2.47–56; 2.3.101–2, 113–14), nor to doing the job completely (for with Malcolm already named Prince of Cumberland and thus heir-apparent, the crown would devolve upon him, not Macbeth).[33] Lady Macbeth apparently lacks sufficient skill for her self-assigned part in the affair, so overdosing the grooms that they are still in a stupor when awakened. We may presume that their having been drugged was so obvious – "they star'd, and were distracted" (2.3.102) – that Macbeth, feigning impetuous rage, was obliged to kill them before they could be interrogated. At any rate, his doing so was not in the plan as we heard it discussed, and it *is* a suspect thing to do, as Macduff's reaction indicates (as also, perhaps, does Lady Macbeth's fainting; 105, 116). Their scheme succeeds only by chance, the timely flight of Malcolm and Donalbain allowing "suspicion of the deed" to be put upon them, thereby compromising Malcolm's claim to succeed his father (2.4.24–7). Add to this the subsequent failure of Macbeth's own design for eliminating both Banquo and his son Fleance, followed by the escape of Macduff, and one can begin to appreciate why he finally despairs of rational planning, vowing to become what might be called 'conscientiously impulsive': "From this moment, / The very firstlings of my heart shall be / The firstlings of my hand" (4.1.146–8).

In short, Macbeth is a strange combination of the contemplative and the impetuous, which may partly explain why we find him so fascinating, intrigued by what he says, appalled by what he does. Because he lacks the prudential judgment to bridge his inner life of reflection and outer realm of action, his frame of things is disjointed and "both the worlds suffer."[34]

Much more could be remarked along these lines, applying Machiavellian prudential analysis to the actions of other characters, and in assessing what actually results. One might reflect on the case of Banquo, for example, who shows how he who helps another to become powerful ruins himself, and why anyone who is perceived to have some "royalty of nature" will sooner or later become suspect to him whom he has assisted.[35] Whereas in Malcolm, who ultimately succeeds in becoming prince, we see demonstrated the right combination of "the fox and the lion," and that "the one who has known best how to use the fox has come out best" (Macbeth relying too much upon the lion; cf. 1.2.35).[36] Having been dispossessed of the princedom of which he was recognized to be the legitimate heir, Malcolm prudently escapes into exile and bides his time, awaiting an opportune moment to return.[37] Unlike Duncan, he is not easily beguiled by appearances, as shown by his elaborate testing of Macduff (4.3.114–20). Although his army is what Machiavelli would have called 'mixed,' Malcolm does command in the field himself, with the foreign contingent being led by a trustworthy member of his own family[38] (5.6.1–6). Especially noteworthy is his pronouncement in the moment of triumph: "We shall not spend a large expense of time, / Before we reckon with your several loves, / And make us even with you." (5.9.26–8). *Even*, notice, not publicly indebted and therefore obliged to anyone (this, too, in marked contrast with his father's behaviour in the wake of victory; 1.4.14–21).

Indeed, one could learn such 'Machiavellian wisdom' (and more) on one's own simply through abstracting the general principles implicit in this concrete portrayal of them. Lady Macduff offers a virtual précis of Machiavelli's central teaching:

> Whither should I fly?
> I have done no harm. But I remember now
> I am in this earthly world, where, to do harm
> Is often laudable; to do good, sometime
> Accounted dangerous folly: why then, alas!
> Do I put up that womanly defense,
> To say, I have done no harm?
> (4.2.72–8)[39]

Ironic, that this stay-at-home mother understands more clearly than her warrior husband that, in this earthly world, foul actions can sometimes be fair and fair ones foul.

Still, it might be objected, Shakespeare obviously does not himself subscribe to the amoral political principles of Machiavelli, for *Macbeth* is a highly moral play. It depicts the treacherous assassination of "a most sainted king" – as Macduff calls him (4.3.109), and Macbeth would seem to agree, worrying that Duncan's "virtues / Will plead like angels, trumpet-tongu'd, against / The deep damnation of his taking off" (1.7.18–20) – a saintly and beneficent king murdered by a pair of cold-blooded usurpers whose only motivation is selfish gain, but who are progressively drawn ever deeper into a morass of evil, who live increasingly tormented lives, and who soon come to a bad end. Good triumphs, and crime is shown not to pay. The play offers a most reassuring answer to the comprehensive question it addresses, namely, what kind of world do we live in? Is human life really (as it seems to the harried Macbeth nearing the end of his tether) "a tale told by an idiot, full of sound and fury, signifying nothing"? That is, incoherent, chaotic, pointless, futile. 'No,' the play as a whole would have us believe; it merely *seems* that way to someone who has destroyed for himself the *ground* of life's meaning and intelligibility.[40] Thus, beware of doing so. *Beware* of living by an amoral Machiavellianism in the service of nothing higher than one's own vanity. And in the final analysis, I believe this interpretation of the play to be correct.

In fairness, however, that 'final analysis' must take into account a couple of the play's other characters, seemingly minor, but who are the keys to its deeper understanding, and who do not allow for quite such a facile dismissal of Machiavellian means to selfish ends. I have in mind "The worthy Thane of Rosse" (as he is introduced by young Malcolm in response to Duncan's "Who comes here?" 1.2.46), and the even more shadowy Lenox (whose name is never mentioned by anyone) – the only two characters who enjoy continuous good fortune throughout the play. Their first speeches function in ironic counterpoint. Malcolm having introduced Rosse, Lenox observes, "What a haste looks through his eyes! So should he look / That seems to speak things strange." And Rosse does say some things that, viewed in retrospect, seem strange indeed, including perhaps the first words he utters: "God save the King!" (1.2.47–8).

So far as the plot is concerned, Rosse is the more important of the two. Still, young Lenox's role is far from negligible. For example, the anonymous messenger who attempts to warn Lady Macduff is almost surely either Lenox or someone sent by Lenox (and given this "homely man's" careful protection of his identity, probably Lenox himself; 4.2.64–72). We can deduce this from the following textual facts. Lenox is present near the Pit of Acheron when Macbeth, learning that Macduff has escaped to England, vows to act upon the very firstlings of his heart, and thereupon announces his vengeful intention to surprise Macduff's castle and "give to th'edge o'th'sword / His wife, his babes, and all unfortunate souls / That trace him in his line" (4.1.146–53).[41] And although Lenox is still in attendance on Macbeth, and dutifully reports the vital news of Macduff's whereabouts brought by the hard-riding messengers, he is no longer loyal to him. For Lenox already knew of Macduff's mission to England, having learned of it in the course of an earlier, apparently conspiratorial conversation with "another Lord" (in which Lenox first refers to Macbeth as a tyrant, and satirizes his versions of the killings of Duncan and Banquo; 3.6.1–22).[42] While at the time of that conversation we could not be sure that Lenox was not an agent of Macbeth charged with ferreting out this valuable information, his evident failure to pass it on makes his position clear in retrospect. Moreover, in the subsequent scene of several Scottish lords en route to meet Malcolm and his English army, Lenox proves that he is in secret communication with Malcolm's party, he alone knowing precisely who is and is not accompanying the invading host (5.2.8–11). Consequently, he is also the most likely source of Malcolm's intelligence about Macbeth's forces (5.4.10–14).

The primary significance of Lenox, however, lies in the contrast he provides for purposes of evaluating Rosse. For both men show comparable Machiavellian 'flexibility,' always on the side (and frequently *at* the side) of whoever is winning – first Duncan, then Macbeth, then Malcolm. Yet once one understands their respective contributions to the events depicted in the play, one's evaluations of them are sure to differ profoundly. In trying to account for *why* one despises Rosse, but not Lenox, one has the opportunity to learn something quite important about the nature of the human soul – about what it finds naturally attractive and what naturally repugnant – if, that is, one agrees that no amount of worldly success Rosse might achieve by his means could possibly make him admirable or enviable.

Uncovering the truth about Rosse entails a labyrinthine exploration of the play. One might pick up the thread amid the confusion following Duncan's murder, for there is a peculiar detail of that early morning scene, seemingly minor, but all the more puzzling for that. Macduff, whether by chance, choice, or necessity, was not billeted in the castle, but had nonetheless been commanded by the King "to call timely on him." Accompanied by young Lenox, he arrives for this purpose, and is greeted by a noticeably laconic Macbeth who shows him the way to the King's chamber. Shortly thereafter, having discovered the dead Duncan, Macduff returns in great passion, and beckons the waiting Macbeth and Lenox to view the horrible sight for themselves. As he proceeds to awaken the rest of the castle, they leave to do so (2.3.70–3). But when moments later they return, they are accompanied (according to the Folio's stage directions) by *Rosse*. Where, we are meant to wonder, did *he* come from?[43] In revisiting the preceding scene, we must presume him to have been one of those lying in the second chamber that Macbeth asks his wife about as he "descended" after murdering Duncan. Recall, he tells her, "There's one did laugh in's sleep, and one cried 'Murther!' / That they did wake each other: I stood and heard them; / But they did say their prayers, and address'd them / Again to sleep" (2.2.22–5). In response to his query, Lady Macbeth mentions only Donalbain as sleeping in the second chamber, and may mistakenly believe (along with most viewers and readers, it would seem) that the conversation Macbeth recounts took place between the King's chamberlains, who she earlier feared might have awakened despite her having doped their night-drinks (1, 9). But this construal cannot be correct. Macbeth already knew about *them* and where they were sleeping; they figure directly in his plan. Moreover, judging from Lenox's report, they were still drugged when forcibly awakened after the discovery of Duncan's murder, seemingly unable to focus either their eyes or their minds: "they star'd and were distracted." Presuming them to be deranged, Lenox adds, "No man's life was to be trusted with them," thereby attempting to explain Macbeth's precipitous killing of them (2.3.102–3).[44] Hence, one may assume that Rosse, dutiful courtier, was also sleeping in the second chamber with Donalbain, and that it was these two who awoke and whose conversation and prayers Macbeth overheard.[45] Consequently, we cannot exclude the possibility of Rosse's knowing more about the assassination of Duncan than he lets on in any scenes *we* are privy to (cf. 2.2.27). Be that as it may, his mysterious – and silent – entrance at his point ought to arouse one's curiosity about him, prompting a review of his other appearances in the play. It does not disappoint.

Start with what turn out to be "things strange" in his first report to King Duncan. Although he enters in company with Angus, apparently he alone attracts notice. This could be an oversight on Malcolm's part; or it could have been intentionally managed by Rosse, wishing to put himself forward as the principal bearer of glad tidings. It would not be the only time he does so. More to the point, why the ambiguity in his speaking of the hero who saved the day at Fife (Macduff's seat; 2.4.36; 4.1.150–1), referring to him only as "Bellona's bridegroom"? Almost everyone, apparently including Duncan, assumes he means Macbeth, but this turns out to be most unlikely. If there *is* a misidentification here, is it merely incidental to Rosse's penchant for ornate but unclear speech? Or does he have some reason for creating confusion as to this champion's identity? Moreover, Rosse is the only person who seems to know anything very definite about Cawdor's part in the rebellions and invasions with which the play begins (claiming that the traitorous Thane openly collaborated with Sweno, Norway's King; 1.2.53–4). This is in marked contrast to Angus, who despite having accompanied Rosse from Fife and then to the site of Cawdor's condemnation, expressly denies knowing just what Cawdor's treason consisted of:

> Whether he was combin'd
> With those of Norway, or did line the rebel [i.e., Macdonwald]
> With hidden help and vantage, or that with both
> He labour'd in his country's wrack, I know not;
> But treasons capital, confess'd and prov'd,
> Have overthrown him.
>
> (1.3.111–16)

How does Rosse know what Angus does not? The fact that Angus heard the account Rosse gave Duncan but *still* professes ignorance himself only makes his disclaimer more emphatic – and Rosse's cognizance more curious. Might Rosse have been on the periphery of Cawdor's conspiracy, prudently avoiding active involvement while awaiting its outcome?

When he, along with Angus, is commissioned by Duncan to "go pronounce [Cawdor's] present death, / And with his former title greet Macbeth," Rosse once again takes upon himself the announcing of the good news to this man whose star is on the rise. Moreover, he prefaces the King's brief message with a twelve-line sychophantic speech that not only goes well beyond anything Duncan authorized him to say, but which actually misrepresents the facts as we saw them

(1.3.89–100). Angus, notice, intervenes in an attempt to restrain Rosse's effusive praise, seeing it as inappropriate to their assigned role: "We are sent, / To give thee from our royal master thanks; / Only to herald thee into his sight, / Not pay thee." Rosse, however, is not to be denied the full profit of their commission, saying, "And, for an earnest of a greater honour, / He bade me, from him, call thee Thane of Cawdor: / To which addition, hail, most worthy Thane, / For it is thine." But Duncan had said nothing about a still *greater* honour, for which the thaneship of Cawdor was mere down-payment. What is Rosse up to? Notice also, Macbeth at this point remains unaware that Cawdor is anything other than "a prosperous gentleman" (108) – making it highly unlikely that it was *he* who, "lapp'd in proof," confronted Cawdor on the battlefield, "rebellious arm 'gainst arm, curbing his lavish spirit"[46] (1.2.55–8). Whoever did, managed to take Cawdor alive (in marked contrast to Macbeth's treatment of Macdonwald, who was "unseam'd" and beheaded without so much as a 'yield or die') and so could scarcely be ignorant of Cawdor's status.

We next hear Rosse speak in conversation with a superstitious Old Man about the unusually dreadful weather during the night of Duncan's murder (2.4.1–10ff). Rosse's initial contribution to the Old Man's catalogue of extraordinary happenings is easily accepted, though his own characterization of it seems inflated: that normally well-behaved horses might be panicked by a storm powerful enough to blow down chimneys (see 2.3.54), far from being "a thing most strange," is altogether plausible. However, when the Old Man reports the rumour he heard: "'Tis said, they eat each other," Rosse replies in a manner that would arouse suspicion of his veracity in anyone less credulous than his immediate interlocutor: "They did so; to th'amazement of mine eyes, / That look'd upon't." Now, are we to believe that Rosse actually saw Duncan's horses *eat each other*? It is not unlikely that confined animals thrashing about in a panic fear might also fight among themselves; and horses bite when they fight – a probable basis for the rumour. But what are we to think about Rosse? That this polished, articulate courtier (simply consider his first two speeches in this scene) is actually as credulous as the Old Man? Or have we here more evidence of his ability to adapt himself to any social situation, and enjoy himself while doing so?[47] Whatever the case, their amusing or bemusing conversation is interrupted by the arrival of Macduff. Rosse's questions to his cousin – about who is believed to have slain Duncan, where he is to be buried, and who has succeeded to the Kingship – suggest that, despite the general agreement, he declined to "meet i'th'hall together" with the others, there to "question this most bloody piece of work" (2.3.125–32). Did he (once again?) keep himself on the periphery of the action until the dust had settled and he could see clearly how things had fallen out? Upon learning that Macbeth has already left for Scone to be invested, Rosse declares his intention to follow him there – in dramatic contrast to the sceptical Macduff, who expressly declines to attend Macbeth's coronation in favour of returning home to Fife (2.4.35–8).

One of the more curious happenings in the play is Rosse's visit to Macduff's castle just prior to the arrival of Macbeth's murder squad. From what we see of his conversation with Lady Macduff, there is no clear purpose to this visit. Macduff is away petitioning Malcolm in England, perhaps at Banquo's urging. For Macbeth's former co-captain has clearly become uneasy about the course events are taking: "Thou hast it now, King, Cawdor, Glamis, all, / As the Weyward Women promis'd; and, I fear, / Thou play'dst most foully for't" (3.1.1–3). Doubtless he is aware of what we can surmise from Macbeth's conversation with the two prospective murderers: that Macbeth's rule thus far has been one of increasing rapacity[48] (76–89; cf. 4.3.57–9). Compromised though Banquo may be by his own involvement in the witches' prophecies (thus his passive complicity in Macbeth's usurpation), he is not without a sense of honour and justice (see 2.1.25–9). Moreover, Macbeth credits him with a "royalty of nature" and "a wisdom that doth guide his valour / To act in safety" (3.1.49–53). Accordingly, Banquo may have intuited Macbeth's fearful suspicion of him, and prudently begun to conceal his own actions. When accosted prior to setting out on his last fateful ride, his replies to Macbeth's queries are evasive (leaving the impression that he is riding just "to fill up the time 'twixt this and supper"). Nevertheless, they are substantial enough to suggest that he has some definite destination in mind, since he knows approximately how long it should take, depending on how his horses hold up (24–7). Might he be riding over to Fife from Scone to have a chat with Macduff?

Be that as it may, Banquo's "Dear Duff" (2.3.87) is not at Macbeth's great feast that night (3.4.127–9) and has since gone south in a hurry – "without leave-taking" of his wife, hence, without informing her of his mission or giving her any special instructions about putting their castle in a state of defensive readiness. As a result, she presumes he simply fled in fear for his life, leaving his family to fend for themselves "in a place from whence himself does fly" (4.2.6–7). Doing so was "madness" in her view (and Malcolm is inclined to agree, contributing to his initial suspicion of Macduff; 4.3.25–8.). In the face of her denunciation of her husband, however, Rosse counsels her to "have patience," and simply trust in her lord's wisdom. He then prepares to leave, adding, "Shall not be long but I'll be here again. / Things at the worst will cease" (4.2.22–5). However, noting with a blessing his "pretty cousin" (the Macduffs' pert young son), he adds, rather enigmatically – might it be the one trace of genuine sentiment he shows in the play? – "I am so much the fool, should I stay longer, / It would be my disgrace and your discomfort: / I take my leave at once." So he does. Again, we are not told why he came, but we can see what in practical terms his advice amounts to: don't worry, sit tight and do nothing – this in dramatic contrast to the anonymous "homely man's advice" given shortly thereafter: "Be not found here; hence, with your little ones" (67–8). Even were Lady Macduff inclined to heed it, however, this warning comes too late, for within moments Macbeth's murderers arrive and the killing begins. Recall, it was at the end of the scene immediately preceding that Macbeth had vowed, "The castle of Macduff I will surprise." The one thing vital to the success of a surprise attack upon a castle is precise knowledge of the state of its defences. And who better to garner such intelligence than a trusted kinsman, someone who can easily gain entrance and see for himself?

Arguably the *most* curious feature of the whole play, however, is the pair of contradictory reports that Rosse, freshly arrived in England, provides Macduff concerning the condition of his family. His apprehension perhaps stimulated by Rosse's evocative description of the general suffering back in Scotland, Macduff asks, "How does my wife?"

> *Rosse:* Why, well.
> *Macduff:* And all my children?
> *Rosse:* Well too.
> *Macduff:* The tyrant has not batter'd at their peace?
> *Rosse:* No; they were well at peace, when I did leave 'em.
> (4.3.176–9)

Yet a moment later, and without any further inquiry from Macduff, Rosse is suddenly moved to announce, "But I have words, / That would be howl'd out in the desert air, / Where hearing could not latch them." His cousin's anxious curiosity aroused as to whom this awful message concerns, he replies, "No mind that's honest [!] / But in it shares some woe, though the main part / Pertains to you alone" (193–9). Warning Macduff to brace himself for what he is sure to find uniquely appalling, Rosse now reports:

> Your castle is surpris'd; your wife, and babes,
> Savagely slaughter'd: to relate the manner,
> Were, on the quarry of these murther'd deer,
> To add the death of you.
> (204–7)

What accounts for this, his first placidly assuring Macduff that his family is safe, only to turn right around and present him with "the heaviest sound" his ears ever heard? Was it just that Rosse initially lacked the courage to tell Macduff the awful truth, but then somehow found sufficient resolve to do so? Is that credible, given that he has travelled all the way from Scotland for the very purpose of soliciting Macduff, this knowledge locked in his breast and knowing full well that he must deal with it one way or another? Would not anyone faced with Rosse's mission have thought through this problem many times, rehearsing in his own mind what he intends to say and how? So, suppose Rosse did so, too. But what if, in the event, he met with a situation wholly unexpected, some development that changed everything, as it were? Let us look, then, at precisely what intervenes between Rosse's contrary accounts.

Macduff's anxiety assuaged by hearing that his family "were well at peace" when Rosse last left them, the conversation turns back to the general state of affairs in Scotland. Rosse reports a rumour to the effect that some active resistance to Macbeth is surfacing, provoking new efforts of suppression, and that what is needed is a great warrior chieftain – namely, Macduff – to galvanize full-scale rebellion: "Now is the time of help. Your eye in Scotland / Would create soldiers, make our women fight, / To doff their dire distresses" (182–8). At this point, Malcolm responds with what he presumes will be comforting news: *both* he and Macduff *are* returning, but not alone; at their backs will be ten thousand English soldiers, led by the best, most experienced general in Christendom, Malcolm's uncle Siward. It is upon learning *this* that Rosse spontaneously offers his second version of the fate of Macduff's family, an account which, though not noticeable at the time, somehow seems strangely detailed and exact: "to relate the manner" (how does he know the manner?); "Wife, children, servants, all that could be found" (not "all that they could find" – a more natural way to describe results of what others have done, seen after the fact, or of what one has merely heard about). Is there not a nuance of complicity, the slightest betrayal of a participant's perspective, in Rosse's mode of expression? Was it indeed "not long" until he returned to Macduff's castle – just long enough to have conveyed the vital intelligence to the awaiting attackers? Did he himself make sure "all that could be found" – all witnesses – were eternally "well at peace" before he "did leave 'em"? Be that as it may, the circumstances under which he belatedly reveals what he knew all along to be the fate of Macduff's family obliges one to consider ulterior motives for his doing so. A plausible one is not hard to find. He has just learned that the jig is up for Macbeth, and that it is time for a prudent man to change sides.

In light of that possiblity, one can re-evaluate his purpose for coming to England in the first place. Ostensibly, Rosse arrives already opposed to Macbeth, eloquent in his depiction of Scotland's suffering, and bent on recruiting Macduff to lead a rebellion against the usurper. But we learned earlier from Malcolm's careful testing of Macduff that "Devilish Macbeth by many of these trains" – that is, sending some pretended opponent of Macbeth to persuade Malcolm to return – "hath sought to win me / Into his power, and modest wisdom plucks me / From an over-credulous haste" (117–20).[49] Perhaps we ought to aspire to such modest wisdom as well, and ask whether now Macbeth, his natural fear of Macduff having been supernaturally amplified at the Pit of Acheron (4.1.71–4), is not trying the same strategem with the Thane of Fife, employing for the purpose someone seemingly above suspicion: Macduff's "ever-gentle cousin" Rosse (as Macduff greets him; 4.3.161). With Macduff's being assured that his family is still safely in possession of his castle, he would mistakenly believe that he is not especially sought after, that he retains a personal stake in the health of his country, and that he has a secure place to which to return.

Still, a question would remain: why does Rosse not simply persist in his first response to Macduff's anxious inquiry, and continue to pretend ignorance of what has actually happened to the Macduff household? Why does his changing sides necessitate his setting the record straight? It must be that someone back in Scotland knows that he knows, and that there is a strong chance it will subsequently be revealed that he was possessed of the truth all along. Having made the return trek to Scotland in company with Macduff and Malcolm, what excuse could he then provide for not earlier owning up to what he knew? If he must come clean sooner or later, then the sooner the better. Moreover, the risk of exposure would be all the more acute if that cognizant person back home is someone likely to survive the ensuing war for the throne. A woman, say. "The Thane of Fife had a wife: where is she now?" How did Lady Macbeth learn about what happened to Lady Macduff? Who provided her this knowledge that only torments her? It may be the thought that more than any other precipitates her madness, the foremost "rooted sorrow" Macbeth wishes plucked from her memory that she might be cured (5.3.40–1). As this atrocity is not the sort of deed a warrior is apt to boast about, or expect to have "applauded" (see 3.2.46), report of it is unlikely to have come from Macbeth himself. Might it have come, then, from some sleek courtier who secretly does not wish her well, perhaps because she dislikes him and so treats him with scant respect (cf. 3.4.51–2, 115–16)? Rosse, of course, had no way of knowing that she would kill herself.

Now, taking all this circumstantial evidence into account, who most likely is the mysterious Third Murderer? In light of this verdict, Rosse's reply to Macbeth at the infamous banquet is not merely more of his sychophancy, but partakes of – if not surpasses – Macbeth's own black irony:

> Here had we now our country's honour roof'd,
> Were the grac'd person of our Banquo present;

> Who may I rather challenge for unkindness,
> Than pity for mischance!
> *Rosse:* His absence, Sir,
> Lays blame upon his promise.
> (3.4.39–43)

Rosse's story may have still more to it, but it is especially important to consider how it ends, with him accompanying Malcolm back to Scotland at the head of a winning army, and toasting the new king in victory.[50] Far from being counted among "the cruel ministers of this dead butcher" (5.9.34), his timely switch in allegiance results in his being elevated to earl along with the other thanes who supported Malcolm. Reflecting upon this outcome, one sees that Rosse is an essential element in Shakespeare's assessment of Machiavellians in political life. They do *not* all get their just come-uppance, as do Lord and Lady Macbeth, at least not in this world. There *are* people like Rosse – ever careful to maintain the proper public face, hence seemingly compassionate, loyal, honest, humane, and above all pious ("God save the King"; cf. 2.4.5–6);[51] adept at subtle flattery (see 5.9.5–13), and at drawing out others while never revealing anything important about themselves; shrewd judges of ever-changing circumstances, thus able always to stay one step ahead of the game[52] – and some of them can be successful in exploiting the vicissitudes of life, at least according to their own lights. Shakespeare apparently believes it important that his more philosophical readers, those for whom the truth is the primary concern, confront this unpleasant fact. But he leaves it to each of us to judge for ourselves whether Rosse's way of life, bereft of all human attachments and of any accomplishment beyond comfortable survival, turns out to have any more meaning than does Macbeth's, or whether it too is not a tale told by an idiot, signifying nothing – a prospect that disturbs Macbeth almost to the point of fury (cf. 5.5.49–52), but which one can imagine Rosse accepting with a shrug of indifference.

Beyond that, we are obliged to see for ourselves the means whereby we make these evaluations. What power of judgment or recognition must humans possess in order so confidently to rank Rosse well below Lenox? This latter is also a 'survivor' who strictly subordinates romantic sentiment to practicality (note his droll response to Cathness's suggestion that, along with Malcolm, "pour we, in our country's purge, each drop of us." Lenox: "Or as much as it needs" 5.2.28–9). But Lenox's Machiavellian duplicity is in the service of something besides just his own survival and prospering, and it this that we approve: his endowing his survival with some purpose beyond itself.[53] Whether Lenox also ranks higher than young Siward, who knowingly risks what eventuates: the sacrifice of himself in pursuit of that same honourable purpose, the defeat and overthrow of this tyrant, is less clear. Perplexing though that issue may be, what does our admiration of nobility per se – expressed as strongly in our regret at seeing it abused and corrupted as in our delight at seeing it victorious or distress at seeing it suffer – what does this tell us about ourselves, about our distinctly human longing for, and appreciation of, something higher in life than mere survival? Nothing that one might imagine happening to Shakespeare's Rosse (and this Rosse is almost entirely his invention, being scarce more than a name in Holinshed) could strike us as tragic. On this point, there can be no real doubt where Shakespeare himself stands. His own creative efforts are the clearest repudiation of the sterility of Rosse's life, regardless of whatever social acceptance and success he might enjoy. Anyone who agrees that Shakespeare aspired to bequeath works of lasting value must see that his reasons for doing so transcend the narrow calculations of self-interest and worldly success that circumscribe the moral horizon of Rosse, though not necessarily of Machiavelli.

No attempt to view the Scotland of *Macbeth* through Florentine eyes would be complete, however, without some attention paid to the matter of religion. Ostensibly, this Scotland is Christian. Macduff, whom we may presume to be more or less representative in this respect, speaks of the King as if divinely anointed, and of his murder as not merely treasonous, but "most sacrilegious" (2.3.66–7). He later refers to Duncan in death as "a most sainted King," and recalls his Queen to have been so assiduous in prayer that she was "oft'ner upon her knees than on her feet" (4.3.109–10). Macbeth also, though contemplating regicide, refers without any evident disdain to Duncan's distinctly Christian virtues, that they "Will plead like angels ... against the deep damnation of his taking off," and that accordingly "Pity ... shall blow the horrid deed in every eye" (1.7.16–24). Christian allusions and formulae are apparent commonplaces ("Golgotha," "In the great hand of God I stand," "God be with you," "the sin of my ingratitude," "God save the King," and so on), including in the speeches of the Macbeths: she refers to Heaven and what is holy even while invoking the powers of Hell and darkness (1.5.21, 53); he also speaks of both Heaven and Hell (2.1.64; 3.1.141), and bitterly of having given his "eternal jewel ... to the common Enemy of man" (68–9). Macbeth reports that the sleepers of the second chamber who awoke while he was murdering Duncan "did say their prayers, and address'd them again to sleep," but that he himself could not add "'Amen,' when they did say 'God bless us,'" despite his then feeling "most need of blessing" (2.2.23–32). So, there can be little doubt that the Christian perspective is the generally recognized and respected one.

However, it is also beyond doubt that this Christianity does not uniformly run deep, and that competing pagan views persist alongside it, or are interwoven with it. As noted, Lady Macbeth fervently petitions "spirits" that tend on mortal thoughts and wait on Nature's mischief (i.e., *not* the Devil's). Her lord, listening for the bell that will summon him to the killing of Duncan, muses how at night "witchcraft celebrates pale Hecate's off'rings" (2.1.51–2), and speaks of "the shard-born beetle" as her agent (3.2.41–2). Under stress, he readily resorts to pagan folk adages:

> It will have blood, they say: blood will have blood:
> Stones have been known to move, and trees to speak;
> Augures, and understood relations, have
> By magot-pies, and choughs, and rooks, brought forth
> The secret'st man of blood.
>
> (3.4.121–5)

Persuaded that the Weyward Sisters do indeed "have more in them than mortal knowledge," Macbeth willingly resorts to them even though he must recognize theirs to be heathen practices (3.4.131). Other characters show that they, too, are less than thoroughly Christianized.[54] The Old Man bids farewell to Rosse with a conventional blessing ("God's benison go with you" 2.4.40); yet his interpreting unusual avian behaviour as a sign presaging "the deed that's done" suggests a mind more in tune with a pre-Christian view of nature. Even Macduff's arsenal of images includes the odd paganism ("and destroy your sight with a new Gorgon" 2.3.70–1). More to the point, though, is his reaction upon learning that Macbeth has slaughtered his family: how quickly and thoroughly he jettisons the Christian principles of forgiveness and 'love thine enemy' in favour of Malcolm's ethos of revenge (4.3.213–15, 230–5; see also 5.2.3). By the time Macduff finally meets Macbeth on the battlefield, pleas to Heaven have been supplanted by prayers to Fortune (5.7.22–3).

Thus, one is obliged to conclude that Medieval Scotland is at most semi-Christian.[55] Now, is that good or bad? The obvious answer is that it is bad, that this Scotland is such a bleak, violent, superstition-ridden place precisely because it is not sufficiently Christianized – simply compare it with the greater refinement and decency of more solidly Christian England, with its miracle-working king (Edward the Confessor) whose heavenly touch cures that disease so poignantly called 'the Evil.' Moreover, according to Malcolm who has been sojourning there for some indefinite but (we must presume) lengthy period of time, "With this strange virtue, / He hath a heavenly gift of prophecy; / And sundry blessings hang about his throne, / That speak him full of grace" (4.3.141–59).[56] That Macbeth despises England as soft and over-refined, derisively dismissing those who "mingle with the English epicures" (5.3.8), would seem only to confirm the superiority of the English regime, including its religious foundation. So, too, the barely veiled contempt he shows for Christian ethics when conversing with the two embittered desperadoes he is recruiting to ambush Banquo:

> Do you find
> Your patience so predominant in your nature,
> That you can let this go? Are you so gospell'd,
> To pray for this good man, and for his issue,
> Whose heavy hand hath bow'd you to the grave,
> And beggar'd yours for ever?
>
> (3.1.85–90)

Further reflection, however, raises doubts as to whether it is a deficiency of good Christian feeling that is Scotland's real problem.

Perhaps it would be best to pose the question in more general terms: what does the play as a whole suggest about the political consequences of the various characters' religiosity (or lack of same)? The most instructive case may well be that of Macduff. His piety certainly seems genuine, being the basis of his loyal, almost worshipful devotion to Duncan. Macduff trusts in God, that God is just and merciful, and accordingly looks after the good, the poor, the innocent – all those that do no harm. Likely it is his view that is voiced by his young son to Lady Macduff: that poor birds are provided for by the bounty of God (4.2.32–6), a clear enough allusion to the Gospel of *Matthew*: "Behold the fowls of the air: for they sow not, neither do they reap, nor gather into barns; yet your heavenly Father feedeth them. Are ye not much better than they?" (6:26). Macduff (and we) are soon set right on that score, however. Initially, he is shocked at learning that all his "pretty chickens, and their dam" have been slaughtered "at one fell swoop" of a Hell-kite: "Did Heaven look on, / And would not take their part?" Without further thought, he blames himself: "Sinful Macduff! / They were all struck for thee. Naught that I am, / Not for their own demerits, but for mine, / Fell slaughter on their souls" (4.3.216–27). Ironically, he is right, but not for the reason he intends: that God makes innocent parties suffer as a means of punishing guilty ones who love them – attributing to God a view of justice not essentially different from that of the First Witch, who boasts that she will torment the sailor husband in retaliation for his wife's refusal to share her chestnuts (1.3.4–10). Macduff's real sin is his culpable naïveté in trusting divine Providence to do what is properly the work of rational prudence backed by courage.[57] As noted above, his wife is a good deal more realistic about conditions in "this earthly world" (4.2.74–6). He should have consulted with her.[58]

But is not the lesson Macduff learns writ large in the play as a whole? Duncan may have borne his faculties with exemplary Christian meekness, but from all we are shown, the meek do *not* inherit the earth; the strong do.[59] God did *not* save the King, nor anyone else. Malcolm and Donalbain save themselves by dint of sound prudential reasoning (2.3.133–44); Fleance is saved by luck (perhaps along with some connivance of the First Murderer; see 3.3.19). And having justice on one's side is not enough – it is by no means irrelevant, as the eventual rebellion against Macbeth's injustices reminds us – but only if justice is sufficiently "with valour arm'd" will it prevail.[60] This basic political truth is first expressed by that anonymous bleeding captain who had fought to prevent Malcolm's capture (1.2.29). Whether it was heeded by Duncan, to whom it was emphatically addressed ("Mark, King of Scotland, mark"), it was not lost on his heir. From the moment he flees his country in the recognition that "there's no mercy left" (2.3.144), Malcolm seems a good deal more inspired by the *Old* Testament view of 'an eye for an eye' than by any teachings of the New. Notice the "comfort" he offers the bereaved Macduff: "Let's make us med'cines of our great *revenge*, / To cure this deadly grief." (4.3.213–15). It is later reported of him as of Macduff, "Revenges burn in them" (5.2.3). In his catalogue of twelve "king-becoming graces" (which fairly begs to be considered in light of Machiavelli's discussion of twelve "Things for which Men and Especially Princes Are Praised or Blamed"),[61] there is no mention of piety per se (4.3.91–4). As for the six virtuous characteristics he swears by "God above" describe *him*, they culminate in his "delight[ing] no less in truth, than life" (120–30).

The issues raised by the various religious (and irreligious) views manifested in the play – about Good and Evil, Right and Wrong, Life and Death, Freedom and Fate – point beyond politics, and can be resolved, if at all, only in light of a comprehensive understanding of the permanent nature of things, the embracing context in which all human living proceeds. Or so Shakespeare, differing perhaps from Machiavelli in this regard, seems to suggest.[62] Therefore, we must turn from a strictly political to a metaphysical consideration of the play.

THE METAPHYSICS OF MACBETH

Macbeth is the only work in the canon in which the word 'metaphysical' occurs. Once one begins to discern some of the play's larger themes, its singular occurrence there cannot be regarded as incidental; neither can the context in which it is introduced and the ideas that are immediately associated with it. Lady Macbeth is musing to herself in response to her lord's report of his strange encounter with those Weyward Sisters, who (he assures her) have "more in them than mortal knowledge." She wishes him speedily returned so that she may pour her spirits in his ear, and subdue his inner impediments to seizing the crown "which fate and metaphysical aid" so clearly seem to have reserved for him (1.5.26–30). Her wish is no sooner expressed than a servant announces, "our Thane is coming" – indeed, so hard and fast that the messenger bringing this news, "almost dead for breath," was barely able to outspeed him. When Duncan arrives with his entourage, he too draws our attention to the speed with which this victorious warrior returned to his wife's side: "We cours'd him at the heels, and had a purpose / To be his purveyor: but he rides well; / And his great love, sharp as his spur, hath holp him / To his home before us" (1.6.21–4; cf. 1.7.25). In this respect, the behaviour of the play's eponym is symbolic. For *Macbeth* is not only the shortest of Shakespeare's tragedies, it is generally acknowledged to be the most fast-paced. And haste suggests that time is of the essence.

The play repeatedly invites its readers to reflect on the basic features of the world in which we find ourselves, including what is distinctive about our own participation in it. It is seasoned from beginning to end with references to nature: to Nature as a whole, to the natures of species and of individuals, to the natural, the *un*natural, and – especially fitting, it would seem – to the *super*natural (Macbeth's characterizing the witches' greeting to him as "this supernatural soliciting" is one of only two uses of the term in the Shakespearean canon). Of special interest, of course, is the play's portrayal of *human* nature, as refracted in the natures of the various characters involved. The fact remains, however, one cannot adequately understand human nature (or natures) apart from some understanding of Nature as such. After all, the term, at least in its superficial meaning, is one of distinction: the natural, as distinct not only from the supernatural and the unnatural, but also from the artificial, from the merely conventional, from the accidental and arbitrary. Before one can truly begin to understand Nature, however, one must see it as a problem – one must become aware of what is *questionable* about the world of immediate experience, what is 'strange' about it (only in *The Tempest* is this word used more often than in *Macbeth*). There are several aspects to this problem of comprehending the world, and I believe the play touches on them all. But it suggests that the *ultimate* metaphysical or cosmological issue concerns how we are to understand the workings of Good and Evil in the natural order of things. And while *Macbeth* seems primarily focused on Evil, on "the instruments of Darkness," on "thick night," on "Night's black agents," on those "murth'ring ministers [that] wait on Nature's *mischief*," it nonetheless shows that the Good is more fundamental, that Evil is unintelligible except in light of the Good, and thus shows why one must see the Good as the ultimate source of *everything* – not simply of Right and Wrong, and Beauty and Ugliness, but of all Truth and Reality, all Knowledge and Intelligibility, even of Being itself.[63]

A tall order, to be sure. And how Shakespeare manages this is perhaps not altogether explicable. It is not difficult, however, to give some indication of the extent to which metaphysical issues pervade the play. Indeed, it begins with tacit reference to three of the most basic. Amid the flashing and clashing of lightning and thunder, "*Enter three* WITCHES" (as the Folio specifies):[64]

> *1st Witch:* When shall we three meet again?
> In thunder, lightning, or in rain?
> *2nd Witch:* When the hurlyburly's done,
> When the battle's lost and won.
> *3rd Witch:* That will be ere the set of sun.
> *1st Witch:* Where the place?
> *2nd Witch:* Upon the heath.
> *3rd Witch:* There to meet with ... Macbeth.

When ... When ... When: the question of Time. *Where the place*: the question of Space. Followed by the answer to an unasked but understood question: *Why*, for what Purpose: to meet Macbeth (which, as is typical, only gives rise to another 'why' question). Time, Space, Purpose. But there is a fourth metaphysical question *we* might wish to ask such strange-looking creatures were we to meet them on some blasted heath, as do Macbeth and Banquo. It is the very question *they* ask. First Banquo:

> – *What* are *these*,
> So wither'd and so wild in their attire,
> That look not like th'inhabitants o'th'earth,
> And yet are on it? Live you? or are you aught
> That man may question?

Then Macbeth: "Speak, if you can: – *what are you*?" (1.3.39–47). What, indeed! That is, what kind of *being* are they? Are they material? Moments later they vanish (as if "the earth hath bubbles, as the water has," according to Banquo; or as Macbeth puts it, "what seem'd corporal, melted as breath into the wind"; 79–82). Are they alive? Are they rational ("aught that man may *question*," and they speak in reply, perhaps explaining themselves)? But first and foremost, are they *real*? If not, *why* not? If so, *how* so? In either case, how can one be sure?

The opening scene, then, incorporates reminders of those essential ontological categories in terms of which we attempt to bring intelligible order out the chaotic flux of immediate experience: Time, Space, Purpose, Being.[65] One might in retrospect add Cause as well, for reflecting back on the play, one wonders whether these three weird and wayward Sisters are in fact the *cause* of anything. As Macbeth later challenges them, "How now, you secret, black, and midnight hags! What is't you *do*?" Their reply, like so many of their pronouncements, is ambiguous: "A deed without a name" (4.1.48–9). The only substantial information we can glean from their initial manifestation – that there is some sort of war going on – partakes of similar equivocality ("When the battle's lost and won"). So too their chant, which concludes this brief but supercharged opening scene: "Fair is foul, and foul is fair ..." – an oblique first reference to the play's (and life's) all-encompassing theme of Good versus Evil.[66]

The second scene, and the first in which appear beings we are sure are human, introduces several more of the metaphyical issues out of which the play is woven: Nature, Fortune, Justice, and Mortality. The first person to speak is the King, presumably recognizable as such by the conventional trappings of his office, and he too begins with a question. With the name 'Macbeth' perhaps still reverberating in the fog and filthy air, he asks, "What bloody man is that?" His son Malcolm, recognizing him whom the King is inquiring about to be "a good and hardy soldier" who helped rescue him from captivity, asks the wounded man for "knowledge of the broil." Whether the battle to which Malcolm refers is the same as that spoken of by the witches is not immediately clear; we soon learn there is more than one. Whatever the case, the gallant captain replies, "Doubtful it stood." Doubtful! An interesting word with which to begin, given that our philosopher-poet has chosen this character – a bleeding warrior of proven virtue – to be the first to mention either Nature or Fortune, doing so with pejorative overtones in both instances: he refers to "the merciless Macdonwald" upon whom "the multiplying villainies of nature do swarm," and then speaks of "Fortune, on his damned quarrel smiling, / Show'd like a rebel's whore" (1.2.10–14). It is also into his mouth that Shakespeare has placed the first reference to Justice, more precisely, "justice ... with valour arm'd" (29). And there is scarcely a sentence he utters that does not remind us of Mortality.

As for the problem that perhaps more than any other gives rise to metaphysical speculation, namely, the relationship – especially the frequent *discrepancy* – between Appearance and Reality, this pervasive issue is represented in the play primarily by its most taxing manifestation: in human beings. The problem is introduced, however, in connection with the three creatures whose humanity – indeed, whose very reality – is at issue: those wither'd, wild-attired, choppy-fingered, skinny-lipped, bearded but otherwise womanish beings of whom Banquo asks, "I'th'name of truth, / Are ye fantastical, or that indeed / Which *outwardly* ye *show*?" (1.3.52–4). Not that it takes an encounter with witches to start one wondering. Every competent person soon learns that often things are not what they seem. King Duncan finds Macbeth's castle at Inverness a pleasant sight; and the air about it "nimbly and sweetly recommends itself unto [his] gentle senses." His senses deceive him. Nor is Banquo's evidence that "the heaven's breath smells wooingly here" to be relied upon (1.6.1–10). In fact, on almost any credible philosophic or scientific analysis, our immediate perceptions of reality virtually *never* correspond to its true character.[67] Thus the innumerable puzzles and mysteries confronting anyone who, like Macbeth, is drawn to ponder the workings of his surrounding world. However, compounding the inherent difficulties with understanding things in general are people's intentional manipulations of appearances, refined to the point of art – several arts, actually, ranging from cosmetics and tailoring to rhetoric and sophistry. We use 'clothing' of all sorts to hide "our naked frailties ... that suffer in exposure" (2.3.124–5). It may be old (2.4.38), it may be new (1.7.34), it may be borrowed (1.3.108–9), it may be stolen (5.2.20–2). And as we know, how well one's clothes fit (1.3.145–7), how well they wear (3.1.106; 4.3.23, 33), how well they suit one's time and place (1.3.40; 2.3.131), depend upon a variety of factors, not least of all one's choice of 'tailors' (1.7.35–6). But as Macbeth's Porter reminds us, not all tailors go to heaven (2.3.13–15).

Duncan first directs attention to the human problem with his rueful lamenting, "There's no art to find the mind's construction in the face." Variations on this theme recur throughout the play. Macbeth, having screwed his courage to the sticking point: "Away, and mock the time with fairest show: / False face must hide what the false heart doth know" (1.7.82–3). Malcolm, conferring with Donalbain in the wake of their father's murder: "To show an unfelt sorrow is an office / Which the false man does easy" (2.3.134–5). Macduff, replying to Malcolm's lecherous pretensions: "you may / Convey your pleasures in a spacious plenty, / And yet seem cold – the time you may so hoodwink: / We have willing dames enough" (4.3.70–3). It may be put to Macbeth's credit, however, that he (like Macduff; 34–7) has neither taste nor talent for dissembling; according to his wife, his face is an open book. A natural warrior, the warrior's code of honour is naturally appealing to him; hence, he prefers direct action and open fighting to treachery (see 1.7.10–16; 5.3.32; 5.5.5–7, 51–2; 5.8.1–3, 27–34). Thus his lady must exhort him, "To beguile the time, look like the time" (1.5.61–3). But he clearly is not comfortable with the necessity of doing so: "Unsafe the while, that we / Must lave our honours in these flattering streams, / And make our faces vizards to our hearts, / Disguising what they are" (3.2.32–5).[68] With all these explicit references to our penchant for masking inner realities with false seemings, one must be that much more alert to the possibilities of various characters – 'good' as well as 'bad' – actually doing so. The play is shot through with duplicity, with double-dealing, but especially with double-meaning, 'equivocal' speech (Shakespeare's use of the various cognates of 'equivocate' is almost exclusive to *Macbeth*). Of course, only because this all-too-human dissembling almost always takes the same direction: vice masking itself with the appearance of virtue (or as Malcolm puts it, "all things foul would wear the brows of grace" 4.3.23), only because people typically endeavour to appear better than they are, not worse, is

Malcolm's deceptive testing of Macduff by means of self-slander as effective as it is.

Granted that all the great metaphysical issues figure thematically in the play, there is one, however, that has a special prominence – signalled in the successive iterations of its very first word: 'When.' *Time* is to *Macbeth's* philosophical story what Tyranny is to its political, and one of the interpretive challenges of the play is seeing why this should be so. All three of the witches are associated with time, the first with the past ("hail to thee, Thane of Glamis," a title Macbeth had earlier inherited), the second with the present ("hail to thee, Thane of Cawdor," a title he has just been granted), the third with the future ("that shalt be king hereafter" – she is the only one of the three that makes predictions; 1.3.48–50; see also 1.1.5; 1.3.67). Thus, it would seem that the Weyward Sisters are, whatever else, unlovely Scottish versions of the three Fates (what Holinshed called in his account, "the goddesses of destinie"). And as they begin the play with the most common question of time, so is Malcolm's concluding speech replete with temporal references: "We shall not spend a large expense of time, / Before we reckon with your several loves ... Henceforth be Earls ... What's more to do, / Which would be planted newly with the time ... by the grace of Grace, / We will perform in measure, time, and place." Every one of the five acts of *Macbeth* begins with an explict allusion to time, as do fully one-half of its original twenty-seven scenes.

Once one makes a point of noticing them, it is remarkable how plentiful – and yet unobtrusive in their context – are the various measures and amounts and locations of time. To cite but one example, the conversation between the Old Man and Rosse begins thus:

> *Old Man:* Threescore and ten I can remember well;
> Within the volume of which time I have seen
> Hours dreadful, and things strange, but this sore night
> Hath trifled former knowings.
> *Rosse:* Ha, good Father,
> Thou seest the heavens, as troubled with man's act,
> Threatens his bloody stage: by th'clock 'tis day,
> And yet dark night strangles the travelling lamp.
> (2.4.1–7)

Then there are the various queries as to what time it is, such as that of Banquo to his son: "How goes the night, boy?" Fleance: "The moon is down; I have not heard the clock." Banquo: "And she goes down at twelve." Fleance: "I take't, 'tis later, Sir" (2.1.1–3). Or Macbeth's to his wife: "What is the night?" Lady Macbeth: "Almost at odds with morning, which is which" (3.4.125–6). And particular characterizations of a given moment in time, such as Macbeth's reaction when the witches disappear after showing him a line of Banquo-fathered kings: "Let this pernicious hour stand aye accursed in the calender!" (4.1.133–4); and Lady Macbeth's apology for her lord's bizarre behaviour at the banquet, as but "a thing of custom ... Only it spoils the pleasure of the time" (3.4.95–7). Add to these the references to Time itself, such as Macbeth's "Come what come may, / Time and the hour runs through the roughest day" (1.3.147–8), or his "Time, thou anticipat'st my dread exploits" (4.1.144), or "these Weyward Sisters saluted me, and referr'd me to the coming on of time" (1.5.8–9); or Banquo's fateful challenge to these same witches: "If you can look into the seeds of time, / And say which grain will grow, and which will not, / Speak then to me" (1.3.58–9). Perhaps not incidentally, then, there are some unusual 'timepieces' mentioned: "the owl that shriek'd, the fatal bellman, which gives the stern'st good-night" (2.2.3–4); the bat whose flight announces dusk, and the "shard-born beetle, with his drowsy hums [that ring] Night's yawning peal" (3.2.40–3); "the wolf, whose howl's his watch" (i.e., of "wither'd Murther" 2.1.52–4) – these natural harbingers of night and sleep supplement Nature's more familiar herald of the dawn and wakefulness, the cock (2.3.24).

Almost every character in the play at some point gives special attention to the 'timing' of actions. There is Macbeth, musing to himself about regicide: "If it were done, when 'tis done, then 'twere well / It were done quickly" (1.7.1–2); and instructing the appointed murderers of Banquo: "Within this hour, at most, / I will advise you where to plant yourselves, / Acquaint you with the perfect spy o'th'time, / The moment on't; for't must be done tonight" (3.1.127–30). Macduff, arriving early in the morning to awaken the King, explains, "He did command me to call timely on him: I have almost slipped the hour" (2.3.45–6). There is Lady Macbeth putting the spurs to her reluctant lord: "Nor time, nor place, / Did then adhere, and yet you would make both: / They have made themselves, and that their fitness now / Does *un*make you" (1.7.51–4). And Rosse – himself the master of timing, switching sides at just the right moment – cynically exhorting Macduff: "Now is the time of help" (4.3.186). Having just learned of their father's murder, Malcolm and Donalbain quickly conclude that then is ***not*** the time to speak in their own defence, but instead to flee for safety (2.3.118–21). Macduff reports that he "was from his mother's womb / Untimely ripp'd" (5.8.15–16). And certainly not to be overlooked are the witches:

> *1st Witch:* Thrice the brinded cat hath mew'd.
> *2nd Witch:* Thrice, and once the hedge-pig whin'd.
> *3rd Witch:* Harpier cries: – 'Tis time, 'tis time.
> (4.1.1–3)

One consequence of all these explicit references to the timing of actions should be a heightening of one's own sensitivity to that very thing. As noted earlier, the solutions to some of the more perplexing features of the play are to be found through analysing the temporal sequence of events.[69]

Several of the most memorable moments and speeches in the play are fairly steeped in the language of time. Consider the chilling conversation between the victorious lord and his lady upon his first arriving home from the wars:

Lady Macb: Great Glamis! worthy Cawdor!
Greater than both, by the all-hail hereafter!
Thy letters have transported me beyond
This ignorant present, and I feel now
The future in the instant.
Macbeth: My dearest love,
Duncan comes here to-night.
Lady Macb: And when goes hence?
Macbeth: To-morrow, as he purposes.
Lady Macb: O! *never*
Shall sun that morrow see!
[Macbeth must visibly react]
Your face, my Thane, is as a book, where men
May read strange matters. To beguile the time,
Look like the time; bear welcome in your eye,
Your hand, your tongue: look like th'innocent flower,
But be the serpent under't. He that's coming
Must be provided for; and you shall put
This night's great business into my dispatch;
Which shall to all our nights and days to come
Give solely sovereign sway and masterdom.
(1.5.54–70)

Then there is the equally time-conscious conversation of Macbeth with Banquo, who unbeknownst to him is about to set off on his final journey:

Macbeth: Ride you this afternoon?
Banquo: Aye, my good Lord.
Macbeth: We should have else desir'd your good advice
(Which still hath been both grave and prosperous)
In this day's council; but we'll take tomorrow.
Is it far you ride?

Banquo: As far, my Lord, as will fill up the time
'Twixt this and supper; go not my horse the better,
I must become a borrower of the night,
For a dark hour, or twain.

...

Macbeth: ... But of that to-morrow,
When, therewithal, we shall have cause of State,
Craving us jointly. Hie you to horse: adieu,
Till you return at night. Goes Fleance with you?
Banquo: Ay, my good Lord: our time does call upon's.
Macbeth: I wish your horses swift and sure of foot;
And so I do commend you to their backs.
Farewell. – [Exit Banquo]
Let every man be master of his time
Till seven at night;
To make society the sweeter welcome,
We will keep ourself till supper-time alone:
While then, God be with you.
(3.1.19–44)

What is so noticeable in speeches such as these is but an intensification of the most distinctive linguistic feature of the play as a whole, namely, the density of terms measuring and positioning things in time: then, now, hereafter, forever, never, always, often, morning, noon, night, nightly, presently, ere, anon, already, while, newly, betimes, henceforth, eterne, momentary, sooner, lated, till, until, sometime, after, since, still, yet, yesterday, today, tonight, tomorrow, olden, modern, at once, early, late (etc.).[70] This sample from our plethora of temporal locators and descriptors – and no fewer than four hundred of the words that compose *Macbeth* refer to time – should remind us of how profoundly, how *essentially*, 'temporal' our very nature is, how 'unconsciously conscious' we are about time (if one may be permitted an oxymoron or two). What accounts for this, our pervasive sensitivity to time? It would seem to be due, in part at least, to our awareness of our mortality, to the realization (always present, however dimly) that we live now but will soon die, that judged in cosmic terms our time here is limited to but the wink of an eye – truth so memorably expressed in the most renowned speech of the play, Macbeth's nihilistic reflection on the ephemerality of human existence, its apparent insignificance in the great expanse of time:

Macbeth: ... What is that noise?
Seyton: It is the cry of women, my good Lord.
Macbeth: I have almost forgot the taste of fears.
The time has been, my senses would have cool'd
To hear a night-shriek; and my fell of hair
Would at a dismal treatise rouse, and stir,
As life were in't. I have supp'd full with horrors:
Direness, familiar to my slaughterous thoughts,
Cannot once start me. Wherefore was that cry?
Seyton: The Queen, my Lord, is dead.
Macbeth: She should have died hereafter:
There would have been a time for such a word. –
To-morrow,
... and to-morrow,
... and to-morrow,
Creeps in this petty pace from day to day,
To the last syllable of recorded time;
And all our yesterdays have lighted fools
The way to dusty death. Out, *out*, brief candle!
Life's but a walking shadow; a poor player,
That struts and frets his hour upon the stage,
And then is heard no more: it is a tale
Told by an idiot, full of sound and fury,
Signifying nothing.
(5.5.7–28)

Fittingly, proud Macbeth, even though dispirited, chooses to end his life with "sound and fury," provoked by Macduff's shrewd threat that, should he yield to capture, he will be made "the show and gaze o'th'time" (5.8.24).

Reflection on the foregoing suggests that, of all the metaphysical questions human beings confront, understanding time – or rather, human existence *in* time – is especially important, or especially challenging, or both. The other prominent themes of the play are each somehow bound up with time. For example, sleep and wakefulness in accordance with the natural rhythms of time, of night succeeding day, and of the practical necessity of nightly rest in the natural economy of life ("the season of all natures, sleep" 3.4.140), and thus of what it means to "Sleep no more," to "murther Sleep" – that is, innocent, secure sleep, the kind that *does* knit up the ravell'd sleave of care, and recreate both mind and body – and to instead "sleep in the affliction of terrible dreams that shake [one] nightly," one's life becoming a murky Hell (2.2.34–9; 3.2.17–19; 5.1.34). It may be worth noting that the first mention of 'sleep' is by the First Witch, boasting of her plan to torment the ronyon's sailor husband by somehow insuring that for eighty-one weeks he shall "sleep ... neither night nor day" (1.3.19–23). Also, the various 'horticultural' allusions (and again, the first comes in conjunction with those three haggish Fates: 1.3.58–9; see also 1.4.28–33; 4.3.76–7, 85, 238; 5.2.30; 5.3.23; 5.5.40; 5.9.31) are so many reminders that all natural growth, and decay, takes time.[71] Or to put the point more generally, that Being is only physically, perceptibly present – which is to say, *naturally* manifested – in its governing the perpetual flux of Becoming in space and time – Time itself being the moving image, the "walking shadow," of Eternity (according to Plato's *Timaeus* 37d–e). Even the oft-noted 'clothing metaphor'[72] is tied into time, as when Banquo observes, "New honours come upon him, like our strange garments, cleave not to their mould, but with the aid of use" (1.3.145–7). And Macbeth protests to his wife, "He hath honour'd me of late; and I have bought / Golden opinions from all sorts of people, / Which would be worn now in their newest gloss, / Not cast aside so soon" (1.7.32–5).

The main focus, however, is on the human *awareness* of time, and the consequences thereof. We all have some appreciation that our present is the result of our past, and that only part of this relevant past is consciously available as memory. Clearly, the particular historical situations in which we are born and nurtured were not of our own choosing or making. How much of our resulting selves, then, can we, should we, must we accept responsibility for? Of the past that produced us, what might we rightfully praise or blame, accept or repudiate, attempt to suppress or to preserve? These are vexing questions, and people differ greatly in how they stand towards these matters. In tacit awareness that the past unalterably closes behind us, that "what's done cannot be undone," we tend to be future-oriented – to such an extent that as our allotment of earthly days dwindles, we may become increasingly inclined to consider an existence beyond the mortal one.[73] It is only in the prime of life, and while dubious of any future life, that one is apt to profess as does Macbeth a willingness to "jump [i.e.,'risk'] the life to come" in return for some great worldly success (1.7.4–7).[74] In any event, the prospects of the future, like the establishments of the past, evoke different sorts of responses in different kinds of people, or even in the same people at different times in their lives. Why this is so, why one individual is confident where another is anxious, seems as much a reflection of a given person's nature, character, and beliefs, as of the objective qualitites of his circumstances.

Here, then, would seem to be the primary dimensions of our temporal nature (obvious enough, to be sure): how one stands towards one's past; how one stands towards one's future; and how one stands towards death. It is the resulting dynamic synthesis of these 'stances' or attitudes that colours and shapes one's ever-moving point of present experience. Reconciliation with human temporality, and especially with one's own perhaps variable but surely finite existence in time, is mainly a matter of having the right attitude towards the various sectors and features of one's temporal horizon. What is entailed in having it right is elliptically indicated in the Macbeths' getting it all wrong. Dogged by their past, morbidly preoccupied with a future finality as elusive as a rainbow, they are unable to enjoy any moment of the present.[75] To understand their mistakes, we need to consider the main alternatives available with respect to each dimension. What does the play suggest these are?

Regarding the Past, Macbeth displays in the extreme what seems to some extent true of many, if not most people: they are more apt to be haunted by their mistakes than gladdened by their successes (rather as Machiavelli suggests they more readily remember grievances than benefactions).[76] Even pleasant remembrances can be tinged with the sadness of things no longer being so. Memory might be conceived as Macbeth's own "sweet remembrancer" describes it: "the warder of the brain" (1.7.66; 3.4.36). But the extent to which it is subject to purposeful control is difficult to determine, and may well vary from person to person.[77] Macduff defends his evident sorrow upon hearing of the death of his wife and children, "I *cannot* but remember such things were, / That were most precious to me" (4.3.222–3). When Macbeth asks of the Scottish physician who has been tending his wife, "How does your patient, Doctor?", he replies, "Not so sick, my Lord, / As she is troubled with thick-coming fancies, / That keep her from her rest." Whereupon Macbeth orders:

> Cure her of that:
> Canst thou not minister to a mind diseas'd,
> Pluck from the memory a rooted sorrow,
> Raze out the written troubles of the brain,
> And with some sweet oblivious antidote
> Cleanse the stuff'd bosom of that perilous stuff
> Which weighs upon the heart?
>
> (5.3.37–45)

No doubt sensing the reflexive possibility of Macbeth's query, the tactful doctor replies, "Therein the patient must minister to himself." Ah, but how? The Porter ("remember the Porter") might have added *forgetfulness* to his catalogue of things that "drink ... is a great provoker of" (2.3.25–9). The effects of this common "oblivious antidote" are variable, however, and not selective, and only temporary unless pursued to mind-destroying lengths. With respect to past mistakes that one regrets, and wishes "were now undone," what ministration is there for the chronic mental discomfort they can cause – which, as the the anguish of Lady Macbeth reminds us, can be so severe as to pall one in the dunnest smoke of Hell, making death seem preferable to life (5.9.35–7)? The play suggests only two alternatives. The first would be to school one's soul to accept, fully and finally, the reasoning so ironically placed in the mouth of the Queen herself (advice applicable to the entirety of life, not merely to one's own mistakes): "Things without all remedy should be without regard: what's done is done" (3.2.11–12). However, abiding by this policy of 'reasoned disregard' presumes a strength of the soul's rational part that is apparently beyond most people. They may have no practical choice but the second alternative: repentance, with the possibility of forgiveness.

Neither disregarding nor repenting are prominent in the play, and least of all by the protagonists most in need of one or the other. Unlike the condemned rebel Cawdor, who according to the report Malcolm passes on:

> ... very frankly he confess'd his treasons,
> Implor'd your Highness' pardon, and set forth
> A deep repentance. Nothing in his life
> Became him like the leaving it: he died
> As one that had been studied in his death,
> To throw away the dearest thing he ow'd
> As 'twere a careless trifle.
>
> (1.4.5–11)

(He – or Malcolm – sounds downright Sokratic,[78] although one must bear in mind that Cawdor's "deep repentance" was born in defeat.) Unlike Cawdor, however, Macbeth merely regrets, never repents. The one time he uses the word, he is lying, or at the least does not mean it in the way he wishes it to be taken; he announces his killing of the blood-badg'd grooms by saying, "O! yet I do repent me of my fury, / That I did kill them" (2.3.104–5). As for his forgetting what once filled his mind with scorpions – the memory of his crimes, along with the fear that he will become the just victim of his own "bloody instructions" – he eventually is successful to a point, but at the price of his humanity. With Banquo's shade at last banished ("Hence, horrible shadow! / Unreal mock'ry, hence!" 3.4.105–6), Macbeth vows to become immune to what he now regards as but guilt-induced delusions: "My strange and self-abuse / Is the initiate fear, that wants hard use: / We are yet but young in deed" (141–3). Having thus committed himself (along with his now passive but worried wife) to becoming habituated – not to bloodshed, which as a seasoned warrior he is inured to from the time we first meet him – but to *atrocities*, he finally succeeds in turning his milk of human kindness to gall. Apparently she does not quite. As his criminal career approaches its climax, Macbeth can muse, "I have almost forgot the taste of fears" (5.5.9). Apparently Lady Macbeth has not. She never expresses repentance ("the access and passage to remorse" perhaps stopp'd, as she prayed it would be; 1.5.44), hence she never seeks what she needs: the kind of self-reconcilation that could come only from a sense of having been forgiven by someone with the power to forgive. As the doctor who witnesses her "slumbery agitation" puts it, "More needs she the divine than the physician. – / God, God forgive us all!" (5.1.71–2). Still, it is evident from her somnambulatory torments and eventual death that Lady Macbeth remains essentially human. Whereas the insensitivity and forgetfulness of Macbeth verges upon that of a beast, not a human being – to "dispute it like a *man*," one must first "feel it *as* a man" (4.3.220–1). The only person who expressly repents his sins is also the only one to pray for Macbeth's forgiveness, albeit on decidedly unChristian terms:

> But, gentle Heavens,
> Cut short all intermission; front to front,
> Bring thou this fiend of Scotland, and myself;
> Within my sword's length set him; if he 'scape,
> Heaven forgive him too!
> (4.3.231–5; cf. 5.7.14–16)

Respecting the Future, the play affirms what common experience would suggest, namely, that the principal factors determining a person's temporal posture are Hope and Fear. A preoccupation with the latter is certainly evident enough. Indeed, there are more mentions of 'fear' and its cognates ('fear'd,' 'fearful,' 'fearing,' 'fears') in *Macbeth* than in any other of Shakespeare's creations. However, its action pivots as much if not more on hopes, especially *false* hopes, we would say, knowledgeable after the fact – "hopes [borne] 'bove wisdom, grace, and fear" (3.5.31) – but our retrospective judgment points to the precise difference at issue: the absolute finality (hence knowability) of the past *versus* the opacity of a future more or less rich with possiblities for good and evil, the final causes of hope and fear. It is the "royal hope" excited by the witches that inspires Macbeth and his lady to act on their black and deep desires. Only in the final minutes of his life does he realize he has been relying on "juggling fiends" who "keep the word of promise to our ear, / And break it to our hope" (5.8.19–22). Macbeth's own first mention of 'hope' comes in a kind of congratulation to Banquo: "Do you not hope your children shall be kings, / When those that gave the Thane of Cawdor to me / Promis'd no less to them?" (1.3.118–20). Banquo does so hope (3.1.5–

10), and it is a prospect Macbeth finds increasingly galling with time. Lady Macbeth's sole reference to hope is in chiding her husband: "Was the hope drunk, / Wherein you dress'd yourself? Hath it slept since? / And wakes it now, to look so green and pale / At what it did so freely?" (1.7.35–8). Her taunting insinuation that he lacks sufficient natural (i.e., sober) courage to act on his – and her – royal hopes has its intended effect. Macduff's hopes in Malcolm are what carry him to England (4.3.24, 114), and Malcolm's hopes in victory carry him back to Scotland (5.4.1–2). It is left to the practical old soldier Siward to remind us that hopes aren't horses, however: "Thoughts speculative their unsure hopes relate, / But certain issues strokes must arbitrate ..." (19–20).

Seeing the future as but through a glass darkly, the rational imagination is to the future what the rational memory is to the past. Macbeth's letters have so stimulated the imagination of his lady that she has been "transported ... beyond this ignorant present, and ... feel[s] now the future in the instant" (1.5.56–8). She has high hopes. Macbeth, too, speaks of the non-existent, merely imagined future as more real than the existent present, but with a distinct foreboding:

> This supernatural soliciting
> Cannot be ill; cannot be good: –
> If ill, why hath it given me earnest of success,
> Commencing in a truth? I am Thane of Cawdor:
> If good, why do I yield to that suggestion
> Whose horrid image doth unfix my hair,
> And make my seated heart knock at my ribs,
> Against the use of nature? Present fears
> Are less than horrible imaginings.
> My thought, whose murther yet is but fantastical,
> Shakes so my single state of man,
> That function is smother'd in surmise,
> And nothing is, but what is not.
>
> (1.3.130–42)

Together, this ambitious couple span the range of humanity's attitudes towards the future, one hoping for what she regards as the best, the other fearing what he imagines could be the worst.[79] Yet, both are contemplating the same prospect: Macbeth's doing whatever might be necessary to seize the kingship.

Precisely because we do not know 'what the future has in store' for us, but often would like to, we have a natural interest in prediction and prophecy – indeed, in some people the eagerness to "look into the seeds of time" and know beforehand "which grain will grow, and which will not" renders them exceedingly gullible. But even a sceptic would be impressed when what seemed a most unlikely prophecy is promptly confirmed. In any event, one can be sure it is no mere coincidence that the first mention of 'prediction' comes in the same speech as the first mentions of *both* 'hope' and 'fear.' The three witches having in turn "all-hail'd" Macbeth, it is Banquo who responds, "Good Sir, why do you start, and seem to fear / Things that do sound so fair?" Then turning back to the witches, he continues, "My noble partner / You greet with present grace and great prediction / Of noble having, and of royal hope, / That he seems rapt withal: to me you speak not" (1.3.51–7). Whereupon he solicits a prediction on his own behalf, and receives their fateful, equivocal answers:

> *1st Witch:* Lesser than Macbeth, and greater.
> *2nd Witch:* Not so happy, yet much happier.
> *3rd Witch:* Thou shalt get kings, though thou be none ...

It is the witches' array of predictions to these two warrior chieftains that sets in motion all the subsequent events of the play.

First, what both Macbeths prefer now to think has been "promis'd" them (1.3.120; 1.5.13, 16) congeals their determination to murder Duncan – and we must notice that this is Lord Macbeth's *immediate* interpretation of "shalt be King hereafter": that it is a suggestion to do something "whose horrid image" makes his heart pound and his hair stand on end. This *despite* the Thaneship of Cawdor being so surprisingly confirmed "without [his] stir." Only afterwards does it occur to him that "Chance" may also as readily crown him King (1.3.144). Almost surely, then, this is *not* the first time Macbeth has thought about regicide. It would hardly be surprising had the temptation of it been troubling his mind as he and Banquo tramped through the foul weather from those desperate battles in which they – not meek Duncan – saved the kingdom. Is this why the witches' pronouncements arouse in Macbeth the rapture which Banquo twice notes (57, 143), and why he is sure they have "more in them than mortal knowledge" – because they have read his mind (cf. 4.1.74)? On the surface, it might seem that Shakespeare's Macbeths merely re-enact The Fall of Man, with the primary responsibility that of the Temptress Eve, in keeping with the traditional account. Examined more closely, however, one detects the author's somewhat different view: his Adam is no innocent, seduced into an act for which he showed no prior inclination.

Second, Banquo's having been implicated in the witches' prophecies has compromised him, thereby facilitating the initial success of Macbeth's bid to gain the crown under a cloak of legitimacy. For Banquo is the one person who is privy not only to the prophecy, but also to Macbeth's suspicious allusion to "that business" the very night of Duncan's murder: "If you shall cleave to my consent, when 'tis, it shall make honour for you" – a conversation cut short by Banquo's guarded "So I lose none in seeking to augment it" (2.1.20–9). Despite having suspicions about Macbeth's involvement in Duncan's assassination (as he later acknowledges), Banquo obviously does not voice them when at his own instigation they all "meet and question this most bloody piece of work, to know it further." Probably it was at this same meeting that Macbeth was named the new Sovereign (2.4.30–32). Banquo's passive complicity is confirmed shortly thereafter in his troubled soliloquy:

> Thou hast it now, King, Cawdor, Glamis, all,
> As the Weyward Women promis'd; and, I fear,
> Thou playd'st most foully for't; yet it was said,
> It should not stand in thy posterity;
> But that *myself* should be the root and father
> Of many kings. If there come truth from them
> (As upon thee, Macbeth, their speeches shine),
> Why, by the verities on thee made good,
> May they not be my oracles as well,
> And set me up in hope.
>
> (3.1.1–10)

That is, Banquo sees the fulfilment of his own prophecy as dependent on the fulfilment of Macbeth's – to validate the witches' predictive powers, at the least, but also quite likely as a necessary step towards his own offspring's eventual success (cf. 15–18).

That would seem to be the way Macbeth sees it, too – and so he resolves to foreclose any such prospect by extinguishing forever Banquo's line, thereby hoping to subvert that part of the witches' prophecy. He may not have noticed it before, but once he has succeeded in becoming King he sees in Banquo a "royalty of nature ... that ... would be fear'd":

> He chid the Sisters
> When first they put the name of King upon me,
> And bade them speak to him; then, prophet-like,
> They hail'd him father to a line of kings:
> Upon my head they plac'd a fruitless crown,
> And put a barren sceptre in my gripe,
> Thence to be wrench'd with an unlineal hand,
> No son of mine succeeding.
>
> (3.1.56–63)

Fearing that Banquo may choose to further the realization of *his* prophecy the same way that Macbeth did, 'wrenching' crown and sceptre with an unlineal hand, he resolves to murder Banquo – the third pivotal consequence of the witches' initial set of predictions. That what Macbeth has in mind is paradoxical, even self-contradictory, should not be lost on us. For Shakespeare means hereby to show the paradox inherent in *all* human interest in prophecy, and consequently in the normal human posture towards the future. For the very possibility of predictive certainty, such that one can have complete confidence in whatever is foretold, presupposes that the future is strictly determined, or 'fated,' and as such cannot be altered. Yet our interest in it stems not simply from curiosity, but from the practical desire to further our own good while avoiding anything bad – which, of course, presupposes that future outcomes are *not* fixed, but subject to discretionary action on our part.[80]

Now, one might object that there is no logical contradiction between the future – and hence all that happens in time – being strictly determined, on the one hand, and our consciously choosing the actions that of necessity lead to those predetermined outcomes, on the other (and that it is simply part of the necessary, determined order of things that we act under the illusion that we are *free* to choose, that we have 'free will'). Consequently, Macbeth is doing nothing illogical in taking an *active* role in pursuing the kingship once it has been "promis'd" him, rather than passively waiting for "Chance" to crown him: this can be seen – even by him – as doing his (predetermined) part to bring the prediction to its fulfilment, having 'of necessity' been moved to do so by its assurance of success. Ah, but what about his efforts to *obstruct* the prophecy regarding Banquo? True, one could argue that logically the cases are the same, that his 'futile' efforts are equally part of the Master Plan, essential to its final outcome. And for the sake of argument, it may be conceded that this might be so. But what about *psycho*-logically? No rational person acts out of a motive to 'fulfill the future' per se, regardless of what it may be. Neither we, nor other living things, are 'neutral' in our nature: we pursue what we perceive to be our *good*, not The Future. Macbeth may have seen his murder of Duncan as simply doing his part to further fate as it has been revealed to him, but he surely cannot see his murder of Banquo in this way. The point is, he, like most people, has a contradictory attitude towards predictions of the future. Those that seem to favour him do not just suggest a possibility, or merely inspire hope; they impart confidence and a sense of legitimacy, a feeling that 'this is how things were meant to be.' Thus, Siward can describe Macbeth ensconced at Dunsinane as "the confident tyrant" (5.4.8; cf. 5.3.2–10). Whereas predictions that threaten him arouse fear *and a will to evade* – not, that is, acceptance, resignation, and despair. This 'double' or 'equivocal' attitude towards predictions reflects his ambivalence about the future itself: sometimes (or in certain respects) regarding it as fixed by fate, other times acting as if it were undetermined, hence, amenable to the influence of human volition.

Several times Macbeth in effect admits as much. When after the Banquo-haunted banquet he resolves purposefully to seek out the Weyward Sisters (a fourth pivotal consequence of his first, apparently chance, meeting with them; 1.3.154), he tells his wife: "More shall they speak; for now I am bent to know, / By the worst means, the worst. For mine own good, / All causes shall give way" (3.4.133–5). He wants to know the worst in order to avoid it, in the pursuit of his own good (as would anyone). The possibility of there being such knowledge before the fact, however, presupposes a determined world-system, as unalterable (hence, predictable) as the planets in their motions – that the "causes" will *not* "give way." When later at the Pit of Acheron the warning of the First Apparition ("beware Macduff") is seemingly contradicted by the exhortation of the Second ("Be bloody, bold, and resolute: laugh to scorn / The power of man, for none of woman born / Shall harm Macbeth"), his response betrays the quite normal, and in that sense, natural doubt in his mind as to whether his should be a passive or an active role in protecting himself:

> Then live, Macduff: what need I fear of thee?
> But yet I'll make assurance double sure,
> And take a bond of Fate: thou shalt not live;
> That I may tell pale-hearted fear it lies,
> And sleep in spite of thunder.
>
> (4.1.82–6)

Having been offered still further "security" by the Third Apparition ("Macbeth shall never vanquish'd be, until / Great Birnam wood to high Dunsinane hill / Shall come against him"), Macbeth insists on the witches telling him one thing more: "shall Banquo's issue ever reign in this kingdom?" Because the answer they "show his eyes" does indeed "grieve his heart" (110), he reacts to their vanishing with a most ironic curse: "Infected be the air whereon they ride; / And damn'd all those that trust them!" (138–9) – for as his confidence almost to the bitter end proves, he continues to trust the parts of their prophecies that he wishes to be true, those that seem to guarantee him protection, and thus free him from fear. He is clearly shaken when Birnam wood comes to Dunsinane ("I pull in resolution; and begin / To doubt th'equivocation of the fiend, / That lies like truth" 5.5.42–4). Still, his "better part of man" is only finally cow'd upon learning that Macduff was not naturally *born* of woman, but "from his mother's womb untimely ripp'd." Too late he realizes how the Instruments of Darkness have played upon his hopes and fears: "And be these juggling fiends no more believ'd, /

That palter with us in a double sense; / That keep the word of promise to our ear, / And break it to our hope" (5.8.19–22).

Perhaps it is worth examining these matters more closely, bearing as they do on this most intimate of metaphysical problems: 'free will' – the very idea of which is so perplexing that one is sometimes tempted to conclude there can be no such thing (not realizing that the alternative is even more perplexing). What must first be addressed, however, is whether or not there really are only two intelligible views about the predictability of the future, and thus about whatever happens in time: that of *strict* 'Determinism' (i.e., that everything is *pre*-determined, 'fated,' 'destined' – and as such, in principle predictable) versus a view which sees a significant role for human freedom in determining actual historical outcomes (with the consequence that precise prediction of what in particular will happen, when, and where, is impossible). Macbeth's speeches and deeds suggest that he is inclined to a third view, a naturally appealing kind of combination of the other two that allows for *both* foreknowledge of the future *and* the possibility of intervening to affect it. That is, he prefers a prospect like the following: knowing what *would* happen in the absence of purposeful action which one might take as a result of such knowing. But upon subjecting such a notion to further examination, one sees that it is naturally impossible. In granting that chosen actions *could* affect actual outcomes, one necessarily concedes that *all* such outcomes are indeterminate before the fact, hence, not predictable. For there is no credible reason to restrict the possibility of free choice to only those situations in which someone somehow has foreknowledge of the future! Either we as reasoning beings have this freedom or we do not. If we do, then such foreknowledge is impossible; if we do not, we could not use it to *alter* preordained outcomes (which must be seen as *including* whatever we come to know and its actual influence upon us).[81]

It is likely that every intelligent person has wondered about this very thing: whether there really is 'free will.'[82] This question is not to be confused with a practically related issue that Shakespeare invites us to think through as well, namely, whether one's choices and efforts really make any difference 'in the long run,' or whether (instead) things would still 'turn out the same.' What he bids us recognize about this latter question is that it is too imprecise to admit of an answer that would advance one's understanding. For it could be truthfully answered 'No,' since in the long run – having strutted and fretted our few hours upon the stage – we're all dead. Or it could as fairly be answered 'Yes,' meaning that one's choices and efforts, be they free or determined, might make all the difference of human importance as to when, where, and in what manner we die – early and bravely on the battlefield, like Young Siward (who "only liv'd but till he was a man; / The which no sooner had his prowess confirm'd, / In the unshrinking station where he fought, / But like a man he died" 5.9.6–9); or old, content, and oblivious in an unsafe bed, like gracious Duncan (2.1.16–17); or pathetically paying the wages of past sin, like Lady Macbeth (who "by self and violent hands took off her life" 5.9.36–7); or dignified in repentance, like Cawdor ("Nothing in his life / Became him like the leaving it" 1.4.7–8).[83] In any event, the issue of free will is not to be conflated with this more ambiguous question, nor with another concerning the impact of individual decisions and actions on large-scale historical outcomes.[84] Young Siward's being vanquished in his confrontation with Macbeth had no effect on the results of the final battle, nor in all likelihood did Macduff's being victorious. Once Macbeth abandoned his strategy of allowing his enemies to exhaust themselves in a siege of Dunsinane[85] ("Our castle's strength / Will laugh a siege to scorn: here let them lie, / Till famine and the ague eat them up" 5.5.2–4; cf. 5.2.12; 5.4.8–10), and instead ventures out to meet them "dareful, beard to beard" (5.5.46), he is effectively doomed by sheer force of numbers. But none of this bears one way or the other on whether Young Siward freely chose to challenge Macbeth to mortal combat, nor on whether Macbeth's change in strategy was destined from the beginning of time ... presuming there was a beginning.[86]

When we analyse our own decisions, we often conclude that we had no 'real choice,' meaning that our reasoning was effectively determined by conditional necessity: if we wished X (e.g., to avoid pain or death, win salvation, get an education, become wealthy, or whatever), then we 'had' to do Y (obey the tyrant, honour God, postpone marriage, defraud our partners, etc.). Thus Macbeth explains to the two prospective murderers why he both can and yet practically cannot openly murder Banquo himself:

> and though I *could*
> With bare-fac'd power sweep him from my sight,
> And bid my will avouch it, yet I must not,
> For certain friends that are both his and mine,
> Whose loves I may not drop, but wail his fall
> Who I myself struck down: and thence it is
> That I to your assistance do make love,
> Masking the business from the common eye,
> For sundry weighty reasons.
>
> (3.1.117–24)

Even granting such Ys to be the only practical means to the sought-after ends, this of course simply moves the issue back to whatever establishes these Xs – virtually never is it something that would qualify as necessity in the strictest sense:

consistent, universal, and inevasible. Erotic 'necessities' may exert a more potent influence over most people's behaviour than do the necessities of geometry,[87] but the latter are a lot more necessary. In their separate ways, both Young Siward and Lady Macbeth remind us that not even fear of death operates with anything like the strict necessity of gravitational force. Nonetheless, having experienced powerful passions ourselves – anger, love, desire, loathing, and especially fear – we are understandably inclined to treat them as 'causing' people to act as they do. When Macduff presents Malcolm "Th'usurper's cursed head," announcing that now "the time is free" (5.9.19–20), he is understood as meaning free from the kinds of pervasive fears characteristic of life under tyranny (see 3.6.33–7) – not, that is, free from any and all forces that might tend to restrain or compel behaviour. Even in those cases where we consciously deliberate and choose among the alternatives that we regard as open to us, we virtually always would acknowledge a variety of antecedent but unchosen factors that either did have or could have had some bearing on our decision. Might such factors, then, either alone or in conjunction with ones we remain unaware of, collectively 'determine' what we decide and actually do in every case? Add to this reasonable suspicion the observation that everything else in our world seems amenable to explanation in terms of antecedent causation; and that the very idea of free will seems to entail the notion of an 'uncaused cause,' something difficult if not impossible to conceive with any sort of clarity – integrating all these considerations together, one may be persuaded that the psychic experience of freely choosing is illusory, and thereupon reject as naïve the belief that humans are uniquely endowed with 'free will,' adopting instead a strictly determined world-view.

However, that brings its own enormous perplexities. The notion that everything I do, no matter how minute or grand – how long I pause to ponder this sentence, or my 'choice' when asked to pick a number between one and seven hundred twenty-nine; my decision as to which of Shakespeare's plays should be addressed in this book, and how much I am able to understand of them – was determined from the beginning of the universe (and from 'before' that if its current configuration represents merely the latest shuffling of the cosmic deck) – and similarly their consequences preordained unto the last syllable of recorded time – for there can be no 'slack' in such a view: if an undetermined effect is deemed a logical absurdity, it is equally so in matters big and small; if *everything* is strictly determined, then all apparent exceptions and aberrations are equally the result of antecedent causes stretching back to the Beginning and beyond – is not this grandiose notion of meticulous Fate every bit as mind-boggling as the idea of free will?[88] Of course, one must reflexively apply the view to one's own deliberations on it. So I must regard my addressing it, and doing so as a necessary consequence of studying this play, as something I was determined to do before I and all my known relatives even existed – indeed before Shakespeare existed, or Adam and Eve, or any other human being, or life itself – and to conclude now *whatever* I conclude (if anything) – which may differ from what I conclude tomorrow (having been determined then to notice something I was determined to overlook today) ... and tomorrow ... and tomorrow, until I am heard no more. And my writing (and your reading) this bemusing sentence, that too was eternally fated, as is my observing that I do so, and my observing that I observe, and so on. One soon feels as if trapped amid cleverly juxtaposed mirrors that reflect a succession of images stretching out, like Banquo's royal offspring, to th'crack of doom.

The infinite reflexivity of this view – surely beyond the mind's power of comprehension – is by no means the most telling objection to it, however. Once one entertains the determinist's contention that one's sense of free will is a determined *illusion*, the floodgates open. For there is no way to contain the implications of this prospect: that though whatever we think is strictly determined, it is not necessarily *true* (as would be freshly confirmed every time one's mind changed about anything). Hence, Determinism as a *positive doctrine*, is self-refuting, since it renders access to the truth, on this or any other question, impossible. Should it happen to be true, there would be no way to *know* it (or to know anything else), nor rational grounds for even suspecting it (or anything else), thus absolutely no reason to believe it, much less have perfect confidence that it is the truth. For upon presuming it to be the case, every assessment of evidence, every distinction one might make, every argument for or against opposing views, every evaluation of those arguments, all so-called reasoning – indeed, the very positing of alternative views, the substance of all conceptions, every ingredient of one's consciousness, must be regarded as determined *irrespective* of the *truth*, to which we have no credible access. Consequently, the very idea of Truth becomes practically meaningless. Accepting such a view is the metaphysical equivalent of having "eaten on the insane root / That takes the reason prisoner." We could (must?) still use all the same words – true and false, probable and improbable, reason and reality, objective, factual, coherent, consistent, contradictory, perceive, suppose, hypothesize, know, speculate, imagine, prove, refute, and myriad others – but they would no longer have their ordinary, 'natural' meaning (as is readily confirmed by consciously comparing one's antecedent understanding of these ideas with the view of them that results from presuming that whatever one thinks is not something oneself 'freely' *decides*, but is strictly predetermined).

Accordingly, it would not be only juggling fiends and Jesuits "that palter with us in a double sense"; for on this view, we are all 'equivocators' with every word we speak – not in the ordinary sense of exploiting ambiguity, but in the far more radical sense of our words being both allegedly referential to, yet irremedially isolated from, 'reality,' the very conception of which is equally 'equivocal.' We could (must?) still exert ourselves investigating, discussing, arguing, assessing, evaluating, and reach whatever conclusions we in fact reach. But if we presume that one is not really *free* to conclude whatever one will from all of this activity, do we not 'necessarily' regard the status of such 'conclusions' – and thus of ourselves – in a radically different light? Would not the resulting equivocal status of thought undercut all intellectual and moral confidence, thereby vitiating practical commitment and resolve – such that we, like Macbeth, "pull in resolution; and begin / To doubt th'equivocation of the fiend, / That lies like truth"? To know one's deed, 'twere best not know oneself.

For anyone who could surrender himself entirely to a strictly determinist view of human nature (and I am frankly dubious whether anyone consistently can), there could be no philosophy or science in the ordinary, 'natural' sense, merely a kind of mock-philosophy or mock-science, which could be taken seriously only so long as one forgets – can forget – that everything one notices, analyses, concludes – or forgets – is in fact determined irrespective of the truth. For the moment one remembers that one is not free to pursue the truth, "from this instant / There's nothing serious in mortality; / All is but toys." Moreover, if one surrenders oneself to the determinist view (whereupon such surrendering must, of course, be seen as itself determined), this mock-philosophizing must be regarded, not as something one *does* (in the natural sense), but as something that happens to, or in, oneself. Surely there is some question whether anyone can really live like that, "in restless ecstacy," becoming accustomed to, even comfortable with, the resulting intellectual schizophrenia: the liability to radical flip-flops in self-understanding, regarding oneself one moment as philosophizing, and the next as being mock-philosophized upon (or within). Liable, that is, to sudden gestalt switches from regarding oneself as autonomous to that of an automaton, and back again – "The fit is momentary; upon a thought / He will again be well" – switching 'purposefully' when one 'chooses' (to lapse into a mode of expression that comes naturally to us, as in discussing these matters one can scarce avoid doing, time and time again), but subject to 'spontaneous' switches as well – though in every case actually determined, presumedly. Thus, one is left with a 'double' view of oneself, that of the natural consciousness with which one begins, and never entirely surrenders; and this endlessly perplexing, artificial view of one's being a determined mechanism, complete with a determined consciousness (whose very perplexity, along with all else, has been pre-determined from the first syllable of Time). Whereupon, the witches' enigmatic chant – "Double, double toil and trouble" – acquires a profoundly metaphysical meaning, and one realizes that Shakespeare has invested speech with heretofore unsuspected equivocality.

The main point, however, is not that the determinist view, strictly adhered to, is apt to be psychically uncomfortable (to put it mildly), but that upon reflexive application, it self-destructs. For upon assuming it, one obviates any and all reasons for believing it. To be sure, the alternative view – that we are in some sense 'free,' and first of all free to think whatever seems true (even if by virtue of our rational nature 'compelled' to interest ourselves in the truth, which entails acknowledging the idea of Truth) – is also perplexing. But it does not carry the same liabilities as does determinism. Applied reflexively, it is not self-refuting, but remains a coherent view – the essential thing, of course. And in squaring with our natural, immediate experience of ourselves, it provokes no chronic psychical distress, no "torture of the mind," such as (I presume) would result from the Sisyphean effort of managing radically irreconcilable views of oneself. Also, it is compatible with a number of vitally important human concerns: with ascribing personal responsibility, as is implicit in the ordinary meaning of morality, and of justice in particular; with the existence of genuine nobility and magnanimity, rightly deserving of admiration; and perhaps most importantly, with self-respect – for we can genuinely, and do naturally, respect a free rational being, as we cannot an automaton (more than any other machine).

So, one may be perplexed whichever way one turns.[89] It is fair to say, however, the view that acknowledges some degree of freedom within the embracing constraints of Nature (the material demands of life and health, the somewhat variable cycles of life, the invariable ones of celestial and terrestial motions, the inflexible rigour of natural forces, and so on) seems truer to our psychic experience.[90] This is, after all, why people believe that they enjoy some freedom of choice and action, and that they are mostly free to think what they will, if not to speak it (that we have what Macbeth calls "free hearts" which we may sometimes choose to express; 1.3.154–6).[91] This is why people distinguish situations in terms of the degree of freedom each offers, seeing some as comparatively open (the basis of Lady Macbeth's taunting her husband for now looking "so green and pale" at what she claims he did "so freely"; 1.7.37–8); whereas other situations practically dictate a single course of action (as in the case of Macbeth's soldiers that Malcolm speaks of: "And none serve with him but constrained things, / Whose hearts are absent too" 5.4.13–14). What Shakespeare helps us to recognize, however, is that, *logically*, it makes no *practical* difference whether one does or does not 'believe in' free will. Provided one is scrupulously consistent in regarding *everything* as (pre)determined, the problems involved in understanding and dealing with the world remain exactly the same. There is no practical difference between asking oneself 'What am I *determined* to do?' (or think, feel, imagine, or whatever) and asking oneself 'What *should* I do?' (however this be construed: as what is 'right' to do, or 'best' to do, or 'best for me' to do, etc.).

However, Shakespeare also prompts us to see that, *psycho*-'logically,' there is an *enormous* practical difference, given that almost no one *is* scrupulously consistent in abiding by the passionless dictates of impersonal logic – indeed, the vast majority of people rarely exert any effort whatsoever to reveal to themselves what these dictates might be. Consequently, the person who prefers to think of himself as 'determined' by antecedent factors tends to give an illegitimate priority to what he is immediately familiar with: his subrational drives and feelings, his particular fears, desires, loathings, and resentments. So far as he is personally acquainted with reason, he has good grounds for regarding it as but a slave of the passions. Thus he insensibly transforms the rationally neutral question, 'What am I determined to do?' into a question that is profoundly biased against the rule of reason: 'What do I really *feel* like doing (hence, am probably going to do anyway, so why make a futile attempt to resist these deepest impulses, feel guilty about giving in to them, etc.)?' – a line of reasoning that terminates in Macbeth's principle of impulsiveness: "From this moment, the very firstlings of my heart shall be the firstlings of my hand."

THE NATURAL WORKINGS OF GOOD AND EVIL

Although spoken by Hecate, self-proclaimed mistress of witchly charms and contriver of all harms, it may nonetheless be the hard truth: that what Macbeth, like most people, longs for – perpetual freedom from all fear – is not really good for beings such as we. It is this very longing which she and her minions exploit to the full:

Upon the corner of the moon
There hangs a vap'rous drop profound;
I'll catch it ere it come to ground:
And that, distill'd by magic sleights,
Shall raise such artificial sprites,
As, by the strength of their illusion,
Shall draw him on to his confusion.
He shall spurn fate, scorn death, and bear
His hope 'bove wisdom, grace, and fear;
And you all know, *security*
Is mortals' chiefest enemy.

(3.5.23–33)

Why so? we might ask. Is it not plain sense and decency to "hope" – as does Malcolm on the brink of his final confrontation with Macbeth – "the days are near at hand, that chambers will be *safe*" (5.4.1–2)? Is it not praiseworthy that Banquo "hath a *wisdom* that doth guide his valour to act in *safety*" (3.1.52–3)? Is it not natural that Macduff's most urgent worry should be for the security of his family, that "The tyrant has not batter'd at their peace" (4.3.178)? And does not Donalbain's reason for his seeking refuge apart from Malcolm seem altogether legitimate: "our separated fortune shall keep us both the *safer*" (2.3.136–7)?[92] Security, 'safety' in its broadest sense, is a pervasive concern of human beings, having some regulatory effect on almost everything we do. We are reminded of this fact with the first explicit reference to it, which comes in Macbeth's rather formulaic pledge of allegiance to Duncan, acknowledging that "our duties ... do but what they should, by doing *everything safe* toward your love and honour" (1.4.24–7). In this we seem but a piece of Nature, 'survival' being one of the two general principles governing the rest of animate creation.[93]

Precisely because the concern for survival, for the safety of oneself and one's own, is such a powerful natural impulse, virtually anyone can appreciate (and envy) courage in the face of death – such as that reported of Macbeth at the beginning of the play. So long as he can count on meeting his enemies in the open, "beard to beard," Macbeth dares do all that may become a man. But from the moment he has reason to fear that his treacherous murder of old Duncan has but provided bloody instructions (and legitimacy) for others to deal with him likewise, he becomes morbidly obsessed with security ("To be thus [i.e., king] is nothing, but to be safely thus" 3.1.47). So, too, Lady Macbeth, whom we hear lament, "Nought's had, all's spent, / Where our desire is got without content: / 'Tis safer to be that which we destroy, / Than by destruction dwell in doubtful joy" (3.2.4–7). Even when Macbeth claims to fear only Banquo (3.1.48–55), he may be deluding himself; his allusion to his and his wife's eating their meals in fear and being shaken "nightly" by terrible dreams leaves one suspecting that his concern for security is more general (3.2.17–19). It comes as no surprise, then, that the murder of Banquo does not release him from the grip of "pale-hearted fear." For now Macduff becomes the focus of his worries (3.4.127–9); warned to "Beware the Thane of Fife," he readily responds, "Thou hast harp'd my fear aright" (4.1.74). Who can believe that were Macduff also eliminated, Macbeth would at last rest easy? Apparently, nothing less than an assurance of invulnerability could free him from his obsession with safety, and it is that which Hecate and her acolytes set about providing.

Still, the benefits of security – beginning with physical security from one's enemies – seem to be so obvious that it is hard to believe security itself might be "mortals' *chiefest* enemy." To begin to see the danger in security, however, we need only reflect on Macbeth. The fact that his security is illusory is irrelevant. The state of his mind is all that matters here: he, like everyone else, acts on the basis of whatever he believes to be the case. So, what effect does the illusion of invincibility have upon him? It does indeed make him even more "bloody, bold, and resolute." But does it make him prudent? Or is the effect quite the opposite: in eliminating all *need* for prudence, it abolishes the primary motivation for acquiring the kind of knowledge – coincident with an awareness of one's ignorance – upon which prudence, including rational foresight (as distinct from 'supernatural' prophecies), can be based? What about the other virtues? Macbeth once had some sense of justice and honour (1.7.6–16). Where is it now? Limited neither by the human wisdom he does not seek nor by the divine grace he has repudiated, all that is left by nature to *restrain* him is animal fear. When liberated from that, he is free to entertain the most extravagant hopes, to indulge his slightest whims, and to act upon every firstling of his vengeful heart, however inhuman or irrational it may be. Take away all of his fears, and there is nothing left to *temper* his desires. But as Macduff with his simple wisdom so plainly puts it: "Boundless intemperance in nature is a tyranny" (4.3.66–7). Moreover is not a germ of such tyranny planted in us all, ready to burst forth "full of growing," unless restrained by wisdom, grace, or fear?[94]

Reflecting upon Macbeth's obsession, we realize that the perfect and final security for which he yearns (as opposed to temporary approximations of it) is not merely a practical impossibility; but also, that the excessive preoccupation with it is unhealthy and destructive. It casts a pall over one's life, even should it not provoke one to the commission of crimes or other extreme actions. Moreover, the paradoxical claim of Shakespeare's Hecate prompts us to see for ourselves that the effects of *pursuing* some practical security, a condition that everyone is necessarily and legitimately concerned about, are quite different from those of actually *achieving* it. To the extent one feels 'perfectly secure,' the utilitarian component of one's motivation for striving after virtue – that is, for the inherently valuable qualities of personal goodness, such as temperance, courage, prudence, justness, and liberality – is diminished, while at the same time an important natural restraint on evil is relaxed.[95]

The preceding discussion of 'Hecate's Hypothesis' could be said to beg a momentous question, however, presuming as it seems an intimate connection, if not outright identification, between *having* the good (the good things, the good life) and *being* good (i.e., virtuous) – as if something, such as 'security' or gaining tyrannical power, could not be truly good for a human being unless its effect was to make one 'good' (with an analogous, and equally questionable, relationship implied between true evils, or 'ills,' and vice). Surely here we must not allow ourselves to be beguiled by language, blithely assuming that there is a single common reality being referred to throughout our profligate uses of the term 'good.' Whatever the truth of the matter, the confusing diversity of our usage is faithfully reflected in Shakespeare's own usage, at least on the surface: the word appears almost three thousand times in his plays, on average (roughly) once every three hundred words. Granted, many of these uses are in greetings and salutations

("Good morrow, both"; "at once, good night") and in modes of address ("my good Lord"; "good doctor"; "good Father"; "good Fleance"). But they are not to be wholly discounted on that score. The fact that these are favourite formulae of polite speech must be regarded as significant, and should make us that much more sensitive to those occasions when they might rightly have been employed, but were not (e.g., 5.5.16; cf. 8). The first three uses of the term in *Macbeth* nicely epitomize its major lexical facets. Malcolm refers to the bleeding Captain who prevented his capture as "a good and hardy soldier" (1.2.4). Banquo addresses his curiosity to Macbeth thus: "Good Sir, why do you start, and seem to fear / Things that do sound so fair?" (1.3.51–2). And with reference to the "prophetic greeting" of the witches, Macbeth muses to himself, "This supernatural soliciting / Cannot be ill; cannot be good" (130–1). Determining whether or not Shakespeare himself sees all these and other uses[96] as intelligible in light of a single solid idea of the Good would require a comprehensive reflection on what the play as a whole shows about the nature and workings of good and evil in our world.

Given the prominence of violent and bloody *deeds* in the play, however, what upon consideration may be most surprising about these matters is Shakespeare's emphasis on *thought* – as if the *power* of thought is the key to understanding everything else important to and about man, not least of all his freedom for good and evil.[97] Understanding thought itself, its mode of being as well as its power over the human soul – hence, over deeds – may present the ultimate metaphysical challenge. Upon the first of the witches' strange pronouncements being confirmed by Rosse and Angus, Macbeth urges Banquo, "Think upon what hath chanc'd; and at more time, / The Interim having *weigh'd* it, let us speak / Our free hearts each to other" (1.3.154–6). When next we see them in conversation, Banquo proves that 'what hath chanc'd' has indeed been on his mind: "I dreamt last night of the three Weyward Sisters: / To you they have show'd some truth." Macbeth's response, verging as it does on the self-contradictory, is scarcely believable: "I think not of them: / Yet, when we can entreat an hour to serve, / We would spend it in some words upon that business, / If you would grant the time" (2.1.20–4).

Similar references and exhortations to thought, and reminders of its intimate relationship with speech (both true and false), recur throughout the play. Macbeth begins the second of what must be three interviews with the prospective murderers of Banquo by inquiring:

> Well then, now
> Have you *consider'd* of my speeches? – *know*
> That it was he, in the times past, which held you

So under fortune, which you *thought* had been
Our innocent self?

(3.1.74–8; see also 137–8)

When Macbeth attempts to question the First Apparition (that of "an armed head"), the First Witch admonishes, "He knows thy thought: / Hear his speech, but say thou nought" (4.1.69–70). The Scottish doctor concludes the sleep-walking episode by confessing, "My mind she has mated [i.e., baffled, confounded – as in 'check-mated'], and amaz'd my sight. / I think, but dare not speak" (5.1.75–6). Endeavouring to explain Macbeth's bizarre behaviour at the banquet, Lady Macbeth first assures her guests, "The fit is momentary; upon a thought he will be well again" (3.4.54–5). And in the wake of Duncan's assassination, she repeatedly warns her Lord against 'inappropriate' thoughts: "A foolish thought to say a sorry sight" (2.2.21); "Consider it not so deeply" (29). "These deeds must not be thought / After these ways: so, it will make us mad" (32–3); "Why, worthy Thane, / You do unbend your noble strength, to think / So brain-sickly of things" (43–5); "Be not lost / So poorly in your thoughts" (70–1) – all of which only draw from a distraught Macbeth, "Methought, I heard a voice cry, 'Sleep no more'" (34); "I am afraid to think what I have done; / Look on't again I dare not" (50–1); "To know my deed, 'twere best not know myself" (72). Later, she protests his increasing isolation thus: "How now, my Lord? why do you keep alone, / Of sorriest fancies your companions making, / Using those thoughts, which should indeed have died / With them they think on?" (3.2.8–11). Having heard out Macduff's eloquent portrayal of Scotland's suffering, a suspicious Malcolm replies, "This tyrant, whose sole name blisters our tongues, / Was once thought honest: you have lov'd him well" Then in response to Macduff's indignant "*I* am not treacherous," he politely suggests an absolving circumstance: "But Macbeth is. / A good and virtuous nature may recoil, / In an imperial charge. But I shall crave your pardon: / That which you *are* my thoughts cannot transpose" (4.3.12–21). All the soliloquies, of course, are but thought rendered aural, and serve to remind us not only that we tend to think in linguistic terms, but that the ability to express one's thoughts precisely and coherently is the surest test of their clarity and validity.[98]

Even more prominent than the manifold references to Thought, however, are those to *Sight*. Perhaps this should not be surprising, given the multifarious relationships – logical, analogical, psychological, metaphorical – between seeing and *knowing*. Presumably, that is the point of this emphasis on sight, especially on seeing for oneself, on things being 'shown,' on truths being literally 'revealed' (unveiled, allowing one to see what is otherwise hidden) – and, correspondingly, on the effect of darkness to hide what eyes might otherwise see, and the beholders thereby presume to know. Despite all the ways in which appearances can be deceiving, especially where humans are involved, there remains an inescapable, irreducible reliance of knowledge on perception. For the many unwary, of course, seeing is believing. In fairness, perhaps they have more reason to trust their eyes than their minds. But to some considerable extent, this remains true for all of us. Our first manifestations of curiosity are with respect to perceptible things, for which perceptual experience suffices – as we are reminded by the Second Witch's childlike enthusiasm for seeing what her first sister is so childishly proud of: "Look what I have." [It's a pilot's thumb!] "Show me, show me" (1.3.26–7). We necessarily continue to believe that often, indeed usually, we *can* see something of the mind's present construction in the face; after all, the feigning of an emotion, such as grief (see 1.7.79; 2.3.134–5; 3.6.11), is parasitic on authentic expressions of it (2.3.62–3ff; 4.3.208–10, 220–1, 228–31). Thus, Banquo invites Rosse and Angus to observe the state of Macbeth's soul: "Look, how our partner's rapt." He is right about seeing rapture, if not about the unseen cause of it (supposing that it is result of the new honours that have so unexpectedly come upon him; 1.3.143–6).

As for the fallibility of sight, and the way we normally cope with this hazard, Macbeth's experience with the "air-drawn dagger" is illustrative:

> Is this a dagger, which I see before me,
> The handle toward my hand? Come, let me clutch thee: –
> I have thee not, and yet I see thee still.
> Art thou not, fatal vision, sensible
> To feeling, as to sight? or art thou but
> A dagger of the mind, a false creation,
> Proceeding from the heat-oppressed brain?
> I see thee yet, in form as palpable
> As this which now I draw.
>
> Mine eyes are made the fools o'th'other senses,
> Or else worth all the rest ...
>
> (2.1.33–45)

Worth all the rest? An arresting thought. What if one had to choose? Would one trade the senses of hearing and smell, taste and touch, for the sole sense of sight? What would existence be like, were sight one's sole perceptual access to the world beyond the mind? Hard to imagine (but revealing to try). As we are presently constituted, however, Macbeth's 'dagger problem,' though seemingly such a bizarre instance, in fact serves perfectly well to show how we cope with the difficulties that can arise from conflicting sensations. Confronted with the visible form of something that is normally graspable – "in form as palpable as this which now I draw" – but which is not "sensible to feeling," Macbeth not surprisingly concludes, "There's no such thing. It is the bloody business which informs thus to mine eyes." That is, he, like almost everyone else, regards the *coherence* of perceptual information as indicative of its reliability; whereas inconsistency – being a violation, not of the physics of perception, but of the fundamental rule of Reason – implies some problem requiring resolution by the intellect.[99] In resolving this one, notice, Macbeth grants priority to tactility for determining what is 'real,' attesting to our normal materialistic prejudice.[100] Generally speaking, however, unless we have grounds for suspecting otherwise (as Macbeth does with the dagger, or as Banquo suggests when the witches suddenly vanish; 1.3.80–5), we trust that what our and other people's senses disclose is the practical truth. Hence, the "one who *saw* him die" was confident that Cawdor did in fact repent, and Malcolm not unreasonably accepts this report as true (1.4.3–7).

So it goes with *most* of what we hear and see and touch for ourselves (and even with much of what others whom we trust report of their own immediate experience): to perceive is to know. Indeed, it is everyone's first paradigm of knowing, and remains the favourite of most people. For them, truth is only fully intelligible and compelling to the extent it can be made visible, audible, tangible. If they are to understand Evil, it will be as Evil Incarnate. Likewise, God, or the Good (see 4.3.140–59). In this respect, Macbeth is typical. Because he believes himself bold enough to "*look* on that which might appal the Devil," he insists, "What *man* dare, I dare" (3.4.58–9, 98; see also 1.7.46–7; 2.2.50–1). When he last visits the witches, insisting that they answer what he asks, and they offer him an option: "Say, if thou'dst rather hear it from our mouths, or from our masters?" Macbeth replies, "Call 'em; let me *see* 'em." And so they do: "Come, high, or low; thyself and office deftly *show*" (4.1.62–8). But preoccupied with what the three Apparitions *say*, Macbeth – ironically – does not recognize what they themselves do so 'deftly show': for the armed head is his own as it will be when severed from his body by the very Macduff it warns him of (scarce wonder it knew his thought, and harp'd his fear aright); the bloody child who assures him that no man of woman born can harm Macbeth was not himself of woman born, being none other than Macduff as he must have looked when "untimely ripp'd" from his mother's womb; the crowned child bearing a tree is, of course, the clever Malcolm, who will manage what Macbeth presumes is impossible: for Birnam wood to come against him at high Dunsinane hill. However, all that Macbeth 'sees' in what he was shown are "Sweet bodements! good!," assuring him that "high-plac'd Macbeth / Shall live the lease of Nature, pay his breath / To time, and mortal custom." Yet still his "heart throbs to ***know*** one thing ... shall Banquo's issue ever reign in this kingdom?" Despite being warned ("Seek to know no more"), he persists, and the witches comply in the most convincing fashion imaginable:

> *1st Witch:* Show!
> *2nd Witch:* Show!
> *3rd Witch:* Show!
> *All:* Show his eyes, and grieve his heart;
> Come like shadows, so depart.
> (107–11)

Whereupon comes "A show of eight Kings" along with a smiling Banquo and a mirror, Macbeth punctuating the procession with his protests: "Why do you show me this? ... Start, eyes! ... I'll see no more ... a glass, which shows me many more; ... Horrible sight! – Now, I *see*, 'tis *true*." In short, Macbeth himself 'shows' *us* – after all, the emphasis on showing is for *our* sake, not his – how strong is the normal human preference for 'perceptible truth' over that which can only be intellected, how much more conviction it carries, thus, why images can be more potent than syllogisms; and generally how much more 'at home' we embodied souls feel in the perceptual world, dealing with things that can be seen and heard and touched and smelled and tasted, than in a purely intelligible realm.[101] But also, how selective we typically are in our perceiving; and how readily we conflate perceiving and knowing.

The equating of seeing with knowing is so natural that we speak of even the invisible logic of arguments as nonetheless 'showing' (meaning 'proving') their conclusions. How more confident are we apt to be, then, of whatever truths seem to have been made at all physically manifest. Once again, it is that "good and hardy soldier," the anonymous bleeding Captain, who first uses such language: "And Fortune, on his [i.e., Macdonwald's] damned quarrel smiling, / Show'd like a rebel's whore" (1.2.14–15). With the Thaneship of Cawdor well settled on Macbeth, Banquo can say to him of the witches, "To you they have show'd some truth." When Rosse asks his cousin, "How goes the world, Sir, now?" Macduff's brusque reply – "Why, *see* you not?" – is (as we say) perfectly 'sensible,' meaning 'intelligible.' Similarly, his parting response to Rosse's decision to attend the investiture of Macbeth at Scone – "may you see things well done there" – does not refer to the punctiliousness of the ceremony (2.4.21, 37). Of course, none of these 'observations' are perceptions in any strict sense. They are the mind's interpretations of the perceptual evidence, seen in the context of the interpreter's antecedent understanding of reality. Thus, this curious multiplicity of references to 'seeing' and 'showing' is of a piece with the equally curious prominence of 'thought.' Both call our attention to the pervasive importance of the human mind. With respect to everything that is, be it perceptible or intelligible, its significance for good or ill is wholly dependent on mind.

However, this is not to say that good and evil are purely subjective. Indeed, nothing could be further from the truth. But it is to suggest that the rational soul is the *medium* through which good and evil work – a different proposition altogether, however likely people are to confuse them. The third scene of the play, that in which Macbeth and Banquo first encounter the Weyward Sisters (prompting, in turn, the first explicit consideration of good and evil), nicely shows this mediating role of the mind. When one part of the witches' "prophetic greeting" to Macbeth is confirmed within moments of its pronouncement, Banquo registers his astonishment: "What? can the Devil speak true?" Notice, for him there is no question but that these hags – whose physical ugliness he so vividly, so pungently describes – are agents of evil. He is accordingly suspicious. Having heard out Angus's explanation of how Cawdor's robes became vacant, he cautions an excited Macbeth, "But 'tis strange: / And oftentimes, to win us to our harm, / The instruments of Darkness tell us truths; / Win us with honest trifles, to betray's / In deepest consequence" (1.3.122–6). Clearly, then, he understands these "instruments" to work their effects by influencing men's thoughts. He turns to question Rosse and Angus further, leaving Macbeth musing to himself. While he gives no indication that Banquo's warning has had any effect, he in his own way bears witness to the reasoning mind as medium for both good and ill (as the emphasized words in his ensuing soliloquy show):

Two *truths* are told,
As happy prologues to the swelling *act*
Of the imperial theme ...
This supernatural *soliciting*
Cannot be ill; cannot be good: –
If ill, why hath it given me earnest of success,
Commencing in a *truth*? I am Thane of Cawdor:
If good, why do I yield to that *suggestion*
Whose horrid *image* doth unfix my hair,
And *make* my seated heart knock at my ribs
Against the use of nature? Present *fears*
Are less than horrible *imaginings*.
My *thought*, whose murther yet is but *fantastical*,
Shakes so my single state of man,

> That *function* is smother'd in *surmise*,
> And nothing is, but what is not.
> (1.3.128–42)

What one notices in this initial scene with Macbeth becomes even more evident upon the first appearance of his wife. Stimulated conjointly by her lord's surprising good news and the announcement of Duncan's imminent visit, Lady Macbeth expressly petitions those "spirits that tend on mortal thoughts" to produce an entire sequence of remarkable effects: to unsex her; to fill her "top-full of direst cruelty"; to make thick her blood; and, to "stop up th'access and passage to remorse" (1.5.40–6).

To repeat, however, there is a world of difference between regarding the mind as the *medium* of good and evil, and regarding it as that which in and of itself dictates what any given person calls 'good' and 'evil' – although many people misinterpret the evidence for the former as implying the latter. Mistaking proximate cause for first cause, they readily approve of Hamlet's assuring Rosencrantz, "there is nothing either good or bad but thinking *makes* it so."[102] The fame of this formula is no mystery, but the kindest assessment of it that can be justified is that the Prince of Denmark is either a careless or a deceptive speaker. For it leaves the false impression that with respect to all evaluation, thought is autochthonous – as if what counts as the "*good* digestion" and "health" Macbeth wishes his guests (3.4.37–8) is entirely a matter of personal preference, having nothing necessarily to do with biochemical processes and the natural design of properly functioning bodies. Or as if the slaughter of Macduff's family would be a good thing rather than a bad if somehow he could just manage to think of it as such (and so regard Macbeth as a benefactor deserving of thanks rather than as a monster to be hated and hunted). As if there were no reason in the nature of the things themselves *why* Macduff's "pretty chickens and their dam" were in fact "most precious" to him; that he has only to 'look on the bright side,' and all will be well with him – though even this absurdity presumes there are objective qualities of things and circumstances that would, if noticed, make them inherently desirable to him, thereby 'brightening' his prospects (fewer mouths to feed, less clutter; more time for himself, perhaps). Or as if any conceivable response one might attribute to the slain chamberlains would serve equally well to answer the question Rosse asks Macduff when told that it was they who murdered Duncan: "Alas, the day! What good could they pretend?" (2.4.22–4).

It is undoubtedly true that most people judge something 'good' because of how they feel about it, that it brings pleasure or comfort of either body or soul (or eases pain and discomfort) – phenomena which are, by definition, experiences of consciousness, or 'thought.' The idea of the Good implicit in this natural hedonism is grossly inadequate, but even so it is sufficient for seeing the inadquacy of a radically subjectivist view. After all, our normal preference for pleasure over pain is not itself something we choose; it is intrinsic to our natural constitution. Similarly, the fact that certain things give pleasure, whereas others cause pain, has as much to do with their natures as it does with ours. We may vary considerably in our capacity to endure excruciating pain, and perhaps partly because some are more able than others to exert 'mind over matter.' But being subjected to the black arts of a skilled torturer is no one's idea of a good time, and the virtually unanimous agreement on which is the torture chamber and which the perfumed garden can hardly be attributed to coincidence. Obviously, there would be no *recognition* of either good or evil were it not for thought (or to speak more precisely, were it not for the rational soul; the only natural beings who show any concern for, or appreciation of, good and evil per se are we humans, distinguished by the rational powers of our souls). Nor, consequently, could any action be consciously undertaken in pursuit of the good or in avoidance of the bad, for there would be no basis upon which the mind could distinguish good from bad, no way of evaluating – hence no rational *choices* to be made, or irrational ones either, for that matter – if none of the actual qualities of things (be they objects, actions, beliefs, people, situations, whatever) were truly good or bad relative to our natures. The question of free will would be pointless. In recognizing that it is through our *awareness* of the existence of such qualities that judgments of good and evil are made, we merely acknowledge mind to be the *medium*, or mediating cause, whereby good and evil operate in our lives. But this is not to conclude that thought alone is what *establishes* good and evil, that "thinking *makes* it so" – as if one could not possibly be mistaken about such matters, believing something to be good that is in reality bad. Macbeth proves otherwise, time and again.

Of course, the mediation of the mind figures in our capacities both as 'recipients' (consciously aware of the world's effect on us), and as 'actors': evil thoughts giving rise to evil deeds, and good ones likewise. As such, we can readily see how the issues involved with free will centre on the question, 'To what extent do I (or can I) control my own thinking?' – and moreover, why *that* matter is especially perplexing. For what is the 'I' here, if not the entirety of one's conscious 'self'? Is thinking something 'I' *do*, or something that *happens* to or in 'me'? What is Banquo praying for when he pleads, "merciful Powers! Restrain in me the cursed thoughts that nature gives way to in repose!" (2.1.7–9). Does the philosopher who says "*I* think, therefore I am" have it right; or should it be "I'm aware of something called thinking going on, therefore ..."?[103] Am 'I' active or passive, cause or effect? Having reflected on the totality of one's experience, one may well want to say, "Some of both, it seems."

Setting aside the problems of establishing *what* precisely the 'I' is, and *why* we all identify more with one part of our conscious self than with another,[104] it seems that I do exercise *some* control over my thinking. When I wish to ignore an intrusive thought, I am sometimes successful, as I sometimes am in directing the focus of my attention, or in remembering something by sheer force of effort, or in making myself concentrate despite my mind's inclination to wander, or in 'facing facts' rather than indulging in wishful fantasies, and so on. On the other hand, it is clear that I am not able to make myself believe just anything I please. In my conception of the real world, I cannot ignore what I am somehow sure is true. Having understood a geometric proof, I seem to have no alternative but to accept whatever it shows; reason itself 'determines' what I shall think. This example perhaps epitomizes the force of pure reason, here unopposed by other conscious forces (such as originate in the passions or appetites). However, there are non-mathematical 'thoughts' that may also be practically impossible to ignore or forget, as the Macbeths serve to remind us: painful memories, morbid fears, vivid images, obsessive desires, terrible dreams, ..."sorriest fancies." That problems without all remedy should be without regard is a purely rational judgment. But the mind seems more like a spiritual cauldron where the various powers of reason meet and contend with the soul's subrational drives, together mysteriously brewing and blending the conscious experience. While usually this 'spiritual chemistry' is to some extent subject to purposeful, wilful manipulation, it rarely if ever is entirely so (although this seems to be a major respect in which people differ: the extent of their control, presumably a function of strength of reasoning joined with will power). If, however, the precise workings of the mind are fated to remain mysterious – and no neurophysiology, regardless of how precisely it may correlate with conscious experience, throws any light whatsoever on the *two*-way communication between mind and body, consciousness and matter-in-motion – then so will a rational understanding of human freedom ever elude us. And we shall continue to believe that which seems more faithful to our experience.

As for the paradox of deliberately 'choosing' to be irrational to whatever extent, it is nicely epitomized by Macbeth's deciding to be ruled by his heart rather than his head. For this is preceded by his providing himself what he judges to be *rational* grounds *justifying* impetuosity. A succession of miscarried intentions has taught him that, in an ever-changing world, the timing of actions is often so crucial that one cannot afford the delay required for careful consideration of one's aims and methods (much less for anguished soul-searching). Nor is this the only facet of Time's implacable tyranny over mortals.[105] Unlike space, where often one may return to a previous position,[106] there's no returning in time – "what's done cannot be undone." Thus, it may seem to Macbeth that he's damned if he does and damned if he doesn't: should he pause to think before he acts, the unique opportunity may be lost; whereas if he acts precipitously, he may do something he will profoundly regret. His predicament is shared by all men of action. And having felt both horns of the dilemma, he (like most men of action) prefers risking the latter. Provoked by learning that Macduff has flown the coop, Macbeth makes his resolution:

> Time, thou anticipat'st my dread exploits:
> The flighty purpose is never o'ertook,
> Unless the deed go with it. From this moment,
> The very firstlings of my heart shall be
> The firstlings of my hand.
>
> (4.1.144–8)

As he sees it, then, his own bitter experience has confirmed what Machiavelli explicitly teaches would-be princes – that in politics "it is better to be impetuous than cautious, because fortune is a woman" who favours the bold and audacious[107] (see 1.2.14–19). The irony is, Macbeth has come to this conclusion *too late* for him to retrieve his own fortunes. And the very first "firstling" of his fretted heart that he vows to act upon would seem to show beyond all doubt the consummate irrationality of 'rationally' choosing to be ruled by passion:

> And even now,
> To crown my *thoughts* with *acts*, be it thought and done:
> The castle of Macduff I will surprise;
> Seize upon Fife; give to th'edge o'th'sword
> His wife, his babes, and all unfortunate souls
> That trace him in his line. No boasting like a fool;
> This deed I'll *do*, be*fore* this purpose cool.
>
> (4.1.148–54)

Having reflected on the example of Macbeth, one may resolve to try always to rule with reason the impulses of one's heart; but one cannot choose to have only those impulses which reason approves, such that rational rule is always effortless.[108] A moment's thought suffices to show how hopelessly paradoxical would be the aspiration to have nothing occur to one unless or until one wishes it to.

Recognizing that no one's mind is entirely free (in the sense of being wholly subject to wilful control), we open ourselves to the possiblity that the power of the Good manifests itself not only in the natural appeal of things that are truly good – which are obviously not identical with whatever things do, or are believed to, bring pleasure – but also in the peculiar "tortures of the mind" that can come from doing evil. In the effort to fathom that possiblity, one necessarily comes to see the nature and relationship of Good and Evil very differently. For on the ordinary view, to eat one's meals in fear of poison, and sleep in the affliction of terrible dreams that shake one nightly; to be taunted by imaginary voices; to feel as if one's mind were full of stinging scorpions; to believe oneself haunted by the ghosts of those one has murdered; to prowl the halls at night while still in fast but restless sleep, futilely attempting to wash clean one's hands and soul, with life on earth having become a murky hell – these are *bad* experiences, 'evils' one could only wish to avoid. But seen as the consequences of one's own wrongdoing, it is readily apparent that these evils, while bad in themselves, actually work to support goodness in human beings (i.e., virtue), and thereby to promote goodness generally in both public and private life. Plainly, then, in cases such as these there is a direct connection between enjoying a good life and being good. The psychic punishments suffered by Lord and Lady Macbeth would suggest that the human soul has no prospect of inner peace or satisfaction unless the person involved abides by certain natural or God-given standards.

This need not be seen as further implying, however, that Shakespeare intends to provide here (or anywhere else, for that matter) a comprehensive catalogue of what these standards of acceptable conduct are. He merely supplies ample food for sobering thought. Several of his characters remind us of certain principles that many human beings, representing long and varied experience with political life, have concluded are divinely ordained, or part and parcel of the natural order of things. These rules supplement and complement those violated by the Macbeths (occasioning their subsequent distress), some of which they allude to themselves. Macbeth, contemplating the murder of Duncan, worries about the "even-handed Justice" whereby his "bloody instructions ... [may] return to plague the inventor" – thus acknowledging a principle basic to almost everyone's reasoning about justice: reciprocity (that what's right for the goose is so for the gander). He recognizes that the King is "here in double trust": that there are obligations towards him arising out of kinship, others out of his being the legitimate ruler ("strong both against the deed"), and still others that arise out of one's role as host (1.7.12–16). Macbeth also acknowledges there to be obligations of gratitude for benefits received (32; cf. 1.4.15), as does his lady when she first welcomes Duncan under her battlements (1.6.14–20). One does not have to be a philosopher to see the 'why' of these principles, how their observance generally improves political life, and how their violation threatens its very possibility. Nor to see why special obligations arise out of the idea of friendship – most cruelly abused by Macbeth in arranging the ambush of Banquo and young Fleance, his radical change of heart towards them masked with shameless flattery and deceit (3.1.20–35, 114–15; cf. 3.2.30–5). Rosse in conversation with his cousin Macduff reminds us of the special opprobrium we attach to parricide, regarding it not simply as immoral, but 'unnatural' (2.4.27–9); for we, unlike beasts, not only recognize who our parents are, but can understand the various grounds of our indebtedness to them, valid irrespective of the affectionate feelings that normally are expected to obtain. Macduff's wife rails against her husband for ignoring the natural obligations of fatherhood in leaving his wife and children unprotected "in a place from whence himself does fly," adding, "He loves us not; he wants the natural touch"; she nonetheless remains loyal, and we soon learn how wrong she is about her husband (4.2.7–9, 80–1; 4.3.176–235). It is only against the fabric of natural expectations regarding fitting behaviour on the parts of parents, children, friends, spouses, rulers, subjects, cousins, and so on, that we can react with appropriate horror at certain things said or done – and not just the great atrocities, the outright murders and betrayals, but seemingly incidental details that contribute to the general atmosphere of evil pervading the play (such as the witches' including in their ghastly stew the "finger of a birth-strangled babe, / Ditch-deliver'd by a drab" 4.1.30–1). These, then, are but some of the allusions to standards of rightful conduct, rules whose violation may bring about a fitting punishment in the soul of an offender, even should he escape the justice of other men. In the words of the Scottish Doctor reflecting on the somniloquence of Lady Macbeth, "Unnatural deeds do breed unnatural troubles" (5.1.68–9).

Clearly the matter is not that simple, however. The casual indifference of an untroubled Rosse to any such standards, and the callousness eventually acquired by Macbeth himself (having so "supp'd full with horrors" that direness has become familiar to his slaughterous thoughts; 5.5.13–14), render dubious, not to say incredible, such an uncomplicated view of natural justice. However salutary a general belief in it may be politically, might it nonetheless be illusory, its alleged effects artificially inculcated by nurture, which someone with sufficient clarity of understanding and strength of mind can – and for his own good, *should* – rise above?[109] After all, remaining vulnerable to such psychic sanctions can only be a liability if neither they nor the standards they support, which might on balance appear to serve more the good of others than one's own, are grounded in natural necessity.

There seems to be no response to this view, either pro or con, that does not perforce rely upon (i.e., trust in) one's power of synoptic judgment. Having brought this power to bear on the various ways people choose to live, one may concede that the result is partly an 'aesthetic' judgment, without thereby intending to imply that it is irrational and merely a matter of subjective taste – as if there were no natural bases for beauty and nobility, hence, no rational basis for praising or blaming Shakespeare's art (since the comprehensive judgment of a play requires this same synthesizing of intellectual, political, moral, and aesthetic considerations). Applying one's judgment to the first case at hand, then, the question simply put is: does one admire Rosse and envy him his success in life, such that placed in his circumstances one would wish to *be* like Rosse? (It *is* a 'package deal'; to have his kind of success – his kind of 'good life' – one has to *be* his kind of person, have his kind of soul, manifest his views and qualities.) What about Macbeth? Of course, for an assessment to be relevant to the point at issue, one must imagine him successful according to his own ambitions: victorious over Malcolm, with whatever Scotland affords being his to enjoy as he would, eventually dying old and in bed, like Agathocles. In becoming a ruthless but enduring tyrant, unrestrained by the ordinary, perhaps merely conventional standards of morality, duty, and decency, and undisturbed by their desecration, does he thereby become "so much more the man" (as his wife assured him he would), or so much less? Is imagining him successful in this manner enough to make him admirable, even noble? Would he, or would he not, still be bereft of that which he acknowledges "should accompany old age, as honour, love, obedience, troops of friends" (5.3.20–8)?

In any event, this much needs be made explicit: one's synoptic judgment of these or any other people's lives need not be based upon how they regard themselves – no more than Duncan's horses have to think themselves "beauteous" and the very "minions of their race" in order for one to judge them so. Obviously, people's own subjective assessments *can* be an important indication of the suitability of the way in which they have actually lived. That a person is happy, and finds his manner of life meaningful and satisfying, would usually be strong evidence in its favour; whereas, nobody sane would wish Lady Macbeth's condition upon himself, and consequently would treat it as a warning against doing as she did. But such feelings are not the be-all and the end-all. There have been lives we would judge eminently worth living that were not distinguished by happiness, as well as lives we would judge debased however pleased were the people that lived them. Would not anyone we could possibly respect rather be Sokrates dissatisfied than a pig satisfied?

Rosse doubtless believes himself wondrously clever, and other men fools for not being as shamelessly self-serving as he; yet it would not be unreasonable to conclude that he is all the worse for that, since it renders him practically incorrigible. In a like vein, one may judge Macbeth a better man when his conscience still plagued him, and for the very fact that it did so: he still had that much goodness in him. To adapt the saying of a subsequent philosopher, himself one of Shakespeare's greatest admirers: "He who despises himself can still respect himself as one who despises."[110] But for these and analogous judgments to have any real value – that is, for one to despise or admire *justly* – it must be possible to discern, however dimly, some natural standards according to which people ought to live, and natural criteria of human goodness or virtue which they ought to aspire to meet. So that when they do not, be it out of ignorance or choice (which includes most of what they choose to regard as 'necessity'), one can truthfully say they are living worse lives than their circumstances allow, whether they are aware of it or not and whether or not their souls are troubled as a consequence. Reaching a positive conclusion as to the possibility of such discernment – again, be it 'yes' or 'no' – may amount to the most comprehensive judgment of all, and presume a synoptic perspective comparable to Shakespeare's own. However, the very presence in most people of something like a 'conscience,' along with the normal human capacities to feel shame and guilt as well as pride and righteousness – all phenomena that are distinctive to human nature, perhaps essential to it – are facts exceedingly hard to explain in the absence of any natural criteria for their being appropriately felt.

About Good and Evil per se: If the ordinary view, which sees a simple opposition between them (and thus tacitly assumes a Manichean duality of independent, and roughly equal, opposing forces at work in the world), is at best superficial, how then are they more correctly understood? One might begin by trying to *think* about evil. After all, does not the play invite such a meditation, filled as it is with evils of all kinds, indeed presenting what are taken to be the powers of evil personified? What one quickly discovers is the natural limitation on conceiving evil as simply the *opposite* of good. It is impossible for evil to be opposite of good in *all* respects, as that culminates in nothingness. For one attribute of good things, beginning with good health, is that they exist; hence, an evil that was in every respect the opposite of good would annihilate itself, leaving only whatever is somehow good. Or alternatively expressed, only nothingness per se could be *absolutely* evil, which implies that existence per se is good (a view towards which we seem to some extent naturally inclined, insofar as we tend to regard premature death, decay, and pointless destruction as generally bad, while regarding life, growth, regeneration, and creativity as generally good). Thus, one must acknowledge all that exists – however repugnant much of it may be to the taste of man, poignantly memorialized by the various ingredients of the witches' brew (4.1.4–38) – as being in some respect or to some extent good, and that the Good is ever triumphant insofar as the natural order continues to be. So, for evil to be a force at work *in* this world, it must exist, hence, cannot be 'pure evil.' How, then, is it to be understood?

Shakespeare's *Macbeth* points us towards a more coherent, thus intelligible view. One might start with a consideration of its portrayal of Evil Incarnate. A convenient juncture at which to begin *that* comes immediately after the ghost of

Banquo has transformed Macbeth's ceremonious banquet into a pageant of "most admir'd disorder" (the spectre first enters at almost the exact midpoint of the drama: 3.4.36; significantly, perhaps, we see it before Macbeth does). What follows this supernatural disturbance is arguably the most *ordered* scene in the play, that in which the Weyward Sisters are given a severe dressing down by Hecate. For not only is the *form* of her speech rigidly metrical, a very paradigm of orderly rhythm and rhyme, its 'matter' is an extended harangue cum demonstration concerning the maintenance of proper order within the hierarchy of evil powers. Indeed, it is only with her arrival that we are given clear indication that any such hierarchy exists, or that there is a consistent rationale guiding its activities.[111] Macbeth had twice earlier referred to Hecate in connection with witchcraft (2.1.51–2; 3.2.41), but the sole "instruments of Darkness" we had actually *seen* were those three sinister hags whose mutual interrogations begin the play. Throughout their subsequent appearances, they seem to be of roughly equal status, suggesting 'thus it is' with all demonic agents. However, from the first words of this scene (a rather anxious "Why, how now, Hecate, you look angerly?" eliciting from the addressee an indignant "Have I not *reason* ...?"), we are obliged to revise radically our understanding of how things stand among the netherworld's various apparatchiks. It turns out the Weyward Sisters do not report directly to Satan. Much less are they a sorority of freelancers, capriciously attacking whatever targets of opportunity happen to cross their crooked paths – or at least they are not supposed to be. Perhaps they do have authority to vent their spite however they can on rump-fed ronyons selfishly mounching chestnuts. But as an angry Hecate soon makes plain, meddling with mighty warrior captains who would be kings – given their great potential for both good and evil – falls well outside the competence of this wither'd trio:

> Have I not *reason*, beldams as you are?
> Saucy, and overbold, how did you dare
> To trade and traffic with Macbeth,
> In riddles, and affairs of death;
> And I, the mistress of your charms,
> The close contriver of all harms,
> Was never call'd to bear my part,
> Or show the *glory* of our art?
> And, which is worse, all you have done
> Hath been but for a wayward son,
> Spiteful, and wrathful; who, as others do,
> Loves for his own ends, not for you.
> (3.5.2–13)

There are several features of Hecate's critique that are worth emphasizing. First and foremost, *reason* is its basis, even if only in the form of instrumental rationality: the witches practice an *art*, of which she is the Grand Mistress and they bare journeymen. The very existence of an art (as opposed to a mere knack) presumes rationally intelligible – and as such learnable and communicable – principles whereby the practitioner pursues the defining end, or *telos*, of his or her art (bountiful crops in the case of a farmer; for a tailor, well-fitting, durable, or perhaps merely fashionable clothes; health for a doctor; savoury food for a cook; beautiful music for a harpist). Moreover, no art of any consequence can be fully acquired in a day; however great one's talent for it, the requisite learning and experience take time. Thus, an art's very existence implies a natural hierarchy of artistic skill among those who would wield its special power, and this further implies rational standards of proficiency whereby to teach, criticize, and superintend others. Competent journeymen, therefore, recognize their own limitations, and so know when to call upon the greater skill of a master artisan. Moreover, if there is a pièce de résistance to be executed, one that will show an art in its greatest glory, this challenge is properly reserved for its most eminent virtuosi.

Thus, Hecate does indeed have reason to be angry with her subordinates, who do not know their place, which would imply also not knowing why they are assigned to that place nor why their place is beneath hers. Or to speak in more general terms, these somewhat childish crones apparently do not really understand why there is an organizational hierarchy at all. They are aware merely that there is one, and that it is maintained by rewards and punishments (beginning with praise and blame; see 4.1.39) which are controlled from above. Their ignorance can be made illuminating, however. If any group, even a society of devils, is to be successful in a *collective* undertaking, its members must act in concert, coordinating their activities, not interfering with each other (much less attacking each other).[112] This requires more than just a rational delineation of responsibilities and authorities, with some agency generally recognized as the ultimate decision-maker and overall supervisor (as Hecate claims to be: the mistress of her underlings' charms and close contriver of *all* harms). It requires as well some shared notion of justice regulating the members' behaviour towards each other, such that the disputes that arise among them can be peacefully adjudicated, the benefits and burdens of association allocated, and transgressions consistently penalized. Nor will just any notion do: it too has to 'make sense,' and seem at least minimally fair. The witches evidently fear Hecate's displeasure, but they presume she is as good as her word, and that consequently they will not be further chastised if they "make *amends* now" by promptly doing as they are told (3.5.14, 36).

Also, however, if a fiendish legion is to succeed in doing its worst, it requires of its members – paradoxical as this may at first seem – a shared conception of their 'common good.' This they apparently have, as we learn when Hecate, attended by three more witches (possible replacements in case the first trio bungled again?), arrives at the Pit of Acheron to supervise the "great business [that] must be wrought ere noon."[113] She congratulates the chastened beldams who have, as ordered, prepared a cauldron of strange brew: "O, well done! I commend your pains, / And every one shall share i'th'gains" (4.1.39–40). *Shared gains* – in this case, the perverse gratification they can all enjoy from their success in luring mighty Macbeth, a man of potentially great nobility, to his final destruction, accompanied by whoever might fall with him. Success in 'doing bad' to or among *others* is their common good, that is, the source of whatever delight, satisfaction, and 'prospering' they are capable of, and as such that for which they strive. Recall with what joyful anticipation all three sisters contemplated the first one's plans for tormenting the ronyon's sailor husband, and how willingly, how "kindly," they contributed their resources towards that end (1.3.11–14). The notion of being consciously *attracted* by something that is in no way gratifying is as self-contradictory as that of a round square. What sense could we make of their collaborating in the pursuit of 'a common bad,' meaning bad for *them*, productive of injury and dissatisfaction? Purposeful action, including intentionally doing evil (whether by devils or men), is intelligible only in light of some idea of the good; and however partial and distorted a representation it may be, this idea necessarily retains certain formal attributes of what is in truth good. Consequently, Evil is subordinate to the Good, and cannot *conceivably* be on a par with it.

Try to imagine any possible way Hecate and her underlings could operate otherwise. Suppose they set about working evil as readily among themselves as among ordinary mortals? What might this consist of? Disrupting the machinations of their colleagues, with the consequence that they actually serve human good? Or, 'better' still, seeking to 'corrupt' and even destroy each other, thus eliminating evil so far as they succeed? Viewed from the Satanic perspective, this clearly will not do. His agents may introduce disorder into the human world; indeed, complete chaos, "confusion," among mortals may be the ideal for which they strive (3.5.29), presuming that a Hobbesian State of Nature – a war of all against all, where every man is enemy to every man – is worse than even the worst tyranny (as Hobbes himself contended). In this connection, we might recall what Macduff exclaims upon his discovering the "Most sacrilegious Murther" of Duncan: "Confusion now hath made his masterpiece!" (2.3.65–6). Malcolm's false impugning of himself strikes a similar note: "Nay, had I power, I should / Pour the sweet milk of concord into Hell, / Uproar the universal peace, confound / All unity on earth" (4.3.97–100). Macbeth several times invokes an image of chaos in issuing his threats (e.g., 3.2.16; 4.1.52–60). The fact that his life is eventually reduced to a meaningless chaos of sound and fury can be taken as evidence that the agents of Evil have been finally victorious over him.

Promoting disorder, chaos, confusion among humans – and even among beasts insofar as this affects the human world (see 2.4.16–18) – is apparently the ultimate goal of their activity.[114] They cannot rationally wish to *destroy* the world, as this would eliminate the only arena in which to pursue that for which they exist: doing evil. Nor can they favour disorder and chaos per se without vitiating their own effectiveness, perhaps to the point of nullity. This is so, even if one conceives evil to be a single unified power rather than a plurality (though why Shakespeare opts for the latter conception is an important issue that must still be addressed). Be it One or Many, however, evil acting randomly, 'chaotically,' cannot be as effective as action in accordance with a discriminating, coherent, efficient, and altogether *rationally ordered* plan. After all, random acts might as readily result in an early exit for bloody Macbeth or compliant Rosse as for pious, gentle Duncan – with a net gain in goodness for Scotland. Moreover, as should be evident, whatever natural limits one discerns in analysing the situation confronted by a cohort of intelligent agents *purposefully* promoting evil (which would seem to guarantee the maximum actualization of evil) must hold true for evil as such.

Hecate's denunciation, however, specifies that the Weyward Sisters are guilty of something "worse" than their violation of the internal principles of rational organization. They have failed to recognize the most basic, most important distinction of practical affairs: 'Us' versus 'Them,' 'friends' versus 'enemies,' 'insiders' versus 'outsiders.' They have dealt with Macbeth as if he were really one of them, dedicated to doing what they are dedicated to: stirring up as much trouble and ill-will among mortals as humanly possible. But this is not so. "Wayward" though he may have strayed from the paths of righteous conduct, spiteful and wrathful as he shows himself capable of becoming, he still "loves for his own ends," which remain those he shares with other sons of man: wealth and power, of course, but also the "honour, love, obedience, troops of friends" that he would prefer accompany his old age. Here, then, is another major clue to understanding evil in human affairs. It is the inevitable consequence of naturally selfish individuals pursuing their own good as they see it (which so often is mistakenly).

Overtly, of course, *Macbeth* centres on evil as we humans experience it, and shows us how it comes to pass. More precisely, Shakespeare concentrates our attention on the sole portion of it that is of *practical relevance* to us: that which is, to whatever extent, the consequence of how we think and act, especially with respect to each other. There are ills that beset us that are no one's doing, and which we are practically powerless to prevent or to remedy once they have happened, ranging from great natural disasters (such as hurricanes) to individual accidents (such as being struck by a falling chimney). But the play is not about the slings and arrows of impersonal fortune, outrageous as they may sometimes be. *Macbeth* does, however, require us to think about the nature of the world in which we find ourselves. As noted earlier, Being 'exists' in space and time only as the Forms of Order immanent in the self-regulating, self-sustaining, self-renewing dynamic hierarchy of perpetual Becoming: the endless flux of specific things that come into being and pass away. To have this material world is to have particular 'instances,' each belonging to some class or *kind* of thing (the various 'species'), these classes in turn belonging to still more inclusive ones, and so on. It may be possible to imagine a world made up of a plurality of idiosyncratic things, but it is not the one we inhabit, as Macbeth's discriminating "catalogues" of dogs and men serve to remind us (3.1.91–102) – to say nothing for now of the elaborate 'ornithology' pervading the play. Nonetheless, ours is a world of *separate* 'beings,' some of which prosper at the expense of others: to eat is good; to go hungry is bad; to be eaten is worse; and to be eaten by one's own kind (as reported of Duncan's horses), 'unnatural' – the idea of species that routinely feed on themselves represents an impossible *ordering* of nature.

Thus, competition with one's own kind for the limited 'good things' in life – beginning with the necessities of life itself – brings some 'bad' into the world. A hierarchy of predation brings some more. Generally speaking, then, much of what we think of as bad, or even evil, is an incidental, but *unavoidable*, consequence of physically separate beings pursuing their own good (the Good as it relates to them), pre-empting, obstructing, depriving, injuring, and even destroying each other in the process. They could not exist as the distinct kinds of beings they are without engaging in their characteristic activities – fleeing from what they flee, hunting if they hunt, eating whatever they eat, fighting when and why they fight, breeding and bearing however they do, each in accordance with its nature. Hence, we cannot understand the 'bads' that beings cause each other apart from the goods they pursue. Human life is of a piece with this competitive universe, though it has several unique features that qualitatively set it apart, all due to the rational powers of the human soul whereby we are (uniquely, so far as we know) *self-conscious* about the good. These powers include that of accurate calculation, not least with respect to gains and losses; of synoptic judgment as to what truly is good and bad; of imagining possible future outcomes, both favourable and not – a capacity as requisite to 'foresight' as is that of calculation (cf. 1.3.137–9; 1.5.57–8, 69–70); and of sympathizing, which enables one to understand other people to the extent they are like unto oneself, each ultimately ruled by a concern for his or her own good (which may be intimately and inextricably bound up with the good of certain others; cf.

4.3.216). It is by means of these various faculties of reason that we can appreciate without experiencing them the evils of tyranny or of some prepolitical 'state of nature' (or practically equivalent extrapolitical condition of civil war), and therefore see how and why people live better lives using their rational powers within a well-ordered polity – that is, one ordered in accordance with a rational idea of justice – than they possibly could outside it: that *this* is the way to maximize the human good.

Thus, we can see that the 'bad' which people do results from the pursuit of what they believe to be their own good. Whatever other limitations Macbeth suffers from, he has a clear enough understanding of this: that he is sacrificing the good of others to what he presumes to be his own good. Early on, this troubles him greatly – that he has no justification for seizing the throne from gracious Duncan beyond his own "vaulting ambition" (1.7.25–7). Later, having gained little but a mind full of scorpions for the pains of his usurpation, and seeing no prospect before him but "on the torture of the mind to lie in restless ecstacy," he professes a willingness to sacrifice the whole universe (this world and any other) to escape the bad that he has brought upon himself and to salvage some good: "But *let* the frame of things disjoint, both the worlds suffer, / Ere we will eat our meal in fear, and sleep / In the affliction of these terrible dreams, / That shake us nightly" (3.2.16–22; see also 4.1.50–60). Some of the bad in our world, then – what we are most apt to regard as truly *evil* – proceeds out of 'evil intentions' of this sort: unnecessarily and unjustifiably, yet knowingly and willingly sacrificing the welfare of others, and even their very lives, in order to gain for oneself a greater share of what one regards to be life's good things. For in the case of humans, unlike beasts, the pursuit of one's own good is *justifiable* only insofar as it is compatible with decent political life (a political environment being the requisite for virtually every person's individual good); and this presumes a polity wherein a concern for the *common* good – beginning with the preservation of the polity itself, but including whatever contributes to political harmony – takes precedence.[115]

Sometimes, maybe most times, those who willingly transgress the bounds of justifiable self-seeking are punished for it, by other men if not by the natural workings of their own souls (as in the cases of Lord and Lady Macbeth). As the example of Rosse shows, however, sometimes they are not. And far from their crimes causing them to lose the balm of innocent sleep – such that life loses all savour, becomes a murky hell, culminating in madness or suicide – they may not feel so much as a twinge of regret; their imperviousness to attacks of conscience might even be an additional source of satisfaction to them. Thus, lacking some universally convincing 'proof positive' of an infallible scheme of divine rewards and punishments, and given the obvious fallibility of all man-made schemes (of "judgment *here*"), evil is a permanent part of the human world. Along with malefactors both greater and lesser, it will always contain some Rosses, successful after their own lights. None are exceptions, however, to the rule that all evil proceeds out of the pursuit of the good. Whatever that which they do may be *called*, they do not themselves really pursue evil as such, but insofar as one can make any sense out of what they do, they must be understood as pursuing their own good as they perceive it. Even when it seems gratuitous spite and malice, it presumably brings them pleasure (which most people treat as the good).[116] Nor should this taking satisfaction in other people's suffering be too hastily denounced as perverse and pointless in all cases, as this would condemn the goodness of revenge. Despite the currency of the adage against 'taking revenge like a beast,' no mere animal seeks revenge; this is a uniquely *human* concern, presuming as it does the rational powers of the human soul. Doubtless, the yearning for revenge can be a source of evil; Macbeth's vengeful slaughter of Macduff's family shows that clearly enough. But it can also be a force for greater good, as it is in the cases of Malcolm and especially Macduff ("Revenges burn in them" 5.2.3; see also 4.3.214). One may wish things otherwise, but with human nature being what it in fact is, there would be much less combatting of evil, much less *active* support for justice, were it not for the spirit of revenge, and the peculiar satisfaction the human soul derives from the thought of evil-doers getting their 'just deserts,' of their having to 'pay' for their crimes in the only currency that seems fitting: by suffering ill effects themselves.

Moreover, it is a revealing feature of human nature that most people would prefer for this to be universally so (usually with tacit exception for their own misdeeds, of course). They may even prefer to believe that there is some supernatural, transcendent power working to this end, punishing the wicked, protecting the innocent, rewarding the good.[117] But insofar as this promotes passivity, Shakespeare shows us that this is a 'bad' mistake, and given its natural consequences, perhaps even an 'evil' one (if in some cases ignorance is culpable). For it, in effect, abets wicked ambition and aids those who would behave in ways more appropriate to beasts than humans – as Lady Macbeth, with unconscious irony, concedes: "What beast was't then, / That made you break this enterprise to me?" (1.7.47–8). Whereas, if goodness in life is to thrive, evil must be actively opposed by "the honest men" who recognize that he who sets out to prey on his own kind is a "traitor, and must be hang'd" (4.2.45–57). Only if justice is "with valour arm'd" will good triumph in one's own corner of the world. Those who believe it sufficient to keep their own hands clean, leaving anything more to what they imagine to be a beneficent god, bear a kind of complicity whenever evil that might easily be thwarted nonetheless succeeds in the vacuum of their own inaction.

INFECTIONS IN THE CASING AIR

Mindful of all this, we can return to a consideration of the apparently supernatural characters of the play, and attempt to determine how they are best understood. We might begin with what is said about them and what they themselves say. Here the most striking thing is their being so consistently associated with *air*. They conclude the opening scene of the play with their equivocal chant, "Fair is foul, and foul is fair: hover through the fog and filthy air." It is not clear just what is to "hover" in the air, but presumably it is the witches themselves. When next they appear, they speak of controlling the winds:

2nd Witch: I'll give thee a wind.
1st Witch: Th'art kind.
3rd Witch: And I another.
1st Witch: I myself have all the other ...
(1.3.11–14)

Thus armed, the First Witch threatens to assault the ronyon's sailor husband ("Though his bark cannot be lost, / Yet it shall be tempest-tost" 24–5). Then, having hailed both warrior captains who come tramping across the blasted heath (though it was only "there to meet Macbeth" that they had arranged their own rendezvous), they suddenly disappear, prompting Banquo to suggest, "The earth hath bubbles, as the water has, / And these are of them. – Whither are they vanish'd?" Macbeth replies, "Into the air; and what seem'd corporal, / Melted as breath into the wind" (79–82). Reporting his experience in the letter to his wife, he says, "When I burn'd in desire to question them further, they made themselves air, into which they vanish'd" (1.5.3–5). Hecate also avows herself "for th'air"; and her little pet spirit "sits in a foggy cloud" (3.5.20, 35). All these pneumatic affinities impart a special coloration to Macbeth's experience with what his Lady calls "the air-drawn dagger" – that which he at the time wondered might be but "a dagger of the mind" (3.4.61; 2.1.38).

Bubbles, breath, wind – what are these 'airy' phenomena? Are they real? Well, "Yes and No," one wants to say – a suitably equivocal answer. A bubble is perceptible, of course, and yet it is not 'really' a *thing* so much as the *absence* of something, a vacant 'shape' or 'shaped vacancy,' a disturbance, a gaseous agitation in something else ("for a charm of powerful trouble, like a hell-broth boil and bubble" 4.1.18–19). The very insubstantiality of a bubble makes it a natural symbol of illusion, and a metaphor for unrealistic beliefs and expectations (hopes dashed, one's 'bubble burst'). As for breath? Mere exhaled air, perhaps made momentarily visible on some chilly moor before melting back into the great boundless sea of "casing air." 'Breath' does not refer to some distinct kind of stuff; it indirectly signifies a particular *use* of quite common stuff. Yet, 'it' is the means of speech, and essential to life itself: the messenger bringing news of Macbeth's homecoming, "almost dead for breath, had scarcely more than would make up his message" (1.5.36–7). Indeed, it is the natural sign of life, and symbol of its divine origin ("heaven's breath," 1.6.5; cf. 4.1.98–100), but also, of what is false, meaningless, impotent: *mere* breath ("mouth-honour, breath, / Which the poor heart would fain deny, and dare not" 5.3.27–8). Similarly, a wind is not really a particular thing that can be loaned or borrowed, there is not really a certain number of them, each with its own distinctive character perhaps ('the cold north wind'); there is only the air, its endless movement, the earthly cycles of time and directions in space ("all the quarters that they know"). Still, there can be much power in the wind, more than enough to blow down the chimneys that Lenox speaks of (along with "lamentings heard i'th'air"; 2.3.54–5). It is the theme of Macbeth's hyperbole when he greets the witches for the last time:

> I conjure you, by that which you profess,
> Howe'er you come to know it, answer me:
> Though you untie the winds, and let them fight
> Against the Churches; though the yesty waves
> Confound and swallow navigation up;
> Though bladed corn be lodg'd, and trees blown down;
> Though castles top on their warders' heads;
> Though palaces, and pyramids, do slope
> Their heads to their foundations; though the treasure
> Of Nature's germens tumble all together,
> Even till destruction sicken, answer me
> To what I ask you.
>
> (4.1.50–61)

Upon being shown the seemingly endless succession of Banquo's regal offspring, Macbeth is left standing in pained amazement. Whereupon, the First Witch (mischievously?) offers to cheer his dashed spirits with her and her sisters' song and dance: "I'll *charm* the *air* to give a *sound*, / While you perform your antic round." When the dance concludes with their once again vanishing, Macbeth pronounces that fatal malediction: "Infected be the air whereon they ride; and damn'd all those that trust them!" (127–39). One suspects, however, that his curse has been anticipated – that the air they ride is ipso facto infected with germs of evil, and that it is the same air he breathes – such that he does indeed "wear [his] health but sickly" (see 3.1.106).

Evil spirits are not the only things that 'ride upon the air,' however. Good ones do, too, although they are more conspicuous by their relative absence in these dark days of Scotland. Even so, Macbeth himself speaks of "heaven's Cherubins, hors'd upon the sightless couriers of the air" (1.7.22–3); and Lenox prays, "Some holy Angel fly to the court of England" (3.6.45–6). Yet most of what flies on the air in this play are not mysterious supernatural beings, but quite familiar natural ones: a splendid variety of birds, as well as the odd bat or beetle. Indeed, were one to assemble all the birds referred to in *Macbeth*, one could populate a respectable aviary: sparrows, magpies, chickens, wrens, crows, kites, hawks, eagles, vultures, ravens, rooks, martlets, owls, falcons, choughs, and geese. Sometimes they serve to illustrate important principles of nature, such as Lady Macduff's noting that "the poor wren, / The most diminutive of birds, will fight, / Her young ones in the nest, against the owl" (4.2.9–11). Other times, their noted presence presumably has some ironic or symbolic function; Macbeth's castle is fairly festooned with nests of "the temple-haunting martlet" (according to Banquo, "no jutty, frieze, / Buttress, nor coign of vantage, but this bird / Hath made his pendent bed, and procreant cradle"; 1.6.4–8). Still other times, birds figure in descriptive analogies, such as the Captain's using the eagle's natural contempt for sparrows to indicate how little Duncan's generals were dismayed by the Norwegians' fresh assault (1.2.35). Whereas, a clear *violation* of the natural avian hierarchy is regarded by the Old Man as a sign of terrible times ahead ("A falcon, towering in her pride of place, / Was by a mousing owl hawk'd at, and kill'd" 2.4.12–13). Birds of ill omen have a special prominence. There is Lady Macbeth's hoarse raven that would croak Duncan's fatal entrance under her battlements (1.5.38–9), and the owl she characterizes as "the fatal bellman, which gives the stern'st good-night" (2.2.3–4); apparently this is the same "obscure bird" that according to Lenox "clamour'd the livelong night" of Duncan's murder (2.3.58–9). We are reminded of the kites that would feed on corpses (3.4.72). Macbeth speaks of certain birds (magpies, choughs, rooks) as being proven instruments of augury (123–4). Nor to be forgotten is his famously chilling: "Light thickens; and the crow / Makes wing to th'rooky wood; / Good things of day begin to droop and drowse, / Whiles Night's black agents to their preys do rouse" (3.2.50–3).

The 'ornithiatrics' of *Macbeth*, however, goes well beyond this plenitude of references to various species of birds, and the recurrent symbolic and analogic and metaphoric allusions to birds. There is also a notable amount of 'birdish' language used in the play. Sometimes it figures in terms of endearment, such as Macbeth referring to his wife as "dearest chuck" (3.2.45), and Macduff's speaking of his beloved family as "my pretty chickens, and their dam" – this upon learning that they have all been killed "at one fell swoop" of the "Hell-kite" Macbeth (4.3.217–19). But as this last reference shows, avine terms are also used pejoratively. Macbeth abuses the "cream-fac'd loon" who brings news of the approaching English army with "Where gott'st thou that goose look?" Whereupon the poor youth, now still more frightened and flustered, stammers, "There is ten thousand – " Macbeth: "Geese, villain?" "Soldiers, Sir" (5.3.11–13). Duncan greets victorious Macbeth with an excuse for his own "ingratitude," explaining, "Thou art so far before, / That the swiftest wing of recompense is slow / To overtake thee" (1.4.16–18). Lenox speaks of "confus'd events, new hatch'd to th'woeful time" (2.3.57–8); and Macbeth of "the flighty purpose" (4.1.145). When ambushed, Banquo exhorts his son, "*Fly*, good Fleance, fly, fly, fly!" (3.3.17). Macbeth repeatedly castigates the "false Thanes" who "fly" from him (5.3.1, 7, 49). However, the most concentrated usage of terms linking the human with the avian world comes in the one scene featuring Lady Macduff. Speaking with Rosse, she repeatedly characterizes her husband's abrupt departure for England as flying ("What had he done, to make him fly the land?" "His flight was madness ... from whence himself does fly? ... where the flight so runs against all reason"). Charging that he lacks the natural paternal instincts, she cites the example set by "the poor wren" defending its young. After Rosse leaves, we see her in conversation with her precocious son:

> *Lady Macd:* Sirrah, your father's dead:
> And what will you do now? How will you live?
> *Son:* As birds do, mother.
> *Lady Macd:* What, with worms and flies?
> *Son:* With what I get, I mean; and so do they.
> *Lady Macd:* Poor bird! thou'dst never fear the net, nor lime,
> The pit-fall, nor the gin.
> *Son:* Why should I, mother?
> Poor birds are not set for.
>
> (4.2.30–6)

He is right, of course – so far as men are rational, that is. Finally, there is her response to the warning of the anonymous "homely man": "Whither should I fly? I have done no harm. But I remember now I am in this earthly world" (72–3). When her grieving husband laments his "pretty chickens, and their dam," he is simply invoking the imagery established at the play's outset. It began with Macbeth being likened to an eagle. It concludes with his resigning his fate to the arbitration of the battlefield: "They have tied me to a stake: I cannot fly" (5.7.1).

As a final curiousity, when Banquo soliloquizes:

Thou hast it now, King, Cawdor, Glamis, all,
As the Weyward Women promis'd; and, I fear,
Thou play'dst most *foully* for't ...

(3.1.1–3)

In the Folio text, the spelling is 'fowly'[118] – that, in contrast with the five uses of 'foul' in the play, all spelt 'foule' in the Folio (as in the witches' "faire is foule, and foule is faire, / Houer through the fogge and filthie ayre").

What is to be made of all this? – the witches as so many bubbles, so much breath, riding the wind, the air, like birds; the human realm, in turn, variously assimilated to the kingdom of birds, with its few eagles and many sparrows, brave little wrens, chattering magpies, lecherous martlets, proud falcons, sinister ravens, scavenging kites, prescient owls, opportunistic vultures, obtuse geese. Might these relationships taken together suggest, albeit indirectly and rather vaguely, that the domain of natural embodied beings coincides with that of 'supernatural spirits'?

This suspicion is reinforced by the direct and unmistakable kinship Shakespeare establishes between the Macbeths and the Weyward Sisters. The first words Macbeth speaks ("So fair and foul a day I have not seen") are an obvious echo of the witches' enigmatic chant that concluded the opening scene. Whereas, Lady Macbeth foreshadows another of these beldams' memorable lines when greeting Duncan before her battlements. He graciously acknowledges his visit's causing her "trouble"; she replies, "All our service, in every point twice done, and then done double" (1.6.14–15) – a clear anticipation of probably the most famous witches' chorus in all of literature: "Double, double toil and trouble" (4.1.10, 20, 35). Macbeth, too, is associated with 'double' and 'quadruple' trouble (as is Banquo!). According to the bleeding Captain, "as cannons overcharg'd with double cracks; so they doubly redoubled strokes upon the foe" (1.2.36–9). Macbeth himself speaks of Duncan's being "here in double trust," but then goes on to cite, not two, but *four* troubling considerations "against the deed" he is contemplating (1.7.12–20) – a deed almost without a name, judging by his (and his wife's) reluctance to speak it (1.5.23, 68; 1.7.31, 48; 2.1.48, 62; 2.2.10, 32, 50, 66, 72; cf. 4.1.49). It is in this context of spiritual associations that one must assess Macbeth's somehow acquiring a mysterious and strangely omniscient adjutant named – of all things – Seyton.[119]

Lady Macbeth, however, is identified with the witches in another, perhaps more revealing way: through her disordered sexuality. Much as Banquo observes to the wither'd hags, "you *should* be women, / And yet your beards forbid me to interpret / That you are so" (1.3.45–7), likewise Lady Macbeth does not seem purely female. One can begin with her fervent praying to the "spirits that tend on mortal thoughts" that she be divested of all feminine softness of soul – indeed, that they quite "unsex" her. While it is doubtful that she truly desires these 'spirits' to go quite that far (not least because it would destroy the distinctly female power she exercises over her husband; 1.7.38–41), any wish to be sexually other than one is would not normally be a sign of harmonious inner integrity and health. Nor should one overlook the possibility that she gets just what she prayed for – and thus more than she really wanted – since by the midpoint of the play her influence over Macbeth has clearly diminished, and we find her complaining of his keeping so much alone (3.2.8–9). Be that as it may, prior to this she several times alleges that her husband is less tough-minded and more compassionate than she: "Hie thee hither, / That I may pour my spirits in thine ear" (1.5.25–6); "Infirm of purpose! / Give *me* the daggers" (2.2.51–2); "My hands are of your colour; but I shame / To wear a heart so white" (63–4); "What! quite unmann'd in folly?" (3.4.72), and so on.[120] She claims to know how it feels to love a suckling child, but apparently none of hers have survived (4.3.216). Though one may doubt that she actually dash'd their brains out, her very capacity to conceive such a horrid image must itself raise some question about the soundness of her femininity. Macbeth, clearly impressed by the cold-blooded manner in which she plots Duncan's murder, makes the point as emphatically as it needs be: "Bring forth men-children only! / For *thy* undaunted mettle *should* compose / Nothing but males" (1.7.73–5). At that juncture, apparently he is still hopeful of his begetting and her bearing viable offspring. Subsequently, however, his brooding over the witches' hailing Banquo as "father to a line of kings" seems to have compromised this hope: "Upon my head they plac'd a fruitless crown, / And put a barren sceptre in my gripe, /... / No son of mine succeeding" (3.1.59–63). His pessimistic appraisal is the more interesting in that nothing the witches said necessarily implied any of this. They gave no indication that the crown would pass *directly* to Banquo's issue – nor does it, as things turn out. Not even Banquo's being "greater" by virtue of begetting a long line of kings need mean that Macbeth begets *none*. But as of yet "he has no children," and now, "fruitless" and "barren," he foresees none.[121]

This issue of 'begetting and bearing' is, of course, intimately bound up with healthy expressions of erotic nature. Whatever else this might entail, it requires that sexual relations be ordered around procreation, and that natural desire not be exploited and perverted to serve primarily ulterior purposes – contrary to what the First Witch hints she intends by way of tormenting the ronyon's sailor husband (with the ultimate purpose of rendering him impotent, thereby denying him to the ronyon):[122]

I'll drain him dry as hay:
Sleep shall neither night nor day
Hang upon his penthouse lid;
He shall live a man forbid.
Weary sev'n-nights nine times nine,
Shall he dwindle, peak, and pine ...
(1.3.18–23)

Though a good deal more subtle, Lady Macbeth insinuates that her husband also might live a man forbid should he not prove the same in "act and valour" as in "desire" (1.7.40–1).[123] Thus far, however, nothing lasting has come from their marital relations – no "strong knots of love," as bind together the Macduffs (4.3.27) – and one suspects that this troubles them both.[124] Could it be that she sought satisfaction from that which could never satisfy her? Established as the Queen she schemed to become, she nonetheless laments, "Nought's had, all's spent, where our desire is got without content" (3.2.4–5). The prominence of other father–son relationships – Duncan and his two sons, Banquo and Fleance, Macduff and his boy, Old and Young Siward – serve to highlight this vacancy in Macbeth's own life, deprived of the natural meaningfulness that children (those "precious motives") impart to all one's labours, accomplishments, and sacrifices. He confirms the natural urge to leave a legacy to his own son in the course of complaining that he will not: "No son of *mine* succeeding ... For *Banquo's* issue have I fil'd my mind" (3.1.63–4).

That Macbeth kills two of these other men's sons, and conspires upon the lives of the rest – as much, one suspects, out of sheer spite and wrath (born of envy and resentment) as from any sense of their posing a danger to him, much less to his non-existent offspring – points to another symptom of diseased *erōs*: the transference of sexual energy from creation into destruction, involving an assimilation of sexual expression and violence. The *association* of sex and violence is found throughout the higher orders of Nature, competition for mates being the primary source of violent conflict within species (confined mostly to males). But humans (again, males in particular) seem peculiarly susceptible to a confusion of means and ends in this business, with the result that humans are prone to all sorts of sexual disorders, including the perverse assimilation referred to above – a sickness that can sometimes assume almost plague proportions. Its possibility, if not its presence, is signalled in the report of the bleeding Captain, when he speaks of "Fortune, on [Macdonwald's] damned quarrel smiling, show'd like a rebel's whore," and then describes Macbeth (whose "brandish'd steel ... smok'd with bloody execution") as "Valour's minion." Rosse continues the association in referring to some great warrior as "Bellona's bridegroom." Macbeth, set on murder as he steals with "ravishing strides" towards the bed of sleeping Duncan, likens himself to Tarquin bent on the rape of Lucrece (2.1.54–6). But it is Lady Macbeth who is most explicit in linking sex and violence when she invites those "Murth'ring ministers" to take possession of her: "Come to my woman's breasts, and take my milk for gall" – suggesting what, exactly? Her willingness to give suck to devils? A desire to mate with murderers? Whatever precisely she has in mind here, it seems clear enough that she too wears her health but sickly, infected with a disease that hovers in the filthy air of an ungentle weal.

When, however, Lady Macbeth calls upon those "spirits that tend on mortal thoughts," there is a nice ambiguity in the choice of words. By 'mortal,' *she* doubtless means 'deadly.' But Shakespeare for his part may be suggesting something more general: that we should regard *all* thoughts of mortals – and thus mortals themselves, insofar as thought is the medium of good and evil – as being attended by spirits of one sort or another, and that there may be as many of them as there are people. These spirits (or *daimones*, as they might have been called in ancient Hellas, the birthplace of Hecate)[125] are not ordinarily visible, of course – not even so fleetingly as bubbles or breath. But there is a sense in which they are at least as real; and given the preference we share with Macbeth for 'perceptible truth,' they are rendered more readily intelligible and credible by being 'shown.' Naturally, we are free to interpret them in a variety of ways. One who is confident that in reality there are no immortal beings of either a saintly or a satanic kind is free to regard those that appear in *Macbeth* as dramatic impersonations of an individual's 'alter ego' (for example), or of archetypal temptations, or archaic remnants of man's childhood, or some such thing. However, they probably should *not* be thought of simply as representations of impulses that *originate* wholly from within a given individual's soul; rather, they seem more like germinal hopes and fears that hover and waft in the very 'atmosphere' of human life, ever ready to take root in congenial psychic soil. We must always remember that *both* Macbeth and Banquo – but *only* they – see and hear the same witches, arguably because each one is secretly animated by the same "black and deep," barely repressed desires, and for reasons that have as much to do with conditions in Duncan's Scotland as with their own natures.[126]

Moreover, the intimation that sterility is associated with evil, and conversely fecundity and creativity with what is good, should not go unremarked. It coheres with the general identification of Nature with Life that pervades *Macbeth*. Reasonable though it might seem to regard death as equally natural, no one in the play does. Rather, Nature is repeatedly *contrasted* with death. Lady Macbeth muses to herself about the sleeping grooms that she has drugged, "Death and Nature do contend about them, / Whether they live, or die" (2.2.7–8). Macbeth, referring to the murdered Duncan, says "his gash'd stabs look'd like a breech in nature / For ruin's wasteful entrance" (2.3.111–12). The First Murderer, reporting Banquo's demise to Macbeth, speaks of "twenty trenched gashes on his head; / The least a death to nature" (3.4.26–7). Such modes of expression suggest that to be fully natural is to be alive, that Nature is *fully* revealed only in living things; 'dead matter' is just that. This being so, to beget and bear, nourish and protect new life are natural acts par excellence, whereas pointless, cold-blooded murder is unnatural in the extreme. That Shakespeare employs both rhyme and reason to conjoin Macbeth and Death perhaps best expresses his final judgment on his protagonist (1.2.66–7; 3.5.4–5).

According to the pattern of evidence the play provides, the most basic distinction *within* Nature is between sleeping and waking. Sleep, according to the distraught Macbeth who fears he has murdered it along with Duncan, is "great Nature's second course, chief nourisher in life's feast" (2.2.38–9) – the 'first course' being wakefulness, obviously. His wife refers to sleep as "the *season* of all natures," presumably meaning the 'spice' or 'salt' that both enlivens and preserves (3.4.140). The most curious aspect of Shakespeare's treatment of these matters, however, is his repeatedly challenging us to distinguish sleep from death. Now, the idea that death might be likened to an endless sleep is an ancient one. It is encountered, for example, in Plato's *Apology of Sokrates* (40d–e). This idea has its echo in Macbeth's observing, "Duncan is in his grave; / After life's fitful fever, *he* sleeps well" (3.2.22–3). He had earlier alluded to the enormous practical difference between sleep and death with his posthomicidal expression of regret: "Wake Duncan with thy knocking: I would thou couldst!" (2.2.73). However, for the most part, the analogy is reversed in the play, with sleep being likened to the *appearance* of death, as in the child's tale of *Sleeping Beauty*. Lady Macbeth, proposing to drug the two chamberlains, is the first to speak in this vein: "when in swinish sleep / Their drenched natures lie, as in a death, / What cannot you and I perform upon / Th'unguarded Duncan?" (1.7.68–71).[127] Having discovered the murdered King, Macduff calls out:

> Awake! awake! –
> Ring the alarum-bell. – Murder, and treason!
> Banquo, and Donalbain! Malcolm, awake!
> Shake off this downy sleep, death's counterfeit,
> And look on death itself! – up, up, and see
> The great doom's image! – Malcolm! Banquo!
> As from your graves rise up, and walk like sprites,
> To countenance this horror. Ring the Bell.
> (2.3.72–9)

Macbeth himself characterizes sleep as "the death of each day's life" (2.2.37) and observes about the darkened, sleeping portion of the globe, "Now o'er the one half-world / Nature seems dead, and wicked dreams abuse / The curtain'd sleep" (2.1.49–51). Lady Macbeth also assimilates the appearances of sleep and death when she admonishes her faltering husband, "the sleeping, and the dead, are but as pictures" (2.2.52–3).[128]

Death *versus* Nature, Sleep *versus* Wakefulness, Sleep as hardly distinguishable from Death in appearance, Thought as something 'spiritual' – if we integrate this with certain other associations the play suggests, such as the one just cited of Macduff: death as "the great doom's image" (2.3.76–7); or that observed by Macbeth: "Good things of *Day* begin to droop and drowse, / Whiles *Night's* black agents to their preys do rouse" (3.2.52–3) – always bearing in mind that though there *are* creatures that prosper at night, in the case of humans living naturally, sleeping and waking are generally coordinated with night and day – taking all of this together, we may discern two contrasting sets of related things. There is Evil, Death, Sickness, Sleep, and Night (on the one hand), and Day, Wakefulness, Health, Life, and Good (on the other). The only placement that stands out as requiring further comment is that of sleep in the first set. Why should it be associated, however remotely, with *Evil*? For that matter, does not characterizing sleep as an image of death betray more than a touch of morbidity? After all, sleep does indeed seem to be great Nature's second course, essential as it is to preserving life. This would seem to imply that what is needed to clarify the relationship between the two sets is an adequate idea of Nature – a matter better pursued in the context provided by *King Lear*. However, reflecting simply on the notion of sleep as itself a kind of temporary death – a condition, moreover, sometimes "provoked" by mind-numbing drink (2.3.27) – one comes to the realization that sleep is *not* something intrinsically good (however much the animal in us might enjoy it). If we did not tire, what good would there be in sleep? Would it not be sheer waste of life? Moreover, as Duncan's fate and Macbeth's anxiety poignantly demonstrate, time asleep can be time of profound, hence worrisome, vulnerability. Nor is this vulnerability with regard only to 'foes' external, as Banquo's rueful prayer reminds us:

> A heavy summons lies like lead upon me,
> And yet I would not sleep: merciful Powers!
> Restrain in me the cursed thoughts that nature
> Gives way to in repose!
>
> (2.1.6–9)[129]

Thus, one can scarce avoid concluding that the *need* for sleep is itself a liability, a kind of weakness inherent in mortality, in being a soul reliant on a body: day by day the body 'sickens' and must be 'healed,' until at last it fails in the finale of death, and one's nature is no more.

The play suggests that to be fully natural is to be alive, and to be fully alive is to be awake, living with one's eyes wide open, as it were. Of course, to see things clearly, there must be sufficient light, and that provided by candles and torches and cooking fires is seldom sufficient. Nothing rivals pure sunlight on a clear day.[130] But even before the moment Lady Macbeth banishes the sun – "O! *never* shall sun that morrow see!" ... nor the morrow after that, consequently, nor any tomorrow – there is precious little natural light in Scotland. Overcast skies, foul weather envelop the place in gloom even before thick Night has cast its blanket of darkness, as the lady prayed it would. The moon is down; and in compliance with Macbeth's black and deep desires, the stars too have hid their fires (1.4.50–1; 2.1.2–5). This is worth noting, however: for all that barbarous Scotland may be more a place of cavelike dusk than is England, neither Macbeth nor his wife seek to take advantage of what light, natural or artificial, it affords – quite the contrary. They wish it, and thus unwittingly themselves as well, still more benighted. Indeed, when Macbeth chooses to leave the overshadowed surface of his everyday world, it is only to descend into an even darker place: the Pit of Acheron. As for Lady Macbeth, she comes to fear the darkness she wished upon herself, and with one pathetic little candle tries to keep at bay the murkiness she now calls Hell. Obviously, neither he nor she had a will to *be* what would normally be regarded as 'good.' What is prior to that, however, and truly fundamental, is that they had no will to 'the light.' Whatever other questions they entertained about their world, they saw no need to be enlightened with respect to the one all-important question: what truly *is* good – confident (as are most people) that they already knew well enough what is good for them. So they pursued it as they did, with the consequences we are shown. Unaware of their profound ignorance with respect to this ultimate source of all truth and being, whence every thought, every deed rightly takes its bearing, they do indeed re-enact The Fall of Man.

As I have endeavoured to show, Shakespeare's *Macbeth* confronts whoever would fully understand it – understand it as its creator himself understood it – with the necessity of thinking one's own way through, so far as one can, certain truly timeless questions, questions that are as inherently intriguing as they are practically important. Shakespeare may ultimately supply some answers, but only through the conscious collaborative effort of his reader, who must first of all be awakened to the questions, seeing *why* they are questions, and why they are worthy of one's time.

In his own way, then, Shakespeare brings one back to the ancient view with which political philosophy is born, personified by Sokrates the Gadfly, that winged spirit divinely ordained to sting Athens and subsequent ages to wakefulness (*Apology* 30e). We humans, in common with other embodied beings, require sleep to recreate body and soul. It would indeed be "A great perturbation in nature, to receive at once the benefit of sleep, *and* do the effects of watching!" But endowed by "bounteous Nature" with the gift of reason, we of all creatures can least fulfil our specific nature in mere "slumbery agitation," sleep-walking through life – much less in "swinish sleep." To be fully alive, we must be roused to full wakefulness, fully self-conscious in what we say and do, having emerged from a day that is like night (2.4.5–10) into true day, its "living light" not obscured by fog and filthy air. Because questions awaken and enliven, whereas answers sedate, Shakespeare is careful never to be overtly didactic. Seldom is he as rude as a gadfly, however. More often like Prince Charming, he awakens with a kiss.

CHAPTER THREE

The Discovery of Nature: Politics and Philosophy in *King Lear*

φυσις κρυπτεσθαι φιλει ("Nature loves to hide")
Heracleitus

King Lear must be among Shakespeare's most profoundly misunderstood plays. The majority of misunderstandings about it begin with a mistaken appraisal of the monarch whose tragedy it depicts. Though usually conceded to have (or to have had) admirable and even endearing qualities, Lear impresses people mainly as some combination of vain, rash, volatile, fickle, egocentric, imperious, obstinate, self-indulgent, unsteady, petulant, irascible – and consequently foolish – old man, whose natural and acquired flaws of character are further aggravated by the whimsy and querulousness so typical of the very aged. This impression, initially gained from his behaviour in the opening scene, is reinforced by his subsequent reactions to its consequences, as well as by what others say about him, and not least by what he says about himself. Given this apparent unanimity of opinion and its congruence with the dramatic evidence, how can one refute it? More to the point, why would anyone wish to? For does he not in a fit of pique disinherit his favourite daughter for her refusal to flatter his vanity; divide what had been a united and peaceful kingdom in such a way as to invite civil war and foreign invasion; then banish on pain of death his most devoted and trustworthy counsellor for protesting what he honestly – and rightly – believes to be acts of "hideous rashness" and "folly"? The assessments privately expressed by his two other daughters, albeit interested participants in these reckless proceedings, are apt to square with those of any neutral spectator, and confirm him in his worst suspicions. Goneril, the elder, sees in this latest episode but more evidence that her father in his agedness is "full of changes," and prone to acts of poor judgment. Her sister Regan agrees that it shows "the infirmity of his age," and adds, "yet he hath ever but slenderly known himself." Goneril continues in a similar vein: "The best and soundest of his time hath been but rash," and warns darkly that besides "the imperfections of long-engraffed condition," they shall now have to cope with "the unruly waywardness that infirm and choleric years bring with them" (1.1.287–98).[1]

Lear himself is the first to speak of his age; and while he never acknowledges that it has made him wayward or choleric, he does clearly imply that his natural powers have greatly declined: "and 'tis our fast intent / To shake all cares and business from our age, / Conferring them on younger strengths, while we / Unburthen'd crawl toward death" (37–40). As his troubles mount, his advanced age is a theme to which he repeatedly recurs (e.g., 2.4.188–91; 3.2.19–24; 3.4.20). So, too, do Goneril and Regan, exploiting every opportunity to stress his dotage and rashness (1.4.323–6; 2.4.143–7, 166–7, 194–5, 199).

Beyond a doubt, there is some truth informing the litany of vices attributed to this aged king. Lear does show signs of vanity, of impatience, of a passionate temper, rather as one would expect would characterize a spirited man long accustomed to praise, to obedience, to having his every desire catered. But these ingrained flaws have little or no bearing on his initiating actions, which actually show him to be a rational, responsible, shrewd statesman.[2] That almost everyone forms a contrary impression of him can hardly be ascribed to coincidence. Creating this misleading appearance must have been part of the author's intention. Hence, I am obliged to amend my opening statement to read '*King Lear* must be among Shakespeare's most superficially understood plays.' My second sentence can stand, however: the superficiality of the common interpretations stems from a profoundly mistaken assessment of the character after whom it is named. Still, one must concede that the author is primarily responsible for the popular view, having made it so very easy to misjudge his oldest and greatest monarch. Why has Shakespeare done this? Why has he so cunningly clothed a king who proves capable of becoming a philosopher in the dress of an octogenarian seemingly on the verge of senility? This is the question that any adequate interpretation of the play must finally confront.

THE PERILS OF POLITICAL IMPROVISATION

The problem begins at the beginning, with Lear's apparently ill-conceived, irresponsible, egotistical, naïve, scarcely credible scheme for divesting himself of the cares – but not the privileges – of his kingship. Coleridge, who greatly admired the play and has some helpful insights into certain of its characters, suggests that one can "omit the first scene in *Lear*, and everything will remain," that this first scene is but a "nursery tale," that it is "prefixed as the porch of the edifice, not laid as its foundation."[3] One could scarcely be more dead wrong: all to the contrary, there may never have been a first scene more truly *fundamental* to the unfolding of a complex but perfectly coherent tragedy. As the scene is fairly long, with more happening than seems generally appreciated, it may be useful to summarize briefly the surface of the action.

The play opens upon two noblemen in mid-conversation. They speak as if they are familiar enough with the King to know his usual preferences, yet they now seem perplexed as to whom of two other noblemen, the Dukes of Albany and Cornwall, he actually favours. One of those conversing, the Earl of Gloucester, is accompanied by a young man whom he introduces in a jocular tone as his bastard son, Edmund, while insisting that he is as dear to him as his other son born in legal wedlock. His friend, the Earl of Kent, politely welcomes the introduction.

At this point, the King arrives, accompanied by an entourage that includes his two married daughters, Goneril and Regan; their husbands (the aforementioned Albany and Cornwall); and his youngest, as yet unmarried daughter, Cordelia. The King's first words command Gloucester to escort hither the Lords of France and Burgundy, who we soon learn are rival suitors for the hand of Cordelia. While awaiting their arrival, Lear proceeds to explain the "darker purpose" for this meeting. Using a map to illustrate his plan, he announces that it is his firm intention to transfer the cares and business of ruling to younger and stronger hands, and with that in mind has divided his kingdom into three parts which are now to be publicly bestowed as doweries on his several daughters. By doing so while he is still the reigning King, he aims to avoid future strife. He will also use this august occasion to settle the question of who wins Cordelia. As for which daughter (and husband) gets the largest and richest part of the kingdom, Lear proposes to award that to whoever of the three loves him most. Moreover, this is to be determined by what each can say here and now to persuade him to that effect.

Goneril, the eldest, is commanded to speak first. She claims to love him more than words can express, that he is dearer to her than whatever is rich or rare, dearer than life itself, as much as any child ever loved a father. Lear seems pleased enough, and awards her and Albany what sounds like quite a rich portion. He then turns to Regan, who naturally tries to outdo her sister by claiming (in effect) to love *only* him, and that her happiness comes exclusively from his love. Again, Lear is apparently satisfied, awarding to her and hers an "ample third of our fair kingdom," of no less worth than that given Goneril. This leaves only young Cordelia to speak; he asks, "what can you say to draw a third more opulent than your sisters?" Cordelia, who throughout her older sisters' professions of love has been privately expressing anxiety at the prospect of having to put into words her feelings for her father, now replies, "Nothing, my lord." Lear is clearly taken aback, and repeatedly invites her to try to do better lest she mar her fortunes. This only succeeds in eliciting from her a precise avowal that she loves him as she is duty-bound to do, followed by an eloquent criticism of her sisters' extravagant claims. This speech does *not* please the King, and once he is convinced that it comes from the heart, he disowns and disinherits her.

This provokes Kent to try to intervene, but Lear rebuffs him most sternly, acknowledging both his anger and disappointment in Cordelia; he had loved her most, and had intended in his retirement to live with her and her husband. He brusquely calls for France and Burgundy to be brought forth, and tells Cornwall and Albany to divide the remaining third part of the kingdom between them. He will monthly alternate his residence with each in turn, he and his establishment of a hundred knights to be sustained by them. He reserves to himself the name of King and the courtesies that attend it, but all other powers, revenues, and responsibilities he now transfers to these two sons-in-law. Again, Kent tries to intervene, beginning with a reminder of his long-proven devotion to the King, but again Lear warns him off. Now, however, Kent refuses to be silenced, insisting it is his duty to speak plainly "when power to flattery bows" and "majesty falls to folly." Kent's protests and the King's annoyance escalate to the point that Lear is on the verge of physically attacking Kent. Indifferent to the threat, he urges Lear to revoke what he has just done. This proposal, unprecedented in his royal experience, so infuriates Lear that he banishes Kent, who obediently takes his leave.

Whereupon Gloucester returns with France and Burgundy. Lear first addresses Burgundy, asking what is the least dower he would require in order to sustain his "quest of love" for Cordelia. Burgundy, understandably puzzled, replies that he expects neither more nor less than was originally offered. He is informed that "her price has fallen" and that now she is dowered with nothing but the King's displeasure. As politely as his astonishment allows, Burgundy protests that such a prenuptial package would not make for a realistic choice. Lear interprets this as a rejection of Cordelia, and turns to France, not to offer Cordelia to him but rather to explain why it would be inappropriate to do so, and to recommend instead that he "avert [his] liking a more worthier way." France, however, attempts to probe more deeply Lear's radical change of heart towards his dearest daughter: he scarce believes she could have done anything "so monstrous" as to justify it. This prompts Cordelia to beseech her father to make clear that his disapproval of her is not due to anything heinous, but merely to her want of the flattering ways she is glad she lacks. The King offers no such assurance, but France is apparently satisfied by what Cordelia herself has said, and after he has elicited a categorical renunciation from Burgundy, claims her for his own. With noticeable ill grace and a further disavowal of her, Lear permits France to take Cordelia, then leaves with Burgundy and most of the court.

And so Cordelia bids farewell to her sisters with barely veiled hints of her distrust of them and consequently of worry for her father's welfare, entrusted as it now is to their suspect love. Goneril and Regan politely but firmly suggest she mind her own business. At France's behest, Cordelia departs with him. Left alone to digest what has just transpired, Goneril takes the lead in criticizing their father, voicing the suspicion that he is apt to prove an awkward burden. Regan agrees, and also agrees that they must consult further to determine a common policy whereby to protect their newly acquired interests.

Given what we are shown, there would seem to be more than a little truth in the diagnosis of Lear provided by his two elder daughters, who we may presume speak from extensive experience in observing and dealing with their father. He does seem decidedly vain, hence, solicitous of flattery and impatient of criticism, imperious, easily angered, and prone to act precipitously – indeed, some would say he behaves more like a pampered child than a wise and august king. His plan for dividing the kingdom appears the height of irresponsibility. First, to divide it at all is a most dubious thing to do. Then to make its actual parsing depend upon which daughter can extemporaneously compose the most flattering profession of love for him – to treat *that* as an indication of "merit" (1.1.52) – seems egomaniacal, if not simply absurd. Even the member of his court who is most selflessly devoted to him, the ever-loyal Kent, here accuses him of "hideous rashness," of bowing to hollow "flattery," of "folly," of acting as if he were "mad" (145–50). Seen in this light, Lear hardly seems capable of truly *noble* suffering; one might judge him more suited for farce than tragedy. His story, then, if one ignores its unjustified sentimentality (as, of course, most people do not) belongs rather with 'The Emperor's New Clothes' than in the company of *Macbeth*, *Hamlet*, or *Julius Caesar*.

However, that same plain-speaking, courageous, ruthlessly honest Kent should give us pause in our judging of Lear. What made Kent think that he could, and should, speak up to his king as he did? Might he be accustomed to speaking his mind, albeit more politely? In any case, he has somehow come to believe, or been led to believe, that it is his "duty" (146). But it is equally apparent that Kent does not regard what he has just witnessed as *typical* of Lear. Quite the contrary: he sees it as calling for an extraordinary protest of unprecedented "plainness" and persistence on his part, which he is honour-bound to provide (148, 164–5). It is not behaviour like this that has won Kent's selfless devotion, such that he can credibly profess, "Royal Lear, / Whom I have ever honour'd as my King, / Lov'd as my father, as my master follow'd, / As my great patron thought on in my prayers" – indeed, vow himself ever ready to sacrifice his life in the interest of Lear's "safety" (138–41, 154–6). Kent's subsequent service in disguise, wherein he continues to practise the plain-speaking he prides himself on, validates several times over the sincerity of what he here publicly proclaims. He is not one of those who plies the "glib and oily art," that Cordelia so despises (223). What does it say about the King that a man such as Kent is among his preferred confidants? Nor, as events prove, is the loyalty of Gloucester, another trusted member of Lear's inner circle, evidence to be despised (see 3.3.17–19). He, too, finds the King's behaviour out of character on this occasion: "And the King gone tonight! prescrib'd his power! / Confin'd to exhibition! All this done / Upon the gad!" (1.2.23–6); "And the noble and true-hearted Kent banish'd! his offense, honesty! 'Tis strange" (113–14). So strange, in fact, that Gloucester can only attribute it to abnormal astrological influences, "these late eclipses in the sun and moon" (100–8).

Is Lear, then, really a vain old man who prefers to be surrounded with flatterers and who is easily angered by criticism when not simply deaf to it? Consider whom he chooses to keep as his "all-licens'd Fool": a clever ironist who apparently is as devoted to the King as is Kent (and whose affection Lear reciprocates; see 3.2.68–73). The Fool's criticism of what Lear has done, beginning well before the evil consequences have begun to accumulate, is relentless (and, I would have thought, insufferable), but Lear never objects. In fact, the only time he flatly promises discipline is when the Fool pleads, "Prithee, Nuncle, keep a schoolmaster that can teach thy Fool to lie: I would fain learn to lie." – to which Lear responds, "And you *lie*, sirrah, we'll have you whipp'd" (1.4.175–7; cf. 108). And what is the most notable characteristic of her who apparently everyone knows was his favourite daughter (including, not least of all, her sisters; 1.1.289; cf. 212–15), the daughter with whom he intended to live out his remaining days? One must ask, whence came Cordelia her contempt for hypocrisy and "a still-soliciting eye?" Could someone of her taste so love her kingly father, as she clearly proves she does, were he really much like the impression he gives a passive observer of this play's opening scene? Judged rather by his preferred associates (birds of a feather, it would seem from both Kent's and the Fool's special relationships with Cordelia; 1.1.150–3; 1.4.69–72; 2.2.161–4; 3.1.46–8), Lear, far from being a fool for flattery, has a decided preference for persons of honesty and truth, and a long-established reputation for reasonableness and prudent governing.

What, then, accounts for what others well acquainted with him, including all those we find most admirable, see as aberrant behaviour on this occasion? Is he *changing* as a natural consequence of aging – more precisely, deteriorating, becoming "wayward," erratic, impulsive, and querulous – more or less as his elder daughters claim? Of course, they are highly biased assessors, inclined to put the worst face on their father, whom we soon learn they do not love at all but rather resent and despise. Not being his favourites, and he a busy man, they may not actually be so intimately familiar with him after all, but have known him only from a distance (as would not be unusual for children of royalty). Moreover, being married, they will have been some time away from the court, living with their husbands. Yet Lear himself, with all his references to his age, might seem to lend credence to these daughters' analysis. Nor can there be any question but that Lear is keenly aware of his not being the man he once was. But what a man that must have been if he can still, though over eighty years old (4.7.61), unassisted kill a serving soldier, presumably with his bare hands (for he was not armed). Well might the officer who escorted him from that scene, the old King (not the officer) bearing the body of Cordelia in his arms, testify in some amazement at the feat: "'Tis *true*, my lords, he *did*." Lear: "Did I not, fellow? / I have seen the day, with my good biting falchion / I would have made them skip: I am old now" (5.3.274–6). Lear may have declined, and declined considerably, from the acme of his natural greatness; he may look on himself as but a shell of his former glory; and the image of him still carried by the likes of Kent and Gloucester (the very image of "authority"; 1.4.27–30) may have been established when he was in his prime – but what a prime that must have been, to have gained and reigned over the whole of Britain for decades, to have brought it peace and prosperity, to have it courted by its most powerful neighbours seeking alliance, and to be still capable of what the opening scene, rightly understood, proves him to be.

To appreciate what Lear is attempting to accomplish, a brief digression is required. If there is one respect in which all the pre-eminent political philosophers would seem to agree with Machiavelli, it is that the *most* difficult political task, and as such the one calling for the greatest statesmanship, is not the founding of a stable, decent regime (enormously difficult though that be), but rather its *perpetuation*. Or, alternatively expressed, only a regime that can perpetuate itself – that outlives its founder, and does not come apart upon his death – is truly well-founded and proves its founder to be a statesman of the highest order. Thus, when Machiavelli speaks of princes who showed the greatest virtue, he names men such as Cyrus, Theseus, Romulus, and Moses, the respective founders of Persia, Athens, Rome, and Israel, great regimes or nations of enduring significance.[4] Plato in his *Republic* has Sokrates make this the first order of business for the rulers of the city they establish "in *logos*": providing for their own replacements. His proposed solution may be comical (intentionally so: requiring that they breed philosopher–kings as they would pedigreed animals),[5] but the problem is real: how to ensure an orderly, peaceful, reliable transfer of power to successors of sufficient quality. Hobbes also recognizes this to be monarchy's greatest problem, and surely history – not least the portion of England's that Shakespeare portrays – bears him out.[6] This is the very problem Lear is facing as the play opens.

The most important practical implication of Lear's agedness, so repeatedly stressed, is that he cannot long continue to delay dealing with this problem. Left unsolved, it will almost surely lead to the "future strife" he wishes to avoid (and which events prove only too real a danger). Although he is amazingly robust for a man of his age (e.g., he still goes hunting with his knights; 1.3.8) – and so the decrepitude he claims for himself, as if barely 'crawling toward death,' may have a rhetorical purpose – the fact remains his demise becomes more likely with each passing day. So, how does Lear intend to ensure that his own political achievement does not perish with him, given that he has no son to have groomed for the task but instead three daughters? What is his plan?

The first confusion to be disposed of concerns the so-called love test – what is the real objective behind it, since it is obviously *not* what Lear pretends it to be. We are alerted to his deception by the first words of the play (though, granted, their significance can be appreciated only in retrospect):

> *Kent:* I thought the King had more affected the Duke of
> Albany than Cornwall.
> *Glouc:* It did always seem so to us; but now, in the division
> of the kingdom, it appears not which of the Dukes he
> values most; for equalities are so weigh'd that curiosity
> in neither can make choice of either's moiety.

These two familiars of the King are privy to part of his plan, but only part. They know he proposes to divide the kingdom into three portions, and know furthermore which portion is to go to Albany (and, incidentally, to Goneril), which to Cornwall (and Regan), and which portion will remain for Cordelia and whoever her husband turns out to be – though they also quite likely, almost surely, know who that is. They are somewhat surprised that Albany does not get more than Cornwall, given that the King always seemed to like Albany better (as well he should, given what we subsequently see of the radical difference in these two Dukes' characters). The King, however, has been scrupulously fair in dealing with them: simply from looking at each one's designated portion, a person could not tell whom he favours. Kent's and Gloucester's assessment squares with what the King himself says in allotting to Regan "this ample third of our fair kingdom, / No less in space, validity, and pleasure, / Than that conferr'd on Goneril." (1.1.79–81). From what they know of the plan (they probably have seen the map upon which the divisions are drawn), neither Kent nor Gloucester seem the least bit upset, and their conversation easily shifts to the young man who will prove the energizer of another, intertwining chain of events, Gloucester's bastard son, Edmund. Specifically, they show no concern over the division of the kingdom – the division as originally planned, that is. Why don't they? Must it not be because they realize it will not have 'divisive' effects?[7]

They are not the only ones who know something of what the King has in mind, however; the Duke of Burgundy does, too. Thus, his surprised response when asked what is the least dower he would require in order to agree to marry Cordelia: "Most royal Majesty, / I crave no more than hath your Highness offer'd, / Nor will you tender less" (190–4). Moments later, "Royal King, / Give but that portion which yourself propos'd, / And here I take Cordelia by the hand, / Duchess of Burgundy" (240–3). Presumably, then, Lear and Burgundy have already agreed upon the details of the match. It is clear that the Duke is Lear's choice, that he has had a concrete indication of the estate with which Cordelia will be endowed, and is well satisfied with it, as Lear is with him. By contrast, the King of France shows no prior awareness of Lear's intentions (though doubtless he is shrewd enough to figure out some of the scheme from what he sees in the shambles left by Cordelia's uncooperative behaviour). Of course, the actual conduct of the love-speech contest itself shows that Lear had no intention of using it to determine who gets what. Instead of waiting for all three daughters to speak and only then awarding his "largest bounty" to whoever he claims has persuaded him that she is the most loving, Lear presents his elder daughters their portion immediately after each speaks. Why he does it that way, why he does not better preserve the facade of its being the contest he proposed (as would have been most easy to do), is a puzzle that must be addressed.

Since it is clear in retrospect that the love test was never what Lear pretended, what purpose was it really meant to serve?[8] To see its role in his plan, one must engage in a bit of speculation – that is, try oneself to think through the political problem as the author presents it. Lear rules a united Britain, which he wishes to pass on. But *how* does he rule it? Not single-handedly, of course, but by means of a hierarchy of loyal subordinates who effectively control their local areas through a network of personal allegiances and familial connections (see 2.1.110–16). The two most powerful of these are apparently Albany and Cornwall, whose names may be presumed to indicate their respective ducal domains: the former, lord of Scotland and northern England; the latter, of what was once called Wessex (the southwest portion of England, which extends far enough to include as a subordinate fief that of the Earl of Gloucester; note 2.1.57–9).[9] Doubtless the King arranged the marriages of his two elder daughters (just as he intends to arrange Cordelia's), and it is a virtual certainty that geopolitical considerations figured hugely in his choices (as they are meant to in the case of Cordelia). By means of these political marriages, both the turbulent North and the remote Southwest are bound to the great Centre, the largest and richest part, where Lear himself holds personal sway. The problem is, sooner or later Lear will be gone. What he is attempting to pass on is the political arrangement as he himself actually manages it. Thus, he 'gives' Albany and Cornwall the portions of the realm they already effectively control, while reserving the centre for Cordelia and the husband he has chosen for her. Retaining the title and prerogatives of King, while turning over the practical administration of affairs to his three sons-in-law, Lear will continue living in the centre where he can continue to employ his prudence in supervising matters however necessary – and most especially, assist Cordelia's husband to establish himself securely as Lear's replacement (1.1.122–3). The longer Lear survives, the more will this new state of affairs gain de facto legitimacy. He does not give up the title of King precisely so that he can bestow it later (though he may make a will to cover the possiblity of his sudden death). Meanwhile the prospect of being chosen his successor will encourage all of his sons-in-law in their best behaviour.

Cordelia's marriage is the last piece of the plan to be fitted into place. Her two suitors, France and Burgundy, are not merely, as Lear puts it, "Great rivals in our youngest daughter's love," they are great rivals – period. We are told they have "Long in our court made their amorous sojourn" (45–6). One suspects that it was not Cordelia who was holding up matters there. Lear has been making his assessment, not of which one is best, but of whether Burgundy is adequate. For while France could not without offence be refused at least the appearance of consideration (an appearance that puts additional pressure on Burgundy), he almost surely was never in the running, for one simple reason: he could not be counted on to fulfil his role in Lear's plan. Already himself a King, he would not leave France to come live in the centre of Britain, an obedient son, apprenticed to strong-willed, ever-demanding Lear (and we must remember, he will have had ample opportunity over his lengthy "amorous sojourn" to assess Lear, and what life is like living with him – a sample of which we, too, are provided upon the King's boisterous return to the "grac'd palace" of Albany and Goneril; 1.4.8–92). Moreover, the part of Britain any French king controlled, and even the whole of Britain should he gain it, would be treated as an appendage of France. We must presume that Lear understands his country well enough to know that Britain is not apt long to remain united and peaceful under an absentee King. By contrast, the prospect of becoming himself a sovereign king would have a powerful appeal for one who is but a duke, and a few years subordination would be a small enough price to pay.[10] Burgundy's existing rivalry with France amplified and his power strengthened by his acquisitions in Britain, he should prove a jealous protector of British interests. The duchy of Burgundy would then become an appendage of Britain, providing a strong continental base from which to harry

France, if necessary, thereby strengthening the French interest in remaining at peace with Britain (a situation not unlike the Angevin Empire under Henry II, or that which existed during the prime of Edward III). The Duke of Burgundy is the only choice, provided he is sensible enough for the job. Apparently Lear has been persuaded that he is, and the one political act we see him perform – rejecting the dowerless Cordelia – tends to validate Lear's judgment of him.

Not that France is a fool to grab her on the rebound, as it were. He must see that the radically altered circumstances present the very opportunity Lear's original plan was intended to deny him. Its having been made clear that the old King was pursuing an alliance tacitly directed against France, he is not to be diverted by Lear's impromptu efforts at dissuasion ("For you, great King, / I would not from your love make such a stray / To match you where I hate; therefore beseech you / T'avert your liking a more worthier way" 1.1.207–10). In ignoring this veiled warning against taking up "what's cast away" (252), France adds injury to the insult implicit in his earlier questioning the sincerity of Lear's "fore-vouch'd affection" for Cordelia (217–22). It comes as no surprise to learn that the two Kings parted "in choler" (1.2.23). France realizes that Lear may have repudiated Cordelia to the fullest extent his words are capable of, but this is not absolute. Nothing can change the natural fact that she is, and everyone knows she is, of royal blood, a true and natural daughter of the reigning house, born in legal wedlock. This retains *some* significance, whatever Lear has the law declare (as would be readily appreciated by anyone aware that England was ruled for almost half a century by a woman who, though the natural daughter of a king married to her mother, had been subsequently declared a bastard; cf. 2.4.127–9). Presumably, this is why later Goneril arranges to have Cordelia killed (5.3.251). So, behind the warm romantic flourish – and loaded irony? – with which France seizes what "chance" has thrown his way ("Fairest Cordelia, that art most rich being poor; most choice, forsaken," etc. 1.1.249–60), there may be the cold calculation of realpolitik. And sure enough, in short order there is a French army on British soil, allegedly to protect her "ag'd father's right," but equally capable of asserting Cordelia's (4.4.28; note 3.1.27–9).

Placed in the context of what Lear originally planned, however, one can readily see the actual purpose of his 'love test.' It is meant to elicit from Goneril and Regan the strongest possible public declarations of their dutiful devotion to him and his will. Certainly, the idea of it would not be alien in a society where pledges of love are a routine part of political life, solicited and duly delivered on all sorts of occasions. A competition among rivals to surpass one another in declarations of love, loyalty, and selfless dedication has been a common feature of court life virtually wherever there have been courts. The daughters' vows of everlasting devotion are meant to reinforce and reaffirm the oaths of fealty we may presume already bind their husbands. Such pledges are hardly bands of steel, but neither are they inconsequential – and least of all in a feudal society, where a failure to stand by one's word to one's superiors gives licence to one's inferiors to treat verbal enactments likewise, and compromises one's credibility with respect to all future undertakings. Thus, there are solid, utilitarian reasons why so much emphasis is placed on 'honour' and 'integrity' in politics generally, but in feudal politics especially. In feudal regimes the actions of all those who count politically are regulated as much by a code of honour as by a code of law; to a considerable degree, the fabric of this way of political life is only as strong as the confidence that can be placed in personal commitments publicly witnessed. With respect to this, the King, being placed highest, must be exemplary – hence Lear's outrage at Kent's insistence that he "revoke" what he had just publicly pronounced on this high ceremonious occasion (perhaps the most important in Lear's long and distinguished reign):

> Hear me, recreant!
> On thine *allegiance*, hear me!
> That thou hast sought to make us break our *vow*,
> Which we durst *never* yet, and with strained pride
> To come betwixt our *sentence* and our power,
> Which nor our nature nor our *place* can bear,
> Our potency made good, take thy reward.
> Five days we do allot thee ...
> ... Away! By Jupiter,
> This shall not be revok'd.
> (1.1.165–78)

This is not to say, of course, that vows and pledges and promises and oaths are never broken. But doing so requires a plausible reason if one's integrity is not to be brought into question. The very fact that everyone not a natural fool is aware that such reasons may be no more than pretexts means that one's alleged justification will be viewed with a suspicion appropriate to one's reputation, and must be able to withstand whatever scrutiny one's fellows care to give it if one's honour – and future effectiveness – is not to suffer.[11]

Bearing all of this in mind, we can see what Lear has sprung on his unsuspecting daughters. It is imperative that they not know in advance what Lear is going to challenge them with, so that they cannot prepare carefully crafted, hence 'crafty,' responses: speeches that are not only polished rhetorical set-pieces, but that employ subtle, equivocal speech and incorporate cleverly concealed loopholes and escape clauses – the sort of thing that is a staple of the diplomatist's art.

If he is to be certain that no hint of what he has in mind reaches his daughters in advance, he must not confide to anyone this feature of his plan.[12] Confronted with the necessity of speaking extemporaneously, and not sure if Lear is serious in his announced intention to award his "largest bounty" according to this egocentric notion of merit (all the more credible to the extent they believe him to have become capricious in old age), their only prudent course is to go all out in telling him what they suppose he wants to hear. Presuming, that is, that each one does indeed desire the largest, most bountiful part, and we must allow Lear to have known his two elder daughters sufficiently well to count on that. (He obviously had no idea of the depths of their baseness, but neither was he simply naïve about their natures; after all, he loved Cordelia best.) Even once Goneril has spoken and immediately been given her share, Regan cannot be sure that the contest is not real; she can see that the best part still has not been awarded, hence, it may still go to the daughter who comes up with that which Lear is waiting to hear. So, both Goneril and Regan play their roles as Lear intended. Having publicly declared that he is their everything, it will be awkward – to say the least – for either of them to seem less than perfectly satisfied with whatever he bestows upon them, or to protest anything else he does or wishes done. Their extravagant professions should be more than sufficient to ensure, as a practical minimum, that they meet conventional standards of filial obligation, especially since he intends to continue residing at the centre of power with the daughter he most loves and trusts.

However, it is with his beloved Cordelia that things go off the rails. The part of his plan to which Lear likely gave the least thought because it seemed so straightforward, so utterly unproblematic, precipates a political crisis whose resolution sends everything spinning off in a new, and far from satisfactory direction. If in retrospect one were to isolate a single crucial mistake Lear made, it was his not taking Cordelia into his confidence and briefing her on the role she must play. Why did Lear not do this? First of all, there seemed no need. In fact, she might better play her part in complete innocence, since her 'role' is simply to be herself. Lear is sure she is the one who truly loves him best. All he is asking of her is that she tell the truth. What could be easier, or more palatable? He neither needs nor expects her to surpass the bombastic flights of her sisters, but merely to give honest expression to her true feelings, to declare publicly the love she has privately indicated a thousand times. Another, and more important, reason was the necessity that the 'love test' be kept secret, and from Goneril and Regan especially if they are to provide the spontaneous hypocrisy his plan requires. It would be best if no one knew for sure that the contest was a charade, since seeing it as a deception undercuts the moral force of whatever professions have been 'deceitfully' elicited. If Lear is viewed as insincere in setting out the contest, he licenses participation in a like temper (which could serve as a pretext for disavowing the things said). Given Cordelia's probity, honesty, and proud sense of honour, might she not balk at taking part in what she is aware from the outset is a sham? Or in the discomfiture of her foreknowledge, betray by word or gesture, even if inadvertently, some hint to her sisters? Lear believes he knows his favourite daughter very well; he thinks of her as kindred in spirit, not merely in body. He is well acquainted with her honesty and her pride, indeed, he probably had a hand in cultivating both. Still, he assumes that, given her intelligence, she will understand what she can see happening as his benevolent intentions unfold before her very eyes, and that she will respond accordingly. But in this he does not make sufficient allowance for her political naïveté, for the natural difficulties involved in learning to 'think politically.'

Lear has been "every inch a King" for so long that the political requirements of his role are second nature to him. He suffers no dissonance from his obligation to behave somewhat differently in public than he does privately among his intimates; he automatically adapts to whatever the circumstances require. His own love of truth and preference for honesty have long since accommodated the fact that fulfilling public responsibilities requires a certain amount of hypocrisy and pretense, to say nothing of outright lies.[13] This willingness to give the common good priority over his personal taste is basic to his political virtue. It has been decades since he made much effort (if he ever did) to distinguish between the respect paid him because he is a powerful king, and that which comes to him on some more personal basis (affection, admiration of his virtues and achievements, or gratitude for benefits bestowed). In short, Lear takes much about the conduct of political life for granted. Almost surely the basis of his relationship with Cordelia, however, has been fashioned in private and concerns only private things. Unless her curiosity runs strongly in a contrary vein – and we have no evidence that it does, and some that it does not – there would be little reason to educate her in the hard, unattractive, *coarsening* necessities of political practice.[14] It may be that Lear so enjoys their relationship precisely because it provides a temporary respite from the often dreary and sometimes unpleasant business of managing everyday affairs, allowing him to dwell in a purer realm more congenial to his nature. Cordelia is obviously bright, reflective, and articulate, as well as considerate and loving; it is no wonder he enjoys being with her, and that doing so full-time would be his preferred retirement. However, with their intercourse having been confined to this higher plane, and with her being responsible thus far for nothing beyond her own integrity, her pure view of life remains unsullied by the truth of what is sometimes involved in dealing with less fastidious people. She is aware, of course, that they exist; but be they ever so vulgar, selfish, scheming, faithless, cowardly, deceitful, or treacherous, she has never yet had to acknowledge in them a reason to adjust her own principles or compromise her own sense of honour. Which is to say, she has never before had to think politically – to understand what is politically required, and why such political necessities deserve respect – and then act accordingly.

As Cordelia is a young unmarried woman, perhaps hardly more than a girl, she has had little or no public role to play. Indeed, this may be the first time she has been required to do something significant in public. Almost anyone would be self-conscious in her circumstances – suddenly, unexpectedly required to make a public speech before the most eminent personages of one's society, a vitally important matter at stake, one's effort to be judged against those of older, more experienced speakers – but a sheltered young woman is apt to be especially so. This is what Lear, so accustomed to public life, apparently failed to appreciate. He presumed that by the time it was Cordelia's turn to speak, the implications of what he had arranged would be as clear as the nose between the eyes on his face; after all, there is only one piece of the kingdom left, it is the largest and richest part, and it has been saved for her. He has sacrificed a degree of his contest's plausibility precisely in order that his true intentions be evident to her at this point. All she has to do is declare her love in sufficiently substantial terms to justify his declaring her the 'winner' – just give him something about which he can plausibly say, "*That's it!* That's what I been waiting to hear!" Her saying "Nothing" is the one thing that will *not* do the trick. Lear believes this would be obvious to a half-wit. In fact, were one purposefully determined to *subvert* his plan, one could be hard put to improve on *that* answer. But Cordelia's asides while her sisters are speaking show that she is completely preoccupied with her own immediate feelings; she's not asking herself what is going on here, what is Father up to, what is the meaning of all this? She is listening to what her sisters say, and ignoring completely what is unfolding before her eyes. One can imagine what effect their sycophancy has on her proud young soul: Goneril's flagrant hypocrisy being distasteful enough, only to be surpassed by Regan's even more preposterous nonsense. She could not possibly outdo them at such a shameful game, but more to the point, she has no wish to try. Nor does she give any indication that she cares much whether or not she gets the "largest bounty"; but she does take professions of love seriously. And so when it is her turn to speak, she in effect abdicates.

Still, one must ask why Cordelia does not make a greater effort to please her father on this occasion. Even granted that she is oblivious to what Lear presumes would be plain to anyone of her intelligence (and so does not, in fact, appreciate the disastrous political consequences of her behaviour), she can hardly be unaware that the King is not happy with her response. Perhaps attempting first to pass it off as a joke, Lear notes that "nothing will come of nothing," and bids her, "speak again." When this merely elicits from her a formula more befitting some logic-chopping lawyer than a tender lover ("I love your Majesty / According to my bond; no more nor less." 1.1.91–2),[15] Lear's response is stronger but still only mildly reproving: "How, how, Cordelia! Mend your speech a *little*, / Lest you may mar your fortunes." Cordelia can be under no illusions at this juncture as to whether the tack she has taken is satisfactory; the King is almost pleading with her to respond in accordance with his cues. But rather than mend her speech the slightest, she continues to express her love in only the briefest, coldest of terms:

> Good my Lord,
> You have begot me, bred me, lov'd me: I
> Return those duties back as are right fit,
> Obey you, love you, and most honour you.
> (94–7)

In effect, "It's my duty to love you, so I love you." One supposes such love is better than nothing, but it would scarce be deeply gratifying. The very manner in which Cordelia makes this profession calls into question the other elements of it as well: it is not a convincing expression of honouring, and could be seen as flagrantly *dis*obedient (as Goneril later tells her, "you have obedience scanted, / And well are worth the want you have wanted" 277–8). Cordelia's quality of speech here begs to be compared with that on other occasions, such as she used in thanking Kent for saving her beloved father ("O thou good Kent! how shall I live and work / To match thy goodness? My life will be too short, / And every measure fail me" 4.7.1–3) and in indicting the cruelty of her sisters (30–42; see also 4.4.1–20). Even on this occasion, what follows her sterile formality proves that she can be passionately articulate when it suits *her* purpose, despite her earlier insistence to the contrary ("Unhappy that I am, I cannot heave my heart into my mouth"):

> Why have my sisters husbands, if they say
> They love you all? Happily, when I shall wed,
> That lord whose hand must take my plight shall carry
> Half my love with him, half my care and duty:
> Sure I shall never marry like my sisters,
> To love my father all.
> (1.1.98–103)

Bad enough that she fail to provide the King a profession of her own love that would be suitable for his plan. Now she taints those which Lear had so cleverly extracted from her sisters. As if he needed her to inform him that what they claimed was not the gods' own truth! Nor for that matter is he apt to enjoy being so bluntly reminded that he will soon be obliged to share his favourite with another man – a fact of life that he may half regret, whereas she looks forward to it "happily." It must be with pained surprise that Lear asks, "But goes thy heart with this? ... So young, and so untender?" There is no word of comfort, no sympathy for him in her lofty (not to say, haughty) answer: "So young, my Lord, and true."

Still, the question remains, why has Cordelia behaved so obstinately? For by all the other evidence in the play, we know she cares for her father deeply. Lear misjudges her because he presumes she has more understanding of what she is doing than she has, and thus he sees far more malice in her action than she intends – indeed, insofar as she intends anything definite, it does not go beyond a tacit protest to her father for putting her in an embarrassing position. Having taken his contest more or less at face value, she is offended by it, nettled by it, and so refuses all but token participation in it. She does not realize there are larger, practically sovereign issues at stake. To explain Cordelia's behaviour, then, one probably need look no further than her pride, the same spirited pride (ironically) as infuses Lear, and not least when in high dudgeon he declaims, "Let pride, which she calls plainness, marry her" (128). Cordelia's later plea to have her offence specified is fairly steeped in pride, and could only exacerbate its offensiveness in her father's eyes: she would *rather* have her lofty disdain of flattery and solicitation than have his "grace and favour," his "liking"; she's "glad" she *lacks* the manner of speech that would please him (222–32).[16]

The human spirit – seat of anger and indignation, as of the other emotions; source of courage and resolve – is ever sensitive to one's status. Manifested in the sense of pride, of honour, of dignity, of self-respect, one's spirit is offended, pained, by all things regarded as shameful, and so is inclined to rebel when required to do anything one sees as demeaning. Thus, high-spirited people balk at lying, at flattering, at being hypocritical merely to gratify the vanity of others. A person such as Kent, in this akin to Cordelia, takes pride in his willingness to "deliver a plain message bluntly" (1.4.33), and radically distinguishes himself from sycophantic courtiers like Oswald ("That such a slave as this should wear a sword, who wears no honesty" 2.2.69–70). Still, once one sees the consequences of Cordelia's prideful 'honesty' for Lear's plan – upon which depends not merely his own remaining happiness (which he is prepared to forfeit; 1.1.124), but what is far more important: the continuing welfare of the polity he rules – one can readily understand why Lear is so upset with her, given his presumption that she realizes what she is doing. It may also colour his displeasure with Kent, who openly takes her part.

For Cordelia has left the King far out on a limb from which it is almost impossible for him to climb back. If she really loved him, loved him more than her own vain pride, she would not, could not have done this to him. Having with due ceremony committed himself to this particular method of distributing the shares of his kingdom, Lear cannot fail to appear to follow through without publicly insulting and thus alienating Goneril and Regan, and what is more important, their powerful husbands who are awaiting their doweries. These two daughters played the game by the rules, dutifully professing what was asked of them; they cannot now be left in the lurch, exposed as dupes, they and their husbands' goodwill seemingly treated with contempt. Moreover, would not almost anyone who witnessed their public humiliation sympathize with these daughters, and regard any future animosity towards their father as justified, and so excuse their failure to respect his will? Thus, what was intended to be an act of highest statesmanship threatens to turn into a first-rate political mess – and all because of Cordelia's persistent, indeed increasing recalcitrance, her stubbornly refusing to accede to her loving father's wishes, despite the dire political and personal consequences of her refusal being so self-evident (just as are the overwhelming benefits that would accrue from her cooperation). Compared with what is at stake, Lear is asking so little of his daughter, almost nothing in fact: just an honest profession of the great love he presumed she genuinely felt for him, variously expressed how many times in private. Or so he had heretofore believed. With his power of judgment distorted by that righteous anger felt most intensely when aggrieved or betrayed by those dear to us,[17] Lear now wonders whether he had all along been misled, deceived. His reserving the best part of the kingdom made clear enough *his* love for *her*. Is it not truly reciprocated? Cordelia's refusal to provide that which he was counting on, what he beseeched her for so far as his kingly dignity would permit, was no act of love. It was at best a prideful, spiteful, selfish indulgence. Is there a side to her that he has never seen before? Might she be a schemer? Perhaps she does not like Burgundy, at least compared with France who would immediately make her a Queen and provide her an escape from the regime of her tiresome old father. Is she thus determined to upset his plan, regardless of its cost to the common good of Britain? If *this* is how it is, she would indeed suddenly seem a stranger to his heart and him (114).

Hence, Cordelia's precipitous fall in Lear's regard, not merely from most to least favourite daughter, but to the status of hated ingrate and imposter, someone who now exposed for what (he mistakenly suspects) she is, deserves *nothing* of his bounty. If she was scheming to arrange her own marriage, his rendering her practically ineligible by refusing her any dowery will be his fitting revenge (see 201–4). When his anger has cooled and he has time to reflect, to remember other considerations that deserve to be weighed in the balance, perhaps coming to realize that she acted out of complete ignorance, he will revise his judgment of Cordelia. Compared with what is ahead at the hands of Goneril and Regan, he will come to see Cordelia's obstinance as a "most small fault," but one which seemed so ugly in the circumstances that it "wrench'd [his] frame of nature / From the fix'd place, drew from [his] heart all love, / And added to the gall" (1.4.264–8). In the crisis of the moment, however, her behaviour is completely if understandably misinterpreted, with the result that the old King, unaccustomed to being either mistaken in his judgments or thwarted in his will, is thrown into a high passion. For Cordelia's surprising response to his carefully crafted piece of political theatre does precipitate a crisis, confronting Lear with having to choose among four unsatisfactory options.

First, Lear could carry through with his original plan. Doing so now, however, would have far different consequences from those which were essential to its basic rationale. Having proclaimed that the daughter who spoke most lovingly was to get the richest part, and then to award it, not to a daughter who clearly complied with his wishes, but to one whose response Lear openly indicated he found wanting – indeed, whose response everyone could see was grudging, and whose behaviour bordered on the disrespectful and disobedient – could only antagonize those who have been publicly treated as pawns. The purpose of the plan was to preserve amity among the major parts of the kingdom; persevering with it now, however, would almost surely have the opposite effect.

Second, the King could do what Kent later implores him to do: revoke everything he has done thus far, suspend further proceedings, and adjourn to reconsider what would be best, given the unexpected turn of events. As we see from Lear's reaction when actually confronted with the suggestion, he finds that idea abominable – not merely because it is unprecedented, but for the reasons *why* it is unprecedented: it is incompatible with both his own proud "nature" and his high political "place" (169–70). The King sets the standard for the entire regime while he lives, and even for his successors after he has died. Any compromise of his honour undercuts the code of honour. His decrees are law, and if the law is to be consistent, his will must be constant.[18] Moreover, Lear lacks admissible grounds for withdrawing at this point – ones, that is, that would not offend the other parties involved, further aggravating the situation. For nothing has happened that would justify his not carrying through his *announced* intention; and he can hardly admit the real reason: that things are not working out according to his covert intention. Whereas, if he does not provide a plausible justification, then the cat is well and truly out of the bag, with no prospect of ever getting it back in again. Then there is the collateral problem of how to deal with the two powerful suitors of Cordelia. Can they be counted upon quietly to endure further postponement? With respect to Burgundy in particular, is he or is he not to be told that the deal is off?

Third, Lear could depart from his declared intention to divest himself *entirely* of "both of rule, interest of territory, cares of state" (48–9) by now announcing that he has decided to retain the largest, most bountiful part of the kingdom for himself. There are obvious objections to this option as well, however. It, too, would amount to a revoking of his publicly expressed will, since his avowed purpose for this ceremonial gathering of the leading magnates of the realm is supposedly his well-considered, therefore "*fast* intent / To shake all cares and business from [his] age, / Conferring them on younger strengths" (37–9). And like the second option, it requires a plausible justification if it is not to poison the very relationships with powers both at home and abroad that a lasting settlement must be based upon. Also, this could only be – and be seen to be – a temporary expedient. Ultimately, Lear must have recourse to either some new version of the first option (which presumes what at the moment seems out of the question: reconciliation with Cordelia); and how, having tipped his hand, the original plan could still be attempted without embittering his other two daughters and their husbands is difficult to see. Or, he must resort to a different arrangement entirely, involving only the two daughters still in favour.

This is the fourth option available to him in the crisis, and the one he chooses, improvising in the heat of the moment a surrogate plan. Of the alternatives available to him at this point, the one he lights upon has little more than simplicity to recommend it. It calls for Albany and Cornwall to divide the remaining third of the kingdom, the largest and richest part, between them. So the prized centre that was to serve as a buffer between the northern and southern duchies now becomes a bone of contention. The King has specified no demarcation, but even if he had, the lands on either side are bound to become the scene of chronic strife (as historically the borders, or 'marches,' of England always were in the absence of a strong central power to suppress it). Lear's only provision to mitigate against this happening is his intention to abide by monthly turns in each duchy, accompanied by a modest armed retinue of a hundred knights. Retaining "the *name* and all th'addition to a king" (which he believes it will still be in his power to bestow later upon whoever proves most deserving), but signing away "the sway, *revenue*, execution of the rest" to his sons-in-law who are to sustain his largely ceremonial court from their now much-expanded resources (131–7), Lear intends by this circulation of his royal person to keep the country stitched together for so long as he lives. He can only hope that this is long enough for some amicable partnership or other stable relationship to become established. As it is an arrangement that neither burdens nor favours one Duke and daughter over the other, Lear presumes he will continue to be recognized as the supreme legitimate authority, and so can serve as a neutral arbiter for any disputes that arise between them. It is here that his failure to distinguish between the respect shown his power and that shown his person, so long melded into one, proves his – and Britain's – undoing. Having signed away his "power, / Pre-eminence, and all the large *effects* / That troop with majesty" (129–31), the distinction will soon be made for him. Given the flaws of Lear's improvised plan, it comes as no surprise that within weeks there are rumours of impending war "'twixt the Dukes of Cornwall and Albany" (2.1.10–11), civil strife that is only temporarily suppressed to make common cause against a foreign invasion hoping to exploit it (3.1.18–29; 4.2.56; 5.1.29–31). The ultimate impracticality of Lear's improvisation is nicely symbolized by what is supposed to "confirm" it: the two Dukes' parting of the coronet that was originally intended for Cordelia's husband-designate (1.1.137–8; cf. 1.4.156–8, 183–4)) – as if half a coronet would rest securely on either one's head.[19]

It is easy to see in retrospect that the second option, for all of its difficulties, would have made the best choice – been the least unsatisfactory way, that is, of dealing with the very bad situation as Lear saw it. And one might blame him for not better knowing the true natures of his elder daughters. Still, they are his daughters, and it is natural that he would prefer to love them and think as well of them as he can.[20] Obviously Kent, Cordelia, and the Fool all harboured darker suspicions of them than did their father (see 1.1.152–3, 183–4, 267–74; 1.5.13–19). But he may never have had a comparable opportunity to observe them. This is a limitation inherent in his (like any) position of great power: determining how people really feel towards him, given the variety of motives for their merely feigning love, for fawning and flattering, for generally telling him what they suppose he wants to hear, and for showing him only what he wants to see. As Lear himself, having undergone his terrible, transforming suffering, will later complain:

> They flattered me like a dog, and told me I had the white hairs in my beard ere the black ones were there. To say 'ay' and 'no' to everything that I said! ... Go to, they are not men o'their words: they told me I was everything; 'tis a lie, I am not ague-proof. (4.6.96–105; cf. 4.1.1–2)

We must not presume, of course, that before this Lear was entirely unaware of the problem. His choosing to favour men like Kent, and to keep the kind of professional Fool that he does, is evidence of his recognizing the need for honest and plain-speaking advisers and critics who have the courage and integrity to tell him what he needs to hear, be it ever so unpleasant. But Lear knows that the basic problem remains; he could hardly have been the prudent ruler his long reign argues he was had he not cultivated an habitual scepticism with regards to how most people behave towards him.[21] While such scepticism would likely remain quiescent in his dealings with proven intimates, it would nonetheless be present, an essential constituent of his posture towards the world. Thus, his susceptibility to becoming suddenly so suspicious of Cordelia.

Somewhat deluded, then, about the basis of his own power as well as about his daughters' true natures, Lear chooses to improvise on the spot a new plan to replace the one scuttled by Cordelia's spirited refusal to perform her assigned part.[22] The balance of the play is a tracing out of the political repercussions of this impromptu change of plans. Suffice it to say, Gloucester's "We have seen the best of our time: machinations, hollowness, treachery, and all ruinous disorders follow us disquietly to our graves" (1.2.109–11) proves only too prescient. From almost every point of view, the political consequences are disastrous. But this is not to say that no good comes of it.

THE PROBLEM OF NATURE

'**Nature**' is a term frequently encountered in Shakespeare's plays, but nowhere so often as in *King Lear*. There it is mentioned thirty-six times, almost 10 per cent of its total uses in the canon. By comparison, it appears twenty times in *Macbeth*, where it is also an important theme, and twenty-seven times in *Hamlet*, the play with the second-most mentions of the word. Together with its cognates – 'natures,' 'natural,' 'unnatural,' 'nature's,' 'disnatur'd' (sole use) – there are over fifty explicit references to Nature in *King Lear* (compared with thirty-one in *Macbeth*).

Beyond this, however, the play is replete with reminders of the luxurious heterogeneity of Nature, the countless varieties of 'natures' that make up the ordered whole of Nature: of bears, sparrows, cuckoos, asses, horses, kites, wolves, rats, mice, geese, monkeys, ants, eels, vultures, hogs, dolphins, owls, lions, worms, sheep, cats, frogs, toads, neuts, tadpoles, nightingales, herring, tigers, crows, choughs, larks, beetles, wrens, fitchews, butterflies, foxes, and serpents, among others. These, along with imaginary or mythical creatures (dragons, centaurs) and an assortment of generic terms (animal, beast, brute, bird, fish, monster, sea-monster, vermin), provide a substantial context in which to reflect upon the various kinds of similarities and differences one may discern in Nature – this by way of attempting to grasp the distinctions and commonalities that are essential to a coherent understanding of it. Not all of the words in everyday use are reliable indicators for this purpose, as the variety of terms pertaining to dogs serves to remind us; some reflect clear and wholly natural distinctions ('bitch'), others do not ('cur,' 'mongrel'). Moreover, the various *breeds* (mastiff, greyhound, spaniel) present a further complication. For they are representative not merely of the fact that there can be important subdivisions within a species (as there are in most domesticated animals), but that their very existence is the result of an 'artificial' manipulation of nature by that most problematic piece of Nature, man. As philosophers have long recognized, the chief obstacle to conceiving an adequate idea of Nature per se is posed by the necessity that it accommodate *human* nature, doing full justice both to what it shares with the rest of nature and to what makes it distinctive.[23]

Bearing on both man's distinctiveness and his commonness regarding the rest of the animal kingdom are the several instances in the play of people being invested with animal traits. Lear refers to Oswald as a "mongrel," a "whoreson dog," and "cur" (1.4.48, 79–80), and calls Goneril "Detested kite" to her face, which he subsequently characterizes as "wolvish" (260, 306). Later, when impugning her treatment of him to Regan, he describes it as "like a vulture" and "most serpent-like" (2.4.132, 158). Kent also associates Oswald with ignoble dogs (2.2.20–1, 77), as well as likening him to a rat and a goose (71, 80). Edmund speaks of man's "goatish disposition," and his father rails against the (falsely) suspected Edgar, "Unnatural, detested, *brutish* villain! *worse* than brutish!" (1.2.124–5, 73–4). The Fool refers to certain men as "asses" (1.5.33) and Lear to others as "gilded butterflies" (5.3.13). Obtuse to its irony, Regan calls Gloucester an "ingrateful fox," who in turn decrys Goneril's "boarish fangs" (3.7.28, 57). Albany describes Goneril and Regan as "Tigers, not daughters" (4.2.40; see also 63). Blinded Gloucester, reflecting on his encounter with Edgar disguised as a mad beggar, observes, "I'th'last night's storm I such a fellow saw, / Which made me think a man a worm" (4.1.32–3). This same Poor Tom provides the most concentrated display of brutish terms being used to characterize human traits; it comes in response to Lear's "What hast thou been?" "... hog in sloth, fox in stealth, wolf in greediness, dog in madness, lion in prey" (3.4.91–2). We have no difficulty understanding the pertinence of such animal imagery; and as a quick review of the above examples reminds us, far more often than not its use is derogatory.[24] Each of these efforts to express one's shame, or to exploit the normal human resentment at being brutishly described, tacitly raises the question of what (if anything) truly and profoundly distinguishes man from beast. Might such shame and resentment themselves be clues? Arguably, the most significant use of animal imagery in the play, however, is Lear's contrasting self-applications of it. Whereas at the beginning he can refer to himself as an angry dragon (1.1.121), by the end he sees himself as a caged songbird (5.3.9). One can scarcely imagine a more prodigious metamorphosis. Something revolutionary must have happened.

Complementing our penchant for animalizing humans is our equally natural tendency to anthropomorphize divinities. Both inclinations, notice, evince our tacit recognition of a natural hierarchy of beings. Speaking of Gods, allusions to them are as plentiful in *King Lear* as are those to Nature. The religious context being pagan, a plurality of higher, supernatural powers is the common presumption. There are some twenty-seven mentions simply of "the Gods," as well as various references to individual deities, and to "the Heavens" in such a way as to mean 'Heavenly Powers.' Of all the personages in the play, Lear himself speaks most often of or to the gods; he also swears by "the sacred radiance of the sun" and "by the power that made [him]," and mentions by name Hecate, Apollo, Jupiter, Jove, and Cupid. Most of the significant characters address gods at least once; the exceptions are Cornwall, Goneril, Regan (her "O the blest Gods" is clearly but a figure of speech; 2.4.166), and the Fool. The roughly equal prevalence of references to both gods and nature might be seen as emblematic of what is arguably the most comprehensive cosmological question humans confront: is the natural world in which we find ourselves ruled by separately existing supernatural powers? Albany's doubts are resolved upon learning that Cornwall was dealt a mortal blow immediately after blinding Gloucester: "This shows you are above, / You Justices, that these our nether crimes / So speedily can venge!" (4.2.78–80). But if they *do* exist and take an interest in us, is it so clearly 'for' and not 'against'? Or might old Gloucester be right when in the despair of his now eternal night he concludes, "As flies to wanton boys, are we to th'Gods; / They kill us for their sport" (4.1.36–7)? Or (as still a third possibility), is the view expressed by his son Edgar correct as to these matters: "The Gods are just, and of our pleasant vices / Make instruments to plague us" (5.3.169–70) – that is, they have so ordered the world that vice is self-punishing? Alternatively, is Nature a self-subsistent realm, the powers or principles that rule it being intrinsic to it, and strictly impersonal?

The Old King is the first to mention Nature. It is somehow central to the rationale he gives for how he shall distribute the shares of his kingdom: "Which of you shall we say doth love us most? / That we our largest bounty may extend / Where nature doth with merit challenge" (1.1.50–2). Lear uses the term twice more before anyone else does (170, 211; see also 218, 234). However, it is only with the play's second scene that the theme of Nature – the *idea* of Nature as something distinct – begins to come into focus.[25] The scene opens with a soliloquy by Gloucester's illegitimate son, Edmund; or, following the Folio's stage direction, "*Enter* Bastard *with a letter.*"[26]

Bast: Thou, Nature, art my goddess; to thy law
My services are bound. Wherefore should I
Stand in the plague of custom, and permit
The curiosity of nations to deprive me,
For that I am some twelve or fourteen moonshines
Lag of a brother? Why bastard? Wherefore base?
When my dimensions are as well compact,

My mind as generous, and my shape as true,
As honest madam's issue? Why brand they us
With base? with baseness? bastardy? base, base?
Who in the lusty stealth of nature take
More composition and fierce quality
Than doth, within a dull, stale, tired bed,
Go to th'creating a whole tribe of fops,
Got 'tween asleep and wake? Well then,
Legitimate Edgar, I must have your land:
Our father's love is to the bastard Edmund
As to th'legitimate. Fine word, 'legitimate'! –
Well, my legitimate, if this letter speed,
And my invention thrive, Edmund the base
Shall top th'legitimate – : I grow, I prosper;
Now, gods, stand up for bastards!

Using Edmund's view as a point of departure – a view with which a great many 'legitimate Edgars' would surely sympathize, and which for that reason might itself be thought natural – we begin with the *distinction* between the 'laws' of Nature and those of men, and thus with the recognition that not everything that exists is equally natural, nor is Nature the only source of order and regularity in the world.[27] What more precisely it is that distinguishes the natural from the non-natural, and on what basis or bases the latter exists, remains to be clarified. Edmund avows himself a devotee of Nature as he understands her, and we get some fuller indication of his conception from his subsequent speeches and deeds.[28] Regardless of their normally resulting from purposeful deliberation, Edmund apparently regards man-made laws as equivalent in basis to customs, such as gentlemen shaking right hands when they meet or rising when a lady enters the room – customs that are but particular, and often peculiar, ways of doing things that could as well be otherwise as not, and that govern people's behaviour only because they allow themselves to be thus imposed upon. In the letter Edmund forges implicating Edgar in a conspiracy against their father, he imputes to his half-brother what we may suspect actually reflects his own belief: "I begin to find an idle and fond bondage in the oppression of aged tyranny, who sways, not as it hath *power*, but as it is suffer'd" (1.2.47–9). His repudiation of the customary precedence given one's elders is later amplified when he voices in private the intention to betray his father to Cornwall: "This seems a fair deserving, and must draw me / That which my father loses; no less than all: / The younger rises when the old doth fall" (3.3.23–5).

Here in his first soliloquy, however, Edmund is castigating two other 'plagues of custom,' both of which are especially prejudicial to him (or would be if the second did not obviate application of the first), and both of which he contends have no rational basis in nature – that in fact run contrary to it. One of these favours the first-born over younger siblings, such that a father bestows his title and estate on his eldest son ('primogeniture'). The other makes a radical distinction between children who are born in legal wedlock (thus called 'legitimate,' from the Latin *legitimatus*, 'declared to be lawful') and those who are not (and are labelled 'bastards'). Both of these particular practices can bear profoundly, pro or con, on the fates of individuals, despite those most immediately affected having nothing to do with what establishes their respective status. Obviously, a person is no more responsible for the temporal order in which he or she is born than for the marital standing of one's biological parents. Nor is there clear evidence that either first-born or legitimate offspring tend to be naturally superior in body or soul, hence more worthy of preference, than those born subsequently or out of wedlock. These would seem to be paradigm cases for illustrating the irrationality and arbitrariness of so much law and custom.

The very fact that primogeniture is far from a universal practice – that there are many other established arrangements, some treating all children equally, some favouring children on another basis than age, and so on – is enough to make its acceptance suspect in those times and places where it does prevail. Whereas the invidiousness consequences of the legitimate–bastard distinction, the comprehensive blight it casts over the lives of innocent individuals, is offensive to reason and a violation of almost any conceivable idea of natural justice. Indeed, it would seem an even clearer exemplification of the contrast between reason and *physis* (nature), on the one hand, and habit and *nomos* (to resort to this useful Greek term for all man-made rules, such as laws, customs, conventions, mores, etc.), on the other. Yet, some recognition of this distinction is well-nigh universal. Moreover, it alone carries a social stigma. The *moral contrast* between these two customary practices, seemingly alike in other important respects, invites further analysis of both. Nobody uses 'you second-born son' as a term of abuse; whereas 'bastard' is a derogatory epithet widely employed, not only to connote vicious and vulgar qualities in people (especially men), but to denominate fraudulent or debased versions of other things as well. The term and its synonym 'whoreson' is used repeatedly in the play: Lear calls Oswald a "whoreson dog" (1.4.79–80), Goneril a "degenerate bastard" (251), and threatens Regan with ex post facto bastardization (2.4.126–9; see also 4.6.114–16). The wonderful catalogue of insults that Kent applies to Oswald several times includes "whoreson," as if fitting company for a "son and heir of a mongrel bitch" (2.2.16, 20–1, 31, 61). In arresting

Edmund, Albany makes a point of labelling him a "half-blooded fellow" (5.3.81); and Kent, conspicuously declining to mention him by name, instead refers to him as "the bastard son of Gloucester" (4.7.89).

Suffice it to say, there is no paucity of evidence as to why Edmund is positively obsessed with the liabilities attached to bastardy, as opposed to the prejudicial consequences of primogeniture – and obsessed he is, returning to the theme time and again.[29] Nor, perhaps, is it a great mystery why he himself behaves like 'a real bastard.' Each time he hears someone use this common term of abuse, to whomever it is applied and whatever the context, he is reminded of the prejudice under which he suffers every day of his life. This is not a formula for bringing out the best in a person; quite the contrary: the constant chaffing could only coarsen his spirit and harden his heart, and the manifest injustice of it would cultivate cynicism in all but the noblest of natures. One can easily sympathize with the resentment Edmund must feel, not only towards individuals, but towards the whole political and legal order that sustains a status so unfair to him. It is hardly surprising, then, that he prefers the order of nature, where he sees no such distinction, to the irrational and perverse arrangements of "whoremaster man" (his term; 1.2.124). Moreover, the recognition of the practical effects of this discrimination on the souls of those who, like him, are made to bear it constitutes yet another argument against its perpetuation. But it should also heighten one's curiosity about its broad, nearly universal prevalence. Is the distinction between legitimate and illegitimate just another instance of the "foppery of the world?" Or is there more to it? What insight does the play itself provide?

Certainly the issue arises early enough: the drama is scarce a minute under way when Kent asks Gloucester, "Is not this your son, my Lord?" We can only guess why he supposes so, given that Kent has not previously met the young man. He may be aware that Gloucester has a son, and simply presumes that this is he. Or, Edmund may noticeably, 'naturally,' resemble his father, as offspring often do. Whatever the case, Gloucester replies:

> His breeding, Sir, hath been at my charge: I have so often blush'd to acknowledge him, that now I am braz'd to it.
>
> *Kent:* I cannot conceive you.
>
> *Glouc:* Sir, this young fellow's mother could; whereupon she grew round-womb'd, and had, indeed, Sir, a son for her cradle ere she had a husband for her bed. Do you smell a fault?
>
> *Kent:* I cannot wish the fault undone, the issue of it being so proper.

Glouc: But I have a son, Sir, by order of law, some year
elder than this, who yet is no dearer in my account:
though this knave came something saucily to the
world before he was sent for, yet was his mother
fair; there was good sport at his making, and the
whoreson must be acknowledged. Do you know this
noble gentleman, Edmund?
Edmund: No, my Lord.
Glouc: My Lord of Kent: remember him hereafter as my
honourable friend.
Edmund: My services to your Lordship.
Kent: I must love you, and sue to know you better.
Edmund: Sir, I shall study deserving.
(1.1.7–30)

The slightly ribald, bantering tone Gloucester adopts would seem to indicate how little significance *he* attaches (or would prefer to attach) to a status he nonetheless feels obliged to make clear. But how would it likely affect Edmund to hear himself and his mother so spoken of? Gloucester attests that he's grown calloused to the shame of having bred a bastard. One suspects it is not so easy to become indifferent to the condition of being one ("Why brand they us with *base*? with baseness? bastardy? base, base?"). Edmund's outer reaction to meeting "noble," "honourable" Kent on these terms is calm and polite, but what must he be feeling? Coleridge has expressed it well:[30]

Edmund hears the circumstances of his birth spoken of with a most degrading and licentious levity, – his mother described as a wanton by her own paramour, and the remembrance of the animal sting, the low criminal gratifications connected with her wantonness and prostituted beauty, assigned as the reason, why 'the whoreson must be acknowledged!' This, and the consciousness of its notoriety; the gnawing conviction that every show of respect is an effort of courtesy, which recalls, while it represses, a contrary feeling; – this is the ever trickling flow of wormwood and gall into the wounds of pride, – the corrosive *virus* which inoculates pride with a venom not its own, with envy, hatred, and a lust for that power which in its blaze of radiance would hide the dark spots on his disk, – with pangs of shame personally undeserved, and therefore felt as wrongs, and with a blind ferment of vindictive working towards the occasions and causes, especially towards a brother, whose stainless birth and lawful honours were the constant remembrances of his own debasement, and were ever in the way to prevent all chance of its being unknown, or overlooked and forgotten ... Need it be said how heavy an aggravation, in such a case, the stain of bastardy must have been, were it only that the younger brother was liable to hear his own dishonour and his mother's infamy related by his father with an excusing shrug of the shoulders, and in a tone betwixt waggery and shame!

However, there is more to be pondered in the play's opening exchange than Edmund's feelings. For example, we should notice that Gloucester is not merely a breeder of bastards; he almost surely is an adulterer. The existence of an older, *legitimate* son implies that he was already married when he begot Edmund, and thus could not have even considered marrying Edmund's mother in the event he got her with child. He could only have intended her to be the fair piece of sport she was, at most a leman.[31] So we are reminded of more distinctions and conceptions unique to human life – fornication versus adultery, wife versus leman or concubine – all equally impertinent to the rest of animate creation (cf. 4.6.109–14). We might also notice that, although Gloucester professes Edmund to be as dear to him as his older, legitimate son (and his having him present on this high public occasion lends credence to his claim), he seems to have provided for the two quite differently. As Gloucester informs Kent just before the King arrives, Edmund "hath been out nine years, and away he shall again" (1.1.31–2). This may be news to Edmund as well as Kent, and it, along with what he sees as the old King's capricious treatment of the daughter he claimed was dearest, may be what precipitates Edmund's plot to supplant Edgar.[32] Whatever the case, Edmund had been sent away to make his fortune elsewhere. Perhaps this arrangement was convenient for him, allowing him to pursue a career (presumably military) in a venue where his dubious lineage would not be such a constant embarrassment. One rather suspects it was at least as convenient for his father, however. The very fact that he could have been parted from this son for nine years, and is prepared to see him leave again, must call into question his claiming to regard him as equally dear (see 3.4.163–7).

Kent, while more gracious and considerate, or at least understanding, of Edmund's sensitivity than his father appears to be, nonetheless subtly attests his adherence to the 'respectable' view: he does not deny that the begetting of Edmund entailed a "fault." And within his seemingly generous "I must love you, and sue to know you *better*," one may detect a more guarded response. The violent readiness with which later he (in disguise) turns on Edmund, who had commanded him to cease his assault on Oswald ("come, I'll flesh ye; come on, young master" 2.2.43–4), suggests that by then he holds an unfavourable view of Edmund. Perhaps more or less immediately upon arriving at Gloucester's residence, he heard of Edgar's alleged treason and flight, as did Cornwall and Regan (2.1.85–8). But Kent, unlike they, may suspect Edmund's role in the affair for something like the reasons Edmund himself expresses in order that they be discredited (66–76). This need not imply that Kent harbours an irrational prejudice against bastards; he may not believe them to be any more self-centred and calculating than people generally. If some prejudice against them does figure in his evaluation of Edmund, it may be entirely rational, based on extensive and even sympathetic observation of how bastards typically turn out, given how they are typically treated. To say that his prejudice may be justified, however, is not to conclude that the sociopolitical arrangement that 'creates' bastards, in both the legal and behavioural sense, is similarly justified. Why, then, is the 'legitimate–illegitimate' distinction practically as widespread as the more commonly noticed (and analysed) 'incest taboo' (still another "curiosity of nations" not observed by the rest of the animal kingdom)? As Shakespeare has provided no character in the play other than Edmund – the injured party – who addresses this issue, and in particular none who expressly defends the prevalent practice or even just openly endorses its rightness, we are left to reason it out for ourselves as best we can.

It is useful for the sake of comparison to try first to see the reasons for and against primogeniture. Here one might glance occasionally towards Lear and his three daughters for concrete illustrations of both its advantages and its liabilities. As noted before, there seems no reason to believe that the eldest child (or eldest son, or daughter) is usually superior in terms of natural qualities, much less invariably so. While Goneril does have some attributes one might wish for in an heir (ambitious, spirited, erotic), few people, and least of all Lear himself, would argue that of his three daughters, she was the most suitable or deserving.[33] What, then, recommends the practice? Its most obvious consequence is the tendency to keep property and power concentrated in fewer hands. And if a *family* is to grow into prominence and then maintain its position, each generation's gains must not be dispersed – literally 'dissipated' – among several siblings. Keeping the family estate, its power and prestige, intact under the control of a single family head not only facilitates its further growth (for up to a point at least, the more power one already has, the easier it is to create and exploit opportunities for gaining still more),[34] that power can also be used to protect and enhance the interests of all 'connected' individuals with any claim on its favour, thereby furthering their own prospects (through marriage, political or clerical appointment, military promotion, commerce, whatever). This, in turn, strengthens the entire family alliance.[35]

Still, this reasoning alone does not dictate that the single inheritor of the family estate be the first-born. So what additional considerations do? A primary concern of any head of family who is bent on perpetuating its relative position is that there *be* an heir to single out. The first child to be born answers that concern, although given the practicalities of political life, the first *son* answers it much better.[36] With his future status known from the outset, the heir-presumptive can be specially nurtured to meet his future responsibilities. Many first-born children would themselves claim that they had a more arduous upbringing than the siblings who followed, had more expected of them earlier, engaged the parents in most of the struggles that establish that family's pattern of parent–child relationship, and that these experiences have made them fitter. A corollary of this is that the last and youngest child, the 'baby' of the family, is often 'babied' (one would not be surprised were this a factor in Lear's relationship with Cordelia or in her sisters' perception of it). Also, the principle of having the eldest (surviving) son be the heir and future head of the family harmonizes with that of respecting and giving precedence to elders generally. Even though primogeniture is not operative with respect to the kingship of Lear's Britain (lacking a son), the normal order of precedence still affects the proceedings: it seems only natural that the eldest daughter be the first to speak. Moreover, having an established, polity-wide formula that takes inheritance out of parents' hands, as it were, can in some ways promote better relations among the family's various members. With there being a kind of impersonal fatality about it all, with everyone knowing where they stand, and why, there is not so much occasion for resentment of parents, siblings need not compete so strenuously for parental approval (as grossly parodied in Lear's love contest), which may allow fraternal feelings to develop more freely.

Yet, there are some considerations that weigh strongly against primogeniture. First, there is the manifest unfairness of one child getting almost everything and the others getting very little. This violates normal parental feelings; even parents who have favourites among their children may nonetheless love them all, and so prefer a more equitable distribution of their legacy (as Lear appears to). Moreover, the practical effect is to cast the less fortunate siblings into a subordinate, socially inferior position, irrespective of their feelings or abilities.[37] But even if one is a hard-headed political realist who gives priority to the concern of building and maintaining family power, and so acknowledges the necessity of there being a single heir, there remain the obvious liabilities of a strict adherence to the rule that it be the first-born. One would prefer that it be the most competent individual for what is inherently a many-faceted task, and determining where such competence is most apt to lie requires the kind of assessment of people that can be made only in their maturity, when all who might be eligible have had a fair opportunity to develop and display their respective abilities. This argues for there being no a priori rule dictating the succession; that it would be better left to the prudential judgment of the current family head.

With the more evident pros and cons of primogeniture being so nearly balanced, it is not surprising that it is nowhere nearly the universal practice. Thus, the contrast that it offers to the legitimate–illegitimate distinction could hardly be more telling. For in the case of this latter 'custom,' whatever beneficial consequences it has for political life are obscure, whereas several strong objections to it are transparent (of which Shakespeare has ensured we take note). Yet adherence to it is very widespread, practically universal among the same societies wherein primogeniture is not. We should take seriously, then, the questions Edmund would prefer to regard as merely rhetorical: "Why bastard? ... Why brand they us with base?" And if we would have answers, Shakespeare leaves us no choice but to raise and examine the various considerations ourselves, having provided a concrete evidentiary context in which to do so.

By way of beginning to understand its prevalence, one might look first at who benefits from this distinction and the discriminating practices that result. And who is that? All legitimate children, obviously, and at the expense of all illegitimate ones – actual or potential – but especially at the expense of any to whom a given legitimate child may be biologically related (as the cases of Edgar and Edmund illustrate). However, such children are beneficiaries of their status long before they are in any position to urge, much less insist upon, its being recognized – indeed, their being benefited virtually from day one of their existence is a major consequence of such status, hence would seem to be an essential aspect of its purpose. So, who speaks for them before they are able to speak for themselves? Again, the answer seems obvious: their lawfully wedded mothers. One might wish to say their fathers, too, and doubtless this often would be true – but not so solidly, nor for precisely the same reasons. For men are much more likely to be fathers of both kinds of children, legitimate and bastard, and thus tend towards the more 'tolerant' view displayed by Gloucester: he loves *both* of his sons for the simple reason that they are both *his*. Were it wholly up to him, were Edmund not a social embarrassment, he would in all probability prefer to ignore altogether the distinction in the legal status of his sons. Moreover, many other men, including some whose children are all legitimate, would sympathize with him, even if they would not be ready to comply with his preference. One suspects, however, that the respective mothers of the two boys, and Edgar's mother especially, would see things very differently.

To the extent a woman, like any other female creature, puts the welfare of her own offspring ahead of those of another, she favours whatever arrangements give her children a comparative advantage. Perhaps if women were as likely to bear children outside of wedlock as within it – if they could do so, that is, without prejudicing those children's welfare – they too might be less fastidious about, if not simply indifferent to, the legitimate–bastard distinction. But there's the hitch. Needing and wanting the various kinds of support that can come only from the more or less consistent presence of a man heading a stable household, and he for his part preferring if not insisting upon giving that support to only those children he is sure are his, women are effectively obliged to conduct themselves in such a way as will provide their men that very assurance. Thus, the heightened importance attached to chastity in women, not least of all *by* the majority of women themselves. The code of sexual morality they seek to maintain is designed primarily to meet the threat to their domestic security posed by the availability of 'loose women,' professional courtesans, and especially of young, unattached women.[38] Consequently, those "honest madams" of Edmund's sarcasm – lawfully wedded, faithful wives, and all women with any intention of becoming so – have a special interest in preserving the idea of 'legitimacy' as an essential constituent, if not the very essence, of the sacred institution of marriage.

To appreciate the broader significance of this idea, one need only ask what marriage would amount to if the offspring that resulted from within it had no special standing in comparison with any engendered outside of it; and what political life would be like given such a diluted conception of marriage and family. One thereby sees that the general recognition of the distinction between legitimate and bastard protects the welfare of 'honest' women's children, and indirectly the women themselves, by endowing them with favoured status; and this, in turn, helps repress any inclination men might feel to leave lawful wives for child-bearing mistresses, or even to share their estate equally with them.[39] Indeed, one might regard the preservation of this distinction as the quid pro quo for the higher standard of chastity demanded of women, given the practical connections between the consequences of these two norms. However, while women as married mothers would seem to be primary beneficiaries of the distinction, once its social recognition is established, men as fathers (and of daughters especially) would also come to count on it, and thus support it. For example, in arranging political marriages for his daughters, Lear presumes that their children will have clear and unchallenged priority over any bastards their husbands might beget. The resulting set of prejudices do not act with anything close to absolute effectiveness, of course, but to the extent that the stigmas carried by bastards and by women of 'easy virtue' do have political consequences, these tend to support the integrity of stable families.

Bearing such considerations in mind, we can readily see why most people, but especially women, would normally make an effort to keep *secret* any adulterous activity that would compromise their own reputation and threaten the sanctity and security of marriage – thus why we are all especially attuned to the slightest nuances indicating such hidden sexual activity (as one is reminded in the course of studying this play). For Goneril quite likely is an adultress, either with or by means of her steward Oswald, even *before* she is captivated by the manly Edmund ("Oh! the difference of man and man" 4.2.26). The most explicit indication is provided by her sister Regan when this same Oswald comes bearing a letter for Edmund, whom Regan (rightly, as we know) suspects Goneril of having designs upon as an eventual replacement for Albany – whereas Regan wants Edmund for herself, as immediate replacement for the dear departed Cornwall. So Regan attempts to seduce Oswald into letting her examine the letter (employing suitably equivocal language for the effort):

Why should she write to Edmund? Might not you
Transport her purposes by word? Belike,
Some things – I know not what. I'll love thee much,
Let me unseal the letter.
Oswald: Madam, I had rather –
Regan: I *know* your Lady does not love her husband;
I am sure of that: and at her late being here
She gave strange œilliads and most speaking looks
To noble Edmund. I know *you* are of her bosom.
Oswald: I, Madam!
Regan: I speak in understanding; *y'are,* I know't:
(4.5.19–28)

But she is not the only one. Kent suspects it, too, which is why he so especially despises Oswald. Thus, in his diatribe upon meeting Oswald at Gloucester's castle, Kent includes, "one that wouldst be a *bawd* in way of good service," as well as "a knave, beggar, coward, *pandar.*" Then, in response to Cornwall's "Why art thou angry?" (i.e., at Oswald): "Such smiling rogues as these, / Like rats, oft bite the holy cords a-twain / Which are too intrince t'unloose" (2.2.70–2). What holy cords could he mean, if not those of matrimony? Rumour of the steward's special services for Goneril seems to have reached Edgar's ears, also. For upon killing Oswald, he observes, "I know thee well: a serviceable villain; / As duteous to the vices of thy mistress / As badness would desire" (4.6.249–51). And what about Edmund? Regan openly accuses him of having carnal knowledge of Goneril:

Now, sweet Lord,
You know the goodness *I* intend upon you:
Tell me, but truly, but then speak the truth,
Do you not love my sister?
Bast: In honour'd love.
Regan: But have you never found my brother's way
To the forfended place?
Bast: That thought abuses you.
Regan: I am doubtful that you have been conjunct
And bosom'd with her, as far as we call hers.
(5.1.6–13)

Must we not presume that Regan knows her sister's propensities and that *that* is the reason she challenges Edmund thus? Be that as it may, apparently Edmund's natural erotic appeal overrules the conventional baseness of his birth, at least in the eyes of these two high-born ladies, and doubtless Shakespeare intends the various implications of this to register.

Regarding the legitimate–bastard distinction itself, however, the fact remains that its recognition is generally tough on bastards, who are made to suffer for faults not their own. And should they turn out (like Edmund) to be 'real bastards,' one might agree that the blame should not fall solely on them.[40] Still, what can be done about it, since we cannot have it both ways? To fail to make any distinction between legitimate and illegitimate children is to divest marriage, and the idea of family which is its natural complement, of most of its significance. Ultimately, the practical consequences of this would be women having children by a plurality of fathers and men by a plurality of mothers. In such circumstances, the radical difference between men's and women's roles with respect to procreation would make itself felt with devastating effects. For while a woman almost always could still be sure of whether or not a child was hers, a man almost never could be sure. The result would be such a bewildering (and utterly impractical) confusion of relationships, and consequently of responsibilites, that no natural basis would exist upon which to found any kind of stable human group in which men (and what they can contribute) were thoroughly integrated. That is, integrated in the way that apparently only 'love of one's own' can generally accomplish, affording children the personal care and discipline they require to maximize their prospects of turning out well. One would be left with a society composed of truncated families (for the most part consisting of only mothers and such surviving children as they could somehow protect, support, and control) immersed in a more or less free-floating (and probably freebooting) population of adult males.[41] It would take an extraordinarily sanguine view of human nature – not to say, a fairy-tale mentality – to suppose that this would constitute a wholesome environment in which to live.

What, then, can be done? The more the stigmatic distinction between legitimate and bastard is softened (and its prejudicial consequences ameliorated), the more this vital, perhaps essential, societal support for stable, two-parent families is weakened. The stability of these groups is inherently vulnerable in so many ways, given normal human 'biology' (especially that of the male, on whom marital fidelity does not always rest easy – as the philandering Gloucester reminds us – whence comes the need for the distinction). Moreover, the general prejudice against bastards is a principal deterent to men begetting, and women bearing, still more of them. To the extent it is obvious that bastards and those who breed them suffer shame and discrimination, and even opprobrium, the temptation for people to produce children outside of marriage is reduced – especially for women, on whom the greater burden and odium usually falls (not least because often almost no one else can be sure who the father is). Still, there is no escaping the fact that, from the standpoint of individual justice, the entire arrangement is unjust to those who happen to be born bastards.

So Shakespeare hereby brings us face to face with one of the hard truths about political life: it cannot, even in principle, even in 'theory,' in all the purity of rational speech, be made perfectly just. The burden of sustaining political life cannot always be as equitably shared as one might wish, much less allocated strictly in proportion to benefits received. Sometimes the welfare of particular individuals, and even the individuals themselves, must be sacrificed (and that would seem the appropriate word) for the good of the whole. This is not only hard on some people, it is hard for any fair-minded person to accept. Yet accept it one must, not only as the price of putting truth before sentiment (a ruling consideration only for lovers of truth, of course – a breed comparatively rare in the best of times), but also because the practical effects of denying it are much worse. For surely any rational person must prefer that only a few live in conditions such as incline them to think like Edmund, than that the circumstances of virtually everyone lead them to approach political life in a spirit akin to his.

Once one understands how basic, and central, the idea of legitimacy is to the inner rationale of families, and thus to the larger political order of which families truly are the primary *atoms*, one can no longer see 'legitimacy' in the terms that Edmund would prefer, as but one more "plague" of irrational custom followed only out of blind habit, just another "curiosity of nations" that could as easily be otherwise as not. From the mere fact that the specific application of this distinction to a particular time and place is established by positive law and reinforced by an array of manners and mores and habits and prejudices, one is not free to conclude that it has no underlying reality, nor that all such 'conventions' are essentially arbitrary, or no less arbitrary than weights and measures.[42] Having seen this much, one can better appreciate *why* Shakespeare has obliged us to consider it – to *think* about bastardy – in the context of the more obvious constituents of family life that bear upon the tragedy of this royal family: the kinds of love and duty, obedience and respect, gratitude, resentment, and rivalry upon which the story turns.[43] The 'natural' expectations, the prejudices and practices regarding these other matters, seem readily understandable, and for the most part rationally defensible. But dealing with the idea of bastardy, so patently unfair and seemingly so unnecessary (indeed, at first blush the very epitome of irrational custom) is far more challenging; sympathy for the plight and thus the perspective of a bastard is only natural. Once the reasons for this prejudicial status are understood, however, the deeper coherence uniting the two interwoven plots of this play, the primary one focused on the family of Lear and the secondary one on the family of Gloucester, is readily grasped. Shakespeare has carefully chosen this idea – this "fine word, 'legitimate'" (which he uses only eight times in all the works we are sure are his, five of them being here in Edmund's ironic speech) – to illustrate a lesson about social arrangements generally: one must not leap to the conclusion that a certain practice, and especially one that is persistent and widespread, is irrational merely because the reasons for it are not obvious. Often in political life, as in nature, the real causes of things are deeply buried, and can be uncovered only through the efforts of persistent inquiry and patient thinking.

Upon sufficient reflection, then, one begins to suspect that the radical opposition between *physis* and *nomos* implicit in Edmund's "Thou, Nature, art my goddess; to thy law my services are bound ..." – the radical contrast he would draw between the laws of Nature and the laws of men – far from showing profound insight, may actually be rather superficial.[44] It is perhaps revealing that Edmund himself is not consistently true to his professed faith. We are several times provided evidence of his apostasy, beginning with his vowing, "Legitimate Edgar, I must have your land." For Edmund tacitly presumes that if his scheme is successful, his 'right' to the property he thereby legally gains will be respected by others, and protected not only by his own strength, but by that of the sovereign power. And in the final scene of the play, we find him proudly alluding to a "rule of knighthood," even while declining the protection it might offer him (apparently this is the same convention that Goneril calls "th'law of war" 5.3.144, 151). Reflecting on Edmund's selective adherence to the laws of Nature as he conceives Her, and his equally selective disdain of the laws of men, one might well wonder whether *anyone* could truly want to be a more assiduous devotee of this Nature than is Edmund. In any event, if Nature is rationally ordered, if there are reasons *why* everything composing the natural order is *necessarily* the way that it is (which would seem to be the precondition of Nature being intelligible to man, as Edmund presumes it to be), then Nature shares a common ground with 'man-made' arrangements to the extent that they, too, reflect rational necessity – as, for example, the maintaining of stable families rationally necessitates not merely recognition of a distinction between legitimate and bastard, but practical consequences that favour the one at the expense of the other.

Still, there would appear to be a major, not to say enormous, difference between the two realms, the natural and the political. Nature seems to be ordered with the kind of strict necessity characteristic of mathematical physics, such that it could *only* be the way that it in fact is. Whereas, one may not claim more than 'conditional necessity' for even the most rational of political arrangements – something to the effect, '*if* people are to live in the kind of *political* setting that is best for them (with "best" having been more or less substantially specified in relation to an understanding of human nature), *then* it must be arranged in this particular way.' One would not be justified in claiming more, that is, provided (first) there is no strict necessity that human beings as such live in some sort of political society regardless, nor (second) any natural impulse compelling humans to concern themselves with which way of life is best. This, then, would be the fundamental *question:* is man, or is he not, *political by nature?* – meaning, is fully human life only possible within some version of a political environment? Or, is it conceivable that humans could live satisfactorily in some other way? For example, directly in accordance with 'laws' of Nature, perhaps in some 'state of nature' akin to that inhabited by other animals, without the distorting mediation of active human governing and the shared ideas of right and wrong, noble and base, good and bad that the various forms of political life ultimately rest upon.

If the latter is not a practical possibility, the radical difference between the 'natural' life of animals and the 'conventionally ordered' life of humans is somewhat illusory. For the 'strict necessity' governing the rest of animate nature is not really as simple as it first seems. While it may be true that each individual animal is strictly ruled by 'antecedent stimuli' (some external to it, others built in), the particular *form* of which it partakes (its species), in conjunction with its actual environmental circumstances, in effect establish for it criteria of conditional necessity, something to the effect: '*if* an individual of this species is to maximize its prospects of surviving and procreating in this here and now, *then* it is best to be configured thus and so, inclined to behave thus and so, etc. (with the forms of the various species themselves – the 'genotypes' – being, according to modern evolutionary theory, the long-term collective consequences of this conditional necessity determining the 'fittest' individuals). Of course, the individual animal, lacking rational awareness and self-control, cannot alter its physique or behaviour accordingly; but this in no way affects the fact that its flourishing is subject to conditional necessity. Similarly, then, if man is (or has now become) 'by nature' a political animal, such that he cannot live in the way for which he is naturally best suited outside of some kind of political society – nor, consequently, *be* fully the kind of being his own species is (or has evolved to be) – then the necessity at work in the two realms, the human and the bestial, is not as profoundly different as it first strikes us. Rather, it points to what *is* different: man's rational ability to *understand* his nature, and the conditions of its flourishing, and to *choose* from among perceived or imagined political alternatives which way to live.[45]

Presuming this to be the case, that man is by nature a political animal, then one cannot regard the natural and the political as radically different, much less profoundly opposed, realms. And so far as laws and conventions are essential to ordering political life (as they certainly seem to be: one can hardly imagine political life functioning without a vast array of shared rules of all kinds, from the rules governing rule-making to those establishing common weights and measures), then there is an important respect in which these things, too, *are natural.* Likewise, then, it would not be correct to think of *physis* and *nomos* as the radically opposed modes of 'being' they seem at first to be. Thus, what one concludes regarding all these matters will depend on how one answers the fundamental question about human nature: whether it is 'political.' And if so, what more precisely that means and entails. But before that question can be usefully addressed, there is more to be considered.

Families, for example, require the most careful thought, especially as to how the underlying fabric of political society is woven out of the various kinds of relations *among* as well as within them. The play is rich in resources for such thinking, beginning with its first scene, which provides more than its allusion to the most troubling distinction pertinent to families, that between a legitimate son and a bastard. When, for example, Lear addresses, "Our son of Cornwall, and you, our no less loving son of Albany," we are reminded of still a third kind of son: a son-in-law. Lear has only partially given away or lost his daughters 'by nature'; and he has in exchange gained sons 'by law.' Of the three kinds of sons mentioned so far, only this last kind is *chosen*, or at least can be, the prospective father having seen what kind of men they have become and what position they hold. We do not know what alternatives Lear may have considered for either Goneril or Regan, but we are made aware that he has taken his own sweet time in choosing a husband for Cordelia – and third son-in-law for himself (1.1.44–7). Cordelia, for her part, indirectly reminds us of the further consequences of marriage: "Happily, when I shall wed, / That lord whose hand must take my plight shall carry / Half my love with him, half my care and duty" (99–101). Even more "happily," her allegiance would not actually be so much 'divided' as *shared*. Hence, it would function as a bond between her original family and the new one she and her husband will create; and as similar remarks apply to her husband, their marriage would constitute a bridge between their respective families of birth. The relational status established by law between those families is meant to foreshadow the anticipated mingling of their blood by nature. Of course, for that to have its intended *political* consequence, the children born within the marriage must be the only ones accorded legitimacy. It is from the interlacing multiplicity of such relationships among many small groups of biologically related individuals that a larger society is formed whose members share a common subjective identity.

These by no means exhaust the kinds of relational status peoples have found useful to recognize in political life. There is, for example, another type of son by law, namely, one who has been somehow 'officially adopted' – as Cornwall perhaps hints to Edmund upon the latter's betrayal of his natural father: "I will lay trust upon thee; and thou shalt find a dearer father in *my* love" (3.5.23–4). In special circumstances, such as the loss of a legitimate heir, this provision can be used to 'legitimize' bastard offspring.[46] Thus, falsely persuaded of Edgar's plot upon his life, Gloucester implies that he will take such legal steps with respect to Edmund: "and of my land, / Loyal and natural boy, I'll work the means / To make thee capable" (2.1.82–4). Nor is this the end of the kinds of 'sons' (or 'daughters') a person may claim. Regan: "What! did my father's godson seek your life? / He whom my father nam'd, your Edgar?" (90–1). So we are reminded that one may have children, not only by nature or law or (as is normal) by both, but also by the rites of religion. Beyond that, one might speak also of 'a spiritual child,' one who despite being related neither by blood, law, nor sacred ceremony, but simply by a kinship of soul, bears towards his 'parent' the kind of true filial affection supposed to characterize a natural, lawful child (and exemplified in a daughter by Cordelia and in a son by Edgar). Lear has such spiritual children, most notably Kent, who protests, "Royal Lear, / Whom I have ever honour'd as my King, / Lov'd as my father" (1.1.138–40) and the Fool (whom Lear treats more as his child than as his servant; see 3.2.68–73).

Regarding this true filial affection, however, we see that often it does not exist where it should. Moreover, even in cases where it is present, it is often alloyed, not to say adulterated, with less genial feelings. Ironically, it is Edmund, of all people, who in the very act of betraying his father's trust expressly refers to "how manifold and strong a bond / The child was bound to th'father" (2.1.46–7). A *manifold* bond, somewhat as Cordelia recognizes, of obedience, of love, and of honour – that in return for nurture, love, and life itself (1.1.95–7). Except that she leaves out what her father would emphasize above all else: *gratitude* – arguably the most basic manifestation of justice, and the least a person can offer in repayment of his or her debts. One may lack every other means of requital, but means of freely acknowledging and expressing gratitude for benefits received are available to everyone.[47] And while the ingratitude of anybody is likely to provoke anger as well as disappointment, that felt in response to the perceived ingratitude of one's own children may have a special intensity.

> Ingratitude, thou marble-hearted fiend,
> More hideous, when thou show'st thee in a child
> Than the sea-monster.
>
> (1.4.257–9)

After all, most children owe their parents so much, especially good, kind parents, the sort Lear believes himself to have been to all of his daughters ("O Regan, Goneril! / Your old kind father, whose frank heart gave all" 3.4.19–20). Thus, to have "a thankless child," one that turns its parent's "pains and benefits to laughter and contempt," might indeed feel sharper than any serpent's tooth (1.4.284–7).

Were one made to endure an extreme instance of such thanklessness, as does Lear, perhaps it would generate such a "tempest in [one's] mind" as to render a person practically insensitive to "all feeling else save what beats there – filial ingratitude!" (3.4.12–14). More than almost any other experience one can imagine, this could so curdle one's milk of human kindness as to produce a general cynicism about human nature per se – such as infuses Lear when, braving the full force of the storm, he calls down destruction upon the entire human race:

> And thou, all-shaking thunder,
> Strike flat the thick rotundity o'th'world!
> Crack Nature's moulds, all germens spill at once
> That makes ingrateful man!
>
> (3.2.6–9)

One wonders, however, whether the pain a parent feels in the face of filial ingratitude (or, for that matter, any other viciousness one's child displays) is entirely the result of deficiencies attributable to the begotten, and none whatsoever to the begetter. Lear may truly (and rightfully) regard himself "a man more sinn'd against than sinning" (3.2.59–60), but does he – *can* he – divest himself of *all* responsibility for how his two elder daughters have turned out? Confronted with the hard evidence of their inhumanity towards him, does not the lurking suspicion that he himself is somehow partly at fault ("a disease ... which I must needs call mine" 2.4.220–1), especially aggravate his torment?

To have a thankless child may feel sharper than a serpent's tooth, but as Lear realizes, one has to be a parent to have any real appreciation of the special anguish it causes. In this instance, as in much else of great importance to human life, there may be no adequate substitute for *felt experience* as a basis for true understanding.[48] Thus, Lear wishes upon Goneril a "child of spleen, that it may live / And be a thwart disnatur'd torment to her!" – a child that will, like so many before it, leave careworn its mother's once youthful face and occasion more tears than joy (1.4.280–3). Of course, children can work these or any other educative effects only so far as a parent truly cares about them. One can easily imagine Goneril, for instance, proving impervious to the normal consequences of maternal experience. The more one loves one's children, however, the more vulnerable one is to being genuinely pained (as well as angered) by their callous disregard. Whereas, the better children are treated, the more readily do a majority of them tend to take such treatment for granted, at least while they themselves remain childless. Comprehending all the practical implications of this natural asymmetry in the parent-child relationship – a manifold asymmetry, typically manifested not only in care and affection, but in honour, power, prudence, dependence, obligation, and almost any other dimension one might name – would seem to be the key to understanding the atomic structure of political life in any given regime.

As the play so effectively reminds us, the feelings, the 'subjectivity' customarily regarded as appropriate to the various biological, social, and legal relationships do not always in fact attend them. Nor are these same feelings exclusive to the objective relationships with which they are normally associated. Sometimes a more distantly related, or even an ostensibly unrelated person proves a better 'child' (or 'parent') than those who are such by both nature and law. Lear's son-in-law Albany shows infinitely more true filial regard for him than does the King's natural-born and -bred daughter whom Albany wived, and whom he berates for just this: her despicable treatment of her father[49] (4.2.31–45, 94–6; see also 5.3.236, 295–9). So does Lear's godson, Edgar (cf. 3.6.59–60). As for Kent, his loyal devotion to Lear matches that of the most dutiful son one can imagine (see 5.3.218–20). But the very intelligibility of this way of speaking presupposes the constellation of feelings and attitudes normally expected to obtain between parent and child – an expectation doubtless somewhat idealized in exhortations and encomiums meant to encourage their realization, but which could not be sustained in the absence of a substantial degree of actual observance.

Still, the basic asymmetry in the parent–child relationship, and especially in their respective *understandings* of that relationship, is a perennial source of tensions and dissatisfactions. All parents have been children, and thus have experienced both sides of the relationship; whereas their children, for so long as they remain childless themselves, have not. As already noted, it can be easy to take benefits for granted. Machiavelli's warning – that most people are far more apt to remember their grievances than the benefactions done them[50] – may apply with special force to children's perception of their standing towards their parents. Moreover, because (as Hobbes teaches[51]) most people find unpleasant the feeling of being indebted (implying as it does an inferiority of status, which offends their pride), they are predisposed to depreciate the motivations of their benefactors. They would prefer to presume that all generosity, all altruism, is somehow self-serving, hence self-rewarding. Edmund's 'naturalism' serves him nicely in this respect. In dramatic contrast to the traditional, decent view of a child's natural regard for his parent (that Edmund publicly expresses, and pretends to act upon; 2.1.43–115), we learn that privately he takes his guidance as to what is natural from the behaviour of animals:

> This seems a fair deserving, and must draw me
> That which my father loses; no less than all:
> The younger rises when the old doth fall.
>
> (3.3.23–5)

Even though Edmund acknowledges that his father loves him (1.2.17), he in effect treats human parental love as no more meaningful than the brute attachment of a bestial parent for its progeny – who as we know do not reciprocate, but (rather) in their turn behave the same towards their own offspring. In most species, as soon as animal young are independent, they no longer show any partiality towards their parents; indeed, they may become rivals of their parents, may even destroy them, ... or mate with them.

Comparisons of the human with the animal world are very much to the point (or animal worlds, perhaps we should provisionally say, recalling the dozens of distinct species mentioned in the play). Moreover, for the purpose of discerning both what we have in common with the rest of animate creation and what distinguishes us – hence, determining the range of phenomena that must somehow be accommodated within a valid idea of Nature – one could scarcely do better than focus on human *families*. For in doing so, one is focusing on the locus of what seems to be the primary task, the pervasive business, the essential work of *all* natures, the *governing purpose* of Nature itself: *reproduction*. Thus, in cursing Goneril, Lear prays:

> Hear, Nature, hear! dear Goddess, hear!
> Suspend thy purpose, if thou didst intend
> To make this creature fruitful!
> Into her womb convey sterility!
> (1.4.273–6)

'Nature, suspend *thy purpose*!' The *telos* of Nature: its end, purpose, fulfillment, 'final cause,' is simply to *Be*. However, this is accomplished only through the practically countless species of life striving, generation by generation, to reproduce themselves. Thus, each of these specific forms of being endures, and thereby 'does its part' to sustain the diversity of nature, including the *ordering* of parts that makes of nature a unified whole. By focusing on how the human form of being perpetuates itself – always within some variation of a family, none of which is structured and led solely by animal impulses – we can begin to appreciate how very distinct we are, how very peculiar is human nature (so much so that we are justified in speaking collectively of all other animal natures in contradistinction to it).

In attempting to understand *why* human families have the specific character they do, we are compelled to acknowledge the large, and apparently irreducible, role of *nomoi* in human life: that various kinds of rules are essential constituents of all the human lives we can actually observe. To speak only of those that bear most directly on families, no other creature distinguishes between bastard and legitimate offspring, or prohibits incest, or insists on chastity, is capable of adultery, has rules of inheritance, sanctifies births and deaths and marriages, may 'arrange' those marriages (and thus matings) with regard to ulterior considerations, expects an offspring to show lifelong respect for its progenitors, acknowledges the relatedness of family members (and not only contemporaries, but ones long since dead or still to be born, such that an awareness of 'lineage' can be an important factor in human life), and so on – all phenomena which both presuppose and are presupposed by 'political' life of some sort. No other creature channels and structures its biophysical impulses, repressing some while amplifying others by means of a self-imposed constellation of obligations, prohibitions, rights, and privileges. Why, then, do humans? And insofar as there is a significant *variety* of ways in which they may do so – again, in contrast to the rest of the animal world, in which a given species' way of life is everywhere and always pretty much the same – are there any criteria whereby the various ways (such as governing inheritance by the principle of primogeniture) can be judged better or worse, right or wrong? Obviously one cannot look to the animal world for such criteria (nor thus to a Nature that is simply identified with the animal world, as in the mind of Edmund), since the need for evaluative criteria is one all-important respect in which the human world differs.

To raise a question about the availability of such criteria, however, is to take an important step along the path that leads ultimately to philosophy, or more precisely, to *political* philosophy. For it implies two quite significant developments in a person's outlook. First, an awareness of the possibility that the established ways of one's own society, the ways in which one was raised, are not the only ways, and consequently may not be simply right, or simply best.[52] Second, to ask whether there exist criteria whereby one may judge alternative ways of arranging political life tacitly presumes that an adequate response to the question (be it yea or nay) is one that is *rationally justified.* Thus, the very raising of the question tacitly grants a certain priority to *reason*. For it is only in light of one's own reasoning that anyone can in seriousness pose the question – see any point in posing such a question. Similarly, it will be in light of one's own reason that one will assess any proferred answer to it. For even if an affirmative answer points ultimately to divine authority, obedience to the will of God certainly would seem rationally defensible, if anything is. Presuming divine will can be clearly determined, that is – which, of course, is where additional problems arise for whoever takes it upon himself to judge these matters by his own reason, by the natural powers of his own soul.

The presumption of judging such questions by one's own natural reason, however, tends to direct one towards the church of St Edmund: "Thou, Nature, art my goddess." But this 'faith' has its own set of problems, for it presumes what is, or should be, at issue: a valid idea of Nature, in light of which one may gain a clear understanding of both human and animal life, including the relationship between them. And to repeat, there are good grounds for suspecting Edmund's idea is *not* valid, despite its commonsense appeal. The search for an altogether adequate idea of Nature is practically identical with philosophy, an insight which the troubled career of King Lear serves to convey. As the disastrous consequences of his political actions drive *him* to reconsider the transpolitical, cosmological context of political life, so too are we led quite naturally from the narrower political issues of human families to the broader philosophical issues of which they partake. What becomes clear upon further reflection is that the political story about families is but an especially interesting and important part of the philosophical story about Nature. Thus, bound up with this treatment of familial relations and the feelings that normally attend them are two other matters whose importance is by no means confined to families, but nonetheless have a special pertinence to them. Both involve manifestations of that most basic and pervasive of philosophical difficulties: distinguishing (mere) Appearance from (true) Reality.

The first of these matters needs no special emphasis or extensive illustration, being sufficiently familiar from everyday life. It concerns the uncertain relationship between people's speeches – their claimed opinions and feelings and intentions – and their thoughts. The frequent discrepancy we observe between a person's words and his actions (which, as we are fond of saying, speak louder than words) requires explanation, and one ready possibility is that it is a consequence of a discrepancy which we can*not* observe, namely, between what that person says and what he really thinks. Hence, the value placed on *honesty*. Lacking any means of directly observing the inner reality of another person's soul, honesty is the quality – or virtue, as it is commonly regarded – that we rely upon to ensure an accurate correspondence between inner being and outer seeming. The difficulty, of course, comes in judging honesty itself. In our assessing of it, we necessarily fall back on the observed correspondence between speech and deed. Moreover, it is normally within the family (where the degree of such correspondence is most readily and regularly observable) that we, as children, first acquire both our practical understanding and our valuation of honesty.

Not that honesty is always in reality as appreciated as a child might suppose from having heard so many people's professed admiration of it. By the time we reach adulthood, we all know from experience that often people would in fact prefer a flattering embellishment of the truth about themselves, or even an outright falsehood, to hearing the plain truth. Thus, many observers of the opening scene, both within the play and without, presume – wrongly, I have argued – that such is the case with Lear. But whatever was then his preference, his hard education at the hands of nature leads him to the bitter reappraisal (noted earlier) of how he was actually treated while still the pre-eminent political power:

> They flattered me like a dog, and told me I had the white hairs in my beard ere the black ones were there. To say 'ay' and 'no' to every thing I said! 'Ay' and 'no' too was no good divinity. When the rain came to wet me once and the wind to make me chatter, when the thunder would not peace at my bidding, there I found 'em, there I smelt 'em out. Go to, they are not men o'their words: they told me I was every thing; 'tis a lie, I am not ague-proof. (4.6.96–105)

Nor in practice is what we *mean* by 'honesty' identical with the simple notions of openness and truth-telling one endeavors to teach children. When in reply to Lear's "What art thou?" Kent claims to be "A very honest-hearted fellow," no one is apt to regard the claim as plainly falsified by his then being disguised in both voice and looks so that he may continue serving the King who banished him, and who he now denies knowing (1.4.1–5, 19–27). Neither is his probity seriously compromised by what seems the one clear exception to the seven things he 'professes,' namely, to fight only when he cannot choose otherwise. Kent's behaviour towards Oswald upon their meeting at Gloucester's castle, and even more his justification for it (being angry "that such a slave as this should wear a sword, who wears no honesty"), surely must raise some question about that profession (2.2.1–44, 67–70). With respect to the others, however, (for example, "to serve him truly that will put me in trust; to love him that is honest" 1.4.13–17), and similarly of the services he claims to be capable of ("keep honest counsel, ... and deliver a plain message bluntly" 31–5), it can fairly be said that Kent's deeds square with his speeches, and thus attest to his having an honest heart.

Similarly, young Cordelia in the end proves herself both tender and true to her aged father (cf. 1.1.105–6). In fact, what she espouses might be regarded as transcending 'mere honesty.' For not only does she deny all facility in "that glib and oily art to speak and purpose not," she goes so far as to claim to reverse the usual order of speech and deed: "since what I well intend, I'll do't before I speak" (223–5). Because she regards her sisters as diametrically her opposites in these respects, it is with scarcely veiled anxiety that she commits the welfare of her beloved father to their "professed bosoms" (267–74). Of course, subsequent events surpass her worst fears: the discrepancy between these elder daughters' public professions of love for Lear and their later treatment of him could hardly be greater, or so one would suppose. But in that, the bastard Edmund eclipses even them. He actively stage-manages deceit in pursuit of his ends, exploiting "A credulous father, and a brother noble, / Whose nature is so far from doing harms / That he suspects none; on whose foolish honesty / My practices ride easy!" (1.2.176–9).

Lear himself, of course, represents a very special case with respect to the relation between speech and deed – or at least he does while still invested with all the powers and responsibilities of kingship. For much more is at stake than simply his own reputation for honesty and the kind of example he thereby sets. As noted earlier, in his capacity as sovereign, his word is law – a fact of which Lear himself is keenly aware. Constrained to appear pre-eminent in both knowledge and resolve by virtue of the "potency" he exercises, and by the necessity that he inspire a sense of almost godlike majesty in his subjects, for him 'to say' is to be committed 'to do' (even when it might otherwise be better to unsay). Because people know from their own experience that ordinarily the connection between speech and deed is so unreliable, cases in which this is never so especially impress them. Thus, Lear can allow nothing "to come between [his] sentence and [his] power," lest the reality of his all-too-human fallibility and vulnerability show through the carefully cultivated appearance of superhumanity (1.1.167–71).

The second matter is closely interwoven with the first, but with other themes as well. It is the special prominence given in the play to two organs that humans naturally invest with great psychic and thus symbolic significance, doubtless derived from but far transcending their more obvious utilitarian importance. These organs are the eye and the heart. There are over fifty references to each in *King Lear.* The one, itself visible, can readily stand for all that is perceptible, not least of all about ourselves. The other, itself concealed but not thereby altogether imperceptible – its palpitations sometimes being tangible and even audible (most noticeably when we are physically or emotionally stressed) – is commonly identified with our real feelings, and with our inner realities generally, as attested by much everyday speech. Shakespeare does employ them here in these familiar metaphorical capacities. He makes them do much more work than that, however, especially the eyes.

Consider first the heart. That it should be Regan who initially mentions it is darkly ironic. Goneril having just finished her profession of love to Lear, Regan begins by declaring – truthfully, as it turns out – "I am made of that self metal as my sister, / And prize me at her worth." Truth ends there, however. What follows, subtly exploiting the priority normally accorded deed over speech, is doubly false: "In my true heart, / I find she *names* my very *deed* of love" (1.1.67–70). The terms of her lie, however, remind us that the heart itself, hidden from view, is the subject of false claims precisely because we regard it as the symbol (if not the actual source) of all loyalty, probity, honesty, and fidelity, the seat of the soul's real posture, of its true disposition towards this world and the things in it – indeed, as the foundation of a person's individual nature. Thus, reference is made to the heart more often in *King Lear* than in any other of Shakespeare's plays. Gloucester refers to Lear simply as "poor old heart" (3.7.60). Urged by her father to "speak again" in profession of love to him, Cordelia responds, "Unhappy that I am, I cannot heave / My heart into my mouth" (90–1).[53] What does then issue from her mouth causes Lear to ask in pained surprise, "But goes thy heart with this?" Confirmed that it does, he declares her "a stranger to [his] heart" (104, 114). Despite Lear's angrily warning him off, Kent protests on Cordelia's behalf: "Thy youngest daughter does not love thee least; / Nor are those empty-hearted whose low sounds / Reverb no hollowness" (151–3). And as the bosom houses the heart, we understand the anxiety Cordelia expresses in committing Lear's welfare to her sisters' "professed bosoms" (271).

This cardiological emphasis established in the first scene continues in the second. Confronted with the forged letter his bastard son has attributed to the legitimate one, Gloucester voices his distress, unaware of how much more pertinent are his words to the son he is addressing: "Had he a hand to write this? a heart and brain to breed it in?" (53–5). Breathing a wonderful mixture of pretences, Edmund assures his father, "It is his hand, my Lord; but I hope his heart is not in the contents" (65–6). This attention to the human heart recurs throughout the play; its concluding scene has no less than ten explicit mentions of the heart. As we traverse the text, we are provided a survey of the manifold significance we customarily attribute to the heart. Truly to know someone is to know his or her heart, as Goneril assures a dubious Albany that she knows Lear's (1.4.329). At various times the heart is treated as the site of both love (267) and lust (3.4.85, 110), of courage (5.3.132), of pride (3.4.80, 83), of anger (128), of one's sense of honour and nobility (5.3.94, 126), and of partisanship (3.7.48). With the heart being identified with the passionate basis of the soul, arguably the very core of one's being, so dire affliction of the soul is expressed in terms of damage, disease, and pain of the heart. Gloucester, describing for Regan the effect on him of Edgar's alleged plot, laments, "O! Madam, my old heart is crack'd, it's crack'd" (2.1.89). Similarly, Edgar finds heart-breaking the sight of mad Lear conversing with blind Gloucester (4.6.140; see also 2.4.283–4; 3.4.4; 5.3.176, 181, 195, 311). Lear associates the onset of his madness with a swelling in or beneath the heart ("O me! my heart, my rising heart! but down!" 2.4.118; cf. 54–6). In the strange lucidity of this madness, Lear asks the most pertinent question of all: "Then let them anatomize Regan, see what breeds about her heart. Is there any cause in nature that makes these hard hearts?" (3.6.74–6). Perhaps that depends upon how one conceives Nature.

Turn now to the eyes.[54] The play reminds us, first, of the great – nay, incomparable – importance we attach to sight, and thus to these most mysterious organs whereby we see, look, behold, descry, observe, discern, view, spy, stare, squint, and so on.[55] For sight is the synoptic sense, showing (visible) things at once in their particularity and in their immediate spatial relations.[56] The potential richness of visual experience is so obvious that we readily approve the notion that a picture can convey more information than could a thousand words. And despite knowing better, time and again we validate the old maxim that 'seeing is believing' – as if seeing for oneself ought to provide a kind of 'proof positive.' Thus, Goneril urges her view of Lear upon Regan: "You *see* how full of changes his age is; the observation we have made of it hath not been little ..." (1.1.287–8). However, it is not only the utility of sight that accounts for the value we place upon it. Sight is also a source of various kinds of pleasure. There is that which comes from visual beauty, such as Nature has endowed Lear's daughters with (artificially enhanced by what they "gorgeous wear'st" 2.4.265–8). And there is the pleasure derived from the mere sight of those we like and love, our dear friends and beloved family members. Indeed, this feature of human life is supposedly so prevalent that it figures in various formulae of politeness, such as that which Lear calls to our attention in taking literally Regan's insincere greeting to him ("I am glad to see your Highness," she says, despite having done everything she could to avoid him; 125). Then there is the pleasure of humorous sights, such as that of Kent in the stocks – or at least Lear's Fool finds it so (the King is not amused; 7–12). Other sights call forth other responses equally unique to humans, most notably *pity* – such as is inspired in Edgar by the attire and behaviour of the deranged Lear ("O thou side-piercing sight!" 4.6.85), as also in Cordelia's gentleman attendant ("A sight most pitiful in the meanest wretch, / Past speaking of in a King!" 201–2; see also 4.7.53–4).

With no more than this in mind, we can readily understand why sight might immediately suggest itself to someone needing a powerful rhetorical comparison, as does Goneril, obliged to persuade Lear of her devotion to him: "Sir, I love you more than word can wield the matter; / Dearer than eyesight" (1.1.54–5; hers is the first mention of either eyes or sight). It is not despite, but because of Goneril's being more conscious than most of the value of sight that she proposes as punishment for Gloucester's alleged treason: "Pluck out his eyes" (whereas Regan had urged, "Hang him instantly" 3.7.4–5). From the perspective of someone bent on doing him the worst, Goneril is 'right': the horror we experience in witnessing the brutal blinding of Gloucester is more terrifying than murdering him could possibly be. Albany's shock upon hearing of it speaks for all decent feeling; and that it brought instant death upon its perpetrator seems to him no less than divine justice (4.2.70–81). His further learning that it was Gloucester's bastard son who brought this outrage upon his father at once fixes Albany's loathing for this "half-blooded fellow" (cf. 5.3.81, 155). And his pledging, "Gloucester, I live / To thank thee for the love thou show'dst the king, / And to revenge thine eyes." (4.2.94–7) effaces the doubt we may have acquired about gentle Albany's character. In her belated recognition that expelling the blinded Earl was a serious mistake, Regan attests to both the value humans place on sight and the power of humane sympathy for pitiful sights: "It was great ignorance, Gloucester's eyes being out, / To let him live; where he arrives he moves / All hearts against us" (4.5.9–11).

However, it is not only what eyes do that makes them so important to us, but also what they *show*. Somehow the eyes have a special power of expression, and ofttimes of attraction or repulsion. Not for nothing have they from Antiquity been called 'windows of the soul' – meaning not merely the portals of the body whereby the soul looks out on the world, but also whereby the world looks in on it. Cordelia speaks contemptuously of those who display "a still-soliciting eye" (1.1.230). Goneril orders her servants to show "colder looks" to Lear's entourage (1.3.23). Kent's "heavy eyes" bespeak his weariness (2.2.166–7). The doctor sees anguish in Lear's eyes (4.4.15). Having divested himself of his political power, Lear finds that Goneril's eyes are "scornful" (2.4.163), and mistakenly believes that they reveal a profound difference between her and Regan: "Thy tender-hefted nature shall not give / Thee o'er to harshness: her eyes are fierce, but thine / Do comfort and not burn" (169–71). The fierceness Lear associates with Goneril's eyes would seem to be why in his madness he greets Gloucester, who has but bloody wounds for eyes, with "Ha! Goneril with a white beard!" (although a moment later, he makes a quite different identification: "I remember thine eyes well enough. Dost thou squinny at me? / No, do thy worst, blind Cupid; I'll not love" 4.6.96, 134–6).[57] Apparently, then, bold Goneril's eyes are more 'honest,' Regan's more beguiling, and one suspects she is using them to seduce Oswald even as she accuses Goneril of enticing Edmund likewise ("at her late being here she gave strange œilliads and most speaking looks to noble Edmund" 4.5.25–6). Reflection on these *erotic* uses of the eyes – announcing sexual interest, sending sexual invitations ('making eyes') – suffices to establish their importance as a means of expression and communication.[58] And is it not remarkable how accurately, and from what a distance, we can judge at what or whom another person is looking?

But there is still a third respect in which the eyes have a special importance for human beings: they are the organs whereby we, and of all creatures only we, *weep*. This unique human capacity to shed tears receives a peculiar emphasis in

King Lear – surely the most heart-rending of Shakespeare's great tragedies (as *Macbeth* is the most reassuring) – and this emphasis is articulated mainly by the play's eponym. Cordelia is the first to speak of weeping, doing so as she bids farewell to her sisters, "with wash'd eyes" (1.1.267). It is not uncommon for family members to cry upon parting, of course, though one doubts that such is the reason in this instance. In any event, sorrow is only one of the states that evokes tears. Pity is another, as moves the disguised Edgar at the sight of Lear's progressing madness: "My tears begin to take his part so much, they mar my counterfeiting" (3.6.59–60). Of course, tears are the normal and thus expected sign of grief (cf. 5.3.256–8). Yet, as the Fool's song reminds us, some people cry when happy, or when relieved of stress: "Then they for sudden joy did weep, / And I for sorrow sung" (1.4.171–2). Others may cry in anger and frustration, such as overcomes Lear in his confrontation with Goneril:

> Life and death! I am asham'd
> That thou hast power to shake my manhood thus,
> That these hot tears, that break from me perforce,
> Should make thee worth them. Blasts and fogs upon thee!
> Th'untented woundings of a father's curse
> Pierce every sense about thee! Old fond eyes,
> Beweep this cause again, I'll pluck ye out,
> And cast you, with the waters that you loose,
> To temper clay.
>
> (1.4.294–302)

In this spirit he had wished daughter Goneril might herself experience the kind of child that would "with cadent tears fret channels in her cheeks." The embarrassment Lear admits to reminds us that, as a rule, only men feel shame at crying, regarding it as a sign of weakness. How keen, then, must be this feeling for one who has always been looked upon (not least by himself) as a mighty king! It is a subject to which he recurs when his daughters make clear their intention to reduce his status to that of an abject dependant. Lear addresses the Gods:

> If it be you that stirs these daughters' hearts
> Against their father, fool me not so much
> To bear it tamely; touch me with noble anger,
> And let not women's weapons, water-drops,
> Stain my man's cheeks! No, you unnatural hags,
> I will have such revenges on you both
> That all the world shall – I will do such things,

What they are, yet I know not, but they shall be
The terrors of the earth. You think I'll weep;
No, I'll not weep:
I have full cause of weeping, but this heart
Shall break into a hundred thousand flaws
Or ere I'll weep.
(2.4.272–84; cf. 3.4.16–17)

Rage on though he might, Lear strikes no fear in these "marble-hearted" daughters. The impotence implicit in grandiose threats he cannot credibly specify only deepens his enemies' contempt for him, while evoking pity in us.

Thus, we are reminded that humans express quite various states of soul by weeping, from grief to joy, from pity to angry frustration. Nevertheless, tears are predominately associated with sadness and sorrow. This is affirmed by the most eloquent description of anyone's weeping, that of Cordelia's, as provided by the unnamed Gentleman who had borne her a message from Kent (cf. 3.1.19–48). Meeting again later, Kent, for reasons not immediately clear, quizzes the Gentleman as to whether his message occasioned in her "any demonstration of grief." Does his curiosity imply that not even he, as a man experienced in the ways of the world, is totally confident of her character? The Gentleman confirms that "now and then an ample tear trill'd down her delicate cheek," but that she struggled most royally to remain "a queen over her passion." Upon Kent's observing, "O! then it mov'd her," the Gentleman replies:

Not to a rage; patience and sorrow strove
Who should express her goodliest. You have seen
Sunshine and rain at once; her smiles and tears
Were like, a better way; those happy smilets
That play'd on her ripe lip seem'd not to know
What guests were in her eyes; which parted thence,
As pearls from diamonds dropp'd. In brief,
Sorrow would be a rarity most belov'd,
If all could so become it.
(4.3.16–24)[59]

Presuming, then, that tears are primarily signs of distress, we still might wonder why humans (uniquely) are moved to shed them. Of all those in the play, only the deranged King – whose strange speeches, as Edgar realizes, consist of "matter and impertinency mix'd; / Reason in madness" (4.6.172.3) – presumes to offer any insight on this question. Having chosen to 'mistake' blind Gloucester, first for Goneril, then for Cupid, Lear eventually addresses his loyal subject thus:

> If thou wilt weep my fortunes, take my eyes;
> I know thee well enough; thy name is Gloucester;
> Thou must be patient; we came crying hither:
> Thou know'st the first time that we smell the air
> We wawl and cry. I will preach to thee: mark.
> *Glouc:* Alack, alack the day!
> *Lear:* When we are born, we cry that we are come
> To this great stage of fools.
>
> (4.6.174–81)

However, even granting this appraisal of man's fate to be sound, it begs the more basic question of why our sorrow, regret, disappointment, or frustration should be made visibly manifest by tears, and for the most part involuntarily. Insofar as these feelings are a consequence of loss or failure or defeat – or to speak more generally, of weakness relative to the challenges one confronts, including that of self-mastery – we can understand why *men*, supposedly the stronger sex, are loath to be seen crying.

But what purpose does crying serve anyone? That a person would welcome the relief provided by discharging uncomfortable passions is easily appreciated. Still, we must wonder why that emotional discharge should be in the form of flowing drops of water from the eyes. Lear's referring to tears as 'women's weapons' may provide one essential clue: the sight of weeping has an effect on other people. Tears evoke pity, draw forth mercy, solicit assistance, and attest to the sincerity of the weeper's misery. And sometimes mere expressions of sympathy from one's fellows are enough to ease the burden of suffering (here it is worth recalling that weeping can itself be an effective form of sympathizing, especially by women). As Lear shows, however, there are situations where one is unwilling to reveal either one's distress or one's lack of sufficient strength to conceal it – especially to those who might relish or contemn it – and so one struggles *not* to weep. Indeed, we feel most at liberty to solicit sympathy when among those we believe care for our well-being; normally this would mean, first and foremost, members of one's own family.

As to why we are moved by crying, why it should be *tears* that work these effects, this may remain a mystery; and perhaps it is a question of no great importance here. Rather, what *is* important is that there be *some* visible sign of a person's inner distress, some trustworthy signal to which others can respond, and tears suffice for this purpose.[60] But to serve this purpose, it is also important that crying normally be regarded as involuntary, thus as a sincere, 'honest' expression of anguish, and not as a manipulable means of exploiting other people's goodwill[61] – though, as Lear's expression 'women's *weapons*' reminds us, the fact remains that tears are sometimes open to the latter interpretation, and with good reason.[62] Generally, however, the fact that human beings (especially women and children) are by nature provided with this ready means of soliciting their fellows' compassion (and especially that of men) would seem to carry certain implications as to how humans are 'by nature' intended to live, namely, in the kind of social setting where such causes and effects can come into play.[63] Moreover, insofar as our range of responses to weeping is graduated, our sympathy typically being intensified where there exist relationships of care and affection, more is implied than mere human gregariousness, to wit, articulated groupings far more complex than those of any herd or flock.

A fourth aspect of the special importance of eyes derives from *seeing* being a natural – arguably, the most natural – metaphor for *understanding*: seeing with the eye of the soul.[64] This extended meaning of 'seeing' first surfaces in the confrontation between Lear and Kent. The King having ordered Kent, "Out of my sight!" Kent replies, "See better, Lear; and let me still remain the true blank of thine eye." (1.1.156–8). Thereafter, variations on such usage are fairly common, much as they are in ordinary discourse (e.g., 1.2.179–80; 1.4.69, 344–5). There are two speeches, however, that most effectively intermingle the two kinds of seeing, that of the body with that of the mind. One is blind Gloucester's reply to the faithful old tenant who has guided him onto the heath, but who is loath to comply with Gloucester's wish that he be left there ("You cannot see your way"):

> I have no way, and therefore want no eyes;
> I stumbled when I saw. Full oft 'tis seen,
> Our means secure us, and our mere defects
> Prove our commodities. Oh! dear son Edgar,
> The food of thy abused father's wrath;
> Might I but live to see thee in my touch,
> I'd say I had eyes again.
>
> (4.1.18–24)

The other comes in the conversation between this same blind Gloucester and the sanely mad Lear, who orders him, "Read thou this challenge; mark but the penning of it."

> *Glouc:* Were all thy letters suns, I could not see.
> *Edgar:* [Aside] I would not take this from report; it is,

And my heart breaks at it.
Lear: Read.
Glouc: What! with the case of eyes?
Lear: O, ho! are you there with me? No eyes in your head,
nor no money in your purse? Your eyes are in a
heavy case, your purse in a light: yet you see how
this world goes.
Glouc: I see it feelingly.
Lear: What! art mad? A man may see how this world goes
with no eyes. Look with thine ears ...
(4.6.137–49)

Read – something else, not that our eyes do, but that we ourselves do by means of the eyes. Restoring Gloucester's sight would allow him to see the letters; but that alone would not enable him to read lest he already knew how. Attempting to account for the difference between merely seeing the letters – as could Gloucester's old tenant; or as could a dog, for that matter, a horse, or a rat – and actually reading what those letters 'say,' points one directly towards that which essentially distinguishes human nature, and moreover does so in such a way as to suggest that this 'essence' is *not* something that is necessarily fully actualized in all cases, nor comes into being automatically (as does, say, sexual maturity). Presumably this is why there is such a plenitude of letters in *King Lear*, figuring so prominently in its plot. Over a dozen letters pass among the various characters, and serve, like invisible threads, to tie together the often widely separated events of the play, events that these same letters sometimes so fatefully affect.

It may be noteworthy that the first letter to figure is a forgery: that which Edmund concocts in Edgar's name and hand, and conspicuously attempts to conceal in order to stimulate his father's curiosity.[65] Next is the letter Goneril writes to Regan, or has her steward Oswald write (but probably just copy) and then deliver, perhaps advising Regan to behave towards Lear as Goneril herself intends to, and informing Regan that she plans to visit her soon (1.3.26–7; 1.4.333–8; cf. 2.4.181–2). Lear also writes to Regan, via the disguised Kent, presumably of his displeasure with Goneril and consequent intention to move in with her and Cornwall immediately (1.5.1–5). The Cornwalls, however, prefer to be 'not at home' to the King and so decamp immediately for an impromptu visit to Gloucester's residence, even "threading dark-ey'd night" to do so. The result of the near simultaneous arrival of the two messengers, Oswald and Kent, is what later precipitates the one-sided brawl that results in Kent being impounded. While Kent sits in the stocks, he reads by moonlight a letter from Cordelia, "who hath most fortunately been inform'd of [his] obscured course" (2.2.161–4). We are told almost nothing of the letter's contents, but it could account for his awareness of French agents and intentions (3.1.22–34). Apparently someone, then, and most likely Kent himself, had previously written to Cordelia, eliciting this letter in reply. Kent sends Cordelia letters about Lear's desperate straits by means of the King's Gentleman whom he had met in the storm (3.1.19–49; 4.3.10 ff).[66] There is the letter that someone has secretly sent to Gloucester bearing on a "worse matter" than the growing division between Albany and Cornwall (almost surely it concerns the landing of Cordelia and her French army at Dover; see 3.7.42). Gloucester's confiding but this much to his bastard son – "I have receiv'd a letter this night; 'tis dangerous to be spoken; I have lock'd the letter in my closet" (3.3.9–11) – seals his fate. Edmund immediately uses it to betray him to Cornwall: "This is the letter he spoke of, which approves him an intelligent party to the advantages of France" (3.5.9–10). Cornwall sends a letter to Albany (it may be, or include, the one he confiscated from Gloucester) apparently for the purpose of urging mobilization against the French invaders (3.7.1–3). And he speaks of several letters to follow: "Our posts shall be swift and intelligent betwixt us" (11–12). Regan sends Goneril a letter by the same messenger who informs Albany of Cornwall's death and Gloucester's blinding (and perhaps of other things as well, for Albany exits with him, saying, "Come hither, friend: tell me what more thou know'st"). As for Regan's letter, all we are told is that it "craves a speedy answer," which Goneril implies she will give, but so far as we know does not (4.2.82ff). She does, however, send a letter to Edmund *via* her loyal if cowardly Oswald, and Regan is decidedly curious about it: "What might import my sister's letter to him?" – "Why should she *write* to Edmund? Might not you transport her purposes by word?" (4.5.6, 19–20). When Regan fails to seduce Oswald into letting her "unseal the letter," she has him convey a letter of her own to Edmund (29). These are the letters, then, that the dying Oswald begs his slayer (the disguised Edgar) give to Edmund (4.6.245–6). But instead Edgar himself reads Goneril's letter, wherein she urges Edmund to kill Albany and wive her, and immediately resolves to show it to the intended victim (257–75). This he does (5.1.40–50), with mortal consequences for both Edmund and Goneril (5.3.153–9). Finally, there is the note that Edmund has the captain carry to the castle where Lear and Cordelia are imprisoned, ordering their death (with the proviso that Cordelia's be made to appear a suicide; 27–38, 244–54).

What is the deeper significance of all this writing and reading? We can easily see what uses are, or can be, made of these various letters – including uses their authors did not intend. But must we not suspect that Shakespeare, by his promiscuous employment of written speeech in this particular play – whose primary, and only persistent, mode of existence (as with all his others) is as *written* speech –

intends to call our attention to something of special importance for what the play as a whole has to teach? As for what that is, perhaps the education of Lear himself provides the clue.

A KING BECOMES PHILOSOPHICAL

A reader suitably acquainted with ancient writings may recognize in *King Lear* a portrayal of the birth of philosophy, inasmuch as philosophy, 'love of wisdom,' practically originates with the search for an adequate understanding of Nature.[67] Beyond that, the play provides an image of the birth of *political* philosophy, incarnate in a king who becomes philosophical – or, rather, an ousted King who is fairly driven to become so. This 'tragical' origin of a *philosophical* consciousness arising out of unhappy political experience[68] is a sobering complement to the 'comical' treatment of a philosopher's rude *political* awakening in Aristophanes' *Nephelai* ('Clouds'). For in that ancient comedy, we are shown how an 'inhumanly' detached, hence, ridiculously imprudent Sokrates brings disaster upon himself and his equally impolitic associates, and so is made to feel the consequences of his contemptuous disregard for the basic nature of the polity upon which he remains dependent.[69] Each of these works, then, may be seen to have an oblique bearing on the two very different possibilities Plato's Sokrates speaks of in the founding work of political philosophy, the *Republic*: "Unless the philosophers rule as kings in the polities or those now said to be kings and lords genuinely and adequately philosophize, and political power and philosophy coalesce in the same place, while the many natures now pursuing either apart from the other are by necessity excluded, there can be no rest from ills for the polities, nor I believe for the human race" (473c–d).[70] In each of these dramatic portrayals, the 'why' of this marriage between philosophical interest and political concern is implicit in the depiction of the ills, for city and man, of their separation.

Philosophy, so far as we understand its history, effectively begins with the 'discovery' of Nature, meaning the recognition that Nature is something distinct: that not everything is natural, that not everything exists in the same way, has the same mode of being.[71] The *natural*, then, is to be distinguished from whatever is presumably *super*natural (especially the divine, the gods and all that belongs to them), but likewise – and firstly – distinguished from what coexists alongside the natural, namely, the *man-made*. Of things in this mortal realm, the character of whatever has a 'nature' comes into being independently of human invention and is everywhere and always the same, whereas that which is humanly contrived is variable with time and place. What exists solely through human making, however, includes two very different kinds of things. As discussed earlier, there is the *conventional*: rules and standards and criteria based on some people's tacit or explicit acknowledgment and acceptance (however eagerly or grudgingly) as regulatory for them. This latter category includes, at least provisionally, all positive laws, but also customs, taboos, manners and mores, as well as currencies, weights, measures, and suchlike – all that the Greeks included under the rubric *nomos*. Second, there is the *artificial*: whatever is produced through the various arts and crafts, the various *technae* people employ.

Both logically and historically, the first attempts to 'philosophize,' that is, to gain sure knowledge deserving of the title wisdom, necessarily focus on discerning a persistent, consistent reality – an ultimate ground of nature – 'beneath' or 'behind' the often-changing and conflicting, hence, confusing, appearances disclosed by the senses and expressed in opinions. Or, rather, to gain knowledge of as much reality as is accessible and intelligible to unaided human reason. Such philosophizing results in what may be termed 'natural philosophy,' or 'philosophy of nature,' or better still, 'physiology' (inasmuch as the aim is to provide 'rational speech,' a *logos*, about 'nature,' *physis*). It is exemplified by the more famous of the so-called pre-Sokratic philosophers, each distinguished by his particular conception of this natural reality,[72] as well as by Aristophanes' portrayal of Sokrates himself in *Clouds*. By virtue of his ambition, the 'natural philosopher' or 'physiologist' is sceptical about human access to anything divine, if not about the divine itself, and disdainful of what is impermanent, transient, variable – all *ephēmera* (which would seem to include everything of merely human origin). If this philosopher of nature studies the Heavens, for example, it is with an eye towards a rational understanding of the celestial architecture and the eternal motions to be observed there. The coming into being of *political* philosophy, however, requires a radical reassessment of the physiologists' tripartite ontology (i.e., Nature *vs* Convention *vs* Art).

It is this logical-historical trajectory from non-philosopher through natural philosopher to political philosopher that we find illustrated in the several phases of King Lear's intellectual transformation.[73] Part of this story has been anticipated in analysing the role of *nomos* in structuring the environment in which the human form of being accomplishes the ruling task common to all of Nature: *reproduction*. For despite the significant variety human life displays, its regular reproduction is invariably carried out in some version of the human family, whose inner structure and external relations are never reducible to just animal impulses. To be sure, families cannot be understood apart from the constellation of distinctly human feelings they typically involve; as only personal experience can teach, families are as much a matter of the 'heart' as of the 'head.' But these feelings are moulded and directed by, thus interwoven with, a lattice of rules and norms whose compliance presumes at least some tacit understanding of them. The moral education that shapes an individual's view of the world and how best to live in it consists largely of learning the code of conduct regulating the behaviour of the people he or she will be associating with, and it invariably requires cultivating sufficient self-control over one's animal nature to be able to abide by that code. As a rule, this education is initiated, and in the best case largely accomplished, within the family.

It is families, then, not their composing individuals, that are the true 'atoms' of their particular political societies. Thus, an understanding of political life logically begins with an analysis of the natural human family.[74] If we are to employ the atomic analogy, physically discrete individuals must be likened to subatomic particles, being incapable as they are of an independent, self-sufficient existence that is fully human – much less of its perpetual reproduction.[75] In working to disclose the underlying rationality of certain of these family-constituting *nomoi*, enough has already been said by way of casting doubt upon the presumption that nature and convention are fundamentally, 'ontologically,' separate. The distinction remains useful, indeed indispensable, but it is not reflective of such a *radical* difference in things as it first seems to be – if, that is, conventions are necessary for humans living fully human lives, according to *their* nature. Granting this to be the case (as by all the evidence we must), a valid idea of Nature, adequate for encompassing *human* nature, similarly must encompass conventions.[76] Much about the particularities of how these or those people live is due to 'mere convention,' but this human capacity to frame and live in accordance with various conventions is not itself conventional: it is natural.

It remains, however, to consider the distinction between Nature and Art (*technē* in Greek), that other class of things that exist only through the activities of man. What is the relationship between the natural and the artificial? As Shakespeare invites us to examine *nomos* primarily in the context of the Gloucester family saga, so we find it similarly expedient to consider *technē* (including everything from pottery to poetry) in the context of Lear's story: the revolution he experiences as a result of being expelled by his daughters from the comparative comfort of a well-constructed human habitation and made to confront the aroused forces of nature on his own – a painful adventure that turns out to be both brutalizing and humanizing.

Nature, represented first of all by the environing weather, dominates the centre of the play. Some times so benign and placid as to be a positive joy, most times sufficiently regular and restrained to be accommodated without undue effort, occasionally it rears up in truly awesome fury and forcefully reminds us of the natural limits to our control over the circumstances in which we live. In the face of these extraordinary outbursts of natural violence, all man can do is seek shelter, as do "the cub-drawn bear ..., the lion and the belly-pinched wolf" (3.1.12–13). The difference in the kinds of shelter they seek, however, provides a further reminder of the essential difference between man and beast.

As a cacophonous obbligato intensifying the stress and turbulence in Lear's soul – the result of his having to confront the truth about his daughters and his own actions – a storm of unusual ferocity attends the opening of the central act. When in the raging night Kent at last finds the old King (reportedly striving "in his little world of man to out-storm the to-and-fro-conflicting wind and rain"; 3.1.10–11), he eloquently attests to the unprecedented virulence with which this tempest is assaulting both body and soul:

> Alas! Sir, are you here? things that love night
> Love not such nights as these; the wrathful skies
> Gallow the very wanderers of the dark,
> And make them keep their caves. Since I was a man
> Such sheets of fire, such bursts of horrid thunder,
> Such groans of roaring wind and rain, I never
> Remember to have heard; *man's nature* cannot carry
> *Th'affliction* nor the *fear.*
>
> (3.2.41–9)

Lear, however, far from fearing and seeking shelter from the storm, is intentionally exposing himself to its blasts, and urging its fury to even greater heights. He calls down destruction – not simply on those who have betrayed his trust and repaid his generosity with hatred and contempt – but on all humanity and the Earth itself: "Strike flat the thick rotundity o'th'world! / Crack Nature's mould, all germens spill at once / That makes ingrateful man!" (7–9). If before he entertained a better estimate of mankind than it deserves, now he goes too far in the opposite direction, forgetting that there are still some who love him and serve him faithfully.

That the tumult inside Lear's soul is worse than the one assaulting his body is attested by his preference for remaining exposed to the latter as a distraction from the former. Kent, having led him to a hovel that would provide some protection, bids the King, "Good my Lord, enter: / The tyranny of the open night's too rough / For nature to endure." But Lear insists he be let alone:

> Thou think'st 'tis much that this contentious storm
> Invades us to the skin: so 'tis to thee;
> But where the greater malady is fix'd,

> The lesser is scarcely felt ...
> ... When the mind's free
> The body's delicate; this tempest in my mind
> Doth from my senses take all feeling else
> Save what beats there – filial ingratitude!
>
> This tempest will not give me leave to ponder
> On things would hurt me more.
> (3.4.6–14, 24–5)

The extraordinary storm to which Lear has been exposed is both the accompaniment to, and the efficient cause of, what is eventually a revolution in his soul. At almost the exact centre of the play, Lear pronounces what must be his most portentous line: "My wits begin to turn" (3.2.67). By the time this turning is complete, he has a radically different view of nature and political life.[77]

Ostensibly, however, Lear is referring to his consciousness of what, for some reason, is his peculiar fear: madness. Of all the losses and sufferings to which humans are susceptible, *his* foremost worry is the loss of his rational faculties. This may be the single most revealing fact about his particular nature. And insofar as we sympathize with the anxiety it arouses in him, it may be the single most revealing fact about human nature per se. Lear first voices this fear to his Fool when, in reaction to Goneril's calculated affronts, he has stalked out on her (and a bewildered Albany), intending to move in with Regan: "O! let me not be mad, not mad, sweet heaven; / Keep me in temper; I would not be mad!" (1.5.42–3). With each new insult to his kingly person, Lear recurs to this peculiar dread. Upon arriving at Gloucester's castle and finding his royal messenger in the stocks, he again gives expression to the threat he feels arising in him: "O! how this mother swells up toward my heart; / *Hysterica passio!* down, thou climbing sorrow!" (2.4.54–5). Then learning that Regan and Cornwall refuse to see him, the feeling returns: "O me! my heart, my rising heart! but, down!" (118–19). Soon thereafter, Goneril arrives to a warm greeting from Regan, and together the two sisters begin to whittle away at his train and his pride, provoking him to issue this part-warning, part-plea to Goneril: "I prithee, daughter, do not make me mad: / I will not trouble thee, my child; farewell. / We'll no more meet, no more see one another ..." (216–18). As he continues, however, his mind begins to oscillate, first acknowledging, "But yet thou art my flesh, my blood, my daughter"; and in the next breath, renouncing her: "Or rather a disease that's in my flesh, ... a boil, a plague-sore, or embossed carbuncle, in my corrupted blood"; followed immediately by, "But I'll not chide thee; let shame come when it will" (219–24). Finally, after Regan has made it clear that she is as callous, contemptuous, and hateful towards him as is Goneril, Lear vows his impotent threats of revenge, insisting that he will not weep though his heart break. As he forsakes the comfort and security of Gloucester's residence, it is with a plaintive, "O Fool! I shall go mad" – this, as "*Storm and Tempest*" is heard for the first time (284).

Because heretofore Lear had always found the world, including people, sufficiently intelligible, thus predictable, he had felt at home in it, his own abilities and powers fully adequate for whatever problems might arise. True, he probably was not cognizant of the extent to which this 'at-homeness' was a consequence of his every wish being catered in deference to his political power. In any event, previously the rightful order of things was adhered to, superintended by just and benevolent gods. Nothing challenged his conventional understanding of the ways of the world, for which his natural shrewdness was more than a match. Although he, like most noble warriors, had always valued truth and honesty, and though he manifests greatness of spirit (as indicated both by his majestic anger and by his kindness and generosity to his followers), we are given no reason to suppose that Lear was any more philosophical than the next man. Not finding this earthly domain perplexing, he was never especially curious, either about its basic ruling principles or man's place in it.

However, precisely because he had such predominately rational expectations about the world, including people (as evident in his plan for passing on his kingdom intact) – precisely because he expected everything to make sense, and people to behave in accordance with rational self-interest, including conventional standards of rightness (or reveal clearly enough to a shrewd observer when they likely would not) – Lear is particularly vulnerable to being deranged by a wholesale overturning of the universe as he has always known it. In his case, the painful psychic tempest that results is immensely magnified by the natural tempest in which he is immersed (for the worse the storm is, the more outrageous becomes his daughters' expelling him to bear the brunt of it; cf. 3.2.21–4). The experience profoundly 'dislocates' him, such that when he at last returns to full possession of his faculties, he knows not where he is ("Where have I been? Where am I?" 4.7.52). But it also unshackles him from all those opinions about people and things that he had never examined, yet trusted implicitly – and given how he had so long lived, as absolute ruler within the horizon of his experience, perhaps nothing less could suffice for this effect.

Lear's straightforward rationality is manifested in the one 'philosophical' proposition we hear him express (though presumably without appreciating its full significance). Cordelia having twice embarrassed him with her "Nothing" answer, Lear uneasily and perhaps half-jokingly protests, "Nothing will come of nothing: speak again" (1.1.89). Lear's claim is the only one that squares with natural human reason: that neither can something come from nothing, nor (as the rational complement of this) can something become nothing.[78] Shakespeare exploits several variations on this theme as the play unfolds. When Gloucester 'happens' upon Edmund pretending to peruse the forged letter, he asks, "What paper were you reading?" Edmund's transparently false reply – "Nothing, my Lord" – prompts his father to rejoin mockingly, "No? What needed then that terrible dispatch of it into your pocket? The quality of nothing hath not such need to hide itself. Let's see: come; if it be nothing, I shall not need spectacles" (1.2.30–5). And when as a result of his half-brother's machinations Edgar has fled into the dark countryside, he resolves to live disguised as Poor Tom, a Bedlam beggar, musing, "That's something yet: Edgar I nothing am" (2.3.21) – that is, Edgar has *not* become nothing simply, but has been transformed into something else. Each of the several times the Fool taunts his master for his injudicious ceding of his power (e.g., "thou hast pared thy wit o'both sides, and left nothing in the middle" (1.4.183–4); and, "I am better than thou art now; I am a Fool, thou art nothing" 190–1), we are to remember Lear's fateful words: nothing will come of nothing. The most interesting exchange in this vein, however, involves Kent as well as the King and his Fool. The latter having offered to teach Lear a speech made up of pithy paradoxes, Kent chides, "This is nothing, Fool." Who replies, "Then 'tis like the breath of an unfee'd lawyer; you gave me nothing for't." Turning to Lear, he asks, "Can you make no use of nothing, Nuncle?" Upon Lear answering, "Why no, boy; nothing can be made out of nothing," the Fool turns back to Kent, "Prithee, tell him, so much the rent of his land comes to: he will not believe a Fool" (1.4.126–32).

Upon reflection, we see that for philosophy to be possible, two conditions must hold true. First, the world must 'make sense,' be intelligible. This, in turn, presumes that it be both *coherent* (everything somehow fitting together, such that it constitutes one world, a uni-verse) and *consistent*. However different people's perspectives and interpretations of it may be, there nonetheless must be but a single reality. This point is easily illustrated by the divergent views of Gloucester and his bastard son Edmund concerning how the world they both inhabit actually works. Gloucester believes that this sublunary realm is subject to astrological influences; hence, he explains the King's extraordinary behaviour, as well as legitimate Edgar's supposed plot against his life: "These late eclipses in the sun and moon portend no good to us: though the wisdom of Nature can reason it thus and thus [as do the 'physiologists'], yet Nature finds itself scourg'd by the sequent effects" (1.2.100–3). Lear would seem also to partake of this view, at least initially, swearing "by the sacred radiance of the sun, / The mysteries of Hecate and the night, / By all the operation of the orbs / From whom we do exist and cease to be ..." (1.1.108–11; cf. 5.3.16–19). Even Kent falls back on this notion by way of trying to account for how such different daughters could come from the same parents: "It *is* the stars, the stars above us, govern our conditions" (4.3.32–3). Edmund, on the other hand, scorns such views:

> This is the excellent foppery of the world, that, when we are sick in fortune, often the surfeits of our own behaviour, we make guilty of our disasters the sun, the moon, and stars; as if we were villains on necessity, fools by heavenly compulsion, knaves, thieves, and treachers by spherical predominance, drunkards, liars, and adulterers by an enforc'd obedience of planetary influence; and all that we are evil in, by a divine thrusting on. An admirable evasion of whoremaster man, to lay his goatish disposition to the charge of a star! My father compounded with my mother under the dragon's tail, and my nativity was under *Ursa major*; so that it follows I am rough and lecherous. Fut! I should have been that I am had the maidenliest star in the firmament twinkled on my bastardizing. (1.2.115–30)

Gloucester's other son also evinces an appropriate scepticism of astrology (see 135–47). But whoever is right about the relationships between the heavenly bodies and human affairs, the basic point is that there is only *one* reality here: only one of these views can be true, the singular truth being reflective of a single reality. Given the pervasive intertwinings of their lives (as in all political associations), Gloucester's life simply *cannot* be subject to astral influences while the lives of his sons are not. Either everybody's is or nobody's is.

Moreover, the principles through which this single reality functions – what we have come to think of as the 'laws of nature' whereby things persist insofar as they do stay the same, thus providing some basis of *identity*, and whereby they move and change, grow and decay, insofar as they do – these principles must be consistent and constant. Only if there is an ultimate *un*changing something that 'rules,' that *causes*, the apparent flux of our ever-changing perceptible world, is there any permanent truth to know about it, thus, any genuine knowledge to be had of it. What possibility could there be of knowing anything, of understanding the 'why' and 'how' of anything, if the principles pertinent to its existence were ever-changing? The observable changes can be understood only in light of unchanging principles of change. Strictly speaking, chaos is unintelligible, and caprice by definition inexplicable. As basic prerequisites of rational intelligibility (the only kind there is, of course): First, it must be impossible that something can come from absolutely nothing or that something can become absolutely nothing.

Such notions would seem to be, quite literally, *inconceivable*. The opposite supposition – that something can only come from something and only nothing can 'come' from nothing – is the precondition of all causal analysis. Second, both X and not-X cannot simultaneously be true: logically contradictory conditions cannot simultaneously coexist. It is our deep intuitive acceptance of this most basic law of reason that lends the zest of paradox to the Fool's concluding his moralizing doggerel with the promise "And thou shalt have more / Than two tens to a score" (1.4.124–5).

The second requirement for the possibility of philosophy – for philosophy itself to 'make sense' – is that human reasoning must be capable of *congruing* with the rationality immanent in the world one seeks to understand. At a minimum, the human mind must function according to the same basic principles; that is, for one's thinking to have any validity, any *possibility* of being true, it also must be coherent, consistent, and non-contradictory. Of course, the coherence of one's thought does not suffice to ensure that it congrues with the coherence of things, hence cannot itself ensure that there actually is a coherence of things. But any alternative is literally unimaginable,[79] for the human imagination is a facet of reason, its clarity and coherence a function of the same principles as displayed in memory, calculation, analysis, and synthesis.[80] There is no rational choice, therefore, but to proceed on the assumption of a natural congruence between mind and reality. To that extent, philosophy rests on the rational faculty of trust, on a necessary faith in reason.[81] What more precisely and substantially having a rational nature entails is a complex and difficult matter. We can get some concrete appreciation of it, however, through a display of its *absence*. We most readily become aware of the rational nature we share, and rely upon, and take for granted, when confronted with someone whose mind is deranged, and so is *not* operating according to the normal rules of human reasoning.[82]

Accordingly, the play provides several variants of madness, each worth comparing with the others as well as with normal human functioning. There is the temporary kind of irrationality we experience when in the grip of some extreme passion, such as Lear's anger at Cordelia, which Kent protests: "be Kent unmannerly, when Lear is mad" (1.1.144–5) – that is, doing something that seems patently irrational, and would be recognized as such (presumably) by the 'madman' himself in a calmer moment (see also 2.2.67, 82; 3.4.162–7; 5.1.60). Then there is the kind of professional craziness of Lear's all-licens'd Fool, although in his particular case it often cloaks a profound sanity. It might be more helpful here to recall the 'class clown' who did silly things simply to make people laugh. Also, there is the feigned madness of Edgar in the guise of Poor Tom a'Bedlam – though here, too, many of his apparent non sequiturs (contrasting with coherent discourse), and even some of his 'nonsensical' babble, actually mask a wisdom he has come to the hard way. Finally, we are shown the profound disruption of Lear's rational faculties resulting from an emotional tempest more stressful and painful than the outer storm that amplifies it. As noted before, this simultaneous assault on his spirit and his senses is the means, or the price, of his ultimate liberation from that dream world in which he has lived for eighty years, a liberation which eventually allows him to see things clearly. However, this clarity is attained only after he has been thoroughly alienated from the familiar, ordinary understanding of political life as he has always lived it, having come to see that life as profoundly false, and the radical opposite of one lived in accordance with nature.[83]

We can discern the distinct stages in Lear's philosophical progress by noting the changes in his attitude towards the great storm engulfing him, which are actually changes in his view about the nature of Nature, and man's relationship to it. When first we see him addressing the warring elements, it is in terms appropriate to the conception of nature and the gods that we see him invoke repeatedly in the first half of the play, primarily in his oaths and prayers and curses. For example, when he rails at Goneril, "But I'll not chide thee; / Let shame come when it will, I do not call it; / I do not bid the thunder-bearer shoot, / Nor tell tales of thee to high-judging Jove" (2.4.223–6). That is, Lear presumes that gods rule the world, and that the forces of nature (epitomized by the thunderbolt) are agencies of the gods whereby, among other things, they punish erring humans. Thus the view here in his first sermon on the storm, culminating with:

> Let the great Gods,
> That keep this dreadful pudder o'er our heads,
> Find out their enemies now. Tremble, thou wretch,
> That hast within thee undivulged crimes,
> Unwhipp'd of Justice; hide thee, thou bloody hand,
> Thou perjur'd, and thou simular of virtue
> That art incestuous; caitiff, to pieces shake,
> That under covert and convenient seeming
> Has practis'd on man's life; close pent-up guilts
> Rive your concealing continents, and cry
> These dreadful summoners grace. I am a man
> More sinn'd against than sinning.
>
> (3.2.49–60)

Accordingly, Lear avers he will bear out the storm with patience ("I will be the pattern of all patience" 37; cf. 2.4.269; 3.6.57–8), since it is not really intended for him. Sinners need fear it, but not one such as he, "more sinn'd *against* than sinning." Doubtless he is unaware of it, but in willing himself patient, he is willing for himself that feminine virtue of the spirit most needful for philosophy:

patience and acceptance, the essential complements to the masculine spirit's virtues of courage, stamina, and indominability.[84]

However, as the storm continues to buffet him, Lear's wits begin to turn, and with this turning comes a new view:

> Poor naked wretches, whereso'er you are,
> That bide the pelting of this pitiless storm,
> How shall your houseless heads and unfed sides,
> Your loop'd and window'd raggedness, defend you
> From seasons such as these? O! I have ta'en
> Too little care of this. Take physic, Pomp;
> Expose thyself to feel what wretches feel,
> That thou mayst shake the superflux to them,
> And show the Heavens more just.
>
> (3.4.28–36)

Previously (as we have just seen), Lear thought of the storm in *moral* terms, that it punished the guilty, but not such as he (although there he is, bearing the brunt of it). Now, however, he realizes that the material forces of nature are *morally indifferent.* That, in truth, the gentle rain waters equally the fields of the righteous and the sinful, and that storms like these fall most heavily – not on guilty sinners – but simply on whoever is poor and vulnerable. As his Fool warned, urging him to seek shelter, "here's a night pities neither wise men nor Fools" (3.2.12–13). Lear now sees that if there is any divine will at work behind these events, it nonetheless requires the active mediation of human intelligence and humane feeling to effect a more just world. And notice, Gloucester's bitter experience teaches him a similar lesson. Unknowingly, he addresses the following to his own son, Edgar, who in the beggar's disguise of Poor Tom has been recruited to lead his blind father to the cliffs of Dover:

> Here, take this purse, thou whom the heav'ns' plagues
> Have humbled to all strokes: that I am wretched
> Makes thee the happier: Heavens, deal so still!
> Let the superfluous and lust-dieted man,
> That slaves your ordinance, that will not *see*
> Because he does not *feel*, feel your power quickly;
> So distribution should undo excess,
> And each man have enough.
>
> (4.1.63–70)

But notice also, Gloucester (unlike Lear) still believes the events of this world to be under the direct, intentional ministration of the divine powers. The fact that he remains shackled to the traditional understanding he inherited along with his lands and his title dictates Edgar's subsequent strategy of treating his despair.

Having just spoken of poor, exposed wretches, Lear now encounters one: this same disguised Edgar (who has taken upon himself "the basest and most poorest shape / That ever penury, in contempt of man, / Brought near to beast" – his face begrimed, nothing but a blanket around his loins, his hair a knotted snarl; 2.3.7–11). Lear's Fool has discovered him huddling inside the hovel to which Kent has led the old King. The indigent condition of this nearly naked 'Poor Tom' being obvious, Lear offers to explain it in terms of his own fixation: "Didst thou give *all* to thy daughters? And art thou come to *this*?" (3.4.48–9). When Poor Tom responds with a string of seemingly incoherent non sequiturs, Lear continues in his own obsessive vein, which now includes a belated recognition of his past mistakes: "What! has his daughters brought him to this pass? / Couldst thou save *nothing*? Would'st thou give 'em *all*?" Kent tries to bring the King back to reality ("He hath no daughters, Sir"), but Lear adamantly persists:

> Death, traitor! nothing could have subdu'd nature
> To such a lowness but his unkind daughters.
> Is it the *fashion* that discarded fathers
> Should have thus little mercy on their flesh?
> Judicious punishment! 'twas this flesh *begot*
> Those pelican daughters.
>
> (3.4.69–74)

Lear now sees both nature and convention differently. 'Proper' familial relations are not determined by nature, but are mere matters of 'fashion'; and fashions, being conventions, are subject to change. Moreover, in seeing what is natural in a different light, his idea of 'natural justice,' is similarly transformed to something more akin to that of Edmund the Bastard, who voiced the view that we must acknowledge ourselves responsible for *whatever* results from our own behaviour. And while this may be a prudent attitude to adopt towards life, it is at best half true, and bespeaks a decidely apolitical notion of just deserts. For however imprudent it was of Lear to have given all to his two elder daughters, and however much one is inclined to blame him for the situation he now finds himself in, this in no way exonerates his daughters and Cornwall to any extent whatsoever. It may be foolish to count unreservedly on the justness of other people, but that is neither here nor there as to what in truth *is just.*

We might notice something else surfacing here, however, and that is Lear's tendency to trace the cause of human folly to human sexuality, to our susceptibility to being ruled by sexual passion. Lear sees his daughters as the bitter fruit of that passion; but here again, preoccupied with his troubles, his is not a balanced view – not a fully *coherent* view – for he has forgotten about a third daughter, that she too was a consequence of that same passion. As Cordelia's Gentleman will later observe, "Thou hast one daughter / Who redeems nature from the general curse / Which twain have brought her [i.e., nature] to" (4.6.202–4). In decrying what he has come to see as the pervasive artificiality and falseness of civilized life, it is with respect to sexual conduct in particular that Lear rails (especially falseness in women, with their pretense of modesty, coldness, and propriety: "Behold yond simp'ring dame ... That minces virtue, and does shake the head / To hear of pleasure's name; / The fitchew nor the soiled horse goes to't / With a more riotous appetite" 116–22). Comporting with his new idea of nature, seeing it as radically distinct from the realm of artifice and convention, Lear expressly dissociates himself from the whole false business whereby human sexuality – the reproduction of human nature – is artificially masked and regulated in the name of orderly political life. Meeting the now blind old adulterer Gloucester, who recognizes the mad King by his voice (and so addresses him), Lear responds:

> Ay, every inch a king:
> When I do stare, see how the subject quakes.
> I pardon that man's life. What was thy cause?
> Adultery?
> Thou shalt not die: die for adultery! No:
> The wren goes to't, and the small gilded fly
> Does lecher in my sight.
> Let copulation thrive; for Gloucester's bastard son
> Was kinder to his father than my daughters
> Got 'tween the lawful sheets. To't, Luxury, pell-mell!
> For I lack soldiers.
>
> (4.6.107–17)

Surely, however, Shakespeare would have us notice that Lear's reasoning in favour of letting human sexuality "thrive" in the manner of the lower animals rests on the utterly false premise that Gloucester's bastard son was kinder to his father than were Lear's legitimate daughters.

Given that the reproduction of natures is the governing business of Nature, it is not surprising that Lear's view of sexuality has come to resemble Edmund's, whose cynicism about human nature also has a strongly sexual coloration ("when we are sick in fortune, often the surfeits of our own behaviour ... drunkards, liars, and adulterers by an enforc'd obedience of planetary influence ... an admirable evasion of whoremaster man, to lay his goatish disposition to the charge of a star ... so that it follows I am rough and lecherous" etc.; 1.2.116–28). Interestingly, however, Gloucester's *other* son seems similarly preoccupied with sexual matters (perhaps heightened eroticism runs in the family). Exposed to raw nature by virtue of the disguise he has adopted, Edgar, like Lear, has been stimulated to reassess life. But perhaps because his point of departure was so very different – that of a reckless, heedless youth who took his pleasure-filled life for granted – he has reached conclusions that differ markedly from those of the erstwhile King (as plainly show through his feigned madness). He responds to Lear's mention of "pelican daughters" with a sexual innuendo, followed by what one suspects is his new catechism: "Take heed o'th'foul fiend. Obey thy parents; keep thy word justly; swear not; commit not with man's sworn spouse; set not thy sweet heart on proud array" (3.4.78–80). What he says apparently arouses curiosity in Lear's overturned but wide-awake mind, for he asks, "What hast thou been?" And, as if this question causes Edgar to lapse momentarily from his mad persona, he replies:

> A servingman, proud in heart and mind; that curl'd my hair, wore gloves in my cap, serv'd the lust of my mistress' heart, and did the act of darkness with her; swore as many oaths as I spake words, and broke them in the sweet face of Heaven; one that slept in the contriving of lust, and wak'd to do it. Wine lov'd I deeply, dice dearly, and in woman out-paramour'd the Turk: false of heart, light of ear, bloody of hand; hog in sloth, fox in stealth, wolf in greediness, dog in madness, lion in prey. Let not the creaking of shoes nor the rustling of silks betray thy poor heart to woman: keep thy foot out of brothels, thy hand out of plackets, thy pen from lenders' books, and defy the foul fiend. Still through the hawthorn blows the cold wind; [followed by seeming nonsense]. (3.4.83–97)

Edgar's description of what he had been (and must we not presume that we are meant to ascribe at least some biographical truth to it, even if he has exaggerated his sins?) is a virtual survey of the human frivolity and decadence only possible in political life. It contrasts most effectively with what Lear now sees before his eyes, crystallizing his new view of nature in relationship to man, prompting him to wonder:

> Is man no more than this? Consider him well. Thou ow'st the worm no silk, the beast no hide, the sheep no wool, the cat no perfume. Ha! here's three on's [i.e., he, Kent, Fool] are

> sophisticated; *thou* art the thing itself; unaccommodated man
> is no more but such a poor, bare, forked animal as thou art.
> Off, off, you lendings! Come; unbutton here. (100–7)[85]

Clothing, to Lear's unfastened mind, represents – or better still, epitomizes – the *artificial*, in contradistinction to the natural. Insofar as it conceals what we really are (merely poor, naked, two-legged animals), and thereby creates a misleading appearance, clothing also stands for everything Lear now regards as false in human life, all that he (ever partial to truth and honesty) accordingly wants to shuck. Lear's efforts to strip off his own artificial lendings and join Poor Tom in what he has come to see as the natural state of man, to become the thing itself – *un*sophisticated, divested of everything owing to the arts whereby we appropriate alien pieces of nature for our own convenience, and thus surrender the natural self-sufficiency characteristic of other natural beings – these efforts are fortunately interrupted by his Fool announcing the arrival of that classic symbol of art: *fire*, gift of Prometheus ('Forethought'), who stole it from the gods. Having just spoken (wishfully, perhaps) of "a little fire in a wild field," likening it to the small spark in "an old lecher's heart," the Fool announces, "Look! here comes a walking fire" (3.4.109–11). It is the loyal old lecher Gloucester, threading dark-ey'd night by the feeble light of a torch.

Gloucester, in direct disobedience to Cornwall and at the risk of his life, has prepared a place for the King "where both fire and food is ready," and come in search of him (150). However, despite his urging Lear to proceed immediately to this secret refuge, the King delays for what must seem the strangest, maddest of reasons: "First let me talk with this philosopher." That is, Lear now regards near-naked Poor Tom (who confesses he lives as an outcast, eating and drinking whatever he can find or scrounge; 126–32) not only as Natural Man, he further concludes that Poor Tom's way of life bespeaks his being a *philosopher*. Why so? Is it because his choosing to reject the falseness of life in human society, and to live instead 'according to nature,' as self-sufficiently as other animals, presumes his having sought and found the truth about Nature? So Lear asks him, "What *is* the *cause* of thunder?"[86] Previously, this was not a question for Lear; he, in keeping with the common view, attributed thunder and lightning to "high-judging Jove" (2.4.225–6; 3.2.5–7, 49–50; cf. 2.1.44–5). Now, apparently, he seeks a purely 'natural' explanation. Edgar has no opportunity to respond, being pre-empted by Kent urging Lear to comply with Gloucester's offer. Still Lear persists: "I'll talk a word with this same learned Theban. What is your study?" Having heard Edgar's reply, Lear makes his enigmatic request: "Let me ask you one word in private" (3.4.157).[87] What does he wish to know of this "unaccommodated" natural man, this "philosopher," this "learned Theban"?[88] What sort of question might appropriately require privacy? Does he not wish to ask, "Are there any gods?"[89] But again Lear's search for knowledge is frustrated by Kent, who sees here only more evidence that "his wits begin to unsettle," and so is even more intent on moving the King's body to the proffered shelter. Rather than abandon his philosopher, however, Lear is prepared to join him in the bare hovel ("Noble philosopher, your company"),[90] and is persuaded to accept instead Gloucester's art-filled sanctuary only on condition that Poor Tom be allowed to accompany him: "Come, good Athenian" (169–77).

In his eagerness to disavow the use of clothing and everything else artificial, to live in accordance with only the natural truth, Lear has missed the import of one little phrase that Edgar keeps repeating: "Poor Tom's a-*cold*"! (3.4.57, 81, 144, 170). This is the more ironic in that the first extended reference to clothing came in the course of Lear's earlier characterizing human nature in terms quite *opposite* to the conception he here adopts. His daughters, insisting that he reduce his train, are challenging his need for having *any* knights:

> O! reason not the *need*; our basest beggars
> Are in the poorest thing superfluous:
> Allow not nature more than nature needs,
> Man's life is cheap as *beast's*. Thou art a lady;
> If only to go *warm* were gorgeous,
> Why, nature need not what thou gorgeous wear'st,
> Which scarcely keeps thee warm.
>
> (2.4.262–8)

Lear's speech here is doubly ironic, in that this, his *pre*-philosophical view of human nature is much closer to the truth of the matter than is the physiologist's view that he later espouses in the midst of his liberating madness. One endlessly important respect in which human life differs from that of beasts is precisely in its being ruled neither by bare necessity nor by strict utility, and that *beauty*, in particular, is a natural human concern: that we wish to go "gorgeous" as well as warm, indeed, may sacrifice the latter for the former, as do these daughters of Lear. However, this is merely a correct opinion at the time Lear utters it, based on quite ordinary, inadequately examined, hence inadequately understood, assumptions. He then had no more genuine understanding of nature, nor consequently of convention, of art, or of their true relationships, than Kent or Gloucester.

What upon reflection one realizes about the arts is that they, too, like conventions, are intrinsic to *human* nature, being manifestations of our reason, our rational powers brought to bear, first of all, on our needs, and those being met, on our wants. It is surely natural that we desire protection for our bodies in the forms of clothing and shelter, that we desire a reliable source of food, safety from whatever threatens us, hence ways of defending ourselves, that we desire health, and beyond that, means of enjoying whatever brings us pleasure, and so on. It is equally natural that we use all of our natural powers, those of our reason as well as those of our bodies, to invent and refine arts whereby these natural needs and wants may be satisfied.[91] In particular, it is natural that we try to enhance our sexual attractiveness artificially (not only by flattering clothing and adornment and scents, but by manner and mannerisms) – it as natural that we use our reason for this sovereign natural purpose of reproduction as that a peacock instinctively spreads his tail to attract a mate and intimidate rivals. As a result of these uses of natural reason to serve needs and wants that are themselves natural, or that at least *arise* naturally (as does the desire for luxury),[92] much of the immediate environment in which humans live is *artificial* – indeed, bearing in mind habitual behaviour in accordance with conventions, much about humans themselves may be seen as 'artificial.' But the human *capacity* for art and artifice (like that of understanding and abiding by conventions) is not itself artificial: it is natural, inherent in our having a rational nature.

In retrospect, one can see that the true relationship of nature, art, and convention is ironically signalled by deranged Lear's first words as he is happened upon by Edgar leading his blind father: "No, they cannot touch *me* for coining; I am the king himself ... Nature's above art in that respect" (4.6.83–6). *Coining money!* using the arts of metallurgy to fabricate tokens for what might seem the most conventional thing of all, money. But as Sokrates shows when constructing in *logos* a *polis* "according to nature" (*kata physis*; *Republic* 428e), the use of money for purposes of economic exchange arises naturally, being a rational response to the needs of political life (371b). However, it has also been understood since Antiquity that the exclusive 'right' to coin money, to establish 'legal tender,' is intrinsic to sovereign political authority, and that (accordingly) counterfeiting – coining by anyone but the 'king' – is necessarily a crime. In this sense, nature – including as it must the political necessities whereby humans may live according to their rational nature – is 'above' both art and convention, encompassing both.

Human rationality is such as can be cultivated to its full potential, and thus human nature fully realized, only in political society, where people can develop their reason 'dialectically': first of all, in this inventing and perfecting of the arts, which though they are not pursued for the sake of refining our rational powers and understanding, *do* incidentally have that effect; second, in people's deliberating with each other about their common business, which entails among other things framing and following the various kinds of rules and conventions – activities that, once again, incidentally develop reason itself; third, by sharing in communal happenings, everything from sports and games to theatricals and religious ceremonies; and, fourth, through jointly pursuing an understanding of things simply for its own sake. In connection with all these employments of reason, but especially the latter ones, Shakespeare's reader is invited to consider further the significance of reading and writing – the consequences, that is, of laws and religious teachings, of histories and dramas and songs, of treatises and treaties, of manuals and formulae, computations and recipes, being fixed in writing, accessible to be read, heeded, and used by anyone literate.

The subsequent references to clothing in the play continue to serve as reminders of the broader significance of this most elementary product of art, and thus of art per se, thereby revealing additional facets of our rational, yet not altogether rational, nature. There is blind Gloucester's requesting his faithful old tenant to provide his new guide, "the naked fellow," some adequate clothing: "And bring some covering for this naked soul" (4.1.39, 44). Ah, yes, our naked souls, our naked frailties that suffer in exposure, as Macbeth expressed it. But with regard to nakedness of bodies, this involves more the body's vulnerability, as Lear's Fool reminds us in his observing about Poor Tom: "he reserv'd a blanket, else we had been all sham'd" (3.4.65). *All*, notice, not merely the naked one. Nature establishes our need for clothing, art supplies the clothing, but convention determines much about its form and use. That, regardless of weather, we cover (more or less) our most sexually distinctive parts, those having to do with procreation, is hardly irrelevant to understanding human nature. Similarly, houses are more than shelters for the body; they are places of privacy and privilege, where in the bosom of the family the soul may find some respite from the subordination to public rules and the stress of public scrutiny inherent in political life (see 3.3.1–6).

On the way to Dover, Gloucester thinks Poor Tom's *voice* is altered, that he speaks "in better phrase and matter" than he did. Edgar replies ironically, "You're much deceiv'd; in nothing am I chang'd / But in my garments" (4.6.7–10). In reminding us that this was the basis of his transforming his *appearance* from that of Noble Edgar to Poor Tom (mainly by clothing and grooming and adornments), we are invited to reflect more generally on how these 'artificialities' figure in sociopolitical status, in setting our expectations of each other (and ourselves?) with respect to sex, age, authority, and station in life. Once Kent is reunited with Cordelia and has given her a report of his recent adventures with old Lear, she wishes him "better suited; / These weeds are memories of those worser hours: / I prithee, put them off." For some mysterious reason, however, Kent does not yet want to set aside his disguise, and he asks her keep his true identity secret (4.7.6–11). And when the sleeping Lear is carried into their presence, Cordelia asks, "Is he array'd?" Recall, while he was romping round the Dover downs (according to Cordelia, "As mad as the vex'd sea"), Lear had arrayed himself in real weeds and wildflowers (4.4.1–6). Now her attending Gentleman answers, "Ay, Madam, in the heaviness of sleep / We put fresh garments on him" (4.7.20–3).

When Lear at last awakens, he is a changed man. And for the first time in this play, he (and we) hear music – pleasing form artfully imposed on sound artificially generated for that purpose.[93] Sleep having cured the "great breach in his abused nature" (for as the doctor had earlier noted, "Our foster-nurse of nature is repose," which he had artificially induced by the art of medicine; 4.4.11–15), Lear at first presumes he has *died* and awakened in the netherworld (4.7.45). Persuaded that he has not, he is still unsure of himself:

> I fear I am not in my perfect mind.
> Methinks I *should* know you and know this man;
> Yet I am doubtful: for I am mainly ignorant
> What place this is, and all the skill I have
> Remembers not these garments.
>
> (63–7)

That Lear no longer rejects these new clothes, however, signals his having passed beyond the pre-Sokratic philosopher's understanding of what is natural and how it relates to political life, with all its arts and conventions. That 'physiologist's' view of Nature (Shakespeare may be seen as suggesting) is a kind of rational madness one necessarily passes through in the natural ascent from an ordinary understanding of the world to that of political philosphy.

Prior to his 'recovery,' his return to a human perspective on human things, Lear expresses a strictly conventional view of justice and law: "see how yond justice rails upon yond simple thief ... change places, and, handy-dandy, which is the justice, and which is the thief? Thou hast seen a farmer's dog bark at a beggar? ... And the creature run from the cur? There thou might'st behold / The great image of Authority: / A dog's obey'd in office" (4.6.149–57). Lear's view here is not unlike that of Thrasymachus in Plato's *Republic* (and of countless moderns): that so-called justice is nothing more than rules backed up by force, made by the powerful to serve primarily their own interests.[94] Apparently Lear had forgotten the example he himself set of a king concerned with natural justice and the common good, one who carried natural authority in his very countenance – at least according to good Kent, who would fain call him master even after being banished by him (1.4.27–30). What would explain the loyalty of a man of Kent's qualities? The Thrasymachean view of justice, like that of 'physiologist's' towards political life in general, is superficial. They delude themselves, believing their understanding to be a profound one, whereas they do not in fact know what they think they know. Lear's recovered sense of *natural* justice is implicit in his sadly confessing to Cordelia, "I know you do not love me; for your sisters / Have, as I do remember, done me wrong: / You have some cause, they have not" (4.7.3–5).

Awakening, and having recovered his wits, Lear avows himself "mainly *ignorant*." As such, he is no longer inclined to make grand pronouncements about nature and politics – quite the contrary: he repeatedly avows he's but a foolish old man (4.7.60, 65, 84). Nor is this awareness of his own ignorance, and that he is of failing memory and mind (63–7), the only 'Sokratic' indication he gives.[95] There is also his "If you have poison for me, I will drink it" (72), and the fact that his judgment is no longer distorted by an aroused spirit, his overpowering anger at the injustice of it all.[96] As the doctor observes to Cordelia, "Be comforted, good Madam; the great rage, you see, is kill'd in him" (78–9). One can detect a Sokratic allusion even in the means whereby Lear assures himself that the hands he beholds are his own ("let's see; I feel this pin prick," 55–6; cf. *Republic* 462c–d, 523e). But perhaps most important is the light-hearted profession of 'disinterested interest' in politics that he expresses when he and Cordelia have been captured:

> Come, let's away to prison;
> We two alone will sing like birds i'th'cage ...
> And pray, and sing, and tell old tales, and laugh
> At gilded butterflies, and hear poor rogues
> Talk of court news; and we'll talk with them too,
> Who loses and who wins; who's in, who's out;
> And take upon's the mystery of things,
> As if we were God's spies: and we'll wear out,
> In a wall'd prison, packs and sects of great ones
> That ebb and flow by th'moon.
>
> (5.3.8–19)

This 'philosophical' attitude towards political life, that of an amused observer of what Sokrates called "our prison home" (*Republic* 517b; see also 515a, 519d), manifests the transcendent perspective to which extraordinary experiences – both felt and thought upon – have carried this large-souled man. It is a perspective beyond tragedy, as indicated by Lear's resolve not to weep regardless of what happens to him (5.3.23–5). But this understanding of the natural human condition that Lear has belatedly come to requires special strength of soul if one is to live in full acceptance of it. It is necessarily a rational aspiration before it can become a full psychic reality. Virtue is knowledge, but the whole soul has to 'know' it, not just the rational part; and schooling the lower parts through habituation, cultivating the requisite spiritual strength, takes time, more time than Lear has left. Perhaps the real tragedy of King Lear is that he came so late to philosophy, too late to do him much good. It's doubtful, however, whether Lear, or any other man of deep feelings, could ever attain such calm acceptance of fate that the wasteful death of beautiful young Cordelia, so good and true, would not move him to howl and curse 'till heaven's vault should crack. Perfect serenity, one suspects, is a privilege of gods (cf *Republic* 603e).

At last we may return to the question with which we began: why the surface of *King Lear* is so misleading as to its deeper story. The answer, not surprisingly, has to do with philosophy – or rather, with *political* philosophy, with philosophizing in a 'politic' way, in a politically responsible, politically effective way. Philosophy's most immediate epistemological problem: distinguishing Opinion from Knowledge (or what ultimately comes to the same thing: Appearance from Reality), is intimately bound up with its most basic ontological problem: distinguishing Nature from non-Nature (equivalent to grasping an adequate idea of Nature per se). The play's thematic concern with nature is fairly explicit; no one who seriously studies the play could miss it. The prior problem, however, is not so much discussed as *shown*. The play as a whole is Shakespeare's most powerful illustration of the appearance–reality problem.[97] He would have been neither surprised nor dismayed by the countless more-or-less superficial interpretations of his masterpiece – all stemming from a massive misjudgment of Lear's mind and actions in the opening scene – since he went to such lengths to invite them. The evidence for a correct interpretation, *his* interpretation, is all there, perfectly 'evident.' But so too are the stimuli for the various prejudices we bring to the play. These prejudices and assumptions, working in conjunction with insufficient care in reading or rigour in thinking, perhaps reflecting in turn insufficient respect for the author as writer or thinker, have consequences perfectly predictable for someone whose understanding of human nature is as deep and broad as the plays show Shakespeare's to be.

In the case of this play, however, more so than in all but a few of his others, there is another factor limiting most people's interpretive efforts: lack of interest in the higher, more abstract philosophical issues, and in philosophy as such. One has to share Shakespeare's philosophical interests to recognize and appreciate this dimension of his creativity, and that in turn presumes that one has at least a 'moiety' of his philosophical nature. Shakespeare understood as well as anyone ever has that this is something most people lack. Accordingly, a story about the birth of philosophy and the making of a philosopher is not the stuff of a theatrical success. It could be of interest only to a precious few, readers who would take delight in their own philosophical efforts to discover it. And so, being a genius of almost unbelievable capacity, Shakespeare politely clothed his story of philosophy within another story, one that resonates with thoughts and feelings and experiences familiar to, and thus of interest to, virtually everyone. Truly a poet for all mankind.

A PHILOSOPHER BECOMES A KING

King Lear is the story of King Lear as *Hamlet* is of the Prince of Denmark. Unlike Shakespeare's other major tragedies, however, it has a so-called Secondary Plot. As I have attempted to show, this Gloucester family saga, provoking as it does a re-examination of the relationship between *physis* and *nomos*, is actually an integral part of the philosophical search for an adequate understanding of Nature. Beyond that, however, the story of an old king's becoming a philosopher is complemented by the similar transformation in a young playboy prior to his becoming a king. The fact that Lear's ascription of 'philosopher' to the disguised Edgar is the recognition of an apparent madman by another madman must not be taken as licence to dismiss its significance. After all, the founder of political philosophy teaches that philosophy itself is a form of 'divine madness,' which might suggest that pronouncements made under its influence can seem as perplexing, even unintelligible, as oracular revelations (*Phaedrus* 244a ff). Safer by far, then, to regard this episode as an example of our philosopher-poet's irony.[98] So taken, the lightly limned story of Edgar's fall from grace and rise to majesty works in conscious counterpoint to the tragedy of Lear.[99] As such it deserves at least a few brief remarks by way of conclusion.

The education of Edgar, the result of his expulsion from political society and first-hand encounter with raw nature, is the complement of Lear's. Its accomplishment is displayed in act 4, and signalled by his father's rueful observation, "'Tis the times' plague, when madmen lead the blind" (4.1.46). For this could be said to symbolize the central teaching of Plato's *Republic*: the vast majority of people (of whom Gloucester is a fair representative) are blind to reality, and the person best suited to lead them is regarded as a madman – while in truth being the only clear-sighted one (cf. 484c, 488a–489c, 516e–517a, 516e–517a, 518a–b).

Reflecting on Edgar's actions over the course of the play, one cannot help but be struck by the multiplicity of roles he chooses to assume. Judging from his later response to Lear's "What hast thou been?" (3.4.82), the young man we first meet in the second scene is something of a careless, irresponsible libertine – a well-coifed 'party animal,' devoted to wine, women, and gambling, living beyond his no doubt considerable means. When forced to flee, however, he transforms himself in the most radical manner imaginable: into a dirty, naked, despised mad-babbling beggar. Then, in taking up the leading of blinded Gloucester, he puts on the clothes of his father's old tenant and becomes a sturdy peasant speaking a rustic dialect. From that he ascends to the status of a gentleman-knight, an anonymous armed champion whose "name is lost" but whose "outside looks so fair and war-like, / And [whose] tongue some say of breeding breathes" (5.3.120, 140–2). Upon defeating his half-brother, he once more reveals himself as Edgar of Gloucester, and shortly thereafter becomes king by default of there being anyone equal or better to assume the responsibility (cf. *Republic* 347c–d).[100] The most significant implication of Edgar's sequence of *personae*, from his having seen (and felt) life from so many distinct perspectives, is its providing the basis for his acquiring a synthetic, transcendent perspective – a philosophical perspective – not unlike Shakespeare's own.

At the play's beginning, however, Edgar manifests a sort of naïve complacency about life. Granted, he shows an intelligent young man's amused scepticism about astrology (and perhaps, by implication, about other popular beliefs as well; 1.2.135–47); still, his perfidious half-brother can lump him with their father as being one "Whose nature is so far from doing harms / That he suspects none; on whose foolish honesty / My practices ride easy!" (176–9). He would seem to exemplify Sokrates' explanation in the *Republic* of "why equitable men, when they are young, look as though they are simpletons, and are easily deceived by unjust men, because they have in themselves no patterns of affections similar to those of scoundrels" (409a–b). Edgar shares several characteristics with Glaukon, Sokrates' favourite young companion in that dialogue, the brother who displays such a natural aptitude for philosophy.[101] Both young men having been accustomed to comparative luxury (curl'd hair, fancy clothes, fine wine, the sporting life; 3.4.83–9), one can easily imagine the pre-philosophical Edgar, just like Glaukon, rejecting the lifestyle of what the latter calls a "city of pigs" (372d). Yet, in adopting the disguise he chooses, that of indigent Poor Tom, Edgar adapts himself to an ascetic life even more extreme than Glaukon endorses for the Guardians of his "Beautiful City" (cf. 415d–417b). Also, Edgar, like Glaukon, proves himself a man of courage, first, in defending his helpless father against the murderous assault of Oswald (4.6.228ff), then in confronting and defeating his bold, politically ambitious brother (5.3.125ff; cf. 368a). Moreover, and equally significant, both Glaukon and Edgar are highly erotic *lovers* (3.4.79–95; cf. 474d). Capping it all, his being victimized by gross injustice at the hands of those from whom he least expected it, implants in Edgar a depth of appreciation for justice – the theme of Plato's *Republic* – such as only unhappy experience can accomplish. There is, then, an ironic truth when at Lear's mock trial of his two evil daughters, he orders the blanket-clad Poor Tom, "Thou robed man of justice, take thy place" (3.6.36).[102]

Once Edgar has rejoined the political society whence he was nurtured –

returned to the 'Cave,' as Sokrates would have it, and reaccustomed himself to the modes of life therein – he not only knows 'the road to Dover,'[103] he knows how to deal most effectively with the multiplicity of people he will encounter along the way, beginning with his own despairing father.[104] We hear no more gibberish from him. As Gloucester notes, "Methinks thy voice is alter'd, and thou speak'st / In better phrase and manner than thou didst" (4.6.7–8). Having reached his own conclusions about this world, Edgar is able to distinguish the valid from the mistaken in the grand political pronouncement of the still-deranged Lear: "O!, matter and impertinency mix'd; / Reason in madness" (172–3). And so, already bearing the name of an illustrious English king,[105] Edgar accedes to the office, not out of desire but out of duty: "The weight of this sad time we must obey" (5.3.322; cf. *Republic* 520e).

CHAPTER FOUR

"Sweet Philosophy": Further Illustrations of Shakespeare's Portrayal of Philosophy in Relation to Political Life

Preposterous ass, that never read so far
To know the cause why music was ordain'd!
Was it not to refresh the mind of man
After his studies or his usual pain?
Then give me leave to read philosophy,
And while I pause serve in your harmony.

The Taming of the Shrew

Nigh on two centuries ago, Coleridge suggested that "our *myriad-minded* Shakspeare" was "the greatest genius, that perhaps human nature has yet produced," and went on to observe:

No man was ever yet a great poet, without being at the same time a profound philosopher. For poetry is the blossom and the fragrancy of all human knowledge, human thoughts, human passions, emotions, language. In Shakspeare's *poems* [*Venus and Adonis* and *The Rape of Lucrece*], the creative power, and the intellectual energy wrestle as in a war embrace. Each in its excess of strength seems to threaten the extinction of the other. At length, in the DRAMA they were reconciled, and fought each with its shield before the breast of the other. Or like two rapid streams, that at their first meeting within narrow and rocky banks mutually strive to repel each other, and intermix reluctantly and in tumult; but soon finding a wider channel and more yielding shores blend, and dilate, and flow on in one current and with one voice ... What then shall we say? even this; that Shakspeare, no mere child of nature; no automaton of genius; no passive vehicle of inspiration possessed by the spirit, not possessing it; first studied patiently, meditated deeply, understood minutely, till knowledge become habitual and intuitive wedded itself to his habitual feelings, and at length gave birth to that stupendous power, by which he stands alone, with no equal or second in his own class ...[1]

If the preceding chapters have fulfilled their intended purpose, they have reaffirmed the credibility of Coleridge's view.

His view and more is implicit in this book's governing thesis: that Shakespeare was not only cognizant of the larger philosophical questions that his political stories raise, but that he crafted his dramas with the intention of showing how those questions arise out of, and bear upon, his stories. Thus, the reader of Shakespeare's plays, as of Plato's dialogues, experiences philosophy arising 'naturally,' that is, out of the diligent pursuit of answers to the problems and questions and perplexities implicit in ordinary political life. This is more than sufficient for Shakespeare's qualifying as a philosophical writer in the primary sense of the word: one whose works are – whatever else – designed to entice a potentially philosophical reader to engage in the humanizing activity of thinking for the sheer satisfaction of understanding. Their effectiveness in this regard need not imply that their author had a fully developed metaphysical 'doctrine,' much less an original one. He may have, but neither doctrines nor originality per se are essential to philosophy, unlike theology or music. Whatever the truth in his case, my hope has been the modest one of providing persuasive evidence, through the detailed analysis of a pair of familiar plays, that Shakespeare was philosophically self-conscious in crafting his dramas, and that he had explored the permanent questions deeply enough to guide us in doing so as well.

A preoccupation with the problem of discerning the truth beneath layers of misleading appearances is obvious in most of the plays we associate with Shakespeare's maturity as a dramatist. While the foreground focus of his plots is upon either innocent misinterpretation or intentional manipulation of appearances, he (or his characters) remind us repeatedly that these are but specifically human complications overlying this most basic of metaphysical problems: understanding the Reality that causes whatever Appears to be. Beyond his preoccupation with this pervasive challenge, however, I am convinced that other, more specific, philosophical issues inspire the way in which Shakespeare fashions the political stories he chooses to tell – as I have endeavoured to show with respect to *Macbeth* and *King Lear*. By way of concluding my attempt to enhance appreciation for this dimension of his art, I shall briefly address aspects of some other plays that I believe further substantiate my claims, but which seem to have gone scarcely noticed heretofore.

In this connection, a point I made at the outset of this study bears repeating. Shakespeare manifests a philosopher's typical self-consciousness about philosophy itself, including its problematic relationship with whatever polity it happens to be dependent upon. And inasmuch as both the essential concerns of philosophy and the requirements of wholesome political life could be said to meet and find their only resolution in Plato's paradoxical idea of a 'Philosopher-King,'[2] Shakespeare is accordingly intrigued by it – or so it seems to me. Exploring the idea from both sides, so to speak, some of his plays depict the political problems that arise because of, or at least are aggravated by, rulers' being insufficiently reflective, that is, lacking in such understanding of their situation as comes only from the kind of sustained, thorough, rigorous, impartial examination that virtually defines philosophy. Whereas other plays portray political problems arising precisely because of a ruler's, or a potential ruler's, philosophical preoccupations. Thus, in this final chapter I have chosen to direct attention to certain of Shakespeare's creations that throw some additional light on his manner of exploring both the nature of a philosopher in his relationship to politics, and the primary questions of philosophy as they bear on human life. Nothing like a full interpretation is intended of the plays I address. Rather, each was selected to illustrate a different facet of Shakespeare's philosophical engagement, and that facet is the primary focus of my remarks. *Othello* exemplifies Shakespeare's way of translating metaphysical issues into the context of political life *via* Platonic psychology. *The Winter's Tale* provides an especially important indication of Shakespeare's relationship to the Platonic literature. *Measure for Measure* is an exposé of the problem at the heart of the Philosopher–King as a political solution.

ELEMENTARY MATTERS IN *OTHELLO*

Shakespeare set two plays in Venice, treating it as the prototype of the modern commercial republic: a tolerant, liberal, pluralistic, outward-looking regime founded on the assumption that its citizens can and will subordinate other personal preferences and concerns to the well-nigh universal love of gain – that wealth and all it stands for can be made the ruling interest of the polity, providing thereby a basis for civic harmony and friendship rooted in mutual economic advantage. Dedicated to the security and prosperity of its composing individuals, the essential characteristics of this regime are embodied in its framework of law, offering equal justice and personal liberty to all residents, regardless of colour, creed, or country of origin.[3] As expressed in *The Merchant of Venice* – appropriately enough, by the sad merchant himself, Antonio:

> The Duke cannot deny the course of law:
> For the commodity that strangers have
> With us in Venice, if it be denied,

> Will much impeach the justice of the state,
> Since that the trade and profit of the city
> Consisteth of all nations.
>
> (3.3.26–31)

This is a viable political conception only to the extent that people do, or can be taught to, rule themselves decisively by rational considerations – or to speak more precisely, by the this-worldly dictates of economic rationality (that 'marginal utility maximization' so dear to modern econometricians) – thus not allowing 'irrational' prejudices and passions to obstruct or distort either public policy or private relations.

The two foremost challenges to the fundamental rationale of the regime come from Race and Religion, that is, from the prejudices and passions that typically attend religious commitments and racial recognition. Few prospects activate such feelings more violently than marriage across sectarian or racial lines. *Erōs* is no great respecter of such lines, but most inhabitants of virtually all polities to some considerable extent are. Accordingly, both Venetian plays feature such marriages, and we are allowed to observe their consequences. In both cases, the fathers of the brides are outraged to the point of disowning their daughters. Desdemona's marriage to 'the Moor' of Venice proves mortal to old Brabantio, as well as to both principals; *Othello* is a tragedy – primarily a 'domestic' tragedy, but the mercenary mentality of its political setting is almost surely meant to be seen as a factor.[4] By contrast, the Jewess Jessica's marriage to a fortune-hunting Christian and its catastrophic effects on her father Shylock is at the crux of what is ostensibly a *comedy* – though the play's most amusing feature may be its depiction of how in practice the Republic's vaunted Rule of Law turns out to be the rule of lawyers, technical experts skilled in exploiting the letter of the law at the expense of its spirit. Set in a Venice ostensibly at peace, *The Merchant* portrays the passion for revenge arising from religious animosity as being strong enough to over-ride any concern for economic advantage, even in a character notoriously preoccupied with money (4.1.84–7; cf. 3.2.271–5). Whereas *Othello*, with Venice at war, shows its reputation-sensitive protagonist being ruled by a jealousy impervious to all rational considerations, not merely economic ones. It may also be pertinent to Shakespeare's assessment of this regime that each play features a character who secretly manipulates events 'behind the scenes,' as it were, producing results significantly at odds with those the regime's principles would otherwise produce. In the one case, a benevolent young woman, wise beyond her years, remedies an evil that the Venetian authorities are powerless to avert. In the other, a cunning and malicious man subverts the opportunity for private happiness that Venice's commitment to equality and liberty are meant to ensure. Together they suggest that this kind of regime is especially susceptible to being manoeuvred – whether for good or ill – in ways perhaps never anticipated, and certainly never intended, by its architects. Moreover, the portrayal of intelligent individuals sufficiently motivated to engage in such manipulating is itself a further corrective to the simplistic assumptions about human nature upon which the regime is premised.[5]

Why Shakespeare has crafted it thus – why he sees religious division (epitomized by the age-old animosity between Christian and Jew) as a fit subject for comedy, whereas racial prejudice is the stuff of tragedy – is an interpretive problem in its own right. With regard to this issue, there is the obvious difference to be noted. One can change, or pretend to change, one's religion (as Jessica does willingly, and perhaps sincerely, but in any case for reasons of love and liberty, not theology; or as Shylock does, not because he was 'born again,' but under a coercive threat to his life and livelihood). However, there is no choosing to change the visible indications of one's race, such as the blackness of one's own face (*Othello* 3.3.267, 393–4), or the "Noses, ears and lips" characteristic of one's race (4.1.42; note 1.1.66). The very fact that friend and foe alike can refer simply to '*the* Moor' (as is done well over four dozen times in the play), and confidently presume that anyone in Venice or Cyprus would know who is meant, attests to Othello's unique visibility amid a fair-skinned populace. Desdemona may have seen "Othello's visage in his mind" (1.3.252), but everyone else sees his visage in his visage. And though the Duke of Venice regards his general as "far more fair than black" (or at least finds it convenient to say so in his present military emergency; 290; cf. 4.1.230–2; 1.1.45–8), he no more than affirms the respectable view – in this case, the rational view – which grants superior importance to character, to the non-material qualities of soul, over body. But the Duke's troubling to express this truism tacitly acknowledges that it is *not* invariably accepted and acted upon. In any event, no one ever forgets the perceptible shape and colour of Othello's material embodiment, least of all Othello himself.

The particulars of *his* body are not the only ones of consequence in this play, however. Othello may be in earnest when, in begging his employers that Desdemona be allowed to accompany him to Cyprus, he insists that it is "not to please the palate of [his] appetite, ... but to be free and bounteous of her mind" (261–5). He expressly stakes his precious reputation on the assurance that his own rational faculties are impervious to the blandishments of "feather'd Cupid" (268–74). His subsequent words and deeds, however, reveal only too clearly that his regard for his young wife is *not* purely one of soul for soul, what is sometimes called 'platonic love.' Later, and in direct contradiction to what he claimed before the Duke and Senators, Othello privately confesses his susceptibility to Desdemona's physical charms: "I'll not expostulate with her, lest her body and beauty unprovide my mind again ..." (4.1.200–2). Othello's preoccupation with Desdemona's body, that it be exclusively his, and his peculiar vulnerability to insinuations and suspicions that it is not, is at the root of his tragedy. Iago's devilish machinations succeed only because of Othello's hypersensitivity on this matter. To be sure, Iago knows his man better than the man knows himself: "I'll pour this pestilence into his ear, / That she repeals [Cassio] for her body's lust." (2.3.347–8). Iago hereby points to the embracive irony of the play. That for all of Othello's reliance on his eye, on "ocular proof," his *ear* is the portal to his vivid imagination, and through it Iago feeds those "dangerous conceits" that "burn like the mines of sulphur" (3.3.330–4), poisonous *images* of copulating bodies, of 'bolstering': "With her, on her, what you will" (4.1.34) – all calculated to prompt Othello's envisioning in his mind what no one could have seen with eyes of the body.

As to *why*, contrary to the delusion in which he indulges to the bitter end, Othello *is* so "easily jealous" – almost absurdly so – this must be regarded as the central puzzle of the plot. And his awareness that he is of an 'alien' race is almost surely relevant to its solution ("Haply, for I am black"), although other bodily liabilities may enter here as well ("declin'd" as he is "into the vale of years"; 3.3.267–70). Whatever factors amplify Othello's anxiety, some germ of his concern is common to most men. We get to watch Iago, who knows men and the importance they invest in women's bodies, exploit the various forms of this proprietary interest throughout the play. He begins by bruising Brabantio's heart through his ear with obscene images of his only child – inerasable verbal pictures of which Iago, with a poet's gift turned "seamy-side without," is such a master conceiver: "an old black ram is tupping your white ewe"; this shy, young virgin "cover'd with a Barbary horse," "making the beast with two backs" (1.1.88–117). Similarly, Iago manipulates the gullible Roderigo through rhetoric which repeatedly reduces sexual relations to attractions and repulsions among bodies: "When she is sated with his body, she will find the error of her choice;" (1.3.351–2); "Her eye must be fed, and what delight shall she have to look on the devil? When the blood is made dull with the act of sport" (2.1.224–5); "Didst thou not see her paddle with the palm of [Cassio's] hand? ... an index and prologue to the history of lust and foul thoughts ... hard at hand comes the main exercise, the incorporate conclusion" (251–9). 'Incorporate conclusion': one imagines the satisfaction with which Iago savours this clever euphemism for his own 'beast with two backs.' And how he must enjoy toying with Cassio's chivalrous idealization of Desdemona: "she is sport for Jove ... I'll warrant her full of game ... What an eye she has! methinks it sounds a parley of provocation ... 'tis an alarm to love" (2.3.16–24).

Iago himself professes contempt for those who allow themselves to be ruled by bodily appetites, and who regard love as more than "merely a lust of the blood, and a permission of the will." This disgruntled 'Ancient,' this perplexing perversion of a philosophical nature[6] – who seems to relish his own black irony as much as his false reputation for honesty; and who, judging from his several asides and soliloquies, is himself utterly free of any racial prejudice he may seek to exploit in others (see 2.1.283–6)[7] – eerily anticipates what another philosopher will famously dub 'Will to Power':

> Virtue? a fig! 'tis in ourselves, that we are thus, or thus: our bodies are gardens, to the which our wills are gardeners, so that if we will plant nettles, or sow lettuce, set hyssop, and weed up thyme; supply it with one gender of herbs, or distract it with many; either to have it sterile with idleness, or manur'd with industry, why, the power, and corrigible authority of this, lies in our wills. If the balance of our lives had not one scale of reason, to poise another of sensuality, the blood and baseness of our natures would conduct us to most preposterous conclusions. But we have reason to cool our raging motions, our carnal stings, our unbitted lusts ... (1.3.319–32)[8]

Drawn in deliberate contrast to his Moor, Shakespeare's Desdemona seems largely indifferent to the nose, ears, and lips of Othello's aging black body. She saw his visage in his mind – or was it, in *her* mind. To explain his strange attraction for her, one must again consider the political context. Why does Venice require the services of an alien warrior, himself an erstwhile barbarian, to protect its commercial empire from barbarian encroachment? Because being dedicated to material prosperity and the refined, gracious, 'cosmopolitan' way of life it makes possible, the Venetian republic does not honour, hence, does not cultivate in its own citizens, that old-fashioned ascetic martial virtue exemplified by the heroes of the Roman republic. It honours moneymaking; its heroes are successful merchants. As Sokrates explains in accounting for how a Timarchy (the regime based upon the love of martial glory) can decay into a property-based Oligarchy, a latent love of wealth becomes increasingly influential in the timocratic elders who, inadequately educated as to the inherent goodness of their virtue and finding they can no longer compete for battlefield distinctions, seek instead the consolations of riches:

> 'Next, I suppose, one sees the other and enters into rivalry with him, thus causing the multitude to become like them.'
>
> 'That's likely,' [Adeimantos] said.
>
> 'Well, then,' I said, 'from there they progress in moneymaking, and the more honourable they think it, the less honourable they think virtue. Or is not virtue at variance with

> wealth, as if each were lying in the scale of a balance, always inclining in opposite ways?'
>
> 'Yes, indeed,' he said.
>
> 'Wealth and the wealthy being honoured in the polity, virtue and the good [men] are less honoured.'
>
> 'Plainly.'
>
> 'And always what is honoured is practiced, whereas what is dishonoured is neglected.'
>
> 'Just so.'
>
> 'Instead of lovers of victory and lovers of honour, they finally become lovers of money-making and lovers of money; and they praise and admire the wealthy [man] and put him in ruling positions, while dishonouring the poor [man].' (*Republic* 550e–551a)

This would seem to fit Venice to a tee. It treats martial virtue as a commodity to be bought and sold, not as something to be cultivated by whoever would pursue eminence in the city. Instead, its highest honours and offices go to wealthy burghers. Within its secure precincts, respectable Venetians fight only with laws (and lawyers). They haul their opponents into court, seeking legal redress, as Brabantio does Othello (whereas there have been and still are societies in which this would *not* be the normal response to one's daughter being abducted). However, might this polite, sophisticated civility of Venice help explain why Desdemona, despite seeming to her father "so opposite to marriage," fell madly in love with Othello? "The wealthy curled darlings of [her own] nation" possessed no erotic appeal for her. But here was a real man, a man among men, virtually a black Odysseus who lived a life of high adventure from one end of the Mediterranean to the other[9] – at least if one credits his own account of himself, as Desdemona evidently did. According to Othello, she was utterly fascinated by it: "this to hear would Desdemona seriously incline"; that she did "with a greedy ear devour up my discourse"; that "often did [I] beguile her of her tears when I did speak of some distressed stroke that my youth suffer'd"; "She wish'd she had not heard it, yet she wish'd that heaven had made her such a man" (a nicely ambiguous line: made her? or made *for* her?). In sum, she assured him that "to tell [his] story ... would woo her" (1.3.145–66). And not surprisingly; as the Duke shrewdly observes, "I think this tale would win my daughter too." By comparison with the cloistered, routinized, vacuous bourgeois fate resulting from marriage to a wealthy Venetian businessman, a life with Othello might seem infinitely preferable to a spirited, romantic girl – well worth the cost of conventional respectability. Thus, she "consecrates" her soul to "his honours, and his valiant parts" (249–54). Othello has at least some inkling of her aspirations, judging from his greeting to her when they are first reunited on Cyprus: "O my fair warrior!" (2.1.182; note 3.4.149).

So, while the outside world may look upon it as a marriage of Beauty and the Beast, its very unconventionality attests to the strength of the attraction on her part. As for Othello, Desdemona would seem ideal: a woman who genuinely appreciates his special qualities and what he has accomplished, who sympathizes with all he has been through: "She lov'd me for the dangers I had pass'd, / And I lov'd her that she did pity them" (1.3.167–8). Yet there may be more to it than that. Cassio, whose ship is the first to beat through the storm to Cyprus, is barely welcomed before he is asked by Montano, "But, good lieutenant, is your general wiv'd?" (2.1.60). Why would Montano think so, unless the last time they served together Othello had mooted some intention of marrying and settling down (35–6)? Perhaps he is not altogether oblivious to the fate that, according to Iago, awaits the "duteous" servant of a bourgeois republic, one who "wears out his time much like his master's ass": that when he is old and thus no longer of use, he will be "cashier'd" (1.1.45–8). Thus, despite his protestations to the contrary, might he have been 'in the market,' as it were, for a suitable opportunity to put his "unhoused free condition ... into circumscription and confine"? That is, to manage a marriage that would insure him a secure place in Venetian society (for so does honest Iago see it: "Faith, he to-night hath boarded a land carrack: if it prove lawful prize, he's made forever" 1.2.50–1). Presuming this to be a factor in his decision, Othello and Desdemona marry at cross-purposes: she, to enter upon a life of adventure; he, to retire from it. And insofar as Ovid is right – that the exotic and forbidden contributes to erotic appeal – one wonders what will happen when he no longer seems so exotic to her. Or whether Iago's prophecy might eventually be fulfilled without any help from him: "When she is sated with his body, she will find the error of her choice; she must have change, she must" (1.3.351–2).[10] There *are* subtle indications that not even Desdemona – seemingly the most 'spiritual' character in the play – is indifferent to bodies. These range from her disappointment that Othello must leave immediately, their marriage unconsummated ("To*night*, my lord?" 1.3.278), to her admiring comments on the Venetian official who attempted to protect her from Othello's abuse ("This Lodovico is a proper man." Emil: "A very handsome man." Desd: "He speaks well" 4.3.35–7).

While still more textual evidence could be adduced, presumably the foregoing is sufficient reminder of the psychological, hence political, importance of *bodies* to the story of *Othello*. The differentiation of kinds of people by means of their respective embodiments, the particular qualities – shape, colour, texture – of the 'matter' that perceptibly individuates them, has a peculiar significance in this play (see 2.1.129–42). So, too, do various material means of both natural and (supposedly) supernatural influence over human bodies. Wine is the material cause of Cassio's undoing, his soul being abnormally susceptible to the pernicious effects of his body's ingestion of alcohol (2.3.30ff): "O god, that men should put an enemy in their mouths, to steal away their brain" (281–3). Poison is Othello's choice for killing Desdemona, before Iago persuades him to use his own body to stifle hers (4.1.200–4).[11] Equally pertinent to the plot are the suspected materials of witchcraft and black magic. Brabantio accuses Othello of having "enchanted" his daughter, "practis'd on her with foul charms, / Abuse'd her delicate youth with drugs or minerals, / That weakens motion" (1.2.63–79), of corrupting her "by spells and medicines, bought of mountebanks' (1.3.60–1), "with some mixtures powerful o'er the blood, / Or with some dram conjur'd to this effect" (104–5). Whereas, the true nature of Othello's charm over Desdemona is perfectly manifested by his convenient *story* of the notorious handkerchief – a strawberry-embroidered piece of silk that he would have her believe has "magic in the web of it." He alleges it to have been sewn by a two-hundred-year-old sibyl and given to his mother by an Egyptian mind-reader as a means of subduing his father, but only if kept physically in her possession (3.4.53–74; cf. 5.2.217–18; 2.1.222). Desdemona seems to credit his claims (3.4.98).[12] Nor to be overlooked in connection with all these 'matters' are the wedding sheets Desdemona specifies to dress her bed and to be used as a shroud for her body when she dies (4.2.107; cf. 2.3.26, 4.3.22–4) – pieces of cloth that, one way or another, might supply Othello all the 'ocular proof' he needs.[13]

Perhaps so much attention to bodies and things of the body explains the curious prominence of 'The Elements' in *Othello* – the four material elements of traditional metaphysics, to wit: Earth, Air, Fire, and Water – regarded as the most basic constituents of the physical realm.[14] When the scene shifts from Venice to Cyprus, these elements are in chaos, as if Nature were "erring from itself." The Cypriots scanning the sea testify to the unprecedented tumult of wind and water assaulting not only the earth's rocky shore but the very fires of heaven:

Montano: What from the cape can you discern at sea?
First Gent: Nothing at all, it is a high-wrought flood,
I cannot 'twixt the heaven and the main
Descry a sail.
Montano: Methinks the wind does speak aloud at land,
A fuller blast ne'er shook our battlements:
If it ha' ruffian'd so upon the sea,
What ribs of oak, when the huge mountains melt,
Can hold the mortise? ... What shall we hear of this?
Sec. Gent: A segregation of the Turkish fleet:
For do but stand upon the banning shore,

The chiding billow seems to pelt the clouds,
The wind-shak'd surge, with high and monstrous main,
Seems to cast water on the burning bear,
And quench the guards of the ever-fixed pole;
I never did the like molestation view
On the enchafed flood.

(2.1.1–17)

When shortly thereafter Lieutenant Cassio arrives with the news that "the warlike Moor Othello" has been sent to be governor of this threatened part of Venice's empire, but is still at risk on the stormy waters, Cassio prays that "the heavens give him defence against their elements" (44–5).

Fittingly, the word 'elements' is mentioned only four times in the play. The other three are in speeches by Iago. Kneeling alongside Othello, who has just vowed a course of vengeance as unfaltering as the "icy current" of the Pontic sea (he has a penchant for expressing himself in hydraulic language,[15] this man who will stifle the fire of Desdemona's life, putting out the light he cannot "relume"), Iago invokes all the stuff of heaven and earth in ratification of his own pledge:

Witness, you ever-burning lights above,
You elements that clip us round about,
Witness that here Iago doth give up
The excellency of his wit, hand, heart,
To wrong'd Othello's service.

(3.3.470–4)

His once referring to Montano and such as "the very elements of this warlike isle" (2.3.53) serves to translate the question of 'basic constituents' into the political realm. However it is his use of the term in reference to Desdemona that is most pregnant with implications, given certain subsequent speeches. It comes in the soliloquy which follows his persuading Cassio to employ Desdemona as mediator with Othello:

And what's he then, that says I play the villain,
When this advice is free I give, and honest,
Probal to thinking, and indeed the course
To win the Moor again? For 'tis most easy
The inclining Desdemona to subdue,
In any honest suit; she's fram'd as fruitful
As the free elements.

(2.3.327–33)

It is his application of 'the elements' to the psychic make-up of Desdemona that provides an Ariadne's thread for exploring the underlying structure of this tragedy.

For this purpose, we must begin at the end, with the play's cataclysmic final scene. Emilia has forced her way into the presence of Othello and the dying Desdemona, whose last words attempt to exonerate him of her murder. Othello, however, repudiates both her and her ultimate act of love:

> She's like a liar gone to burning hell,
> 'Twas I that kill'd her.
> *Emilia:* O, the more angel she,
> And you the blacker devil!
> *Othello:* She turn'd to folly, and she was a whore.
> *Emilia:* Thou dost belie her, and thou art a devil.
> *Othello:* She was false as water.
> *Emilia:* Thou as rash as fire,
> To say she was false: O, she was heavenly true!
> (5.2.130–6)

False as water (presumably referring to her woman's tears; cf. 4.1.240–1), rash as fire (cf. 1.1.76). When Iago arrives with Montano and Gratiano, and the truth about his role in precipitating the disaster begins to emerge, he commands his wife, "Zounds, hold your peace." But Emilia refuses: "'Twill out it will: I hold my peace, sir, no, / I'll be in speaking, liberal as the air" (219–21).[16] False as water, Rash as fire, Liberal as the air. What then of earth? Alas, all four mentions of 'earth' refer to the planet, not the stuff of which it is mostly made. What then about common synonyms for this stuff? The possibility is quickly confirmed. Emilia, rejecting Othello's pathetic rationalizing of his action, berates him with "O gull, O dolt, as ignorant as dirt" (164–5).

False as Water, Rash as Fire, Liberal as the Air, Ignorant as Dirt. Are not these psychic correspondents the 'elements' of character that figure most importantly in this tragedy? And are they not the very constituents out of which Othello's jealousy is compounded? Might they also be the common human qualities that most dangerously compromise the instrumental rationality upon which the modern commercial republic is founded?

Falseness, as opposed to honesty, fidelity, truthfulness, openness, being what one seems – of which so much is made in this play, especially by its most duplicitous character: "Men should be what they seem, / Or those that be not, would they might seem none!" (3.3.130–1). Iago is such a skilful deceiver that not even his wife suspects that he is other than the blunt, honest soldier he is supposed to be (3.3.3–4, 5.2.170–6; cf. 2.3.209–15, 237–9, 3.3.121–8, 5.1.31–3). Yet, at the very outset Iago declares to his walking purse, the endlessly gullible Roderigo, a sovereign contempt for "honest knaves" and an admiration for those who, merely "trimm'd in forms, and visages of duty, / Keep yet their hearts attending on themselves." He professes himself likewise: "not I for love and duty, / But seeming so, for my peculiar end" (1.1.49–60). Ironically, he is as good as his word here. Knowing the Moor to have "a free and open nature ... that thinks men honest that but seems to be so," he proceeds to lead him "by the nose, as asses are" (1.3.397–400; cf. 1.1.47, 2.1.304). As is normally the case when a person is especially skilled at something, Iago positively enjoys staging the destruction of his victims. But he is not the only deceiver in this play. All the principal characters tell lies at some point. Cassio is considerably less than forthright with Bianca. Desdemona lies to Othello about losing the handkerchief (3.4.81). More importantly, as Iago rightly observes and Othello agrees, "She did deceive her father, marrying you" (3.3.210; cf.1.3.293). Emilia lies benignly to Othello about Cassio and Desdemona never having whispered nor been left alone together (4.2.1–10; cf. 2.1.168, 3.1.52–6); and despite knowing the deep distress it is causing her mistress, perniciously lies about not knowing what happened to the handkerchief (3.4.20). Imagine how differently things would have developed had Emilia come clean at this point, thereby exonerating Desdemona and Cassio while implicating Iago.[17] Othello also lies. Apart from the embroidered account of his past life (as if someone descended "of royal siege" would have been consigned to the army since age seven, been captured and sold into slavery rather than ransomed, much less himself seen "men whose heads do grow beneath their shoulders";[18] 1.2.21–2; 1.3.83, 137–45), he lies to Desdemona about the origin of the handerchief he gave her (see 5.2.215–18) and privately admits lying about his jealous condition ("O, hardness to dissemble!" 3.4.30). The extent that deception pervades the play is thrown into relief by the frequency with which the characters speak of honesty. The words 'honest' or 'honesty' occur no less than fifty-two times (far more than in any other of Shakespeare's plays) and roughly three times as often as the word 'false.' A high proportion of the uses have to do with sexual fidelity.

Rashness, as opposed to patience, to waiting upon "dilatory time." The action *of* the play proceeds with its oft-noted rapidity largely because of impatience on the part of so many *in* the play. The elopement with which the play begins manifests impatience on the part of either Othello or Desdemona, or both. Rather than undertake the long, perhaps uncertain, but by no means impossible 'wooing' of Brabantio (by Othello's own testimony, "Her father lov'd me, oft invited me, still question'd me the story of my life"; 1.3.128–9), Othello exploits Venice's military emergency to confront the old father with a fait accompli; (see 1.1.147–53, 1.2.36–47; 1.3.44–9, 221–8). The Duke, who is clearly impatient with anything causing a delay in Othello's attending to the Republic's business (whose "affairs cry haste, and speed must answer" 1.3.276–7), nonetheless counsels Brabantio, "What cannot be preserv'd when fortune takes, / Patience her injury a mockery makes" (206–7). Othello is content to leave his bride behind, asking only that suitable accommodation be provided her. When the Duke suggests her father and he refuses, only then does Othello also decline the suggestion, as does Desdemona: "I would not there reside, / To put my father in impatient thoughts" (236–42). 'Impatient Thoughts': a fitting title for the catastrophe that ensues. Desdemona herself is impatient to enjoy the marriage she has sacrificed so much for, and begs leave to accompany her husband: "let me go with him" (259). Were it not for her importuning, the tragic events on Cyprus would never have taken place. Belatedly, Othello seconds her plea, but – interestingly – does *not* take her with *him*. Instead, he consigns her conveyance to the ship bringing the officer he chooses to leave behind (285). This Othello, whose precipitous descent into insane jealousy is propelled by impatience as he leaps from one rash judgment to another[19] – who is indeed a "rash and most unfortunate man" in everything *else* concerning Desdemona (5.2.284) – proves himself strangely patient as to enjoying the "fruits" of his "purchase." When the Duke tells Othello he "must hence tonight," Desdemona responds with evident dismay ("To*night*, my lord?"), but Othello answers, "With all my heart" – indeed, he allows himself "but an hour" to spend with her along with getting ready for a hasty departure of uncertain duration, insisting "we must obey the time" (1.3.277–8, 298–300; cf. 2.3.9–16, 241–5). Might there be a connection between the 'patience' he shows in delaying the consummation of his marriage and the rashness with which he plunges into an all-consuming jealousy? Once Iago has successfully planted the evil seed in such fertile soil, he can counsel patience, knowing it will have the opposite effect: "My lord, I would I might entreat your honour / To scan this thing no further, leave it to time" (3.3.248–9). All too soon, Othello is meditating revenge: "O, blood, Iago, blood!" To this Iago falsely pleads, "Patience I say, your mind perhaps may change" (458–9). The effect intended, of course, is to solidify Othello's commitment, thereby hastening him to immediate action – just as it does.

Then there is Cassio. Iago is right about him, at least when he is inflamed by liquor: "Sir, he is rash, and very sudden in choler" (2.1.267; see also 2.3.287–8). Iago easily exploits the rashness of Cassio's fiery temper to get him cashiered, then as readily preys upon his impatience to be restored to Othello's good favour. Though assured by Desdemona that Othello will remain estranged no longer than politically required, Cassio worries:

Ay, but, lady
The policy may either last so long,
Or feed upon such nice and wat'rish diet,
Or breed itself so out of circumstance,
That I being absent, and my place supplied,
My general will forget my love and service.
(3.3.13–18)

Cassio's anxiety is effectively communicated to Desdemona, who assures him, "my lord will never rest, / I'll watch him tame, and talk him out of patience" (22–3). Sure enough, scarce moments later she begins her imprudent campaign of nagging and wheedling for Cassio's immediate rehabilitation, oblivious to the impropriety of her intervening, much less to any suspicions it might arouse.[20] Later, Iago, working all three principals like marionettes, exhorts Cassio to renew suing Desdemona. Chaffing under the uncertainty of his situation, Cassio complies, confessing to her "I would not be delay'd" (3.4.111). Desdemona can offer him no comfort, finding herself out of favour with her much-changed lord: "you must awhile be patient" (126). Herself in need of both comfort and counsel, she turns to Iago, pleading, "O good Iago, what shall I do to win my lord again?" He advises patience: "I pray you, be content, 'tis but his humour, / The business of state does him offence / ... Go in, and weep not, all things shall be well" (4.2.150–1, 167–73). As for the hapless Roderigo, who apparently lives to be a fool, Iago encourages him with promises of expedition ("So shall you have a shorter journey to your desires." 2.1.272–3), and suppresses his anaemic fits of rebellion with exhortations to patience, preaching him this bit of wisdom:

How poor are they that ha' not patience!
What wound did ever heal, but by degrees?
Thou knowest we work by wit, and not by witchcraft,
And wit depends on dilatory time.
(2.3.360–3)

Perhaps it often does, but the time it takes for Iago's witchcrafty wit to wound Othello's exposed spirit is anything but dilatory.

Liberality, as oppposed to – what, exactly? For the status of liberality, traditionally regarded as a virtue, is rather ambiguous in this text. Whereas we might expect 'liberal' to denote a laudable openness and generosity of nature, of being free with one's possessions, time, effort, and very self, in some contexts (or in some minds) it can connote 'too much so,' as transgressing prudence, decorum, and even decency. Thus, Desdemona playfully disparages Iago for his risqué bantering: "how say you, Cassio, is he not a most profane and liberal counsellor?" (2.1.163–4). Othello, his jealous suspicions activated, plays upon the ambiguity of the term when observing that Desdemona's hand is moist: "This argues fruitfulness, and a liberal heart; / Hot, hot and moist, this hand requires / A sequester from liberty ... / A liberal hand." (3.4.32–42). There are several points worth noting about this speech. 'Fruitful' is the term Iago also used to describe Desdemona, seemingly in what we would regard as a complimentary way ("she's fram'd as fruitful as the free elements"). Moreover, the qualities by which Othello characterizes her hand are not only the sensations indicative of two of these basic elements, fire and water; but according to the metaphysical view of the day, those same qualities imposed together on basic matter are what constitute air.[21] Hence, Desdemona's hot and moist hand is "liberal," like the air in Emilia's analogy ("I'll be in speaking, liberal as the air"). In ascribing liberality to the air, however, it is invested with liberality's ambiguous moral status as well: "The bawdy wind, that kisses all it meets" (4.2.80). While the word 'liberal' (like 'rash') is used only four times, the sometimes synonymous term 'free' is used more generously. Othello alludes to his own liberality as well as Desdemona's in professing his desire "to be free and bounteous of her mind" (1.3.265). And Iago, in praising her to Cassio, observes: "she is so free, so kind, so apt, so blessed a disposition, that she holds it a vice in her goodness not to do more than she is requested" (2.3.310–13). In private, Iago acknowledges something similar to be true of Othello, that he also is "of a free and open nature" (1.3.397). The trust and goodwill typically inherent in such natures, often accompanied by a naïveté about people differently constituted, is precisely what Iago so skilfully exploits, even as he pretends to warn Othello of the danger: "I would not have your free and noble nature / Out of self-bounty be abused" (3.3.203–4).

Ignorance, as opposed to knowledge, or wisdom – especially the wisdom of 'knowing thyself,' the prime requisite to the rational pursuit of true self-interest. Honest Iago early on observes how uncommon such self-knowledge is: "I ha' look'd upon the world for four times seven years, and since I could distinguish between a benefit and an injury, I never found a man who knew how to love himself" (1.3.311–13). Taking him at his word, one wonders whether Iago truly loves *himself*.[22] Be that as it may, it would be difficult to catalogue all of the kinds of ignorance and ways they figure in this play. Probably in no other does what the audience knows, and the characters do not, so draw the former into the action, arousing a wish to intervene with the information that would avert the tragedy it so easily foresees.[23] And, one might add, the efforts of the tragedy's two main victims to inform themselves are invariably misdirected and misconceived. Desdemona pleads with Othello, "Alas, what ignorant sin have I committed?" (4.2.72) None, of course – that is not the knowledge she needs to extricate herself from her troubles. Or none at least that Othello would himself call a sin had he actually learned the truth from his prejudiced investigations, as he wrongly thinks he surely has: that Desdemona is "a subtle whore" and "false as hell" (4.2.21, 40), that Cassio has carnal knowledge of her ("Now do I see 'tis true" 3.3.451), just as he is sure that Iago is "wise" and "full of love and honesty" (3.3.122; 4.1.74).

But it is with respect to self-knowledge that Othello would most justly be characterized "ignorant as dirt." Having deluded himself that his murder of Desdemona is motivated by justice rather than a vengeful jealousy (5.2.1–6, 17, 138–40; see also 4.1.205), he can pose as "an honourable murderer," offering in extenuation of his guilt, "For nought did I in hate, but all in honour" (5.2.295–6). His last speech shows him facing but a small part of the truth behind the tragedy he has brought about, and even that is distorted by his irrepressible desire to romanticize himself:[24]

> When you shall these unlucky deeds relate,
> Speak of them as they are; nothing extenuate,
> Nor set down ought in malice; then must you speak
> Of one that lov'd not wisely, but too well:
> Of one not easily jealous, but being wrought,
> Perplex'd in the extreme.
>
> (342–7)

Jealousy is but one of a family of base qualities that disfigure the human soul. Not surprisingly, the others – spite, envy, resentment – are also at work in this story. Brabantio's warning to Othello, for example, is surely motivated more by spite and resentment than benevolent regard ("Look to her, Moor, have a quick eye to see: / She has deceived her father, may do thee" 1.3.292–3). Indeed, one may have to invoke this entire quartet of misanthropic passions in explaining what energizes Iago's malignity. But the action focuses upon jealousy, and in seeking to explain its arising in Othello's soul *when* it does – the efficient cause, as it were – we can see this as primarily the result of Desdemona's liberality, Iago's falseness, and Othello's own rashness and ignorance. The presence of these same 'elements' in others are also factors, to wit, Cassio's rashness and impatience, and Emilia's falseness, along with Othello's own liberality and Desdemona's own falseness and ignorance of human nature (see 4.3.60–2). Still, their composite effect presumes a soul antecedently disposed to find in "trifles light as air ... confirmations strong as proofs of holy writ," at least where sexual fidelity is in question. Thus, one is directed to the deeper problem of jealousy. For until one understands the natural basis of this passion, one can understand neither why Othello in particular is so easily but so irrationally jealous (personifying this disfigurement for all subsequent time), nor why he – but not only he (3.4.22–7) – *thinks* he is *not*. Ironically, the clue may be found in his very concern that he not be made what he turns out to be: "A fixed figure, for the time of scorn / To point his slow unmoving fingers at" (4.2.54–6). Prepared to bear every sort of *bodily* affliction and privation (49–52; cf. 5.2.278–81), he cannot bear the thought of thus stigmatizing the core of his soul.

Jealousy manifests a lack of confidence in one's own 'lovability,' which is to say, in one's self-worth. For the perfectly confident man, a woman's failing to return his love, or to remain faithful to him, is a prejudicial reflection on her, rendering her to that extent not *worthy* of his love, hence, less loved.[25] Othello attempts to adopt that posture in response to Iago's warning about "the green-ey'd monster":

> Think'st thou I'd make a life of jealousy?
> To follow still the changes of the moon
> With fresh suspicions? No, to be once in doubt,
> Is to be resolv'd ...
>
> Nor from mine own weak merits will I draw
> The smallest fear, or doubt of her revolt,
> For she had eyes, and chose me. No, Iago,
> I'll see before I doubt, when I doubt, prove,
> And on the proof, there is no more but this:
> Away at once with love or jealousy!
> (3.3.181–96)

Later in soliloquy, he still insists that should she prove "haggard," he would "whistle her off, and let her down the wind, to prey at fortune" (3.3.264–7). However, Othello cannot carry through this pledge without its profoundly undercutting his vulnerable sense of his own worth. This is betrayed by his recurring to his race, his rustic manners, and his advancing age in the very midst of trying to persuade himself that his "relief must be to loath her" (271–2). But mere loathing or despising will not suffice him, for he lives in other people's eyes. His self-confidence is fatally dependent on the confidence others have in him, his self-respect based on the respect they show him, on the honour they accord him, on reputation. Iago, knowing his man, steadily works this vein:

> Good name in man and woman's dear, my lord;
> Is the immediate jewel of our souls:
> Who steals my purse, steals trash, 'tis something, nothing,
> 'Twas mine, 'tis his, and has been slave to thousands:
> But he that filches from me my good name
> Robs me of that which not enriches him,
> And makes me poor indeed.
>
> (3.3.159–65)

In short order – remarkably short – Iago has Othello bemoaning what he sees as the intolerable consequence of being cuckolded: "my name, that was as fresh as Dian's visage, is now begrim'd, and black as mine own face: ... I'll not endure it" (392–6). It is his 'name,' his reputation, his honour that matters most to him. That is, honour in the sense of its being *shown* him by others, not a purely internal sense of honour.[26] His tormentor plays upon the distinction between the two senses of the word, and on the imperfect coincidence between the external appearance and the inner reality, observing that "honour is an essence that's not seen, / They have it very oft that have it not" (4.1.16–17).

Iago, by contrast, is a 'materialist' in every sense of the word. Preferring money in his purse, non-material 'essences' – such as honour, loyalty, honesty, generosity, affection – are of no concern to him, since only the perceptible appearances of these spiritual qualities have any utility in his world. Judging from all the evidence we are shown, he lives by the truth about reputation that he provides the distraught Cassio, and not by the eloquent encomium of it that he feeds the receptive Othello. Responding to Cassio's "I ha' lost the immortal part, sir, of myself, and what remains is bestial; my reputation, Iago, my reputation!" Iago mocks surprise:

> As I am an honest man, I thought you had receiv'd some bodily wound, there is more offense in that than in reputation: reputation is an idle and most false imposition, oft got without merit, and lost without deserving. You have lost no reputation at all, unless you repute yourself such a loser. (2.3.258–63)

The extent to which Iago appreciates that what actually motivates him is some equally non-material 'essence' of his soul – some malice-inducing compound of envy, resentment, spite, and jealousy, imparting a destructive preference to his curiosity and will to power – is unclear.[27]

What are we meant to conclude from this elaborate interplay that Shakespeare has fashioned between the material elements of the human body and the spiritual elements of the human soul, with blood being treated as the mysterious medium of communication between these two radically different constituents of our existence, body and soul?[28] As the play so forcefully reminds us, there is a world of difference between detecting and identifying the various forms of *matter* – all the directly perceptible stuff of which things are made: the glossy silk of a handkerchief, the tempered steel of a Spanish blade, the rough quarried granite of a fortress, the smooth alabaster of some monument, the oak ribs of a man-o'-war, the fermented grapes of wine, the gold of a purse full of crusadoes, the brass of a housewife's skillet, the pitch of birdlime – and rightly determining the mutable qualities of character and states of *soul*: probity, justness, respect, love, confidence, gratitude, goodwill, piety, patriotism, and dozens of other such things, as well as their opposites. Whereas recognition of the one is a matter of direct observation, subject to 'ocular proof,' discerning the other relies far more on our fallible powers of interpretation and judgment. Hence, the latter is far more subject to external influences, especially what has rightly been dubbed 'the power of suggestion' – a power as immaterial as the means it employs: the *intelligibility* of speech. Since the medium transmitting this power is (mainly) air-borne sound, the bodily sense of greater importance, at least in this tragedy, is not that of sight (upon which Othello reposes such faith), but of hearing. Fittingly, Iago – a "busy and insinuating rogue" nonpareil (4.2.133), one whose use of insinuation shows it to be far more effective than direct suggestion – refers to audition in the first line he speaks: "'Sblood, but you will not hear me." The hearing of intelligible speech is the basis of both Othello's charm and Iago's poison. Its importance is subtly emphasized by the conversations Othello witnesses but cannot hear, and so imagines in accordance with what Iago had led him to expect (4.1.74–87). Had he actually heard and thereby truly known what passed between Cassio and Iago or Cassio and Bianca (4.1.100–57), the effect would have been the very opposite of what Iago intended.

Othello can with his own eyes inspect the fortifications on Cyprus, seeing all there is to see, understanding what he sees more-or-less immediately, and appraising it according to the adequacy of his own military expertise (3.2.3–6). That is a straightforward matter compared with the necessity of interpreting what he sees of Cassio's embarrassed departure from his soliciting Desdemona, or the significance of Desdemona's assiduous importuning on Cassio's behalf – assessments all too open to bias from Iago's prejudicial insinuations (3.3.35–41, 249–56). These misinterpreted episodes, in turn, are the tainted ingredients upon which Othello's passion-warped power of synoptic judgment assesses the honesty and loyalty of both his lieutenant and his wife. Othello can feel Desdemona's moist, warm hand (3.4.30–9), taste her lips (3.3.347), smell her balmy breath (5.2.16; cf. 4.2.69–70), hear her faltering voice (120), see her fair skin and charming eyes (5.1.35, 5.2.4–5). But his soul yearns for what in the nature of things cannot be supplied:

comparable "proof" of her fidelity. For although it is framed as a demand for proof of *in*fidelity (3.3.365–6) – something in principle possible, difficult as it may be in practice to catch them in the very act of 'bolstering' – what Othello actually seeks is perfect assurance that Desdemona is exclusively his, body and soul, body chaste because soul faithful. And this, strictly speaking, is *not* possible. For no quantity of failures to prove infidelity amounts to a proof of fidelity.

Moreover, the inductive implication such failures might otherwise have is compromised by the presumption that strenuous efforts are taken to conceal infidelity, that (as elsewhere) "In Venice they do let God see the pranks / They dare not show their husbands" (3.3.206–7). Thus, Othello's interrogation of Emilia ("Have you seen nothing, then?" Emil: "Nor ever heard, nor ever did suspect"), and her emphatic endorsement of Desdemona's character ("I durst, my lord, to wager she is honest, / Lay down my soul at stake ..."), merely deepens his suspicions:

> She says enough, yet she's a simple bawd
> That cannot say as much: this is a subtle whore
> A closet, lock and key, of villainous secrets,
> And yet she'll kneel and pray, I ha' seen her do it.
> (4.2.20–3)

While the problem Othello is grappling with has a peculiar complexity and salience for men and women, it shares essential features with all the many situations in which we have reason to suspect people may not care to, or dare to, express the truth of what they think and feel, and instead manipulate appearances to the contrary. Inspiring the black irony of Iago's feigned reluctance to allow Othello access to what he disarmingly admits is a dirty mind (3.3.150–2), and "give the worst of thought the worst of word," are several truths of which any competent adult is at least tacitly aware:

> Good my lord, pardon me;
> Though I am bound to every act of duty,
> I am not bound to that all slaves are free to;
> Utter my thoughts? Why, say they are vile and false:
> As where's that palace, whereinto foul things
> Sometimes intrude not? who has a breast so pure,
> But some uncleanly apprehensions
> Keep leets and law-days, and in session sit
> With meditations lawful?
> (3.3.137–45)

Iago's taunting retort to Othello's insistence ("By heaven, I'll know thy thought") simply affirms the inherent privacy of the human mind: "You cannot, if my heart were in your hand, / Nor shall not, whilst 'tis in my custody" (167–8). The security of this personal citadel depends solely upon the control one exercises over whatever one outwardly expresses by word or demeanour – that is, upon a will power Othello has never cultivated, but which is the very cornerstone of Iago's character. As he assures the obtuse Roderigo at the play's beginning:

> Heaven is my judge, not I for love and duty,
> But seeming so, for my peculiar end.
> For when my outward action does demonstrate
> The native act, and figure of my heart,
> In complement extern, 'tis not long after,
> But I will wear my heart upon my sleeve,
> For doves to peck at: I am not what I am.
> (1.1.59–65)[29]

He maintains this credo to the very end. When his guilt is at last discovered, and the disconsolate Othello requests Cassio that he "demand that demi-devil / Why he hath thus ensnar'd my soul and body," Iago remains defiant: "Demand me nothing, what you know, you know, / From this time forth I never will speak word" (5.2.302–5). 'Why *hath* he?' we too want to ask. Shakespeare, as silent here as his Iago, leaves it for us to puzzle out ourselves.

To understand either this play or the world it reflects, one must grant that the interiority of a human soul – not only the phenomena of consciousness, but whatever hopes and fears may lie and stir beneath the level of awareness – is at least as real and causative as the body it invests.[30] The change that overcomes Othello, transforming devoted love into vengeful hate, is not in the first instance a change in his material make-up, caused by (say) a blow on the head, or something he ate. It proceeds from a change in his understanding, in how his *mind* 'sees' things. The presumption that this, in turn, is nothing but a mechanical event, fully explicable in terms of matter and its motions, is the merest prejudice, of which there neither is nor could be any possible proof. The perceptual evidence of Cassio's slinking away remains constant (3.3.30–3), but we watch Othello's interpretation of it change from simple curiosity to deep suspicion. To be sure, Iago's diabolical psychology is instrumental in accomplishing this transformation.[31] However, the resulting 'subjective' state of Othello's mind is as much a part of the reality of this tragedy as are the 'objective' circumstances about which he is so pathetically mistaken. For even were one dogmatically convinced that his consciousness is somehow but an epiphenomenal 'effect' of material causes in the brain, the consciousness itself is not something material, any more than is the magnetic field of a lodestone or the gravitational force of a planet (cf. 2.3.173; 5.2.110–12). The 'fruitfulness' of Desdemona that Iago speaks of, likening it to the "free elements" of material nature, refers to the constituents of her soul, whatever in her psychic make-up inclines her to respond favourably to "any honest suit." After all, the *non*-material status of these psychic elements is the point of resorting to the analogy, whether or not Iago realizes the full implication of his own words. The belief that liberality or honesty in character, or rashness in temperament, is *caused* by peculiar configurations of 'matter' – be it earth, air, fire, and water; or protons, neutrons, and electrons – could only be an article of the Materialist Faith; there is not a shred of direct evidence for it, either in Shakespeare's world or ours. The *grounds* of the 'reputations' that so concern both Cassio and Othello, and that figure so prominently in the 'meritocracy' of a commercial republic (see 1.1.35–7), are criteria and preferences and beliefs (including prejudices) in the *minds* of other people. And these assessments are subject to change, as Lodovico's opinion of Othello changes in consequence of witnessing his violent treatment of Desdemona ("Is this the noble Moor, whom our full senate / Call all in all sufficient? This the noble nature, / Whom passion could not shake?" 4.1.260–2). If, in turn, these mental phenomena somehow become physically manifested in people's brains (as I presume they do), the relationship between mind and matter cannot be a one-way street.

When one reflects sufficiently upon such phenomena, as time and again *Othello* provides occasion to do, one comes to see why a strictly materialistic ontology can never be adequate, even setting aside the perplexities that matter itself and its causal efficacy gives rise to. Nor, if the lessons of Shakespeare's Venetian plays are sound, can any 'materialistic' theory of political practice be other than superficial.[32] Can one simply discount the possibility, or even the likelihood, that Shakespeare, having expressly established certain psychic correlates of the material elements – the rashness and ignorance, falseness and liberality upon which he makes this tragedy turn – did not *intend* that a thoughtful reader do this very thing: reflect upon the metaphysical mysteries posed by the reciprocal communication between these radically different, apparently irreducible modes of being, body and mind, whose *interaction* is as incomprehensible as it is undeniable? And thereby come to appreciate that of all the metaphysical problems to which one may direct one's mind, the most bewildering is incarnate in one's very existence, in being an embodied soul?

THE TRUE TEST OF A WISE POET: *THE WINTER'S TALE*

The first quality that strikes an innocent viewer or reader of *The Winter's Tale* is apt to be this: the radically different tone and temper of the first half of the play from that of the second, and a consequent feeling of perplexity about the whole of it – that it is, to say the least, a rather strange play. As a recent editor of the text, having reviewed scholarly opinion, observed: "It has long been noted that the play ... could be divided into two parts, and references to its 'first' and 'second' parts are common" – that, in fact, "It has even been described as consisting of two 'plays.'" Summing up the history of its criticism, he concludes, "There used to be almost general agreement that the structure was clumsy, the play loosely, even carelessly, put together, and the opinion is still held, although the quite contrary, and surely correct view, that the play is a masterpiece of skillful construction, is gaining ground."[33] The bases upon which critics have argued for this latter assessment, however, are quite various, and may not all be compatible with one another. Reliance upon allegorical and symbolic interpretation is prominent among defenders of the play; but whereas some regard it as classical or pagan in its inspiration (e.g., as a reworking of the Demeter–Persephone myth), others emphasize its implicit ratification of Christian doctrine.

It is easy to see how various scholars have found sufficient evidence for quite divergent views. The play is a cunning synthesis of disparate elements, and its author may have had more than one purpose in so very carefully crafting his story. He may, for that matter, be telling more than one story. The dramatic context of the play is ostensibly pagan – the most famous shrine of Antiquity, the Delphic Oracle,[34] being crucial to the plot – and most of the characters' names are fittingly of classical origin. But there is also a plenitude of allusions to the Christian experience: the doctrine of Original Sin (1.2.73–5; see also 178), and of the forgiveness of sins (3.3.119–20); references to "churchyards" (2.1.30), to the persecution of heretics (2.3.114–15), psalm-singing puritans (4.3.44), the Prodigal Son (93–4), and to the sale of "hallowed" trinkets (4.4.602–3); the Clown acts the 'good Samaritan' to the feigning Autolycus (4.3.54ff); and, of course, there is the 'death' and 'resurrection' of Hermione, with Paulina as a Saint Paul through whose mediation the repentant Leontes is 'reborn.' I am persuaded that a meticulously detailed Christian allegory provides one structural dimension of the play, though I have nothing of consequence to say about that.[35] However, I am convinced that there is also a Platonic inspiration behind *The Winter's Tale* – indeed, that herein lies the explanation for the play's peculiar bifold character – and the balance of my remarks will be confined to expounding this thesis. It requires a brief digression.

The most famous philosophical text on love is Plato's *Symposium*. The dramatic setting of this dialogue is quite complex, being the recounting through a series of intermediaries of a dinner party hosted by a famous young tragedian, Agathon, and given in honour of his gaining a victory at Athen's Lenaeon festival with his first tragedy.[36] The banquet is attended by several of Athens's most renowned residents, including the greatest of its comic poets, Aristophanes, and the founder of political philosophy, Sokrates. Other notables include Phaedrus, a connoisseur of rhetoric and traditional stories (*mythoi*); Pausanias, an amateur sociologist of law; and Eryximachus, a physician wonderfully enamoured (as doctors so typically are) of the power of medicine and 'physiological' explanations. The atmosphere throughout the evening is one of good humour, with much witty bantering and teasing, comic trickery and horseplay; Sokrates in particular is here shown at his most urbane. After finishing their meal, the host and his invited guests agree to refrain from heavy drinking – several of them still suffering the effects of the previous day's festivities – and instead to entertain each other with speeches in praise of the God of Love: *Erōs*. Not surprisingly, the succession of encomia that result reflect the personae and perspectives and preferences of the respective encomiasts (cf. *Laws* 637d–650b). For example, Sokrates' contribution is in the form of his recounting a dialogue (or dialogues) he claims to have had with an otherwise unknown woman, "Diotima of Mantineia," whom he credits with having taught him *erotika* (201d) – the one and only thing in which he admits being knowledgeable (177e). At the very moment when this program is completed (all the invited celebrants having taken their turn), the party is crashed by Athens's most problematic politician, the notoriously erotic and wonderfully talented warrior–demogogue, Alkibiades. Himself apparently quite inebriated, and dissatisfied with the comparative sobriety of the others – a 'sym-posium' is, after all, literally a 'drinking-together' – he promptly appoints himself their dictator with respect to drinking, thereby overturning the earlier democratic resolution in favour of moderation; no one protests (213e). Invited to add his contribution in praise of *Erōs*, he refuses, pleading the impossibility of his praising anyone but Sokrates, and so he offers to do that instead. His encomium, however, turns out to be but another variation on the proposed theme in that his appraisal focuses upon the philosopher's peculiar kind of erotic nature. Within moments of Alkibiades' concluding, more unruly revellers arrive uninvited, and what was originally a genteel, decorous gathering soon dissolves into drunken disorder. In all, then, the dialogue comprises seven speeches offering seven distinct perspectives on *erōs*, with Aristophanes' comic portrayal of 'being in love' happening to be the central one (his would have been the third, but an apparent 'chance' case of hiccups caused his speaking out of order).

The account of all this – upon which we eavesdrop – is presented by an enthusiastic young admirer of old Sokrates named Apollodorus ('Gift of Apollo') to some unnamed companions who request it of him. He prefaces his response by informing them that he happens to be well prepared to comply, as only the day before yesterday he had done the same for another interested solicitor named

Glaukon ('Gleaming' or 'Brilliant'), who had heard about this feast of erotic speeches from a certain Phoenix. Glaukon, however, was confused as to when the illustrious gathering took place, thinking it to have been quite recent. Apollodorus had to clarify for him that it was many years ago, when he and Glaukon were but boys.[37] Hence, he was not himself an eyewitness to the events of that distant evening. Nor did he get his account directly from Sokrates, although he says the philosopher subsequently confirmed certain details. Rather, Apollodorus' original source was the same person who told Phoenix, namely, a little man called Aristodemus ('Best of the People') who was at that time most enamoured of Sokrates, even going about barefooted in imitation of him. An unusually spruce Sokrates had chanced to meet Aristodemus on the way to Agathon's house, and spontaneously invited his scruffy little disciple to accompany him to the poet's select gathering. Thus it happened that Aristodemus was present, and some account of the evening preserved. But only incompletely: some speeches he simply could not remember well enough to recount at all (180c); of the other speeches, he could not remember everything that was said, nor in turn does Apollodorus remember all he was told (178a; cf. 201d); and later, after the heavy drinking began, Aristodemus fell asleep (223b–c). Perhaps this incompleteness in our account is indicative of something important about *erōs* itself (cf. 192e–193a). Be that as it may, when Aristodemus finally awoke, everyone else had either left or was sleeping, except Agathon, Aristophanes, and Sokrates. The tragedian, the comedian, and the philosopher were sharing a large cup of wine and discussing. Aristodemus, having missed the beginning of their conversation and being still somewhat dazed from sleep and drink, either did not grasp or could not remember much of what was said: "However, the main point, he said, was that Sokrates was compelling them to agree that the same man should know [*epistasthai*] how to make a comedy and a tragedy, and that he who is a tragic poet by art [*technē*] is also a comic poet" (223d).

This "main point" is the more interesting in that it appears diametrically opposed to what Plato has Sokrates argue in his *Republic* (albeit to a very different kind of interlocutor): "Nor even in two imitations that seem to be like each other, such as making a comedy and a tragedy, are the same [men] capable of imitating [both] well at the same time [*hama*]" (395a). It is worth noting, however, that the respective theses Sokrates argues in these two dialogues are not really contradictory, as one claim is prescriptive and the other descriptive. Their deceptive compatibility nicely illustrates the especially close and complementary relationship between these two dialogues, *Symposium* and *Republic*, as is indicated by a number of dramatic features. Both begin with accounts of their respective narrators being "caught sight of from afar" (*kattadōn ... porrōthen*) as each was travelling up to the city proper from one of its coastal ports (Apollodorus from the older Phalerum, Sokrates from the newer Piraeus). Sokrates tells us this happened "yesterday"; Apollodorus, "the day before yesterday" – perhaps indicating some sort of priority with respect to each dialogue's theme, that *erōs* is in some sense 'prior' to justice. In each case, the narrator travels with someone named Glaukon. Both offer accounts of gatherings that last all night, concluding the next morning. But the symmetrical *contrasts* between the two dialogues are as indicative of their relationship as are their similarities. The *Symposium* begins with the participants unanimously resolving that their evening not become a drinking bout, and instead be devoted to conversing with each other about love (176e); subsequently, however, this agreement is quite openly repudiated, and the party turns into a drunken rout. The *Republic* begins with a resolution to eat, drink, and make merry all night on the town (328a), but this agreement in words is silently supplanted by one in deed to remain at home, soberly, hungrily, discussing that question of questions, justice (cf. 450a). We are told that by the end of Agathon's symposium, everyone except Sokrates had either left or fallen asleep. So far as we know, apart from old Kephalos, who departs before the discussion is well under way, none of the rest of those gathered at his house either leaves or sleeps (331d; cf. 344d).

It is most important to appreciate, however, that even if our report of the symposiasts were complete to the last detail, the account of *erōs* provided by that dialogue would remain radically incomplete precisely because they are all enjoined to make speeches in *praise* of love. That is, staying within the bounds of legitimate eulogizing that Sokrates specifies, namely, confining oneself to the truth (as he complains the preceding speakers did not), a *eulogy* does not call for the *whole* truth – as the philosopher tacitly acknowledges. According to him, one selects for the purpose the most beautiful parts of the truth and arranges them in the seemliest manner (198d). No wonder, then, that it is mainly the light, attractive, creative, intoxicating side of *erōs* which is presented in Plato's *Symposium*. What one learns there must be mated with the far more sobering treatment it receives in his *Republic*, which tends to emphasize the dangerous and destructive side of *erōs*, showing it to be the principal threat to reason and justice in both the polity and the individual human soul – that the daimōn, *Erōs*, is a tyrannical power which, left unbridled, is the cause of tyranny in both public and private life (571a–580a).[38]

One more point of comparison: Plato's *Republic*, his just appraisal of the just life, is set in summer (see 350d); whereas his *Symposium*, his lovely and loving account of love, takes place in the winter – it is, one might say, his 'winter's tale.'[39]

Sokrates would have had no difficulty persuading Shakespeare of his "main point": that a poet who is truly knowledgeable and possessed of a genuine dramatic art should be able to make both comedies and tragedies. This and more Shakespeare had himself amply proven several times over. Thus, he might well have imagined that an even finer test of a philosophical poet – a still greater challenge for his own unique powers – would consist of working in both imitative modes *hama*: "at the same time." That is, attempt to make a single play that is half tragedy and half comedy, and yet is both dramatically effective and intellectually coherent.[40] Might he, moreover, have chosen for unifying themes the very same ones as structured the dialogues whence he could have come by his inspiration: erotic love and justice? Certainly it would be difficult to find two topics of more profound or pervasive importance, or ones more intimately connected. *Erōs* in its various manifestations would seem the key to understanding human nature, if not Nature as a whole, being (as 'Diotima' teaches) the immanent force propelling life itself. Whereas the idea of *justice* is of necessity architectonic, being that in light of which human life is rightly structured and ordered, everything allotted its proper place and everyone treated as they deserve. So Shakespeare wrote *The Winter's Tale*, the first half a tragedy showing the dark side of *erōs* perverting justice, the second half a comedy with love benign and justice triumphant.

The first half of the play (acts 1 through 3) shares the perspective on erotic love of Plato's *Republic*: that it is a constant threat to justice, both in the city and the man. Of the eleven references to justice in the play, ten are in this first half – as is the only mention of injustice, which conveniently marks the turning point in the drama (3.2.147); if one includes 'justified,' there are two allusions to justice within the play's first nine lines. We are invited to ponder why and how the passionate form of love (*erōs*), so intensely particular and selfish, hence naturally possessive of the beauty that attracts it, has the power to uglify as well as beautify the lover. And how it can overwhelm and destroy the generous, selfless form of love (*philia*) that animates friendship, such as Camillo and Archidamus attest has existed between their respective princes since childhood (1.1.21–34).[41] Once his jealousy is activated, King Leontes – who, to judge by the qualities of those who admire and serve him, was a good ruler, husband, father, and friend – becomes instantly suspicious and angry towards anyone, including trusted advisers of long standing (1.2.235ff), who so much as questions his judgments or wishes. Distorting all of his perceptions and reasonings, inspiring imaginary faults and offences, jealousy transforms Leontes' affection for both his wife and his lifelong friend to deadly hate.

The possibility that such a radical reversal of feelings and evaluations could occur almost instantaneously – a sort of '*gestalt* switch' of the whole soul – and be triggered by words and actions seemingly so harmless, must be basic to what Shakespeare would have us recognize about erotic love and its relation to reason and judgment (Leontes' jealousy is subsequently quelled as quickly as it was aroused, resulting in still another psychic revolution).[42] Doubts of Hermione's fidelity having taken root, even his estimation of young Mamillius, his only son and heir to the throne, is tainted (1.2.126ff; 208–11, 330–1) – and the future of the polity to that extent endangered (1.1.34–40; 1.2.335–41; 5.1.23–34). Meanwhile, as this jealousy increasingly tyrannizes Leontes' soul, his spiritual isolation deepens, and he betrays signs of metamorphizing from a just king into a wilful tyrant: ordering the covert assassination of his friend and guest (1.2.312ff); summarily imprisoning his queen and forbidding her access to their son, while declaring "guilty" anyone who would dare speak in her defence (2.1.59–60, 103–5); renouncing any need to be advised, claiming for himself the "prerogative" to be ruled by the strong impulses of his own "natural goodness" (161–70); staging a public trial in which he clearly intends his queen to be found guilty, while audaciously proclaiming, "Let us be clear'd / Of being tyrannous, since we so openly / Proceed in justice" (3.2.4–6). Paulina is the first to speak of "his tyrannous passion" (2.3.28), and confronts him with:

> I'll not call you tyrant;
> But this most cruel usage of your queen –
> Not able to produce more accusation
> Than your own weak-hing'd fancy – something savours
> Of tyranny, and will ignoble make you,
> Yea, scandalous to the world.
>
> (115–20)

At her trial, Hermione also implies he is acting tyrannically (3.2.30–2), concluding her defence with "if I shall be condemn'd / Upon surmises, all proofs sleeping else / But what your jealousies awake, I tell you / 'Tis rigour and not law" (111–14). However, it remains for the Oracle of Delphi to declare flatly, "Leontes [is] a jealous tyrant" (133).

In short, Leontes' soul is profoundly sickened, and his view of the entire world jaundiced (see 1.2.198–207), by this erotic disease called jealousy. For so Shakespeare treats it, perhaps taking his cue from Dr Eryximachus's account of *erōs* in Plato's *Symposium*, that love has a "double" nature, that "one love presides over the healthy state, and another over the sickly" (186b). In any case, it is in terms of illness that everyone affected speaks of it. Leontes himself complains of a tremor of the heart and an "infection of [his] brain" (1.2.110, 145), and laments, "Physic for't there's none" (200). He also refers to Hermione as "infected" (305), which is the term she uses to characterize her own treatment: "like one infectious" (3.2.97–8). Camillo urges Leontes, "Good my lord, be cur'd / Of this diseas'd opinion" (1.2.296–7), and later warns Polixenes:

There is a sickness
Which puts some of us in distemper, but
I cannot name the disease, and it is caught
Of you, that yet are well.
(384–7)

When Paulina forces her way into the King's presence, she professes herself his "physician," insisting that she comes "with words as medicinal as true, / Honest, as either, to purge him of that humour / That presses him from sleep" (2.3.37–9, 54). Unfortunately, it takes much stronger medicine than Paulina brings (the despised baby Perdita) to cure Leontes: nothing less than the death of his beloved son, heir of his life and throne, surrogate for immortality.[43]

Fortunately, the King is curable. Nor was he ever wholly tyrannical. His willingness to submit his judgment to the oracle – even while claiming it is only to "Give rest to th' minds of others" (2.1.189–93) – bespeaks his continuing respect for something higher than his own will. And though he threatens punishment for anyone who takes the queen's part, he tolerates the several lords of his court who do, and moreover endures some strong criticism from them, responding with nothing worse than expressions of contempt for their views (126–68). When Paulina charges that his treatment of the Queen "savours of tyranny," he rightly responds, "Were I a tyrant, / Where were her [Paulina's] life? she durst not call me so, / If she did know me one" (2.3.121–3). Leontes is no rival to Agathocles, the ancient Sicilian tyrant endorsed by Machiavelli for his effective use of cruelty.[44]

A few concluding observations about this first half: The very mention of the Oracle at Delphi brings to mind Sokrates, inasmuch as the pronouncement which became by far its most famous concerned his 'wisdom': that no one was wiser. This utterance he claimed to have found so puzzling as to make its investigation the basis of his life, at least according to his ironic *Apology*, that timeless statement of the relationship between the Philosopher and the Polity (21a ff). Second, the presiding deity of Leontes' Sicily is Apollo, as his consultation of the Delphic Oracle indicates (cf. 2.3.199; 3.2.115–18, 146). Recall, the accounts of love we are provided in Plato's *Symposium* come courtesy of Apollo, 'Gift of Apollo' (*Apollodoros*) being our narrator. Apollo is also the ruling deity of the city that Sokrates 'makes' (*poiēsei*) in Plato's *Republic* (427b-c). And (third), prior to his leading his young friends in that making of a 'city in *logos*' wherein they will search for what justice essentially is, Sokrates explains his rationale by means of an image that involves reading the same message, one writ large and one small (368d). Interestingly, Paulina uses a similar image in arguing for the just recognition that Perdita is indeed Leontes' legitimate daughter: "Behold, my lords, / Although the print be little, the whole matter / and copy of the father" (2.3.97–

9). That the claimed resemblance is apparently false (Perdita turns out to look like her mother; cf. 5.1.226–7; 5.2.36–7) need not affect our interest in the rhetorical figure Shakespeare here provides Paulina. A final point: one might say that this first half of the play justifies the concern for managing *erōs* that is evident throughout the *Republic*, while the second half shows why the comical solution of familial communism (outlined in its Book V) would inevitably fail. *Erōs* will not submit to management according to the rational formulae of passionless mathematics (cf. 458d, 546a–547a).

The second half of the play, expressly set apart from the first by personified Time proclaiming that a "wide gap" of sixteen years separates the events previously portrayed from those we are now to witness, shows a very different view of love in relation to justice. Thoroughly pervaded by a pastoral spirit of romance, it is apt to remind one of the praise of *erōs* in Plato's *Symposium*, especially Agathon's, with his emphasis on love's being young and beautiful as evidenced by its decided preference for the young and beautiful, fleeing (!) from what is old and faded (195a–b); and that as love is itself soft and tender and supple, it dwells within and amid whatever is likewise, such as souls and fragrant, blooming flowers (195c–196b); that love's ways are non-violent, commanding everyone willingly through its being the source of the strongest pleasure (196c); and that love is a poet of such wisdom that he inspires poetry and song in all those he touches (196d–e).[45]

Appropriately enough, the heart of the play's latter half is the central of the seven scenes it comprises. One of the longest scenes in all of Shakespeare, it too is a feast of celebration for which its participants have especially attired themselves. Featuring an abundance of ballads, guests being greeted with bouquets of flowers, and a dance of satyrs (Alkibiades had likened Sokrates to the satyr Marsyas, claiming the philosopher charmed with his speeches as the satyr did with his songs; *Symposium* 215b–e), this scene first introduces the pair of lovers whose story dominates the second half. Florizel,[46] the Crown Prince of Bohemia, has fallen in love with Perdita, living as the daughter of a humble shepherd. One might see in them a reminder of the origin Sokrates attributes to *Erōs* himself (as per the teaching of "wisest Diotima"; 208c), namely, that Love is the offspring of a father rich in resources (*Porus*) and a penurious mother (*Penia*; 203b–c).[47]

As is so often the case in love, Florizel and Perdita met by chance. The Prince was out hunting with his falcon, whose flight led him to the old shepherd's vicinity (4.4.14–16). Indeed, Shakespeare has made liberal, not to say lavish, use of Chance throughout this tale of love – perhaps taking his cue from the Platonic Aristophanes' 'comical' account of *erōs*, more precisely from his explanation of falling in love as one's happening upon one's 'missing half' (cf. *Symposium*

192b–c).[48] The first words of *The Winter's Tale* refer to chance, and Perdita's fate is subject to chance happenings virtually from birth, some exceedingly unlikely. When Leontes rejects the baby as Polixenes' bastard, he commands Antigonus to take it away "to some remote and desert place, quite out of our dominions," adding, "As by strange fortune / It came to us, ... commend it strangely to some place / Where chance may nurse or end it" (2.3.175–82). Precluded from disposing of the baby in Sicily, but with no destination specified, Antigonus puts to sea, whereon he happens to dream that a weeping Hermione pleads with him to leave it at some remote spot in Bohemia (3.3.31–2). Presuming that this confirms Polixenes as the child's father, Antigonus obeys, providing the child with some pieces of treasure: "there these, which may, if fortune please, both breed thee, pretty, and still rest thine" (43–9). That no sooner done, he, rather than the helpless child, is accosted and eaten by a bear, while at the same time the ship awaiting him offshore has the misfortune also to be "swallowed," it by a raging sea – thus leaving no one in Sicily aware of the child's disposition. The babe, however, is promptly found by a shepherd searching for sheep, and an especially benevolent shepherd at that, who exclaims "Good luck" upon first spotting the child (68). Meanwhile, his son has just happened to witness the end of both Antigonus *and* the ship that brought him, and so is apprised of knowledge that will eventually prove vital in establishing Perdita's true identity (5.2.62–72). The shepherd having been fortuitously foretold that he would be made rich "by the fairies," regards the accompanying treasure as "fairy gold" which requires him to keep secret its origin if he is to enjoy his good fortune ("We are lucky, boy; and to be so still requires nothing but secrecy" 116–24). Thus, he is also obliged to conceal his true relationship to Perdita, passing her off as his own daughter.

Chance continues to both haunt and help the young lovers. Perdita worries that Florizel's father, the king, "by some accident should pass this way" and so discover their affair (4.4.18–20). The Prince assures her that he will remain hers regardless, and she pleads, "O lady Fortune, / Stand you auspicious!" (51–2). Once Polixenes, having with Camillo attended the feast in the disguise of an old man, reveals his angry awareness of their intentions, issuing dire threats to all concerned, Florizel resolves to flee with his beloved. He informs Camillo of his determination to "let [himself] and fortune / Tug for the time to come." Moreover, as luck would have it, the Prince has a ship nearby "most opportune to [their] need" (493–503). When Camillo inquires, "Have you thought on a place whereto you'll go?," Florizel responds:

Not as yet:
But as th' unthought-on accident is guilty
To what we wildly do, so we profess

Ourselves to be the slaves of chance, and flies
Of every wind that blows.

(538–42)

And so they are. For had not Autolycus intercepted the shepherd and his clownish son on their way to inform the King, and led the pair to Florizel's ship instead, the lovers might have been intercepted by Polixenes. Nor would shepherd and son have been so conveniently available in Sicily to help establish Perdita's true identity. Thus, though immediately prior to his deliverance Florizel is complaining of "Fortune, visible an enemy" (5.1.215), the truth is quite the contrary.

Given the conspicuously heavy reliance upon luck in both the plot and the dialogue of *The Winter's Tale*, one can scarce avoid concluding that Shakespeare means thereby to indicate something significant concerning his view of erotic love. Indeed, might this itself be the most important thing to appreciate about love: that the ways of *Erōs* are so mysterious and unpredictable precisely because from birth on – or even before – chance plays such a large role?[49] That just as in war, one does indeed need much luck to be lucky in love.

Names are another feature of this play that links it to Plato's dialogues. Shakespeare uses none of the names of his characters' counterparts in the primary source story (Greene's *Pandosto*), instead choosing ones which we must presume suit his purposes. Consider the first character to speak, Archidamus, who after his brief conversation with Camillo in the first scene is never heard of or from again. Having provided us vital information, we are allowed to forget him, much as we forget our original informant in the *Symposium*, Aristodemus ('Best of the People'). But only a reader of the play could notice the similarity in these names, since that of Archidamus ('Ruler of the People'; *damos* is the Dorian variant of the Attic *dēmos*) is never mentioned. Presumably he returns to Bohemia with King Polixenes (from *Polyxenos*, 'hospitable'; literally, 'of many guests/strangers'), but there it would seem his position – which he indicates corresponds to that of Camillo in Sicily (1.1.2–3) – is filled (usurped?) by Camillo. It is enough to make one wonder about Camillo, so deceptively clever. The King of Sparta at the outset of the Peloponnesian War was named Archidamus, and there are other subtle indications that we are meant to regard Bohemia as more 'Spartan,' Sicily more 'Athenian.' Archidamus begins the play by emphasizing to Camillo the "great difference between our Bohemia and your Sicilia," manifested by the "magnificence" of Sicilian entertainment compared with that available in rustic, bear-infested Bohemia. And the Dorian root of Florizel's pseudonym ('Doricles') is obvious. The coming together of the two kingdoms with the marriage of Florizel and Perdita might be seen to symbolize the same synthesis Sokrates attempts in the regime he outlines in the *Republic*, blending the virtues of both Athens and Sparta.

Then there is Leontes, the king whose aroused spirit – seat of anger and indignation, pride and shame, love and jealousy – overrules his and everyone else's reason, with (seemingly) such tragic consequences. His spirit in charge, he lusts for revenge (2.3.19, 22), openly threatens subordinates with his "wrath" (138), while insisting with perfect sincerity that he seeks only justice (179, 204; 3.2.6, 89–90). Leontes provides the perfect illustration of what Plato's dialogue teaches concerning the threat the spirit poses to justice when either it is not tamed and rendered obedient to reason, or the reason is not knowledgeable and thus competent to rule. The name Leontes, like that of Leontius in the *Republic*, derives from the Greek (and Latin) for 'Lion' (*Leōn*; genitive: *Leontos*, 'of the Lion'), proverbial 'King of the Beasts' and the natural symbol for spiritedness. Sokrates uses it as such in moulding his image of the human soul (588d). As for Leontius, the story told about his anger provides the basis for Sokrates' distinguishing the spirit from the other parts of the human soul in his abbreviated psychology (439e–440a).[50]

Consider also Autolycus, that "rogue" most fittingly named (as he is the first to insist): "My father named me Autolycus; who, being as I am, littered under Mercury, was likewise a snapper-up of unconsidered trifles" (4.3.24–6). The name goes back to Homer, being that of Odysseus's maternal grandfather, "who surpassed all humans in thievery and swearing oaths" (*Odyssey* XIX, 395–6). In later accounts (e.g., Ovid's *Metamorphoses*), a divine descent from Hermes (Rome's Mercury) is attributed to him. Sokrates refers to this same Autolycus and this very line in the course of exposing the inadequacies of Polemarchos's definition of justice (which seemed to imply that a just guardian was necessarily also potentially a clever thief), adding, "and I'd venture you learned this from Homer. For he is fond of Autolycus, Odysseus's grandfather on his mother's side, and says he surpassed all humans in stealing and swearing oaths" (*Republic* 334a–b; cf. 4.4.267–72, 283–5, 712–13, 5.2.154–7).

Speaking of oaths and swearing, they have a curious prominence in *The Winter's Tale*, along with vows, promises, pledges of faith, contracts, and such. Hermione is the first to mention any of these morally fraught species of language. Invited by Leontes to try persuading Polixenes to extend his visit, she complains to her husband of his proceeding "too coldly," as more apt to have "drawn oaths from him *not* to stay." Then obliquely addressing Polixenes, she suggests that a longing to see his son would justify his insistence on departing: "But let him *say* so then, and let him go; / But let him *swear* so, and he shall not stay" (1.2.29–36). This is not the last time in the play that a distinction is drawn between merely saying, and positively swearing (see 3.2.203; 5.2.156–63). Having elicited from Polixenes the vague "I may not, verily," Hermione rejects his "limber vows," countering with her own 'verily' and the claim that "a lady's Verily's / As potent as a lord's" (45–51). From this point on, there are well over five dozen instances of, or references to, avowals of one sort or another. Whereas many are isolated, others are concentrated, such as in connection with Camillo's warning Polixenes of Leontes's plot against him and the reason for it (1.2.414–46); Hermione and various lords attesting to her innocence (2.1.63, 95, 130–46); Antigonus's being made to "swear by this sword" to carry out the disposal of the baby Perdita (2.3.167–8, 183; 3.3.30, 53); the trial scene wherein the ambassadors to Delphos, Cleomenes and Dion, are required to "swear upon this sword of justice," and do so (3.2.124, 130); and Paulina's (duplicitous?) insistence that Hermione has died in court: "I say she's dead; I'll swear't. If word nor oath / Prevail not, go and see" (203–4). All these are in the play's 'first half,' and have mainly to do with the sexual crime Leontes unjustly supposes to have been committed and his reaction to it. By contrast, those of the 'second half' are mainly in connection with pledges of love, some in the songs and banter of the clown and his shepherdess girlfriends (4.4.236–41, 300–9), but most having to do with Florizel's commitment to Perdita (368–91, 418, 461, 478, 487–92; 5.1.203). And there is the peculiar oath Paulina extracts from Leontes: "Will you swear/ Never to marry, but by my free leave?" (69–72, 82).

Is there any explanation other than the obvious one for Shakespeare's liberal seasoning of this play with so much swearing of oaths? Namely, that these things have a special – but quite disparate – pertinence to both matters of justice and expressions of love? The gravity with which we naturally treat justice imparts the highest importance to truthfulness on the part of anyone and everyone practically involved in its administration, whether as accusers, defenders, judges, witnesses, or even mere recorders. Hence, it is typically the case that oaths enjoining people to uphold the truth are mandatory in courts of law, requiring them to accept, explicitly and self-consciously, a special moral obligation not simply to 'say' they speak the truth so far as they know it, but to *swear* that they do, and preferably in the name of something they would fear to offend or disgrace (even if only their own honourable reputation; see 1.2.407, 442; 2.1.146; 2.2.65; *Republic* 443a, 368b–c).

In oaths of love, by contrast, we are apt to have quite different expectations. As Bacon observes, here hyperbole is the rule, not the exception. The extravagance of language in pledges of exclusivity and constancy is in lieu of the possiblity of any more substantial guarantees. Praising *erōs* in the *Symposium*, Pausanias goes still further, contrasting what is acceptable in love pursuits with all other activities:

For if in wishing to take money from someone, or to hold [political] office, or any other power, [were one] to do as lovers do towards their beloveds – making all sorts of supplications and entreaties, swearing oaths, sleeping on doorsteps, willing to slave in a slavery that no slave would endure – he would be hindered from acting thus by both friends and enemies ... But a lover doing all of this is granted grace ... And what is most terrible [*deinotaton*],[51] as the many say, for him alone is there pardon from the gods for departing from his sworn oath. For they say there is no oath in matters of sex [*aphrodision*]. (183a–b)

The common saying 'All's fair in love and war' makes Pausanias's point more succinctly. As to why people are apt to regard the making and breaking of love oaths as warranting special indulgence, presumably this is in recognition of certain basic truths about *erōs*. For example, that intense erotic love is a kind of 'possession,' as by a demon, rendering lovers not really responsible for what they say and do. How many popular songs are on the theme of 'that old black magic called love'? Polixenes would seem to share this understanding in warning off Perdita: "And thou, fresh piece of excellent witchcraft ... And you, enchantment" (4.4.423–4, 435). According to Diotima (that wise foreign woman from whom Sokrates claims to have learned all about 'love matters,' *erotika*), there is some truth in the popular view; she teaches that *Erōs* is "a great *daimōn*" whereby the commands of supernatural powers are communicated to mere mortals (202e–203a). Most people also concede that, no matter how sincerely one tries, or how emphatic or exalted one's oaths, there is no way to bind the heart: that falling in – and out – of love is something that happens, not something one does. That love is a mysterious power, perhaps beyond human understanding and control – this also is confirmed by Diotima, who warns Sokrates that he may not be able to comprehend the upper reaches of her account (209e ff).

The idea of a statue that comes to life reminds one of the legendary Daedalus, and indirectly of Sokrates inasmuch as he (ever the ironist) claimed descent from this cunning craftsman of statues so lifelike they moved, or at least seemed to (*Alkibiades Major* 121a, *Euthyphro* 11c–e, 15b; see also *Meno* 97d, *Greater Hippias* 281d–282a). Also the idea of a dear departed wife that comes back to life may recall the ancient story of Alcestis that figures importantly in the speeches of both Phaedrus and Diotima (*Symposium* 179b–c, 208d). Despite its proven dramatic effectiveness, the lack of credibility in Shakespeare's 'trick' with Hermione – having her *seem* to die and be buried, then live in seclusion for sixteen years, only to appear as a (suitably aged) statue of herself in order to stage a theatrical reentry to public life – all this has been the target of much criticism, and understandably so. What has perhaps not been sufficiently appreciated, however, and contributing to both its dramatic force and its philosophical significance, is that this episode makes concrete a profound yearning in human nature. As a sympathetic scholar so aptly expressed it:

> The teasing realism in which life is made to seem like stone, and stone to suggest life, indicates the true function of the statue scene. One of the deepest of all mysteries is that of the difference between thought and thing, between mind and matter. Much of human desire is and always has been a longing to animate the inanimate. We need discuss neither anthropological formulations such as Tyler's animism, nor the speculations of philosophers ... because the realization of the difference between thought and thing, and the desire to animate the inanimate, are part of the fabric of all men's awareness. The longing to reconcile the two realms, and the knowledge of their utter difference, reach their greatest urgency at that almost universally suffered moment when a human being, living, stands beside the loved statue that is a corpse and experiences the abyss of separation between the living and the inanimate.[52]

Finally, a numerical peculiarity of *The Winter's Tale* provides an esoteric link with Plato's dialogues, and the *Symposium* in particular. This play is the only one in the canon in which the term 'twenty-three' appears, and not once, but twice.[53] The sight of his son Mamillius moves Leontes to "recoil / Twenty-three years" to his own childhood[54] (1.2.154–5). And at the surprise announcement that the embassy to the Delphic Oracle has so soon returned ("their speed hath been beyond account"), Leontes responds, unaware of the irony of his words:

> Twenty-three days
> They have been absent; 'tis good speed; foretells
> The great Apollo suddenly will have
> The truth of this appear.
>
> (2.3.197–200)

This is the more interesting in that it is a purposeful departure from Shakespeare's source, Greene's *Pandosto*, in which the outward journey to the oracle was "within three weeks." The special significance of the number twenty-three derives from Plato's having established its symbolic association with *Erōs* in the Sokrates–Diotima dialogue which the philosopher recounts in the *Symposium* (201d–212a), wherein this 'daimonic being' is referred to by name that many times.[55] This numerical association is indirectly confirmed in *Apology of Sokrates*, the dialogue portraying his response to the capital crimes on which he was brought to trial: "corrupting the young, and not believing in the gods in whom the City believes, but in other *daimonia* ['daimonic things / beings'] that are new" (24b–c). In this 'defence speech,' the philosopher's public accounting of himself and his way of life, he explains that "the god" has commanded him "to live philosophizing and examining [himself] and others" (28e; see also 33c). Altogether, he refers to "the god" twenty-three times in his apology. And though once early in his speech he cleverly implies that this "god" is Apollo (offering as his witness "the god in Delphi" whose Pythia proclaimed that "no one was wiser" than he; 20e–21a), Sokrates never actually *says* 'Apollo' – and he *is* on *trial* for *not* believing in the gods the city recognizes. Subsequently, moreover, he speaks of "something divine and daimonic, a voice that comes to [him]," and who acts as a censor over all he says and does (31c–d; see also 37e, 40c). In his prior argument with his accuser Meletus, he reminded him and everyone that the poetic tradition offers alternative conceptions of *daimones* ("And do we not believe that *daimones* are either gods or offspring of gods?" 27d). So, putting two and two together – that *erotika* is the only thing in which he is expert (*Symposium* 177e; cf. *Theages* 128b), that he is ruled by a daimonic sign, that *Erōs* is a great *daimōn*, and that *daimones* are either gods or sons and daughters of gods (demi-gods) – are we not invited to identify the "the god," which Sokrates refers to twenty-three times, with *Erōs*? Thus, not only is the numerical symbolism established in the *Symposium* ratified in the *Apology*, but also this same number's association with philosophy.[56]

It seems that *The Winter's Tale* is meant to be seen as at once Christian and Pagan, with its easily recognizable Christian allusions being conspicuously imbedded in a Classical setting. Careful analysis of the text, however, reveals a much more elaborate, artful interweaving of these two intellectual traditions that have shaped the West, the one associated with Athens, the other with Jerusalem, each identified with one of the two most famous trials in history and indelibly coloured by the martyrdom of its founder. Relevant to their comparison, it is reported that Jesus wept but there is no record of his having laughed, whereas Sokrates laughed but was never known to cry (cf. *Phaedo* 115c). As to why Shakespeare chose to bring them together as he does in this hybrid story – part sad-serious as suits winter, part happy comedy of summer (2.1.25; 4.4.80) – a story centring upon the chance meeting and marrying of the heirs of two kingdoms, I suspect that love is the answer. If the most famous and influential philosophical teaching about love and justice is Plato's, the most famous and influential religious teaching about love and forgiveness is that of Jesus. Perhaps, then, our philosopher–poet saw a special suitability in crafting a tale that, drawing upon elements of both teachings, would provide his reader that much more to think about.

HIGH-MINDED NEGLIGENCE IN *MEASURE FOR MEASURE*

It has become common in modern times for certain of Shakespeare's creations to be categorized as 'problem plays,' meaning that they pose more than the usual problems of interpretation, partly perhaps because of the sorts of problems addressed within them, but also because of something problematic about the plays themselves. While agreement as to which plays qualify is far from universal, *Measure for Measure* is on the list of virtually everyone who acknowledges the category.[57] However, there is nothing like unanimity as to what is questionable about it. While ostensibly a comedy, and certainly having its amusing moments, some judge it defective because its central story is just too dark, serious, and disturbing for comic treatment.[58] On this view, the attempt is simply a misbegotten idea. Other critics, whose conception of comedy is more purely formal (any drama that allows its audience to delight in a happy outcome involving the overcoming of adversity), nonetheless contend that *Measure for Measure* is defective because the manipulations required to bring about its joyful resolution are too incredible to accept: it is not a *human* triumph with which one can identify.[59] Still others argue that the main problem with the play is primarily one of dramatic structure, that it is compounded of disparate parts differing in temper and tone, or that it suffers from an incompatibility between plot and character.[60] As such, these critics contend, it fails to be either intellectually or poetically satisfying. Nor do complaints about the play end here.

There is, however, a problem within the *plot* of the play that goes largely unnoticed, yet which if addressed goes far towards enhancing one's appreciation of this uncomfortable comedy. It is this: *Why* has the moral climate of Vienna been allowed so to degenerate that drastic measures are required to reform it? Notice, it is only against the need for these radical, draconian measures that the precipitating action of the plot (the arrest of Claudio on a technical violation of the law prohibiting fornication) becomes plausible. Once this question is raised, however, a second immediately suggests itself. Why has reform been ordered *now*; what induced the effort to reinstitute strict rule of law at this time? To see what is behind this story, determining its course as it unfolds, one must consider carefully the first three scenes, especially the third.[61]

The first word in the play, spoken by the man ultimately responsible for the negligent ruling of Vienna during its past decade and a half, is rather peculiar. It is a *name*, but not a German name, nor a Christian, nor even a biblical name; it is a Greek name: Escalus. Albeit differently spelled than that of the first great tragedian (Aeschylus, as it is usually transliterated), this is no more noticeable when spoken than is the variant spelling of Macbeth's late-appearing adjutant (Seyton). What significance might one attach to the fact that the ruler's agreeable assistant (described in the Folio's list of actors as "an ancient Lord") bears the name of a famous poet? This, however, is not the only oddity attending the names in this play. Despite its Viennese setting, there is a strange preponderance of Roman-Italian names, though at least two are of Greek origin (i.e., Angelo, from *aggelos* 'messenger,' 'herald,' 'envoy'; Lucio, from *lukē,* 'light,' whence *lux*, lucid, etc.). Also, two names are supplied in the Folio's list that are never spoken in the text: Francisca ("a Nun"), and that of the reigning duke, Vincentio. Thus, only a reader of the play would be aware that the Duke bears a name meaning 'conqueror,' or 'victor.' A final curiosity: it is not before the play's closing scene that anyone – auditor or reader – learns the pseudonym the Duke assumed while disguised as a friar ('Lodowick'; 5.1.128).[62]

The first subject raised is politics, again addressed from the Duke to this "ancient" servitor, Escalus:

> Of government the properties to unfold
> Would seem in me t'affect speech and discourse,
> Since I am put to know that your own science
> Exceeds, in that, the lists of all advice
> My strength can give you.

As the Duke immediately makes clear, the political 'science' he ascribes to Escalus is distinctly parochial:

> The nature of our people,
> Our city's institutions, and the terms
> For common justice, y'are as pregnant in
> As art and practice hath enriched any
> That we remember.

All the more interesting, then, that the Duke should be turning over full governmental power during his supposed absence, not to Escalus, but to another, and much younger subordinate, a certain Lord Angelo, with "Old Escalus, though first in question, [his] secondary" (1.1.18–21, 42–6). Escalus, however, is given his own "commission," along with an explicit warning that he not "warp" from it (13–14). We know nothing of its provisions, and our puzzlement is only deepened by his telling Angelo, "A power I have, but of what strength and nature / I am not yet instructed" (79–80). It would seem he expects such instruction from the as yet unread commission. Still his announcement, coupled with the Duke's warning, is somewhat curious; and given the astuteness the Duke ascribes to him, perhaps one ought not assume that everything Escalus tells Angelo is to be taken at face value. Angelo also is provided a written commission, about which likewise we are told nothing (47). However, we are allowed to witness the oral instructions the Duke provides, and note that they are strictly formal: "Your scope is as mine own, / So to enforce or qualify the laws / As to your soul seems good" (64–6). Presumably, then, Angelo is expected to rule according to the established institutional and legal structure, but within those broad limits he is given carte blanche. At this point, there is no indication that anything is amiss in Vienna, nor that Angelo's is other than a routine assignment.

We might nonetheless wonder why the duke must leave Vienna in such haste, and – what is more surprising – unaccompanied (62–4, 67). Apparently the official story put about is that he is on a mission of military diplomacy to Poland (1.2.1–5; 1.3.14–16). Somehow the credibility of that explanation is soon compromised, and thus his actual whereabouts is the subject of continuing speculation throughout the play (3.2.83–90; 4.1.60–5). As the puzzlingly well-informed Lucio explains to Isabella:

> The Duke is very strangely gone from hence;
> Bore many gentlemen – myself being one –
> In hand, and hope of action: but we do learn,
> By those that know the very nerves of state,
> His giving out were at an infinite distance
> From his true-meant design.
>
> (1.4.50–5)

The matters about which we *know* Lucio is right – as in this instance (cf. 4.3.154–7) – should make us question whether there might be some truth in certain of his other claims. As his name could suggest, he may shed more light on the play's dark corners than is generally appreciated.

The contrast in tone between the first scene and the second could hardly be greater. Following hard upon the sober, grave, responsible, well-mannered formality that pervaded the Duke's parting from his two senior officials comes a display of Viennese street life. We do not know how long the Duke has supposedly been gone – it could be days, could be weeks – but it has been long enough for certain public speeches to have been made, proclamations issued, and threatened actions taken (1.2.71–4). To judge by the trio of young bachelor soldiers we now meet (denominated 'gentlemen,' only one of whom is named, the irrepressible Lucio),[63] Vienna is in a condition of advanced moral degeneracy, characterized by lewd impiety, widespread sexual promiscuity, and (consequently) by widespread venereal diseases – symbolic, perhaps, of the polity itself being sick in ways that threaten its very continuation. This unholy trinity is soon joined by the proprietor of an establishment where one can "purchase" such diseases, the well-named Mistress Overdone. From her, they (and we) learn that a legal crackdown on fornication is under way, moreover one of extreme severity. Among the first to feel its effects is Claudio, a friend of Lucio, who is being taken to prison where he is to be decapitated within three days. Lucio leads his fellow gallants off to investigate this report, whereupon the good madam, left lamenting the decline in her trade, is joined by her part-time tapster, part-time pimp, Pompey, who tells of another such case (later, upon being imprisoned himself, Pompey indicates that he feels quite at home as the jail is filled with the erstwhile denizens of his mistress's establishment; 4.3.1–20). Pompey provides more evidence that a general clean-up is being undertaken: it has been proclaimed that all the brothels in Vienna's suburbs are to be demolished. As for those in the city itself, they too were to have been pulled down, "but that a wise burgher put in for them" (85–95). Apparently, then, illegitimate dealings in Vienna are not confined to people's sexual relations, but infect other dimensions of political life as well. Be that as it may, what is behind this surprising new rigour in law enforcement? That is the question which we bring to the play's crucial next scene.

The third scene consists entirely of the middle of a conversation between the supposedly absent Duke and a friar named after the doubting disciple. The Duke's relationship with this Friar Thomas is apparently a long-standing one of some confidence and familiarity, as he reveals to him at least part of his secret plan and enlists his assistance in carrying it out. However, it is interesting – to say the least – that the Duke must first assure Thomas that his desire for a "secret harbour" is not for the purpose of an amorous escapade. Why would this friar, well acquainted with the Duke's character (according to the Duke's own testimony; 7–10), need such assurance? Is this, perhaps, not the first time the Duke has secretly withdrawn from public life? Thomas's supposition squares suspiciously with Lucio's suspicion (3.2.127–32). Here, however, the Duke insists that he is impervious to those passions more appropriate to "burning youth," that no "dribbling dart of love can pierce [his] complete bosom" – much as later in his clerical disguise he challenges Lucio's allegation that "He had some feeling of the sport; he knew the service" with "I have never heard the absent Duke much detected for women; he was not inclined that way" (115–19). A strange rebuttal, when one thinks about it: that he was not "much *detected* for women." Was he was more 'detected' than he realized? In any event, there is no contradiction between having a "feeling for the sport" and being immune to romantic infatuations.

Assuring his friar friend that he pursues "a purpose more grave and wrinkled [i.e., winding, sinuous, convoluted]," the Duke proceeds to speak of it:

My holy sir, none better knows than you
How I have ever lov'd the life remov'd,
And held in idle price to haunt assemblies,
Where youth, and cost, witless bravery keeps.
I have deliver'd to Lord Angelo –
A man of stricture and firm abstinence –
My absolute power and place here in Vienna,
And he supposes me travell'd to Poland;
For so I have strew'd it in the common ear,
And so it is receiv'd. Now, pious sir,
You will demand of me, why I do this.
Friar: Gladly, my lord.
Duke: We have strict statutes and most biting laws,
The needful bits and curbs to headstrong jades,
Which for this fourteen years we have let slip;
Even like an o'er-grown lion in a cave
That goes not out to prey. Now, as fond fathers,
Having bound up the threatening twigs of birch,
Only to stick it in their children's sight
For terror, not to use, in time the rod
Becomes more mock'd than fear'd: so our decrees,
Dead to infliction, to themselves are dead,
And Liberty plucks Justice by the nose,
The baby beats the nurse, and quite athwart
Goes all decorum.

(1.3.7–31)

Vienna is ostensibly a principate, but judging from its prince's own description, in practice life in his regime more closely resembles that of a quasi-anarchic democracy. Indeed, it is reminiscent of Sokrates' hyperbolic indictment of the democratic regime in Plato's *Republic*: "And isn't the city full of freedom and free speech? And isn't there license in it to do whatever one wants?" (557b). Following upon the absence of compulsion is a reversal in the natural relations of authority between rulers and ruled, masters and servants, parents and children ("a father habituates himself to become like his child and fear his sons, and the son [becomes like] the father, and has neither shame nor awe of his parents"), teachers and students ("a teacher fears and fawns upon the students" (562e–563a). Sokrates speaks of men condemned to death, nonetheless living on "as if no one cared or saw" (558a ff – rather like the case of Barnardine? – 4.2.126–35). "And we almost forgot to mention the legal equality and freedom in relations of women with men and men with women" (563b). The Duke's general assessment of the Viennese situation accords perfectly with prison-bound Claudio's more particular response to Lucio's inquiring, "Whence comes this restraint?"

> From too much liberty, my Lucio. Liberty,
> As surfeit, is the father of much fast;
> So every scope by the immoderate use
> Turns to restraint.
>
> (1.2.117–20)

This, too, reminds one of Sokrates' account of democracy, specifically of how the increasing immoderation of people can lead to tyranny. That just as the oligarchs' unrestrained desire for more wealth ultimately results in the collapse of their regime and the loss of all their wealth, so in a democracy the people's greed for freedom – understood, not as rational self-rule, but simply as the absence of political-legal restraint, licensed by a belief in the equality of all desires (560e–561c) – results in the regime's steadily spiralling downward into licentious anarchy that sooner or later, one way or another, will bring forth an autocratic regime and the loss of freedom (562b ff).

The Duke having stated the problem, Friar Thomas interjects, implicitly raising two obvious questions: "It rested in your Grace / To unloose this tied'up justice when you pleas'd; / And it in you more dreadful would have seem'd / Than in Lord Angelo." (1.3.31–4) That is: Why has the Duke not addressed this problem sooner – for that matter, why did he allow it to arise at all? And why is he now turning the task of reformation over to Lord Angelo, since he could as effectively carry it out himself. Notice, the Duke's response addresses only the latter question.

> I do fear, too dreadful.
> Sith 'twas my fault to give the people scope,
> 'Twould be my tyranny to strike and gall them
> For what I bid them do: for we bid this be done,
> When evil deeds have their permissive pass,
> And not the punishment. Therefore indeed, my father,
> I have on Angelo impos'd the office;
> Who may in th'ambush of my name strike home,
> And yet my nature never in the fight
> To do in slander.
>
> (1.3.34–43)

This turns out to be only half of his answer, however – what might be called the overtly *political* half. While it includes several points worthy of expansion, what must first be noted is that Duke Vincentio's plan amounts to a variation on what is probably the most memorable illustration of political sagacity in Machiavelli's *The Prince*. It concerns how Cesare Borgia, also known as Duke Valentino, went about pacifying Romagna:

> Once the duke had taken over Romagna, he found it had been commanded by impotent lords who had been the readier to despoil their subjects than to correct them, and had given their subjects matter for disunion, not union. Since that province was quite full of robberies, quarrels, and every other kind of insolence, he judged it necessary to give it good government, if he wanted to reduce it to peace and obedience to a kingly arm. So he put there Messer Remirro de Orco, a cruel and ready man, to whom he gave the fullest power. In a short time Remirro reduced it to peace and unity, with the very greatest reputation for himself. Then the duke judged that such excessive authority was not necessary, because he feared that it might become hateful; and he set up a civil court in the middle of the province, with a most excellent president, where each city had its advocate. And because he knew that past rigors had generated some hatred for Remirro, to purge the spirits of that people and to gain them entirely to himself, he wished to show if any cruelty had been committed, this had not come from him but from the harsh nature of his minister. And having seized this opportunity, he had him placed one morning in the piazza at Cesena in two pieces, with a piece of wood and a bloody knife beside him. The ferocity of this spectacle left the people at once satisfied and stupified.[64]

Machiavelli prefaces this story with his judgment that it is "deserving of notice and of being imitated by others."

Apparently Shakespeare agreed. The parallels between Duke Valentino's plan, including the motive behind it, and this much of Duke Vincentio's are obvious enough. But it is pertinent to reflect upon the two most important differences. First, Vincentio (unlike Valentino) is by his own admission responsible for the current state of disorder. It has been his failure to enforce his regime's laws, despite acknowledging them "needful" for curbing and directing people's normal inclinations, that has resulted in the laws becoming "more mock'd than fear'd," with justice and appropriate standards of conduct deteriorating accordingly. He expressly notes that the failure to punish transgressions is interpreted not merely as permitting, but as practically encouraging, the very behaviour that is supposedly outlawed. Second, Shakespeare's version has a much gentler outcome. Remirro, who served Cesare strictly in the manner that was expected of him, was sacrificed to political expediency: summarily executed to provide the populace a spectacle both cathartic and awe-inspiring (while also – not so incidentally –

eliminating a dangerous potential usurper). Whereas Angelo, although guilty of a serious abuse of power and breach of trust, is but momentarily threatened with death, and is instead subjected to an humiliating public exposure, then made to marry a woman he scorned but who nonetheless loves him madly. Especially in light of Cesare Borgia's ferocious disposal of de Orco, the finale Duke Vincentio arranges seems a salutary illustration of justice tempered with mercy. Nor is there evidence that he ever intended any treatment more severe. Indeed, given the lengths to which he goes to preserve Angelo's reputation while his offence was confined to attempted sexual extortion (see 3.1.150–66; 4.2.77–83), one sees that Lucio is likely correct in claiming, "The Duke yet would have dark deeds darkly answered: he would never bring them to light" (3.2.170–2). That being so, Vincentio must have planned from the outset to deal privately with any transgressions Angelo might commit. Only when Angelo shows himself capable of judicial murder does the Duke resolve to chasten him with public humiliation (as well as taking certain precautions for his own safe return and resumption of power; note 4.5.6–13). Be all this as it may, we can see a connection between the two respects in which Shakespeare's 'imitation' departs from the Machiavellian original. More specifically, that the first difference at least partly accounts for the second – presuming what seems indubitable: that Shakespeare intended that his duke be clearly seen as more *just* than was Cesare Borgia.

The fact remains, however, that the basic rationale behind Duke Vincentio's plan is essentially the same as Duke Valentino's: he has some dirty work that needs doing, and he wants it done without his own reputation being sullied (appreciating, as Machiavelli teaches, that a prince's good reputation is an essential constituent of his power).[65] In his conversation with Friar Thomas, the Duke openly acknowledges his concern that no "slander" accrue to him. But he also expresses a concern to avoid acting tyrannically, noting that having given "the people scope," it would be his "tyranny" to punish them for what he in effect bade them do. Of course, the notion that turning over the task to Angelo absolves the Duke of the responsibility for what he characterizes as acts of tyranny is plainly sophistical, even allowing for the fact that he gave Angelo no specific instructions, merely leaving him to "enforce or qualify the laws as to [his] soul seems good" (1.1.65–6). For the Duke knew his chosen deputy to be a martinet: cold, rational, passionless, hard, "a man of stricture and firm abstinence" – doubtless this is precisely why the Duke chose "precise" Angelo for the task, rather than knowledgeable but indulgent old Escalus (see 2.1.241–53). Here one might note that his secret awareness of Angelo's treatment of Mariana, revealed only later, in no way compromises Angelo's fitness for the job – quite the contrary: the purely mercenary attitude implicit in Angelo's action, of instrumental rationality impervious to sentiment, further confirms it. The Duke wishes the job done; perhaps it has become a matter of political necessity that it be done. Doubtless he knows that if it is to be done, 'twere well it were done quickly and thoroughly. If this be tyranny, it is unavoidable – in which case, his concern to avoid tyranny necessarily reduces to a concern to avoid the infamy of tyranny.

However, the question of what truly constitutes tyranny would seem to be an important issue in this play, if only because so many characters express opinions about it. Claudio is the first to use the term. Reflecting upon his being arrested on orders of a newly appointed deputy newly enforcing what had been a practically defunct statute, he wonders, "Whether the tyranny be in his place, or in his eminence that fills it up" (1.2.152–3). That is, Claudio readily, and understandably, regards what has happened to him as an act of tyranny – much as the Duke anticipated people would. For there is no way that suddenly beginning to enforce laws previously neglected, especially ones carrying such heavy sanctions, will not seem capricious and arbitrary. Both Claudio and his sister wonder why *he* must be the first to feel the full force of this sudden legal stringency (2.2.107–8). And there is no reason, necessarily, other than the fact that somebody has to be first, and whoever it is will feel the same way and have the same response ('Why me?'). Thus, anyone who undertakes this task of restoring respect for the laws in a decadent regime will almost surely be seen as acting tyrannically. Claudio's reaction is typical. The only question in his mind is whether such behaviour is intrinsic to a new governor's need to establish his authority, or whether it derives from the particular nature of the person doing so (146–51).

Faced with the evidence of Mistress Overdone's incorrigibility, even patient old Escalus muses that certain individuals leave one no recourse but tyranny: "Double and treble admonition, and still forfeit in the same kind? This would make *mercy* swear and play the tyrant" (3.2.187–9). Isabella seems to think that tyranny consists of employing disproportionate power: "O, it is excellent / To have a giant's strength, but it is tyrannous / To use it as a giant" (2.2.108–10). We might imagine Hobbes replying, "No, my dear, this is just what Leviathan must be, and how it must act, if it is to guarantee the peace, order, and security we all desire." It is from a similar perspective that Angelo accuses Isabel of (wrongly) treating strict law enforcement – that is, unqualified by pity or indulgence for common human failings – as being in itself tyrannical: "You seemed of late to make the law a tyrant" (2.4.114). Whereas Angelo has a quite different conception in mind when he subsequently threatens to "prove a tyrant" by executing Claudio in a manner that "shall his death draw out to ling'ring sufferance" (165–8) – the implication being that it is the use of torture and excessive cruelty that is characteristic of tyranny.

The Duke is the last to speak of tyranny, and brief though it is, his is the fullest discussion. Responding to the Provost's scepticism as to the prospects of a reprieve for Claudio ("It is a bitter deputy"), Vincentio expresses a view that may be sound, despite the irony in his implying that it exonerates Angelo:

> Not so, not so; his life is parallel'd
> Even with the stroke and line of his great justice.
> He doth with holy abstinence subdue
> That in himself which he spurs on his power
> To qualify in others: were he meal'd with that
> Which he corrects, then were he tyrannous;
> But this being so, he's just.
>
> (4.2.77–83)

While one can never assume that a particular character is Shakespeare's spokesman (having written all the parts, presumably his wisdom is in the whole), one may treat the Duke's views with special regard, since he is portrayed as being the inner 'director' of this play. Moreover, there are grounds for suspecting that the problem of tyranny – of being clear as to what is and what is not tyranny – has a special pertinence for him.

So, drawing together his speeches and deeds, what does the Duke seem to believe constitutes tyranny? It is not simply a matter of exercising great, or overwhelming, or even absolute power. After all, this has been historically a father's natural relation to his children, but this power can (and, of course, should) be exercised in a kingly, not a tyrannical, manner. And in certain rare cases there may be a comparable natural entitlement to one man's justly exercising absolute power over an entire polity.[66] Nor does tyranny consist in the strictness or rigidity with which the laws are enforced, untempered by mercy; there may be other criticisms to be made of such a policy, but it is not tyrannical per se – it can be just, if the conditions require it. Nor even is tailoring the laws to one's own taste, using one's own likes and dislikes as the 'measure' against which all others will be measured, in itself tyrannical; were a ruler himself a noble and good man, his tastes may indeed be a fitting touchstone for what the law ought to be.[67] Rather, according to the Duke's pronouncements, tyranny results from two things, though they may be seen as stemming from a single root. First, gross inconsistency in what one requires of those one rules, permitting one day what is forbidden in the next. Along with the unpredictability, hence, anxiety, that this introduces into people's lives, it is at odds with law-abiding behaviour becoming habitual. Second, not abiding by the rules one imposes on others; that is, despite having the power to set the rules however one wishes, nonetheless departing from them oneself whenever one feels like doing so. Both of these practices may be seen as reflecting the rule of personal caprice; so, whatever else might be involved, capricious rule is essentially tyrannical.[68]

Tyranny, however, or what at least will seem like tyranny to those who suffer from the radical change in the character of rule, is what Vienna requires in its present disorder. The spirit of licentious freedom that has evolved out of the Duke's own political negligence is a sickness that will require extreme medicine to cure. And the Duke wants it cured, but without his own reputation being tarnished in the process. Indeed, as a consequence of what people will have suffered under his deputy, he almost surely will enjoy an increase in their love upon his public resumption of power. But, as noted earlier, this political purpose is only half of his rationale for delegating his ducal authority to Angelo, and in itself does not require his secret presence in Vienna.

The other half does. It is somewhat more difficult to characterize immediately, and is only partially revealed in our hearing. But what we can make of it throws considerable light on Friar Thomas's prior question: why the Duke allowed the political problem to arise in the first place. We have already heard enough to eliminate one possible answer: that he is simply soft, weak, full of pity, and as such overindulgent by nature. Quite to the contrary, his 'cynical' use of Angelo proves him fully capable of Machiavellian cunning (and all the toughness of soul that implies; see 3.2.96). His subsequent actions, moreover, show that he can be cruel if it serves a good end (as does the mental cruelty to which he subjects several characters, especially Isabella), and that he is flexible, capable of quickly modifying his schemes as changing circumstances require. It may well be that he is also part-lion (cf. 1.3.22; 3.2.140–2), but we can be sure he is part-fox, and that (as Machiavelli recommends) he relies more on vulpine than leonine qualities. Indeed, his entire plan is based on the fox's favourite trick: leaving a trail off in one direction in order to double back on it.[69] As he proceeds to explain this secret plan to Thomas, we learn why the Duke wished to leave his city unaccompanied: to facilitate his returning incognito. For he continues:

And to behold [Angelo's] sway,
I will, as 'twere a brother of your order,
Visit both prince and people. Therefore, I prithee,
Supply me with the habit, and instruct me
How I may formally in person bear
Like a true friar. Moe reasons for this action
At our more leisure shall I render you;
Only this one: Lord Angelo is precise;
Stands at a guard with Envy; scarce confesses

That his blood flows; or that his appetite
Is more to bread than stone. Hence shall we see
If power change purpose, what our seemers be.
(1.3.43–54)

So, whatever else, whatever "moe reasons" he may have (cf. 5.1.536), the Duke is *curious* – in particular about his acting-Prince Angelo, how he will bear up under the temptations inherent in exercising sovereign power; but also about people in general.[70] He gives no indication of intending to intrude at any point; rather, he returns to his city in the pose of foreign visitor (3.2.211–14), hence, a 'disinterested' observer – a mere "looker-on here in Vienna" (5.1.315), a stranger to the place.[71] For the purpose of his investigation, he adopts an especially felicitous disguise: that of a cleric, thereby availing himself of people's trust in his beneficence (2.3.3; 3.1.197), and of the special access it provides to their very souls (see 2.3.19ff; 3.1.150ff; 3.2.224ff; 4.1.53–5, 66–7; 4.2.168ff).

This expression of broad curiosity is not the only peculiar feature of Shakespeare's Duke, however. Notice, he begins his explanation to his sceptical friar friend with a reminder of how (as the friar well knows) he has "ever lov'd the life remov'd," and of what a waste of time and money he regards all those "assemblies" dominated by people on the make ("where youth, and cost, witless bravery keeps"). He prefers privacy, perhaps shared with a few select friends (which we know he has, all bearing distinguished ancient names;[72] cf. 4.5.12–13) In this connection, recall his earlier admission to Escalus and Angelo of his distaste and distrust of public ceremony (while acknowledging its political utility):

I'll privily away. I love the people,
But do not like to stage me to their eyes:
Though it do well, I do not relish well
Their loud applause and *Aves* vehement;
Nor do I think the man of safe discretion
That does affect it.
(1.1.67–72)

Despite the persona he has adopted, the teaching he later provides Claudio: "Be absolute for death" (3.1.5–41), is hardly a model of Christian doctrine; in particular, there is no reference to death being but the portal to a blissful afterlife, or any other suggestion that the individual soul is immortal. Instead, it contains unmistakable echoes of the Sokratic view (whence the Stoic derives) that death is not something to be feared, but is to be likened to sleep (cf. *Apology* 40c–e).[73] Indeed, it has been a maxim of philosophers since antiquity, and of philosophical poets such as Horace and Lucretius, 'That to Philosophize Is to Learn to Die.'[74] And when in his clerical disguise he queries his old adviser "of what disposition was the Duke?" Escalus replies:

> One that, above all other strifes, contended especially
> to know himself.
> *Duke:* What pleasure was he given to?
> *Escalus:* Rather rejoicing to see another merry, than merry
> at anything which professed to make him rejoice.
> A gentleman of all temperance.
>
> (3.2.225–31)

Note also, the Duke claims an 'Aristotelian' attitude towards passionate, 'romantic' love[75] (see 3.1.239–43) – that it is appropriate only for youths – whereas no "dribbling dart of love can pierce [his] complete bosom." This is in no way disproven by his subsequent interest in Isabella. In fact, prior to his rather astonishing two-line proposal to marry her (sandwiched among a half-dozen other pieces of business; 5.1.489–90), the Duke gives no evidence that he is the least bit smitten by the young lady. His reiteration of his proposal ("Dear Isabel, / I have a motion which much imports your good" 531–2) would leave any girl speechless. The Duke's behaviour is in marked contrast to Angelo's, who is quite overpowered by his passion for her. Add to all of this the Duke's distrust of the charm of music (4.1.14–15), and his preferring irony to hypocrisy (see 5.1.10–14), but with a purely utilitarian attitude towards both honesty and deceit[76] – as his entire disguised presence in the city attests (see esp. 3.1.257–9; 3.2.270–5; 4.1.73–5) – and a fairly clear conclusion emerges: that however he became the ruler of the city (presumably by accident of birth), he is by nature a philosopher.[77]

This, apparently, is why the city has gone to seed: sheer neglect, owing to its ruler's preoccupation with the life of study, with matters intrinsically more important and personally more engaging and enriching than what mostly makes up everyday political life, dominated as it is by the petty affairs of petty people.[78] We are provided a vivid illustration of what this can entail in the highly comic courtroom scene that begins act 2. The Duke, presumably, would have even less patience with such time-wasting, mind-numbing – but nonetheless quite necessary – business than has Angelo (2.1.133ff). In fact, Angelo may to some extent share a side of the Duke's nature. According to our best 'behind-the-scenes' informant, the joyfully irreverent Lucio, Angelo "doth rebate and blunt his natural edge / With profits of the mind, study, and fast" (1.4.60–1). Whatever the truth about Angelo, the Duke, preferring "the life remov'd" (which may of course, include dialogue with a few like-minded friends), while finding much about 'society' and public ceremony positively distasteful, has allowed himself to become detached from practical day-to-day ruling. Public administration being left to the likes of soft-hearted Escalus (see 3.2.185–9), and law enforcement to bozos such as Elbow (and this "poor Duke's constable" is indeed the constable of a poor-performing duke – whereas, again according to Lucio, "Lord Angelo dukes it well ... he puts transgression to't" 91–2), the decay of law and order, and thus of morality, is hardly surprising.

The political problem, then, as Shakespeare presents it here, is somewhat as follows. The man who could be expected to have the requisite understanding of the most important matters (including the basic principles of effective political rule) – namely, the philosopher[79] – and who would not be morally corrupted by the opportunities inherent in wielding political power, mainly because he is more-or-less indifferent to the sorts of 'goods' most men find so tempting – would prove over the long run a negligent ruler because the activity which defines him (manifesting the desire that rules him) – the only pursuit that can possibly be self-justifying: philosophy – tends to be all-consuming to the extent one is by nature drawn to it. Moreover, this quest for wisdom need have only a minimal dependence on the polity; so long as its continued existence is not endangered, and thus the environment in which to philosophize threatened, whatever else happens in political life need not concern a philosopher who is content to live privately.[80] Might this explain why the Duke has undertaken to reform his city now, and in a hurry: the very survival of his polity is at risk? Apparently the threat of war is on the horizon, and his dissolute, ill-disciplined populace is in no fit condition to meet it (see 1.2.1–5, 75).

In sum, a philosopher by virtue of his wisdom and immunity to corruption would make an ideal ruler, were he not preoccupied with what he regards as higher matters, hence, negligent of the public's business.[81] On the other hand, anyone who can take political life seriously enough to accord it the importance its successful management requires – which is to say, anyone whose idea of the good life turns primarily on the goods and bads the polity distributes (privileges and rewards of status and wealth; punishments of pains and privations) – such a person, however practically knowledgeable, and however steeled in sense of duty and ethical scrupulousness, is corruptible. Such people (which includes almost everybody) are susceptible to having their obligation to the common good compromised, either in a way comparable to that which Angelo displays, exploiting one's office to favour oneself and one's friends. Or in a way that may only seem more benign but actually be more dangerous, exemplified perhaps in old Escalus: by nature generous and sympathetic, his will to be firm but fair simply becomes worn down by prolonged exposure to the Sisyphean labour of trying to correct human failings. As a result, he has become lax by default, at times indulgent almost to the point of practical indifference. One can imagine a rueful shrug of the shoulders and shake of the head to be his most characteristic gesture.

The preceding, however, may be an oversimplification of what Shakespeare means to show in *Measure for Measure.* For it presumes that Duke Vincentio is the same at the conclusion of the play as at the beginning. Yet this clearly is not so. To mention only the most obvious difference, he is a bachelor at the start – giving no indication of any intention not to remain so – but as good as married by the end. Might this change in his personal status signal something of more general consequence? Something he has learned as a result of his sojourn among the people? While he makes no promise in the play's busy finale not to return to his negligent ways, he does leave the clear impression of his taking a more active role in the governing of his city. Yet, it is most unlikely that a man such as he, one by nature drawn to philosophy, would ever give it up. Has he learned, then, both why and how he must combine the two, political responsibility and love of knowledge – that it is not sufficient for him to be a philosopher: he must become a political philosopher?

If so, one might see the Duke as recapitulating the experience of Sokrates, who first learned the necessity – the *philosophical* necessity – of 'bringing philosophy down from the heavens and into the cities' (as Cicero credits him with doing).[82] The action of the play does suggest something like that in the Duke's case. For he comes down from his citadel, his ivory tower, into the very bowels of the city, into its darkest, most shadow-steeped place: its cavernous prison, where most of the inhabitants are – quite literally – prisoners. Much as Sokrates 'returns' to the Cave of the City, not as a Guardian charged with ruling it, but as a participating observer, so too for now does the Duke, whose religious disguise provides him a kind of 'Gygean' invisibility so far as his true identity is concerned.[83] In the course of his tour through the lower city, he discovers for himself what Sokrates explicitly taught: that unrestrained *erōs* is both a tyrannizing and an anarchizing force – and as such, the most dangerous threat to the justice of a polity, indeed to its very continuation – and thus why the laws regulating sexual relations are fundamental, truly *constituting* laws.[84]

From what he (and we) see, too many Viennese have adopted one of two unwholesome ways of dealing with their sexual natures: either indulging more-or-less indiscriminately in fornication, or retreating into complete abstinence. The only character that we meet who has pursued the reasonable middle way between these extremes, that of lawful marriage, is a dunce: Constable Elbow.[85] And while Claudio and Juliet have planned on marrying legally, they have jumped the gun, so to speak, and it is all too likely that the permissive atmosphere of Vienna tacitly encouraged their doing so. Upon reflection, one sees that sexual disorder is at the root of general political decadence. It is the irresponsible, practically impossible fantasies of sexual liberation that are behind most people's desire for "too much liberty." Sexual decadence is the worst kind of decadence – thus it is the appropriate epitome of decadence per se – because it naturally tends towards ever lower, ultimately bestial, modes of expression. Unlike, say, Epicureanism, which can lead to greater refinement of taste, sexual hedonism naturally spirals downward. Once sexual excitement and gratification becomes generally accepted as ends in themselves – rather than as the means to fulfilling the natural purpose of reproduction, the only conceivable source of a natural 'measure' – there is hardly any limit to how low people may sink in pursuit of fresh stimulation. Behaving little better than beasts, they come to accept without shame a corresponding view of themselves.[86] Even Constable Elbow dimly foresees something of the ultimate consequence of all this (3.2.1–4). Escalus says more than he realizes in chiding Pompey, "Troth, and your bum is the greatest thing about you; so that, in the beastliest sense, you are Pompey the Great" (2.1.214–16, 249–53). The Duke, made of sterner stuff, does not leave it at chiding:

> Do thou but think
> What 'tis to cram a maw or clothe a back
> From such a filthy vice. Say to thyself,
> From their abominable and beastly touches
> I drink, I eat, array myself, and live.
> Canst thou believe thy living is a life,
> So stinkingly depending?
>
> ... Take him to prison, officer:
> Correction and instruction must both work
> Ere this rude beast will profit.
>
> (3.2.20–32)

However, not everyone reacts to the declining standards of sexual behaviour by acceding and conforming to them. Some people, judging sexual relations as such by what they see of the ambient practices, are repelled by the ignobility inherent in the shameless pursuit of mere bodily gratification. Such people, and they are for the most part a clearly better if smaller class, accordingly prefer to have as little as possible to do with the sexual side of life. They do not usually go so far as Isabella, who regards illicit sex as the most abhorent of vices (2.2.29), who presumes her brother would (and should) die twenty times rather than she be a party to it (2.4.178–81), and who withdraws into a nunnery that does not allow its members to so much as speak with a man unsupervised (with she wishing it imposed an even "more strict restraint"; 1.4.4, 10–11).[87] But like Angelo, they are more repulsed than attracted by flagrant solicitation and wanton behaviour (2.2.183–5). Abstemious, prim, prudish, severe, narrow, and contemptuous of anyone who is not – in short, what we have come to call 'puritanical' – they can be as serious a political problem as the profligates. In their self-righteousnes, they are intolerant, and resistant to any arguments that their overall view of life – that it is something to be endured rather than enjoyed – is not a wholesome one. Libertines, by contrast, may congratulate themselves on being liberated from 'irrational inhibitions' and silly moral rules that obstruct their enjoying life's pleasures; but they cannot pretend even to themselves that as a consequence they occupy higher moral ground. Like Lucio, they know well enough why they prefer the "foppery of freedom," and that indulging one's desires is easy, anyone can do it, whereas denial requires strength of character. By the same reasoning, puritans can take pride in their asceticism (as Angelo privately confesses; 2.4.9–10), bespeaking as it does self-control over the baser appetites, and imparting a sober dignity and gravity to one's life. The Angelos see no cause to doubt their moral superiority to the Lucios of this world. Presumably, this is what the Duke is counting on in putting Angelo in charge, that the one kind of extremism will cure the other. But perhaps he is also aware that the puritan's rigid self-control, entailing so much repression of nature, is of a brittle sort: that subjected to sufficient temptation, it cannot bend, only break. Is he also, then, counting on Angelo's compromising himself to such an extent as will force a moderating of his character, tempering his strong but almost-mechanical sense of justice (2.1.27–31; 2.2.101–5; 5.1.365–72) with some compassionate understanding born of experiencing normal human weaknesses? The Duke may agree with what Mariana has somewhere heard: "They say best men are moulded out of faults, / And, for the most, become much more the better / For being a little bad" (5.1.437–9).

The punishment to which Duke Vincentio subjects Angelo seems infinitely more humane than that administered to Remirro de Orco by Duke Valentino. But Angelo *is* made to suffer, and most painfully, in publicly surrendering his posture of obdurate moral fastidiousness, his 'precision.' He professes to find his humiliation a fate worse than death (5.1.472–5). Like all rational punishment, however, its aim is to make him a better man – and perhaps not incidentally, make him still more useful to the Duke. As noted earlier, the lengths to which Vincentio was prepared to go to protect Angelo's reputation suggest a concern to preserve, and if possible enhance, his political utility. Isabella, too, is put through a painful ordeal: made to feel the loss of a brother, publicly confess to fornication, be adjudged mad, sent to prison, and finally beg mercy for her enemy. As Angelo is possibly transformed into a more useful political auxiliary by his suffering, the high-spirited Isabella is definitely transformed into a more suitable prospective wife (and the Duke never need worry about *her* chastity!). These two saintlier-than-thou characters having been brought down from the pedestals they created for themselves and obliged to concede their common humanity, they are now open to a moral posture superior to that of rigid asceticism: rational moderation, in which sexual gratification (along with other pleasures) has its proper place. That place is mainly within marriage and for the sake of family, no other arrangement being compatible with healthy political life. Thus, this uncomfortable comedy concludes in a spree of marriages, with the Duke himself leading by example as well as by fiat.

'By fiat' – for that is the first point worth noting about these otherwise so very different marriages: all four, including his own, are *mandated* by this philosopher–ruler – much as Sokrates assures Glaukon that truly just rulers would "marry wherever they want, giving [in marriage] to whomever they will" (*Republic* 613d). The managing of suitable marriages in their imagined city was the central piece of business Sokrates addressed in book 5 of that dialogue (458e ff),[88] and the mismanagement of marriages cited for the eventual decay of their city (546a–d). A second point: the legalization of three of these marriages is after the fact, so to speak, as they have already been consummated (to be sure, each under radically different moral circumstances). That in only one of the three cases does the man intend to regard his 'natural marriage' as permanently binding shows the necessity of there being laws to govern these matters. This implies the third point: two of the marriages are 'political' in the extreme, being punitive – for the grooms, surely, and quite possibly for the brides as well. A final point: in the case of one union, that upon which most attention is focused and about which most questions would naturally be raised – Angelo's coerced wedding of Mariana – the Duke resorted to an elaborate deception to bring about its 'premarital' consummation, which he then uses to justify the coercion (5.1.417–20; cf. *Republic* 459b–460a).

So, as nuptial festivals go, this one is passing strange. What might we conclude from it? That none of the four marriages would seem to be anyone's 'ideal' may itself be relevant to what the play has to teach on the subject: that there shall be marriages, regardless of their seldom being ideal. They may nonetheless be fitting, and can be made to work tolerably well, given a determined effort by the principals and a sufficiently supportive political context. The Duke, in publicly demonstrating that he can and may choose when and with whom his subjects will marry, tacitly encourages them to pre-empt this option by a timely choosing of mates for themselves lest they (like Lucio and Angelo) are mandated marriages they might regard as 'worse than death.' There would seem no need for such a heavy-handed management of *erōs* in a decent society – which means, first and foremost, sexually decent – but perhaps nothing less will suffice to restore decency to a polity as corrupt as Vienna had become.[89]

As the result of his descent into the lower city, Vincentio has learned that being privately virtuous is not sufficient for being reputed virtuous:

> No might nor greatness in mortality
> Can censure 'scape. Back-wounding calumny
> The whitest virtue strikes. What king so strong
> Can tie the gall up in a slanderous tongue?
> (3.2.179–82)

While acknowledging the practical impossibility of eliminating all disparagement of his person, the Duke sees the need to use his power publicly to discourage it so far as is possible, since his doing so is in the public interest.[90] Even supposing that Lucio's bawdy insinuations about "the old fantastical duke of dark corners" have no basis in fact,[91] Vincentio must realize that his dwelling in relative seclusion while widespread sexual misconduct goes unchecked has made it that much easier for such rumours to circulate, and in doing so, further validate the licentious behaviour of his subjects. The best way to lay such rumours to rest is by regularizing the sexual dimension of his own life through a public marriage, especially to a beautiful, spirited young woman known to have *very* strict views on the matter.

The importance of his setting a salutary example of sexual conduct is not all that the Duke learned through his secret visit to the depths of his city. His experience has also brought home to him the broader truth of his own admonition to Angelo:

> Thyself and thy belongings
> Are not thine own so proper as to waste
> Thyself upon thy virtues, they on thee.
> Heaven doth with us as we with torches do,
> Not light them for themselves; for if our virtues
> Did not go forth of us, 'twere all alike
> As if we had them not.
> (1.1.29–35)

Living comfortably insulated in his citadel while relying upon his subordinates, the Duke had only a remote, abstract appreciation of the consequences of his negligent attitude towards law enforcement. Coming face to face with the everyday reality, the evidence steadily mounting of its degeneracy – "Still thus, and thus: still worse!" (3.2.51; 216–22) – seeing "corruption boil and bubble / Till it o'errun the stew" (5.1.316–17) – has been a sobering revelation. He cannot continue serenely to regard himself as *just* while permitting what he has seen to continue (or recur), since it is in his power to ensure that it does not. Unlike Sokrates, Vincentio cannot justly claim for himself the luxury of a private citizen to engage in political activity only so much or so little as he pleases. Thrown by fortune into a position of sovereign political responsibility, which he must either exercise or abdicate, he is obliged to make the best of it. And he cannot fool himself that abdication would be making the best of it, given the qualities that he alone could bring to the task of ruling – truths all the more pressing if he takes seriously his professed "love ... in doing good" (3.1.197). Thus, he must now return to the 'Cave' that is his city as its Guardian, as truly the soldier-statesman he claims to be, not merely as the detached scholar he might prefer to be (3.2.142).[92] Having learned that he must become more actively involved in the ruling of his regime – mainly by becoming and remaining better acquainted with the characters and doings of *all* his various subordinate officers, that indispensible cohort of intermediaries through whose agency he will actually rule (cf. 3.2.5; 4.2.84–5; 5.1.527–8) – he can take comfort in knowing his task will be made the easier by virtue of his enjoying a reputation for almost godlike omniscience (5.1.365–8).

What is perhaps most important, however, Duke Vincentio has learned that he has much to learn from participating more directly in political life, and not least of all, about himself. He had prided himself on being a skilful judge of people's natures (4.2.154), but Angelo's proving capable of judicial murder clearly caught him off guard. The not-so-clever 'bed trick' presumed – rather naïvely, as it turned out – that Angelo would stand by his immoral bargain. Confident that he knew his man, it apparently never occurred to the Duke that, having agreed to pardon Claudio, Angelo would nonetheless order his execution simply to ensure himself against future revenge (4.4.26–30). To the very instant the Provost reads Angelo's special writ dashing all hope of commutation, the Duke is predicting clemency ("This is his pardon, purchas'd by such sin / For which the pardoner himself is in"; 4.2.106–7). Thus the Duke learns that it is *he* who needs "to practise his judgment with the disposition of natures" (3.1.162–3) – as can be done only in the midst of political life, exposing oneself to the entire spectrum of human nature in all conditions of living.[93]

The Duke may also have learned that he still has something to learn about justice. And justice is the question of questions for political philosophy.[94] But a full appreciation of the practical problems justice poses can be acquired only 'in action,' as it were, since only then are the *feelings* involved with justice displayed.[95] There are those necessary but dangerous expressions of the spirit that energize the demand for justice: anger, indignation, outrage even – such as Isabella becomes so over-filled with, losing all sense of proportion; but also feelings of sympathy and pity for erring humans, especially for those who truly feel shame and remorse. One's feelings, however, will be only as appropriate, hence as reliable, as the understanding that guides them. And gaining a correct understanding of justice is a challenge that few can meet on their own, for reasons the play helps us appreciate. We are reminded of some of the practical complexities of justice in the argument between Angelo and Escalus (2.1.1–31): the inevitable unevenness of its actual application ("What's open made to justice, *that* justice seizes"), and the inevitable imperfections of those who administer it – neither of which considerations must be allowed to compromise a polity's best efforts, as that would result in the complete triumph of injustice. Angelo reminds us of the most important practical distinction of all: between thought and deed ("'Tis one thing to be tempted, Escalus, / Another thing to fall"). For we are all subject to temptation; that is why laws are needed. And the entire play reminds us of a degree of 'relativity' inherent in practically administering justice; that is, of the need for much stricter enforcement and much harsher penalties to instil or restore order among a dissolute, ill-disciplined populace, compared with what is required to maintain order in a responsible, law-abiding community of people.

It is in the two confrontations between Angelo and Isabella, however, that some of the more fundamental issues concerning justice itself are raised. Precisely because we acknowledge the practical imperfections Angelo is prepared to accept in administering the law, we readily see why justice cannot be equated with the rule of law, however perspicacious lawgivers might be. Moreover, there will always be 'legitimate exceptions,' as the case of Claudio is intended to show. Although technically in violation of the law, "He hath but as offended in a dream" (so the unhappy Provost puts it; 2.2.4). But this means there must be something higher than the law, an idea of justice in light of which one judges *both* the normal justness of the law *and* the legitimacy of the exception.[96] Hence, even in 'theory' justice is not reducible to strict legality. Nor, of course, is justice to be confused with mercy, which is commonly regarded as an alternative to, or at least a qualification upon, strict justice.[97] However, presuming that being merciful is sometimes itself the just thing – that a person may for some reason *deserve* mercy (having previously performed an especially valuable service, for example, perhaps at some risk or cost to himself) – then clearly the matter is more complicated than the 'Justice *vs* Mercy' schema allows.

If Duke Vincentio (or any reader) believed he already possessed an adequate understanding of justice, the issues involved in regulating people's sexual conduct provide the perfect test.[98] In his troubled soliloquy after first meeting Isabella, Angelo expresses a convenient entry point to the array of problems involved, asking, "What's this? What's this? Is this her fault, or mine? / The tempter, or the tempted, who sins most, ha?" (2.2.163–4). Not an easy question, at least insofar as neither the one *intended* to be tempting nor the other to be susceptible. So, one might say 'both'; or one might say 'neither,' and instead blame Nature. But this natural dialectic of tempting and being tempted is endlessly repeated throughout political life, only further complicated by the various degrees and permutations of intentionality, ambivalence, and awareness. Thus, it presents a range of problems all regimes must deal with, which means they must confront the very question Angelo asks. Whatever way a given polity answers it will have profound implications for its entire ordering of life. In attempting to manage people's sexual natures, channelling them in ways that will maintain a decent civic order, generation by generation, should the laws focus primarily on minimizing the temptations by restraints and restrictions on the temptresses? Or should the onus be primarily on the tempted, with laws, morals, and manners arranged so as to stiffen their resolve to resist temptation? Virtually all regimes address the problem from both directions, so to speak, encouraging to some degree both female modesty and male self-restraint. But within this broad range of possibilities, they differ widely, both as to how they balance their efforts, and as to the overall extent to which they endeavour to control such matters. There are regimes which are extremely permissive, like Vienna at the beginning of *Measure for Measure* (to say nothing of Sodom and Gomorrah), others extremely puritanical, with most regimes somewhere in between. What is the best and most just arrangement, one wonders?

Suffice it to say, it is a problem (and there are numerous others) presenting challenges worthy of a philosopher, as Duke Vincentio has come to realize. Having thus discovered that an openness to political life can serve his philosophical interests, he can to some considerable extent – within measure – reconcile his political responsibilities with his higher love, doing justice to both his city and himself.

FINAL REMARKS ON SHAKESPEARE AS PHILOSOPHER-POET

An obvious implication of my analyses of the plays addressed in this book is that Shakespeare was an assiduous student of philosophical texts and problems, especially of Plato's texts and problems, and most especially those having to do with the relation between philosophy and political power. His appreciation of Machiavelli's hard-nosed, clear-eyed, forked-tongue realism about power was part and parcel of that larger interest. While I am hardly the first to attribute profound philosophical understanding to Shakespeare, it is a view of him that runs counter to certain assumptions that are widely held today about the man and his art. Accordingly, I have tried to present some of the evidence for it more fully and thoroughly analysed than has been done heretofore.[99]

However, there might seem to be an enormous objection to Shakespeare's having the close relationship with Plato that I claim for him, an objection based upon Plato's being famous – or infamous – for his scathing criticism of poetry, condemning it as both morally unwholesome and intellectually shallow, thus banishing it, or at least all of the more pleasing and powerful forms of it, from the "beautiful city"(*kallipolis*, 527c) described in his *Republic*. Although one could reply that this common understanding of Plato's view of poetry is decidedly superficial,[100] the objection based upon it cannot be simply dismissed. Moreover, in considering Plato's critique, one goes some way towards clarifying both what poetry is, and its relationship to philosophy.

Any defence of poetry, to be adequate, must one way or another address the ironic attack upon it that Plato ascribed to his own greatest dramatic creation, 'Sokrates' – a fictitious character presumably true to the nature of the historical man, but (by Plato's own admission; *Second Ltr* 314c) made "handsome and young," or "noble and new" (*kalou kai neou*), by art. Although the "ancient quarrel" between poetry and philosophy is referred to only belately in his *Republic* (607b), one sees in retrospect that the dialogue is preoccupied with the inherent tension between these rival authorities, literally from its beginning to its ending in an exemplary piece of philosophical poetry, the magisterial 'Tale of Er.' This being so, a just exposition of its teaching about poetry would require a book unto itself (at least). What follows, then, is but the beginning of such an exposition, but adequate I hope for the present limited purpose.[101]

The first criticism of poetry is implicit in Sokrates' first reference to poets. He has inquired of his very old host, a wealthy arms merchant named Kephalos, as to the source of his considerable wealth: was it inherited or earned? Having heard the old man's reply ('some of both'), the philosopher explains the reason for his question: that unlike most bigtime moneymakers, but instead like those who do *not* regard their wealth as of their own earning, Kephalos does not seem to be "overly fond" of money. Whereas those who mainly earn it themselves are doubly attached to it, valuing it for its utility (as other people do), but also as their own accomplishment. "For just as poets are fond of their own poems and fathers of their children, so too are moneymakers serious about their money, as being their own product [work, deed; *ergon*]" (330c). That is, the poet as such, manifesting the special 'love of one's own' that is a well-nigh univeral trait of human nature, is inclined to have a favourable opinion of his own poetry simply because it is his – and not, that is, because of its actual qualities. Being not merely an enjoyer but the 'maker' (the original, literal meaning of *poiētēs*, 'poet'), indeed the Maker par excellence who can claim credit for both the form and the matter of the poems he makes – the progeny of his soul, one could say – the poet may be suspected of caring more for his own subjective experience and personal perspective on things than for the truth. The implication would seem to be that the poet (and thus the 'poetic' constituent in each of us) values his own 'creativity' more than knowledge, ranks 'originality' higher than validity, and lives life accordingly.

The philosopher's second remark about the poets carries with it another criticism of them. It comes in the course of a discussion with Kephalos's son, Polemarchos, who invokes the authority of the poet Simonides in support of his and his father's view of justice, citing the poet's succinct definition: that it is just to give to each what is owed (331e). Sokrates presses the young man to explain more substantially what this high-sounding, pithy maxim actually means. Under the philosopher's gentle prodding, Polemarchos interprets it to mean: doing good to friends and bad to enemies, this being what is "fitting." Whereupon Sokrates observes that apparently, then, Simonides "made a *riddle*" in his "poetically" (*poiētikōs*) saying what is just, using the expression 'what is owed,' but leaving it to us to figure out that this means treating people in whatever way is fitting or appropriate (332a–c). The implication is that a poet's seemingly wisest pronouncements are typically ambiguous, equivocal, oracular, 'riddling.' Such utterances being open to a variety of interpretations, a person can invest them with whatever meaning seems wisest to him. The poet's reputation is enhanced accordingly, being admired by a diversity of people who would by no means agree on precisely what is the 'wisdom' the poet expresses.

These initial observations about poets are delivered en passant, as it were. However, poetry is twice the explicit focus of extended criticism in the dialogue. The perspective of the first critique (end of book 2 through middle of book 3) is overtly political; that of the second, philosophical (book 10). The first arises out of the need to educate the prospective Guardians and rulers in both 'music' (in the original sense of the word: all that falls within the jurisdiction of the Muses) and 'gymnastic' (i.e., athletics). It thus entails an appraisal of the already established musical education, which means primarily the great poets (especially Homer) who provide people their basic architecture of beliefs about the most important matters: about the divine powers and their relations with the mortal realm, hence, about the nature of the world and man's place in it; about death and Hades, and so the fate of the human soul; and about heroes, that is, models of human excellence. The traditional poets are blamed, not because the tales they tell are lies, but because the lies they tell are not fine ones (377d) – that is, they have pernicious political and personal consequences. For example, how can one expect citizens to remain at peace with one another, or cultivate self-control, or the young to respect their elders, if they have been nurtured since childhood in the belief that even the gods war among themselves, and mutilate their parents, and destroy their own offspring, and are carried away by their passions (378b–d, 388b–c, 390b–c)?

Left to tell whatever tales they please, much of what poets make will be politically pernicious because, first of all, they are not sufficiently aware of their own ignorance concerning that about which they speak, much less of the more remote consequences of people believing the stories they fashion. But inasmuch as they say things in the beautiful way that the majority of people find persuasive and pleasing (397d) – rather, persuasive because pleasing (which nicely complements a poet's natural fondness for his own poems) – poets readily imagine themselves wise, being unaware of what a long, strenuous, all-consuming effort the pursuit of true wisdom requires (494d, 535d; cf *Apology of Sokrates* 22a–c). And to the extent a poet is desirous of fame (and fortune too, of course, if possible), he is disposed to gratify the tastes of those who bestow recognition and appreciation, irrespective of whether doing so strengthens propensities in people that ought not be indulged, or weakens those most in need of being amplified (395d ff).

Thus, in the interest of nurturing a virtuous citizenry, and of creating and maintaining a generally wholesome political environment, poets must not be free to make whatever they will. Instead, all tale-makers must be supervised by rulers who do have the requisite knowledge, and whose first concern is the good – not of themselves, much less of the poets – but of the polity as a whole (377b, 401b, 412d), and who thus will allow poets to produce only politically salutary fare. Moreover, to be acceptable, poets must forgo the modes and techniques that most people naturally find most pleasing: those which invoke and depict, hence ratify and encourage, extremes of passion and action (399e ff). So, should even a great poetic genius come to the city – one who has "the power by wisdom" to imitate virtually anything and everything – offering to display himself and his poems, he should be worshipped as "sacred, wonderful, and pleasing," but nonetheless not be allowed entry. To the extent we are concerned with the health of a polity and its people, we are obliged by nature to be content with "a more austere and less pleasing poet" (398a).

Lurking in the justification of this policy, however, is a disturbing acknowledgment. Namely, that not only are ignorant, lying, self-aggrandizing poets politically pernicious; but that a poet could be politically dangerous precisely because he may know, and so may tell, *the truth*, truths that are politically unsettling – ugly truths about human nature, for example, about the depths of the human soul, or about the limits of most people's prospects, truths which are perhaps especially evident to someone by virtue of the very gifts whereby he is capable of creating immortal poetry. Presuming this to be so, one can see inherent in the relationship between even great poetry and great politics a tension correspondent to that between the pursuit of knowledge (or love of truth) and the promotion of wholesome politics (or love of life), a tension that gives rise to distinctly *political* philosophy. Can there be a poetry comparably regardful of the requirements of decent political life – which the poet, like the philosopher, remains dependent upon – a poetry that can command the respect of truth-lovers and yet be salutary for citizens?

Plato's *Republic* concludes with a return to the subject of poetry. In this dialogue that repeatedly 'begins' (327a, 368b ff, 451b, 543c) – and which expressly cautions "that the beginning [*archē*] is the most important part of every work [*ergon*]" (377a) – the fresh beginning of book 10 stands out: it is the only one that is in no way imposed upon Sokrates (cf. 327c, 357a, 449b ff, 544b). It is Sokrates' sole voluntary extension of the night's long conversation. Indeed, the discussion would seem to be complete with book 9, the superiority of the just life having been established to the satisfaction of the interlocutors who challenged the philosopher to prove just that. But rather than leave well enough alone, Sokrates offers his summary judgment that the city they set out to "make in speech [*logos*]" (369c) is "entirely correct," and not least with respect to poetry (595a). Thus is initiated what turns out to be a philosophical critique of poetry, assessing its *intellectual* adequacy as a fit educator of human beings – a critique that apparently complements the earlier political or moral one, confirming it from a higher, transpolitical perspective.

On the surface, the case is fairly straightforward. The poet, insofar as he is primarily if not simply a poet – a maker of moving speeches – does not apprehend Reality, that is, the singular forms (eidē; 596a, 597c) that are the ultimate sources (*archai*; 511b) of the essential identities of their many respective instantiations. Not having sought, much less found, these truly divine things, the poet cannot model his making directly on them (as might a philosopher; 500c–e). Rather, his making is only an imitation of the various appearances (*phantasmata*) of these instances (598a–b). As such, what the poet makes is but a shadow or reflection of a phantom of Reality, thrice removed from reality itself (597e, 599a); and this is especially so with respect to his portrayal of human excellence (600e). Moreover, his plausibility as a knower rests on kinds of deceitful ornamentation (metre, rhythm, harmony) that are rationally irrelevant to assessing what is true and false, but nonetheless "by nature possess great charm." As a charming deceiver, the poet is a kind of wizard, who thereby seems "all-wise" (*passophos*) to those who do not know how to test for true knowledge (598d, 602d). Were his makings stripped of their artificial beauty, their cosmetic finery, his views would be seen for the prosaic things they actually are (601a–b) – mere endorsements of the common opinions and prejudices to which he necessarily defers, not knowing any better himself (602b). In this respect, the poet is indistinguishable from a sophist (see 493b–d). Moreover, insofar as his makings, his 'poetry,' appeal not to reason, but to the subrational parts of the soul (603a–b, 605a) – to the hopes and hates, desires and dreads, to the envies and vanities and resentments familiar to everyone – they in effect give people licence to indulge and thereby strengthen passions that decent people would otherwise be ashamed to express in public, all at the expense of reason's capacity to rule (602a, 605b–e). Indeed, the greatest charge against poetry is that it has this power to maim the souls of all but the very few, very best sort of people – everyone, that is, who lacks solid knowledge both of the matters about which the poet speaks, and of how imitation works its thought-deceiving, soul-deforming effects (605c; cf. 595b). For poetry preys especially upon a passion that is basic to one's very humanity, its role essential to both the philosophical and the political sides of human nature: *pity* – the capacity, through the power of the rational imagination, to *feel* what others feel (thus, 'sym-pathy,' 'com-passion,' 'com-miseration'). Without pity, one would have neither understanding of, nor care for, other people. A man, or a woman, without pity is a monster, an alien being who merely appears human. But pity is also an especially dangerous passion precisely because it seems so benign, so decent, so 'humane.' For left unchecked, it subverts justice by excessive mercy, and subverts self-control by encouraging self-pity: "For having fed strong the pitying part, it is not easily restrained in one's own sufferings" (606b).[102] This applies mainly to tragedy. But something similar holds for comedy as well. Giving way to that in one which wants to laugh, irrespective of whether or not reason confirms a thing to be truly laughable, strengthens excessively a base tendency in people to act more like apes than humans (606c; cf. 452d). So it goes for the other desires and passions; imitative poetry fosters what ought to be allowed to wither – establishing as rulers in the soul what ought to be ruled, namely, pleasure and pain (606d, 607a).

This, in short, is the political philosopher's ostensible case against the poet: that he is mired in his own subjectivity; that he thrives through speaking ambiguously; that he does not actually know what he is talking about; and that he undermines both moral character and reason's ability to rule in the soul by strengthening passions and distorting judgment.

These are over and above the criticisms Sokrates makes elsewhere about the inadequacies of the art of writing in general: that it weakens memory; that unlike live conversation, it is static and thus cannot be questioned in order either to clarify or justify what it says, but simply keeps saying the same things over and over again; that it is inherently imprudent speech, unable to discriminate when and to whom to speak, when and before whom to be silent; that instead, being accessible to whoever can read, it says the same things to everyone, be they young or old, sensible or foolish, friend or enemy (*Phaedrus* 274b–278d). Of course, one is obliged to reflect on the fact that the philosopher's criticisms of writing have all been given in writing, and so must be applied reflexively to it. It is a peculiar piece of writing in that it appears to imitate live conversation, and includes the acknowledgment that wise men and women from old have indeed conveyed some of their wisdom in writing (235b). It even provides explicit criteria whereby to judge a well-wrought piece of written discourse, one manifesting 'logographic necessity': that it be organized like a living being, in which each part is necessary and proportioned to fit with every other part, and the parts together are sufficient (264b–c; cf. 263b, 277b–c).[103]

Every serious student of Shakespeare's plays, just as of Plato's dialogues, will attest that they amply fulfil these 'logographic' requirements, and moreover are immune to Sokrates' general criticisms of written speech: studying them does not weaken but instead exercises, thus strengthens one's memory; they do not on successive readings keep saying the same things; nor do they say the same things to everybody, regardless of qualities of character, mind, and experience (no doubt they remain essentially silent to some); and they can be questioned, and when read more closely, often will clarify and even justify themselves to a reader who is willing to expend the effort it takes to understand them as did their author. But what about that author's understanding? Can Shakespeare be as easily defended against Sokrates' criticisms of the poet as such? For the philosopher's indictment is a powerful one, and doubtless valid with respect to the vast, *vast* majority of tale-makers. There may be other considerations that offset Sokrates' criticisms, but who could with a straight face defend as wise, as profoundly knowledgeable concerning the things about which they write, today's most popular, fashionable, or successful 'poets' – all our makers of novels, plays, and scripts for television and movies? Or that the political and personal effects on the people exposed to their 'poetry' is generally salutary, that their makings raise and refine the general level of culture and encourage virtue? Or who would deny that these 'poets,' along with other so-called artists, are not enamoured of their own subjectivity, and see their products as primarily a means of 'self-expression,' and regard complete freedom for such expression – regardless of consequences – as a natural right? Or that given a free political environment, the most successful makers (that is, who garner the most fame and fortune) are mainly those who most wilfully and skilfully pander to people's lower desires, especially their almost insatiable appetites for vicarious lust and mayhem?

But is what is true about the vast majority of poets necessarily true about *all* poets, true about poetry as such? If not, might some poets, the very best poets, even agree with the philosopher's criticism of the poetry made by the many inferior poets? First, however, one might wonder whether the surface of Sokrates' critique is the whole story. The fact that Sokrates himself describes it as an "apology" for their decision to expel imitative poetry from the city they made in speech is perhaps indicative of its partial, even partisan, character (607b; cf. 595a). For taken literally, an *apology* is a 'defence speech,' and as such may be construed as a piece of rhetoric, implicitly understood to be *not* a full and impartial exposition of the issues. Moreover, in virtually the next breath, Sokrates admits to there being "an ancient quarrel between philosophy and poetry," citing several examples of poets' criticisms of philosophers as evidence of "this old opposition." He then opens the door to the possibility of there being arguments (or speeches; *logon*) showing imitative poetry and its pleasures to have a rightful place in a well-ordered polity, adding that he would be delighted for it to be recalled from exile, if rationally persuaded that doing so was consonant with the truth (607c). And despite his earlier warning about its dangerous charm (601a), he is even prepared to accept an "apology" for poetry rendered in *metre*, as well as listen benevolently to any "friends" or "lovers of poetry" (*philopoiētai*) who can show in prose "that it is not only pleasant but also beneficial to regimes and human life" (607d). However, in the absence of such an apology for it, and aware of its natural erotic appeal, he shall continue to chant his argument against it as a countercharm (608a).

Accepting the philosopher's tacit invitation to reconsider his critique of poetry, one might begin by more carefully examining the examples he cites as evidence for the veracity of his claims. The primary one is Homer, described as the teacher and leader of all the beautiful, noble things of tragedy (595b–c, 598d), and commonly credited as "the poet who educated Greece" (606e). (Until some way into the twentieth century, Shakespeare would have been for English speakers the closest counterpart to Homer.) Allusions and references to Homer, by no means all of them expressly acknowledged, pervade the dialogue from beginning to end; he is mentioned by name – the first of forty-three times – in Sokrates' conversation with Polemarchos (334a), while Homeric features and characters figure prominently in the concluding 'Tale of Er.' Although elsewhere in the dialogue he is cited with approval (and even his authority invoked; e.g., 468c–d), aspects of his portrayal of gods, heroes, and Hades, as well as his imitative technique, are the principal targets of the earlier political critique of poetry in books 2 and 3. Suffice it to say, a comprehensive examination of whether Sokrates' actual treatment of Homer squares with his philosophical critique of poetry is a task virtually coextensive with that of interpreting the whole dialogue. However, simply reflecting upon the references to Homer within the philosophical critique itself may serve adequately to test or qualify it.

It effectively begins with Sokrates' confessing that, since he was a child, he has felt towards Homer "a certain friendship [*philia*] and modesty [or shame; *aidōs*]" (595b; see *Apology* 22b). Still, the truth must be told: "for a man must not be honoured ahead of the truth." Having argued that the imitative artist, of which the painter would seem the paradigmatic example, is thrice removed from reality and the truth; and that the same can be said, then, about the maker of tragedies, "*if* he is an imitator" 597e) – that done, Sokrates turns to an extensive consideration of Homer. For there are those who contend that he is "all-wise," "knowing all arts and all things human pertaining to virtue and vice, and things divine as well" (598d–e). (One is reminded of the many admirers of Shakespeare who have claimed as much for him, including a broad array of technical knowledge.) The people who believe this simply presume that such knowledge is the prerequisite of making beautiful poems that seem 'realistic.' But in this perhaps they are deceived, and that it is actually easy to create what will merely *appear* true to those who do not themselves know what *is* true. So this is what must be tested: do "good poets" really *know* the things about which people believe them to speak so well (599a)? Note, the philosopher concedes this to be a practical possibility, at least in the case of good poets; indeed, knowing that about which he speaks might be what distinguishes a truly good poet. Given, however, that the poet is not available to be directly examined, rigorously questioned in order to determine whether or not he can give an adequate rational defense of his views (cf. 531e), how is this to be tested?

The indirect test that Sokrates suggests is somewhat curious, for it rests on a set of premises that are suspect (to say the least). First, that a person who was able to do or make *both* the thing that is imitated *and* its imitation would not be seriously interested in the latter, nor regard that as his best accomplishment. Thus, second, anyone who was "in truth a *knower* of that which he can also imitate" would be more intent on doing the actual *deeds* such knowledge makes possible than in producing imitations of them. For, third, noble deeds are more fitting memorials of oneself than are the laudatory descriptions of such deeds. And, fourth, that given the choice, anyone would rather be the eulogized than the eulogizer (Glaukon supposes so, since the respective "honour and benefit are not equal"; 599b). *Ergo*, anyone who has made only imitations of the deeds, but not done the deeds himself, must be presumed to lack the knowledge requisite for doing the deeds. And since not even the expert Homeridae, who would be the first to insist that Homer is the greatest of the poets, credit their favourite with having done any of the great deeds he memorializes – he restored no one's health, as he tells us Asclepius did, nor accomplished any other technical feat; he commanded no armies, won no great victories in war; is not famed with being any city's lawgiver, nor with having provided any city with good governance; no significant inventions or clever schemes are attributed to him; nor could he boast of any great educational accomplishments (he founded no school, much less established a distinct way of life, as did Pythagoras) – we must conclude that making imitations of deeds was the best he could manage, because he lacked sufficient knowledge for doing the deeds themselves (599c–600e).

Now, there are a variety of objections one can raise by way of rebutting the case of the philosopher-turned-prosecutor – in fact, a variety of *kinds* of objections. For instance, one can cite 'empirical evidence' against it: actual people who stand as unproblematic counter-examples with respect to one or more of the premises. Plato's contemporary and fellow eulogizer of Sokrates, Xenophon, who played a leading role in the events he memorialized in his *Anabasis of Cyrus*, clearly placed a higher value on this and his other writings than on his or most other men's deeds. Similar remarks pertain to Thucydides and his *History* of the Peloponnesian War (and who, incidentally, treats Homer's account of the war between the Greeks and the Trojans as the only serious rival to the story he tells; and since his historical purpose is completed and extended by Xenophon's *Hellenika*, one must assume that Xenophon shared Thucydides' estimate of the work's importance). Or one might invoke the authority of certain modern novelists, men such as Melville and Conrad who acquired expert knowledge of life at sea upon which they based works of permanent value, and which doubtless they regarded as the finest accomplishments of their lives (and which, for that matter, eventually brought them far greater honour, and even a bit more fortune, than did the experiences themselves). These men, then, while proven capable of engaging in the actions about which they write – at least so far as knowledge is the issue – chose to write about them as well, or instead.

'So far as knowledge is the issue.' But with respect to deeds, virtually never is their doing solely a matter of knowledge. Many other factors enter into determining who can do what; to mention but some of the more important: qualities of body (no blind poet, however knowledgeable, can lead troops into battle, or engage the enemy's champion in personal combat); other qualities of soul (the knowledge of a surgeon is beside the point if he cannot stay sober); opportunity (it is difficult to prove oneself the greatest general if there are no wars); material resources (what use knowing how to build cathedrals if there is no stone, or no men to work it?); social standing (what chance a glover's son from Stratford becoming King of England, be he ever so knowledgeably suited to rule?). Even performing noble deeds of education entails more than simply being knowledgeable in what is to be taught: additional skills of explicating and motivating, the desire to teach, access to suitable students, liberty. Suffice it to say, even were one to grant the dubious claim that doing noble deeds is inherently preferable to telling about them – 'imitating' them, if that is quite what it is – there are any number of reasons why someone profoundly knowledgeable about them might not choose, or be able, to do them. Hence, Sokrates' case against Homer's, or any other poet's, being knowledgeable proves far from conclusive.

Of course, there is something at least slightly paradoxical about exalting the *honour* that accrues to the doer of noble deeds in comparison with the praiser of them, given that the former is so largely dependent upon the latter. Beyond that, however, here too there is some important empirical evidence to the contrary. One thinks immediately of that ironic line (though presumably not intended as such) in Lincoln's 'Gettysburg Address': "The world will little note, nor long remember, what we say here, but it can never forget what they did here" – whereas the opposite has turned out to be true: Lincoln's words have become immortal, while the individuals who perished in that pivotal battle are otherwise all but forgotten. In this respect, the famous 'Funeral Oration' of 'Pericles' is doubly ironic: the dead whose deeds are praised are completely forgotten except for this oration, which in turn would be forgotten (and the orator's reputation considerably diminished) were it not preserved in Thucydides' artful imitation. How many noble Greeks and Romans owe the world's recollection of them primarily to Shakespeare's favourite classical source, Plutarch, who continues to enjoy more renown today than all but a few of those whose lives he depicts?

Still more ironic, however, is Sokrates' treatment of Homer as Educator. Having considered and dismissed any claim to his having done great public deeds, Sokrates turns to the private sphere, asking whether there is any evidence of Homer's being a leader in educating individuals, people who cherished the opportunity to be with him, and patterned a way of life based on his (as in the case of Pythagoras, and some of the famous sophists). According to the traditional accounts of him, the contrary was true: that he suffered great neglect, and was obliged to gain his living as a lowly, wandering rhapsode. But if he was actually knowledgeable and not just an imitator, if he were "really able to educate human beings and make them better," would he not have acquired a company of comrades who would have jealously kept him with them, or accompanied him wherever he went? (600a–d). Of course, the best evidence supporting this claim is provided – not by the various sophists cited – but by the historical example of the man here portrayed as making it. However, one can be a great educator without enjoying direct, personal contact with one's students – as a hundred generations of grateful readers of Plato's dialogues, in which the image of the living man is preserved, would testify. It is in this sense that Homer "educated Greece," as the "the praisers of Homer" were wont to say (606e). Until, that is, his heroic portrayals were supplanted by a new one: that of Plato's Sokrates.[104] The evident power of these ever-young and beautiful 'imitations' of the man who founded political philosophy, and who by his martyr's death gained at least grudging acceptance for its presence in the polity, prompts one to re-examine 'his' account of "what imitation generally is" (595c ff).

It begins with a notion of imitation as image-making in the most literal sense: using an actual mirror to produce images of everything made by manual artisans, along with all that grows naturally from and on the earth, including humans, and the earth itself, and even the heavens. But when Sokrates adds, "and gods and everything in heaven and everything in Hades under the earth," surely one is meant to object. One could use a mirror to 'make' images of existing visible images of such things (statues and paintings, or of actors impersonating gods or the dead in Hades), but not the things themselves. Or is the philosopher subtly suggesting there are no such things, but only imagined representations of them? Be that as it may, his own account of 'divine things' (cf. 500c–d) – of the eternal, unchanging beings that truly cause and rule the ever-changing realm of perishable, perceptible things – stresses that they are intelligible but not perceptible (507b ff). No actual mirror can show the forms of dog or man, or of the virtues, much less of the ultimate ruler of all that is: the Good (see 508e–509b). Nor does the mirror provide a conception of imitation that can be straightforwardly applied to Homer, proving him to be a mere imitator, thrice removed from reality. Even his most detailed 'word-pictures' (such as his famous description of Achilles' shield) do not correspond to some object in the way that a reflection in a mirror does to the thing reflected.

Following from this mirror-image idea of imitating visible things, Sokrates introduces the painter (596e). Insofar as the images a painter makes are themselves visible, and can be accurate portraits of visible things he sees (such as the picture of an actual couch, one of many made by a couchmaker in 'imitation' of his grasp of the singular idea of 'couchness'; 597a), it initially seems plausible to assimilate painted images to those produced by mirrors. But a moment's thought dispels the plausibility. For the painter can also make images that correspond to nothing he has ever laid eyes on. That is, he may paint what he has only imagined, perhaps stimulated or inspired by what he has heard or read. For example, having been nurtured on Homer, he may 'envision' Odysseus visiting Achilles in Hades, and render it visible to others on a painted surface. In this case, is his 'imitation' thrice removed from Reality? It would seem to depend on what counts as the pertinent 'reality.' The actual visit? Homer's account? Or the painter's own vision (which need not be based on someone else's description)? In any event, what he does is closer to that of Homer than is that done by a man with a mirror. Yet it still is not an idea of imitation that works to explain what Homer made, those epics that read *as if* they are merely descriptive accounts, 'imitations,' of what other men have actually done – as Sokrates here pretends to treat them – but which cannot conceivably be so simply characterized.

A vital clue to what is inadequate (if not simply wrong) with the treatment of Homer's poetry here in the centre of Sokrates' philosophical critique is its being radically inconsistent with his own earlier political critique – as, of course, we must presume him to be fully aware. Plato implicitly challenges the reader to rub the two critiques together and thereby generate a third view that coherently synthesizes both the political and philosophical considerations in a just assessment of poetry's proper place in human life (cf. 435a). One might begin by noting that in the earlier political critique, Sokrates rejected some of what Homer presents on the grounds that it is simply not true – so it could hardly be a mirror-like reflection of anything (cf. 379c–d, 391d). But the main point is that Sokrates censors feature after feature of the Homeric presentation of gods, Hades, and especially heroes as unsuitable to be heard, believed, and thereupon imitated by the Guardians and other citizens of his "beautiful city" – a city that exists in the same way as does Homer's Troy: in speech. That is, far from Homer's poetry providing merely a superficial record of other men's doings, his making it is itself a deed, a deed whereby he provides the bases for potentially countless imitations. Charmed by what he has made, actual men and women will attempt to model themselves in mind and character on the views and behaviour of his beautiful, larger-than-life heroes and heroines.

So, what is it, then, that radically distinguishes Homer's 'imitating' from that of any and all painters and sculptors? Sokrates expressly warns against trusting the mere "likelihood" that poetry is a paltry kind of imitating analogous to painting, but instead to consider directly what imitating human beings consists of, and to what part of the the mind poetic imitation appeals. He suggests that the poet "imitates humans performing forced or voluntary actions, and as a result of the actions supposing themselves to have done well or badly, and in all this feeling pain or joy." He asks whether there is any more to poetic imitation than this (603c). The correct answer is, "Yes, much more." For he has left out the most important thing: *logos*, 'rational speech.' Both Homer's medium and much of what he is imitating is *speech* – which, contrary to what Sokrates implies (603b), not only must be *heard* (or as written speech, seen), but *understood.* Only a maker who works in speech can possibly imitate human beings *doing* the most distinctly human things, those which 'bespeak' a rational soul: cursing and blaming, praying and pleading, exhorting and excusing, commanding and conceding, prescribing and pronouncing, praising and denouncing, apologizing and forgiving, but especially, conversing, arguing, persuading, justifying, and explaining – all the kinds of 'reasoning' that provide insight into *what* is being done (or attempted), and *why*. That is, the poet's appeal is necessarily in the first instance to the rational part of one's soul, that which understands what is described or spoken, out of which one's own imagination (itself a rational faculty; 511d–e) can then generate plausible characters to populate the story, and to which one may emotionally respond. It is primarily in light of all this that we pass judgment on the people 'imitated,' be they partly real or wholly fictitious.

Of course, to the extent they are imaginary 'people,' it is misleading to characterize them as imitations in the sense of mirror-like images. True, to be of interest, they must be credible, and that means being faithful imitations of possible human lives, acting as they probably would. But in an important respect, they are – or at least can be – also original 'makings,' no further removed from reality than a couchmaker's couch. It would depend upon whether the maker models his makings simply on the people he has actually observed, treating them as the ultimate reality; or whether (alternatively) he has seen *through* them to their archetype, and beyond these to the permanent human nature of which each and every one participates yet but partially instantiates: so many refracted 'images' or 'phantoms' of the singular form of human being. It would depend upon whether the maker accepts the opinions of his historical locale, his 'Cave' – the ambient beliefs about virtue and vice, about happiness and goodness, about the sacred and the profane, about the nature of things – as authoritative; or (alternatively) regards them as but ever-shifting shadows and reflections of facets of the truth, lacking the depth or solidity of genuine knowledge. It would depend upon whether he simply presumes that his ability to make imitations that most of his contemporaries find persuasive proves the adequacy of his general understanding of things; or whether (alternatively) he has come to see the entire perceptible realm as problematic, and thus to realize that if his makings, his poetry, are to have any lasting value, any true worth, he must first pursue knowledge.

Interestingly, Sokrates observes that for each thing that is made, there are three arts: the User's art, the Maker's, and the Imitator's (601d). Moreover, that insofar as each thing's "virtue, beauty, and correctness" is related exclusively to its *use*, the user, who learns through experience how well something serves its intended purpose, is the ultimate authority with respect to its being properly made. So the user has knowledge, and the maker who is necessarily advised by him, has correct opinion (whereas the mere imitator need have neither). Bearing in mind that the poet is so pre-eminently the 'maker' (*poiētēs*) that he simply goes by that name, one may see in the philosopher's taxonomy a tacit acknowledgment that the true poet – one *worthy* of the name, capable of genuinely creative imitation – enjoys a closer relationship with reality than those so-called poets who merely imitate the appearances of things. It is worth noting that this natural relationship between maker and user fits precisely with the relationship between poet and ruler that was established in the course of Sokrates' making a 'city in speech' (401b). What is more significant, however, it suggests that when the maker is himself the user, he is his own ultimate authority.

Such might be the case, for example, when an author's makings are intentionally crafted to serve an educational purpose. This is obviously so of Plato's dialogues, his dramatic imitations of philosophical discussions, which we must presume were used by the students of the Academy he founded (and carefully preserved by his successors, who followed the way of life he established). But we know that the dialogues had a far broader public circulation, and there is every reason to believe that this was also part of Plato's intention: to educate not merely those whom he could personally supervise in his own brief lifetime, but similarly to educate those among the succeeding generations who had whatever it takes to read his dialogues with understanding, especially the desire to enter into dialogue themselves with these 'imitations of Sokrates.'

Applied reflexively, the dialogue's critique of poetry is self-correcting. Upon recognizing that its criticism of the poets does not extend to poets who are genuinely philosophical, much less to a poet who is himself a political philosopher and who can make poetry truly capable of educating mankind, the obvious objection to a 'Platonic Shakespeare' is potentially nullified. But no more than potentially, since Plato's recognition of the possibility of such a poet – and proven possible by Plato himself – does not, of course, establish that Shakespeare likewise is such a poet. In order to determine that, so far as anyone can, the final court of appeal must be the plays themselves, taken as wholes, manifesting both 'logographic necessity' and philosophic profundity.

So, *can* as much be said for Shakespeare? That he wrote his wonderfully entertaining plays to serve a higher purpose than simply that of providing theatrical recreation? Might he also be rightfully spoken of as an Educator – and not just incidentally or inadvertently (as anyone might be), but self-consciously, with perfect awareness of what he was making and why: that his making was part of a doing, ruled by a pedagogical purpose?[105] What is of prior importance, however, is whether he agreed with the deeper implications of Sokrates' criticisms of poetry: that only to the extent a poet is first of all a philosopher can he make poetry of lasting value, or have a natural right to attempt to educate human beings – both intellectually and morally – by means of his poetry. No serious person, of course, would wish to argue that it is a matter of complete indifference as to whether a poet knows whereof he speaks. However beautiful the music he makes, it cannot be so beautiful as to justify a complete disregard for the truth, insofar as it bears on his poetry. That what he beautifully says be *true* can only make it still more beautiful. Hence, the ability to employ the charms of poetry to shape the subrational parts of the soul so as to harmonize with an understanding of the truth addressed to the rational part would seem to define poetical excellence of the highest kind: that which is both moving and enlightening. The real point at issue concerns what is entailed in becoming knowledgeable. Is it a relatively straightforward matter, at least for a person who is intelligent, observant, sensitive, and serious; or (at the other extreme), is arriving at a true understanding of the world, or any significant part thereof, invariably difficult, requiring an enormous, perhaps almost total investment of one's time and energy? Does Shakespeare agree with the Platonic Sokrates on this and the other matters that figure in the philosopher's deeper critique of poetry?

With such questions in mind, one might examine the entire corpus of writings attributed to Shakespeare, searching for evidence that could in any way bear on them. One might start, for example, with Hamlet's famous advice to the players, that they "o'erstep not the modesty of nature," but rather "to hold as 'twere the mirror up to nature" (3.2.19–22). In saying this, we can be sure that whatever exactly Hamlet means by it, he does not mean it in the literal sense that Sokrates does at the outset of his inquiry into 'what is imitation.' As I hope I have shown, Plato's Sokrates is fully aware that Homer's – and Shakespeare's – *mimesis* has only the most remote connection with this kind of physical image-making. But however one understands Hamlet's advice, Hamlet is not Shakespeare. Nor is any other character from his three dozen plays we might find speaking to the subject. Consequently, even the most comprehensive assemblage of textual evidence we can imagine, while it would doubtless be suggestive (perhaps to the point that one found it practically conclusive), would still in principle leave one short of positive knowledge of Shakespeare's own views, and fundamentally reliant upon what one sees exemplified by the plays themselves. The play's the thing.[106]

Accordingly, the plausibility of my own view: that Shakespeare was a political philosopher – indeed, one of the greatest – rests on the persuasiveness of interpretations I have herein set forth, which, whatever else, purport to show that these familiar dramas have a philosophical depth not generally recognized, and that this is manifested in (among other ways) the evident relationship between the plays and Plato's dialogues. While I believe the interpretive analyses presented here are sufficient to make the case, the work of other scholars addressing other plays significantly augments it, such as those who have explicated the relationship between Plato's *Republic* and *The Tempest*, or the Roman plays, or between Plato's *Laws* and *A Midsummer Night's Dream*.[107] Perhaps even more intriguing is the contention that Shakespeare's Falstaff is clearly meant to recall Plato's Sokrates. There are several recent exponents of this view who point to a number of the parallels between the two characters, beginning with the strikingly similar descriptions of their deaths (e.g., with their going cold and numb from the feet upwards; *Phaedo* 117e–118a, *Henry V* 2.3.20–5), but including most importantly their both being accused of practicing sophistry: Falstaff of "wrenching the true cause the false way" (*2nd Henry IV* 2.1.108–9), Sokrates of "making the weaker argument [appear] the stronger" (*Apology* 18b–c, 19b–c, 23d).[108] Another scholar, also taking his cue from the similarity of the death scenes, has explored the relationship more fully, and notes that Shakespeare has signalled his intention by the many hints he has dropped *before* the death of Falstaff, including especially the identical charge against Falstaff ("That villainous abominable misleader of youth"; *1st Henry IV* 2.4.446–7) as was mortally applied to Sokrates (*Apology* 24b).[109] More examples could be cited, but I would hope that these suffice to assuage any remaining skepticism regarding the possibility of a special kinship between these two great political philosophers, Plato and Shakespeare.

As I observed at the outset of this study, our lack of unproblematic biographical knowledge precludes establishing positively what Shakespeare did and did not know, what he could and could not do, or why he undertook to do that which he did. The evidence that the plays themselves provide, though I believe it to be so substantial as to be practically conclusive, is nonetheless circumstantial and open to a variety of interpretations. As another admirer of both Plato and Shakespeare conceded, "it is uncertain how much of Plato Shakespeare might have read," and it is therefore "impossible ... to establish conclusively that Plato 'influenced' Shakespeare." He goes on, however, to cite "the enormous regard for Plato that obtained in the Renaissance":

> In Sidney's influential *Defense of Poesy*, for instance this kind of testimonial occurs: "But now indeed my burthen is great, that Plato his name is laid upon me, whom, I must confess, of all philosophers I have ever esteemed most worthy of reverence, and with good reason, as of all philosophers he is the most poetical." Indeed, reverence for Plato, and the sense that Plato conformed most closely to the interests of poetry, were not attitudes restricted to cultivated noblemen like Sidney: for example, Shakespeare's fellow-dramatist, fellow-poet, and fellow-commoner, Chapman, in the preface to his translation of Homer, says that "as the contemplative life is most worthily and divinely preferred by Plato to the active ... so much preferre I divine Poesie to all worldly wisdom." So despite the lack of conclusive evidence, it should not be assumed that Shakespeare was necessarily ignorant of or uninterested in Plato. The converse seems more likely ...[110]

In conclusion, however, I wish to emphasize that it is the depth of Shakespeare's own understanding of the great philosophical questions, evident I believe in all of his greatest plays, that is of primary importance for us students, seeking our own understanding. Whether he furthered his through first-hand acquaintance with Plato's texts, or second-hand, or through study of other texts, or achieved it simply through his own careful observation, patient inquiry, and rigorous analysis of the world, is a secondary matter. Strictly speaking, *how* he acquired his wisdom is a biographical question, and as such, philosophically irrelevant – except insofar as we can do likewise. Should one's own careful, patient, rigorous study of Shakespeare's texts reveal him to have profited from the study of his predecessors, one may wish to follow his example: to be an imitator of Shakespeare in this most important respect.

Notes

1: The Political Philosopher as Dramatic Poet

1 The popularity of Shakespeare in Japan reportedly surpasses even that of Beethoven. Akira Kurosawa's acclaimed film adaptations of *Macbeth* (*Throne of Blood*) and *King Lear* (*Ran*, 'Chaos') are merely representative of Shakespeare's extensive penetration of Japanese culture. Similarly, Grigori Kozintsev, one of Russia's most eminent stage and film directors, acquired his international reputation mainly on the basis of his cinematic productions of *Hamlet* and *King Lear* (featuring musical scores by Shostakovitch, whose opera *Katerina Ismailova* was originally titled *Lady Macbeth of Mtsensk*). There have been film versions of most of Shakespeare's plays, and in several different languages (*Hamlet* has been rendered over two dozen times).

2 Allan Bloom, introducing a selection of his Shakespeare commentaries in *Love and Friendship* (New York: Simon and Schuster, 1993), 270–1.

3 Gary Schmidgall, *Shakespeare and Opera* (New York: Oxford University Press, 1990).

4 As if health were not as 'objectively' *good* as it is real, the desire as well as the standards for it – for living at the peak of one's powers – determined by nature. As if the self-mastery implicit in personal virtues (e.g., temperence, courage, prudence, and liberality whereby one exercises control over one's desires, fears, attachments to one's property) was not *intrinsically* desirable, regardless of one's chosen or allotted way of life. As if 'ought' (supposedly a 'value' ontologically independent of 'fact') were not inextricably bound up with 'can' (with what is physically, psychologically, and politically possible – factual matters, one and all). A sufficiently detailed analysis showing the invalidity of this distinction, and the disutility of the very concept of 'values,' is provided in an endnote of my book *The War Lover: A Study of Plato's Republic* (Toronto: University of Toronto Press, 1994), 326–36.

5 Harbingers of the sorts of views currently in vogue, loosely associated under the rubrics 'historicist' and 'postmodern,' first appeared at the end of the nineteenth cen-

tury. But it was only near the end of the twentieth that they came to dominate the critical study of literature. That the accounts their proponents provide of thought, language, and things (and their relationships) are paradoxical to the point of incoherence make it difficult to believe that anyone could take them seriously, but there is a plenitude of people who write as if they did. And the study of great literature has suffered accordingly. Not that the theoretical rationales supposedly grounding these critical postures have gone unchallenged, but it seems that the challengers have gone conveniently unread by most devotees of the New. A.D. Nuttall, for instance, provides one of the more thorough and rigourous refutations by way of beginning his excellent renovation of the old-fashioned, naturalistic, commonsensical approach to reading premodern literature, *A New Mimesis: Shakespeare and the Representation of Reality* (London: Methuen, 1983). On these matters and several others, I shall quote him at length:

> My argument is directed against formalism, that is, against the resolution of matter into form, reality into fiction, substance into convention ... I am conscious that my target is in a way unreal; no one can really live with the kind of fundamental, epistemological formalism which this book attacks. But current critical discourse has adopted a certain style. This style admits or even welcomes metaphysical absolutes, and these absolutes themselves directly imply a wholly disabling conclusion. Meanwhile one of the immemorial ways of praising a writer, that is by saying that he or she is true to life, has become obscurely tabu, as if it involved some fundamental misconception of the nature of literature and the world. In such circumstances it seemed fair to take the fundamental postulates a little more seriously than they are often taken by their proponents. My own position ... is that the word *reality* can be legitimately used without apologetic inverted commas and that literature may represent that same reality ... (vii–viii)
>
> [Speaking about these 'obscure tabus' of the structuralist/poststructuralist movement,] empiricism is rejected, and so is truth-to-life and the free creative sovereignty of the author over his own work. Instead we have certain Gallic epigrams: literature writes itself, people are read by the books they suppose themselves to be reading, thought (not people) thinks, speech speaks and writing writes. (6)
>
> Tell your structural anthropologist that his structural anthropology is a subjectively generated myth (subjective, that is, to his culture) and he, or she, will often commit the highly venial sin of resistance, will show signs of wishing to claim objective truth, of the old-fashioned kind, for structural anthropology if for nothing else. And at once the trap closes. Either the absoluteness of *verum factum* ['truth is made'] must go, or else must its claim to be believed.
>
> For if the anthropologist did not claim objective truth, did not avail himself of

the usual twentieth-century strategem whereby the expert exempts himself from the noncognitive determination which enslaves all the rest, we should once more be confronted by the spectacle of the self-dismantling philosophy. (10–11)

Meanwhile the cardinal truth stands: specific demonstrations of subjective or ideological modification always presuppose an objective referent against which they are plotted. One may show subjectivity in musical taste by the fact that Jane likes Tchaikovsky though Jill does not. But this demonstration presumes that in the 'hard phenomenal' sense they are hearing the same thing. (18)

What might be called 'the objectivist correlative' remains inescapable. If you want to say that a society imposes its cultural forms on reality, you must have a conception of reality with respect to which the imposition is detected ...

Certainly Bacon was wrong in suggesting that we could put our notions to one side and attend to 'things' in themselves; 'thing' is a normative concept; we decide what counts as a thing or it is decided for us by our inherited perceptual apparatus ...

The shapes we bring to bear on the world are interrogative rather than constitutive. We trawl with the human net and therefore catch only what can be caught in its mesh, but it does not follow that we are the sole inventors of the catch. I and the history of my species may decide what counts as a chair, but if I then 'trawl' for chairs in this room I shall find so many, and no more. Human astronomy is perspectival in the sense that it is from a given point of view, but this does not imply that the knowledge so gained cannot be objective. A whale would, I imagine, be unlikely to notice my ears, but may conversely be aware of gradations in the character of sea water of which we are unconscious, but this does not mean that my ears are an anthropocentric fiction or conversely that the gradations of the sea are a myth of the whale race, a phallaenocentric fiction. (20–1)

It is indeed odd that so many people these days (and especially those who supposedly think for a living) have such difficulty grasping the basic point: that there is simply no way for a radical relativism to be protected from the annihilating effects of its reflexive application. Treating it as a mere 'hypothesis' won't work, since it's no more coherent as an hypothesis (or guess, or suspicion) than as a positive claim. It is similarly incoherent as an article of 'faith' (what exactly is it that one has faith in? that relativism is the absolute truth?). Postmodernists sometimes speak as if, by their 'accepting' the manifest irrationality of their position as itself evidence of the irrationality of the world and/or the illusory character of Reason, they had thereby disarmed all criticism. And yet, they purport to have arrived at their position by the most rigourous reasoning about the nature of language and its relationship to thought and existence – every step of which presumes the basic validity of the law of contradiction: that self-contradictory claims are ipso facto wrong.

6 Whereas it is just here – ironically – that historicists and cultural relativists betray their selective faith in the potential objectivity of knowledge, including that of the most problematic kind: *historical* knowledge, where there is no possibility of directly observing the thing to be known.

7 Samuel Schoenbaum must be as familiar as anyone with the historical evidence bearing on the case, and has taken the greatest pains to distinguish that which has some solid empirical basis from the mass of subsequent mythical accretions and problematic guesswork. As he summarily states, "Yet, if it would be an exaggeration to say that the materials concerning the dramatist deny matter enough for a page, they hardly amount to a great deal, and they are fraught with perplexities for the biographer." *Shakespeare's Lives* (New York: Oxford University Press, 1970), 72. Having surveyed virtually all biographical efforts with any claim to our attention, Schoenbaum concludes:

> Perhaps we should despair of ever bridging the vertiginous expanse between the sublimity of the subject and the mundane inconsequence of the documentary record. What would we not give for a single personal letter, one page of diary! Hardy expressed what many have felt when he wrote:
>
> Bright baffling Soul, least capturable of themes,
> Thou, who display'dst a life of commonplace,
> Leaving no intimate word or personal trace
> Of high design outside the artistry
>   Of thy penned dreams,
> Still shalt remain at heart unread eternally.
>
> A certain kind of literary biography, rich in detail about (in Yeats's phrase) the momentary self, is clearly impossible. (767–8)

8 *Forewards and Afterwards* (New York: Vintage, 1974), 90.

9 'What's in a Name,' *Réalitiés* (Nov. 1962) 41. Over the intervening centuries, the various portraits once supposed to have been of Shakespeare have all been proven derivative (of the Martin Droeshout engraving that adorns the title page of the *Folio*, and which almost surely was not taken from the life as the engraver was only fifteen in 1616 when Shakespeare of Stratford died), or otherwise spurious (e.g., to have been painted long after his death, or of someone else entirely). About young Droeshout, Samuel Schoenbaum wryly observes, "How he obtained the commission we do not know – perhaps his fee was as modest as his gifts":

> The portrait has not gone entirely without admirers. 'What a powerful impression it gives,' enthuses Dr. Rowse: 'that searching look of the eyes understanding everything, what a forehead, what a brain!' But the engraver has not depicted the

brain, only the forehead, described by another observer as that 'horrible hydrocephalus development.' Droeshout's deficiencies are, alas, only too gross. The huge head on the plate of a ruff surmounts a disproportionately small tunic. One eye is lower and larger than the other, the hair does not balance at the sides, light comes from several directions. It is unlikely that Droeshout ever sketched Shakespeare from the life. Probably he worked from a line drawing supplied to him. Still the Folio editors, who knew Shakespeare well, did not reject the likeness, and Jonson was able to bring himself to supply a few perfunctory lines of commendation, printed on the adjoining flyleaf. No doubt only an over-subtle reader will detect a latent irony in Jonson's conclusion – 'Reader, looke / Not on his Picture, but his Booke' – but the advice is sound enough. *William Shakespeare*: *A Documentary Life* (New York: Oxford University Press, 1975), 258

10 Letter to William Sandys, 13 June 1847, in *Letters of Charles Dickens*, G. Hogarth and M. Dickens, eds. (London: 1893), 173.

11 "It is difficult, of course, indeed it is apparently impossible, to keep Shakespeare's writings and the facts of his life in separate compartments, and few have resisted the temptation to see in his works the reflection of developments in his inner life as the outcome of conjectural experiences." So C.J. Sisson notes, by way of ironically introducing some suspect examples in his chapter entitled 'Shakespeare,' in *Shakespeare: The Writer and His Work*, Bonamy Dobrée, ed. (London: Longmans, 1964), 17. Bloom in *Love and Friendship* addresses the main issue here in his comments on *Troilus and Cressida* ("perhaps the bleakest of all Shakespeare's plays"):

> The atmosphere is very different from that of *Antony and Cleopatra*, so different that many interpreters can render the change intelligible only by supposing disappointments in love undergone by the Bard. Such explanations appeal to modern readers, who, under the persisting influence of Romanticism, understand writers as chroniclers of their own personal histories or their moods, sublime reproductions of the way most of us approach things. The notion that a writer overcomes his particular experience or feeling in the name of a more comprehensive and less personal view of things is rejected and treated as antipoetic, although this suggestion is annunciated by Shakespeare himself and discussed even in this play. It is more a commentary on ourselves that we take the autobiographical explanation as truth, when it is little better than an assertion, and an implausible one at that. (347)

12 Whether the scholars who take this view are aware of it or not, they are hereby reiterating the depreciation of the dramatic poet that Plato places (so ironically) in the mouth of his own dramatic creation, Sokrates: that the poet is a mere imitator thrice removed from reality (*Republic* 597e ff). For example, Alfred Harbage, in *Conceptions of Shake-*

speare (New York: Shacken, 1968), disparages the various claims for Shakespeare's having all sorts of professional expertise, and assures us that "the plays and poems, in indicating that their author was well informed – an excellent observer, especially of nature – are also indicating that he possessed specialized knowledge of nothing, except how to write plays and poems. The notion of his prodigious 'knowledge' is attributable in part to his skills as an *illusionist*" (24; emphasis added). Harbage pursues the point further, and a bit more generously, in 'Shakespeare and the Professions,' in *Shakespeare's Art: Seven Essays,* Milton Crane, ed. (Chicago: University of Chicago Press, 1973), 11–28.

One may agree with Harbage in discounting the likelihood of Shakespeare's possessing all the kinds of technical expertise that various admirers have attributed to him over the centuries, but what bears emphasizing is that politics and philosophy must not be regarded as comparable specialities. While presupposing astute observation, the great truths to which the philosopher aspires are accessible to no one except through rigorous *thinking*. Thus, if one wishes to share whatever wisdom Shakespeare has embedded in his plays, one must be willing and able to think for oneself the thoughts that structure them.

13 So we are assured by no less an expert on textual matters than Fredson Bowers, in *On Editing Shakespeare* (Charlottesville: University of Virginia Press, 1966): "Indeed, on the evidence, Shakespeare felt little incentive to worry about the form of his plays in print. Plays were not regarded as 'literature'; when Shakespeare in his early days wrote two narrative poems that were respectable literary forms, he seems to have taken some care to assure himself that they were carefully printed. But not the plays on which – at the time – anything that could be called a literary reputation could rest" (109).

We are to believe this, despite the – inescapably reflexive – sentiments concerning the enduring significance of such literature expressed in the plays themselves? And despite both authorized and so-called pirated editions of particular plays having sold successfully for years? (For what purpose? home theatre?) And despite Shakespeare's name even being used to peddle works of which he was *not* in fact the author (as by William Jaggard in publishing his 1599 edition of *The Passionate Pilgrim*)? And in striking contrast to the extravagant eulogies that preface the First Folio, which boasts that it alone offers authentic texts of his entire dramatic corpus, and which counts upon the author's name being sufficient to ensure a ready market for this quite expensive volume (as did Thomas Thorpe in publishing a book entitled *Shake-speares Sonnets* a decade and a half earlier)? Why would anyone propose to publish the Folio, emphasizing its textual accuracy (albeit not altogether warranted, it seems), if Shakespeare had not established a 'literary reputation,' that is, for producing plays worth *reading*? In short, are not Bower's claims, though widely accepted these days, rather unlikely? Obviously, Ben Jonson did not subscribe to them, having published a Folio volume of his own works some seven years previous. The fact that much playwrighting of his time was not taken seriously, and rightly so, is neither here nor there. As Jonson would be the first to insist, it's solely a question of quality. Since antiquity, dramatic poetry of requisite quality has been regarded as 'respectable literature,' and preserved accordingly; the mere mention of Aeschylus, Sophocles, Euripides, Aristophanes, Seneca, Plautus, Terence – all known to the Renaissance – adequately establishes the point. Not for nothing did Jonson rank Shakespeare with "thund'ring Aeschilus, Euripides, and Sophocles," as Britain's one dramatist equal to "all, that insolent Greece, or Haughtie Rome sent forth," reminding us that Shakespeare (like his ancient predecessors) will remain "alive still, while [his] Book doth live, and we have wits to read [!], and praise to give." For, as Jonson famously observed, "He was not of an age, but for all time!"

14 Anthony Burgess expresses these assumptions as forthrightly as anyone could wish: "Shakespeare's main aim was, I think, to make money, not to bequeath deathless plays to posterity ... Making money was a means of becoming a gentleman with a fine cloak" *Urgent Copy: Literary Studies in Search of Shakespeare the Man* (New York: Norton, 1968), 159–60.

15 Kenneth Muir, in his 'Introduction' to the Arden edition of *Macbeth* (London: Routledge, 1988, xxv), assures us: "In all Shakespeare's plays there are loose ends, references to scenes which were deliberately left unwritten, and conflicting impressions of motives and characters." Muir would have us see this as a virtue, however: "Nor are these dramatic weaknesses, but rather devices to create the illusion of life. Attempts to improve on Shakespeare by turning him into a naturalistic dramatist should be resisted." As Muir's position is doubtless shared by many today, it is worth careful dissection. For example, if by 'unwritten scenes' one means no more than that characters allude to conversations or actions we are not shown, this poses no problems – and is perfectly consistent with Shakespeare's being 'naturalistic,' since we don't see and hear much of what goes on in our own corner of the world either, and accordingly must infer what we can from the evidence that *is* available. Indeed, I shall argue that this, along with the integrating of 'conflicting impressions' of characters, is not merely legitimate but mandatory for any adequate understanding of the plays. What is troubling in Muir's position is the business about 'loose ends,' as this in effect provides an interpreter the licence to disregard any details that don't fit into his interpretation: they are merely examples of those loose ends that Muir somehow divines are "in all of Shakespeare's plays." How does one distinguish a loose end from a feature one does not (yet) understand, or a detail whose significance one has not (yet) seen, but which one might were one to persist in trying, instead of dismissing it as just another of those 'lifelike' loose ends?

16 While I do not always find Johnson to be the best interpreter of Shakespeare, he has famously expressed a general viewpoint which I readily endorse: "Shakespeare is above all writers, at least above all modern writers, the poet of nature; the poet that holds up

to his readers a faithful mirrour of manners and of life. His characters ... are the genuine progeny of common humanity, such as the world will always supply, and observation will always find. His persons act and speak by the influence of those general passions and principles by which all minds are agitated, and the whole system of life is continued in motion." 'Preface to Shakespeare,' in *A Johnson Reader*, E.L.McAdam, Jr. and George Milne, eds. (New York: Pantheon, 1964), 317.

To this one might add the testimony of Coleridge: "Another excellence in Shakespear [*sic*], and in which no other writer equalled him, was in the *language of nature*, so correct was it that we could see ourselves in all he wrote"; and that of Hazlitt: "The striking peculiarity of Shakspeare's [*sic*] mind was its generic quality, its power of communication with all other minds – so that it contained a universe of thought and feeling within itself, and had no one peculiar bias, or exclusive excellence more than another. He was just like any other man, but that he was like all other men." From 'Lectures on the Characteristics of Shakespear' and 'On Shakspeare and Milton,' both as excerpted in *The Romantics on Shakespeare*, Jonathan Bate, ed. (New York: Penguin, 1992), 131, 181.

Given the preoccupations of our time, however, some would no doubt take issue with these writers on grounds of sex. In this regard, it is worth reading de Quincey, who distinguishes Shakespeare from his Greek and Roman predecessors precisely in his being the first dramatist to present "female characters that had the appropriate beauty of female nature; woman no longer grand, terrific, and repulsive, but woman 'after her kind' – the other hemisphere of the dramatic world; woman running through the vast gamut of womanly loveliness; woman as emancipated, exalted, ennobled, under a new law of Christian morality; woman the sister and co-equal of man, no longer his slave, his prisoner, and sometimes his rebel." From his article 'Shakespeare' in the *Encyclopaedia Britannica*, 7th ed. [1842], excerpted in *De Quincey as Critic*, John E. Jordon, ed. (London: Routledge and Kegan Paul, 1973), 232. One can find support for de Quincey's assessment among more recent, and certifiedly female, perspectives, e.g., that of Clara Claiborne Park, in her essay entitled 'As We Like It: How a Girl Can Be Smart and Still Popular,' in *The Woman's Part: Feminist Criticism of Shakespeare*, C.R.S. Lenz, G. Greene, and C.T. Neely, eds. (Urbana: University of Illinois Press 1983), 100–16:

> Shakespeare liked women and respected them; not everybody does ... He is not afraid of the kind of assertiveness and insistence on her own judgment that Eve displays when she gets busy bringing death into the world and all our woe; the evidence of the plays is that he positively enjoyed it.
>
> From Mrs Jameson on, critics, male and female, have praised Shakespeare's women. 'The dignity of Portia, the energy of Beatrice, the radiant high spirits of Rosalind, the sweetness of Viola' ... Shakespeare's girls and mature women are

individualized, realized, fully enjoyed as human beings. His respect for women is evident in all the plays, but it is in the middle comedies that the most dazzling image recurs. (101–2)

What catches his imagination ... is a young woman ... who, by her energy, wit, and combativeness, successfully demonstrates her ability to control events in the world around her, not excluding the world of men. (102)

17 There are many useful surveys, or partial surveys of modern Shakespearean criticism, e.g., Sisson in 'Shakespeare,' Derek Traversi, 'Introduction' to the 3rd ed. of his *An Approach to Shakespeare* (London: Hollis and Carter, 1969); Alfred Harbage in the title essay of his *Shakespeare without Words* (Cambridge: Harvard University Press, 1972); Kenneth Muir, his chapter entitled 'The Betrayal of Shakespeare,' in *Shakespeare: Contrasts and Controversies* (Norman: University of Oklahoma Press, 1985). A detailed recounting of the rise to prominence of an especially important approach, that of the '*Scrutiny* Critics' (F.R. Leavis, G. Wilson Knight, L.C. Knights, Derek Traversi, among others), is S. Viswanathan, *The Shakespeare Play as Poem: a Critical Tradition in Perspective* (Cambridge: Cambridge University Press, 1980).

18 Although commonly traced back to the influence of Coleridge (and before him to that of Pope, Dryden, and others), the 'character analysis' school of interpretation is invariably associated today with A.C. Bradley, in his *Shakespearean Tragedy* (London, 1904), the most frequent target at which subsequent opponents of that school take aim.

19 In addition, there were many examples of fanciful character elaboration without any textual justification beyond that of providing ad hoc plausibility for otherwise implausible interpretations of particular plays. Of course, inept or stupid applications do not invalidate a critical approach properly employed, though citing them can be (and has been) rhetorically effective in undermining respect for that approach.

20 Caroline F.E. Spurgeon, *Shakespeare's Imagery and What It Tells Us* (Cambridge: Cambridge University Press, 1935), is usually credited with initiating, or at least heralding, a fresh spate of scholarship that takes its bearings from patterns of symbols and images. Two important examples of this genre that bear directly on the plays with which I am primarily concerned are Cleanth Brooks, 'The Naked Babe and the Cloak of Manliness,' in *The Well Wrought Urn* (New York: Harcourt, Bruce and Company 1947) and Robert B. Heilman, in *This Great Stage: Image and Structure in King Lear* (Baton Rouge: Louisiana State University Press, 1948).

21 To be sure, there has never been an absence of prominent voices combating the more simplistic kinds of historicist reductionism. G. Wilson Knight, in the 'Prefatory Note' he saw need to add to the 1951 edition of *The Imperial Theme* (originally published by Oxford University Press, 1931; reprinted by Methuen: London and New York, 1985), diagnoses the basic issue: "Let me yet once again emphasize that the correct procedure is to interpret an age in the light of its great books and men of visionary genius, not the

men of genius in light of their age. Our academic tradition has got it the wrong way round" (xii). In a similar vein, Derek Traversi, in *An Approach to Shakespeare*, while praising the constructive contribution of the "increased modern interest in Elizabethan thought," goes on to observe:

> The criticism that has followed from this approach has shown itself apt to ignore the element of essential *discontinuity* which separates a genius from the commonplaces of his age. A writer of Shakespeare's stature is of his time in the ideas he uses, and we shall always be unwise to forget this; but he uses these ideas in ways of his own, which are not necessarily of his time alone. Shakespeare's plays on English history, for example, lean heavily on contemporary notions concerning such subjects as monarchy, its origins, its *rôle*, and its justification; but to interpret the series of chronicles from *Richard II* to *Henry V* as no more than exercises in Tudor patriotic propaganda is, in my submission, seriously to under-estimate their originality. What truly emerges from these plays ... is a thoroughly personal vision, increasingly tragic in its implications, of man as a political being; so that, properly read, they speak to us not less than they did to the late sixteenth-century, and speak to us moreover in ways that very few minds of that age – with the possible exception of Machiavelli – would have fully understood. To compare Shakespeare, as a mature dramatist, to almost any other Elizabethan writer is to be made aware of the degree to which he evades, escapes from the current Elizabethan limitations. Such a writer, in other words, and to adapt a critical commonplace, both is of his time and transcends it. (10–11)

Robert Ornstein, 'Historical Criticism and the Interpretation of Shakespeare,' in *Shakespeare Quarterly* 10 (1959) 3–9; as reprinted in *Approaches to Shakespeare*, Norman Rabkin, ed. (New York: McGraw-Hill, 1964, 172–82), expounds the logical case for the strict subordination of all kinds of historical scholarship to the direct experience produced by the plays themselves, concluding:

> Thus while scholarship can make the interpretation of Shakespeare more scientific, it cannot make of interpretation a science based upon factual information. The dichotomy of scholarly fact and aesthetic impression is finally misleading because the refined, disciplined aesthetic impression *is* the fact upon which the interpretation of Shakespeare must ultimately rest; that is to say, all scholarly evidence outside the text of a play is related to it by inferences which must themselves be supported by aesthetic impressions. The attempt of historical criticism to recapture (in so far as it is possible) Shakespeare's own artistic intention, is, or should be, the goal of all responsible criticism. But we must insist that that intention is fully realized in the play and can be grasped only from the play. (180–1)

Of those I've encountered, one of the finest exemplifications of the contribution historical knowledge can make to our contemporary understanding of Shakespeare is that of Roland Mushat Frye in *The Renaissance* Hamlet: *Issues and Responses in 1600* (Princeton: Princeton University Press, 1984). Taking his cue from Hamlet's advice to the Players, Frye explains:

> By holding up a mirror to reflect the age and body of the time he knew best, he transmuted the problems, attitudes, and concerns of his own age into something rich, fresh, and marvelous, transcending any one cultural epoch. It is this successful combination of effects that sets him apart ... [T]he words Shakespeare's characters speak still voice our concerns, and their problems merge into our problems ...
>
> Marvelously universal though they are, however, Shakespeare's plays originated in his own time and place. It could not be otherwise, because even a great genius must begin by perceiving, reflecting upon, and transmuting what is immediately before him. Hamlet's description of the players as 'the abstract and brief chronicles of the time' underscores that point (2.2.512). What Shakespeare knew that is relevant to all men and to every society was learned in his own period and place, and was timelessly expressed in the language of his own age. If we are to understand his universality, we can scarcely better begin than with his particularity. (4–5)

Frye neatly illustrates his point with a brief discussion of what 'mirror' meant to Elizabethans (and expands on this in Appendix A, 281–92), hence what they might make of Hamlet's "purpose of playing": "to hold, as 'twere, the mirror up to nature." Frye begins by informing us that "as artifacts, Elizabethan mirrors were small instruments," and then proceeds to trace out the implications of this fact for the proper interpretation of Hamlet's trope (6). But Frye nonetheless argues against those who would see Shakespeare as providing merely a reflection of his own time and place:

> ... Shakespeare did not write his plays to advise crown, court, parliament or people as to what should be done about this, that, or another problem of state. If we expect such 'timeliness' in Shakespeare we will miss the point of his peculiar greatness, and if we never go beyond Elizabethan frames of reference in interpreting him, we shall miss his universality. Shakespeare neither can nor should be confined within a straight jacket of Elizabethan opinions, nor should we reduce the majesty of his words to the commonplaces and clichés of his time. Here balance and moderation are as important to the interpreting scholar as to the interpreting actor: Hamlet's advice to the one should also apply to the other, 'that you o'erstep not the modesty of nature.' Or, as one distinguished historian of drama has put it, knowledge and tradition 'must be used with all the skill and caution with which one handles edged tools.'

> But if we are to appreciate Shakespeare's plays fully, we should not omit any practical means for seeing them in their nascent environment. (7)

> Such an historical approach can provide safeguards against the precarious subjectivisms of individual critics and the provincialisms of critical schools ...
>
> But while protecting us from that danger, historical approaches typically expose us to others. Scholars can be betrayed by historical reductivism as readily as by any other form of oversimplification. While studying historical backgrounds, we must remind ourselves that a great creative writer like Shakespeare used the materials his culture made available to him, but that he refused to be used by those materials. Instead, he transcended and transmuted them. (8)

Throughout his book, Frye does an especially fine job of showing "Elizabethan uncertainties, ambiguities, doubts, and disagreements," as well as "agreements and consensuses." This heterogeneity of views pervading all classes of the Elizabethan population is worth emphasizing, since it is often conveniently ignored by historicist-minded interpreters of Shakespeare. As Graham Bradshaw observes in *Misrepresentations: Shakespeare and the Materialists* (Ithaca: Cornell University Press, 1993), "One problem with historicist readings, old and 'New,' is their unhistorical readiness to think of the Original Audience as some fabulous beast with many bodies but one obediently loyal heart, and one unimpressive mind" (34). When one thinks about it, of course, this homogenization of Shakespeare's audience is hardly plausible since the plays themselves present such a variety of people – from superstitious rustics to thoroughgoing nihilists – representing such a diversity of beliefs and perspectives.

22 Harley Granville-Barker is usually given credit for leading the charge here with his succession of volumes of *Prefaces to Shakespeare*, originally published between 1927 and 1947, since reprinted (Princeton: Princeton University Press, 1974).

23 The extent of Shakespeare's classical learning has long been a matter of debate. The issue is in no wise clarified by Ben Jonson's ambiguous eulogizing:

> *And though thou hadst small* Latine *and lesse* Greeke,
> *From thence to honour thee, I would not seeke*
> *For names; but call forth thund'ring* Aeschilus,
> Euripides, *and* Sophocles *to us ...*

For if Jonson – reputedly a classical scholar of the first rank – used himself as the standard of comparison, even a practical fluency in Latin might seem 'small.'

Of the various investigations of Shakespeare's plays undertaken with an eye towards assessing his access to and familiarity with classical literature, Paul Stapfer's sober treatment of the questions, itself something of a modern classic, remains well worth reading: *Shakespeare and Classical Antiquity*, Emily J. Carey, trans.; originally published in 1880, reissued by Burt Franklin, New York, 1970. Stapfer concludes, "Shakespeare, we need not doubt, knew Latin as well as any man of his time; and in his time the educated portion of the public knew it better than they do now" (100). As for Greek, Stapfer is sceptical: "Even admitting that he may have learned the declensions and verbs at school, such knowledge would have been quite insufficient to enable him to read a Greek author in the original" (104). Supposedly, then, Shakespeare – like those famous philhellenes, Goethe and Schiller – relied on translations. It is Stapfer's view that "the English" attach far more importance to this philological question than it deserves: "If we take the word 'learning' in its large and liberal sense, and no longer reduce the question to a miserable pedantic wrangling over his more or less of Greek and Latin, then, of all men that ever lived, Shakespeare is one of the most learned" (105).

Concerning the grammar school education of Shakespeare's day, the exhaustive study by T.W. Baldwin entitled *William Shakspere's Small Latine & Lesse Greeke* (Urbana: University of Illinois Press, 1944) remains authoritative. Summing up in the final chapter of this massive two-volume work, Baldwin writes:

> The evidence appears to be conclusive that Shakspere had such knowledge and techniques as grammar school was calculated to give. We have no direct evidence that he ever attended any grammar school a single day. Rowe was probably merely reporting an inference when in 1709 he said, "His Father ... had bred him, 'tis true, for some time at a Free-School." But the inference is an inevitable one, amounting almost to a certainty. Those nearest the time either knew or assumed that Shakspere had attended the grammar school at Stratford. It is reasonably certain that he did attend school there for some period of time. The internal evidence and such external evidence as survives conspire together to indicate that Shakspere pretty certainly had at Stratford the benefits of the complete grammar school curriculum ...
>
> Most important of all, if Shakspere had this grammar school training, he had the only formal literary training provided by society in his day. University training was professional, with literary training only incidental and subsidiary ...
>
> If William Shakspere had the grammar school training of his day – or its equivalent – he had as good a formal literary training as had any of his contemporaries. At least, no miracles are required to account for such knowledge and techniques from the classics as he exhibits. Stratford grammar school will furnish all that is required. The miracle lies elsewhere; it is the world-old miracle of genius. (vol. 2, 662–3)

24 For reasons that I hope to make clear in the following chapters, it has become axiomatic for me that Shakespeare (like Ben Jonson) wrote with the intention that his plays would be read as literature, as well as performed in theatres. I am well aware that this conviction is at odds with several elements of what might be called the standard scholarly view today regarding Shakespeare's relationship to his plays (proprietary and oth-

erwise – e.g., that he was careless of their fate, that they didn't in any sense 'belong' to him, etc.). I am to that extent 'doubtful' about this standard view. And it seems to me that an unprejudiced reading of Heminge's and Condell's prefatory letter in the Folio, 'To the great Variety of Readers,' itself casts considerable doubt on the standard view:

> It had bene a thing, we confesse, worthie to haue bene wished, that the Author himselfe had liu'd to have set forth, and ouerseen his owne writings; But since it hath bin ordain'd otherwise, and he by death departed from that right, we pray you do not envie his Friends, the office of their care, and paine, to haue collected & publish'd them; and so to haue publish'd them, as where (before) you were abus'd with diuerse stolne, and surreptitious copies, maimed, and deformed by the frauds and stealthes of iniurious imposters, that expos'd them: euen those, are now offer'd to your view cur'd, and perfect of their limbes; and all the rest, absolute in their numbers, as he conceiued the[m] ... But it is not our prouince, who onely gather his works, and give them you, to praise him. It is yours that reade him. And there we hope, to your diuerse capacities, you will finde enough, both to draw, and to hold you: for his wit can no more lie hid, then it could be lost. Reade him, therefore; and againe and againe: And if then you doe not like him, surely you are in some manifest danger, not to understand him. And so we leaue you to other of his Friends, whom if you need, can bee your guides: if you neede them not, you can leade your felues, and others. And such Readers we with him.

So, it might reasonably have been expected that Shakespeare would have himself 'set forth' and 'overseen' the publication of a complete edition of his plays, corrected as he saw fit ('cur'd'). He had some sort of *right* to do so, which was vacated by his (untimely) dying. In his stead, his friends now make them available – every last one, they stress, as if even his least estimable work were nonetheless valuable – that none may be lost, but enjoyed by being *read.* Indeed, by being read again and again, as only great literature deserves to be (or so I should have thought). As for those who do not appreciate the true worth of these plays, it is probably because they do not understand them, and so could profit from the efforts of a competent interpreter.

25 The author is L.C. Knights, who in my opinion has produced some of the better commentary on Shakespeare written in this past century. The essay of his that I am referring to was originally issued as a monograph in 1933, but was subsequently included with only slight changes in his collection entitled *Explorations* (New York: New York University Press, 1964). And while Knights offers a couple of qualifications on the essay in the Preface to this later volume, they do not affect the points with which I here take issue. The case he makes has been made by others, too, but no better; and his version of it has a certain canonical status. His main target was the then dominant 'character analysis' school, which he judged guilty of encouraging extravagant flights of irrelevant fancy:

> For some years there have been signs of a re-orientation of Shakespeare criticism ... The present, therefore, is a favourable time in which to take stock of the traditional methods, and to inquire why so few of the many books that have been written are relevant to our study of Shakespeare as a poet. The inquiry involves an examination of certain critical presuppositions, and of these the most fruitful of irrelevancies is the assumption that Shakespeare was pre-eminently a great "creator of characters." So extensive was his knowledge of the human heart (so runs the popular opinion) that he was able to project himself into the minds of an infinite variety of men and women and present them "real as life" before us. (15)

It is partly because I am in such strong agreement with this once more broadly endorsed 'popular opinion,' which Knights here disparages, that I take issue with what I understand to be the intended practical implications of this line of criticism.

26 Ibid., 19, 52.

27 Ibid., 20, 45. G. Wilson Knight also insists that it is a basic mistake to praise Shakespeare for his realism. As Wilson Knight writes in 'Tolstoy's Attack on Shakespeare,' included in the revised edition of *The Wheel of Fire* (London: Methuen, 1949): "The Shakespearian world does not exactly reflect the appearances of human or natural life. The events in his world are often strange to the point of impossibility. Whoever knew the sun go out? What man has ever acted as did King Lear ...?" (270). On this last point, suffice it for now to reply that Wilson Knight finds Lear's behaviour unrealistic because he doesn't understand the real reasons for it, having been misled by the apparent reasons with which Shakespeare has so skilfully overlain them. But according to Wilson Knight, the whole naturalism/realism issue is bound up with the excessive emphasis on 'characterization': "Shakespeare is a great poet. We have, misled by nineteenth-century romantic criticism, regarded him rather as a great novelist ... [As did an eminent twentieth-century novelist, D.H. Lawrence – 'Why the Novel Matters,' in *Phoenix* (New York: Viking 1936), 536.] We have not understood Shakespeare. And our error has been this: a concentration on 'character' and realistic appearances generally, things which do not constitute Shakespeare's primary glory; and a corresponding and dangerous, indeed a devastating, neglect of Shakespeare's poetic symbolism" (271–2).

28 Knights, 'How Many Children' (op. cit.), 18. Knights himself revisited the issues he raised in the 'How Many Children' essay, notably in 'The Question of Character in Shakespeare' in Norman Rabkin, *Approaches to Shakespeare* (New York: McGraw-Hill, 1964, 47–65). And once again, much of what he says there strikes me as quite sound. Yet, by way of providing some guidance as to how far character analysis is legitimate, Knights maintains that this "is true of all the characters of Shakespeare": "we know about them only what the play requires us to know ... [H]owever we define for ourselves a character and his rôle, there is a strict criterion of relevance: he belongs to his play, and his play is an art-form, not a slice of life" (58). Considered as an abstract for-

mula, this might be acceptable. But the practical issue is, how much are we required to 'make' of what we 'know' in order to arrive at a valid understanding of a given play. Clearly, Knights is ready to dismiss as 'irrelevancies' certain speculations about characters that seem to me both relevant and plausibly surmisable from the textual evidence, e.g., the claim that "Macbeth's tendency to ambition 'must have been greatly strengthened by his marriage'" (51).

29 Knights, 'How Many Children,' 17–18. As noted above, scholars who agree with Knights in his disallowing speculations beyond the letter of the text are not difficult to find. Harold Jenkins, e.g., in his editorial notes to the Arden edition of *Hamlet* (London: Methuen, 1982) has this to say about the Prince's addressing his mother the Queen, "I must to England, you know that?" (to which she responds, "Alack, I had forgot. 'Tis so concluded on." 3.4.202–3): "As to how Hamlet knew of it, since the text, as eds. note, is silent, speculation is invalid. The 'difficulty' passes unnoticed in the theatre, and such inventiveness as making Hamlet search Polonius's pockets is misplaced" (331). I agree that particular invention is inappropriate, but only because there is a much more plausible and straightforward assumption: Hamlet's speech is meant to inform *us* (not Gertrude) of something that has happened but which we were *not shown*, and about which we're free to wonder, namely, his having been informed by someone of the King's plan for him (it could have been Polonius, Rosencrantz, Guildenstern, or anyone else – other than the Queen or the King [cf. 4.3.47] – who got wind of it; and it could have happened incidentally, or purposefully). But the beginning point is, Hamlet knows, and also knows that his "two schoolfellows, whom [he] will trust as [he] will adders fang'd" are to accompany him, that they (not he) will be carrying the documents of the mission, and accordingly he suspects that there's mischief afoot. And so he wonders how much his *mother* knows about this business. Might she even be a party to it? Whereupon we, along with him, learn that she too has somehow been apprised of his mission. We never saw when this happened either, but Jenkins raises no objection to it. Surely if we are to assume that husbands and wives talk to each other off-stage, other characters do likewise.

In one of his longer notes appended to this text (discussing various theories about the King's reaction/non-reaction to the so-called dumb show of the 'mouse-trap' scene), Jenkins expresses more fully his interpretive principle: "The trouble with all these theories is that they make additions to the text, or at least assumptions for which the text gives no warrant. They all apply to imaginary events the kind of rational inference appropriate only in the real world. In a work of fiction what we do not know because the fiction does not tell us cannot be presumed to exist" (502). As I have just argued, taken literally one simply *cannot* accept the latter claims, on pain of reducing the plays to incoherence. The real issue here concerns what sorts of assumptions Shakespeare allowed for, and Jenkins provides no evidence that he knows Shakespeare's mind in this regard.

There is a subtle but crucial difference between Knights's and Jenkins's position and that of Norman Rabkin in *Shakespeare and the Common Understanding* (New York: Free Press, 1967) when he observes: "We cannot answer some questions – 'How much did Gertrude know about Claudius' crime?' 'What was her relationship with Claudius while her husband still lived?' – because Hamlet himself cannot answer them, and our doubts intensify our sympathies with a hero who must act on insufficient knowledge" (2–3). While I'm not sure that Rabkin's exemplary questions would defy all interpretive efforts to answer them, his general point here is a valid one.

30 In sum, I must agree with Nuttall's judgment in *A New Mimesis* concerning the position Knights stakes out in his 'How Many Children' essay: "It is strange that so coarse a piece of reasoning should have passed for a great stroke of destructive theory. Knights's singular presumption that humane inference is inapplicable to drama is simply mistaken. When a character sits up and yawns we infer that he has been sleeping ... All our inferences and suppositions with regard to fictitious persons are in terms of probability, not fact" (82–3).

The theoretical analysis Nuttall provides re-establishes a solid basis for interpreting fictional literature mimetically – an approach at least as old as Aristotle's *Poetics*, as he reminds us: "the central, classic statement of *mimesis* [is] Aristotle's observation that, while history tells us 'what Alcibiades did,' poetry tells us 'the kind of thing that would happen' (*Poetics*, 1451a)." Whereas, it is precisely the failure to appreciate this subjunctive quality of dramatic poetry that compromises various modern and postmodern approaches, from that of Knights to Derridean deconstructionism. "Probability is the missing factor, and its importance was plain to Aristotle more than 2000 years ago" (55).

For analytic purposes, Nuttall suggests one can discern among scholars a basic dichotomy of critical postures. There are those whose approach involves:

> a severe separation of critic and reader (or spectator). The critic knows how the conjurer does the tricks, or how the tricks fool the audience, and is thereby excluded, by his very knowingness, from the innocent delight of those who marvel and applaud. Such criticism can never submit to mimetic enchantment because to do so would be to forfeit critical understanding of the means employed.
>
> [Scholars using the approach he argues for instead are] less afraid of submission, feeling that enchantment need involve no submersion of critical faculties, but that on the contrary without such a willingness to enter the proffered dream a great many factors essential to a just appreciation may be artificially excluded from discussion ... They know that Ophelia is not a real woman but are willing to think of her as a possible woman. They note that Shakespeare implicitly asks them to do this, but they do more than note the request; they comply with it. (81)

Obviously, any critic worth reading can and does first experience the work naturally, then technically analyses it. But the fact remains, he hasn't *fully* experienced it if he hasn't opened himself up to all reasonable inferences, treating the characters as possible persons – rather than acceding to Knights's view that Falstaff "is not a man, but a choric commentary." Surely Nuttall's position is the more sensible: "Falstaff is quite clearly presented, through fiction, as a human being. To strive to dislodge such fundamental and evident truths as this is a kind of critical idiocy" (100). See also J.I.M. Stewart, *Character and Motive in Shakespeare* (London: Longmans, 1949), 113.

31 For reasons which I presume are sufficiently clear by now, I ignore most postmodern criticism since it tends to be overtly historicist and ideological, and aimed more at exposé than sympathetic understanding. In my view, this is an injustice to the quality of Shakespeare's mind. Such a prejudiced approach closes one to the very possibility that the author has anything important to teach the reader, that he might in fact be philosophically superior. As Graham Bradshaw observes in *Misrepresentations*, his penetrating – and often amusing – examination of some of the leading practitioners in the field of postmodern Shakespeare criticism:

> Many materialist critics dismiss any concern with dramatic intentions: the search for 'imaginary coherence' or 'unity' is derided as a 'humanist' illusion, or as part of the cultural conspiracy to conceal ideological inconsistencies within the text. Yet as soon as we attend with any closeness to their readings and their language, we find them all implying or assuming some intention – usually a single intention, and often an ugly intention ... (30)
>
> If our response is so far determined by what 'conservative' or 'radical' prejudices we bring to the show, before we have even seen it, it is not obvious what studying literature and drama can ever teach us. (31)

Must we not expect that 'critiques' which show little more than that past authors did not share the orthodoxies these critics currently favour will themselves soon fall victim to the very historicism they endorse?

32 His case, as presented in Plato's *Apology of Sokrates*, provides what is still the best initiation into political philosophy. As Leo Strauss observes, "the *Apology of Socrates* is the portal through which we enter the Platonic kosmos." See 'On Plato's *Apology of Socrates* and *Crito*,' in *Essays in Honor of Jacob Klein* (Annapolis: St John's College Press, 1976), 155.

33 Neither of these essential characteristics seem to be appreciated by T.S. Eliot as he rejects the idea that Shakespeare is a philosopher in his 'Introduction' (1930) to G.Wilson Knight's *The Wheel of Fire*:

> I have always maintained, not only that Shakespeare was not a philosophical poet in the sense of Dante and Lucretius; but also, what may be more easily over-

> looked, that 'philosophical poets' like Dante and Lucretius are not really philosophers at all. They are poets who have presented us with the emotional and sense equivalent for a definite philosophical system constructed by a philosopher – even though they may sometimes take little liberties with the system. To say that Shakespeare is not a philosophical poet like these is not to say anything very striking or important. (xiii)
>
> I once affirmed that Dante made great poetry out of a great philosophy of life; and that Shakespeare made equally great poetry out of an inferior and muddled philosophy of life. (xv)

I suppose there are few who could advance these judgments with more plausible authority than Eliot. But still, and as I hope to go some way towards showing, here he has *greatly* underestimated Shakespeare. The problem begins, however, with Eliot's identifying 'philosophy' with fully articulated 'metaphysical systems.' It is to such system-builders that he contrasts the poet.

> The poet has something to say which is not even necessarily implicit in the system, something which is also over and above the verbal beauty ... [What Eliot, borrowing an image from Henry James, calls a 'pattern of the carpet.'] And of this sort of 'pattern' the most elaborate, the most extensive, and probably the most inscrutable is that of the plays of Shakespeare. (xiii)
>
> [Given that] Dante's pattern is the richer by a serious philosophy, and Shakespeare's the poorer by a ragbag philosophy, I should say that Shakespeare's pattern was more complex, and his problem more difficult than Dante's ... But our first duty as critics or 'interpreters,' surely, must be to try to grasp the whole design, and read *character* and *plot* in the understanding of this subterrene or submarine music ... For Shakespeare is one of the rarest of dramatic poets, in that each of his characters is most nearly adequate both to the requirements of the real world and to those of the poet's world. (xix)

I readily agree with Eliot's last point here, but contend (and will endeavour to demonstrate) that such 'grasping' and 'reading' necessarily involve one in philosophical activity. However, Eliot is clearly suspicious of all 'interpretations' of poetry (while conceding that the impulse to interpret is quite natural), and seems to reject the idea that the author's meaning can be the criterion of correct interpretation, given that there are so many possibilities of meaning (xvi):

> But our impulse to interpret a work of art ... is exactly as imperative and fundamental as our impulse to interpret the universe by metaphysics. Though we are never satisfied by any metaphysic, yet those who insist dogmatically upon the impossibility of knowledge of the universe, or those who essay to prove to us that the term 'universe' is meaningless, meet, I think, with a singularly unanimous

> rejection by those who are curious about the universe; and their counsels fall more flat than the flimsiest constructions of metaphysics. And Bradley's apothegm that 'metaphysics is the finding of bad reasons for what we believe upon instinct; but to find these reasons is no less an instinct,' applies as precisely to the interpretation of poetry. (xvii)

In short, by identifying 'being philosophical' with having a fully articulated metaphysical view, Eliot overlooks the fact that philosophy is first of all, both logically and psychologically, a self-conscious commitment to an *activity*, to rigorous and persistent thinking, in the recognition that the *questions* – not the answers – are *primary*. Hence, whenever an author endeavours to provide (whatever else) a deeper appreciation of the questionableness of the questions, he is thereby encouraging philosophical activity in others, at least to the extent they too are naturally inclined to it. Whereas, on Eliot's view (which is by no means unique to him), the Sokrates of the *Apology* would not qualify as a philosopher.

Here, then, I emphatically agree instead with L.C. Knights in 'The Question of Character in Shakespeare' who recommends "we take seriously Coleridge's remark that Shakespeare was 'a philosopher'; the vision of life that his plays express is, in a certain sense, a philosophic vision. But at the same time we remember ... that the plays are not dramatizations of abstract ideas, but imaginative constructions mediated through the poetry" (53). It is sufficient for philosophical purposes to see each of the plays as does Bradshaw in *Misrepresentations*, "as a highly organized matrix of potential meanings, rather than as a chaotic site," and thus be more "concerned with how the play thinks or sets us thinking, not with what the play 'really' thinks or tells 'us' to think" (31).

In this connection, however, there is a danger in concluding with Robert H. West, in *Shakespeare and the Outer Mystery* (Lexington: University of Kentucky Press, 1968), that Shakespeare purposefully left things mysterious because that's just how they are in reality: "He does not prescribe a metaphysical ground for the superhuman evil in *Macbeth* any more than he sets forth a social theory about miscegenation in *Othello* or a theory of class struggle in *Coriolanus* ... By indefiniteness about the Sisters and the phenomena related to them Shakespeare preserves awe and mystery and at the same time expresses our general assurance of the existence of a thing that we may sense to loom above us but whose economy we have no means really to know" (79). The hazard is this: in presuming that Shakespeare everywhere found the universe *incorrigibly* mysterious (or every bit as mysterious as West does), one will not strive as hard as one might to uncover whatever insights into its intelligibility the philosopher-poet may have provided. It is more prudent to presume that he saw more deeply into things – including their deeper coherence – than the rest of us do. That is, after all, the point of studying him.

I do not wish to imply that I am the first to argue that Shakespeare is a political philosopher. However, I do believe that the case I make in this book differs somewhat from any other I am acquainted with, and that it goes considerably farther in demonstrating the extent of Shakespeare's philosophical ambitions. Be that as it may, I mean it to supplement and complement that which Allan Bloom presents in the Introductory chapter of *Shakespeare's Politics* (New York: Basic Books, 1964) and likewise that of Howard B. White, in *Copp'd Hills toward Heaven: Shakespeare and the Classical Polity* (The Hague: Martinus Nijhoff, 1970). I have learned much over the years from David Lowenthal's essays on various plays (now collected in *Shakespeare and the Good Life,* Lanham, MD: Rowman and Littlefield, 1997), especially concerning the transpolitical philosophic issues they address. See also the exemplary essays in John E. Alvis and Thomas G. West, eds., *Shakespeare as Political Thinker* (Wilmington, DE: ISI Books, 2000) and in Joseph Alulis and Vickie Sullivan, eds., *Shakespeare's Political Pageant* (Lanham, MD: Rowman and Littlefield, 1996).

34 For treatments that *do* address the reason for Antonio's sadness, see Barbara Tovey, 'The Golden Casket: An Interpretation of *The Merchant of Venice*,' in *Shakespeare as Political Thinker*, 261–87; and, Allan Bloom, 'On Christian and Jew: The Merchant of Venice,' in his *Shakespeare's Politics*, 13–34.

35 Some scholars, such as the editor of the second Arden edition, T.S. Dorsch (siding he tells us "with most recent editors"; 106n), have found this apparent 'inconsistency' so perplexing that they've taken refuge in that omnibus explanation for any feature that resists ready explanation: a mangled text. In this case, we are to suppose "that the copy from which the Folio was printed contained two versions of the account of Portia's death, of which one was a revision, and that both were printed by mistake." This is a typical instance of 'interpretation by re-editing,' a tactic too frequently employed precisely because its legitimacy has become so widely accepted. Its use in this case is particularly unfortunate, since it results in ignoring the single most important piece of evidence Shakespeare provides as to the true character and deeper motivation of Brutus. There are several very good studies of this play, including that of David Lowenthal, 'Julius Caesar,' in *Shakespeare and the Good Life*; Allan Bloom, 'The Morality of the Pagan Hero,' in his *Shakespeare's Politics*, 13–34; Jan Blits, *The End of the Ancient Republic* (Durham: Carolina Academic Press, 1982); Michael Platt, *Rome and Romans According to Shakespeare* (Salzburg: Studies in English Literature, *Institut für Englische Sprache und Literatur*, 1976), 173–245.

36 From what I have seen of scholarly as well as more popular literature on what are regarded as the greatest plays – including especially *Macbeth* and *King Lear* – rather few people do understand 'what's *really* going on' in them. And this should not be taken as a failure on Shakespeare's part (i.e., an inability to make his meaning clear), but quite the contrary: *success* in concealing his fuller thoughts from all but his favourite few. Only those who recognize the author's philosophical stature, and who are both willing and able to subordinate themselves to him in order to learn what he has to teach (which may include truths that will never be acceptable to, or for, the vast major-

ity of people) permit themselves the opportunity to communicate with him at this deeper level. The rest of his audience is provided edification and entertainment more to their needing and liking. I agree with Traversi in *An Approach to Shakespeare*, vol. 2, 20 when he writes:

> Shakespeare's greatest plays have, in reality, something of the universal appeal of myth, of the expression of a universal consciousness deeply implanted in the popular mind and accessible, though in varying degrees and ways, to all levels of society. They appeal in different fashions to different levels of understanding, related to one another by the very fact of their common participation, but not identical. There is something in these great plays for the illiterate as for the intellectual, and it is part of their greatness that the immense field of experience they offer to the latter is still intimately related to the primary emotions which constitute the chief popular appeal of the drama.

I think this is exactly right, and that it is essential to an understanding of Shakespeare's political aspirations: to provide a differentiated and yet communal experience that binds together "all levels of society." What bears emphasizing here, however, is that the real problem of appealing to "*all* levels" occurs at the *upper* end of the intellectual scale, not the lower. If Shakespeare is to provide something for everyone, he must prove that he is equal to the best, challenging the intelligence and spirit of the most intelligent and spirited few.

37 My appreciation of this point has been enhanced by Nuttall's more extensive discussion in *A New Mimesis* (75–80); as he observes:

> The artist, as artist, deals occasionally in realities and therefore is concerned with knowledge. This does not mean, however, that good mimetic art must present us with fresh knowledge, should teach us things we did not know before. From antiquity the commonest praise of the mimetic artist is that he has truly rendered some readily available, known subject. We praise a work of scholarship when it adds to our stock of information, but that has never been important in the mimetic tradition ... We therefore bestow no especial praise on the person who merely states a known truth accurately. We reserve praise for such things as minute, highly detailed or unexpectedly pointed accuracy of description and the power to 'realize' or 'give life' to the object of the mimesis. Thus we find that there are two ways of using words (two ways which are frequently mingled but are nevertheless distinguishable). We can use words merely to summarize or refer to known material. Or we can use words to elicit an imaginative awareness of the known material. (74)

As Nuttall rightly emphasizes, the dramatic poet need not supply fresh information to have an educative effect. But as I argue below, he may do this as well.

38 Bradshaw, *Shakespeare's Scepticism* (Ithaca, NY: Cornell University Press, 1987), 230.

39 Thus, I believe there is more going on beneath Alfred Harbage's example of Shakespeare's moral teaching in *As They Liked It* (Philadelphia: University of Pennsylvania Press, 1972) than Harbage himself allows for when he asks us to imagine a father and daughter returning home after a performance of *King Lear*:

> They know what the play was about. It is a terrible thing, perhaps the most terrible of all things, when a father turns against his own child, or the child against its own father. They knew this before they came to the theatre, Shakespeare knew that they did, and he left them in firm possession of a truth which life, infinitely more powerful than art as a teacher, has taught them. He has given their homely truth a wonderful, a beautiful investiture ... Shakespeare is a dramatic artist, and the relation of dramatic art to the moral nature of man is about that of wind to the surface of water. It keeps the surface agitated, spanking it into sunny little ripples or driving it into powerful surges, but it does not trouble the depths. Dramatic art neither raises nor lowers the level, and the business of the dramatic artist is to know the height of the surface upon which he works. (56–7)

I am far from convinced of Harbage's basic point: that life is always "infinitely more powerful than art as a teacher." I rather suspect that great drama can sometimes crystalize in a single powerful example a vast amount of disparate, diluted life experiences whose import was not previously recognized, hence had not 'sunk in.' Whereas I *am* reasonably sure that neither Shakespeare's ambition nor his actual effect on his audience is limited to ratifying moral truisms, and that he manages to penetrate (and 'trouble') some souls far more deeply than Harbage allows for. Here again, Nuttall in *A New Mimesis* helps explain how Shakespeare manages this, and thus how he stimulates and quickens philosophic activity in readers naturally inclined to think about what they see and hear and read:

> Again, if we think of experiential rather than propositional knowledge, we shall be less embarrassed by the persistent tendency of literary works, even those which lodge a claim to be realistic, to blur outlines, to bury information and to withhold clues. Experiential knowledge is naturally involved with emotional commitment and withdrawal, is naturally dynamic. It is deepened or intensified by the overcoming of difficulties. Thus a work which stimulates (even by temporarily frustrating) the faculty of apprehension will engage us more fully than one which blandly displays its material. (78)

With this in mind, much of what Bertrand Evans shows in *Shakespeare's Tragic Practice* (Oxford: Clarendon Press, 1979) – of how Shakespeare creates 'gaps' in knowledge between characters, and between characters and audience, which he then exploits for dramatic-ironic effect – can also be seen as serving the philosophical purpose of stimulating thought. But the kind (and depth) of re-thinking involved can also have profound moral and political consequences, as Nuttall observes in speaking of *The Merchant of Venice* in *A New Mimesis*:

> It is true, of course, that certain archetypes operate powerfully in the play. But it is not true that they are the only thing there, that the mind should be arrested at their level of generality, that there is nothing behind them. It is Shakespeare's way to take an archetype or a stereotype and then work, so to speak, against it, without ever overthrowing it. Shakespeare himself darkens the pristine clarity of these ethical oppositions ... (124)

> [But] Shakespeare will not let us rest even here. The subversive counter-thesis is itself too easy. We may now begin to see that he is perhaps the least sentimental dramatist who ever lived. We begin to understand what is meant by holding the mirror up to nature. (131)

> Shakespeare, more perhaps than any other writer, creates a cloud of alternative or overdetermining explanations round his figures. One begins to sense that there are two ways of using the intelligence: to solve difficulties and to start them. Those who assume that intelligence is essentially concerned with solutions find themselves at a stand when they are asked to explain the intelligence of Shakespeare: no problems were solved by him. (180)

This 'starting difficulties,' making us see the interesting questions behind the commonplace answers, and this preclusion of our explaining people and what they do in causally simplistic terms, is (I contend) basic to the philosophical pedagogy of the plays.

40 The first Churchill, John, Lord Marlborough, avowed that the only English history he ever read was Shakespeare's. And his most famous descendant, Winston, while still a boy at Harrow, "could quote whole scenes from Shakespeare and had no hesitation in correcting the masters if they misquoted." A.L. Rowse, *The Churchills: From the Death of Marlborough to the Present* (New York: Harper & Brothers, 1958, 253).

41 This is splendidly borne out by Rabkin in his *Shakespeare and the Common Understanding*, despite what would seem to be his explicit claim to the contrary. Rabkin provides persuasive evidence for his view that what consistently distinguishes Shakespeare's plays is "a characteristic mode of vision, a view of the world as problematic in ways which, though infinitely various, share a common pattern," namely, that of allowing for – if not requiring – diametrically opposed conclusions on virtually every question of consequence. Rabkin contends that this apprehension of the world as essentially problematic, in which we are forever confronted with having to choose between incompatible views of seemingly equal validity:

> is what puts Shakespeare's plays out of the reach of the narrow moralist, the special pleader for a particular ideology, the intellectual historian looking for a Shakespearian version of a Renaissance orthodoxy. Indeed it is that mode of vision that puts the plays beyond philosophy and makes them works of art. They cannot be reduced to prose paraphrase or statements of theme because the kind of "statement" a given play makes cannot respectably be made in the logical language of prose, where it will sound merely paradoxical. Paradox is not the kind of formulation the rational mentality has traditionally been happy with, and for good reason. But the kind of "statement" a play like *Hamlet* makes, paradoxical only when translated into discursive prose, represents the state of intellectual and spiritual tension which makes art. Informing such verbal constructs as the plays of Shakespeare, this approach to experience makes them essentially non-verbal because it makes them supralogical. It enables the plays to create illusory worlds which, like the world we feel about us, make sense in ways that consistently elude our power to articulate them rationally and yet seem to represent the truth better than rational articulation. Shakespeare's habitual approach makes his plays definitive embodiments of our knowledge that we live in a world which though it makes sense to our intuitive consciousness cannot be reduced to sense, and which though palpably coherent is always more complicated than the best of our analytic descriptions can say. (12–13)

However, in contending that all this "puts the plays beyond philosophy," Rabkin is mistaken: it merely puts them beyond the modern, derivative conception of philosophy (as being a set of doctrines), with its impoverished conception of reason (as practically equivalent to logic). The sort of endlessly thought-provoking challenges Rabkin so convincingly shows the plays provide are precisely what make them philosophical in the original sense of the word. I'm not convinced that Shakespeare saw the paradoxes as unresolvable, but I can easily agree that he makes us aware that their resolution, if possible at all, is exceedingly difficult. At the least, then, he shows us why the great questions remain questions for human beings generally. And this is sufficient to justify Rabkin's arguing that faithfully portraying "the unresolvable tensions that are the fundamental conditions of human life" is the mimetic basis of Shakespeare's art (27).

42 The potential conflicts between the unrestricted pursuit of knowledge and the requirements of wholesome political life – epitomized in Plato's portrayal of the life and death of the historical Sokrates – is what the idea of a regime ruled by a philosopher-king is meant to resolve. For a fuller exploration of that idea as Plato first presented it, See my analysis in *The War Lover: A Study of Plato's Republic* (ch. 7). Among the most useful treatments of the perennial problems entailed in the uneasy relationship between philosophy (including science) and politics – or what often comes to the same thing, between philosophy and religion – is that found in the writings of Leo Strauss. See

especially the 'Introduction' and title essay in Strauss, *Persecution and the Art of Writing* (Glencoe: Free Press 1952), 'On a Forgotten Kind of Writing,' in *What Is Political Philosophy* (Glencoe: Free Press, 1959), 'Exoteric Teaching,' in *The Rebirth of Classical Political Rationalism*, Thomas L. Pangle, ed. (Chicago: University of Chicago Press, 1989).

43 For all the quantity of material written about Shakespeare, one seldom encounters much appreciation of this aspect of his plays. L.C. Knights, in *Some Shakespearean Themes,* is one of the exceptions: "Indeed the distinguishing mark of Shakespeare's handling of political actions is the clarity with which he sees them, not in terms of 'politics' (that word which, perhaps as much as any, is responsible for simplification and distortion in our thinking) but in terms of their causes in human fears and desires and of particular human consequences. His interest in politics was of a kind that led, inevitably, beyond them, and the insights that made possible *Coriolanus* were developed outside the bounds of a merely political concern" (29).

44 The textual problems arising from the difference between the Quarto and Folio versions (the mock trial is not in the latter) will be addressed later. That the whole scene was in the original (i.e., Quarto) version is sufficient for my purpose here: indicating a special relationship between the two plays. The text I shall be using, that of the second Arden edition, is (like most modern editions) a composite of the two versions. Its editor, Kenneth Muir, discusses the recent criticism of this standard practice of conflating the two versions in 'The Texts of *King Lear*: An Interim Assessment of the Controversy,' in *Shakespeare: Contrasts and Controversies* (Norman: University of Oklahoma Press, 1985, 51–66). The larger theoretical – and political – issues at stake in Revisionists' efforts to de-throne the composite version in favour of the much shorter Folio version are trenchantly dissected by Paul A. Cantor, 'On Sitting Down to Read *King Lears* Again: The Textual Deconstruction of Shakespeare,' in *The Flight from Science and Reason*, Paul R. Gross, Norman Levitt, and Martin W. Lewis, eds. (New York: New York Academy of Sciences, 1996, 445–58). Incidentally, because Cantor judges "the mock trial Lear conducts of Goneril and Regan" to be "absolutely integral to the structure of *King Lear* as a whole," he too prefers retaining "some form of conflated text of the play" (451). Beyond that, he argues that "recent developments in the editing of *King Lear* are emblematic of everything that has gone wrong in literary studies today":

> But I am more struck by the way the new editorial approach conforms to the general mood in literary studies today. Is it any wonder that precisely the generation of critics raised on deconstruction as a critical theory has chosen to decompose the single greatest masterpiece of Western literature? In a narrow sense, deconstruction as a movement in literary theory shows signs of having reached a dead end. But in a larger sense deconstruction has changed the whole landscape of literary study and survives and indeed flourishes in such transformations as the

New Historicism, which is really a kind of a deconstructed Marxism. Above all, deconstruction has succeeded in transforming the basic attitude of critics toward a text, from a kind of respectful awe that issues in a desire to learn from the work to a barely suppressed hostility that reflects a desire to control and dominate it. During the reign of the New Criticism, critics had a respect, almost a blind faith, in the integrity of literary texts, what was often referred to as their organic wholeness ...

All this has changed in the postdeconstruction era, in the wake of relentless assaults on the wholeness of works of literature and in particular the systematic debunking of the idea that the author's consciousness stands behind and undergirds the text, supplying it with the integrity and coherence of an intentional artifact. A generation of critics has been brought up on the deconstructive principle that a work of literature can always be shown to mean something other than its author intended, perhaps reflecting some unconscious pressure on him or a buried division in his psyche or a contradiction inherent in his subject and/or his medium. An approach that fragments works into multiple versions is the appropriate editorial counterpart of this brand of criticism. (452–3)

2: Living in a Hard Time

1 Unless otherwise indicated, textual references are to the second Arden edition of *Macbeth*, Kenneth Muir, ed. (originally published by Methuen and Co., London 1951, revised in 1971 and 1984; reprinted London and New York: Routledge, 1988). My infrequent departures from this text in favour of the Folio text or my own emendations are easily recognized as such. Also, I occasionally quote snippets of verse as prose, when doing so facilitates readability.

2 But as Jane Adamson rightly observes in her *Troilus and Cressida* (Boston: Twayne, 1987): "The fact that [*Troilus and Cressida*] includes an unusual amount of abstract language and rather abstruse analytical argumentation does not in itself make it any more 'philosophical' than, say, the Tragedies, nor any more profound than, say, the late plays ... Nor should the substance and style of the play's own thinking be confused with the characters' frequent philosophizing, which is always biased by their having a personal axe to grind and is often infested with illogicalities. The distinction between the way the play is 'thinking' and the way the characters think, feel, act, and express themselves is obviously a central one in all Shakespeare's plays, though it works differently in each ..." (28).

3 Wilbur Sanders, in one of the better essays on the play, '*Macbeth*: What's Done, Is Done' in *Shakespeare's Magnanimity*, Sanders and Howard Jacobson (New York: Oxford University Press, 1978) expresses a refined version of this view in the portrait he provides of barbarous Scotland: "It doesn't seem arbitrary there ... to inter-

pret '*prediction* / Of noble having, and of royal hope' as a 'supernatural *soliciting*' to crime. Even the civilized Banquo is pretty prompt to name the solicitors as 'instruments of darkness,' and to wonder whether the whole thing isn't some devilish trap for the unwary. He counters, that is to say, one superstition by appealing to another" (62).

4 What to make of Shakespeare's name for these three crones – or names, rather – is a matter of some controversy, bearing as it does on how one conceives them. The first three times it is given as 'Weyward' (1.3.32; 1.5.8; 2.1.20); the last three times as 'Weyard' (3.1.2; 3.4.132; 4.1.136). In the fourth instance, the term modifies 'Women'; in all other cases, it is coupled with 'Sisters.' That the Folio text was set by two different compositors has been suggested as a possible explanation of the irregular spelling, which presumes that one compositor consistently misread the original text. In any event, these are the only uses of either version in the canon (whereas 'wayward' appears fourteen times, including once in *Macbeth*: Hecate speaks of Macbeth as himself "a wayward son"; 3.5.11). Most editors regard Shakespeare's term(s) as an early alternative spelling of 'weird' – and so use that as a replacement – no doubt influenced by the fact that this is the word that appears in Holinshed's text: "that these women were either the weird sisters, that is (as ye would say) the goddesses of destinie, or else some nymphs or feiries" (reproduced in Appendix A of the Arden edition, 171–2). For the Arden text, Muir chose Theobald's variation, 'Wëird.' But the very fact that Holinshed is obviously a primary source for Shakespeare should make one pause. Is it not prudent to presume that Shakespeare has some reason for departing from his source whenever he chooses to do so? He could easily have employed Holinshed's term (or spelling, if one prefers) had he wished to. Garry Wills' discussion of Shakespeare's names for the witches includes some interesting information about the meaning of 'wayward' in Wycliffe's translation of the Bible: *Witches and Jesuits: Shakespeare's Macbeth* (New York: Oxford University Press, 1995). Wills suspects that Shakespeare has invented an "exotic form" meant to evoke both 'weird' and 'wayward' (161). For an informative account of the 'social reality' in which the belief in witchcraft flourished (c. 1450 to 1750), exploding many of the myths and stereotypes current today, see Robin Briggs, *Witches and Neighbors* (New York: Viking, 1996).

Believing the witches to be vitally important to Shakespeare's intentions in the play, and bearing in mind Marvin Rosenberg's excellent discussions of the various interpretations of these three strange creatures and their activities in *The Masks of Macbeth* (Newark: University of Delaware Press, 1978), 1–36, 52–7, 490–6, 501–26, I am persuaded that it is best to stick with 'Weyward.' I agree it may well be a word Shakespeare himself coined, meaning to synthesize the associations of both 'weird' and 'wayward.' There is no evidence of its existence prior to the Folio text of 1623. The Oxford English Dictionary, Compact ed., treats 'weyward' as equivalent to 'weyard,' both being obsolete variants of 'weird' (Oxford: Oxford University Press,

1971; 3731 and 3746); but the only evidence cited for these conclusions is Shakespeare's *Macbeth*.

There is one more curiosity connected with the 'Weyward' name. It is a perfect rhyme for the name of Malcolm's uncle and cousin as it is spelled throughout the Folio text: Seyward (not 'Siward,' as it appears not only in most modern editions, but also *in Holinshed*)!

5 Modern historians, even more so than those upon which Shakespeare relied, can be invoked in Macbeth's defense, though one candidly admits that a certain construal of events, "which were copied from the Scottish into the English histories, and invested by Shakspere [sic] with a power that makes historical reality shrink before it like a mendacious culprit," result in Macbeth being "so deeply branded by the poet as a usurper that no skill can remove the stigma." See the first volume of Rev. Thomas Thomson, *A History of the Scottish People*, 3 vols. (London: Blackie and Sons, 1896), 84.

6 Here using the term 'theoretical' in its original sense (from the Greek *theōria*, 'contemplation'); in this sense, 'theoretical' knowledge is that which serves primarily if not solely to satisfy the human desire to know.

7 No one whose opinion is worth considering would deny that Shakespeare has both the means and the intention to show some of his characters to be more intelligent than others, or more reflective than others. Thus, to allege that Macbeth displays some quasi-philosophical inclination raises no problems in principle (whether or not one would agree that there is sufficient evidence to justify the claim in his case). But to suggest that Macbeth has something of a *poet's* soul is another matter. For there are those who deny that it is ever legitimate to attribute such a quality to a character, that however vivacious the imagery he employs, however 'moving' his speeches, the poetry is all Shakespeare's; and that, strictly speaking, *all* of his characters are 'poetic.' Even granting that he has carefully qualified it, Muir states this position clearly enough in his 'Introduction' to the Arden edition of Macbeth: "If we go further and pretend that this poetic imagery is proof that Macbeth had a powerful imagination, that he was in fact a poet, we are in danger of confusing real life and drama. Every character in a poetic play may speak in verse, may speak poetry: but this poetry does not necessarily reflect their poetic dispositions – it is merely a medium" (1).

Because the issue is of major importance with respect to interpreting Shakespeare generally, and for this play in particular, I must treat it at some length. There are several ways one may wish to challenge Muir's view, but what seems most crucial to me is that it in effect denies that Shakespeare's art is capable of portraying what I suspect he (like me) would regard as one of the most important respects in which people differ, namely, in their poetic capacities (or, in what often comes to the same thing, their rhetorical powers). So, for example, if there is any truth to the romantic idea that falling in love can inspire poetry, on this view Shakespeare could not *show* it; at most, he could have someone claim it, albeit quite 'poetically.' A character's lacklustre language prior to falling must be understood to be every bit as poetic as his later flights of fancy spoken under love's influence. A moment's reflection on any of several plays is sufficient to render such a notion highly dubious. One can agree that Iago has only the words that Shakespeare gives him. But if we cannot see that what *distinguishes* Iago is his extraordinary ability to conjure poisonous images – that it is this perverse poetic talent, working in conjunction with his deep understanding of human nature – that constitutes his evil genius, we could never understand what Shakespeare presumably wishes to teach us: the basis of Iago's diabolical power. Are we not meant to recognize the great difference in the rhetoric with which Shakespeare has endowed Brutus compared with that of Marc Antony when they successively address the crowd, and see it as reflective of differences in the two men themselves? Suffice it to say, I believe Muir is quite mistaken in his insisting that we not give Shakespeare's characters any credit for the poetry he has issue from their mouths.

L.C. Knights in *Some Shakespearean Themes* (London: Chatto and Windus, 1960) singles out *Macbeth* for the power of its poetry. He judges *King John* to be "a good play, containing some admirably vigorous poetry," but goes on to say: "Not only is the verse of *Macbeth* more fluid, more vivid and compressed than the verse of *King John*, the mind of the reader or spectator is more fully activated, and activated in different ways. The compression, the thick clusters of imagery (with rapidly changing metaphors completely superceding the similes and drawn-out figures to be found in the earlier plays), the surprising juxtapositions, the over-riding of grammar, and the shifts and overlapping of meanings – all these, demanding an unusual liveliness of attention, force the reader to respond with the whole of his active imagination" (18–19).

I would simply add that most of the best illustrations of what Knights here describes are to be found in the speeches Shakespeare has provided his Macbeth. There is only one speech in the entire play whose poetic power rivals any of a half dozen that one could cite of Macbeth's, and that is Lady Macbeth's "The raven himself is hoarse ..." (1.5.38–54). W.H. Auden in *The Dyer's Hand and Other Essays* (New York: Vintage, 1989) makes an intriguing observation about Macbeth's poetry. Contrasting this tragic figure with Falstaff ("a character whose true home is the world of music," thus is easily translated into opera), he suggests, "If Verdi's *Macbetto* fails to come off, the main reason is that the proper world for Macbeth is poetry, not song; he won't go into notes." (183).

Rosenberg has especially useful assessments of both the poetic and philosophic qualities of Macbeth in *The Masks of Macbeth*, 97–103. With respect to 'Macbeth as Poet,' he says:

> But the poetry is an essential part of the characterization. We are awed and taken with Macbeth, as we are not by Coriolanus, for instance – or in this play, by Mal-

> colm – not only because of what Macbeth does, or even what he feels, but also because of how he can describe what he does and feels. The sensitivity of the poetic language belongs to the man; it is he who finds words to glimpse his self and world in metaphors that make them achingly real and recognizable. Macbeth's verbal visions that open his soul to us validate his dread of committing murder, and the impact on him of the horror that follows. The poet-Macbeth establishes the identity of the man of action who loves words, caresses them, savors their sounds, invokes their magic for narcotic or spur. Even in his greatest stress, the song of his speech is some extenuation for him – a major source of our empathy with so terrible a man. (98)

Bertrand Evans in *Shakespeare's Tragic Practice* (Oxford: Clarendon Press, 1979) goes even further, making the extraordinary quality of Macbeth's poetry the basis of a radical thesis about the play as a whole:

> Our hardest question ... is how it can be that *Macbeth* has so regularly been characterized as the tragedy of an 'essentially good man' whose principles give way to overmastering ambition and who thereafter undergoes moral deterioration, experiencing all the while those agonies of conscience that, indeed, only an essentially good man can experience ...
>
> Two explanations suggest themselves. The first has to do with the quality of poetry that Shakespeare gives Macbeth to speak ... Macbeth's language is everywhere richly imaginative, vivid in the extreme. It teems with figures of every sort and with ideas that erupt, stage pyrotechnical displays, then yield to new eruptions – all with such rapidity that the effects dazzle eye, ear, and mind alike ... He sees, feels, thinks, and speaks habitually as a poet – not, indeed, like one who self-consciously coins clever phrases and devises extravagant conceits, ... but like one who is literally possessed by a poetic demon, who could never speak dully if he tried. (218)

[H]is utterances wildly spill from his intoxicated brain because it is filled to overflowing. His imagination is not under his control; he is its creature. It drives him not only to pour out striking images and splendid sounds in profusion but to see visions, hear voices, conceive bizarre and inexplicable ideas ...

But for all its charm, Macbeth's poetic power does not fool Macduff, who is not even 'in' on his secret, as we are; and perhaps it should never have deceived students of the play. Yet there can be no question but that Macbeth's spellbinding power of language has contributed much to the deception of generations of critics who have found him to be better than he is – to be, indeed, possessed of moral sense and inner goodness that in plain fact he lacks. Totally self-centred, judging all that lies in past, present, and future in terms of consequences to himself only,

> he has thrust his sensations upon us in such dazzling images that we have been hoodwinked ... (219)

As I shall argue more fully later, Evans profoundly misjudges Macbeth, partly because he applies an anachronistic (and utterly utopian) conception of morality. Also, he never considers the possibility that Macbeth's words captivate us because he must have *thought* about things (albeit unsystematically and perhaps even unwillingly, considering puzzling phenomena in isolation and as they intrude into his consciousness), and that it is this fascination and perplexity that have inspired his poetry.

It is worth noting in this connection that martial societies have *typically* been distinguished by their high regard for beautiful and powerful speech, and not infrequently by their being sources of immortal poetry: the Homeric epics of the Greeks, the *Sagen* of the Norsemen, Tales of Knights Errant, the Ballads of the Troubadours. Pre-eminence in a warrior society is never simply a matter of martial prowess; of equal importance is the ability to speak well in counsel, which reveals the qualities of mind. Achilles is tutored in both fighting and speaking, and shows it; whereas mighty Ajax is the butt of jokes. Typically, terse but pithy, dense and arresting speech is favoured, leading naturally to poetry. This is nicely illustrated in the Japanese Samurai tradition, which is filled with stories of poetic warriors, such as those recounted by S.R. Turnbull in *The Samurai: A Military History* (New York: Macmillan, 1977), for example:

> Yorimasa's suicide, though not the first in Japanese history ... was performed with such finesse that it served as a model of the noblest way by which a defeated samurai could take his leave of the world. While his [mortally wounded] sons held the gate the septuagenarian samurai calmly wrote a farewell poem on the back of his war-fan, which read:
>
> Like a fossil tree from which we gather no flowers
> Sad has been my life, fated no fruit to produce.
>
> He then thrust the point of his dagger into his abdomen, and cut himself open. He was soon dead. (47)

8 As Hazlitt observes "[Macbeth's] speeches and soliloquies are dark riddles on human life, baffling solution, and entangling him in their labyrinths. In thought he is absent and perplexed, sudden and desperate in act, from a distrust of his own resolution," as reprinted in Jonathan Bate, ed., *The Romantics on Shakespeare* (New York: Penguin, 1992, 424).

Paul Cantor, in an essay entitled '*Macbeth* and the Gospelling of Scotland,' *Shakespeare as Political Thinker*, John E. Alvis and Thomas G. West, eds. (Wilmington: ISI Books, 2000), argues that Macbeth is partly attracted to (and compromised by) Christianity because he "is questing for what I will call the Absolute Act, what he calls 'the be-all and the end-all,' a single deed that will give him everything he desires and give it to him securely and forever" (329).

While basing their analysis on a more general theory of the relationship between Shakespeare's tragedies and Protestant Christianity, C.L. Barber and Richard P. Wheeler, *The Whole Journey: Shakespeare's Power of Development* (Berkeley: University of California, 1986), seem to reach a somewhat similar view of Macbeth (in what they judge to be "the most intense of all the tragedies"): "Macbeth expects the achievement of some absolute, total state of being by being crowned, yet in the process is unmanned" (33).

9 It is pertinent to recall in this connection that the founder of political philosophy reputedly heard voices (see Plato's *Euthyphro* 3b, *Apology of Sokrates* 31c–d, *Theages* 128d ff, *Phaedrus* 242c), was given to rapt absorbtion in his own thoughts, and even to day-and-night-long trances (cf. *Symposium* 174d–175b, 220c–d). That philosophy is born of *wonder* is an ancient view. As Aristotle teaches: "For it is owing to their wonder that humans both now begin and at first began to philosophize; they wondered originally at the obvious perplexities, then progressed gradually to being thoroughly perplexed about the greater things" (*Metaphysics* 982b 12–15, my translation). Unless otherwise indicated, translations from Plato's dialogues are my own. In the case of his *Republic*, however, my rendering is indebted to the translation by Allan Bloom, *The Republic of Plato* (New York: Basic Books, 1968).

10 Since antiquity, the accurate and precise 'dividing' (*diairesis*) of the world's phenomena in one's thought and speech, along with their 'collecting' (grouping into categories; *sunagōgē*) has been regarded as the basis of *dialectical reasoning*, which in turn is the distinguishing power of a genuine philosopher. See Plato's *Phaedrus* 266b–c; *Republic* 531d–532b, 534b–c, 537b–c.

11 See Craig, *The War Lover: A Study of Plato's Republic*, 54–5.

12 Given the overt mystery of the Third Murderer of Banquo, it is hard to understand how anyone could claim, as does Evans, in *Shakespeare's Tragic Practice*: "*Macbeth* is not at all a 'mystery' play, a play of suspense, for the question of who killed King Duncan hardly even figures as an issue" (189–90). In his discounting the importance of the rational plot in favour of other poetic factors, G.Wilson Knight (*The Wheel of Fire*) is mistaken in the opposite way:

> The story and action of the play alone will not carry us far. Here the logic of imaginative correspondence is more significant and more exact than the logic of plot.
>
> *Macbeth* is a desolate and dark universe where all is befogged, baffled, constricted by the evil. Probably in no play of Shakespeare are so many questions asked. (141)

He is right about the questions, but not in implying that they defy answering, or that everyone in the play is quite so baffled as they seem to him (142–3). In particular, Rosse is *not* "at a loss as to Macduff's flight," nor is the "mysterious messenger" who warns Lady Macduff meant to remain a mystery to us.

13 Machiavelli, *The Prince*, Harvey C. Mansfield, ed. and trans. (Chicago: University of Chicago Press, 1985), ch. 2: "I say, then, that in hereditary states accustomed to the bloodline of their prince the difficulties of maintaining them are much less than in new states" (6); ch. 3: "But the difficulties reside in the new principality" (7); ch. 17: "And of all princes, it is impossible for a new prince to escape a name for cruelty because new states are full of dangers" (66); ch. 24: "he has a double shame who, having been born prince, has lost it through his lack of prudence" (96–7; subsequent page references are to this edition of *The Prince*).

14 See ibid., ch. 17: "And men have less hesitation to offend one who makes himself loved than one who makes himself feared; for love is held by a chain of obligations, which, because men are wicked, is broken at every opportunity for their own utility, but fear is held by a dread of punishment that never forsakes you" (66). "Since men love at their convenience and fear at the convenience of the prince, a wise prince should found himself on what is his, not on what is someone else's" (68).

15 See ibid., ch. 14: "Francesco Sforza, because he was armed, became duke of Milan from a private individual; and his sons, because they shunned the hardships of arms, became private individuals from dukes. For, among the other causes of evil that being unarmed brings you, it makes you contemptible, which is one of the infamies the prince should be on guard against ... For there is no proportion between one who is armed and one who is unarmed, and it is not reasonable that whoever is armed obey willingly whoever is unarmed, and that someone unarmed be secure among armed servants. For since there is scorn in the one and suspicion in the other, it is not possible for them to work well together. And therefore a prince who does not understand the military, besides other miseries, cannot, as was said, be esteemed by his soldiers nor have trust in them" (58).

In this connection, it is worth noting the report in Holinshed of the "railing tants this Makdowald uttered against his prince, calling him a faint-hearted milkesop, more meet to governe a sort of idle moonks in some cloister, than to have the rule of such valiant and hardie men of warre as the Scots were." Holinshed himself later speaks of Duncan's administration as "feeble and slouthfull" (as quoted in Appendix A of the Arden edition of *Macbeth*, 168, 173). Muir notes Holinshed's depicting Duncan as a "feeble ruler," but believes this to be one of a dozen ways that Shakespeare departed from his source: "By making the victim old and holy, and by passing over his weakness as a ruler, Shakespeare deliberately blackened the guilt of Macbeth" (xxxvii). Muir relies implicitly on what is said in the play, not seeing for himself what is *shown*. Graham Bradshaw in *Shakespeare's Scepticism* (Ithaca, NY: Cornell University Press, 1987) gets it right: "Shakespeare has retained and developed – not eliminated – Holinshed's sketch of a king who is saintly, feeble, and necessarily cunning" (246).

Shakespeare may also have consulted John Leslie's *De Origine, Moribus, et Rebus Gestis Scotorum* (1578), who writes of Duncan that he was "a man whose nature was unmarked by any roughness, resentment or bitterness, he was of the sort which does not retaliate even when provoked by the most grievous outrage" (C. Collard, trans., as excerpted in Appendix C of the Arden edition, 187).

16 *The Prince*, ch. 18: "Men in general judge more by their eyes than by their hands, because seeing is given to everyone, touching to few" (71).

17 Ibid., ch. 15, where Machiavelli contrasts being "fierce and spirited" with "effeminate and pusillanimous"; and ch. 19: "What makes him contemptible is to be held variable, light, effeminate, pusillanimous, irresolute, from which a prince should guard himself as from a shoal" (72).

18 Here one might recall the warning with which that subtle and refined (and much experienced) Machiavellian, Francis Bacon, begins his essay 'Of Ambition' in *The Works of Francis Bacon* vol. 6, Jame Spedding, Robert Ellis, and Douglas Heath, eds. (London: Longmans, 1870). "*AMBITION* is like a choler; which is an humour that maketh men active, earnest, full of alacrity, and stirring, if it be not stopped. But if it be stopped, and cannot have its way, it becomes adust, and thereby malign and venomous. So ambitious men, if they find the way open for their rising, and still get forward, they are rather busy than dangerous; but if they be checked in their desires, they become secretly discontent, and look upon men and matters with an evil eye" (465).

19 On this point, the usually sure-footed Derek Traversi stumbles badly, *An Approach to Shakespeare* vol. 2 (London: Hollis and Carter, 1969), and his interpretation of the play never recovers. He would have us believe that Scotland is in a state of *harmony* "under its lawful king" until Macbeth's murder of Duncan disrupts it. He finds the early scenes of the tragedy to be "light-drenched." And when Macbeth first meets Duncan after the opening battles, Traversi thinks that he still speaks "as the loyal general" – though in the immediately preceding scene we saw him contemplate *murdering* Duncan! And Malcolm is no sooner named Prince of Cumberland than Macbeth is privately musing, "That is a step / On which I must fall down, or else o'erleap, / For in my way it lies" (1.4. 42–50). In Macbeth's lifeless, formulaic pledge of allegiance, Traversi judges "his poetry attains, though fugitively and imperfectly, a breadth, a completeness of emotional content, that it will never recover" (123, 127). Inexplicable. G. Wilson Knight in *The Imperial Theme* (129) has similarly substituted a fairy-tale kingdom for the one Shakespeare depicts: "At the start, we saw courage, unity, honour, under the gracious rule of Duncan." *Unity?* Again, Bradshaw in *Shakespeare's Scepticism* sees far more clearly into the political situation that Shakespeare actually depicts:

> In the opening scenes the 'multiplying Villainies' are everywhere in evidence; but Order is not. From every seeming comfort 'Discomfort swells.' Acts of appalling

savagery obliterate any steadying, sustaining sense of the values which are ostensibly being defended ... But then, if this is so, why should so scrupulously attentive a critic as A.P.Rossiter refer to 'the breakdown of ordered nature' which is 'released by Duncan's murder'? ...

The strange thing is that we do indeed have an impression of something being 'released' through Duncan's murder – even though this 'Scotland' has afforded no strong impression of 'ordered nature,' and 'disorder' would be a tame word for the initial havoc. (222)

20 The problem is akin to that of relying on mercenary captains. Cf. *The Prince*, ch. 12: "Mercenary captains are either excellent men of arms or not: if they are, you cannot trust them because they always aspire to their own greatness, either by oppressing you, or by oppressing others contrary to your intention; but if the captain is not virtuous, he ruins you in the ordinary way. And if one responds that whoever has arms in hand will do this, mercenary or not, I would reply that arms have to be employed either by a prince or by a republic. The prince should go in person, and perform himself the office of captain" (49).

21 Ibid., ch. 15, 61.

22 Philosophers from Plato to Nietzsche have noted the special susceptibility of martial men to the blandishments of women. See *Republic* 420a, 548a; Aristotle's *Politics* 1269b 24–9; Bacon's essay 'Of Love,' wherein he observes, "I know not how, but martial men are given to love. I think it is as they are given to wine; for perils commonly ask to be paid in pleasures" (*The Works* ... vol. 6, 398).

23 Most notably, concerning the murder of Banquo: "Be innocent of the knowledge, dearest chuck, till thou applaud the deed" (3.2.45–6) – after all, that was her idea of manliness: "When you durst do it, *then* you were a man; / And, to be more than what you were, you would / Be so much more the man" (1.7.49–51).

24 Many critics, beginning with Hazlitt, credit Lady Macbeth with greater inner strength than the play shows her to have. Coleridge sees through her more clearly (from Bate, *The Romantics on Shakespeare*): "Lady Macbeth, like all in Shakespeare, is a class individualized: – of high rank, left much alone, and feeding herself with daydreams of ambition, she mistakes the courage of fantasy for the power of bearing the consequences of the realities of guilt. Hers in a mock fortitude of a mind deluded by ambition; she shames her husband with a superhuman audacity of fancy which she cannot support, but sinks in the season of remorse, and dies in suicidal agony" (418).

25 See *The Prince*, ch. 3 [speaking of princedoms habituated to princely rule]: "and to possess them securely it is enough to have eliminated the line of the prince whose dominions they were ... And whoever acquires them, if he wants to hold them, must have two concerns: one, that the bloodline of their ancient prince be eliminated; the other, not to alter either their laws or their taxes" (9).

26 Ibid., ch. 8: "Hence it should be noted that in taking hold of a state, he who seizes it should examine all the offenses necessary for him to commit, and do them all at a stroke, so as not to have to renew them every day and, by not renewing them, to secure men and gain them to himself with benefits. Whoever does otherwise, either through timidity or through bad counsel, is always under necessity to hold a knife in his hand; nor can one ever found himself on his subjects if, because of fresh and continued injuries, they cannot be secure against him. For injuries must be done all together, so that, being tasted less, they offend less; and benefits should be done little by little so that they may be tasted better" (38).

27 Ibid.

28 Ibid., ch. 16: "Among all the things that a prince should guard against is being contemptible and hated" (65); ch. 17: "The prince should nonetheless make himself feared in such a mode that if he does not acquire love, he escapes hatred" (67).

29 Ibid., ch. 8, 35.

30 We needn't accept her assessment as altogether accurate in order to see in it some large measure of truth. J.I.M. Stewart in *Character and Motive in Shakespeare* (London Longmans, 1949) makes an important general point in speaking about Lady Macbeth's awareness here of "forces in [Macbeth's] nature that may militate against her designs": "These she does not review 'objectively' but magnifies in passion and scorn. And this should be clear to us. For we already know that Macbeth has murder in his thoughts, and 'black and deepe desires'; he has been on stage declaring these only a matter of seconds before ... Lady Macbeth, then, when she censures him as having too much of the softness of common humanity and nothing of the ruthlessness ambition requires, reveals herself as a woman so apt for evil that she regards her husband's near-black as an inadequate grey! ... Lady Macbeth's whole monologue ... is passionate. And in passionate speech – particularly in passionate upbraiding – not the simplest audience will expect only objective appraisal. The overstating or distorting of a case is natural under such conditions, and Shakespeare follows nature" (58).

31 *The Prince*, ch. 14. The learning of such prudence is the principle underlying *both* modes of 'exercise' Machiavelli recommends. Although he speaks as if one mode were 'with deeds,' upon reflection it is clear that the 'geography' lessons learned while on hunts and maneuvers is as much an exercise 'with the mind' as is the study of great historical predecessors (59–60).

32 Ibid., 'Dedicatory Letter'; cf. ch. 20, 85.

33 In fairness to Lady Macbeth, however, she may not be aware of this last point: there was no mention of it in Macbeth's letter to her. Nor did he say anything there about "what greatness is promis'd" *Banquo* by the Weyward Sisters (1.5.1–14).

34 Timothy Fuller recognizes something like this to be "a central aspect of Macbeth's character ... The intense conflict between thought and action, or, to put it another way, the necessity for Macbeth to reject thought in order to act in the manner he

wishes to act. As I see it, the argument of the play is not that thought and action are opposed, but for a man like Macbeth they must be opposed." See 'The Relation of Thought and Action in *Macbeth*,' *Shakespeare's Political Pageant*, Joseph Alulis and Vickie Sullivan, eds. (Lanham, MD: Rowman and Littlefield, 1996), 211.

35 *The Prince*, ch. 3: "From this one may draw a general rule that never or rarely fails: whoever is the cause of someone's becoming powerful is ruined; for that power has been caused by him either with industry or with force, and both the one and the other of these two is suspect to whoever has become powerful" (16).

36 Ibid., ch. 18. To this Machiavelli immediately adds, "But it is necessary to know well how to color this nature, and to be a great pretender [or 'hypocrite'] and dissembler" (70). With that in mind, one should probably view with some skepticism Malcolm's dealing with Macduff.

37 Ibid., ch. 2: "And should he be deprived of [his state], if any mishap whatever befalls the occupier, he reacquires it" (7).

38 Ibid., ch. 13.

39 This view could be synthesized from any number of parts of Machiavelli's teaching, beginning with the pivotal ch. 15 of *The Prince*: "for it is so far from how one lives to how one should live that he who lets go of what is done for what should be done learns his ruin rather than his preservation" (61); "for if one considers everything well, one will find something appears to be virtue, which if pursued would be one's ruin, and something else appears to be vice, which if pursued results in one's security and well-being" (62). Add this from ch. 18: "And if all men were good, this teaching would not be good; but because they are wicked and do not observe faith with you, you also do not have to observe it with them" (69); and from ch. 19: "And here one should note that hatred is acquired through good deeds as well as bad ones; and so ... a prince who wants to maintain his state is often forced not to be good" (77).

40 Or as Leo Strauss more guardedly suggests in *The City and Man* (Chicago: Rand McNally, 1964), 59: "In order to know what Shakespeare, in contradistinction to his Macbeth, thinks about life, one must consider Macbeth's utterance in light of the play as a whole; we might thus find that according to the play as a whole, life is not senseless simply, but becomes senseless for him who violates the sacred law of life, or the sacred order restores itself, or the violation of the law of life is self-destructive; but since that self-destruction is exhibited in the case of Macbeth, a human being of a particular kind, one would have to wonder whether the apparent lesson of the play is true of all men or universally; one would have to consider whether what appears to be a natural law is in fact a natural law, given the fact that Macbeth's violation of the law of life is at least partly originated by preternatural beings."

41 Most editors, including Muir in the Arden edition, follow Samuel Johnson in presuming that this speech is an 'aside.' But apart from whatever dramatic awkwardness this

might cause, there is no good reason to presume it, given that Macbeth must reveal his intentions to his henchmen if they are to act accordingly, and that he obviously regards Lenox as a loyal attendant. In any case, we must somehow be able to explain the "homely man's" warning.

42 Many commentators have managed to make heavy weather of this scene, finding in it all sorts of inconsistencies with what precedes and succeeds it. But it poses no real difficulties. We can understand its conversation to have taken place in the wake of the Banquet that Macbeth's bizarre behaviour caused to break into "most admir'd disorder." As the various lords disperse, virtually expelled by Lady Macbeth ("At once, good night: – / Stand not upon the order of your going, / But go at once" 3.4.117–19), Lenox and this other Lord, perhaps travelling together or lodging together, have begun exchanging their respective misgivings in cautious circumlocutions. The way in which the scene opens would suggest that Lenox has taken the lead, as he is apparently alluding to matters which directly connect with what he subsequently says ("My former speeches have but hit your thoughts / Which can interpret farther"); while the other Lord's reference to freeing "from our feasts and banquets bloody knives," and so on, suggests that he too witnessed the strange happenings of that fateful evening. As for his affirming that Macduff was expressly sent for by Macbeth, but curtly refused the 'invitation' (39–43), this squares with what Macbeth tells his wife after all their guests have departed: "How say'st thou, that Macduff denies his person / At our great *bidding*?" She asks, as if seeking confirmation, "Did you send to him, Sir?" His reply must be read with tones of sarcasm and menace: "I heard it by the way; but I *will* send" – that is, 'messengers' that this time will *not* be rebuffed (3.4.127–9).

Once one correctly understands Lenox's role in the unfolding of events, one sees that speculation about this scene being out of order (e.g., that it ought to follow, not precede, scene 1 of act 4, for the various reasons Muir gives in his 'Introduction' to the Arden edition, xxxiv) is groundless.

43 This has so puzzled some editors (including Kenneth Muir of the Arden edition) that they have followed Capell in suppressing it, thereby eliminating a vital clue for fathoming the play's deeper story, as well as dismantling the visual triptych it allows for: Macbeth flanked by two young Machiavellians of contrasting moral colour. My analysis of the 'politics' of *Macbeth*, and of Rosse's role in particular, owes much to insights gleaned from the excellent essay by David Lowenthal on *Macbeth* in *Shakespeare and the Good Life* (Lanham, MD: Rowan and Littlefield, 1997).

44 Lenox later revises his interpretation both of their killing and of what he saw, speaking of the awaked grooms as being "the slaves of drink and thralls of sleep" (3.6.11–16).

45 Some commentators presume that Macbeth was merely 'hearing voices,' as when shortly thereafter he reports, "Methought, I heard a voice cry, 'Sleep no more! Macbeth does murder Sleep,'" which leads on to his troubled musings about the signifi-

cance of sleep. But in carefully comparing the two parts of their conversation (i.e., lines 2.2 14–33 and 34–43), one cannot help but be struck by the practical concreteness of the first (note the tone of Lady Macbeth's interjections) and the guilt-induced distractedness of the second (to which she responds in utter puzzlement). And whatever one's view, it must accommodate the mysterious presence of Rosse.

46 Macbeth's puzzlement here echoes his earlier reaction to the witches' hailing him 'Thane of Cawdor': "But how of Cawdor? The Thane of Cawdor lives, / A prosperous gentleman" (1.3.72–3). As for the 'him' that was "confronted" and the 'his' whose "lavish spirit" was curbed in Rosse's original report, this could only intelligibly refer to Cawdor, as obviously the Norwegian King was not captured (being still free to ransom his dead), nor could *his* arm be described as "rebellious."

47 Holinshed includes among the "monstrous sights" that were reported in the year following Donwald's killing of King Duff, "horsses in Louthian, being of singular beautie and swiftnesse, did eate their own flesh, and would in no wise taste anie other meate" (quoted in Appendix A of the Arden edition, 166). That Shakespeare avails himself of this bizarre story (along with that of "a sparhawke also strangled by an owle") cannot be taken to mean that he regarded it as credible.

48 Contrary to what Machiavelli advises in *The Prince*, ch. 17: "being feared and not being hated can go together very well. This [a prince] will do if he abstains from the property of his citizens and his subjects, and from their women; and if he also needs to proceed against someone's life, he must do it when there is suitable justification and manifest cause for it. But above all, he must abstain from the property of others, because men forget the death of a father more quickly than the loss of a patrimony. Furthermore, causes for taking away property are never lacking, and he who begins to live by rapine always finds cause to seize others' property" (67). The fact that later Malcolm "grants" that Macbeth is "luxurious" (i.e., lascivious), and then (falsely) alleges against himself an even greater, indeed bottomless "voluptuousness" (4.3.57, 60–1) may be taken as suggesting that Macbeth did not abstain from other men's women any more than from their property.

49 Given the self-preserving character of this 'modest wisdom' of Malcolm, king-to-be, it seems akin to that which Macbeth attributes to Banquo, soliloquizing about his "royalty of nature": "He hath a wisdom that doth guide his valour to act in safety" (3.1.48–53). That is, more than once in this play, Wisdom and Kingship are affiliated (see also 4.3.129–30).

50 That is, according to the Folio's scene divisions and directions, Rosse enters with Malcolm, Siward, and other unspecified "Thanes" at the point in the final scene when it is clear that victory has been "cheaply bought" (most modern editors divide the Folio's seventh and final scene into three separate scenes, using this entrance to signal the beginning of 5.9). Rosse is conspicuous by his absence, however, from our two brief looks at Malcolm's entourage just prior to battle (5.4 and 5.6). Absent also is Lenox,

despite his informative presence among the rebel thanes marching to join up with Malcolm's English army (5.2.8–11). Is he still falsely serving with Macbeth, providing Malcolm with intelligence about the tyrant's dwindling forces (cf. 5.4.11–14)? Muir, as do many editors, adds both Rosse and Lenox to the others named present at 5.4.

51 Cf. *The Prince*, ch. 18: "to see him and hear him, he should appear all mercy, all faith[fulness], all honesty, all humanity, all religion. And nothing is more necessary to appear to have than this last quality" (70–1).

52 Ibid., ch. 25: "for if he would change his nature with the times and with affairs, his fortune would not change" (100).

53 It is with respect to these two characters, and Lenox in particular, that I am most strongly in disagreement with Jan H. Blits's frequently insightful treatment of the play, *The Insufficiency of Virtue:* Macbeth *and the Natural Order* (Lanham, MD: Rowman and Littlefield, 1996). He notes that "Rosse's actions and motives throughout *Macbeth* are largely mysterious" (91), that he's "a man surrounded ... by mystery and intrigue" (17), that his actions are "often puzzling" (147). Blits directs attention to much of what is suspicious concerning Rosse, yet – rather strangely – backs away from the conclusion to which the pattern of evidence points (159). But it is in assimilating Lenox to Rosse (129) that I believe Blits obscures a matter of major importance for understanding Shakespeare's teaching. The thematic focus of Blits's book, as well as its form (a scene-by-scene commentary), is very different from mine, resulting in but a limited amount of overlap in substance. It came to my attention only after my chapter on *Macbeth* was virtually completed, and served mainly as a stimulus to review (and as it turned out, on the whole to confirm) my own interpretation.

54 Ronald Mushat Frye in *Shakespeare and Christian Doctrine* (Princeton: Princeton University Press, 1963) examines the religious views and behaviour in *Macbeth* in light of the pronouncements of various Christian authorities influential in Shakespeare's day, and shows quite convincingly that they can all be fitted into the contemporary Christian *Weltanschauung* (see esp. 140–6, 150–2, 174–6, 237–9, 254–9). But in a sense, this begs the question, for by the late Sixteenth Century Christianity had practically absorbed many persisting primitive 'folk' and pagan elements, resulting in beliefs that one would be hard-pressed to justify on strict Biblical authority (as in their different ways the various emerging 'reformists' were to emphasize). Such may well have been Shakespeare's assessment also, and his intention in this play, set in a more primitive time and place, to show something of how this absorbtion (or contamination) could have happened. Be that as it may, by never connecting the pagan Hecate (nor any of her subordinate "instruments of darkness") directly with Satan, he has left open alternative interpretations. We may choose to see the struggle between Good and Evil in purely Christian terms (i.e., as God *versus* Satan contending for the souls of men); or, we may view Eleventh Century Scotland as a battleground where radically different theologies struggle for supremacy. As Frye concludes:

The patterns of a Christian understanding of sin seem to have contributed in marked ways to the development of Macbeth's characterization. The recognition of these patterns as they are exemplified in our representative theologians should thus help us to appreciate more adequately Shakespeare's dramatic protagonist. I would suggest once again, however, that we must not allow our attention to be diverted from Macbeth on the stage, for that is where we find him. Shakespeare could have placed him in a Dantesque or Miltonic hell, but he did not do so, and neither should we. In Macbeth, Shakespeare has created one of the most magnificent presentations of the degeneration of the human soul which our culture affords, and he has done so in reference to Christian theology, but his purpose is still to keep the mirror up to *nature* and to show the course of human life in *this* world. (255; my emphasis)

55 Paul Cantor, '*Macbeth* and the Gospelling of Scotland,' sees Scotland's transition to Christianity as a primary theme of *Macbeth* (and indicative of Shakespeare's own view of history): the strange things that happen to a community of noble warriors when it is Christianized. One might add that the mixture of conflicting religious views further exemplifies the general turbulence in Duncan's Scotland. Blits, *The Insufficiency of Virtue*, sees the clash of two conceptions of virtue, "manly" or "warrior virtue" versus "Christian virtue," as one of two related themes structuring the play (the other being the tension between virtue per se and living well): "The first tension, then, involves the unreconciled forms of virtue practiced and esteemed in Macbeth's Scotland and, ultimately, the different conceptions of human life underlying them. The second tension, though less apparent, is still deeper. It is the tension within nature between virtue or order, on the one side, and life, on the other. Where the first tension involves the coherence of virtue, the second involves the coherence of nature itself" (4).

56 Not that anything Malcolm says need imply he is himself a believing Christian (there's some evidence he is not); but he knows it is effective rhetoric with Macduff, who has just testified to his own Christian views in his chastizing of Malcolm (4.3.106–11).

57 As Machiavelli rather amusingly argues in the final chapter of *The Prince*: "God does not want to do everything, so as not to take free will from us and that part of the glory that falls to us" (103). A thoughtful reading of ch. 25, however, suggests that Machiavelli is a skeptic who subtly equates 'Fortune' and 'God': "It is not unknown to me that many have held and hold the opinion that worldly things are so governed by fortune and by God, that men cannot correct them with their prudence, indeed that they have no remedy at all; and on account of this they might judge that one need not sweat much over things but let oneself be governed by chance. ["If Chance will have me King, why, Chance may crown me, without my stir."] When I have thought about this sometimes, I have been in some part inclined to their opinion. Nonetheless, in order

that our free will not be eliminated, I judge that it might be true that fortune is arbiter of half of our actions, but also that she leaves the other half, or close to it, for us to govern" (98). What happened to God, one wonders.

58 Bradshaw expresses a similar view in *Shakespeare's Scepticism*: "The incidental but pointedly complementary tragedy of Macduff is that his initially unquestioning commitment to a natural and supernatural order must be paid for – both by the loss of his 'pretty Chickens, and their Damme,' and in that moment when he is driven to pronounce that a rightful king is unfit to govern and unfit to live ... The instinctive, pious patriotism which the earlier Macduff represents is explored in its natural and unnatural aspects. It is seen as unnatural by Lady Macduff, and in relation to the Nature that is red in tooth and claw, the natural world of eagles and wrens, martlets, kites, chicks and eggs. It is natural, as an expression of higher *human* aspirations, and of the human needs which the early Macduff acknowledges without question but which Macbeth cannot credit" (242–3).

59 Or as Machiavelli puts it, armed prophets conquer and unarmed ones are ruined (*The Prince*, ch. 6). It may be worth noting that Macbeth's reference to Duncan's exemplary Christian meekness, and the special pity his assassination would therefore elicit, is immediately prefaced by Macbeth's own worry about being the recipient of "even-handed justice" (1.7.7–25). That is, Shakespeare has brought together in Macbeth's train of thought allusions to both the Old Testament doctrine of justice (with its naturally appealing principle of reciprocity: an eye for an eye) and the New Testament doctrine of meekness and compassion (with which goes mercy, forgiveness, and love of one's enemies). And he has done so, moreover, in such a way as to remind us of what their actual practical relationship is most apt to be: Macbeth never presumes that the response to his murder of Duncan would be one of Christian forgiveness; if anything, Duncan's Christian virtue will only intensify the animosity felt towards the perpetrator of "the horrid deed."

60 Ibid., ch. 12: "The principal foundations that all states have, new ones as well as old and mixed, are good laws and good arms. And because there cannot be good laws where there are not good arms, and where there are good arms there must be good laws, I shall leave out the reasoning on laws and shall speak of arms" (48). Machiavelli speaks in a similar vein about the utility of 'friends' in defending oneself from external powers (ch. 19): "One is defended with good arms and good friends; and if one has good arms, one will always have good friends" (72). So, according to Machiavelli, good laws, good arms, and good friends go together, perhaps along with what seems to others to be good luck.

61 Ibid., ch. 15, 61–2.

62 Once one appreciates the extent to which *Macbeth* is an illustration – and partial endorsement – of Machiavellian political science as presented in *The Prince*, one must

question Alvin Kernan's conception of Shakespeare as a court propagandist for King James' 'Divine Right of Kings' doctrine, in *Shakespeare, the King's Playwright: Theater in the Stuart Court 1603–1613* (New Haven: Yale University Press, 1995). Obtuse to what the play actually *shows*, Kernan contends: "Shakespeare's play dramatizes this critical point in the Stuart Myth, when Duncan names as his successor his son, Malcolm, prince of Cumberland, and Malcolm later creates the rank of earl, thus establishing the true principles of succession and hierarchy that, as natural law, had been struggling all along to emerge from the desperate events of Scottish history.

History was tidied up considerably in the process of staging this ideology of legitimacy. The information that Macbeth was Duncan's cousin with equal 'right' to the throne and that Duncan was a weak king while Macbeth was strong and effective was suppressed. Banquo's complicity in the murder of Duncan was also ignored" (78).

63 Much as Plato has Sokrates attest in the *Republic* 509a–c.

64 This may be as fitting a place as any to note a stylistic feature of *Macbeth*: it abounds in triads. For in addition to the three witches who "All hail" Macbeth three times (1.3.48–50), then likewise thrice "Hail" Banquo (prefacing their three-part prophecy regarding him; 62–7), and whose magical chants and charms involve multiples of three ("Thrice to thine, and thrice to mine, / And thrice again, to make up nine" – 35–6; and, "Thrice the brinded cat hath mew'd." "Thrice, and once the hedge-pig whin'd" – 4.1.1–2); there are Macbeth's three titles (Glamis, Cawdor, King), and his three portrayed crimes (the murder of Duncan, the ambush of Banquo, the slaughter of Macduff's household). Several triads figure in the Porter's scene: his repeated "Knock, knock, knock" (2.3.3, 12–13); his welcoming three sinners to Hell (farmer, equivocator, English tailor); the "three things" he reminds us that drink "is a great provoker of" (25–7). There is the surprising return of a trio (Macbeth, Lenox, and Rosse; 88), whereas only two left to view the site of Duncan's murder. There are three murderers who set upon Banquo and Fleance. Macbeth alludes to three avine instruments used by "Augures" (magpies, choughs, rooks; 3.4.124). There are Malcolm's three false self-accusations (lust, avarice, and a lack of all "king-becoming graces"; 4.3.60, 78, 91). It is on his third night of watching that the Scottish Doctor at last views the somnambulent, somniloquent Lady Macbeth (5.1.1–2). When Hecate arrives at the Pit of Acheron, she is accompanied by three more witches (4.1.38). And at the Pit, Macbeth sees a succession of three "Apparitions," offering three prophecies (each of the first two begin "Macbeth! Macbeth! Macbeth!"; to the second, Macbeth confusedly replies, "Had I three ears, I'd hear thee" – 77–8). Macbeth calls three times for Seyton before he finally appears (5.3.18, 20, 29). According to the Folio text, the play comprises twenty-seven scenes, i.e., 3^3. This triadic pattern lends further support to the surmise that there must be, not two, but three battles referred to at the beginning of the play, involving all three great warrior captains (Macbeth, Banquo, and Macduff).

As for what significance one might see in this pattern, several possibilities suggest themselves. For example, one might suspect a kind of 'black' counterpart to Trinitarian Christianity. But it also reminds one of the 'threeness' so evident in the most famous Platonic dialogues (i.e., the *Apology of Sokrates* and the *Republic*). And given the prominence of Time in the play (a matter to be discussed at length in this examination of the play), its manifold triads are stylistic echoes of the ever-moving sectors of Past, Present, and Future. T. McAlindon, in *Shakespeare's Tragic Cosmos* (Cambridge: Cambridge University Press, 1991), begins his useful discussion of the symbolic dimension of the play by observing: "One of the most remarkable features of this tragedy is the way in which number symbolism cooperates with nature symbolism in the process of signalling key ideas relating to the tragic theme of disunity and chaos. This may be largely due to the fact that here, as in *Julius Caesar*, Shakespeare the tragedian shows a more than usual interest in time, the movement of the heavenly bodies, and history. The tradition of numerical symbolism and the temporal sensibility were closely related in literature since there was a natural connection between the time sense, astronomy, and the art of exact measurement according to number" (200). McAlindon stresses especially "the traditional association of the number three with the rituals of witchcraft."

65 Each of the play's first three scenes begin with one of these questions: 'When,' 'What,' 'Where.' The first explicit use of 'why' is Banquo's query upon noticing Macbeth's reaction to the witches' all-hailing him: "Good Sir, why do you start, and seem to fear things that do sound so fair?" (1.3.51–2). Good question.

66 Knights, in *Some Shakespearean Themes*, also views the witches' chant as announcing the play's primary thematic focus, but construes it somewhat differently: "In none of the tragedies is there anything superfluous, but it is perhaps *Macbeth* that gives the keenest impression of economy. The action moves directly and quickly to the crisis, and from the crisis to the full working out of plot and theme. The pattern is far easier to grasp than that of *Lear*. The main theme of the reversal of values is given out simply and clearly in the first scene – 'Fair is foul, and foul is fair'; and with it are associated premonitions of the conflict, disorder and moral darkness into which Macbeth will plunge himself" (122).

However, Bradshaw, in *Shakespeare's Scepticism*, questions whether the 'main theme' is really that simple and clear: "Yet 'Faire is foule' is ambiguous. Instead of providing an indirect confirmation of the conceptual abstractions it may assert their *unreality*, in relation to the elemental 'Hurley-burley' (that word suggests amoral Chaos rather than immoral Evil), and to the obscene, elemental savagery of battles which are (in a comparably ambiguous way) 'lost and wonne'" (223).

67 This is easily illustrated by the unreliability of sensory evidence with respect to the reality of Matter, which according to any plausible account (from those of Plato or Aristotle to that of modern physics) is *very* different from what we perceive it to be. According to modern physicists, this 'too solid flesh' is anything but: were the bodies

of the earth's entire human population fully compressed in the gravitational field of a 'black hole,' the resulting 'solid matter' (they tell us) would scarce fill *one fortieth of a tablespoon*!

68 Wilson Knight, in *The Wheel of Fire*, sees this as the root cause of both his torment and his vice: "Whilst Macbeth lives in conflict with himself there is misery, evil, fear: when, at the end, he and others have openly identified himself with evil, he faces the world fearless: nor does he appear evil any longer. The worst element of his suffering has been that secrecy and hypocrisy so often referred to throughout the play ... Dark secrecy and night are in Shakespeare ever the badges of crime. But at the end Macbeth has no need of secrecy" (156).

69 The dramatic effectiveness of Shakespeare's oft-remarked 'trickery' with time, not noticeable to spectators but puzzling to reflective readers, is itself revealing about human temporality: how the felt experience of time need not correspond to 'objective' measures of time; and how much freedom the rational imagination allows in the manipulation of time.

70 Francis Berry, in an essay entitled '*Macbeth:* Tense and Mood,' calls attention to a related grammatical feature of the play in *Essays in Shakespearean Criticism*, J.E. Calderwood and H.E. Toliver, eds. (Englewood Cliffs, NJ: Prentice-Hall, 1970, 521–9): "The Form of the Verb of *Macbeth*, that which controls the whole plot, is peculiarly striking. It is, of course, the Future Indicative. But the dominant form of the Verb 'in' *Macbeth*, that which animates not the main outlines but the detail of passage, is also significant. It is the Subjunctive. The Verb Form 'of' *Macbeth* and the Verb Form 'in' *Macbeth* struggle against each other, and from this struggle issues the tragedy" (521).

Berry goes on to observe, "Indeed, the whole play is Future minded, thus →. Unlike *Hamlet* and *Othello* there are in it no temporal flashbacks, no protracted memories of earlier generations, no narrations of past events, but it purely and avidly pursues a Future, and that is why reader and audience derive from it a sensation of rapidity or hurrying" (522). As for Macbeth himself, he exists mainly "in the subjunctive realm of *possibilities* – the realm of hopes and dreads; of 'if's' and phantasies; of what may be and may not be; of what ought to be and what ought not to be. The Subjunctive is a private realm" (523).

71 Michael Davis, in his article entitled 'Courage and Impotence in Shakespeare's *Macbeth*,' in *Shakespeare's Political Pageant*, Joseph Alulis and Vickie Sullivan, eds. (Lanham MD: Rowman and Littlefield, 1996), points to the broader connections and implications of Banquo's challenge to the witches ("If you can look into the seeds of time ...") by observing: "The witches must represent time past, present, and future because the future is not independent of the past. Time has seeds. Events done in the present grow in the soil of past events and have consequences for the future ... The entire play subsequent to the regicide may be described in terms of Macbeth's struggle against the consequences of his earlier actions. His battle is not so much a bat-

tle for a specific future as a battle against the past. And yet his every attempt to right the situation sinks him deeper into enslavement by the past" (231).

72 Examined at length in Cleanth Brooks's influential (and controversial) essay, 'The Naked Babe and the Cloak of Manliness,' in *The Well Wrought Urn* (New York: Harcourt, Brace and Co., 1947).

73 Epitomized by old Kephalos in Plato's *Republic* 331d–e.

74 As Howard White puts it in his essay entitled "Macbeth and the Tyrannical Man," *Interpretation* 2 (Winter 1971, 148), "I submit that the difficulty with Hamlet is similar to the difficulty of Macbeth. They are not sure whether they believe or not." Macbeth's famous soliloquy (1.7.1–28) reveals the conflicting feelings at war within his soul. Wilson Knight, in *The Wheel of Fire*, however, sees Macbeth's confusion as more formless than it is: "With Macbeth it is almost impossible to fit clear terms of conceptual thought to the motives tangled in his mind or soul. Therein lies the fine truth of the *Macbeth* conception: a deep, poetic, psychology or metaphysic of the birth of evil. He himself is hopelessly at a loss, and has little idea as to why he is going to murder Duncan. He tries to fit names to his reasons – 'ambition,' for instance – but this is only a name. The poet's mind is here at grips with the problem of spiritual evil – the inner state of disintegration, disharmony and fear, from which is born an act of crime and destruction" (121).

F.R. Leavis, in *Education and the University* (Cambridge: Cambridge University Press, 1979; originally published 1943), seems to have a better grasp of what essentially is going on beneath the puzzling, yet strangely effective imagery Shakespeare provides Macbeth in this soliloquy:

> It is a speech that exhibits Shakespeare's specific genius – an essentially poetic genius that is at the same time essentially dramatic – at its most marvelous. The speech is that of the intensely realized individual, Macbeth, at the particular, intensely realized moment in the development of the poem. Analysis leads us directly to the core of the drama, its central, animating interests, the principles of its life. The whole organism is present in the part. Macbeth, weighing his hesitation, tells himself that it is no moral or religious scruple, deriving its disturbing force from belief in supernatural sanctions. His fear, he says, regards merely the chances of lasting practical success in this world. His shrinking from the murder expresses, he insists, a simple consideration of expediency. Then he proceeds to enlarge on the peculiar heinousness of murdering Duncan, and as he does so that essential datum concerning his make-up, his ignorance of himself, becomes plain. He supposes that he is developing the note of inexpediency, and picturing the atrocity of the crime as it will affect others. But already in the sentence invoking the sanctity of hospitality another note begins to prevail. And in the next sentence the speech achieves its unconscious self-confutation ...

> What we have in this passage is a conscience-tormented imagination, quick with terror of the supernatural, proclaiming a certitude that 'murder will out,' a certitude appalling to Macbeth not because of consequences on 'this bank and shoal of time,' but by reason of a sense of sin – the radical hold on him of religious sanctions. (80–1)

This is an opportune point at which to address Evans's radical contention in *Shakespeare's Tragic Practice* that in *Macbeth*, Shakespeare uses his powerful poetry to 'hoodwink' us into believing that it is "the tragedy of an 'essentially good man' whose principles give way to overmastering ambition and who thereafter undergoes moral deterioration, experiencing all the while those agonies of conscience that, indeed, only an essentially good man can experience" (218). Whereas Evans insists that:

> What sets [Macbeth] most significantly below our level of vision is the fact that the idea of murder has invaded his mind. It is noteworthy that the witches have not mentioned murder or suggested any wrongful act ...
>
> His plane is in fact not one of moral awareness, but of moral ignorance; and from this plane he never rises. From beginning to end of the action he remains oblivious of murder as a moral fault. (200)
>
> *Macbeth* is not the tragedy of a good man's moral deterioration, but of a man who lives and dies without knowing what moral sense means. (208)

As for the famous soliloquy (1.7.1–28) Leavis so insightfully analysed, Evans sees in it only evidence of Macbeth's "fatal limitation: his lack of moral sense" (201). "Macbeth's flaw is not a defective moral mechanism that gives in to his overweening ambition; it is rather his total lack of a moral mechanism" (204). And in sum, "The crucial gap between Macbeth's awareness and ours is simply that we have a moral sense and he has none" (204); he is a "moral cripple" (221), a "moral idiot" (222). Much of Evans's chapter on *Macbeth* is devoted to explaining away textual evidence that could be interpreted as showing some moral concern – and he resorts to some dubious 'practices' of his own in doing so – but the real issue here is Evans's hypertrophied Kantian conception of what it means to be moral: something utterly divorced from consequences, such that every time Macbeth shows himself concerned with his actions' effect on him (e.g., his reaction to the thought of murdering Duncan, 200; his revulsion in the immediate wake of Duncan's murder, 206; his plea to the Doctor to cure Lady Macbeth, 212), it is discounted as having any genuine moral content – as if a perfectly respectable response to 'Why be moral?' is not 'Because otherwise you will experience relentless psychic torment.' Indeed, according to Plato's *Republic*, the effect of one's actions on one's own soul is the natural *ground* of what properly defines that which we call 'moral' (443c–e). But Evans, who seems unaware that his implicit Kantianism is anachronistic when applied to Shakespeare, apparently believes that every whole human being has a distinct 'moral sensibility' that is supposed to judge and rule without regard to consequences (blithely conflating it with 'conscience'; 217) – that thereby everyone not radically defective 'knows' murder is just wrong (220). Consequently, even to ask 'Why be moral?' is evidence that one *is* defective. Evans simply could not take Machiavelli seriously, i.e., as possibly being right. Hence his chapter has a value he never intended, namely, that of demonstrating how radically impractical, thus impolitic – indeed utopian – this conception of morality actually is.

75 In an essay pervaded by Shakespearean allusions, 'On the Uses and Disadvantages of History for Life,' *Untimely Meditations*, R.J. Hollingdale, trans. (Cambridge: Cambridge University Press, 1983), Nietzsche observes:

> In the case of the smallest or of the greatest happiness ..., it is always the same thing that makes happiness happiness: the ability to forget or, expressed in more scholarly fashion, the capacity to feel *unhistorically* during its duration. He who cannot sink down on the threshold of the moment and forget all the past, who cannot stand balanced like a goddess of victory without growing dizzy and afraid, will never know what happiness is – worse, he will never do anything to make others happy. Imagine the extremest possible example of a man who did not possess the power of forgetting at all and who was thus condemned to see everywhere a state of becoming: such a man would no longer believe in his own being, would no longer believe in himself, would see everything flowing asunder in moving points and would lose himself in this stream of becoming ... (62)

76 *The Prince*, ch. 17: "For one can say this generally of men: that they are ungrateful, fickle, pretenders and dissemblers, evaders of dangers, eager for gain. While you do them good, they are yours, offering you their blood, property, lives, and children ... when the need for them is far away; but, when it is close to you, they revolt. And that prince who has founded himself entirely on their words, stripped of other preparation, is ruined; for friendships that are acquired at a price and not with greatness and nobility of spirit are bought, but they are not owned and when the time comes they cannot be spent" (66). Also relevant is what is said in ch. 7: "And whoever believes that among great personages new benefits will make old injuries be forgotten deceives himself" (33).

77 Jane Austen provides the heroine of *Mansfield Park* a pertinent observation on this matter. Fanny Price is reflecting on the humble topic of domestic landscape:

> 'Every time I come into this shrubbery I am more struck with its growth and beauty. Three years ago, this was nothing but a rough hedgerow along the upper side of the field, never thought of as anything, or capable of becoming anything; and now it is converted into a walk, and it would be difficult to say whether most valuable as a convenience or an ornament; and perhaps in another three years we

may be forgetting – almost forgetting what it was before. How wonderful, how very wonderful the operations of time, and the changes of the human mind!' And following the latter train of thought, she soon afterwards added: 'If any one faculty of our nature may be called *more* wonderful than the rest, I do think it is memory. There seems something more speakingly incomprehensible in the powers, the failures, the inequalities of memory, than in any other of our intelligences. The memory is sometimes so retentive, so serviceable, so obedient – at others, so bewildered and so weak – and at others again, so tyrannic, so beyond our controul! We are to be sure a miracle every way – but our powers of recollecting and forgetting, do seem peculiarly past finding out.' (vol. 2, ch. 4)

78 The view 'that to philosophize is to learn how to die' could be said to originate with Sokrates. Cf. *Apology* 29a, 40c–41d, *Republic* 486a, 500b–c, 604b–c, 608c–d. See also Montaigne's essay of that title (No. 20 of Book One in *The Complete Essays of Montaigne*, Donald Frame, ed. and trans., Stanford: Stanford University Press, 1958).

79 That Macbeth does not altogether welcome the "suggestion" which his own irrepressible ambition forces upon his imagination lends credence to R.S. Crane's view of his character, 'Monistic Criticism and the Structure of Shakespearean Drama,' in *Approaches to Shakespeare*, Norman Rabkin, ed. (New York: McGraw-Hill, 1964), 99–120: "For the essential story of *Macbeth* is that of a man, not naturally depraved, who has fallen under the compulsive power of an imagined better state for himself which he can attain only by acting contrary to his normal habits and feelings; who attains this state and finds that he must continue to act thus, and even worse, in order to hold on to what he has got; who persists and becomes progressively hardened morally in the process; and who then, ultimately, when the once alluring good is about to be taken away from him, faces the loss in terms of what is left of his original character" (116).

Paul A. Cantor also emphasizes the importance of imagination in determining the behaviour of the Macbeths in his article entitled 'Shakespeare's *The Tempest*: The Wise Man as Hero,' *Shakespeare Quarterly* (Spring 1980), 64–75:

> The theatrical imagery of prologues and acts points to the element common to the real usurpers of *Macbeth* and the would-be usurpers of *The Tempest*: the way they plot out their crimes with the imagination of a playwright ... Antonio tempts Sebastion in just the way the Witches and later Lady Macbeth tempt Macbeth, by making him imagine himself already a king ... A 'strong imagination' seems characteristic of Shakespeare's usurpers: they can leap ahead in their minds to picture themselves already possessed of what they most desire ...
>
> The usurper's strong imagination is what makes him potentially forceful as a character. Believing that what his imagination shows him is real, the usurper can proceed with strength and conviction to achieve his goals. But to impress us, the usurper must in fact act ... The mere desire to rule proves nothing: to distinguish

> oneself, one must show the force of one's desires by acting upon them. As the term is ordinarily understood, one can be heroic only in deed, not in thought. Macbeth and Lady Macbeth undergo the heroic test of translating their thoughts into deeds. Though they both bend under the strain of trying to realize their dreams, and Lady Macbeth eventually cracks, they do have a chance to establish their heroic stature. They are not run-of-the-mill human beings; they are great-souled figures, if only in the single-minded determination with which they pursue their ambitions. (69)
>
> The treatment of usurpation in *Macbeth* and *The Tempest* reveals the limitations in the usurper's imagination, the way the force of his desires deceives him about reality. He thinks he knows what his crime will entail, but in his eagerness he underestimates the obstacles that stand in his way and overestimates his ability to live with the consequences of his deed. (71)

80 Michael Davis ('Courage and Impotence') recognizes that Macbeth's behaviour is contradictory, but doesn't quite get to the source of its inconsistency:

> On the surface, one who disdains fortune should have no truck with fortune-tellers. Macbeth feels this tension, and so his attitude toward the witches is throughout the play equivocal. On the one hand, he acts out of the belief that what they say is true; on the other hand, he acts on his own in order to be doubly sure ... This attitude is certainly understandable – no use taking chances. At the same time, however, it is patently ridiculous. To know one's fate is to neutralize chance. To think that prophecy needs assurances is to doubt that it is prophecy ... He believes [the witches] enough to worry about Banquo, but not enough to give up all attempts to forestall the future they predict. He doubts and does not doubt that what they say about the future is correct. (226)

But this is not the root of the problem. One can be *dubious* about prophecy, hence 'cover one's bet,' without being caught in a contradiction, so long as one is consistent. As we shall see, Macbeth's real confusion is about Time itself, and all that happens 'in time,' such that he finds security in some pronouncements while undertaking to forestall others. Davis goes on to speak of what he regards as "a more serious difficulty with Macbeth's view of prophecy. He traffics with preternatural beings, beings who do things no man can do, and yet it does not occur to him for a moment that, having defied the ordinary course of nature in one respect, they might well be able to do so in other respects." Again, this is not strictly so; if the natural order is determined, *knowledge* of the future would in principle be possible without violating any natural laws (though gaining such knowledge may be beyond ordinary human capacities). However, in observing that "Foreknowledge, which appears to ensure courage, in the end makes it impossible to consider oneself courageous" (228), Davis does make an important point in as much as Macbeth's self-esteem is based on his courage.

81 Thus, the imagined (but naturally impossible) situation would be no less perplexing *with respect to free will* than is any other situation. For one would still wonder whether the recipient's response to such a prophecy (i.e., 'of what will happen unless ...') was 'free,' or determined by this foreknowledge.

82 The question has attracted the attention of philosophers since antiquity (see Aristotle, *Nicomachean Ethics*, books 3 and 8). In our era of academic philosophy, it has generated an enormous scholarly literature, and standard arguments pro and con figure prominently in textbook introductions to philosophy. *Macbeth* raises the issue in a wholly natural way, inviting the reader to think the problem through afresh for himself. My own comments make no pretense to be anything more than an example of such an effort.

83 As Brutus expresses it in *Julius Caesar*, "That we shall die, we know; 'tis but the time / And drawing days out, that men stand upon" (3.1.99–100).

84 This is not to say that there might not be a theoretical position which integrates both issues (i.e., that of free will, and that of the historical impact of individual actions). Based especially on his study of the Napoleonic Wars, Leo Tolstoy seems to have arrived at such a theoretical conclusion, arguing (by no means clearly) for a fairly sophisticated but strict historical determinism regarding the great collective events of history. He begins the second volume of his *War and Peace*, Louise and Aylmer Maude, trans. (Norwalk, CT: Easton, 1981), with an extended consideration of the matter, concluding:

> We are forced to fall back on fatalism as an explanation of irrational events (that is to say, events the reasonableness of which we do not understand). The more we try to explain such events in history reasonably, the more unreasonable and incomprehensible do they become to us.
>
> Each man lives for himself, using his freedom to attain his personal aims, and feels with his whole being that he can now do or abstain from doing this or that action; but as soon as he has done it, that action performed at a certain moment in time becomes irrevocable and belongs to history, in which it has not a free but a predestined significance.
>
> There are two sides to the life of every man, his individual life which is the more free the more abstract its interests, and his elemental hive-life in which he inevitably obeys laws laid down for him.
>
> Man lives consciously for himself, but is an unconscious instrument in the attainment of the historic, universal aims of humanity. A deed done is irrevocable, and its result coinciding in time with the actions of millions of other men assumes an historic significance. The higher a man stands on the social ladder, the more people he is connected with and the more power he has over others, the more evident is the predestination and inevitability of his every action.

'A king's heart is in the hands of the Lord.'

A king is history's slave.

History, that is, the unconscious, general, hive-life of mankind, uses every moment of the life of kings as a tool for its own purposes. (part 9, ch. 1)

85 A sound strategy, according to Machiavelli, provided a prince has "fortified his town well" *and* that he "is *not* hated by the people" (*The Prince*, ch. 10, 43).

86 Of the great philosophical artists with which I am acquainted, only Herman Melville compares with Shakespeare in the subtlety with which he treats the inter-related problems of time, chance, free will, and determinism. Consider, for example, the reflections he attributes to his protagonist narrator, the novice whaleman Ishmael, in ch. 47 of *Moby-Dick*. Ishmael and his friend (the savage harpoonist Queequeg) are weaving what is called in the leviathan-hunting trade a 'sword mat' (an item used in the whaleboat):

> I was the attendant or page of Queequeg, while busy at the mat. As I kept passing and repassing the filling or woof of marline between the long yarns of the warp, using my own hand for the shuttle, and as Queequeg, standing sidewise, ever and anon slid his heavy oaken sword between the threads, and idly looking off upon the water, carelessly and unthinkingly drove home every yarn: I say so strange a dreaminess did there then reign all over the ship and all over the sea, only broken by the intermitting dull sound of the sword, that it seemed as if this were the Loom of Time, and I myself were a shuttle mechanically weaving and weaving away at the Fates. There lay the fixed threads of the warp subject to but one single, ever returning, unchanging vibration, and that vibration merely enough to admit of the crosswise interblending of other threads with its own. This warp seemed necessity; and here, thought I, with my own hand I ply my own shuttle and weave my own destiny into these unalterable threads. Meantime, Queequeg's impulsive, indifferent sword, sometimes hitting the woof slantingly, or crookedly, or strongly, or weakly, as the case might be; and by this difference in the concluding blow producing a corresponding contrast in the final aspect of the completed fabric; this savage's sword, thought I, which thus finally shapes and fashions both warp and woof; this easy, indifferent sword must be chance – ay, chance, free will, and necessity – no wise incompatible – all interweavingly working together. The straight warp of necessity, not to be swerved from its ultimate course – its every alternating vibration, indeed, only tending to that; free will still free to ply her shuttle between given threads; and chance, though restrained in its play within the right lines of necessity, and sideways in its motions modified by free will, though thus prescribed to by both, chance by turns rules either, and has the last featuring blow at events.
>
> Thus we were weaving and weaving away when I started at a sound so strange,

long drawn, and musically wild and unearthly, that the ball of free will dropped from my hand, and I stood gazing up at the clouds whence that voice dropped like a wing. High aloft in the cross-trees was that mad Gay-Header, Tashtego. His body was reaching eagerly forward, his hand stretched out like a wand, and at brief sudden intervals he continued his cries. To be sure the same sound was that very moment perhaps being heard all over the seas, from hundreds of whalemen's lookouts perched as high in the air; but from few of those lungs could that accustomed old cry have derived such a marvelous cadence as from Tashtego the Indian's.

As he stood hovering over you half suspended in the air, so wildly and eagerly peering towards the horizon, you would have thought him some prophet or seer beholding the shadows of Fate, and by those wild cries announcing their coming.

"There she blows! there! there! there! she blows! she blows!"

That Melville writes with Shakespeare and the whole philosophical tradition on his mind is indicated in a hundred ways, large and small. A minor example is found in his chapter 'Cetology' (no. 32), which provides a wonderful caricature of Baconian natural history based on all the reported varieties of whales except those omitted because Melville "can hardly help suspecting them for mere sounds, full of Leviathanism, but signifying nothing."

Incidentally, 47 just happens to be the number of chapters in that other great book about "a full-grown Platonian Leviathan" (as Melville calls "the living whale, in his full majesty and significance, [as] is only to be seen at sea in unfathomable waters; and afloat the vast bulk of him is out of sight, like a launched line-of-battle ship"; ch. 55), namely, that of Thomas Hobbes. And as chance would have it, Hobbes and Shakespeare are indirectly related *via* the Old Testament *Book of Job*, whence Hobbes borrowed the name for his own great book and the civil state depicted therein ("Upon earth there is not his like, who is made without fear. He beholdeth all high things: he is a king over all the children of pride" – 41:33–4, King James version). By the time Macbeth confronts young Siward (or 'Seyward,' as this name is spelt throughout the Folio text), Shakespeare has him speak lines that unmistakeably recall the Biblical description of this same terrifying "leviathan" ("The sword of him that layeth at him cannot hold: the spear, the dart, nor the habergeon ... He esteemeth iron as straw ... The arrow cannot make him flee ... Darts are counted as stubble: he laugheth at the shaking of a spear" – 41:26–9).

Yo. Siward: What is thy name?
Macbeth: Thou'lt be afraid to hear it.
Yo. Siward: No; though thou call'st thyself a hotter name
Than any is in hell.
Macbeth: My name's Macbeth.

Yo. Siward: The devil himself could not pronounce a title
More hateful to mine ear.
Macbeth: No, nor more fearful.
Yo. Siward: Thou liest, abhorred tyrant: with my sword
I'll prove the lie thou speak'st.
[They fight, and young Siward is slain]
Macbeth: Thou wast born of woman: –
But swords I smile at, weapons laugh to scorn,
Brandish'd by man that's of a woman born.
(5.7.4–13)

87 As Glaukon assures Sokrates; *Republic* 458d.

88 I am aware that on the standard ('Copenhagen') interpretation of Quantum Theory, certain subatomic events are regarded as indeterminate. Suffice it to say, such interpretations raise enormous metaphysical problems, and allege phenomena that are literally inconceivable – or at least no more easily conceived than either free will or eternal fate. This is freely conceded by several of the leading architects of the theory. Niels Bohr observed that anyone who is not shocked by Quantum Mechanics obviously does not understand it. And Erwin Schrödinger described the claims of this theory as not quite as meaningless as a triangular circle, but much more so than a winged lion.

89 Philip Carey, the protagonist in Somerset Maugham's *Of Human Bondage*, attempts to have it both ways; despite its being obviously illogical, his is a position with which many a thoughtful person might sympathize:

> But Philip's unlucky words engaged him in a discussion on the freedom of the will, and Macalister, with his well-stored memory, brought out argument after argument. He had a mind that delighted in dialectics, and he forced Philip to contradict himself; he pushed him into corners from which he could only escape by damaging concessions; he tripped him up with logic and battered him with authorities.
>
> At last Philip said:
>
> 'Well, I can't say anything about other people. I can only speak for myself. The illusion of free will is so strong in my mind that I can't get away from it, but I believe it is only an illusion. But it is an illusion that is one of the strongest motives of my actions. Before I do anything I feel that I have a choice, and that influences what I do; but afterwards, when the thing is done, I believe that it was inevitable from all eternity.'
>
> 'What do you deduce from that?' asked Hayward.
>
> 'Why, merely the futility of regret. It's no good crying over spilt milk, because all the forces in the universe were bent on spilling it.' (end of ch. 67)

For his own reasons, then, Philip practically agrees with Lady Macbeth when she counsels her husband, "Things without all remedy should be without regard: what's done is done." This remains rationally sound advice irrespective of one's view about human freedom.

90 Rosenberg, in *The Masks of Macbeth*, relates the 'Free Will *vs* Determinism' issue to the of evaluation of Macbeth, and does so in a way that is both plausible, and revealing about human nature: "The more Macbeth is seen as a victim of external forces, a relative innocent, seduced, or driven, or even fated to misdo, the more we may feel for – with – him. Conversely, the more he chooses violence of his own free will, embracing it more than resisting it, the more he evokes alienation. No really distinguished interpretation, critical or theatrical, locates Macbeth at either end of the free will vs compelled spectrum. Most more or less recognize an ambiguity of motivation" (67). Of course, applied at the metaphysical level, such 'ambiguity' could only mean confusion, as there is no half-way point between free will and fatalism. To allow that Macbeth's actions result from a *mix* of the freely chosen and the compelled is to acknowledge the existence of free will.

Knights in *Some Shakespeare Themes* well expresses the depicted relationships among darkness, reason and freedom: "To listen to the witches, it is suggested, is like eating 'the insane root, That takes the reason prisoner' ... Both Macbeth and his wife wilfully blind themselves ('Come thick Night,' 'Come seeling Night'), and to the extent that they surrender the characteristically human power of intellectual and moral discernment they themselves become the 'prey' of 'Night's black agents,' of the powers they have deliberately invoked. Automatism is perhaps most obvious in Lady Macbeth's sleep-walking, with its obsessed reliving of the past, but Macbeth also is shown as forfeiting his human freedom and spontaneity" (139).

91 A full understanding of ourselves as free rational beings – free because rational – may remain ever elusive. The interaction of reason and 'non-rational factors' may ever remain myserious to us, much as does the interaction between mind and matter, consciousness and body. But if we consult our actual experience, we do not *feel* 'unfree' in having our thoughts determined by reason. Quite the contrary: in assenting to reason, we feel we do so freely, even when we are acceding to a conclusion we regret that we 'must' accept – for in such cases, it is not the *accepting* we regret, but whatever we feel obliged by reason to accept, regretting that it should be so (many of Machiavelli's generalizations about people would likely qualify). We feel free in accepting the 'dictates' of reason, for we are aware that not everyone does, nor do we ourselves all the time. Many people many times reject conclusions, not because they can fault the reasoning that leads to them (nor do they even trouble to try), but simply because they do not *like* the conclusion at issue; they have opinions they prefer to hold, irrespective of the truth. Thus, we tacitly recognize that this acceptance of whatever reason determines is itself a manifestation of our free will. Reason alone cannot make us *heed* reason, since all reason can do is provide rational arguments for heeding reason. But if we are deaf to

reason, choose to ignore reason, such arguments are impotent (a severe limitation on the power of a philosopher who is not also a poet). The natural relationship between freedom and reason presumably explains why, generally speaking, we are prouder of ourselves when we choose to be rational: then we regard ourselves as at our best, fulfilling our true nature (animated, as we uniquely are, by a soul whose rational part is by nature suited to rule), thus most fully human. We *choose* to be rational, so far as we are. Or more to the point, we *will* ourselves to be rational, for we abide by what we rationally choose only so far as we have sufficient 'will power.' If we attend to our actual, 'natural' experience of ourselves, we notice that we do not ordinarily feel that our will is either free or unfree. Rather, as Nietzsche observes, "in real life it is solely a question of *strong* and *weak* wills" (*Beyond Good and Evil*, aph. 21).

92 I do not mean to imply that we should necessarily take him at his word here. The possible distrust between the brothers, that neither knows for certain that the other isn't involved in their father's murder, might better explain their "separated fortune." It would still be an issue of safety, of course, but with an eye to more than one threat. That Malcolm chooses comparatively civilized England, whereas Donalbain prefers semi-barbaric Ireland, may indicate something of their respective natures (2.3.135–6; 3.1.29–30). Later, an explicit point is made of the fact that Donalbain will *not* be accompanying Malcolm's conquering army back to Scotland (5.2.7–8). Though he has no opportunity to mention it, Shakespeare may well have in mind "Donalbain's future role as the murderer of Malcolm's son" (so suggests Bradshaw in *Shakespeare's Scepticism*, 229).

93 At least according to modern Evolutionary Theory. On this view, every persisting physical and behavioural feature of a given species is ultimately a reflection of the balance struck between the requirements of individual survival and those of reproduction.

94 In a more ordinary, limited, and obvious way, Duncan also shows how one's sense of security can be inimical to one's own well-being. By contrast, his son Malcolm has cultivated a prudential suspicion, a "modest wisdom" that guards against credulity and congenial assumptions.

95 In a roundabout way, Hecate's claim about security is supported by Glaukon's version of the fabled 'Ring of Gyges,' and the uses to which (he claims) would be put its power to render one invisible. Protected by the security of invisibility, everyone not a natural fool would take whatever they want, do whatever they want, kill or liberate whomever they want, and altogether live "as equal to a god among humans" (*Republic* 359c–360c).

96 One might distinguish still a fourth facet of 'good' in Macbeth's letter to his wife (the fourth circumstance in which the word is used): "This I have thought good to deliver thee" (1.5.10–11) – that is, 'good' as 'useful.' There is some practical utility in distinguishing what is 'instrumentally good' from what is inherently good, but this kind

of goodness must ultimately be derived from some inherent goodness either *for* or *in* humans (as are the formulaic uses in titles and greetings).

97 To be sure, there is ample emphasis on deeds, on doing, on not being able to undo what's been done or do later what was left undone. As Blits notes in *The Insufficiency of Virtue*, "While many words resound throughout *Macbeth*, none echoes so frequently or so significantly as 'done.' Nor is any word more equivocal. What Macbeth does is never quite done in one sense ... yet is completely done in another ... His deeds are at once irreversible and incomplete" (11; cf. note 10, 205). T. McAlindon, commenting on the First Witch's "I'll do, I'll do, and I'll do," makes a similar point: "[Her] promise of vindictive action against the captain of the *Tiger* isolates the play's key word, 'do/deed,' and anticipates, and numerically emphasizes, the tragic pattern whereby Macbeth's 'horrid deed' traps him in a hell of torturing, sterile, restless, and endless activity" (*Shakespeare's Tragic Cosmos*, 207).

98 Cf. *Republic* 531e, 534b–c.

99 Cf. ibid. 523a–524d.

100 It is this prejudice that Machiavelli rhetorically exploits when observing, "Men in general judge more by their eyes than by their hands, because seeing is given to everyone, touching to few. Everyone sees how you appear, few touch what you are" (*The Prince*, ch. 18, 71).

101 Although I believe he underestimates the intellectual component of the play, here I would none the less endorse the insistence of Wilson Knight, in *The Wheel of Fire*: "Analysis must not be directed to the story alone, but to the manifold correspondencies of imaginative quality extending throughout the whole play. The *Macbeth* vision is powerfully superlogical. Yet it is the work of interpretation to give some logical coherence to things imaginative. To do this, it is manifestly not enough to abstract the skeleton of logical sequence which is the story of the play ... [I]t expresses its vision not to the critical intellect, but to the responsive imagination" (158).

102 *Hamlet* 2.2.249–50, Arden edition. The passage cited is in the Folio version, but not in the earlier Quartos.

103 See Nietzsche, *Beyond Good and Evil*, aph. 16.

104 Cf. *Republic* 430e–431b. This and other relevant passages are extensively analysed in Craig, *The War Lover*, ch. 4.

105 Knights in *Some Shakespearean Themes* contends that this is a theme threaded pretty much throughout Shakespeare's writings, from the Sonnets (which are generally presumed to come from early in his creative career) to the last plays. As he puts it in 'Time's Subjects':

> Great poetry demands a willingness to meet, experience, and contemplate all that is most deeply disturbing in our common fate. The sense of life's tragic issues comes to different men in different ways. One of the ways in which it came to

Shakespeare is not uncommon; it was simply a heightened awareness of what the mere passage of time does to a man and all created things. (45)

From the Sonnets to *The Tempest* Shakespeare's progress as a dramatist is not to be summed up as a series of adventures of the soul; like that of all great artists it is a directed exploration. True enough, it is only when we begin to see the whole pattern that we can realize how completely Shakespeare was committed, for in each new venture there is freedom as well as commitment, and nothing could be further than these plays from the compulsive following of an idea. But the imagination has its responsibilities, and Shakespeare found his when, in a deeply personal experience, he confronted the power of Time. (51)

106 Cf. *Republic* 516e.

107 *The Prince*, ch. 25, 101.

108 Cf. *Republic* 558d–559a, 571a–d.

109 In this connection, one might have to consider more seriously than one would prefer Nietzsche's 'immoral'/anti-moral perspective on Macbeth, and Shakespeare, as expressed in aphorism 240 of *Daybreak: Thoughts on the Prejudices of Morality*, R.J. Hollingdale, trans. (Cambridge: Cambridge University Press, 1982):

On the morality of the stage. – Whoever thinks that Shakespeare's theatre has a moral effect, and that the sight of Macbeth irresistibly repels one from the evil of ambition, is in error: and he is again in error if he thinks Shakespeare himself felt as he feels. He who is really possessed by raging ambition beholds this its image with *joy*; and if the hero perishes by his passion this precisely is the sharpest spice in the hot draught of this joy. Can the poet have felt otherwise? How royally, and not at all like a rogue, does this ambitious man pursue his course from the moment of his great crime! Only from then on does he exercise 'demonic' attraction and excite similar natures to emulation – demonic means here: in defiance *against* life and advantage for the sake of a drive and idea. Do you suppose Tristan and Isolde are preaching *against* adultery when they both perish by it? This would be to stand the poets on their head: they, and especially Shakespeare, are enamoured of the passions as such and not least of their *death-welcoming* moods – those moods in which the heart adheres to life no more firmly than does a drop of water to a glass. It is not the guilt and its evil outcome they have at heart, Shakespeare as little as Sophocles (in Ajax, Philoctetes, Oedipus): as easy as it would have been in these instances to make guilt the lever of the drama, just as surely has this been avoided. The tragic poet has just as little desire to take sides *against* life with his images of life! He cries rather: 'it is the stimulant of stimulants, this exciting, changing, dangerous, gloomy and often sun-drenched existence! It is an *adventure* to live – espouse what party in it you will, it will always retain this character!' – He speaks thus out of a restless, vigorous age which is half-drunk and stupifies by its excess of blood and energy – out of a wickeder age than ours is: which is why we need first to *adjust* and *justify* the goal of a Shakespearean drama, that is to say, not to understand it. (140–1)

110 Nietzsche, *Beyond Good and Evil*, aph. 78.

111 Again, it is a consequence of the failure to understand the metaphysical dimension of the play that has led various commentators to suspect that the Hecate scenes are interpolations by an alien hand. See, e.g., Kenneth Muir in his Introduction to the Arden edition (xxxiii–v); and Granville-Barker's 'Preface' to *Macbeth* (in *More Prefaces to Shakespeare*), where he begins his analysis by asserting, "Hecate may be ruled out with hardly a second thought. If this be not true Middleton, it is at least true twaddle, and Shakespeare – though he had his lapses – was not in a twaddling mood when he wrote *Macbeth*" (60). While I would be chary of speaking about Shakespeare's "lapses," I have no such reluctance to pronounce this one of Granville-Barker's worst. Rosenberg (*The Masks of Macbeth*) includes a useful review of the various reasons critics have adduced for regarding the 'Hecate Scene' (i.e., 3.5) as 'unShakespearean,' but nonetheless argues for its authenticity – and shows much perspicacity, I believe, in analysing its dramatic and poetic qualities. As he observes, "Hecate appears in the play immediately after the 'other woman' in Macbeth's life begins to lose control of his direction; though he seems to need no further guidance, she will take him to deeper, darker assurances than Lady Macbeth did" (492). Rosenberg concludes:

> The scene was there because it intensified the climate of terror with remarkable spectacle. It worked ...
>
> Shakespeare's Hecate represents a dimension of evil more deliberately malicious, more intent on destruction, than in the ambiguous witches; she appears at a crucial time, when Macbeth leaves his Lady to visit the Sisters; and any possibility that the Three may mean him well is threatened by the counter commands of the fearful goddess. We now know better than Macbeth what danger lies ahead. (496)

As I hope my analysis makes clear (which is especially indebted to that of David Lowenthal's 'Macbeth' in *Shakespeare and the Good Life*), Hecate's role is crucial.

112 Cf. *Republic* 351c–d.

113 The place Hecate appoints for her and her subordinates' final rendezvous with Macbeth, the Pit of Acheron (3.5.15), further indicates her netherworldly status. According to ancient tradition, the entrance to Hades is at the source of the river *Acherōn*, the name of which is derived from the word meaning 'ache,' especially an ache or pain of the mind (*achos*).

114 This view of good and evil is the same as in the natural theology preached by the Savoyard Vicar in Rousseau's *Emile*, Allan Bloom, trans. (New York. Basic Books,

1979): "General evil can exist only in disorder, and I see in the system of the world an unfailing order." And, "the goodness of God is the love of order; for it is by order that He maintains what exists and links each part with the whole" (282, 285).

As Knights in *Some Shakespearean Themes* notes about Macbeth himself, "He has directed his will to evil, towards something that of its very nature makes for chaos and the abnegation of meaning. The solid natural goods – ranging from food and sleep to the varied mutualities of friendship, service, love – are witnesses to the central paradox of evil, that however terrible its power it can only lead to 'nothing'" (141). But this needs to be clearly understood: the 'evil' Macbeth *consciously* pursues is a false *good*, false partly because of the true goods it precludes.

Incidentally, if we understand evil in terms of disorder, we can hardly admire Duncan's rule of Scotland (see note 19 above).

115 As the implications of this claim are easily confused, it is worth further comment. First of all, it does not necessarily imply an egalitarian arrangement; historically, a variety of regimes have proven to be compatible with decent political life, including that of prudent kingship. Whereas it is highly dubious whether a radically egalitarian arrangement, one in which everyone has an equal share of wealth, power, and status, offers much prospect of long-term political harmony. Second, the issue is not what people actually do, but what they can fully *justify* doing. And because everyone who subsists within a polity – even, indeed especially, those such as thieves, frauds, extortionists, beggars, and all others who pursue parasitic livelihoods – has a stake in its preservation, whether or not one realizes it and whether or not one is willing to accept any responsibility for it, one can not rationally justify favouring oneself in ways that are in principle incompatible with the indefinite preservation of that polity. This is what Macbeth sees clearly in alluding to "this even-handed Justice" (1.7.10): that there is no convincing justification he could give, to himself or anyone else, for violating with respect to Duncan the rules pertaining to host, kin, and subject that would not simultaneously justify their violation with respect to him.

116 Even consciously self-destructive behaviour, in so far as we can make any sense of it (i.e., that it partakes of reason at all), presumes that the person believes he would be 'better off' dead.

117 Bradshaw, in *Shakespeare's Scepticism*, sees this as the key to what is most unsettling about the play:

> In *Macbeth* as in *Lear*, the vividly apprehended reality of these pressing *human* needs and aspirations does not of itself guarantee the existence of a corresponding moral and spiritual order; it may leave man all the more terrifyingly 'unaccommodated.' *Macbeth* terrifies, not by denying the existence of 'order' in some dogmatically sceptical or nihilistic way, but by making its reality so alarmingly uncertain. (224)

> In conceptual terms, the opposition between a world of Day and a world of Night or between two halves of nature promises a degree of clarity, like the opposition between Good and Evil ... But it seems more important to notice the disparity between the *conceptual* clarity such oppositions seem to promise, and the *experiential* uncertainty the play provokes. (225)

> It is one thing to say that Macbeth shows a 'fatal ignorance' of his own nature, but can we also say ... that he fails to perceive the world – his world – as it really is? It is one thing to suppose that Macbeth's actions are inevitably self-destructive because he is the man he is; but has anybody ever supposed that some reassuringly inevitable process will ensure that the men who butcher Banquo or Macduff's family feel a corresponding mental agony? (233–4)

118 The word is used only four times by Shakespeare, once here, once each in *Measure for Measure* (2.2.173) and *All's Well that Ends Well* (5.3.154), where also it is spelt 'fowly,' and once in *Henry VI (Part One)*, spelt 'fouly' (1.3.154). 'Fowl' is not used in *Macbeth*, but elsewhere in the folio it is spelled 'Fowle' (e.g., in *Measure for Measure* [2.2.85; 3.1.91]).

119 Although modern editors typically provide him an exit and re-entry in response to Macbeth's question at 5.5.7, the Folio has him present throughout the scene, indicative of his knowing without inquiring the answers to Macbeth's questions.

120 To this one might add the observations of Timothy Fuller ('The Relation of Thought and Action in *Macbeth*'):

> Lady Macbeth ... fears Macbeth's nature, because he is too full of the milk of human kindness. She fears, in short, the femaleness of Macbeth or femaleness in general. It might also be said that Macbeth is a failure for her insofar as he is pregnant with thought – presumably the milk of kindness relates reflectiveness to the female as opposed to the violent, unreflective life of the warrior-king. She wishes to be unsexed to achieve 'direst cruelty' ... She wants Macbeth to unify desire and act.
>
> Macbeth tries to put her off by asserting, 'I dare do all that may become a man.' This is suitably ambiguous in that what is becoming to a man and what a man is able to become are in tension here. It is what a man is able to become that interests Lady Macbeth and she engages to try to alter what a man is: 'What beast was't then / That made you break this enterprise to me?' She thinks he was more a man when a beast in his first thoughtless enthusiasm. The confusion of beast and man follows when there is the subsumption of the female into the male, so that all becomes male. (214–15)

121 Some would have us see Malcolm as the antecedent of 'he' in 'he has no children' (4.3.216) – reading it to be Macduff's dismissing what they regard as Malcolm's

insensitive importuning of him to seek revenge. But this squares with neither Malcolm's reaction nor the readiness Macduff shows seconds later in acceding to the same exhortation (229–35), nor with the passage wherein Macbeth contrasts his and Banquo's status with respect to descendants (3.1.59–69). Nor does it make any sense for Macduff to appeal with such an observation to Rosse who (so far as we know) has no children either, and thus would be no better prepared than Malcolm to sympathize fully with Macduff's loss. It is far more plausible that Macduff is explaining aloud, and primarily to himself, Macbeth's otherwise inconceivably vicious act.

122 Thereby accomplishing 'ligature,' as it is called in technical legalese – a crime often associated with sorcery. On this and related issues, see Dennis Biggins, "Sexuality, Witchcraft, and Violence in *Macbeth*," *Shakespeare Studies* 8 (1975) 255–77.

123 Blits (*The Insufficiency of Virtue*) points to the larger sigificance of this seemingly incidental vignette: "There is a striking similarity between the fate the Witches intend for the sailor and the fate awaiting Macbeth. Just as the Witches will drain the shipmaster dry as hay, Macbeth will find that his own life has become withered and dry ('[M]y way of life / Is fallen into the sere, the yellow leaf' ...). And just as they will prevent the sailor from sleeping, so Macbeth will hear a voice cry, 'Sleep no more!' ... and become afflicted by 'these terrible dreams, / That shake us nightly' ... That the two men's sufferings have something to do with their wives, and particularly with what their wives say, only increases the resemblance" (22).

124 Despite this incompleteness in their marriage, Kay Stockholder, wielding a bewildering mode of psychoanalysis over both Shakespeare and his characters, would have us view them as the philosopher-poet's model couple: "Lady Macbeth and Macbeth, from whose marital intimacy radiate the widening circles of bloody crimes, constitute Shakespeare's closest approach to dramatizing a mature, married and childbearing, though significantly childless couple. They have verisimilitude" (*Dream Works: Lovers and Families in Shakespeare's Plays*, Toronto: University of Toronto Press, 1987, 4). But for ideology-engendered critical obtuseness, it would be hard to surpass Joan Larsen Klein, who interprets Lady Macbeth's maliciously ironical "He [Duncan] that's coming must be provided for" as evidence of her domestic preoccupation! See her essay entitled 'Lady Macbeth: "Infirm of Purpose,"' in *The Woman's Part: Feminist Criticism of Shakespeare*, 246.

125 Cf. *Republic* 617d–e, 620d–e.

126 As Robert H. West (*Shakespeare and the Outer Mystery*) notes: "After three hundred years of discussion Shakespeare critics are not sure – or at least not agreed – about this evil, not even agreed, in spite of the witch and devil symbols, that it *is* a superhuman evil. Is it fundamentally distinguishable from the cosmic violence and indifference of the storm in *King Lear* or from the mortal cunning and malice of Iago? ... The case for demonic agency in *Macbeth* probably has to stand or fall with the meaning the

Weird Sisters can have. All the other phenomena of evil in the play are possibly attributable to human fears and passions. But it is hard to show that the Sisters are not best understood as discrete beings moved by malice at once personal and non-human" (70).

127 Here Shakespeare apparently took his inspiration from Homer, endowing Lady Macbeth with powers akin to Circe, who also employed potions that turned some men into swine, others into lions and wolves (*Odyssey* book 10), 212, 233.

128 Shakespeare employs an ingenious inversion of this 'sleep-death' likeness with the 'statue' of Hermione in *The Winter's Tale,* having Paulina present it, saying, "But here it is: prepare / To see the life as lively mock'd as ever / Still sleep mock'd death" (5.3.18–20).

129 Cf. *Republic* 571c–572b; *Hamlet* 3.1.64–8.

130 Cf. *Republic* 507d–508d.

3: The Discovery of Nature

1 Textual references are to the second Arden edition, Kenneth Muir, ed. (originally published in 1952, reprinted by Routledge, London and New York, 1989). A third Arden edition, edited by R.A. Foakes (Walton on Thames: Thomas Nelson and Son, 1997), appeared after this chapter had been substantially completed. It has some advantages over its predecessor, but as I learned in the course of attempting to change all my textual references so as to comport with it, more disadvantages (at least for the kind of analysis I pursue here). Expressly in response to the recent controversy over the two versions of the text, that of the best Quarto and the Folio's (briefly discussed below), Foakes has attempted "to offer an edition that seeks to give an idea of the work, while making the major differences between the versions easily recognizable" (119). But often this results in a redundant, awkward, and/or inflated text, and so a commentator is obliged to make the editorial choice, then note his departure. To illustrate with a simple example. At 1.5.43–4, Muir chooses to follow the Folio's wording ("O! let me not be mad, not mad, sweet heaven; / Keep me in temper; I would not be mad!"), relegating the Quarto's alternative to the notes. Foakes, however, combines them, while signaling with superscripts which parts are unique to which versions ("O let me not be mad, [F]not mad[F], sweet heaven! [Q]I would not be mad.[Q] / Keep me in temper, I would not be mad."). Thus, where one wishes to quote 'the text,' I find Muir's preferable (I also generally prefer his spellings and punctuation, which renders the meter more obvious). Since for the most part Foakes's lineation is close enough to Muirs's (rarely more than two lines off), textual citations keyed to the latter's edition should cause no special bother to anyone using the former's. The most important difference in the editions is in the scenic divisions of act 2. Muir, following an editorial tradition begun by Capell, divides what is a single second scene in both Quarto and Folio versions into

three separate scenes (treating Edgar's soliloquy as a scene unto itself, i.e., 2.3.1–21). Foakes re-integrates them into a single long scene (and provides sound arguments for doing so), but conveniently includes in brackets the alternative lineation as per the traditional three-scene version.

Because Muir's text, then, like most modern editions (including Foakes's), is a composite of the best Quarto version (the Second, which although dated 1608 like the First, textual scholars now believe to be a corrected copy actually printed in 1619) and that of the Folio (which deletes some three hundred lines of the Quarto, and adds another hundred along with numerous other verbal alterations), the interpreter of this play confronts special problems almost entirely absent from a consideration of (say) *Macbeth*. Moreover, the legitimacy of what has long been the standard practice, this combining of the two versions, has recently come under attack. Stanley Wells, general editor of the Oxford edition of the *Complete Works*, favours printing each text separately (as Oxford Press has done): "The disentangling of the two versions reveals plays that are clearer and simpler to read and to perform than the conflated version. It ought to enhance appreciation of the play; some of the structural defects that have troubled readers of the past can now be seen to be the creation of Shakespeare's editors rather than of the playwright himself' (*Shakespeare: A Life in Drama*, New York: W.W. Norton, 1995, 264). I cannot agree that greater clarity results from keeping the two versions separate. I presume that the lines omitted from the Folio were cuts that could be made without essentially changing the story, and were done simply in order to shorten performance, whereas the additions were seen as needed to enhance dramatic force and/or clarity. But the material omitted from the Folio version does provide details that enrich our understanding of the characters, and makes the underlying rationale of the play clearer. Muir, in "The Texts of *King Lear*: an Interim Assessment of the Controversy," summarizes the issues involved and defends the established practice (satisfactorily, to my mind). For a much more politically astute analysis of what is actually at stake in the controversy, see Paul Cantor, 'On Sitting Down to Read *King Lears* Again: The Textual Deconstruction of Shakespeare,' quoted previously, note 44, ch. 1.

Fortunately, the differences in the two versions of the play do not much affect most of what I see to be centrally involved in arriving at an adequate interpretation of it. Where such differences do bear, I shall of course duly note them. And as in the case of *Macbeth*, I occasionally quote bits of verse as prose.

2 With respect to my subsequent defence of this claim and much else about the play, I am indebted to the analysis by Harry Jaffa, entitled 'The Limits of Politics: *King Lear*, Act I, scene i' in Allan Bloom, *Shakespeare's Politics* (New York: Basic Books, 1964).

3 *Coleridge's Shakespearean Criticism*, Thomas Middleton Raysor, ed. (Cambridge: Cambridge University Press, 1930), 55; Bate, *The Romantics on Shakespeare*, 389. Similarly, Hazlitt, who judged *King Lear* "the best of all Shakespear's plays," seems also to have

misunderstood its first scene, seeing only the subrational determinates of Lear's behaviour (*The Romantics on Shakespeare*): "The character of Lear ... is the only ground on which such a story could be built with the greatest truth and effect. It is his rash haste, his violent impetuousity, his blindness to everything but the dictates of his passions or affections, that produces all his misfortunes, that aggravates his impatience with them, that enforces our pity for him. The part that Cordelia bears in the scene is extremely beautiful: the story is almost told in the first words she utters" (394–5).

So far as I've been able to determine, all of the most influential Shakespeare scholars of the past century have misjudged Lear, and accordingly failed to understand what he is actually attempting in the first scene. Like Coleridge, they still have valuable insights to contribute, but their overall interpretations of the play are invariably compromised. To mention only a few of the best: A.C. Bradley, *Shakespearean Tragedy* (London: Macmillan 1963; orig. pub. 1904): "Lear's intention [is] a mere form, devised as a childish scheme to gratify his love of absolute power and his hunger for assurances of devotion" (204). G. Wilson Knight, *The Wheel of Fire*: "From the start, the situation has a comic aspect. It has been observed that Lear has, so to speak, staged an interlude, with himself as chief actor, in which he grasps expressions of love to his heart, and resigns his sceptre to a chorus of acclamations. It is childish, foolish – but very human. So, too, is the result" (161). Derek Traversi, *An Approach to Shakespeare*, vol. 2: "Old age has weakened [Lear's] capacity for self-control, making him as soon as he is crossed the prey of an anger definitely rooted in the 'blood'" (148). Harold C. Goddard, *The Meaning of Shakespeare* vol. 2 (Chicago: University of Chicago Press, 1951): "Lear, at the beginning of the play, possesses physical eyesight ... as perfect as Gloucester's. But morally he is even blinder. He is a victim, to the point of incipient madness, of his arrogance, his anger, his vanity, and his pride. A choleric temperament, a position of absolute authority, and old age have combined to make him what he is" (147). Bertrand Evans, *Shakespeare's Tragic Practice*: "Kent's angry speeches ... serve a vital function by delineating the features and dimensions of the monumental egotism, vanity, and plain obstinacy by which Lear is blinded, his mind impenetrably insulated from the truth"; "he is even more wilful than blind, and would be quite capable, if it came to that, of literally cutting off his nose to spite his face" (150–1). René Girard, *A Theater of Envy* (New York: Oxford University Press, 1991): "The king invites his three daughters to exhibit their love for him, each one in turn; instead of preventing all mimetic competition among them, as his role demands, he foolishly incites it: he proposes himself as an object of competitive desire ... he turns the satisfaction of his unspeakable appetite into some kind of obligation for his daughters, and the ceremony he organizes to this effect cannot fail to coincide with his abdication. By acting as he does, Lear effectively resigns as father and king" (181).

Marvin Rosenberg in *The Masks of KING LEAR* (Newark: University of Delaware Press, 1972, 17–18) conveniently catalogues the various interpretations, in performance and scholarly criticism, of what motivates Lear:

The design of Lear's motivation is as complex as any in drama; when it is narrowed to simplified "correlatives," the character is savagely diminished. Yet a synthesis of all major critical and theatrical interpretations begins to match the dimensions of the role. Here, simplified, are the main ones:

Lear is a barbarian, with primitive, untamed impulses.

Lear is senile.

He is old – with all the frailties, physical and mental, of age.

He is mad from the first.

He is not mad – but capricious: angry, impetuous, spoiled, wilful, unnatural, revengeful, proud, stubborn, tyrannical, implacable, lacking imagination, etc.

He is a slave of passion (wrath); though the very greatness of his passion reveals the greatness of his soul.

He is wise, loving, magnanimous, a tender father upset by ingratitude.

He is conditioned to rule, he cannot adjust to the rule of others, especially others whom he once dominated.

He is an archetypal king figure, living out its inevitable fate.

He is a troubled Everyman in the robes of a king.

He is selfish, narcissistic – needs love desperately, but cannot himself give love.

He is masochistic, self-hurting (moved even by a death wish), self-pitying.

He has a repressed incestuous attachment to his daughters, particularly Cordelia or Goneril.

He is regressive, mainly in the direction of a return to the womb, the shelter of the mother (here, too, the element of death wish).

His motivation is mysterious. (Sometimes an alternative for: Shakespeare failed.)

Alvin Kernan, *Shakespeare, the King's Playwright* (New Haven: Yale University Press, 1995), is therefore unusual in his recognizing Lear to be Shakespeare's "most magisterial image of the true king," one who "towers above his subjects, a titanic personality, 'every inch a king,' a man who has in his countenance an inalienable authority that his followers 'would fain call master.' His will is locked, commanding, fearless, autocratic in every way" (96–7).

4 *The Prince*, ch. 6, par. 2–3.

5 Cf. *Republic* 412a, 459a ff.

6 *Leviathan*, ch. 19 (last six paragraphs).

7 The significance of their calm acceptance here of the planned division can scarcely be exaggerated. Simply compare it with Kent's reaction later, after Lear has spontaneously ordered a quite different division: "Cornwall and Albany, with my two daughters' dowers digest the third" (1.1.126–7). Kent erupts and will not be silenced, calling Lear "mad," and insisting: "Reserve thy State" (148). Anyone with any understanding of politics generally, and especially anyone at all acquainted with the history of Britain, would readily appreciate the over-riding importance of keeping the Kingdom united.

And as for the play's own historical context, recall that James VI of Scotland had only recently ascended the throne of England, thereby uniting the kingdoms – to the great relief of most English politicians familiar with the chronic problems attendant to an independent Scotland.

8 What purpose it serves in the plot, that is, as distinct from its purpose in the theatre. The popular appeal of folk tales and literature featuring three daughters (the elder ones evil, the youngest one good but abused), a 'love test,' and so on, suggests there is some psychic appetite such stories satisfy, and may account for Shakespeare's use of it to clothe the deeper, more challenging tale he herein tells.

9 As Foakes notes in his 'Introduction' (95), Holinshed, who is the probable source for the titles of Shakespeare's two dukes, specifies that 'Albania' is that part of Britain north of the Humber (including Scotland).

10 In Shakespeare's own time, Englishmen apparently were prepared to accept (albeit grudgingly) foreign princes as rulers on the condition that they marry with the royal blood and become resident kings – this being the common expectation during the first half of Elizabeth's reign.

11 It is true that Machiavelli begins ch. 18 of *The Prince* ('In What Mode Faith Should Be Kept by Princes') with what would seem a contrary view: "How laudable it is for a prince to keep his faith, and to live with honesty and not by astuteness, everybody understands. Nonetheless one sees by experience in our times that the princes who have done great things are those who have taken little account of faith and have known how to get around men's brains with astuteness; and in the end they have overcome those who founded themselves on loyalty." Machiavelli makes clear by the end of this chapter, however, that this advice only works so far as one's duplicity goes unrecognized, at least for the foreseeable future: "A prince should thus take great care that nothing escapes his mouth that is not full of the above-mentioned five qualities and that, to see him and hear him, he should appear all mercy, all faith, all honesty, all humanity, all religion" (68–70). In this, as in all respects, the truly successful 'Machiavellian' is never suspected of being one. Perhaps needless to add, there are *very* few people who can manage this, since but one slip can destroy the entire facade.

12 In the earlier *King Leir* that was an important source of inspiration for Shakespeare's masterpiece, the King explicitly acknowledges that this is to be a "sudden strategem" with a secret purpose (as quoted in Muir's Introduction to the Arden edition of *King Lear* xxv):

> I am resolu'd, and euen now my mind
> Doth meditate a sudden strategem,
> To try which of my daughters loues me best:
> Which till I know, I cannot be in rest.
> This graunted, when they iointly shall contend,
> Each to exceed the other in their loue:

Then at the vantage will I take *Cordella*,
Euen as she doth protest she loues me best,
Ile say, then, daughter, graunt me one request,
To shew thou louest me as thy sisters doe,
Accept a husband, whom my selfe will woo.

This Leir, however, takes his counsellors into his confidence, and that confidence is betrayed by one of them (Skalliger) who reveals the strategem to Gonorill and Ragan. They, consequently, have the opportunity to prepare and rehearse the sort of speeches as will beguile their father with what they know he wants to hear.

The difference between the two plays provides an excellent illustration of Shakespeare's practice of leaving implicit in his plot – there for his readers to discern for themselves – features and rationales that were explicit in his sources. His depiction of King Duncan in *Macbeth* compared with Holinshed's description of Duncan works likewise.

13 Cf. *Republic* 382c–d, 414b ff.

14 That I see no indication of Cordelia's having received the kind of political education that would prepare her actually to rule is the first reason that I cannot agree with David Lowenthal's interpretation of what Lear is attempting in the first scene (*Shakespeare and the Good Life*). He suggests that Lear's "foremost objective was to pass on the greatest share of his power to Cordelia" (77), contending that "he had in mind an actual division of the kingdom, and not a temporary or merely apparent division ... He implies that something like a tripartite council of state would give unity to the rule of Britain" (76). This makes for a rather foolish Lear, and a most implausibly complacent Kent and Gloucester discussing the King's intention (in dramatic contrast to Kent's violent reaction to Lear's impromptu alteration of his original plan). In this connection, one might recall the notorious tripartite indenture executed by Percy, Mortimer, and Glendower whereby England was to be partitioned into three petty kingdoms upon the overthrow of Henry IV (Shakespeare's unflattering portrayal of the three principals arguing over the details begins Act III in *King Henry IV, Part 1*). Thus I must side with Jaffa, 'The Limits of Politics,' with regard to the deciphering of Lear's plan for his succession. That said, however, I find myself mainly in agreement with most of what Lowenthal argues in the rest of his excellent essay on this play, and have profited much from his entire discussion.

15 There are those who, like Louis Auchincloss, in *Motiveless Malignity* (London: Gollancz, 1970), "consider her definition of filial love to be an exact and appropriate one" (15). But 'definitions' are not what are called for here. Imagine a wife soliciting reassurance from her husband, "Do you love me, dear?" – only to be told, "I love you as much as you deserve, neither more nor less." A memorable response, no doubt, but hardly for reasons the wife would treasure.

16 The judgment of Harley Granville-Barker (*Prefaces to Shakespeare* vol. 1) regarding the

Cordelia we see in the first scene seems right: "It will be a fatal error to present Cordelia as a meek saint. She has more than a touch of her father in her. She is as proud as he is, and as obstinate, for all her sweetness and her youth" (303).

17 Cf. Aristotle, *The Art of Rhetoric* II, ii, 15–16 (1379b 3–8).

18 Cf. *The Book of Daniel* 6:8–15.

19 Given Lear's opting for some new arrangement that would still be consistent with his declared "fast intent" to confer all the practical business of government on others, one might wonder why he doesn't simply endow Albany here and now with the strategic 'Cordelia portion,' given his (justified) preference for Albany. But we must bear in mind that Lear is trying to prevent "future strife" (1.1.43–4). *We* may approve of Albany's being made the dominant power, but would the "hot Duke" Cornwall acquiesce in being relegated to subordinate status (bear in mind Lear's fastidious efforts to treat both dukes equally, and Gloucester's reminder to Lear: "You know the fiery quality of the Duke; how unremovable and fix'd he is in his own course" 2.4.89–91). Cornwall's temper and ambition, combined with the perceived "milky gentleness" of Albany – as Goneril early chides him, "You are much more attax'd for want of wisdom than prais'd for harmful mildness" (1.4.342–3; see also 4.2.1); and later, "Milk-liver'd man! / That bear'st a cheek for blows, a head for wrongs" (4.2.50–1) – is not a formula for perpetual peace. Admittedly, events prove that Albany's made of sterner stuff than others give him credit for (and least of all his wife; 12–14), but there may be good reason he has not acquired a reputation that strikes fear into bold men's hearts. And even after he has shown his mettle, there remain grounds for suspecting that he is *not* an ideal successor to Lear. One simply need consider how ready he is at the play's conclusion to surrender his "absolute power," first to old Lear, then to Kent and Edgar (5.3.297–9, 318–19). I would not go so far as Joseph Alulis in saying, "Albany is virtuous, but his virtues are those of loyalty and decency only," in 'Wisdom and Fortune: The Education of the Prince in Shakespeare's *King Lear*,' *Interpretation* 21 (Spring 1994) 373–89; 376. But Alulis is correct in recognizing that Albany is a man who does not really *want* to be king badly enough to make a go of it. Cornwall, on the other hand, is a vicious scoundrel.

20 Shakespeare's sources stressed the love he bore for all his daughters. The earlier, anonymously authored *King Leir* has the King declare:

> How deare my daughters are vnto my soule,
> None knowes, but he, that knowes my thoghts and secret deeds.
> Ah, little do they know the deare regard,
> Wherein I hold their future state to come:

Similarly, Holinshed reports: "It is written that he had by his wife three daughters without other issue, whose names were Gonorilla, Regan, and Cordeilla, which daughters he greatly loued, but specially Cordeilla the youngest farre aboue the two elder" (both sources as quoted in Appendices to Muir's edition of *King Lear*, 207, 220).

21 Shakespeare shows us the more youthful King Henry V learning this – or at least claiming to – from the conspiracy by three of his intimates to kill him on the eve of his embarking for the conquest of France. Addressing especially his boon companion, Lord Scroop of Masham:

> O how hast thou with jealousy infected
> The sweetness of affiance! Show men dutiful?
> Why, so didst thou. Seem they grave and learned?
> Why, so didst thou. Come they of noble family?
> Why, so didst thou. Seem they religious?
> Why, so didst thou. Or are they spare in diet,
> Free from gross passion or of mirth or anger,
> Constant in spirit, not swerving with the blood,
> Garnished and decked in modest complement,
> Not working with the eye without the ear,
> And but in purged judgment trusting neither?
> Such and so finely boulted didst thou seem:
> And thus thy fall hath left a kind of blot
> To mark the full-fraught man and best endued
> With *some* suspicion. I will weep for thee,
> For this revolt of thine, methinks, is like
> Another fall of man. (2.2.126–42)

22 As Graham Bradshaw observes in *Shakespeare's Scepticism* by way of introducing an especially helpful discussion of the issue, "The question, 'Why does Cordelia die?' is rightly regarded as fundamental in *Lear*-criticism" (87). And doubtless Dr Johnson spoke for untold thousands in his famously confessing his dissatisfaction with the play's final scene: "Shakespeare has suffered the virtue of Cordelia to perish in a just cause, contrary to the natural ideas of justice, to the hope of the reader, and, what is yet more strange, to the faith of the chronicles." But I would suggest that those who accede to Johnson's criticism of the play have failed to appreciate Cordelia's not altogether innocent part in precipitating the entire tragedy. No one, of course, would argue (absurdly) that she only gets what she deserves, but neither can she be exonerated from all responsibility for what happens. The challenge of comprehending the tragical ending Shakespeare crafted is made more thought-provoking – if not necessarily as Johnson found it, the "more strange" – by an awareness that it is a radical departure from all the 'source' texts.

23 John F. Danby, *Shakespeare's Doctrine of Nature: A Study of King Lear* (London: Faber and Faber, 1948), wrong though I believe him to be in several important respects (including the crucial first scene and the role of Cordelia's pride in initiating the tragedy; 128–33), nonetheless provides a valuable exploration of the play and what he rightly sees as its central theme: "*King Lear* can be regarded as a play dramatizing the

meanings of the single word 'Nature.' When looked at in this way it becomes obvious at once that *King Lear* is a drama of ideas – such a drama of ideas not as the morality play had been, a drama of abstractions; nor such a drama of amusing talk about theses as Bernard Shaw's is; a drama of ideas, however, none the less, and Shakespeare's own creation: the real *Novum Organum* of Elizabethan thought" (15).

Danby is concerned to explicate the view of Nature informing all of Shakespeare's major plays (well over a dozen figure in the book besides *King Lear*, although he focuses especially on it), and his analysis is distinguished by his familiarity with major works of modern political philosophy (e.g., Hooker, Hobbes, Bacon, Machiavelli). He contends that the play's main characters are first and foremost representations of various conceptions of Nature: "It is how they stand with regard to Nature that gives each character whatever importance it carries in the play" 121. My general approach is quite different from Danby's, however, focusing more on philosophy itself in relation to the problem of Nature. Moreover, Danby's is unabashedly historicist, and to that extent precludes granting Shakespeare's work genuine philosophical status (i.e., as presenting a view of things that might be simply true): "The universal work 'grows up from the deeps of Nature, through the noble sincere soul who is a voice of Nature.' We have tried to show that 'the deeps of Nature' underlying Shakespeare's work include the nature of the society and 'the times' into which Shakespeare was born. *King Lear* elucidates the human plight at a particular phase of its historical unfolding. We have also tried to show, besides this, how *King Lear* explains Shakespeare's own development" (196).

24 Discussing the tensions within human nature, Russell A. Fraser makes good use of the animal imagery that pervades this and other plays in his *Shakespeare's Poetics in Relation to King Lear* (London: Routledge and Kegan Paul, 1962, 85–102). According to Rolf Soellner, (*Timon of Athens: Shakespeare's Pessimistic Tragedy*, Columbus: Ohio State University Press, 1979), *Timon*, a play frequently linked with *Lear* by the theme of ingratitude, has more "comparisons of men in general to animals" than has any other of Shakespeare's dramas: "This imagery underlines human beastliness" (106).

25 At this point, we are confronted by a second conception of Nature, very different from the one Lear tacitly alludes to in the preceding scene. As Robert B. Heilman observes in his renowned treatment of the play, *This Great Stage: Image and Structure in King Lear* (Baton Rouge: Louisiana State University Press, 1948; reprint, Seattle: University of Washington Press, 1963):

> *King Lear* presents a two-fold view of nature, or, perhaps more accurately, shows men holding two contradictory views of nature. The characters in the play say a good deal about nature; but the characters differ morally, and their differences extend into their philosophies of nature ... To most of the characters in the play, nature is a fundamental principle of order; it is the *lex naturalis*, the divinely ordered cosmic scheme; it implies a distinction between good and evil, and the

operation of an eternal justice. On the other hand, nature is understood simply as vital force, the physical drive and the impulses of the individual, the totality of unfettered and uncriticized urgencies. The two senses compete with each other; thus they set up a special tension; and this tension qualifies the total dramatic statement. (115)

Danby (*Shakespeare's Doctrine of Nature*) makes a similar point in commenting on Lear's proposal to "anatomize Regan" so as to determine whether there is "any cause in nature that makes these hard hearts": "'*Nature*' here is pushed across an important threshold. The physical nature of science (the Nature Bacon mostly confines himself to in *Novum Organum*) is made to encroach on the territory of moral corruption. For strict orthodoxy the Fall of Man rather than anatomy should have been brought into the explanation" (49). Neither Heilman nor Danby, however, appear to see the intimate connection between the complex problem of 'nature' and political philosophy, which I contend – and am attempting to show – is the deeper story in this play.

26 The almost universal practice of modern editors, replacing the term 'Bastard' with 'Edmund' in all stage directions and speech attributions, is highly questionable, given the importance of the 'legitimate–illegitimate' issue in the play. Suffice it for now to note that Edmund's compromised social status is much more emphatically impressed upon a reader of the Folio, and even more so of the best Quarto (the Second), than it is upon those who encounter the play only in modern editions. Edmund appears in ten scenes. According to the Folio's stage directions, in five of these scenes (seven in the Quarto) his entrance is indicated by "Bastard'," and in the others by "Edmund." However, *all* of the speech attributions are to "Bast." except Edmund's three brief speeches in act 1, scene 1 (totalling thirteen words) and his final three speeches in this second scene.

27 The expression 'law of nature' itself reflects an anthropomorphic view of Nature – and 'bad philology,' this confused coupling of *physis* and *nomos* – as Nietzsche so amusingly exposes in *Beyond Good and Evil*, aph. 22.

28 The 'mundane' perspective of Edmund is suggested by the very name Shakespeare chose for him. Although it is a respectable Old English name (meaning something like 'happy protection') and was borne by some eminent Saxon kings, it nonetheless suggests the Latin *mundus* ('world').

29 On this point, along with many others of importance, one could hardly be more mistaken than is Stanley Cavell, in *Disowning Knowledge in Six Plays of Shakespeare* (Cambridge: Cambridge University Press, 1987): "In [his] soliloquy, Edmund rails equally against his treatment as a bastard and as a younger son – as if to ask why a younger son should be treated like a bastard. Both social institutions seem to him arbitrary and unnatural. And nothing in the play shows him to be wrong" (49). *Equally?* After the mere mention of his being younger than his half-brother – a moot point, given his

other liability – Edmund goes on for sixteen lines questioning the baseness of bastardy and the moral priority attending that "Fine word, 'legitimate'."

30 As quoted in Bate, *The Romantics on Shakespeare*, 386–7.

31 This presumes that Edgar's mother was still alive at the time Edmund was conceived. The tone and spirit in which both Gloucester and Edmund discuss the young man's begetting certainly suggest that she was.

32 Contrary to the stage directions of some modern editions, including the second Arden used here, there is no indication in the Folio or Quarto versions that Edmund is not present throughout the whole of the first scene. That Foakes in editing the third Arden has returned to the Folio's singular "Exit" is a marked improvement, and his note addressing the possible significance of Edmund's presence is very much to the point.

33 Melville provides an interesting interpretation of her by means of the 'Goneril' he has included in ch. 12 of *The Confidence-Man*:

> It appeared that the unfortunate man had had for a wife one of those natures, anomalously vicious, which would almost tempt a metaphysical lover of our species to doubt whether the human form be, in all cases, conclusive evidence of humanity ...
>
> Goneril was young, in person lithe and straight, too straight, indeed, for a woman, a complexion naturally rosy, and which would have been charmingly so, but for a certain hardness and bakedness, like that of glazed colors on stone-ware. Her hair was of a deep, rich chestnut, but worn in short, close curls all around her head. Her indian figure was not without its impairing effect on her bust, while her mouth would have been pretty but for a trace of moustache. Upon the whole, aided by the resources of the toilet, her appearance at distance was such, that some might have thought her, if anything, rather beautiful, though of a style of beauty rather peculiar and cactus-like.

All of this, to my mind, shows Melville's considerable insight into Shakespeare's Goneril, as especially does his endowing his own with "large, metallic eyes, which her enemies called cold as a cuttlefish's, but which by her were esteemed gazelle-like; for Goneril was not without vanity"; and his assuring us that "Goneril brooked no chiding," such as might be brought on by her penchant for "touching, as by accident, the arm or hand of comely young men."

34 As Hobbes puts it in *Leviathan*, ch. 10, par. 2, "For the nature of Power, is in this point, like to Fame, increasing as it proceeds; or like the motion of heavy bodies, which the further they go, make still the more hast."

35 Mark Girouard, in his chapter entitled 'The Power Houses,' provides a succinct description of the general rationale underlying this practice in *Life in the English Country House* (New Haven: Yale University Press, 1978):

> This power was based on the ownership of land. But land was not important

> to country house owners because they were farmers ... The point of land was the tenants and rent that came with it. A landowner could call on his tenants to fight for him, in the early days of the country house, and to vote for him – or his candidate – in its later ones. He could use the money which they paid in rent to persuade even more people to fight or vote for him, either by hiring them to do so, or by keeping up so handsome and impressive an establishment that they felt it was to their interest to come in on his side. Anyone who had sufficient resources and followers, and displayed them with enough prominence, was likely to be offered jobs and perquisites by the central government in return for his support. Acceptance produced money, which could be turned into more land, more power and more supporters. The more a landowner prospered, the more anxious his fellow landowners were to be connected with him. Through good connections and marriages with heiresses he or his descendants acquired the leverage for still more jobs and perquisites. Such, at any rate, was the ideal route to power; and although there were many pitfalls on the way, it was a route that led often enough to broad estates, a peerage, and the establishment of a dynasty. (2)

Discussing the Irish origins of transportees in his "epic of Australia's founding" (*The Fatal Shore*, New York: Alfred A. Knopf, 1987), Robert Hughes speaks summarily of the discriminatory penal laws to which Irish Catholics were subject, including: "They were disabled in property law, which was rewritten to break up Catholic estates and consolidate Protestant ones. Protestant estates could be left intact to eldest sons, but Catholic ones had to be split between all the children. Thus Catholic landowning families degenerated into sharecropping ones within a generation or two" (182).

36 Primogeniture, which was the rule in England from Norman times until abolished in 1926, applied to sons; if one had only daughters as heirs, one's estate was divided equally among them. Hence, the contrast between the dispositions of Lear's and Gloucester's estates.

37 One might consider here what Bacon says in his essay 'Of Parents and Children' (*The Works of Francis Bacon* vol. 6, James Spedding, Robert Ellis, and Douglas Heath, eds., London: Longmans, 1870):

> The difference in affection of parents towards their several children is many times unequal; and sometimes unworthy ... A man shall see, where there is a house full of children, one or two of the eldest respected, and the youngest made wantons; but in the midst some that are as it were forgotten, who many times nevertheless prove the best. The illiberality of parents in allowance towards their children is a harmful error; makes them base; acquaints them with shifts; makes them sort with mean company; and makes them surfeit more when they come to plenty. And therefore the proof is best, when men keep their authority towards their children, but not their purse. Men have a foolish manner (both parents and school-

masters and servants) in creating and breeding an emulation between brothers during childhood, which many times sorteth to discord when they are men, and disturbeth families. (390)

38 See, in this connection, the exhortation to republican women with which Rousseau concludes the Dedicatory Letter 'To the Republic of Geneva' of his *Discourse on the Origin and Foundations of Inequality among Men*, in *The Discourses and Other Early Political Writings*, Victor Gourevitch, ed. and trans. (Cambridge: Cambridge University Press, 1997):

> Could I forget that precious half of the Republic which causes the other's happiness, and whose gentleness and wisdom preserve its peace and good morals? Amiable and virtuous Citizen-women, it will always be the lot of your sex to govern ours. How fortunate when your chaste power, exercised in conjugal union alone, makes itself felt solely for the State's glory and the public happiness: This is how women commanded at Sparta, and this is how you deserve to command at Geneva. What man would be so barbarous as to resist the voice of honor and reason from the mouth of a tender wife; and who would not despise vain luxury upon seeing your simple and modest attire which, by the radiance it owes to you, seems to complement beauty most. It is up to you, by your amiable and innocent dominion and your ingratiating wit, always to preserve the love of the laws in the State and Concord among the Citizens; by happy marriages to reunite divided families; and above all, by the persuasive gentleness of your lessons and the modest graciousness of your conversation, to correct the misconceptions our young Men acquire in other countries ... among lost women ... Therefore always be what you are, the chaste guardians of morals and the gentle bonds of peace, and continue at every opportunity to assert the rights of the Heart and of Nature on behalf of duty and virtue. (121–2)

39 While wives may not always be able to prevent their husbands from philandering, they can deny respectability to those women with whom they philander by excluding them from the company of decent women. This, in turn, typically has a pronounced influence on the behaviour of men. Gloucester seems to take a rather cavalier attitude towards his own adultery, but notice he does speak of Edmund's mother as a whore, and it is unlikely that he would expect his wife to accept any such woman's company.

40 Neither, of course, does their status simply exonerate them. Many people have to cope with the same or other prejudices equally burdensome, and do so without becoming vicious. The ranks of bastards include men whose virtues have carried them to great distinction, such as William the Conqueror, Erasmus, and T.E. Lawrence.

41 Edmund provides a concrete illustration of how the better, the stronger, of unattached, hence self-centred men are apt to think, and accordingly approach life. Such a

scenario likely sounds more familiar than one should wish, as there are localities in North America that already approximate this degenerate state of 'matriarchy amidst anarchy.' I imagine one would find there, particularly amongst the beleaguered women and all of the elderly, a most sympathetic appreciation of Hobbes's teaching about political life: that any regime which can effectively enforce law and order is preferable to this 'state of nature.' As Rousseau hinted in the passage quoted above (note 38), women have a special interest in the rule of law. If there is one prospect we 'postmoderns' should have no difficulty imagining, it is the nightmarish political and personal consequences of the breakdown of monogamous marriage and the resulting deterioration of the stable family life so essential to the healthy maturation of children, especially boys.

42 Conrad gives this point a special twist in having the narrator of 'The Informer' (*The Works of Joseph Conrad*, vol. 9, London: Heinemann, 1921) observe, "Anarchists, I suppose, have no families – not, at any rate, as we understand that social relation. Organization into families may answer to a need of human nature, but in the last instance it is based on law, and therefore must be something odious and impossible to an anarchist" (93).

43 It is a *family* tragedy; not only Lear, but his entire family is destroyed – his "mould" cracked and broken, his "germens" spilled and lost forever (cf. 3.2.8).

44 As Paul Cantor observes in his 'Nature and Convention in *King Lear*,' *Poets, Princes, and Private Citizens*, Joseph M. Knippenberg and Peter A. Lawler, eds. (Lanham, MD: Rowman and Littlefield 1996, 213–33), "Indeed, the problem of nature and convention is at the heart of *King Lear*" (218): "One should never underestimate the explosive potential of trying to distinguish between the natural and the conventional. As Lear's regime shows, any social order to some degree rests upon a confusion of the natural and the conventional. For a community to function smoothly, its citizens must become naturalized to the conventions by which it operates. Hence, rejecting convention in the name of nature always has a profoundly unsettling if not subversive effect on a community" (223).

45 The centrality of this issue has perhaps been best expressed by John E. Alvis in his 'Introductory' essay to the volume *Shakespeare as Political Thinker* ('Shakespearean Poetry and Politics'):

> Every Shakespearean character lives within a political regime governed by laws and shaped by distinctive institutions. How a character acts and how he perceives his deeds is affected, sometimes crucially affected, by his participation in the corporate life of a city or a realm. We might infer from his political focus that Shakespeare conceives the political context as a necessary condition for displaying, and hence also for understanding, human nature. Quite apart from the instinct of sexual love that brings man to woman or the need to exchange affection that keeps men and

women together and extends to kindred, and perhaps apart from the innate sociability that causes men to congregate on any terms, Shakespeare presents human beings seeking their completion within associations that maintain community by combining affection and compulsion. Shakespeare provokes his serious readers to consider in what sense this propensity to live in political community is natural to human beings. Is it natural merely in the sense of instinctual, habitual, or given; or is it natural in the sense of proper to the realization of the essential? The omnipresent political bearings of the plays invite, one may say, this first question of political philosophy. To pursue it at all satisfactorily, one is obliged to consider other questions relating to the view of human nature that appears to underlie the poetry. Politics does not exhaust Shakespeare's subject. We see political life transacted within horizons that enfold other activities; principal among these are sexual love, friendship, divine worship, the interactions of kinsmen, personal combat, and, in rare instances, the pursuit of private contemplation. We may discern the place of the political theme within Shakespeare's subject by gauging the weight of politics in relation to the other ends the dramatist allots to his characters. The estimate depends upon an assessment of what for Shakespeare constitutes a human life. Do his plays and poems imply a view of what essentially defines human beings?

The subject which for Shakespeare subsumes all others and which appears to be the distinctly human province is the activity of making choices. His characters deliberate towards choice, implement their decisions, and reflect upon the consequences of having chosen one possibility in preference to another. Every play builds toward, then moves from, an important act of choice which stands as a fulcrum transferring momentum of complication to momentum of resolution ... It appears that for Shakespeare the distinctly human mode of being – though not necessarily man's highest mode of being – reveals itself in acts of choice. Men are what they elect to do. (4–5)

46 Such legitimation after the fact figured hugely in the Tudors' shaky claim to the English throne, Henry Tudor tracing his descent from the House of Lancaster *via* its Beaufort line, which originates from John of Gaunt's adulterous liaison with Catherine Swynford (who later became his third wife, after both their previous spouses had died). Their bastard offspring were by Gaunt's request to his nephew, Richard II, granted legitimacy by Act of Parliament in 1397. However, at the instigation of Henry IV (one of Gaunt's legitimate sons by his first marriage), this Act of Legitimation was subsequently amended by royal decree so as expressly to exclude the Beauforts from the line of succession – unsuccessfully, as it turned out.

47 Cf. *Republic* 338b. This may not always suffice to ensure that one's benefactor "have no reasonable cause to repent him of his good will" (as Hobbes enjoins in laying down his "fourth Law of Nature" requiring gratitude in *Leviathan*, ch. 15, par. 16), but it may be all that can be reasonably required in some circumstances.

48 Great art, however, may provide a surrogate 'felt experience' upon which to base some

understanding. As Mark Schwehn observes, "The very best poetry does not simply instruct us *and* move us; it instructs us *by* moving us"; in '"King Lear Beyond Reason": Love and Justice in the Family,' *First Things* (36) (October 1993), 25.

49 At least this is made explicit in the Quarto version. Much of the relevant confrontation between Albany and Goneril was cut from the Folio version, beginning with his most pertinent – indeed, crucial – observation:

> I fear your disposition:
> That nature, which contemns its origin,
> Cannot be border'd certain in itself;
> She that herself will sliver and disbranch
> From her material sap, perforce must wither
> And come to deadly use. (4.2.31–6)

50 *The Prince*, ch. 17, par. 3–4. To this might be added Machiavelli's famously cynical explanation for advising the prince against taking the property of his own citizens and subjects: "because men forget the death of a father more quickly than the loss of a patrimony" (67).

51 *Leviathan*, ch. 11, par. 7

52 Obviously, it is much easier for we moderns to come to such an awareness than it would be for someone raised in a pre-modern, traditional, more-or-less closed society, barely aware that there *are* alternative ways. By contrast, the museum mentality of contemporary culture and the encyclopedic spirit of contemporary education (so brilliantly dissected by Nietzsche in *The Use and Disadvantage of History for Life*) is primarily dedicated to cultivating such an awareness – not that most people actually are brought to question the basic opinions of their own time and place, but they certainly are provided both opportunity and encouragement to do so.

53 Foakes, in the third Arden edition, points out that the first half of Cordelia's name alludes to 'heart' (as in 'cordial,' 'heartiness'; cf. Fr. *coeur*, from the Greek *Kēr* or *Kardia* via L. *cor*), but also that the second half is an anagram of 'ideal' (31, 96).

54 At the outset, however, we might note a curious complication in Shakespeare's treatment of eyes and the sense of sight. It has to do with the nose and the sense of smell, and the metaphoric uses to which they are put in the play (as in life). We encounter one such use prior to any mention of sight: Gloucester concludes his punning account of Edmund's conception by asking Kent, "Do you smell a fault?" (1.1.14–15). And that falseness, especially that of flattery, also has a smell to it seems to be implied by the King's Fool: "Truth's a dog must to kennel; he must be whipp'd out when the Lady's Brach may stand by th'fire and stink" (1.4.109–11). Lear claims to have "smelt out" the flatterers who told him he was everything (4.6.103). And when blind Gloucester begs to kiss his hand, Lear responds, "Let me wipe it first; it smells of mortality" (4.6.132). Most of the references to noses and smelling, however, are in immediate conjunction with eyes and sight, and directly invite reflection on these two so very dif-

ferent senses and the kind of perceptual access to the truth about the world they each provide. The Fool asks his master "why one's nose stands i'th'middle on's face," and then himself provides the not altogether foolish answer, "Why, to keep one's eyes of either side's nose, that what a man cannot smell out, he may spy into" (1.5.19–23). Later, replying to fettered Kent's query as to why the King is accompanied by "so small a number," the Fool offers this further piece of realism: "All that follow their noses are led by their eyes but blind men; and there's not a nose among twenty but can smell him that's stinking." (2.4.61–9). Regan, having urged her husband to put out the second of Gloucester's eyes, then facetiously suggests that he smell his way to Dover (3.7.91–2) – a nice confirmation of her vicious nature, as one could hardly mark the difference between these two senses more poignantly.

What are we to make of these juxtapositions of sight and smell, of visible objects and invisible odours, and their respective roles in disclosing the truth of things? At the least, they serve to remind us that while sight is the most useful of the senses, we don't know *what* we see without considerable learning; whereas, smell seems to be the most 'instinctive' sense, at least of the three that disclose objects at a distance – that prior to any learning or experience, we find the odour of certain things attractive (nutritious things, for example, and flowers, such as those Lear decks himself in; 4.4.2–5), and the odour of other things repellent (noxious things, such as toxic substances, body wastes, and decay). These instinctive sensations are the basis, of course, for our metaphoric use of olfactory language. It is with such considerations in mind that we comprehend the sermon "preached" by a disillusioned Lear: "the first time that we smell the air we wawl and cry" in lamentation "that we are come / To this great stage of fools" (4.6.177–81). Perhaps in light of that, one might ponder the larger significance, both political and philosophic, of perfume (cf. 3.4.103).

55 Heilman (*This Great Stage*) devotes a chapter to 'The Sight Pattern,' and as with the other thematic patterns he identifies in the play, he does an admirably thorough job of assembling the textual evidence. On its basis, he contends, "By a full and varied use of all the functions of men's eyes Shakespeare has achieved a rich, multivalued symbolic expression of man's moral make-up" (62). I more than agree with this judgment, since I see still more dimensions to the significance than those Heilman explores. He is mainly concerned to draw the contrast between sight and insight, and in that vein makes some important connections (e.g., "Cordelia exemplifies the human being who sees because she does feel ... She feels compassion and cries; the tears come from the eyes; feeling and seeing are identified" 61). But in judging that with respect to the state of Lear's mind and temperament in the play's opening scene the elder sisters "see things only too clearly," he shares their mistake, and it compromises much of his overall analysis (58).

56 Given sufficient light, that is; cf. *Republic* 507c–508e.

57 This is another point about which, I believe, Cavell grossly misunderstands the text,

seeing Lear's words as "the only active cruelty given to Lear by Shakespeare, apart from his behavior in the abdication scene. But here it seems uncaused, deliberate cruelty inflicted for its own sake upon Gloucester's eyes" (*Disowning Knowledge*, 50–1). Far from this being so, Lear's apparently disjointed remarks elicited by the sight of disfigured Gloucester express the old King's deeper preoccupation with sex and its consequences that surfaces repeatedly throughout this scene (4.6).

58 James Shreeve, in *The Neandertal Enigma* (New York: William Morrow, 1995) reports:

> Human mate recognition systems are overwhelmingly visual. 'Love comes in at the eye,' wrote Yeats, and the upright, bipedal posture provides a lot of sexual signals for the eye to take in ... But the locus of the human body that lures, captures, and holds the eye most of all is the face. In one recent study, when American women were asked what part of a man's body they looked at first, 77 percent answered either the face or the eyes ...
>
> Human faces are exquisitely expressive instruments. Behind our facial skin lies an intricate web of musculature, concentrated especially around the eyes and mouth, evolved purely for social communication – expressing interest, fear, suspicion, joy, contentment, doubt, surprise, and countless other emotions. Each emotion can be further modified by the raise of an eyebrow or the slight flick of a cheek muscle to express, say, measured surprise, wild surprise, disappointed surprise, feigned surprise, and so on. By one estimate, the twenty two expressive muscles on each side of the face can be called on to produce ten thousand different facial actions or expressions.
>
> Among this armory of social signals are stereotyped formal invitations to potential mates. The mating display we call flirtation plays the same on the face of a New Guinean tribeswoman as it does on the features of a *lycienne* in a Parisian café: a bashful lowering of the gaze to the side and down, followed by a furtive look at the other's face and the coy retreat of the eyes. (203–4)

59 This entire scene is absent from the Folio version. It, and the scene it hearkens back to (3.1) – both of which in the Quarto version provide so much important detail as to the broader political context – go far (in my opinion) towards justifying the long-established practice of integrating the two versions, at least for purposes of reading.

60 As already noted, the eyes are expressive in many ways, and accordingly we pay special attention to each other's eyes. Moreover, the 'mechanism' for producing tears is already in place, since the eye requires regular lubrication for normal functioning. There may be no more to the mystery of 'why tears' than this. But means of producing tears do not explain weeping; many animals have tear ducts.

61 Tears work for this purpose precisely because most people cannot cry at will, whereas with but a little practice almost anyone can imitate the *sounds* of sadness and distress – the sighs and moans and "wawls" – as well as the gestures. This is true of most passion-

ate states: anger, joy, fear, excitement. Perhaps the other expression of the soul most difficult to imitate convincingly is laughter: the kind of spontaneous body-shaking, soul-dominating reaction to perceived absurdity that (strangely) can also terminate in tears, though of a very different kind. Tears and laughter, like tragedy and comedy, would seem to bracket the range of human response to their world. That there is so little to laugh at in *King Lear*, that even its official Fool is a "bitter fool" (1.4.132–48), may be taken as indicating the incompleteness of the view of human life it offers.

62 Among students of the play, Albany's brusque "No tearing, lady" (5.3.156) is usually construed as meaning 'no ripping' of her letter with which he has just confronted Edmund ("Hold, sir; / Thou worse than any name, read thine own evil: / No tearing, Lady; I perceive you know it"). This is a likely interpretation, but given the two meanings of 'tear,' it is possible that it is instead a rejection of a cynical appeal for sympathy by Goneril.

63 Surely one of the most curious features of Rousseau's *Second Discourse* is his seeming to argue that humans are by nature compassionate (indeed, that pity or commiseration is one the two primary motors of the human *psychē*, second only to self-regard), while also maintaining that humans are by nature solitary beings possessed of only the passions they need. This 'paradox' may serve to alert his reader that things are not at all what they first seem in that book. Also relevant here is Rousseau's discussion in *Emile* of the significance of a baby's tears (New York: Basic Books, 1979, 65–9; see also Allan Bloom's Introduction, 10–11).

64 An idea figuring in philosophical literature at least since Plato's *Republic*; cf. 518b–519b, 533c.

65 Here, as so often in reading Shakespeare, one is reminded of the *Essays* of Francis Bacon, who includes the following example in his discussion 'Of Cunning': "Some procure themselves to be surprised at such times as it is like the party that they work upon will suddenly come upon them; and to be found with a letter in their hand, or doing somewhat which they are not accustomed; to the end they may be apposed of those things which of themselves they are desirous to utter" (*The Works* ... vol. 6, 430).

Recall, when Gloucester asks Edmund about the letter, "When came you to this? Who brought it?" Edmund replies, "It was not brought me, my Lord; there's the *cunning* of it; I found it thrown in at the casement of my closet" (1.2.57–9). And we can see that this is indeed "the cunning of it," for it is a lie in which Edmund risks no possibility of exposure, regardless of whether or not it succeeds in its intended purpose. And yet, it is a most unlikely – hence implausible – conspiracy. What's in it for Edgar? If he were willing to do away with his father, why would he be willing to share the proceeds with his illegitimate brother? But nobody, beginning with old Gloucester himself, seems to notice this.

66 See note 59 above.

67 There are more mentions of 'wisdom' in *King Lear* (ten) than in any other of Shake-

speare's plays; *Macbeth* is second with eight; *Hamlet* has seven (or eight, if we include the mention of 'wisdoms' at 1.2.15). And while the sheer diversity of the contexts in which the word is used tacitly raises the question of what wisdom truly is, surely heading the list of possibilities must be that contained in Gloucester's naïve "These late eclipses in the sun and moon portend no good to us: though the wisdom of Nature can reason it thus and thus, yet Nature finds itself scourg'd by the sequent effects" (1.2.100–3). Ah, yes – "the wisdom of Nature" as a basis for reasoning.

68 One might see some shadow of Lear's hard lesson in the political experiences of Xenophon and Thucydides, which similarly resulted in their lives taking a philosophical turn – fortunately for them and us, at a much earlier age. In Plato's *Republic*, the seducements of political life are treated as the primary threat to those rare natures best suited for philosophy (490e–495b), though Sokrates concludes his analysis with four or five ways that a few fitting candidates none the less remain "to consort with philosophy in a way that is worthy" – the first, being forced into political exile (496a–c).

69 While citing neither the prodding of Aristophanes nor any other untoward personal experience, Sokrates in Plato's *Phaedo* explains why he eventually found the kind of philosophizing depicted in *Clouds* to be unsatisfactory, hence why he turned his attention back to political life in his search for wisdom of use to human beings. In doing so, he thereby (as Cicero observes) "called philosophy down from the heavens and established her in the cities" (*Tusculan Disputations* V.4.10). And according to T.W. Baldwin, in *William Shakspere's Small Latine & Lesse Greeke* vol. 2 (Urbana: University of Illinois Press, 1944), there is ample evidence in the plays (especially *Hamlet*) for concluding "that Shakspere had learned his *Tusculan Disputations* in the way that a learned grammarian was supposed to have learned them"; moreover, that he had read them in the original Latin (607–8, 610; cf. 601–10).

70 Cf. *Republic* 474b–c, 487e, 498e, 501e, 499b–c, 502a, 503b, 540d, 543a, 592a–b.

71 So far as I know, the best treatment of this matter is found in Leo Strauss, *Natural Right and History* (Chicago: University of Chicago Press, 1953), ch. 3.

72 At the very least, Shakespeare was acquainted with certain of the characteristic doctrines of some famous pre- and post-Sokratics. Paul Stapfer, in his astute appraisal of 'Shakespeare's Classical Knowledge' in *Shakespeare and Classical Antiquity*, Emily J. Carey, trans. (1880; reprint, New York: Burt Franklin, 1970, ch. 4), conveniently summarizes some of relevant dramatic evidence (93–4):

> Pythagoras is several times mentioned in Shakespeare, and always with some ironical allusion to his doctrine of the transmigration of souls. The lively Gratiano, in the 'Merchant of Venice,' tells Shylock that he must have been a wolf in a former existence (Act IV., Sc. 1); Rosalind, in 'As You Like It,' has a confused recollection of having once been an Irish rat (Act III., Sc. 2); and in 'Twelfth Night,' the clown, when mocking and jeering at Malvolio, advises him not to kill

a woodcock lest he should thereby dislodge the soul of his grandmother (Act IV., Sc 2). The authority of Pythagoras is invoked by name in each of these three passages.

Shakespeare alludes to Heraclitus, though without mentioning his name, in Act I., Sc. 2, of the 'Merchant of Venice,' in which Portia says of one of her suitors, the melancholy and morose County Palatine, that when he grows old he will become like the weeping philosopher.

Epicurus is only treated as the voluptuous materialist of common tradition, and is thus presented in 'Antony and Cleopatra' (Act II., Sc. 1); in 'King Lear' (Act I., Sc. 4); in 'Macbeth' (Act V., Sc. 3) and in the 'Merry Wives of Windsor' (Act II., Sc. 2).

Where or how Shakespeare acquired whatever he knew of these and other ancient thinkers, whether it was by means of his own allegedly "small Latine and lesse Greeke," or merely heard or read about them from others, God only knows. According to Herbert S. Long's Introduction to the modern Loeb edition of Diogenes Laertius, *Lives and Opinions of Eminent Philosophers*, "The first parts of Diogenes to be printed were the lives of Aristotle and Theophrastus, included in the Aldine Aristotle of 1497. The *editio princeps* of the whole Greek text was published by Froben at Basel in 1533 ..." (1925 originally published; reprint, Cambridge: Harvard University Press, 1980, xxiv). Aristotle's discussions of his predecessors' views in various treatises, available in Latin translations as well as in the original Greek, is another possibility (*Nicomachean Ethics* was the only Aristotle text available in English translation in Shakespeare's day; allusion to it in *Troilus and Cressida* [2.2.166–8] is one of the oft-cited 'anachronisms' of that play).

We get a clear indication from the works of Shakespeare's contemporaries that a fairly broad acquaintance with the ancient philosophers was somehow a practical possibility in his day. Francis Bacon, for example, was familiar with the doctrines of Heraclitus, Democritus, Leucippus, Anaxagoras, Parmenides, Empedocles, Pythagoras, Zeno, Epicurus, Xenophanes, Philolaus, as well as with the writings of Plato and Aristotle. This much is evident from references to them in his *New Organon*; see, e.g., aphorisms 42, 51, 57, 63, 65, 67, 71.

73 It is with respect to this dimension of the story that I find myself in closest agreement with David Lowenthal's analysis in *Shakespeare and the Good Life.* I have long since lost track of what particulars in my own account are owing to his insights, but I'm sure they are many. Also very useful here is Paul Cantor's 'Nature and Convention in *King Lear.*'

74 This is well illustrated in book 1 of Aristotle's *Politics.*

75 Contrary, that is, to the accounts of political society such as one finds in Hobbes and Locke, which are based on conceptions of the 'atomic individual.' However, it is worth noting that in his *Second Treatise of Government*, Locke (like Aristotle) discusses familial relations immediately before his chapter 'Of Political or Civil Society' (ch. 7).

76 Suffice it to note that the meanings of virtually all words exist 'by convention.' Thus, if one agrees that the use of speech is natural to human beings, and that it is the countless uses of rational speech that essentially distinguishes us from dumb brutes, then an adequate conception of Nature must comprehend conventions.

77 Cf. *Republic* 515c, 518d–519a, 521c.

78 One might see in this a tacit challenge to Catholic Christianity's interpretation of the account of the origin of the world given in *Genesis*, that it is to be understood not merely as God imposing order on a chaos of elements, but as *creatio ex nihilo*, this being a reflection of God's omnipotence. That such a view is rationally *inconceivable* for the human mind, that it could be believed only as an article of faith (and in recognition of the inadequacy of the human mind for dealing with ultimate questions), points to the essential difference between religion and philosophy, rival intellectual authorities for human beings throughout history (cf. 1.1.220–2).

79 In substantial terms, that is. For any such attempt to imagine the world (or 'reality') tacitly concedes its 'oneness,' which implies some minimum of coherence – that 'it all hangs together' somehow. Whereas attempting to imagine the world actually cohering in a manner different from that of one's coherent account of the world can at best produce but another (i.e., alternative) coherent *account* of the world, generated by the same rational means as the first, thus presuming – rather than proving – the congruence of human reason with the world.

80 It is worth remarking that one's evaluation of this particular creation of Shakespeare's imagination, his *King Lear*, depends fundamentally on discerning *its* rational coherence, which involves more than simply matters of logic. It includes an appreciation of its *psycho*-logical and 'musical' coherence: the interplay between passion and reason in the characters, the harmony of its poetic and symbolic elements with its plot. And similar considerations apply, of course, to assessing the adequacy of any interpretation of the play. Whatever persuasiveness it carries will be primarily a function of its coherence.

81 Cf. *Republic* 509d–511e.

82 Deranged, or 'mad,' is not the same as 'retarded,' meaning underdeveloped, and thus more child-like than irrational – although retardation and immaturity can also be revealing about the nature of human rationality.

83 It is noteworthy in this connection that Sokrates, in telling his 'Cave Allegory,' speaks repeatedly of how *painful* one is apt to find liberation from the comfortable shackles of cave life (*Republic* 515c–516a).

84 Cf. ibid, 503c–d; Bacon's *New Organon*, aphs. XLVIII, XLIX, LIII, LV.

85 Lear's conclusion here, that man is but "a poor, bare, forked animal" is unmistakably reminiscent of the definition reached through the almost mechanical kind of 'dialectical analysis' practiced by the Eleatic Stranger in Plato's *Politikos* ('Statesman'): that man is essentially a 'featherless biped' (266e). The Eleatic School is understood as having

originated with the pre-Sokratic philosopher Parmenides of Elea, but is also closely identified with his pupil, Zeno, famous for his paradoxes.

86 Cf. Aristophanes, *Clouds* 374ff.

87 Of this pregnant moment, Paul Cantor observes ('Nature and Convention in *King Lear*,' 215): "The stage is thus set for what might well be the most profound dialogue in all of Shakespeare's plays, a king and a philosopher enquiring into the principles that govern nature and into how those principles might be related to the curing of human ills. But Shakespeare tantalyzingly denies us access to the most profound conversation in the central scene of his greatest play. Lear and his philosopher drift away from center stage, and whatever words they exchange are drowned out by the noise of the storm and Gloucester's conventional observations to the disguised Kent. Nevertheless, the very fact of their meeting points to a larger question raised by the play as a whole: what is the relation of wisdom and political power? Perhaps *King Lear* as a whole offers what III.iv seems to deny us: a dialogue about philosophy and kingship."

88 There are no really famous pre- or post-Sokratic philosophers associated with Thebes (though there is a minor figure named Crates [*Kratēs*], who was born in Thebes, but came to Athens where he adopted Cynicism under the tutelage of Diogenes). But might Shakespeare's King Lear have in mind King Oedipus, who not only solved the riddle of the Sphinx – and remember: the answer is 'man' – but whose infamous deeds involving his father and his mother are fully allowable according to Edmund's conception of Nature (which is now Lear's, if only temporarily), though they provoked Jocasta to hang herself and Oedipus to blind himself?

89 Virtually from its origins, philosophy has been associated with atheism. In defending himself against the prejudicial rumours that have circulated about him in particular – that he thinks about things aloft and investigates things beneath the earth – Sokrates explicitly links them to atheism: for people who hear about such investigators suppose that they "do not believe in gods" (*Apology of Sokrates* 18b–c; see also 26c).

90 Here one might be reminded of the hovel in Aristophanes' *Clouds*, the so-called Thinkery (*phrontistērion*) wherein dwelled the unkempt, shoeless, and "miserably unhappy" Sokrates, who also is solicited by an old man seeking a certain wisdom.

91 Shakespeare signals the basic relationship between our natural needs and the coming into being of the arts by having Lear speak of "the art of our necessities" (3.2.70). According to Plato's Sokrates, this relationship between the multiplicity of human needs and the various technical specialities devoted to meeting them is the practical basis of the political association, and the resulting mutual interdependence of citizen-artisans is a reflection of man's political nature (*Republic* 369b–370c).

92 Cf. ibid., 372c–e.

93 Or so it is in the Quarto version. This symbolically important detail was cut from the Folio, along with the presence of the doctor (his lines being given to the anonymous Gentleman). As does clothing for the body, so music for the soul nicely illustrates the

entwining of art, nature, and convention. The music is artificially generated, but the harmony of the sounds is natural (indeed, amenable to mathematical analysis); and often convention determines what sort of music is appropriate (compare marriages with funerals, Christmas with Olympic Games).

94 *Republic*, 338c–e. Thrasymachus's view anticipates several prominent modern variants, notably that of Marxism and Legal Positivism.

95 Cf. *Apology of Sokrates* 38c, 41d; *Crito* 53d–e.

96 Cf. *Republic* 536b–c; *Apology of Sokrates* 35e.

97 That facets of the problem (especially people's intentional manipulation of appearances) figure more or less overtly in most if not all of his plays attests to Shakespeare's own appreciation of its pervasive, inescapable importance.

98 Paul Cantor's prescient observation (cited earlier, note 87) is here worth reviewing. Heilman, *This Great Stage*, also speaks of "the philosophical Edgar" (44). Foakes in the third Arden edition *King Lear* on the other hand, rather depreciates Edgar and his significance for the play, generally finding his "moralizing" shallow and inappropriate (cf. e.g., 49, 364). It is not clear, however, that Foakes and the sources he cites in support of his view truly understand quite what Edgar is saying, much less why he says it. Danby, in *Shakespeare's Doctrine of Nature*, offers a more insightful assessment (189–91).

99 It is with respect to Edgar's story that the difference in the two versions of the text is of some importance, especially in the attribution of the last speech in the play. For reasons I hope to make clear, the Folio's attributing it to Edgar is to be much preferred over the Quarto's giving it to Albany. I do not believe it represents a change so much as a clarification in Shakespeare's conception of the play.

100 Danby, *Shakespeare's Doctrine*, credits Edgar with "a virtue of duplicity" that is equally Machiavellian but more than a match for the "pleated cunning" of the elder sisters:

> Edgar, therefore, slips from role to role. Poor Tom is followed by the peasant, the peasant by the gentleman, the gentleman by the shining champion, until finally Edgar is himself again, and, with Kent, is made King of England. The roles in their sequence suggest two things: the singleness of the essential nature of man at every level and in every social function; second, the ability of the seed of 'natural honesty' to quicken the Beggarman and transform the beggarman into a King. Edgar at the end of the play is the national champion of the Falconbridge tradition; the Kingly nature as inherent in the stuff of valiant humanity rather than in any dynastic title to a throne. (190–1)

Good points, but needing amendment. We know that Kent, of course, declines any share of the royal power, and dies more or less immediately. And Danby leaves out of this sequence the 'role' of wealthy playboy, which (according to Edgar's own account, 3.4.83–96) is his status at the play's beginning.

101 Adeimantos, Sokrates' other primary interlocutor, is a full brother to Glaukon, and –

in contrast to Edgar's half-brother Edmund – is an excellent young man in his own right. But he is inescapably wedded to political life, and as such, is at most and best a sympathetic friend to philosophy, a gentleman open to being advised by a philosopher. For a detailed comparison of the natures of Glaukon and Adeimantos, see Craig, *The War Lover: A Study of Plato's Republic* (Toronto: University of Toronto Press, 1994), ch. 5.

102 This parody of a trial is one of the least-accepted omissions from the Folio version.

103 'Dover' – a name that occurs only twelve times in the canon, ten of them being in *King Lear* – apparently has a symbolic meaning in this play, which the reader is challenged to ascertain. It's special significance is signaled by the thrice-asked question, "Wherefore to Dover?" (3.7.51–4).

104 Edgar's continued refusal to reveal himself to his father even after having cured him of his despair (exploiting the old man's beliefs in order to teach him a truth: "Thy life's a miracle" 4.6.55) has long been a scholarly crux. The explanation for it, I suspect, is implicit in what happens to Gloucester when Edgar – going to do battle-to-the-death with Edmund, "Not sure, but hoping, of this good success" – finally does reveal himself: Gloucester immediately dies (5.3.192–8; cf. 4.1.23).

105 According to *The* History Today *Companion to British History* (London: Collins and Brown, 1995), Edgar, King of the English from 959 to 975, also had first to wrest his dominion from his brother, but that his reign "was apparently largely peaceful and successful" (267).

4: "Sweet Philosophy"

1 James Engell and W. Jackson Bate, eds., *Biographia Literaria* vol. 2 (Princeton: Princeton University Press, 1983), 19, 25–7.

2 This being the familiar abbreviation of the formula first enunciated at 473c–d of Plato's *Republic*: "Unless the philosophers rule as kings in the polities or those now said to be kings and lords genuinely and adequately philosophize, and political power and philosophy coalesce in the same place, while the many natures now pursuing either apart from the other are by necessity excluded, there can be no rest from ills, dear Glaukon, for the polities, nor I believe for the human race."

The best exploration of the inherent tension between philosophy and politics remains that of Plato in his treatment of the life and fate of Sokrates. The essentials of the problem are presented in his *Apology of Sokrates*, and extensively analysed in his *Republic*, which Allan Bloom so aptly deemed "the true *Apology* of Socrates." As he observes in *The Republic of Plato* (New York: Basic Books, 1968) by way of beginning the 'Interpretive Essay' which accompanies his translation of the dialogue: "Only in the *Republic* does [Socrates] give an adequate treatment of the theme which was forced on him by Athens' accusation against him. That theme is the relationship of the philosopher to the political community" (307). How the idea of a philosopher-king attempts to reconcile the various problems philosophy and politics present each other, and why it is none the less paradoxical, is treated in detail in my study of the *Republic*, *The War Lover*.

3 John Russell Brown ed., in the Arden edition (whose version of the text I generally rely upon), supplies the following in his note on the term 'commodity': "Clarendon quoted Thomas, *History of Italy* (1549), Z1: 'Al men, specially strangers, haue so muche libertee there, that though they speake verie ill by the Venetians, so they attempt nothyng in effecte against theyr astate, no man shall controll them for it ... If thou be a Jewe, a Turke, or beleeuest in the diuell (so thou spreade not thyne opinions abroade) thou arte free from all controllement'" (93).

4 Indeed, might Shakespeare's own ironic judgment be encapsulated in his eponym's bitter, "I cry you mercy, / I took you for that cunning whore of Venice, / That married with Othello" (4.2.90–2)? And this, in turn, connect with his earlier private musing: "this is a subtle whore, / A closet, lock and key, of villainous secrets, / And yet she'll kneel and pray, I ha' seen her do't" (21–3)? Be that as it may, one can scarce avoid suspecting that Othello's insecure status in Venice influences much of what he says and does and feels, beginning with the dubious way he manages to marry into one of the leading houses of Venice, carrying off a Senator's daughter in the middle of the night. While it would grossly undervalue his standing to regard him as just another "knave of common hire" (cf. 1.1.125), he doubtless is aware that he's of little use – hence importance – to Venice in peacetime. His situation reminds one of Hobbes's discussion in *Leviathan* of how the worth of a man is relative to circumstance, at least in the sort of 'bourgeois' polity Hobbes outlines and Venice exemplifies: "The *value*, or WORTH of a man, is as of all other things his Price; that is to say, so much as would be given for the use of his Power: and therefore in not absolute; but a thing dependant on the need and judgment of another. An able conductor of Souldiers, is of great Price in time of War present, or imminent; but in Peace not so. A learned and uncorrupt judge, is much Worth in time of Peace; but not so much in War. And as in other things, so in men, not the seller, but the buyer determines the price. For let a man (as most men do,) rate themselves as the highest Value they can; yet their true Value is no more than it is esteemed by others" (ch. 10, par. 16.).

Thus, despite having been idle the past nine months (1.3.84), Othello does not choose to elope with Desdemona until political events once more make indispensible expertise such as his (1.1.147–53; cf. 1.3.44–6). From beginning to end, Othello speaks as if he believed that his past labours leave Venice morally indebted to him: "My services, which I have done the signiory, shall out-tongue [Brabantio's] complaints"; (1.2.18–19; cf. 5.2.340), but his actions suggest a somewhat more realistic understanding of his situation. Still, Iago quite likely has Othello in mind when he ridicules loyal service:

You shall mark
Many a duteous and knee-crooking knave.
That, doting on his own obsequious bondage,
Wears out his time much like his master's ass,
For nought but provender, and when he's old, cashier'd,
Whip me such honest knaves ... (1.1.44–9; see also 1.3.400; 2.1.304)

A decidedly mercantile, if not mercenary mentality manifests itself in the language of both Venetian plays. In *The Merchant of Venice*, money is a major factor in both Bassanio's and Lorenzo's choice of marriage partners, and Gratiano speaks of marriage itself as solemnizing "the bargain of your faith" (3.2.193). Even Portia uses such language, remarking to Bassanio, "Since you are dear bought, I will love you dear" (312). Othello leads Desdemona away with "come, my dear love, / The purchase made, the fruits are to ensue, / The profit's yet to come 'twixt me and you" (2.3.8–10). According to W.H. Auden in *The Dyer's Hand*, since "love and understanding breed love and understanding ... with the rise of a merchantile economy in which money breeds money, it became an amusing paradox for poets to use the ignoble activity of usury as a metaphor for love, the most noble of human activities" (230).

Pamela Jensen provides an especially useful analysis of the modern Venetian republic's way of maintaining civilian authority over its military, contrasting it with the ancient Roman republic's arrangement: '"This is Venice": Politics in Shakespeare's *Othello*' in *Shakespeare's Political Pageant*, Joseph Alulis and Vickie Sullivan, eds. (Lanham, MD: Rowman and Littlefield, 1996), 155–87.

All my textual references to *Othello* are to the Arden edition, M.R. Ridley, ed. (London: Methuen, 1958).

5 Not so incidentally, *The Merchant of Venice* can be read as an allegory illustrating the proper relationship between philosophy and politics, which necessarily also involves considering the relationship between philosophy and religion. Portia, dwelling in a higher, fairer place (Belmont), and explicitly linked to her ancient namesake (daughter of the the philosopher Cato; 1.1.165–6), represents classical philosophy. And when she goes down into The Cave of the Polity (Venice) to set things right, she goes incognito, adopting the appearance and manners of a man in order to be accepted in the masculine realm of politics, where force competes with reason. Not herself ruled *by* the law, she uses it – and if necessary, misuses it – to bring about a more equitable outcome and restore something like civic harmony to the city, reaffirming and even strengthening its established religion, but at a cost perhaps not altogether just to a conflicting religion. Shylock's coerced conversion symbolically points to what wisdom determines is politically most salutary: a single religion as the basis for a unified polity (cf. *Republic* 427b–c). The mode of her intervention in Venice complements the way she also rules at Belmont: indirectly. While ostensibly abiding by the 'rules,' she cleverly manipulates matters so that things turn out as they should (i.e., as she wants). Shakespeare here por-

trays what he understands is the deeper teaching of Plato's *Republic*: philosophical kingship being at best a most remote possibility, the more practical way philosophy *can* 'rule' is indirectly, not in its own name and identity but through intermediaries (officially Portia-as-Balthazar is merely a 'technical advisor' to the Duke). In this sense, philosophy's actual mode of rule is 'feminine' in character.

But Portia/philosophy goes down into the city for a second purpose: to release and lead out of the Cave a suitable young man (Bassanio is described as both a lover of learning and a warrior – "a scholar and a soldier"; 1.2.109 – that rare combination of qualities requisite in one genuinely suited for philosophy; cf. *Republic* 503b–d) in order that he, too, can enjoy contemplating the heavenly things from the vantage of Belmont, and do so moreover with a clear conscience. Precisely because *The Merchant of Venice* manifests this feminine rule of Wisdom, it is a comedy. And because a comparable rule is absent in *Othello*, and a perversion of it active in its place (see following note), this other Venetian play is a tragedy. For a similar and somewhat fuller treatment of *The Merchant of Venice* as an allegory relating philosophy and politics, see Barbara Tovey, 'The Golden Casket: An Interpretation of *The Merchant of Venice*,' in *Shakespeare as Political Thinker*, 2nd ed., John E. Alvis and Thomas G. West eds. (Wilmington, DE: ISI Books, 2000), 261–87.

6 It is doubtless with Coleridge's famous dismissal of Iago's expressed motivation in mind ("the motive-hunting of a motiveless malignity") that Hazlitt argues instead (as quoted in Jonathan Bate, *The Romantics on Shakespeare*):

> The character of Iago is one of the supererogations of Shakespear's genius. Some persons, more nice than wise, have thought this whole character unnatural, because his villainy is *without a sufficient motive*. Shakespear, who was as good a philosopher as he was a poet, thought otherwise. He knew that the love of power, which is another name for the love of mischief, is natural to man. He would know this as well or better than if it had been demonstrated to him by a logical diagram, merely from seeing children paddle in the dirt or kill flies for sport. Iago in fact belongs to a class of character common to Shakespear and at the same time peculiar to him; whose heads are as acute and active as their hearts are hard and callous. Iago is to be sure an extreme instance of the kind; that is to say, of diseased intellectual activity, with the most perfect indifference to moral good or evil, or rather with a decided preference for the latter, because it falls more readily in with his favourite propensity, gives greater zest to his thoughts and scope to his actions ... 'Our ancient' is a philosopher ... who plots the ruin of his friends as an exercise for his ingenuity, and stabs men in the dark to prevent *ennui*. (491–2)

In a somewhat similar vein, Stanley Wells, in *Shakespeare: A Life in Drama* (New York: W.W. Norton, 1995), observes "Irony is an intellectual quality, and *Othello* is an intellectual play in the sense that Iago's mind and intuition work overtime as he intrigues to bring about Othello's downfall; his insistence on the power of reason over passion, or instinct, is indeed a sign of his villainy" (246). I certainly believe that Hazlitt goes too far in denominating Iago a philosopher, as does Wells in regarding a character's preference for reason over passion to be a sure sign of villainy in Shakespeare. But we can agree that Iago is very intelligent, energetic, an astute observer unclouded by sentiment, with deep insight into human nature (especially human weaknesses), one who "knows all qualities, with a learned spirit, of human dealing" (3.3.263–4) – the better to exploit them. He is amused by his power to manipulate others, for causing psychic effects. He positively revels in the discrepancy between his appearance ("honest, honest Iago") and his reality ("I am not what I am"). Indeed, he is far and away the most intelligent and practically knowledgeable character in the play – one who "works by wit, not witchcraft" – and has a boldness to match. All this is what makes him such a puzzle. One might crystalize the issue by asking, 'Why *isn't* he a philosopher? what's missing?'

With Iago in mind, one might consider Sokrates' explaining why the perversion or corruption of the philosophic nature is the rule, not the exception: "Concerning every seed or thing that grows, either from the earth or animals, ... we know that the more vigorous it is, the more it is deficient in its own properties when it doesn't get the food, climate, or place fitting for it. For bad is more opposed to good than to not-good ... Won't we say for souls too ... that, similarly, those that are best-natured become exceptionally bad when they get bad education? Or do you suppose that great injustice and unmixed villainy come from a paltry nature, and not from a lusty one corrupted by its rearing – whereas a weak nature will never be a cause of great things, neither good nor bad?" (*Republic* 491d–e).

I believe Auden is right to contend, "Any consideration of the Tragedy of Othello must be primarily occupied, not with its official hero but with its villain" (*The Dyer's Hand*, 246). Auden's own analysis leads him to suggest what must be one of the most arresting interpretive possibilities: "For is not Iago, the practical joker, a parabolic figure for the autonomous pursuit of scientific knowledge through experiment which we all, whether we are scientists or not, take for granted as natural and right?" (270). Insofar as Iago is simply curious, and wishes to discover what effects he can cause (thereby exerting the power of his will), the image fits. But since his interests are exclusively destructive, it is not sufficient to identify him with the neutral, 'objective' pursuit of all knowledge; ostensibly, the preponderance of modern science remains committed to the Baconian formula: the relief of man's estate. Iago's preference for acquiring knowledge for doing evil remains to be accounted for.

7 It seems that most modern, and practically all postmodern, critics of the play regard Iago as its leading racist, seeing this as at least part of the explanation for his hatred of Othello. But the evidence typically cited comes from his speeches to other characters, which in this as in all other respects are tailored to work upon *their* susceptibilities.

The fact that in his private speech he refers to Othello as 'The Moor' shows nothing, since everyone in the play does so, including Desdemona – indeed, speaking in his presence she calls him 'The Moor' twice before ever using his name (1.3.189, 248, 252). The Duke is the first to address Othello by name ("Valiant Othello"; 48), and is the only character who does so exclusively. The thirteenth century Mongol rulers of China may have been racially prejudiced along with their subjects, but one would want more evidence for this conclusion than Marco Polo's being frequently referred to as 'The Venetian.' There can be little doubt, I believe, that Shakespeare fully anticipated the general presumption that Iago shares the racial prejudice he so skillfully arouses and exploits in others. But mightn't Iago's actually being free of this particular human stupidity be one more indication of his superior intelligence?

Since the matter of race and the various prejudices that typically attend its recognition are so obviously pertinent to this play (as anti-Semitism is to *The Merchant of Venice*), a few cautionary remarks are in order – especially since so many of the more recent writers who address this play seem to have chosen it mainly as a vehicle for exposing (with suitable condescension and indignation) the 'pervasive racism' (and 'sexism,' of course) of Shakespeare and/or the culture for which he wrote, and/or represented, and/or sought to legitimate. While some of these critics simply dismiss all the white male characters as racist, others judge this epithet applicable to but a subset of them, agreeing that it includes old Brabantio as well as Iago and Roderigo, whoever else. Yet, is the fact that Brabantio is vehemently opposed to his daughter marrying Othello, and scandalized by the very thought of it, necessarily evidence that he is a racist? To be sure, he is exceedingly angry with Othello, and says some very harsh things to him, including some pejorative allusions to his race. But who wouldn't be angry to find his generous hospitality so abused? and harshly critical of any man luring away his daughter in the middle of the night with no better excuse than anticipation of the father's refusal of the match? Brabantio finds the idea of such a marriage *unnatural* (1.3.62), not only on grounds of racial difference, but of Desdemona's previous disinclination to marry ("So opposite to marriage, that she shunn'd / The wealthy curled darlings of our nation"; 1.2.67–8), of temperament, of culture, social standing, and gross disparity of age:

A maiden never bold of spirit,
So still and quiet, that her motion
Blush'd at her self: and she, in spite of nature,
Of years, of country, credit, everything,
To fall in love with what she fear'd to look on?
It is a judgment maim'd, and most imperfect,
That will confess perfection so would err
Against all rules of nature ... (1.3.94–101)

Othello would not, and does not, dispute a word of this; his later explict recognition of its truth ('And yet how nature erring from itself –') encourages Iago to reiterate several of Brabantio's points:

> Not to affect many proposed matches,
> Of her own clime, complexion, and degree,
> Whereto we see in all things nature tends;
> Fie, we may smell in such a will most rank,
> foul disproportion; thoughts unnatural. (3.3.231–7; cf. 267–70)

These three very different men apparently share the view of what is natural with respect to *mating*: all things mate with their own kind. There are hundreds of varieties of sparrows genetically capable of interbreeding, but they almost never do. Similarly, there are dozens of kinds of ducks, but mallards mate with mallards, not canvasbacks. Recognition of these facts of nature carries no implications for judging one kind of duck or sparrow to be superior to the other – it is simply 'the natural way' of all things. Similarly, then, accepting the applicability of such a view of the natural to human beings needn't imply any beliefs about racial superiority or inferiority (after all, that seems an unlikely attribution to Othello, whatever one may suspect of Brabantio or Iago). For most animals, of course, the visible 'look,' along with sounds and smells, is of paramount importance in identifying their 'own kind.' Perhaps needless to say, these perceptible qualities of *bodies* are not necessarily of such over-riding importance to human beings (which is not to insist that they are of no importance whatsoever). Nor, to repeat, does Brabantio himself reduce the issue of 'natural suitability' to the colour and shape of Othello's (or anyone else's) body. But on a variety of grounds, he judges the marriage between Othello and his daughter to be unnatural, 'monstrous' (to use a term that occurs most frequently in this play), to such an extent that he would rather have Desdemona wed Roderigo, whom he despises and has forbidden access (1.1.95–8, 176), than Othello (whom he liked well enough to have "oft invited"; 1.3.128). Doubtless Brabantio's conception of Nature, and the standard of rightness implicit in it, is inadequate. But, it doesn't make him a racist, anymore than is the wise Portia in *The Merchant* (cf. 1.2.121–5; 2.1.13–22; 2.7.78–9), whose attitude contrasts so tellingly with Desdemona's.

Virginia Mason Vaughan provides a convenient sampling of recent critical views regarding the racism in, or of, the play in *Othello: A Contextual History* (Cambridge: Cambridge University Press, 1994), esp. ch. 3 ('Racial discourse: black and white'). As she observes, "Note that this assortment of critics from varied backrounds and perspectives agrees on one thing – the stereotype is there, deeply embedded in the text of Shakespeare's play. Their disagreement lies in the analysis of how Shakespeare's text exploits that stereotype" (65). Vaughan's own judgment mimics Othello's equivocal assessment of Desdemona's 'honesty': "I think this play is racist, and I think it is not.": "The wonder of *Othello* is that Shakespeare was able to exploit the full complexity of

[Cinthio's] discourse, showing expectations gone topsy-turvy with a white villain opposed to a black man of heroic proportion. Even though the predominant typology of white over black is only temporarily subverted in fits and starts within the play, that subversion is itself an incredible artistic triumph" (70).

8 For whatever reason, Iago's 'will to power' (as noted above) is dedicated exclusively to moral destruction: to spoiling others' happiness, and sowing as much hate and discontent as he sees means to. Iago has the soul of a pyromaniac, who lights fires just to watch them burn (note 1.1.75–7). Unlike Nietzsche, he never by word or deed gives any indication that he practices destruction in the name of creation, or that he uses others as a means to some higher purpose.

9 On this point and several which follow from it, I am indebted to Paul A. Cantor, 'The Erring Barbarian among the Supersubtle Venetians,' in *Southwest Review* (Summer 1990), 296–319, who argues that Othello is "the most Homeric of all Shakespeare's characters, the one most devoted to a career of martial adventure and hence most remote from ordinary domestic life. The result is that of all Shakespeare's tragic heroes, Othello is the most alien to the world he moves in" (298).

10 Here the Folio version is more pointed, prefacing the line quoted with "She must change for youth."

11 Martin Elliot, in *Shakespeare's Invention of Othello* (New York: St Martin's Press, 1988) draws attention to the fact that Shakespeare "departs radically from Cinthio" in this matter of how Desdemona is killed. Whereas in Cinthio she is clubbed to death, Shakespeare has Othello say, "yet I'll not shed her blood, / Nor scar that whiter skin of hers than snow, / And smooth, as monumental alabaster" (5.2.3–5).

> The cause of this reluctance to scar her – expressed in a far more complex language than is the simple reluctance to shed her blood – is linked not at all to Othello's resolve, earlier, that Desdemona should be strangled. It is, instead, an aversion from spoiling, blemishing a body which, it might have been thought, expresses a concomitant purity of spirit in the accustomed neo-Platonic manner. Othello's 'Be thus when thou art dead, and I will kill thee, / And loue thee after' refers to the exorcism he will have achieved in the execution of his wife. He will have despatched the devil from her along with her soul; so that the purity of her body, *post mortem*, will truly reflect the (new) purity of her soul in heaven. The body will be the earthly representative of a heavenly inhabitant – which is a status roughly equivalent to Othello's. The pure whiteness of the skin, therefore, must not be discoloured. (190)

12 Hers is the only name Shakespeare took from the story that he transformed into this quite different play. In Cinthio's original version, the name is Disdemona, which is obviously derived from the Greek δυσδαιμων, and means 'ill-fated,' 'unfortunate' (as Brabantio refers to her: "O unhappy girl"; 1.1.163; or, as Othello himself addresses

her: "O ill-starr'd wench"; 5.2.273) – literally, 'attended by a bad/evil/hard *daimōn* (the δυσ prefix would usually be transliterated 'dys,' and is the source for both our prefixes 'dys' and 'dis'; its antonym is ευ, 'eu,' meaning 'good,' 'well,' 'felicitous'; hence, the Greek term we usually translate as 'happiness': *eudaimonia*). But Shakespeare's slight alteration in the name opens up another possibility: *deisidaimōn*, 'superstitious.' This was Shaftesbury's preferred etymology for the name in this play, and Allan Bloom concurs, discussing the issue at length in note 44 of his seminal essay 'Cosmopolitan Man and the Political Community,' in *Shakespeare's Politics* (New York: Basic Books, 1964, 72–3). Certainly the credulity Desdemona shows here towards Othello's tale of the handkerchief, much like her acceptance of his fanciful biography (cf. 1.3.134–65; 2.1.222), would tend to substantiate this alternative, or additional, interpretation of her name.

13 Whether their marriage was ever *physically* consummated – or ever could be – is a question that affects profoundly one's interpretation of this play. This, and the various other interpretive issues entwined with it (e.g., dramatic trickery with Time), are sensibly analysed by Graham Bradshaw, in *Misrepresentations: Shakespeare and the Materialists* (Ithaca: Cornell University Press, 1993), 151–68.

14 Although Aristotle in *Metaphysics* (948 a 7–11) credits Empedocles with first arguing for the equal primacy of all four elements, they are more famously associated with his own scientific writings, figuring in several of his treatises. For example, in *Physics*: "Of things that exist, some exist by nature, some of other causes. By nature, the animals and their parts exist, and the plants and the simple bodies (earth, fire, air, water) – for we say that these and the like exist by nature" (192 b 9–11). And in *De Meteorologia*:

> We have already laid down that there is one principle which makes up the nature of the bodies that move in a circle, and besides this four bodies owing their existence to the four principles, the motion of these latter bodies being of two kinds: either from the centre or to the centre. These four bodies are fire, air, water, earth. Fire occupies the highest place among them all, earth the lowest, and two elements correspond to these in their relation to one another, air being nearest to fire, water to earth. The whole world surrounding the earth, then, the affections of which are our subject, is made up of these bodies." (339 a 11–20)
>
> So we must treat fire and earth and the elements like them as the material causes of the events in this world (meaning by material what is subject and is affected) ... (28–30)
>
> Fire, air, water, earth, we assert, come-to-be from one another, and each of them exists potentially in each, as all things do that can be resolved into a common and ultimate substrate. (339 a 37 – b 2)

In *De Respiratione* Aristotle observes, "For some [animals] have a greater proportion of earth in their composition, like plants, and others, e.g. aquatic animals, contain a larger amount of water; while winged and terrestial animals have an excess of air and fire respectively. Each has its station in the appropriate regions." (477 a 27–30). Unless otherwise indicated, quotations of Aristotle are from the translations in *The Complete Works of Aristotle: The Revised Oxford Translation*, Jonathan Barnes, ed. (Princeton: Princeton University Press, 1984).

15 Cf. 1.2.26–8; 59; 3.3.460–7; 4.2.49–62; 5.2.268–9.

16 In this instance, one must agree with Ridley that the text of First Quarto is obviously superior to the practically unintelligible Folio substitution ('liberal as the north'). Its place in the present analysis should remove any doubt as to which is the correct reading.

Thomas L. Berger, in the essay entitled 'The Second Quarto of *Othello*,' in *Othello: New Perspectives*, Virginia Vaughan and Kent Cartwright, eds. (Rutherford, NJ: Fairleigh Dickinson University Press, 1991), 26–47, provides an interesting review of the textual problems posed for editors by the extensive differences between the strangely late Q1 (1622) and the Folio (1623) texts, and argues that the usually ignored *second* Quarto (1630) can be a useful source in producing the best conflation of the other two (for as he rightly observes, "conflate we will"; 30).

17 This fact is conveniently ignored by Carol Thomas Neely, who would have us believe that Emilia "is dramatically and symbolically the play's fulcrum" – see her essay entitled 'Women and Men in *Othello*,' as revised for inclusion in *The Woman's Part: Feminist Criticism of Shakespeare*, C.R.S. Lenz, G. Greene, C.T. Neely, eds (Urbana: University of Illinois Press, 1983), 211–39. Thus, Neely explicitly adopts the perspective of this character in order to "perceive [the play] with something like her good-natured objectivity" (213). And I readily agree that Neely's own 'good-natured objectivity' is pretty much on a par with Emilia's (whose jaundiced view of men is – not surprisingly – the natural complement to Iago's cynicism about women). Neely sees nothing untoward in Desdemona's vowing to Cassio that she'll nag Othello constantly until he grants Cassio's suit; it merely "reveals her sense of her own persistence and force" (227). As for Othello's fictional origin of the handkerchief: his account, "and its part in the plot reveal that it is a symbol of women's civilizing power" (228). In speaking summarily about the men and women in the play, she offers this nicely balanced piece of good-natured objectivity: "The women, for all their affection, good sense, and energy, fail to transform or be reconciled with the men. The first reason for this is that the sexes, so sharply differentiated in the play, badly misunderstand each other. The men ... persistently misconceive the women; the women fatally overestimate the men ... The men see the women as whores and then refuse to tolerate their own projections. The women recognize the foolishness of the men's fancies but are all too tolerant of them" (228). There is a mingling of truth in Neely's prejudiced assessment, but she has steadfastly ignored untoward evidence in order to morally glamourize the women and depreciate the men, resulting in a grossly distorted understanding of the play.

Bearing in mind the obvious parallels between Emilia's protesting the similarity of women's desires to those of men (implying, as she sees it, the right to behave sexually as men do: 4.3.86–103) and Shylock's more famous assertion of Jews' right to behave as do Christians (hence seek revenge: *Merchant* 3.1.52–66), it may well be argued that *Othello* is as much an exploration of the sexual distinction as of the racial. Indeed, as Shakespeare invites us to recognize, the two sets of issues intersect so provocatively in inter-racial marriage, and the touchy subject of miscegenation. The immediate perceptual basis for both distinctions, sex and race, is the body. This, it is worth noting, is what both Emilia's and Shylock's arguments mainly rest upon: similarity of *bodily* needs, desires, powers, and vulnerabilities – which ignores precisely what distinguishes a Christian from a Jew: the posture of the soul as a consequence of differing religious educations and beliefs. With that in mind, one might ask what this play shows about the differences in the *souls* of men and women. Here, I think, one thing stands out: the men's greater preoccupation with women's bodies (however, see 4.3.35–9; 1.3.390–6). Bradshaw, in *Misrepresentations*, is on the right track in observing:

> [T]he ensemble of characters is a means of exploring representative attitudes to sex, the other sex, and marriage, and if we are responding to the contrasts between the three *couples*, we are more likely to see Emilia's hostility to men as the counterpart of her husband's misogyny. In this perspective, her attitude to 'Affections' and 'Desires' seems as limited as her husband's, so that the contrast between the couples is likely to increase our sympathy for Othello and Desdemona's vulnerably isolated attempt at a more enduring, mutually loving relationship. However, in the Shakespearean nexus of contrasts the three couples are also presented as two male-and-female *trios*, so that Desdemona, Emilia, and Bianca make up a triad of women who all suffer from their men and from a disquietingly representative range of male attitudes; in this perspective, we are more likely to warm to Emilia's speech as a perceptive crypto-feminist denunciation of a double code. (172)

18 It is true that some early explorers returned with tales this fabulous, but they were met with the incredulity they deserved. And Shakespeare would have been the last person to believe there actually were *men* whose heads grew "beneath their shoulders," contrary to the bodily structure of every known vertebrate, be it mammal, bird, reptile, or fish! Suffice it to say, such a phenomenon would make racial differences seem pretty picayune.

19 In Cinthio's story, neither 'the Moor' nor his officers are identified by personal names. Thus the ones used in this play are of Shakespeare's choice or invention. 'Othello,' given a Spanish pronunciation ('Oh-THEH-yoh') – a not utterly capricious notion in light of: the historical connection of the Moors with Spain; Othello's possessing a Spanish sword; that the name of his comrade, Iago (or 'Jago,' as Rymer refers to him) is

a Spanish variation of 'Jack'; and, the fact that he is a Christian (see Barbara Everett, 'Spanish Othello: The Making of Shakespeare's Moor,' *Shakespeare Survey* 35, 1982, 101–12) – might have been suggested to Shakespeare by the Greek ωθεω (*ōtheō*): literally, 'I force,' 'thrust,' 'push,' 'shove,' 'press forward'; idiomatically, 'I hurry,' 'I rush matters along.' This certainly fits the character, the very picture of precipitous judgment and action.

20 Montano's reaction to the sight of Cassio's "infirmity" (2.3.121–34), Othello's reaction to the "foul rout" it causes: "What, in a town of war ... on the court and guard of safety? 'Tis monstrous." (204–7), and Cassio's own assessment of his "indiscretion" (269–73), all serve to emphasize what a serious breach of military discipline he has committed – a matter about which we must presume the cloistered Desdemona to be utterly incompetent to judge.

21 The four perceptible elements are constituted by distinct pairings of qualities imposed on a common basic matter (which as such is truly the 'basis' of their being transmutable into one another); thus earth is cold and dry, water cold and moist, fire hot and dry, air hot and moist. Cf. Aristotle, *De Caelo*: "Now in fire we observe a destruction of two kinds: it is destroyed by its contrary when it is quenched, and by itself when it dies out ... The elements of bodies must therefore be subject to destruction and generation" (305 a 9–13). "The elements therefore cannot be generated from something incorporeal nor from a body which is not an element, and the only remaining possibility is that they are generated from one another" (31–3). This, of course, is the basic premise of alchemy, an arcane science of matter that may have its psychological counterpart. As Jensen observes ("'This Is Venice'"): "Iago sees himself as the perfect alchemist, who can transmute everything (including himself) into its opposite at will ... As his own 'blackest sins' can be hidden by 'heavenly shows,' so Desdemona's pure white virtue can be turned into 'pitch'" (167).

22 According to the Platonic Sokrates, true self-love is a *consequence* of a justly ordered soul: "And the truth was, as it seems, that justice is something of this sort; however, not with respect to one's minding one's external business, but with respect to what is within, with respect to what truly concerns him and his own, not letting each part in him mind the business of others, nor the classes in the soul meddle with each other; but really disposing his own house well, he rules himself, and orders himself, and becomes his own friend" (*Republic* 443c).

23 One measure of this is the number of anecdotes about people in the audience actually intervening during performances of it, shouting warnings and admonitions to the actors on the stage. Once when Edmund Forrest was playing Iago to Edmund Kean's Othello, someone in the audience was overheard to say, "You damn'd lying scoundrel, I would like to get a hold of you after this show is over and wring your infernal neck." My favourite is probably apocryphal, but I hope not. During one performance by a company touring the Old West, a member of the audience took out his pistol and shot

the actor who was playing Iago. He was buried beneath a tombstone bearing the epitaph, "Here lies the greatest actor." Versions of these two episodes are included in Norrie Epstein, *The Friendly Shakespeare* (New York: Penguin, 1993, 379–80).

As Evans has observed in *Shakespeare's Tragic Practice*: "*Othello* is a tragedy of unawareness ... [T]he participants stand ... ignorant of Iago's malign nature and intent, and Iago uses their ignorance as means to enmesh and destroy them all." Thus, Evans contends in this play "unawareness is more than merely a dramatically useful condition the exploitation of which yields various spectacular but incidental effects ...; it is the open road to catastrophe" (115).

24 Here, then, I am in basic agreement with T.S. Eliot's famously controversial assessment of Othello's character, anticipated by Thomas Rymer and to varying degrees concurred in by F.R. Leavis, Robert B. Heilman, and Jane Adamson, among others. In his essay 'Shakespeare and the Stoicism of Seneca' (1927), *Selected Essays* (New York: Harcourt Brace, 1950), Eliot writes:

> I have always felt that I have never read a more terrible exposure of human weakness – of universal human weakness – than the last great speech of Othello ... What Othello seems to me to be doing in making this speech is cheering himself up. He is endeavouring to escape reality, he has ceased to think of Desdemona, and is thinking about himself. Humility is the most difficult of all virtues to achieve; nothing dies harder than the desire to think well of oneself. Othello succeeds in turning himself into a pathetic figure, by adopting an *aesthetic* rather than a moral attitude, dramatising himself against his environment. He takes in the spectator, but the human motive is primarily to take in himself (110–11).

My only reservation – as to whether humility is truly a virtue (cf. Aristotle, *Nicomachean Ethics* , 1123 b 2–30) – is (at most) tangential to the issue of Othello's character. Robert B. Heilman, *Magic in the Web* (Lexington, KY: University of Kentucky Press, 1956) writes, "we can see that Othello was so easily deceived, so easily taken in by appearances and the false physician and the honesty game, because he had such a great talent, and even a need, for self-deception" (155). And referring to Othello as "the romantic historian of self," Heilman judges him to be "the least heroic of Shakespeare's tragic heroes. The need for justification, for a constant reconstruction of himself in acceptable terms, falls short of the achieved selfhood which can plunge with pride into great errors and face up with humility to what has been done" (166). F.R. Leavis, in *The Common Pursuit* (London: Chatto and Windus, 1952), offers this droll assessment of Othello's 'Whip me, you devils' rant: "When he discovers his mistake, his reaction is an intolerably intensified form of the common 'I could kick myself' ... But he remains the same Othello; he has discovered his mistake, but there is no tragic self-discovery" (150). Heilman agrees in both substance and tone: "He somehow conveys the impression that his big mistake was not so much murder and revenge as it was depriving himself of Desdemona; he less repudiates the violence than deplores the silly mistakes which wiped out a very nice girl" (165). Rightly recognizing that the play *is* none the less a tragedy, not mere melodrama, Jane Adamson in *Othello as Tragedy: Some Problems of Judgment and Feeling* (Cambridge: Cambridge University Press, 1980), finds the issues here somewhat more complicated: "Once we notice how transparent Othello's self-dramatizations are, we also recognize how crucially necessary they are to him: without them, he could not survive ... The 'sentimentality' is Othello's own, not Shakespeare's, and what Shakespeare imaginatively grasps and dramatizes and makes us respond to are the vital reasons for, and the vital reality of, this man visibly straining *not* to recognize how idealizing and sentimental – indeed, how false – his extenuating self-images are" (288–9).

As for Othello's claim to being "an honourable murderer," Adamson finds that "The bravado and the self-justification are preposterous" (292). Martin Elliot in *Shakespeare's Invention of Othello*, apparently wanting to put some distance between such views and his own, draws the following distinction: "My term 'self-publication' differs from 'self-dramatisation' and from 'histrionics' – another popular description of Othello's speech – in eschewing any idea of insincerity, of falsity; and also in emphasising Othello's extraordinary need to impress himself upon his listener" (108). Elliot none the less concurs that Othello is "deluded" in his claim to having "a non-jealous nature" (229).

25 For a fuller analysis of the inner 'rationale' of jealousy, developed in the context of this play, see Allan Bloom's 'Cosmopolitan Man and the Political Community,' in *Shakespeare's Politics*, 51–4.

26 The nature of Othello is readily understood within the context of Platonic psychology as it is discussed and displayed in Plato's own dramatic creation, his *Republic*. The basic evidence and arguments for humans having a tripartite soul (i.e., comprising a rational part, a spirit [*thumos*], and an appetitive part) is sketched in book 4 (435c–441c), then amplified and refined in the balance of the dialogue. In light of this basic account, one can distinguish several archetypes of souls (or 'natures'), according to which part of the soul is strongest and therefore rules in a given person. One of these archetypes Sokrates calls 'timocratic' (the name derives from the Greek term for honour, *timē*); it refers to an especially manly, honour-loving type of man who is ruled by the spirited part of his soul, that being the part to which honour and glory appeal. Timocrats tend to be men of action more than reflection, more concerned with the practical than the theoretical, not much concerned with polish of either speech or manner (cf. 1.3.88–90, 3.3.268–9). The essentials of the timocrat's nature, and of the distinctive characteristics of a regime in which this class of men – the warrior class – rules, is explicitly treated (along with the other, inferior types of cities and souls) in book 8 (547a–550b). The type of man at his best is exemplified in the dialogue by

Adeimantos, though in a rawer form by Thrasymachos. (Explicating Plato's psychology, and of the crucial significance of the spirited part of the soul for both philosophy and politics, is the guiding purpose of my analysis of the *Republic* in *The War Lover*; see esp. chs. 4 and 5.)

Othello, too, is a genuine 'Timocrat': honour, status, respect, reputation mean more to him than any other goods that political life affords. Traditionally, the highest honours accorded men *as men* are those won on the battlefield. Thus Othello's preference for and pride in the martial life he has led:

The tyrant custom, most grave senators,
Hath made the flinty and steel couch of war
My thrice-driven bed of down: I do agnize
A natural and prompt alacrity
I find in hardness, and would undertake
This present wars against the Ottomites. (1.3.229–34; cf. 1.3.81–7, 129–39)

Thus, also, his despondence in fearing that he has lost all he has lived for ("Farewell the plumed troop, and the big wars, / That makes ambition virtue: ... Farewell, Othello's occupation's gone!" 3.3.353–63). Thus, his majestic – and easily inflamed – anger, his readiness to resort to violence to impose his will (cf. 2.3.195–200), his rashness, his overwhelming sense of indignation and desire for revenge at what he believes to be the betrayal of Cassio and Desdemona, and his insistence to the bitter end that he be regarded as "an *honourable* murderer" ("For nought did I in hate, but all in honour" 5.2.295–6). Cassio is a lesser version of the Timocrat ("Reputation, reputation, I ha' lost my reputation! I ha' lost the immortal part, sir, of myself, and what remains is bestial" 2.3.254–6). And Iago, having served many years among such men, and with Othello in particular (1.1.27–30), knows them inside out.

Sokrates warns that though the timocrat when he is young despises money (to say nothing of money-grubbing), when he grows older and can no longer compete so successfully for martial glory, he begins to concern himself more with comfort and wealth and a more secure status, and so tends to degenerate into a moneylover (549a–b; cf. 548a–b). Might this help explain Othello's belated interest in a marriage that promises financial and social security ("Faith, he to-night hath boarded a land carrack: / If it prove lawful prize, he's made for ever" 1.2.50–1)?

27 Better men than he have similarly failed to see the reflexive inadequacy of their own materialistic accounts. Aristotle in his *Metaphysics* speaks of his materialistic predecessors, observing: "After these [men] and their principles, which were found insufficient for generating the nature of things, [men] were compelled by the truth itself, as we said, to inquire into the next first principle [*archēn*]. For surely it is likely that things being or becoming good and beautiful [*eu kai kalōs*] is neither from fire nor earth nor any other such [material element], nor that they should have thought such to be the

cause; nor again is it a deed [*pragma*] nobly [*kalōs*] ascribed to spontaneity and chance. Hence when someone said mind [*noun*] to be within [*eneinai]* – throughout nature as in the animals, the cause of the world and arrangement of everything – he appeared like that of a sober [man] in contrast to the haphazard talk of his predecessors" (984b 8–18; my translation).

28 Fully half of the two dozen references to blood associate this bodily fluid with psychic phenomena, and often as the medium whereby matter affects consciousness, or vice versa. For example: Brabantio treats Desdemona's willingness to run away in the night as "treason of the blood" (1.1.169), and suspects that Othello has overcome his daughter's natural modesty and taste "with some mixtures powerful o'er the blood" (1.3.104); Iago associates "sensuality" with "the blood and baseness of our natures," and regards conscious love as "merely a lust of the blood" (328–35; see also 5.1.36); he assures Roderigo that awareness of beauty is needed to "inflame" it once "blood is made dull with the act of sport" (2.1.225–9); he privately gloats that his poisonous insinuations are "Dangerous conceits ... / Which at the first are scarce found to distaste, / But with a little act upon the blood / Burn like the mines of sulphur" (3.3.330–4); confronted with Othello's irrational treatment of his wife, Lodovico wonders whether the written communications he has brought from Venice may have unsettled Othello's wits: "did the letters work upon his blood ...? (4.2.271); when an immediate explanation is not provided of the ruckus involving Cassio and Montano, Othello warns, "My blood begins my safer guides to rule, / And passion having my best judgment collied / Assays to lead the way." (2.3.196–8); he subsequently speaks of his "bloody thoughts" (3.3.464), and Desdemona worries that "some bloody passion shakes [his] very frame" (5.2.44).

29 The frankness with which he reveals himself to Roderigo suggests that it was always Iago's intention eventually to do away with this hapless fool – after, that is, he had mulcted him of all the money in his purse.

30 Obviously there can be no *demonstration* that the body is 'more real' than consciousness, since all evidence and arguments for the claim presuppose conscious acceptance and assessment, hence the prior reality of consciousness *per se*. Nor can it be even hypothesized as such, since the same reasoning applies as readily to the hypothesis as to any putative demonstration. The ontological status one grants to conscious experience must be extended also to whatever may be antecedently accessible to or influential upon consciousness, such as memories and repressed anxieties.

31 One might even credit him with having originated the paradox that currently enjoys such popularity amongst a certain sect of literary scholars, something like that of Nietzsche's ironic formulation: "There are no facts, only interpretations." To appreciate its regressive incoherence, one need only ask, "Of what, pray tell?" Or one might simply rejoin, "Oh, *really*? Is that a fact?"

32 Thus, there is a nice irony in *Othello* being a favourite target for Cultural Materialists

to practice their reductionist analyses on, happily oblivious to the possibility that the play itself is meant to show the *inadequacy* of any attempt to explain the world in purely materialistic terms. Of course, in practice what Cultural Materialists and their New Historicist cousins mean by 'materialism' has little to do with *matter* as such, nor (consequently) with the question of how matter can be causally determining; their 'material factors' invariably refer to *formed* matter, all of whose qualities are due to the form, not the matter. As they use the term, 'materialism' is meant to imply a hard-nosed 'realism' about what truly counts in this world, thereby giving their favourite reductionist theory – never fully formulated or defended, but usually at root politico-economic in character – a rhetorical advantage over the (allegedly hypocritical) 'idealism' and 'humanism' that they profess to expose. Bradshaw in *Misrepresentations* provides a convincing demolition of the various representative exponents of this approach, showing that their perspectives on this play are at least as crass as anything I would have attributed to Iago.

33 J.H.P. Pafford, in his Introduction to the Arden edition of the play used here (London: Methuen, 1963), liv. That *The Winter's Tale* is often labelled a 'romantic tragi-comedy' further attests to its perplexing character. Pafford prefers to see the play as having three parts (distinguishing the quality of happiness experienced upon the return to Leontes' court in act 5 from that found in the Bohemian portion), while nonetheless insisting: "But *The Winter's Tale* is not a dramatic curiosity consisting of separate parts; it is a whole, and its unity has the rhythm and vitality of a great work of art. In spite of the fact that it is spread over a wide area and many years, the plot is perfectly clear. It is true that the first period, at Court, is almost wholly an unhappy time where mad jealousy threatens absolute disaster; that the second, coming after sixteen years in another country and different milieu and largely with different people, is, for its first half, extremely happy; and that the last period, again at Court, is chiefly one of mellow happiness and reconcilation. But all these parts belong to and complete each other" (liv–lv).

Pafford, however, concerns himself almost exclusively with the play as it would be seen in performance, dismissing all puzzling features about it as "matters [that] cannot occur to an audience ... and therefore do not arise in an appreciation of it" (li). Whether or not one should speak of Shakespeare's 'audience' in such undifferentiated terms, this is not adequate for establishing the *intellectual* coherence of the play – a unity that will stand up to rational scrutiny. My brief treament here is meant to contribute to that end.

34 Apparently there was confusion in Shakespeare's day between the island of Delos (also known then as Delphos), and Apollo's temple at Delphi, which overlooked the Gulf of Corinth, and was regarded as the supreme oracle of all Greece.

35 Of all the 'Christianizing' interpretations of the play I've encountered – and their abundance attests to the conspicuity of its Christian motifs – one of the most intriguing (and, to me, most compelling) is that which John Orrell has sketched in an essay, 'The

Measure of *The Winter's Tale*,' which unfortunately has yet to be published. Based on a numerological analysis of the lines of verse, Orrell argues that the play has a precise arithmetical design, at once liturgical and musical. That such could be the case is by no means as improbable as it might at first seem to many contemporary readers, for recent scholarship has established beyond doubt that numerological and geometrical and calendric structuring is fairly common in Renaissance and Elizabethan poetry (see, e.g., Alastair Fowler, *Triumphal Forms: Structural Patterns in Elizabethan Poetry*, Cambridge: Cambridge University Press, 1970; Christopher Butler, *Number Symbolism*, London: Routledge & Kegan Paul, 1970; Maren-Sofie Røstvig, 'Structure as Prophecy: The Influence of Biblical Exegesis upon Theories of Literary Structure,' in *Silent Poetry: Essays in Numerological Analysis*, Alastair Fowler, ed., London: Routledge & Kegan Paul, 1970). The sheer volume of numerical references in this play (over 90) itself invites numerological speculation, as do certain curiously – and otherwise pointlessly – detailed speeches, such as that of Antigonus defending the fidelity of Hermione:

> Be she honour-flaw'd,
> I have three daughters: the eldest is eleven;
> The second and third, nine and some five:
> If this prove true, they'll pay for't. By mine honour
> I'll geld 'em all; fourteen they shall not see
> To bring false generations ...
>
> (2.1.143–8)

Despite the extensive part played by their mother, nothing more is heard of these daughters. And what is one to make of the shepherd's musing?

> I would there were no age between ten and three-and-twenty, or that youth would sleep out the rest; for there is nothing in the between but getting wenches with child, wronging the ancientry, stealing, fighting – Hark you now! Would any but these boiled-brains of nineteen and two-an-twenty hunt this weather? (3.3.59–65)

Or of the "four threes of herdsmen," each one of whom can jump at least "twelve foot and a half" (4.4.336–9; cf. *Republic* 337b).

Suffice it to say, there are grounds for suspecting Shakespeare of employing principles of numerology that are traceable back to Plato, especially his *Timaeus*, and beyond him to Pythagoras (Butler provides a convenient summary of the rudiments in the first chapter of his *Number Symbolism*). Obviously, to the extent one is unfamiliar with the symbolic meanings of various numbers (e.g., of the association of 3 with Time, and the union of male and female; of 4 with Space, the Elements, and Justice; of 7 with God,

Nature, Magic, Completion, and the union of body and soul). Or with the sense in which only *prime* numbers are *real* – having no factors, they are unique unto themselves – or with the order of primes. Or with the often amazing properties of numbers themselves, defining special categories of numbers: 'triangular,' 'square,' 'perfect' (i.e., equal to the sum of their divisors, e.g., 6, 28), 'deficient,' 'abundant,' 'circular,' etc. To that extent, one is not prepared to interpret the possible significance of Shakespeare's use of numbers.

36 We know this to have been the year 416 BC. The competition of tragedies was part of the festival known as *Dionysia ta epi Lēnaiō*, and held on the twelfth day of the month of Gamelion (late January to early February). Agathon was the most renowned successor to the 'big three' of Attic tragedy (Aeschylus, Sophocles, and Euripides). None of his plays survives, though Aristotle refers to him, crediting him with certain technical innovations (*Poetics* 1456 A; cf. 1451 B, 1454B). He was born c. 445, and emigrated from Athens to the court of Archelaus, tyrant of Macedonia, in 407, where he died c. 401.

37 Given the dates of Agathon's victory and Sokrates' death (399 BC), seventeen years is the longest interval historically possible between the original banquet and this account of it. Presumably it is something less, but not much less, given Apollodorus's emphasizing that the dinner party was long before he began consorting with Sokrates some three years ago, that Agathon has been gone "many years" (172b–c), and Glaukon's acknowledging it to have been "a very long time ago" (173a). A "wide gap" of fifteen or sixteen years might be a reasonable guess.

38 The dangerous and domineering nature of *erōs* runs like a scarlet thread through the *Republic* virtually from its beginning to its end. It first appears in the form of a man's sexual lust for womens' bodies, Kephalos professing to find his old age a blessed release from this "frenzied and savage master" (328c–d). It is last discussed in the form of a passionate but unwholesome love of poetry (607e–608b; cf. 619b–c). The musical education of the Guardians is aimed especially at moderating their susceptibility to the attraction of sexual pleasure (it being not only the greatest and keenest, but also the maddest of the pleasures, at least according to Glaukon; 402d–403c). At the dialogue's centre, it is affirmed that "erotic necessities" are far more compelling with most people than are logical necessities (458d). Erotic love is repeatedly associated with inebriation, madness, sickness, and irrationality (e.g., 395e, 396d, 439d, 573b–c, 578a, 586c).

39 As noted above, the contest for tragedians in which Agathon was victorious was part of a winter festival. Aristodemus, in explaining his sleeping so late, refers to the nights' then being long (223c). The *Republic* takes place on the day the worship of Thracian goddess *Bendis* was first introduced in Athens (327a, 354a); her day of worship was the 19th of the Thargelion month (late May to early June).

40 Thus the judgment of many modern scholars that this play, along with *Cymbeline*, *Pericles*, and *Henry VIII* – all regarded as among the last of Shakespeare's plays – is 'exper-

imental' precisely because it does not fit neatly into any of the established dramatic forms. Pafford, in his Introduction to *The Winter's Tale* conveniently surveys some of the leading proponents of this view (xxxix–xliv).

Thomas McFarland, analysing the play in his *Shakespeare's Pastoral Comedy* (Chapel Hill: University of North Carolina Press, 1972), links it to both *Pericles* and *King Lear* by the common motif of separation and reunion of father and daughter: "But where *Lear* is true to the tragic fact of death, though the language nevertheless holds out the possibility of heavenly reunion, both comedies retreat into their genre's typical artificiality and typical reluctance to face the reality of death. They thereby achieve a unique position in Shakespeare's art, for they combine tragic intensity with comic wellbeing. The combination in each case is achieved at a certain cost, that of probability, but the cost is debited to comedy's special account with the artificial" (141).

41 According to Polixenes' recollection, they shared an idyllic time of "innocense" ("we knew not / The doctrine of ill-doing, nor dream'd / That any did"), which sexual maturity brought to an end. With the advent of "stronger blood," they became subject to "temptations," resulting in their taking wives. To this, Hermione responds:

> Grace to boot!
> Of this make no conclusion, lest you say
> Your Queen and I are devils. Yet go on;
> Th' offence we have made you do, we'll answer,
> If you first sinn'd with us, and that with us
> You did continue fault, and that you slipp'd not
> With any but us. (1.2.80–6)

Hermione's use of the present tense ("*are* devils") indicates that Polixenes' queen is alive at the time, and raises the question as to why she has not accompanied her husband on a visit of such duration. Whatever explanation he might give, the fact that he is willingly apart from her so long (nine months!) – not on state business, but a mere pleasure trip – hardly attests to his having a deep attachment to his wife. One's curiosity on this point is only heightened by Hermione's earlier suggestion that an eagerness to see his *son* would be an understandable reason for his insistence on departing (34–6). And Polixenes' subsequent declaration of extreme fondness for his "young prince" ("If at home, sir, / He's *all* my exercise, my mirth, my matter"; 165–6) only throws into relief his resounding silence about his wife. Then there is the unfortunate fact that Hermione's use of the plural in speaking of 'offenses' and 'sinning' and 'slipping' and 'faults' may be interpreted (even if only subconsciously) as the 'royal we.' All of this, however innocent, lends plausibility to Leontes's suspicion.

42 The fact that Shakespeare departed so markedly from his source (Robert Greene's *Pandosto*) in this very respect – the precipitousness with which Leontes descends into his jealous suspicions – must be treated as significant for correctly interpreting this play.

He was certainly capable of making a drama that shows jealousy growing by stages, as *Othello* proves (where the hero's transformation, rapid enough to be sure, is both activated and hurried along by the clever machinations of a trusted subordinate). Many critics judge Leontes' sudden onset of jealousy as insufficiently justified, hence psychologically implausible, and so regard it as a serious defect in the play. Others, wishing to defend the play, gloss the problem as dramatically irrelevant in performance. Allan Bloom in chapter 11 of *Love and Friendship* is one of few who treats it as an important interpretive problem, and provides a plausible explanation for it. He sees Shakespeare as using it to call attention to a troubling possibility:

> The sudden explosion of angry jealousy brings to light a problem about a married woman's blameless friendship with a man. The suspicions aroused make it impossible to have that confidence required for men and women to be together without tincture of erotic involvement. Moreover their new condition of marriage also raises doubts about the possibility of friendship between married men. (376)

It is also useful to consider the suddenness of Leontes' jealousy in the context of McFarland's judgment in *Shakespeare's Pastoral Comedy* that "The most persistent theme in all Shakespeare, in fact, is that of human faithlessness" (127): "The mysterious rage of Leontes is another expression of this persisting view of the probability of baseness in human relationships. The dual potentiality of man, either to be like the animals or like the angels, was often insisted on by Shakespeare's philosophically minded predecessors in the Renaissance ... Leontes' rage, following so suddenly on the benign scene appropriate to comedy, is a sort of reflection of the Renaissance emphasis on man's multiple possibility. To it, moreover, must be added darker thoughts, from Augustine and Calvin, about man's inherent corruption. All such thoughts receive their validation from experience: in Shakespeare's life, about which we can only speculate, or in our own, about which we can be certain" (129).

As for the tension between *erōs* and Reason, it is exemplified as clearly in Florizel as by Leontes. The young prince insists, "[Had I] force and knowledge / More than was ever man's, I would not prize them / Without her love" (4.4.375–7). And when later urged by Camillo, "Be advis'd," he responds, "I am: and by my fancy. If my reason / Will thereto be obedient, I have reason; / If not, my senses, better pleas'd with madness, / Do bid it welcome" (483–6).

Thus Bacon begins his tenth essay, 'Of Love,' by observing: "The stage is more beholding to Love, than the life of man. For as to the stage, love is ever matter of comedies, and now and then of tragedies; but in life it doth much mischief; sometimes like a siren, sometimes like a fury. You may observe, that amongst all the great and worthy persons (whereof the memory remaineth, either ancient or recent,) there is not one that hath been transported to the mad degree of love: which shows that great spirits and great business do keep out of this weak [i.e., weakening] passion ... It is a strange thing to note the excess of this passion, and how it braves the nature and value of things, by this; that the speaking in a perpetual hyperbole is comely in nothing but love" (cf. *Symposium* 183b).

Bacon goes on to say, "For there never was a proud man thought so absurdly well of himself as the lover doth of the person loved; and therefore it was well said, *That it is impossible to love and be wise*" (cf. *Troilus and Cressida*, 3.2.154–5). This is the problem explored at such length and breadth and depth in Plato's *Republic*: the tension between *erōs* and sound judgment, equally troubling to both Justice and Philosophy. But, as noted before, the account there must be integrated with that of the *Symposium*, wherein is emphasized the productive, creative, elevating potential of *erōs* – that (according to Plato's Sokrates' Diotima) the erotic longing for the beautiful in some strong souls leads ultimately to philosophy (210d ff).

43 As Diotima teaches, "This practice [*pragma*], pregnancy and bringing to birth, is divine, and it is immortal in the mortal animal" (*Symposium* 206c). And, "the mortal nature seeks as far as possible to be always, and immortal. It is capable only in this way, through generation, because it is always leaving behind another that is young to replace the old" (207c–d).

44 *The Prince*, ch. 8, 35, 37.

45 There are any number of details in Shakespeare's play that might be seen as correlates of things said in Plato's *Symposium*. For example, the old shepherd's "thou met'st with things dying, I with things new-born" (3.3.112–13) conforms with Diotima's description of *Erōs*: "And by nature [or, birth] neither immortal or mortal, but sometimes on the selfsame day he flourishes and lives, whenever well-resourced, and sometimes he is dying, but comes to life again through the nature of his father" (203e). And the noble forebearance of Florizel in his loving of Perdita (4.4.146–53; 5.1.202–8) would seem to justify Pausanias's distinguishing a higher, 'heavenly' form of *erōs*, in which the loving is done "correctly and nobly," from the lower, baser, 'Pandemian' form (181a). Similarly, the disguised Polixenes' observation to his disguised son, "Your heart is full of something that does take your mind from feasting" (4.4.347–8) instantiates Diotima's reminder that a lover in the presence of his beloved prefers "neither to eat nor drink," but only to behold and be with the one he loves" (211d–e). And Dr Eryximachus attributes the divergent qualities of Summer and Winter (cold versus hot, dry versus moist) to the interaction of the two forms of *erōs* (188a).

46 Florizel's name itself suggests flowers (*Flora* being the Roman goddess of flowers and Spring [see 4.4.2]; *floridus* means 'flowery'), and adds a special piquancy to the discussion between his kingly father and Perdita concerning the roles of Art and Nature in the breeding of flowers (4.4.80–108). Even more pointed is the irony of Perdita's rejection (and Polixenes' promotion) of "streak'd gillyvors / Which some call nature's bastards," given Leontes' original insistence that she is Polixenes's bastard (2.3.160).

47 This possibility is further strengthened by the etyma of the two names: 'Perdita,' from *perdo* ('wretched,' 'miserable,' 'abandoned'); 'Penia' (πενια, 'impoverished,' 'needy').

48 However, the Tragedian's account of *erōs* is also pertinent inasmuch as Agathon contrasts the ways of *Erōs* with those of Necessity (195c). Nor should one overlook the fact that the record of the entire erotically charged evening is supposedly due to chance: Aristodemos's lucky encounter with Sokrates.

49 This would seem the summary conclusion implicit in Sokrates' explanation of the eventual decay of the 'city in *logos*' constructed by him and his companions. Offering to imitate the Muses as speaking "tragically," but only in jest (i.e., comically; *Republic* 545e), he articulates one of the most famous (or notorious) numerological cruxes in all of philosophical literature:

> Although they are wise, the ones you educated as leaders of the city will none the less fail to hit upon the prosperous birth and barrenness of your kind with calculation aided by sensation, but it will pass them by, and they will at some time beget children when they should not. For a divine birth there is a period encompassed by a perfect number; for a human birth, by the first number in which root and square increases, comprising three distances and four limits, of elements that make like and unlike, and that wax and wane, render everything conversable and rational. Of these elements, the root four-three mated with the five, thrice increased, produces two harmonies. One of them is equal an equal number of times, taken one hundred times over. The other is of equal length one way, but is an oblong; on one side, of one hundred rational diameters of the five, lacking one for each; or if of irrational diameters, lacking two for each; on the other side, of one hundred cubes of the three. This whole geometrical number is sovereign of better and worse begettings. And when your guardians from ignorance of them cause grooms to live with brides out of season, the children will have neither good natures nor good luck. (546a–d)

The obscurity of this so-called Nuptial Number being proverbial, there are few with the temerity to offer anything like a full interpretation of it. But it would seem safe to suppose that the 3 : 4 : 5 proportions of the perfect Pythagorean triangle, basic to both geometry and harmony, are somehow involved.

50 See Craig, *The War Lover*, 96–111.

51 It is a quirk of the Greek language that this word can also mean 'most clever,' which imparts an irony to Pausanias's claim.

52 McFarland, *Shakespeare's Pastoral Comedy*, 142.

53 However, the expression "three and twenty" occurs three times: once in *Hamlet* (5.1.167), once in *Troilus and Cressida* (1.2.238), and once here (3.3.59–60).

54 Is not his 'recoiling' rather peculiar in its precision – not the more casual 'it takes me back twenty years' (as might explain the discrepancy between Time's exactness and

Camillo's approximation, 4.2.4), but precisely twenty-three? This, as Leontes muses upon his child, itself the result (according to Diotima) of Leontes's own erotic striving for "immortality, remembrance, and happiness for all future time" (*Symposium* 208e).

55 At least so far as I know, it is Plato who established it, though it is quite possible that it was already part of, say, the Pythagorean's hermetic doctrine. As for why he (or whoever) chose twenty-three to represent *erōs*, I have no suggestions worth sharing. Apparently certain subsequent philosophers picked up on it, however (e.g., Bacon, Descartes, Rousseau, Nietzsche), as well as on the view that philosophy is the highest expression of *erōs* (*Symposium* 204b, 210d–212a; *Republic* 403a, 499b–c).

Given this number's connection with love matters, it may not be the merest coincidence that in a symbol-ladened pastoral romance 'which is so much concerned with dreams and with moonlight,' with love and magic, there are "twenty-three references to the moon in *A Midsummer Night's Dream*, more than in any other Shakespearean play" (this according to Howard White in *Copp'd Hills toward Heaven*, 51).

56 Cf. Descartes, *Discourse on Method*, final paragraph of part 2 with regard to the "fable" he tells of his life; also, the twenty-third paragraph of Part One of Rousseau's *Discourse on Inequality*. The first part of Nietzsche's *Beyond Good and Evil: Prelude to a Philosophy of the Future* is entitled 'On the Prejudices of the Philosphers,' and has twenty-three aphorisms; in the twenty-third, he introduces that which in his psychology equates with or supplants *erōs*, namely, 'will to power.' Once one has taken into account its irregular numbering, the whole book is found to comprise 299 aphorisms (23 x 13). The twenty-third section of Nietzsche's exceedingly strange 'autobiography,' *Ecce Homo*, is all about love and sexuality; in its center is this provocative question and answer: "Have there been ears for my definition of love? it is unique, the one worthy of a philosopher. Love – in its means, war; at base [*Grunde*], the mortal hatred of the sexes." (my translation). See also aphorism 23 of *The Antichrist*. Nietzsche was a prodigy in classical philology, and (as virtually every book he wrote bears witness) knew his Plato like few before or since.

57 According to Peter Ure's 'The Problem Plays' (in *Shakespeare: The Writer and His Work*, Bonamy Dobrée, ed., London: Longmans, 1964), "The term 'problem plays' was first applied to *All's Well, Measure for Measure*, and *Troilus and Cressida* by F.S. Boas (who associated *Hamlet* with them) in 1896. It is not a term which bears too rigorous an examination" (239). In the Introduction to his published lectures entitled *Shakespeare's Problem Plays* (London: Chatto and Windus, 1950), E.M.W. Tillyard also admits his dissatisfaction with the term, and warns that he uses it "vaguely and equivocally; as a matter of convenience." He further suggests:

> To achieve the necessary elasticity and inclusiveness, consider the connotations of the parallel term 'problem child.'
>
> There are at least two kinds of problem child: first the genuinely abnormal child, whom no efforts will ever bring back to normality; and second the child

who is interesting and complex rather than abnormal: apt indeed to be a problem for parents and teachers but destined to fulfilment in the larger scope of adult life. Now *All's Well* and *Measure for Measure* are like the first problem child: there is something radically schizophrenic about them. *Hamlet* and *Troilus and Cressida* are like the second problem child, full of interest and complexity but divided within themselves only in the eyes of those that have misjudged them. To put the difference in another way, *Hamlet* and *Troilus and Cressida* are problem plays because they deal with and display interesting problems; *All's Well* and *Measure for Measure* because they *are* problems. (9–10)

Vivian Thomas in *The Moral Universe of Shakespeare's Problem Plays* (London and New York: Routledge, 1991) devotes his introductory chapter to surveying, quite helpfully, various critics' attempts to explicate what is 'problematic' about certain sets of plays.

As is hardly surprising, the good Dr Bowdler found *Measure for Measure* problematic in a way that critics today could scarce take seriously, namely, in its being – uniquely – 'beyond bowdlerization'; that is, impossible to alter such that it too could (as his *The Family Shakespeare* advertised) "with propriety be read aloud in a family." Thus he felt obliged to provide it a special editorial preface warning of its dangers – so Jonathan Bate recounts in *The Genius of Shakespeare* (London: Picador, 1997), 294–8. According to Rolland Mushat Frye, in *Shakespeare and Christian Doctrine* (Princeton: Princeton University, 1984) an indication of early Catholic attitudes towards this play is provided by the so-called Valladolid Folio (an ordinary copy of the second Folio [1632], but "censored under the authority of the Inquisition by an English Jesuit" to be used "as reading matter for students in the English College at Valladolid, Spain"): "The censorship was customarily exercised with pen and ink and consisted in the blacking out of particular words, phrases, and lines. The one exception to this method of expurgation is the total removal of *Measure for Measure* from the volume, the pages having been neatly cut out with a sharp instrument" (275–7).

58 Derek Traversi, observes in *An Approach to Shakespeare*, 3rd ed. (London: Hollis and Canter, 1969), 65: "'Most of the difficulties derive ultimately from the discrepancy which is generally felt to exist between the play's formal assumptions and a prevailing spirit which is, for the greater part of its development, notably incompatible with them. Formally speaking, *Measure for Measure* is a comedy ... The most individual episodes, on the other hand, are notably uncomic, dedicated not to reconciliation but to the exploration of insoluble conflicts and sombre moral realities."

59 Norman Rabkin in *Shakespeare and the Common Understanding* (New York: Free Press, 1967) is one of those who find its 'happy ending ... imperfectly convincing' (104). He also contends, "For modern audiences what seems most problematic is how to respond to Isabella's demand that her brother Claudio sacrifice his life rather than allow Angelo to violate her chastity" (101). He goes on to argue, unconvincingly to me but in accor-

dance with his general thesis about Shakespeare's view of the world, "There is no answer to Isabella: she is right. But there is likewise no answer to Claudio, who is right in his own terms" (104).

60 Granville-Barker in *More Prefaces to Shakespeare* (Princeton: Princeton University Press, 1974) observes, "That for all the beauty and ruthless wisdom of the play, [Shakespeare] is not working happily. And in doing his duty by the plot, truth to character has to suffer violence at the end" (151). F.R. Leavis in *The Common Pursuit* bucks the trend by offering an unqualified defense of *Measure for Measure* against those (such as L.C. Knights) who challenge its dramatic integrity: "My own view is clean contrary: it is that the resolution of the plot of *Measure for Measure* is a consummately right and satisfying fulfillment of the essential design; marvellously adroit, with an adroitness that expresses, and derives from, the poet's sure human insight and his fineness of ethical and poetic sensibility" (169). Suffice it to observe, a marvelling sense of 'satisfying fulfillment' is *not* the 'common' experience of most viewers or readers of the play.

61 As per most modern editions, that is, such as the Arden edition of *Measure For Measure* J.W. Lever, ed. (London: Methuen, 1965) used here. The only original text of the play, that of the Folio, divides the modern Second Scene into two separate scenes at line 107. This has some potential importance for one's interpretation. The Folio's division more clearly implies that Pompey's "Yonder man is carried to prison" (79) does *not* refer to Claudio – and thus that Mistress Overdone's response is not a textual anomaly (as Lever too readily concedes in his Introduction, xix–xx) – and that, rather, we are to understand that Angelo's dragnet is catching several, perhaps many, similar cases (see 4.3.1–20).

62 'Lodowick' may be a slight 'Germanization' of Lodovico; see *Othello*, and Machiavelli's *Discourses on Livy* III, 11. Its belated introduction is as puzzling as the name supplied for the disguised Kent at the end of *King Lear* ('Caius'; 5.3.282), but it is perhaps worth noting that 'Lodovico,' like 'Vincentio,' refers to victory.

63 We subsequently learn from the interrogation of Master Froth what the title 'gentleman' is worth in Vienna (2.1.144–208).

64 This story is the central paragraph of the seven that make up chapter 7 (Mansfield translation, 29–30). Bloom, in his essay on the play in *Love and Friendship*, and Harry V. Jaffa, 'Chastity as a Political Principle: An Interpretation of Shakespeare's *Measure for Measure*' (in *Shakespeare as Political Thinker*, 203–40), are two of very few treatments in which the parallel with this notoriously 'Machiavellian' episode is even noted, much less discussed. Their analyses are also unusual in the attention given to the broader political significance of the sexual disorder in Vienna. And while I have some important points of disagreement with both authors (as they have with each other), I am indebted to their many insights, which I have tried to incorporate and further develop in my own interpretation.

65 Having explained why a prince cannot always actually practice 'all those things for which men are held good,' Machiavelli goes on to observe:

> And so he needs to have a spirit to change as the winds of fortune and the variations of things command him, and ... not depart from the good, when possible, but know how to enter into evil, when forced by necessity.
>
> A prince should thus take great care that nothing escape his mouth that is not full of the above-mentioned five qualities and that, to see him and hear him, he should appear all mercy, all faith, all honesty, all humanity, all religion. And nothing is more necessary to appear to have than this last quality. (*The Prince*, ch. 18, par. 5–6, 70)

66 As Aristotle argues in his *Politics* 1259b 10–18, 1287b 37ff.

67 This seems to be the goal of the education given the Guardians in Plato's *Republic*: their souls having been properly tuned, internally harmonized, by an appropriate mixture of music and athletics, they would have a natural sense of grace and harmony, thus the sharpest sense of what isn't finely made by art or by nature, and "being displeased correctly, would praise the fine things" (401d–402a).

68 As Machiavelli teaches, consistency is necessary both for the people's sense of security in their obedience, and for the prince's projection of strength: "What makes him contemptible is to be held variable, light, effeminate, pusillanimous, irresolute, from which a prince should guard himself as from a shoal." In this same context, Machiavelli argues that the ruler "should insist that his judgments in the private concerns of his subjects be irrevocable" (*The Prince*, ch. 19, par. 1; 72) – a principle Angelo clearly appreciates. But one cannot help wondering whether the Duke's failure to enforce the laws respecting sexual conduct does not derive from a different concern with consistency, namely, his unwillingness to impose on others what he does not abide by himself. It is certainly a theme he recurs to often enough (3.2.249–51, 258–63; 4.2.77–83; 5.1.111–15, 402–14).

69 The *Prince*, ch. 18, par. 3, 69–70. In this connection, it is worth recalling that Machiavelli's most famous comedy, *Mandragola*, also involves a 'bed trick,' though his features a switch in the male, rather than the female, participant.

70 Anyone familiar with *The Prince* is apt to be reminded here of Machiavelli's Dedicatory Letter wherein he observes, "To know well the nature of peoples one needs to be a prince, and to know well the nature of princes one needs to be of the people." Machiavelli's treatise, however, makes clear that being a successful prince actually requires both kinds of knowledge.

71 That is, the Duke poses as what the Greeks called a *xenos* (foreigner, stranger, guest). This is the term by which Sokrates in his *Apology* refers to himself in relation to the Athenians he is addressing (17d). The term also stands in place of a name for the two Sokrates-like philosophers who serve as the leading interlocutors in four Platonic dialogues not led by Sokrates, i.e., the *xenos* from Elea (the so-called Eleatic Stranger) in

Sophist and *Statesman*, the Athenian Stranger in *Laws* and *Epinomis*. Also, Friar Peter's oddly qualified explanation of 'Friar Lodowick's' absence from the Duke's homecoming celebration ("he is sick ... of a strange fever"; 5.1.153–4), gains special pertinence in light of Sokrates' famously cryptic insinuation that, from the philosopher's perspective, life itself is a sickness (*Phaedo* 118a; 59b).

72 Most bear names of famous ancient Romans or Roman *gens* (Crassus, Flavius, Valencius, Varrius); 'Rowland' is Shakespeare's spelling of Childe Roland, legendary son of King Arthur. (see also *King Lear*, 3.4.179).

73 G. Wilson Knight, in his famous essay, '*Measure for Measure* and the Gospels' in *The Wheel of Fire*, sees the play as Christian through and through: "There is thus a pervading atmosphere of orthodoxy and ethical criticism, in which is centred the mysterious holiness, the profound death-philosophy, the enlightened human insight and Christian ethic of the protagonist, the Duke of Vienna" (76). But while Knight adduces many interesting parallels between the texts of the play and of the Gospels, he has to resort to misrepresentation to make his case. For example, he tells us, "After rebuking Pompey the bawd very sternly but not unkindly, he [the Duke] concludes: 'Go mend, go mend.' His attitude is that of Jesus to the woman taken in adultery: 'Neither do I condemn thee: go, and sin no more.'" Hardly so, for Knight has conveniently ignored both Pompey's response and what is in fact the Duke's *concluding* benediction on Pompey: "Take him to prison, officer: / Correction and instruction must both work / Ere this rude beast will profit" (3.2.30–2)

Speaking more generally, however, Wilson Knight's entire analysis is compromised by an all too typical error: mistaking the fact that Shakespeare's Duke rules a Christian city, and thus employs Christian rhetoric and supports Christian morals, for clear evidence that he is Christian himself. Similar remarks, of course, apply to Shakespeare as well.

74 This practical definition of philosophy imparts a whole other meaning to the Duke's advising, 'Be absolute for death.' Its meaning is nicely encapsulated in his 'consoling' Isabella, "That life is better life, past fearing death, / Than that which lives to fear" (5.1.395–6). Shakespeare's dear Montaigne generously documents the distinguished lineage of this formula in his essay devoted to the subject. In fact, his discussion may provide the clearest insight into what the Duke is attempting to accomplish with his advice to Claudio.

> The body, when bent and bowed, has less strength to support a burden, and so has the soul; we must raise and straighten her against the assault of this adversary. For as it is impossible for the soul to be at rest while she fears death, so, if she can gain assurance against it, she can boast of a thing as it were beyond man's estate: that it is impossible for worry, torment, fear, or even the slightest displeasure to dwell in her ...
>
> What does it matter when it comes, since it is inevitable? To the man who told

Socrates, 'The thirty tyrants have condemned you to death,' he replied: 'And nature, them.'

The translation is that of Donald M. Frame in *The Complete Essays of Montaigne* (Stanford: Stanford University Press, 1985), 63–4.

75 Cf. *Prior Analytics* 68 b 4–7; *Nic. Ethics* 1116 a 10–15; 1156 a 31–b 6; *Politics* 1252a 24–30; 1334b 29 – 1335a 35; 1335b 38 – 1336a 2.

76 Cf. *Republic*, 601b, 398a–b, 399e; 382c–d, 389b, 414b ff.

77 Cf. ibid., 499b–c.

78 Cf. ibid., 346e. Both Bloom and Jaffa (see note 64 above) recognize in the pattern of evidence Shakespeare provides that his Duke is a philosopher, and that the previous years of his misrule are attributable to this fact. So does Barbara Tovey in 'Wisdom and the Law: Thoughts on the Political Philosophy of *Measure for Measure*,' in *Shakespeare's Political Pageant*, 61–75). Tovey, however, argues (63), "A philosophical nature may unfit a person for political rulership in at least two distinct ways." In addition to being negligent by virtue of his philosophical preoccupations, he may be incapable of sufficient anger, and thus of the harshness necessary for law enforcement, because in acquiring self-knowledge he perforce must recognize his own faults and failings. Hers is a tempting suggestion, and certainly worth considering, but I'm not persuaded it serves to explain (as it is apparently intended) the Duke's earlier permissiveness, since it makes his sudden willingness to crack down all the more puzzling. In any case, none of the these three authors really undertakes to explain why or how the Duke's attitude towards his political responsibilities *changes*, thus leaving something of a paradox at the center of their respective analyses: Vienna is a political mess because its ruler is a philosopher, and Vienna is salvaged because its ruler is a philosopher.

79 Cf. *Republic*, 485d–e.

80 As the philosopher Rousseau so honestly confesses in his *Discourse on Inequality*: "It is reason that engenders amour propre [i.e., vanity], and reflection that reinforces it; reason that turns man back upon himself; reason that separates him from everything that troubles and afflicts him: It is Philosophy that isolates him; by means of Philosophy he secretly says, at the sight of a suffering man, perish if you wish, I am safe. Only dangers that threaten the entire society still disturb the Philosopher's tranquil slumber and rouse him from his bed." From *The Discourses and Other Early Political Writings*, 153. Cf. *Republic*, 596a–597e.

81 Here, then, I believe Shakespeare exposes the central problem with the idea Plato introduces in his *Republic*: that of the philosopher-king – not that Plato was unaware of it himself, as carefully expositing the implications of the most pertinent passages makes clear (especially 519b–521b, but see also 540a–b, 592a–b).

82 *Tusculan Disputations* V.4, 10.

83 I refer here, of course, to the richest, most famous image in all of philosophical litera-

ture, Plato's so-called Allegory of the Cave (*Republic* 514a–521c; see also 529a–d), along with another well-known story from that dialogue, Glaukon's version of the Gyges legend (359d ff).

84 The entirety of Plato's *Republic* is relevant to this point, but note especially 402e–403a, 458d, 571b–576c. Book 5 of the dialogue is itself a comedy highlighting the most serious dimensions of the problem posed by *erōs* (see the 'Interpretive Essay' that accompanies Allan Bloom's translation of the dialogue, 379–97; also Craig, *The War Lover*, ch. 6).

85 Technically, I suppose, one must include Mistress Overdone amongst the married set, but surely the madam of brothel who's gone through nine husbands (so far) is in a class by herself – and *not* representative of a reasonable alternative.

86 In the very course of reproaching himself, Claudio's language betrays a trace of this: "Our natures do pursue, / Like rats that ravin down their proper bane, / a thirsty evil" (1.2.120–2). Traversi in *An Approach to Shakespeare* (vol. 2) provides an especially useful analysis of how this speech works poetically (66).

87 Amusing though his characterization is, Wylie Sypher goes too far in dismissing her as "that hysterical virgin" in his essay entitled 'Shakespeare as Casuist: *Measure for Measure*,' in *Essays in Shakespearean Criticism*, J.E. Calderwood and H.E. Toliver, eds. (Englewood Cliffs, NJ: Prentice Hall, 1970), 324. But certainly Isabella shows more than a trace of fanaticism on the subject, and one must wonder what's behind it. Her own powerful but repressed sexual desire is the most likely candidate. As has frequently been noted, at least since William Empson publicly directed attention to it, Shakespeare has provided her a language whose ambiguities are redolent of sexual possibilities. Jonathan Bate in *The Genius of Shakespeare* briefly reprises the importance of Shakespeare in general, and this play in particular, for Empson's new approach to appreciating and analysing poetry (302–11).

88 As Sokrates explicitly notes, "The amount of the marriages we'll leave to the rulers in order that they may most nearly preserve the same number of men, taking into consideration wars, diseases, and everything of that sort" (460a). Is it altogether fanciful to see a shadow of this in Mistress Overdone's complaining, "Thus, what with the war, what with the sweat [i.e., sickness], what with the gallows, and what with poverty, I am custom shrunk" (1.2.75–7)?

89 Much of my appreciation for just how strange is this orgy of marrying that the Duke has instigated comes from having the opportunity to read an as yet unpublished essay by Tobin L. Craig, entitled 'Measured Marriages.'

90 This is of such importance that Hobbes makes it the third of the ten political commandments in which he would have all subjects of Leviathan educated: "They ought to be informed, how great a fault it is, to speak evill of the Sovereign Representative, (whether One man, or an Assembly of men;) or to argue and dispute his Power, or any way to use his Name irreverently, whereby he may be brought into Contempt with his

People, and their Obedience (in which the safety of the Common-wealth consisteth) slackened" (*Leviathan* ch. 30, par. 9).

91 It is at least interesting that in the Folio's list of characters, Lucio himself is described as "a Fantastic." As for Lucio, I believe he is subject to more abuse by commentators than he deserves. Barbara Tovey ('Wisdom and the Law') is especially hard on this rascal that I find as engaging as Falstaff: "Lucio is an instance of the most dangerous sort of human being, a highly intelligent person who is nevertheless devoid of morality. It is not inappropriate to think of him as a comic equivalent of Iago. *Othello* is a tragedy because it is ruled by intelligent malevolence. *Measure for Measure* is a comedy because it is ruled by intelligent benevolence. Lucio is a greater threat to the duke and to the city as a whole than any other character in the play. This is why he receives the harshest treatment" (65).

In order to accede to such a judgment, one has to overlook: (a) that Claudio regards him as a "good friend" (1.2.182); (b) that he proves to be a good friend, genuinely distressed at Claudio's predicament (64–5); (c) that he not only, as requested, promptly informs Isabella of her brother's danger, but overcomes her reluctance to attempt to help (1.4.68–84); (d) that he accompanies her on her mission of mercy, and but for his insistent prodding and coaching she would have given up after only the most perfunctory effort (2.2.43–7, 70, 90, 111, 125, 130, 133); (e) and that he attempts to protect her from what he supposes to be the Duke's impending wrath by shifting the blame from her to the "meddling friar" Lodowick, attesting that he saw her being suborned by him ("a saucy friar, a very scurvy fellow"; 5.1.130–9). As for the "treatment" to which Shakespeare's has him be subjected by the Duke, I would agree that being made to marry a whore upon whom one begot a child is not a kindness (at least to the begetter), but I am not persuaded that it is harsher than that to which Angelo is subjected (cf. 516–18).

92 Here one might compare what Plato has Sokrates tell Adeimantos in *Republic*:

> "Then the philosopher, associating with the divine and orderly, becomes orderly and divine, to the extent it is possible for a human being. But there is much slander everywhere."
>
> "That is entirely so."
>
> "If some necessity arises," I said, "for him to practice putting what he sees there into the characters [ēthē] of humans, both in private and in public, instead of forming only himself, do you suppose he'll prove a poor craftsman of moderation, justice, and all kinds of ordinary virtue?" (500c–d)

Sokrates had earlier suggested that "in a suitable [regime, the philosopher] himself will grow more, and save the common things along with the private" (497a).

93 As Nietzsche observes in *Beyond Good and Evil*, aph. 26:

Every choice [or 'chosen'; *auserlesene*] human strives instinctively for a citadel and a secrecy where he is *liberated* from the crowd, the many, the majority, where he may forget the rule 'Human,' being the exception – excluding only the one case in which he is pushed straight to such people by a still stronger instinct, as a seeker after knowledge in the great and exceptional sense. Anyone who, in intercourse with people, does not occasionally glisten in all the shades of distress, green and grey with disgust, satiety, sympathy, gloom, and loneliness, is certainly not a human of elevated taste; supposing, however, that he does not take all this burden and disgust upon himself voluntarily, that he persistently avoids it, and remains, as aforesaid, quietly and proudly hidden in his citadel, one thing is certain: he was not made, not predestined, for knowledge. If he were, he would one day have to say to himself, 'The devil take my good taste! but the rule is more interesting than the exception – than me, the exception!' – and he would go *down*, and above all, he would go 'inside.' The study of the *average* human being, long, serious, and with much dissembling, self-overcoming, familiarity, bad company – all company is bad company except that of one's equals – : this constitutes a necessary part of the life-history of every philosopher, perhaps the most unpleasant, malodorous, and disappointing part. (my translation)

94 Thus, the dialogue Plato devoted to plumbing the question of justice to its very roots, his *Republic*, is also the dialogue in which he gives his fullest account of political philosophy. For an extensive analysis of the special relationship between justice and philosophy, see Craig, *The War Lover*, passim.

95 However, as Shakespeare's plays so amply prove, well-wrought works of art may provide a surrogate experience insofar as we react to what is portrayed as we would in 'real life.'

96 Cf. *Republic* 331c–d.

97 For all of the prominence given to Justice *versus* Mercy in *The Merchant of Venice* (being central to its studied contrast between Old Testament and New Testament 'world-views'), these two terms are actually more frequently mentioned in *Measure for Measure*: 'justice' 26 times (one seventh of its total uses in the canon; it occurs 15 times in *Merchant*); 'mercy' 17 times (13 in *Merchant*).

98 Cf. *Republic* 444a, 449c–d ff.

99 In various notes appended to my main text, beginning with note 35 of my introductory chapter, I have cited a number of recent efforts to rehabilitate Shakespeare's standing as a political philosopher. Here I might add that these analyses are the work of scholars trained extensively if not primarily in political philosophy, and who are thus the better prepared to recognize this dimension of Shakespeare's dramas.

100 This is a superficiality, one should add, common to the vast majority of both Plato's

attackers and his defenders. For a typical example of the former, see René Girard, *A Theater of Envy*, 64. G.M.A. Grube's chapter 'Art' in *Plato's Thought* (Indianapolis: Hackett, 1980) is fairly repesentative of the standard view, which simply takes Plato's Sokrates at his word without any attempt to see how Plato's use of the dialogue form, itself dramatic imitation, might qualify, even partially repudiate, what his Sokrates says – or rather (ever the ironist) *seems* to say, often by asking leading questions. And while more expansive in her treatment of the topic, Iris Murdoch likewise does not really see beyond the surface of Sokrates' critique, *The Fire and the Sun* (Oxford: Oxford University Press, 1977). Similarly, Hans-George Gadamer's exposition, though philosophically more interesting, remains constrained by a 'non-dialogical' understanding of Sokrates' various criticisms, 'Plato and the Poets,' *Dialogue and Dialectic: Eight Hermeneutical Studies in Plato*, P. Christopher Smith, ed. and trans. (New Haven: Yale University Press, 1980). More nearly adequate is Julius A. Elias, *Plato's Defence of Poetry* (Albany: State University of New York Press, 1984).

101 There are a goodly number of more ambitious treatments of the subject, though (as I noted above) it is rare to find one whose author has a sufficient appreciation of the dramatic and reflexive subtleties of Platonic dialogues – of how comprehensive is their *irony* – and consequently of the special challenges they present to interpretation. Many scholars (a solid majority, I suspect) are put off by the very idea that determining Plato's (or Shakespeare's) views might not be the straightforward matter they would prefer it to be. Such, for example, is Thomas Gould in *The Ancient Quarrel between Poetry and Philosophy* (Princeton: Princeton University Press, 1990), whose very detailed and wide-ranging exposition is premised on certain dialogic characters (mainly Sokrates) being in effect direct and frank spokesmen for Plato. Gould is clearly troubled by those who presume otherwise, and devotes a portion of a chapter ('Was Plato Serious') to refuting students of the dialogues who see in Plato anything other than an implacable hostility to poetry: "Many [studies] propose ways to absolve Plato of the charge of having been (seriously) opposed to the (whole) poetic tradition. The best are those that start from a consideration of Plato's own dramatic artistry, his use of profound and vivid myths, his elevation of beauty to the object of highest knowledge, his thoughts about pleasure, and his appreciation of love and other kinds of inspired energy. The most exasperating are those that claim to detect playfulness or irony in Plato's criticisms" (219).

What scholars such as Gould find exasperating, readers more genuinely philosophical – more akin, that is, to Plato – would find exhilarating: the challenge of interpreting a text that faithfully imitates the challenge of interpreting the world, in which almost nothing is as straightforward as it first seems. As I emphasized in my Introduction, it is questions, puzzles, perplexity (whether encountered in the study of a text or in the direct observation of everyday life) that most effectively stimulates philosophical *activity*, inviting the reader-observer to provide for himself a coherent interpretation of what initially appears to be confusing and contradictory.

102 A careful reading of Rousseau's *Discourse on Inequality*, one of the most persuasive endorsements ever of the importance of pity for human life, confirms that he too regards pity as both reliant upon and properly subordinate to reason: "Mandeville clearly sensed that, for all their morality, men would never have been anything but monsters if Nature had not give them pity *in support of reason*; but he did not see that from this single attribute flow all the social virtues he wants to deny men" (pt 1, par. 37, my emphasis; *The Discourses and Other Early Political Writings* 153).

103 Sokrates' criticisms of writing are the guiding theme of the Prologue 'On Reading a Platonic Dialogue' which prefaces my study of Plato's *Republic*, in Craig, *The War Lover*. For a more detailed analysis, see Ronna Burger, *Plato's* Phaedrus: *A Defense of a Philosophic Art of Writing* (University: University of Alabama Press, 1980).

104 Cf. Nietzsche, *The Birth of Tragedy*, sects. 13–15 in Walter Kaufmann, ed. and trans. *Basic Writings of Nietzsche* (New York: Modern Library, 1968).

> He went to his death with the calm with which, according to Plato's description, he leaves the Symposium at dawn, the last of the revelers, to begin a new day, while on the benches and on the earth his drowsy table companions remain behind to dream of Socrates, the true eroticist. *The dying Socrates* became the new ideal, never seen before, of noble Greek youths: above all, the typical Hellenic youth, Plato, prostrated himself before this image with all the ardent devotion of his enthusiastic soul. (89)

> The Platonic dialogue was, as it were, the barge on which the shipwrecked ancient poetry saved herself with all her children: crowded into a narrow space and timidly submitting to the single pilot, Socrates, they now sailed into a new world, which never tired of looking at the fantastic spectacle of this procession. Indeed, Plato has given to all posterity the model of a new art form, the model of the *novel* – which may be described as an infinitely enhanced Aesopian fable, in which poetry holds the same rank in relation to dialectical philosophy as this same philosophy held for many centuries in relation to theology: namely, the rank of *ancilla*. This was the new position into which Plato, under the pressure of the demonic Socrates, forced poetry. (90–1)

> Anyone who has ever experienced the pleasure of Socratic insight and felt how, spreading in ever widening circles, it seeks to embrace the whole world of appearances, will never again find any stimulus to existence more violent than the craving to complete this conquest and to weave the net impenetrably tight. To one who feels that way, the Platonic Socrates will appear as the teacher of an altogether new form of "Greek cheerfulness" and blissful affirmation of existence that seeks to discharge itself in actions – most often in maieutic and educational influences on noble youths, with a view to eventually producing a genius. (97)

105 John E. Alvis is in no doubt on this point ('Introductory: Shakespearean Poetry and Politics' in *Shakespeare as Political Thinker*): "The plays invite their audiences (in theaters or studies) to continue the action of the plays by applying the moral principles affirmed in the fiction to their own existence. Insofar as these principles are political, Shakespearean drama performs a political function. Somewhat like Prospero, Vincentio, and Theseus, the dramatist arranges spectacles that may have a beneficial effect upon the public life. However, although the art is political in content and in effect, the wisdom which informs the art may suggest a life beyond politics" (23)

106 Or as John E. Alvis observes (ibid): "The sort of intellectual excellence Shakespeare attributes to the superior human being consists of a blending of theoretical principle with intuitive tact responding to particulars. The plays do make us aware of a more exclusively contemplative possibility available to the speculative poet, but this awareness is conveyed by reminders of the presence of the dramatist overseeing his creations rather than embodied in any of the staged characters" (14).

107 As Howard White in *Copp'd Hills Toward Heaven* says flatly (and, I believe, rightly), "*The Tempest* is a play about a philosopher king." (113). See also Paul A. Cantor, 'Prospero's Republic: The Politics of Shakespeare's *The Tempest*' (in *Shakespeare as Political Thinker*, 239–55); Diana Akers Rhoads, *Shakespeare's Defense of Poetry* (Lanham, MD: University Press of America, 1985), and more recently, David Lowenthal in *Shakespeare and the Good Life*, 21–70.

In analysing the Roman plays, both Michael Platt and Cantor rely heavily upon the psychology adumbrated in Plato's *Republic*. Platt, *Rome and Romans According to Shakespeare* (Salzburg: Institute For English Language and Literature, 1973), speaking of Coriolanus, observes, "His character springs from the exclusive and peculiar development of single part of the soul, the θυμοσ. In him Shakespeare has abstracted the *thymetic* or spirited man. *Thymos* – we adopt this term from the *Republic* ..." (128). Cantor suggests in *Shakespeare's Rome: Republic and Empire* (Ithaca: Cornell University Press, 1976), "A reading of Plato's discussion in the *Republic* of *erōs* and *thumos*, the two irrational parts of the soul, is very helpful for understanding the relationship between *Antony and Cleopatra* and *Coriolanus*" (213).

Howard White has documented the connections between Plato's *Laws* and *A Midsummer Night's Dream* in *Copp'd Hills towards Heaven* (43–64).

108 See, e.g., Thomas McFarland, *Shakespeare's Pastoral Comedy*, 179–84.

109 Michael Platt, 'Falstaff in the Valley of the Shadow of Death' in *Interpretation* vol 8, no. 1 (January 1979), 12–13. Platt notes as well that both characters do their military service on foot rather than mounted on horseback (in contrast to their famous companions, Hal and Alkibiades). Both are notoriously capable of consuming much drink. Moreover, "Falstaff asks the Socratic question, what is a thing? With his question, what is honor?, Falstaff calls into question the life of the gentleman ... Falstaff says he is witty and the cause of wit in other men (*2 Henry IV* 1.2.6); the friends of

Socrates think that he is wise and the cause of wisdom in themselves ... Neither Falstaff nor Socrates is beautiful, yet both exercise an extraordinary attraction upon other men." Moreover, Platt argues that within the garbled account of Falstaff's death given by Hostess Quickly, we may discern that Falstaff was attempting to recite the Twenty-third Psalm (8ff), and that this points to the major difference between the two deaths: "the terror of Falstaff and the equanimity of Socrates" (14).

Allan Bloom also addresses the Falstaff-Sokrates parallels in *Love and Friendship*:

> Hal and Falstaff are a pair for whom nothing is sacred, at least in speech. They insult each other without any of the elaborate formalisms that characterize the court. Their insults are the courtesies of this world and are more honest than those in use among the nobles ... Law and religion are the first targets of these free spirits ...
>
> The impious relationship of Hal and Falstaff, and the pious relationship between Hal and his father, pretty much represent the essential tension between philosophy and obedience to the ancestral so central to the life of Socrates. Falstaff is indeed Henry IV's rival. Hal knows that, although Henry IV does not ... [In playing King], the real son of the father epitomizes the father's role by an extreme attack on Falstaff, whom he calls "that villainous abominable misleader of youth" ... This is the complaint of the fathers against Socrates. And this charge, corrupting the youth, is really what brought Socrates down. He is the rival of the fathers in the education of their children, a function that belongs to the fathers in all traditional social orders, orders that are changed by the success of Socrates.
>
> Socrates' questioning of the sons inevitably leads sons to question their fathers. The Hal-Falstaff relationship is not entirely unlike the one between Socrates and Alcibiades. (406–7)

110 Thomas McFarland, *Shakespeare's Pastoral Comedy*, 181. He also observes: "In this context, the similarity of Falstaff and Socrates interlocks with a pervasive similarity that exists between the structure of the pastoral and that of Platonism. Indeed, as a recent commentator has argued at length, 'Platonism' is the 'informing philosophy of pastoral literature from its Greek origins to the Renaissance [*sic*] and after.'" McFarland's reference here is to Richard Cody, *The Landscape of the Mind: Pastoralism and Platonic Theory in Tasso's* Aminta *and Shakespeare's Early Comedies* (Oxford: Clarendon Press, 1969), 18.

Wesley Trimpi's analysis of Sidney's treatise on poetry shows it to be based especially on Platonic philosophy ('Sir Philip Sidney's *An Apology for Poetry*,' *The Cambridge History of Literary Criticism*, vol. 3, *The Renaissance*, Glyn P. Norton, ed., Cambridge: Cambridge University Press, 1999, ch. 18). One can easily believe that Shakespeare would have agreed with Sidney's view as Trimpi summarily presents it:

"First for Sidney, the exemplary *imago* has the power to overcome the limits of [didactic] philosophy by rendering its truth visible to 'the sight of the soul' (107.16), and this palpability has a far greater and more immediate effect upon moving the emotions than abstract conceptions do ... The poetic image, or the confluence of *imagines* in a fictional narrative, may also overcome the ethical limits of history through the poet's power to reveal the 'universal' by choosing exemplary figures and thereby supplying causes for effects in the 'imaginative ground-plot' of his 'profitable invention.' By means of the poetic image, that is, philosophy becomes apprehensible, history comprehensible" (197).

Bibliography

The following is a list of works cited. It does not include, however, classics of literature and philosophy (such as Plato's dialogues or Hobbes's treatises, or Shakespeare's plays and poems, or the novels of Melville or Jane Austen) unless reference has been made to a specific edition.

Adamson, Jane. *Othello as Tragedy: Some Problems of Judgment and Feeling.* Cambridge: Cambridge University Press, 1980.

–. *Troilus and Cressida.* Boston: Twayne, 1987.

Alulis, Joseph. 'Wisdom and Fortune: The Education of the Prince in Shakespeare's *King Lear*,' *Interpretation* 21/3 (Spring 1994).

Alulis, Joseph, and Vickie Sullivan, eds. *Shakespeare's Political Pageant.* Lanham, MD: Rowman and Littlefield, 1996.

Alvis, John E. 'Introductory: Shakespearean Poetry and Politics.' In *Shakespeare as Political Thinker.* 2nd ed. Edited by John E. Alvis and Thomas G. West. Wilmington, DE: ISI Books, 2000.

Alvis, John E., and Thomas G. West, eds. *Shakespeare as Political Thinker.* 2nd ed. Wilmington, DE: ISI Books, 2000.

Aristotle. *The Complete Works of Aristotle: The Revised Oxford Translation.* Edited by Jonathan Barnes. Princeton: Princeton University Press, 1984.

Auchincloss, Louis. *Motiveless Malignity.* London: Gollancz, 1970.

Auden, W.H. *Forewards and Afterwards.* New York: Vintage, 1974.

–. *The Dyer's Hand and Other Essays.* New York: Vintage, 1989.

Baldwin, T.W. *William Shakspere's Small Latine & Lesse Greeke.* Urbana: University of Illinois Press, 1944.

Barber, C.L., and Richard P. Wheeler. *The Whole Journey: Shakespeare's Power of Development.* Berkeley: University of California Press, 1986.

Bate, Jonathan, ed. *The Romantics on Shakespeare*. New York: Penguin, 1992.

–. *The Genius of Shakespeare*. London: Picador, 1997.

Berger, Thomas L. 'The Second Quarto of *Othello*.' In *Othello: New Perspectives*. Edited by Virginia Vaughan and Kent Cartwright. Rutherford, NJ: Fairleigh Dickinson University Press, 1991.

Berry, Francis. '*Macbeth*: Tense and Mood.' In *Essays in Shakespearean Criticism*. Edited by J.E. Calderwood and H.E. Toliver. Englewood Cliffs, NJ: Prentice-Hall, 1970.

Biggins, Dennis. 'Sexuality, Witchcraft, and Violence in *Macbeth*.' *Shakespeare Studies* 8 (1975).

Blits, Jan H. *The End of the Ancient Republic*. Durham: Carolina Academic Press, 1982.

–. *The Insufficiency of Virtue:* Macbeth *and the Natural Order*. Lanham, MD: Rowman and Littlefield, 1996.

Bloom, Allan. *Shakespeare's Politics*. New York: Basic Books, 1964.

–. *The Republic of Plato*. New York: Basic Books, 1968.

–. *Love and Friendship*. New York: Simon and Schuster, 1993.

Bowers, Fredson. *On Editing Shakespeare*. Charlottesville: University of Virginia Press, 1966.

Bradley, A.C. *Shakespearean Tragedy*. London: Macmillan, 1904.

Bradshaw, Graham. *Shakespeare's Scepticism*. Ithaca, NY: Cornell University Press, 1987.

–. *Misrepresentations: Shakespeare and the Materialists*. Ithaca, NY: Cornell University Press, 1993.

Briggs, Robin. *Witches and Neighbors*. New York: Viking, 1996.

Brooks, Cleanth. 'The Naked Babe and the Cloak of Manliness.' In *The Well Wrought Urn*. New York: Harcourt, Brace and World, 1947.

Brown, John Russell, ed. *Merchant of Venice*. 2nd Arden Shakespeare ed. London: Methuen, 1959.

Burger, Ronna. *Plato's* Phaedrus: *A Defense of a Philosophic Art of Writing*. University, AB: University of Alabama Press, 1980.

Burgess, Anthony. *Urgent Copy: Literary Studies in Search of Shakespeare the Man*. New York: Norton, 1968.

Butler, Christopher. *Number Symbolism*. London: Routledge and Kegan Paul, 1970.

Cantor, Paul A. *Shakespeare's Rome: Republic and Empire*. Ithaca: Cornell University Press, 1976.

–. 'Shakespeare's *The Tempest*: The Wise Man as Hero.' *Shakespeare Quarterly* (Spring 1980).

–. 'The Erring Barbarian among the Supersubtle Venetians.' *Southwest Review* (Summer 1990).

–. 'Nature and Convention in *King Lear*.' In *Poets, Princes, and Private Citizens*. Edited by Joseph M. Knippenberg and Peter A. Lawler. Lanham, MD: Rowman and Littlefield, 1996.

–. 'On Sitting Down to Read *King Lears* Again: The textual Deconstruction of Shakespeare.' In *The Flight from Science and Reason.* Edited by Paul R. Gross, Norman Levitt, and Martin W. Lewis. New York: New York Academy of Sciences, 1996.

–. '*Macbeth* and the Gospelling of Scotland.' In *Shakespeare as Political Thinker.* 2nd ed. Edited by John E. Alvis and Thomas G. West. Wilmington, DE: ISI Books, 2000.

Cavell, Stanley. *Disowning Knowledge in Six Plays of Shakespeare.* Cambridge: Cambridge: University Press, 1987.

Coleridge, Samuel Taylor. *Biographia Literaria.* Edited by James Engell and W. Jackson Bate. Princeton: Princeton University Press, 1983.

Conrad, Joseph. *The Works of Joseph Conrad.* London: Heinemann, 1921.

Craig, Leon Harold. *The War Lover: A Study of Plato's Republic.* Toronto: University of Toronto Press, 1994.

Crane, Milton, ed. *Shakespeare's Art: Seven Essays.* Chicago: University of Chicago Press, 1973.

Crane, R.S. 'Monistic Criticism and the Structure of Shakespearean Drama.' In *Approaches to Shakespeare.* Edited by Norman Rabkin. New York: McGraw-Hill, 1964.

Danby, John F. *Shakespeare's Doctrine of Nature: A Study of* King Lear. London: Faber and Faber, 1948.

Davis, Michael. 'Courage and Impotence in Shakespeare's *Macbeth.*' In *Shakespeare's Political Pageant.* Edited by Joseph Alulis and Vickie Sullivan. Lanham, MD: Rowman and Littlefield, 1996.

Diogenes Laertius. *Lives and Opinions of Eminent Philosophers.* Translated by R.D. Hicks. Cambridge, MA: Harvard University Press, 1925.

Dobrée, Bonamy, ed. *Shakespeare: The Writer and His Work.* London: Longmans, 1964.

Elias, Julius A. *Plato's Defence of Poetry.* Albany: State University of New York Press, 1984.

Eliot, T.S. *Selected Essays.* New York: Harcourt Brace, 1950.

Elliot, Martin. *Shakespeare's Invention of Othello.* New York: St Martin's Press, 1988.

Epstein, Norrie. *The Friendly Shakespeare.* New York: Penguin, 1993.

Evans, Bertrand. *Shakespeare's Tragic Practice.* Oxford: Clarendon Press, 1979.

Everett, Barbara. 'Spanish *Othello*: The Making of Shakespeare's Moor.' *Shakespeare Survey* 35 (1982).

Foakes, R.A., ed. *King Lear* 3rd Arden Shakespeare ed. Walton-on-Thames: Thomas Nelson and Son, 1997.

Fowler, Alastair. *Triumphal Forms: Structural Patterns in Elizabethan Poetry.* Cambridge: Cambridge University Press, 1970.

Frame, Donald, ed. and trans. *The Complete Essays of Montaigne.* Stanford: Stanford University Press, 1958.

Fraser, Russell A. *Shakespeare's Poetics in Relation to King Lear.* London: Routledge and Kegan Paul, 1962.

Frye, Roland Mushat. *Shakespeare and Christian Doctrine*. Princeton: Princeton University Press, 1963.

–. *The Renaissance* Hamlet: *Issues and Responses in 1600*. Princeton: Princeton University Press, 1984.

Fuller, Timothy. 'The Relation of Thought and Action in *Macbeth*.' In *Shakespeare's Political Pageant*. edited by Joseph Alulis and Vickie Sullivan. Lanham, MD: Rowman and Littlefield, 1996.

Gadamer, Hans-George. *Dialogue and Dialectic: Eight Hermeneutical Studies in Plato*. Edited and translated by P. Christopher Smith. New Haven: Yale University Press, 1980.

Gardiner, Juliet, and Neil Wenborn, eds. *The* History Today *Companion to British History*. London: Collins and Brown, 1995.

Girard, René. *A Theater of Envy*. New York: Oxford University Press, 1991.

Girouard, Mark. *Life in the English Country House*. New Haven: Yale University Press, 1978.

Goddard, Harold C. *The Meaning of Shakespeare*. Vol 2. Chicago: University of Chicago Press, 1951.

Gould, Thomas. *The Ancient Quarrel between Poetry and Philosophy*. Princeton: Princeton University Press, 1990.

Granville-Barker, Harley. *Prefaces to Shakespeare*. 2 vols. Princeton: Princeton University Press, 1974.

–. *More Prefaces to Shakespeare*. Princeton: Princeton University Press, 1974.

Grube, G.M.A. *Plato's Thought*. Indianapolis: Hackett, 1980.

Harbage, Alfred. *Conceptions of Shakespeare*. New York: Schocken, 1968.

–. *As They Liked It*. Philadelphia: University of Pennsylvania Press, 1972.

–. *Shakespeare without Words*. Cambridge: Harvard University Press, 1972.

–. 'Shakespeare and the Professions.' In *Shakespeare's Art: Seven Essays*. Edited by Milton Crane. Chicago: University of Chicago Press, 1973.

Heilman, Robert B. *This Great Stage: Image and Structure in King Lear*. Baton Rouge: Louisiana State University Press, 1948.

–. *Magic in the Web*. Lexington, KY: University of Kentucky Press, 1956.

Hogarth, G., and M. Dickens, eds. *Letters of Charles Dickens*. London: 1893.

Hughes, Robert. *The Fatal Shore*. New York: Alfred A. Knopf, 1987.

Jaffa, Harry. 'The Limits of Politics: *King Lear*, Act I, scene i.' In *Shakespeare's Politics*. With Allan Bloom. New York: Basic Books, 1964.

Jenkins, Harold, ed. *Hamlet*. 2nd Arden Shakespeare ed. London: Methuen, 1982.

Jensen, Pamela. '"This is Venice": Politics in Shakespeare's *Othello*.' In *Shakespeare's Political Pageant*. Edited by Joseph Alulis and Vickie Sullivan. Lanham, MD: Rowman and Littlefield, 1996.

Jordon, John E., ed. *De Quincey as Critic*. London: Routledge and Kegan Paul, 1973.

Kernan, Alvin. *Shakespeare, the King's Playwright: Theater in the Stuart Court 1603–1613.* New Haven: Yale University Press, 1995.

Klein, Joan Larsen. 'Lady Macbeth: "Infirm of Purpose."' In *The Woman's Part: Feminist Criticism of Shakespeare.* Edited by C.R.S. Lenz, G. Greene, C.T. Neely. Urbana: University of Illinois Press, 1983.

Knight, G. Wilson. *The Wheel of Fire.* London: Methuen, 1949.

–. *The Imperial Theme.* London: Methuen, 1965.

Knights, L.C. *Some Shakespearean Themes.* London: Chatto and Windus, 1960.

–. *Explorations.* New York: New York University Press, 1964.

–. 'The Question of Character in Shakespeare.' In *Approaches to Shakespeare.* Edited by Norman Rabkin. New York: McGraw-Hill, 1964.

Knippenberg, Joseph M., and Peter A. Lawler, eds. *Poets, Princes, and Private Citizens.* Lanham, MD: Rowman and Littlefield, 1996.

Lawrence, D.H. *Phoenix.* New York: Viking, 1936.

Leavis, F.R. *The Common Pursuit.* London: Chatto and Windus, 1952.

–. *Education and the University.* Cambridge: Cambridge University Press, 1979.

Lever, J.W., ed. *Measure for Measure* 2nd Arden Shakespeare ed. London: Methuen, 1965.

Lowenthal, David. *Shakespeare and the Good Life.* Lanham, MD: Rowman and Littlefield, 1997.

Machiavelli, N. *The Prince.* Edited and translated by Harvey Mansfield. Chicago: University of Chicago Press, 1985.

McAdam, E.L., Jr, and George Milne, eds. *A Johnson Reader.* New York: Pantheon, 1964.

McAlindon, T. *Shakespeare's Tragic Cosmos.* Cambridge: Cambridge University Press, 1991.

McFarland, Thomas. *Shakespeare's Pastoral Comedy.* Chapel Hill: University of North Carolina Press, 1972.

Muir, Kenneth. *Shakespeare: Contrasts and Controversies.* Norman: University of Oklahoma Press, 1985.

–, ed. *Macbeth.* 2nd Arden Shakespeare ed. London and New York: Routledge, 1988.

–, ed. *King Lear.* 2nd Arden Shakespeare ed. London and New York: Routledge, 1989.

Murdoch, Iris. *The Fire and the Sun.* Oxford: Oxford University Press, 1977.

Neely, Carol Thomas. 'Women and Men in *Othello.*' In *The Woman's Part: Feminist Criticism of Shakespeare.* Edited by C.R.S. Lenz, G. Greene, C.T. Neely. Urbana: University of Illinois Press, 1983.

Nietzsche, Friedrich. 'The Birth of Tragedy.' In *Basic Writings of Nietzsche.* Edited and translated by Walter Kaufmann. New York: Modern Library, 1968.

–. *Daybreak: Thoughts on the Prejudices of Morality.* Translated by R.J. Hollingdale. Cambridge: Cambridge University Press, 1982.

–. *Untimely Meditations.* Translated by R.J. Hollingdale. Cambridge: Cambridge University Press, 1983.

Nuttall, A.D. *A New Mimesis: Shakespeare and the Representation of Reality*. London: Methuen, 1983.

Ornstein, Robert. 'Historical Criticism and the Interpretation of Shakespeare.' *Shakespeare Quarterly* 10 (1959).

Pafford, J.H.P., ed. *The Winter's Tale*. 2nd Arden Shakespeare ed. London: Methuen, 1963.

Park, Clara Claiborne. 'As We Like It: How a Girl Can Be Smart and Still Popular.' In *The Woman's Part: Feminist Criticism of Shakespeare*. Edited by C.R.S. Lenz, G. Greene, C.T. Neely. Urbana: University of Illinois Press, 1983.

Platt, Michael. *Rome and Romans According to Shakespeare*. Salsburg: Institute für Englische Sprache und Literatur, 1973.

–. 'Falstaff in the Valley of the Shadow of Death.' *Interpretation* 21/1 (January, 1979).

Rabkin, Norman. *Shakespeare and the Common Understanding*. New York: Free Press, 1967.

–. ed. *Approaches to Shakespeare*. New York: McGraw-Hill, 1964.

Raysor, Thomas Middleton, ed. *Coleridge's Shakespearean Criticism*. Cambridge: Cambridge University Press, 1930.

Rhoads, Diana Akers. *Shakespeare's Defense of Poetry*. Lanham, MD: University Press of America, 1985.

Ridley, M.R., ed. *Othello*. 2nd Arden Shakespeare ed. London: Methuen, 1958.

Rosenberg, Marvin. *The Masks of* King Lear. Newark: University of Delaware Press, 1972.

–. *The Masks of* Macbeth. Newark: University of Delaware Press, 1978.

Røstvig, Maren-Sofie. 'Structure as Prophecy: The Influence of Biblical Exegesis upon Theories of Literary Structure.' In *Silent Poetry: Essays in Numerological Analysis*. Edited by Alastair Fowler. London: Routledge and Kegan Paul, 1970.

Rousseau, J.J. *Emile*. Translated by Allan Bloom. New York: Basic Books, 1979.

–. *The Discourses and Other Early Political Writings*. Edited and translated by Victor Gourevitch. Cambridge: Cambridge University Press, 1997.

Rowse, A.L. *The Churchills: From the Death of Marlborough to the Present*. New York: Harper and Brothers, 1958.

Sanders, Wilbur, and Howard Jacobson. *Shakespeare's Magnanimity*. New York: Oxford University Press, 1978.

Schmidgall, Gary. *Shakespeare and Opera*. New York: Oxford University Press, 1990.

Schoenbaum, Samuel. *Shakespeare's Lives*. New York: Oxford University Press, 1970.

–. *William Shakespeare: A Documentary Life*. New York: Oxford University Press, 1975

Schwehn, Mark. '*King Lear* beyond Reason: Love and Justice in the Family.' *First Things*, no. 36 (October, 1993).

Shreeve, James. *The Neandertal Enigma*. New York: William Morrow, 1995.

Sisson, C.J. 'Shakespeare.' In *Shakespeare: The Writer and His Work*. Edited by Bonamy Dobrée. London: Longmans, 1964.

Soellner, Rolf. *Timon of Athens: Shakespeare's Pessimistic Tragedy*. Columbis, OH: Ohio State University Press, 1979.

Spedding, James, Robert Ellis, and Douglas Heath, eds. *The Works of Francis Bacon*. London: Longmans, 1870.

Spurgeon, Caroline F.E. *Shakespeare's Imagery and What It Tells Us*. Cambridge: Cambridge University Press, 1935.

Stapfer, Paul. *Shakespeare and Classical Antiquity*. Translated by Emily J. Carey. New York: Burt Franklin, 1970.

Stewart, J.I.M. *Character and Motive in Shakespeare*. London: Longmans, 1949.

Stockholder, Kay. *Dream Works: Lovers and Families in Shakespeare's Plays*. Toronto: University of Toronto Press, 1987.

Strauss, Leo. *Persecution and the Art of Writing*. Glencoe: Free Press, 1952.

–. *Natural Right and History*. Chicago: University of Chicago Press, 1953.

–. *What Is Political Philosophy*? Glencoe: Free Press, 1959.

–. *The City and Man*. Chicago: Rand McNally, 1964.

–. *The Rebirth of Classical Political Rationalism*. Edited by Thomas L. Pangle. Chicago: University of Chicago Press, 1989.

Sypher, Wylie. 'Shakespeare as Casuist: *Measure for Measure*.' In *Essays in Shakespearean Criticism*. Edited by J.E. Calderwood and H.E. Toliver. Englewood Cliffs, NJ: Prentice-Hall, 1970.

Thomas, Vivian. *The Moral Universe of Shakespeare's Problem Plays*. London and New York: Routledge, 1991.

Thomson, Rev. Thomas. *A History of the Scottish People*. 3 vols. London: Blackie and Sons, 1896.

Tillyard, E.M.W. *Shakespeare's Problem Plays*. London: Chatto and Windus, 1950.

Tolstoy, Leo. *War and Peace*. Translated by Louise and Aylmer Maude. Norwalk, CT: Easton, 1981.

Tovey, Barbara. 'The Golden Casket: An Interpretation of *The Merchant of Venice*.' In *Shakespeare as Political Thinker*. 2nd ed. Edited by John E. Alvis and Thomas G. West. Wilmington, DE: ISI Books, 2000.

–. 'Wisdom and the Law: Thoughts on the Political Philosophy of *Measure for Measure*.' In *Shakespeare's Political Pageant*. Edited by Joseph Alulis and Vickie Sullivan. Lanham, MD: Rowman and Littlefield, 1996.

Traversi, Derek. *An Approach to Shakespeare*. 2 vols. 3rd ed. London: Hollis and Carter, 1969.

Trevor-Roper, Sir Hugh. 'What's in a Name?' *Réalitiés* (November, 1962).

Trimpi, Wesley. 'Sir Philip Sidney's An Apology for Poetry.' In *The Cambridge History of Literary Criticism*, vol. 3, *The Renaissance*. Edited by Glyn P. Norton. Cambridge: Cambridge University Press, 1999.

Turnbull, S.R. *The Samurai: A Military History*. New York: Macmillan, 1977.

Ure, Peter. 'The Problem Plays.' In *Shakespeare: The Writer and His Work*. Edited by Bonamy Dobrée. London: Longmans, 1964.

Vaughan, Viginia Mason. Othello: *A Contextual History*. Cambridge: Cambridge University Press, 1994.

Viswanathan, S. *The Shakespeare Play as Poem: A Critical Tradition in Perspective*. Cambridge: Cambridge University Press, 1980.

Wells, Stanley. *Shakespeare: A Life in Drama*. New York: W.W. Norton, 1995.

West, Robert H. *Shakespeare and the Outer Mystery*. Lexington: University of Kentucky Press, 1968.

White, Howard B. *Copp'd Hills toward Heaven: Shakespeare and the Classical Polity*. The Hague: Martinius Nijhoff, 1970.

–. 'Macbeth and the Tyrannical Man.' *Interpretation* 2/1 (Winter 1971).

Wills, Garry. *Witches and Jesuits: Shakespeare's* Macbeth. New York: Oxford University Press, 1995.

Index of Names

Note: With the exception of Sokrates, characters in Plato's dialogues or in Shakespeare's plays are not included unless they are historical persons referred to as such in the text.

Achilles, 262, 300n7
Adamson, Jane, 295n2, 369n24
Aeschylus, 230, 275n13, 280n23, 374n36
Aesop, 389n104
Agathocles, 35, 91, 221
Ajax, 300n7, 327n109
Alulis, Joseph, 289n33, 306n34, 314n71, 338n19, 358n4
Alvis, John E., 289n33, 300n8, 345–6n45, 359n5, 390nn105, 106
Anaxagoras, 352n72
Archelaus, 374n36
Aristophanes, 168–9, 216, 275n13, 351n69, 354nn86, 90
Aristotle, 12, 18, 242, 285n30, 301n9, 304n22, 313n67, 320n82, 338n17, 352nn72, 74, 75, 364–5n14, 367n21, 368n24, 370n27, 374n36, 382n66, 384n75
Asclepius, 259
Auchincloss, Louis, 337n15
Auden, W.H., 5, 298n7, 358n4, 360n6
Augustine, 376n42
Austen, Jane, 317–18n77
Autolycus, 225

Bacon, Sir Francis, 18, 226, 271n5, 303n18, 304n22, 322n86, 340n23, 341n25, 343n37, 350n65, 352n72, 353n84, 360n6, 376–7n42, 379n55
Baldwin, T.W., 281n23, 351n69
Barnes, Jonathan, 365n14
Bate, Jonathan, 276n16, 300n8, 304n24, 333n3, 342n30, 359n6, 380n57, 385n87
Bate, W. Jackson, 356n1
Barber, C.L., 301n8
Beethoven, Ludwig van, 269n1
Berger, Thomas L., 365n16
Berry, Francis, 314n70
Biggins, Dennis, 331n122
Blits, Jan H., 289n35, 309n53, 310n55, 326n97, 331n123
Bloom, Allan, 269n2, 273n11, 289nn33, 34, 35, 329n114, 333n2, 350n63, 356n2, 364n12, 369n25, 376n42, 381n64, 384n78, 385n84, 390n109
Boas, Frederick S., 379n57

Bohr, Niels, 323n88
Borgia, Cesare (Duke Valentino), 236–7, 246
Bowdler, Dr Thomas, 380n57
Bradley, A.C., 277n18, 334n3
Bradshaw, Graham, 280n21, 286n31, 288n33, 291n38, 302–3n15, 303–4n19, 311n58, 313n66, 325n92, 329n117, 339n22, 364n13, 366n17, 372n32
Briggs, Robin, 269n4
Brookes, Cleanth, 277n20
Brown, John Russell, 357n3
Burger, Ronna, 389n103
Burgess, Anthony, 275n14
Butler, Christopher, 373n35

Calderwood, J.E., 314n70
Calvin, John, 376n42
Cantor, Paul, 294–5n44, 300n8, 310n55, 318–19n79, 333n1, 345n44, 352n73, 354n87, 355n98, 363n9, 390n107
Capell, Edward, 307n43, 332n1
Carey, Emily J., 280n23, 351n72
Cartwright, Kent, 365n16
Cato, Marcus Porcius, 358n5
Cavell, Stanley, 341n29, 348n57
Chapman, George, 267
Churchill, Lord John, 1st Duke of Marlborough, 292n40
Churchill, Winston, 292n40
Cicero, Marcus Tullius, 244, 351n69, 384n82
Cinthio, Giovanni Battista Giraldi, 363nn7, 11, 12, 366n19
Cody, Richard, 391n110
Coleridge, Samuel Taylor, 113, 139, 192–3, 276n16, 277n18, 288n33, 304n24, 333–4n3, 359n6
Collard, C., 303n15
Condell, Henrie, 282n24
Conrad, Joseph, 260, 345n42
Craig, Leon Harold, 269n4, 293n42, 301n11, 326n104, 356n101, 357n2, 370n26, 378n50, 385n84, 387n94, 389n103
Craig, Tobin L., 385n89
Crane, Milton, 274n12
Crane, R.S., 318n79
Crates, 354n88
Cyrus, 118, 260

Daedalus, 227
Danby, John F., 339–40n23, 341n25, 355nn98, 100
Dante Alighieri, 286–7n33, 310n54
Davis, Michael, 314–15n71, 319n80
De Quincey, Thomas, 276n16
Demeter, 215
Democritus, 352n72
Derrida, Jacques, 285n30
Descartes, René, 18, 379nn55, 56
Dickens, Charles, 6, 273n10
Dickens, M., 273n10
Diogenes the Cynic, 354n88
Diogenes Laertius, 352n72
Dobrée, Bonamy, 273n11, 379n57
Dorsch, T.S., 289n35
Droushout, Martin, 272–3n9
Dryden, John, 277n18

Edward III, 122
Elias, Julius, 388n100
Eliot, T.S., 286–8n33, 368n24
Elizabeth I, Queen, 5, 336n10
Elliot, Martin, 363n11, 369n24
Ellis, Robert, 303n18
Empedocles, 352n72, 364n14
Empson, William, 385n87
Engell, James, 356n1

Epicurus, 245, 352n72
Epstein, Norrie, 368n23
Erasmus, Desiderius, 344n40
Euripides, 275n13, 280n23, 374n36
Evans, Bertrand, 291n39, 299–300n70, 301n12, 316–17n74, 334n3, 368n23
Everett, Barbara, 367n19

Foakes, R.A., 322n1, 336n9, 342n32, 347n53, 355n98
Forrest, Edmund, 367n23
Fowler, Alastair, 373n35
Frame, Donald, 318n78, 384n74
Fraser, Russell A., 304n24
Fuller, Timothy, 305–6n34, 330n120
Frye, Roland Mushat, 279–80n21, 309–10n54, 380n57

Gadamer, Hans-Georg, 388n100
Gaunt, John of, 1st Duke of Lancaster, 346n46
Girard, René, 334n3, 388n100
Girouard, Mark, 342–3n35
Goddard, Harold C., 334n3
Goethe, Johann Wolfgang von, 281n23
Gould, Thomas, 388n101
Gourevitch, Victor, 344n38
Granville-Barker, Harley, 280n22, 328n111, 337n16, 381n60
Greene, G., 276n16, 365n17
Greene, Robert, 224, 228, 375n42
Gross, Paul R., 294n44
Grube, G.M.A., 387n100

Harbage, Alfred, 273–4n12, 277n17, 291n39
Hardy, Thomas, 272n7
Hazlitt, William, 276n16, 300n8, 304n24, 333n3, 359–60n6
Heath, Douglas, 303n18
Heilman, Robert B., 277n20, 340–1n25, 348n55, 355n98, 368–9n24
Heminge, John, 282n24
Henry II, King, 122
Henry IV, King, 346n46
Henry VII (Henry Tudor), King, 346n46
Heracleitus, 112, 352n72
Hobbes, Thomas, 18, 95, 118, 238, 322n86, 335n6, 340n23, 342n34, 345n41, 346n47, 347n51, 352n75, 357n4, 385–6n90
Hogarth, G., 273n10
Holinshed, Raphael, 48, 56, 296–7n4, 302n15, 308n47, 335n9, 336n12, 338n20
Hollingdale, R.J., 317n75, 327n109
Homer, 225, 253, 258–63, 300n7, 331n127, 363n9
Hooker, Richard, 340n23
Horace, 242
Hughes, Robert, 343n35

Isolde, 327n109

Jacobson, Howard, 295n3
Jaffa, Harry, 333n2, 337n14, 381n64, 384n78
Jaggard, William, 274n13
James VI/I, King, 3, 5, 335n7
James, Henry, 287n33
Jameson, (Mrs) Anna, 276n16
Jenkins, Harold, 284–5n29
Jensen, Pamela, 358n4, 367n21
Jesus, 229, 383n73
Jocasta, 354n88
Johnson, Samuel, 7, 275n16, 306n41, 339n22
Jonson, Ben, 273n9, 274–5n13, 280n23, 281n24
Jordon, John E., 276n16

Kant, Immanuel, 316–17n74
Kean, Edmund, 368n23
Kernan, Alvin, 312n62, 335n3
Klein, Joan Larsen, 331n124
Knight, G. Wilson, 277nn17, 21, 283n27, 286n33, 301n12, 303n19, 314n68, 315n74, 326n101, 334n3, 383n73
Knights, L.C., 277n17, 282–6nn25–30, 288n33, 294n43, 298n7, 313n66, 324n90, 326–7n105, 328n114, 381n60
Knippenberg, Joseph M., 345n44
Kosintsev, Grigori, 269n1
Kurosawa, Akira, 269n1

Lawler, Peter A., 345n44
Lawrence, D.H., 283n27
Lawrence, T.E., 344n40
Leavis, F.R., 277n17, 315–16n74, 367–8n24, 381n60
Lenze, G.R.S., 276n16, 365n17
Leslie, John, 303n15
Leucippus, 352n72
Lever, J.W., 381n61
Levitt, Norman, 294n44
Lewis, Martin W., 294n44
Lincoln, Abraham, 261
Locke, John, 352n75
Long, Herbert, 352n72
Lowenthal, David, 289nn33, 35, 307n43, 328n111, 337n14, 352n73
Lucretius, 242, 286–7n33

Machiavelli, Niccolò, 25, 30–8, 48, 51, 62, 88, 118, 153, 221, 236–7, 240, 251, 278n21, 302–3n13, 303nn14–18, 304nn20–1, 25, 305nn26–9, 31–2, 306nn35–9, 307n43, 308n48, 309nn51–2, 310–11n58, 311nn58–61, 311–12n62, 317nn74, 76, 321n85, 324n91, 326n100, 327n107, 335n4, 336n111, 340n23, 347n50, 355n100, 377n44, 381nn62, 64, 382nn65, 68–70
Mandeville, Bernard de, 389n102
Mansfield, Harvey, 302n13, 381n64
Maude, Louise and Aylmer, 320n84
Maugham, William Somerset, 323–4n89
McAdam, E.L., 276n16
McAlindon, T., 313n64, 326n97
McFarland, Thomas, 374n40, 376n42, 378n52, 390n108
Melville, Herman, 260, 321–2n86, 342n33
Milne, George, 276n16
Milton, John, 3, 276n16, 310n54
Montaigne, Michel de, 318n78, 383n74
Moses, 118
Muir, Kenneth, 275n15, 277n17, 294n44, 295n1, 296n4, 297–8n7, 302n15, 306n41, 307nn42–3, 309n50, 328n111, 332–3n1, 336n12, 338n20
Murdoch, Iris, 388n100

Neely, Carol T., 276n16, 365n17
Nietzsche, Friedrich, 18, 304n22, 317n75, 325n91, 326n103, 327–8n109, 328n110, 341n27, 347n52, 363n8, 371n31, 379nn55–6, 386–7n93, 389n104
Norton, Glynn P., 391n110
Nuttall, A.D., 270–1n5, 285–6n30, 290n37, 291–2n39

Odysseus, 199, 225, 262
Oedipus, 327n109, 354n88
Orco, Remirro de, 236–7, 246
Ornstein, Robert, 278n21
Orrell, John, 372–3n35

Ovid, 200, 225

Pafford, J.H.P., 372n33, 375n40
Park, Clara Claiborne, 276–7n16
Parmenides, 352n72, 354n85
Pericles, 261
Persephone, 215
Philoctetes, 327n109
Philolaus, 351n72
Plato, 2, 16–19, 24, 108, 118, 168, 186, 189–90, 193–4, 215–18, 234, 251–69, 273n12, 286n32, 293n42, 301nn9–10, 304n22, 312n63, 313nn64, 67, 315n73, 316n74, 318n78, 322n86, 325n95, 326n104, 327nn106, 108, 328n112, 331nn125, 129–30, 335n5, 337n13, 346n47, 348n56, 350n64, 351nn68–70, 352n72, 353nn77, 81, 83–5, 354nn89, 91–2, 355nn94–6, 356–7n2, 358–9n5, 359–60n6, 367n22, 369–70n26, 373n35, 374nn37–9, 377nn42–5, 379nn54–6, 382nn67, 71, 384nn76–81, 386n92, 387nn94, 96, 98, 387–8n100, 388n101, 389nn103–4, 390nn105, 107, 109
Platt, Michael, 289n35, 390nn107, 109
Plautus, 275n13
Plutarch, 261
Polo, Marco, 361n7
Pope, Alexander, 277n18
Prometheus, 182
Pythagoras, 260–1, 351–2n72, 373n35, 378n49, 379n55

Rabkin, Norman, 278n21, 283n28, 285n29, 292–3n41, 380–1n59
Raysor, Thomas Middleton, 333n3
Rhoads, Diane Akers, 390n107
Richard II, King, 346n46
Ridley, M.R., 358n4, 365n16
Robin Hood, 6
Romulus, 118
Rosenberg, Marvin, 296n4, 298–9n7, 324n90, 328n111, 334–5n3
Rossiter, A.P., 304n19
Røstvig, Maren-Sofie, 373n35
Rousseau, Jean-Jacques, xi, 18, 328n114, 344n38, 345n41, 350n63, 379nn55–6, 384n80, 389n102
Rowe, Nicholas, 281n23
Rowse, A.L., 272n9, 292n40
Rymer, Thomas, 366n19, 368n24

Sanders, Wilbur, 295–6n3
Sandys, William, 273n10
Schiller, Friedrich von, 281n23
Schmidgall, Gary, 269n3
Schoenbaum, Samuel, 272n7, 272–3n9
Schrödinger, Erwin, 323n88
Schwehn, Mark, 347n48
Seneca, 9, 275n13
Sforza, Francesco, 302n15
Shaftesbury, 1st Earl of, 364n12
Shaw, George Bernard, 340n23
Shostakovich, Dimitri, 269n1
Shreeve, James, 349n58
Sidney, Sir Philip, 267, 391–2n110
Simonides, 253
Sisson, C.J., 273n11, 277n17
Smith, P. Christopher, 388n100
Soellner, Rolf, 340n24
Sokrates, 63, 91, 111, 118, 168–9, 184, 187, 189–90, 198, 216–18, 234–5, 241, 244, 247, 249, 252–65, 266–7, 273n12, 288n33, 293n42, 312n63, 318n78, 323n87, 351nn68–9, 353n83, 354nn89–91, 356n2, 360n6, 367n22, 369n26, 374n37, 377n42, 378nn48–9, 382–3n71, 384n74,

385n88, 386n92, 388nn100–1, 389nn103–4, 390n109
Spedding, James, 303n18
Spurgeon, Caroline F.E., 277n20
Stapfer, Paul, 280–1n23, 351–2n72
Stewart, J.I.M., 286n30, 305n30
Stockholder, Kay, 331n124
Strauss, Leo, 286n32, 294n42, 306n40, 351n71
Sullivan, Vickie, 289n33, 306n34, 314n71, 358n4
Swynford, Catherine, 346n46
Sypher, Wylie, 385n87

Tchaikovsky, Piotr Ilyich, 271n5
Terence, 275n13
Theobald, Lewis, 296n4
Theophrastus, 352n72
Theseus, 118
Thomas, Vivian, 380n57
Thomson, Rev. Thomas, 274n13
Thucydides, 260–1, 351n68
Tillyard, E.M.W., 379–80n57
Toliver, H.E., 314n70, 385n87
Tolstoy, Leo, 283n27, 320n84
Tovey, Barbara, 289n34, 359n5, 384n78, 386n91
Traversi, Derek, 277n17, 278n21, 290n36, 303n19, 334n3, 380n58, 385n86
Trevor-Roper, Sir Hugh, 5
Trimpi, Wesley, 391n110
Tristan, 327n109
Tudor, Henry. *See* Henry VII
Turnbull, S.R., 300n7

Ure, Peter, 379n57

Valentino, Duke. *See* Borgia, Cesare
Vaughan, Virginia Mason, 362–3n7, 365n16
Verdi, Giuseppe, 297n7
Viswanathan, S., 277n17

Wells, Stanley, 332–3n1, 359–60n6
West, Robert, 288n33, 331n126
West, Thomas G., 289n33, 300n8, 359n5
Wheeler, Richard, 301n8
White, Howard B., 289n33, 315n74, 390n107
William I (the Conqueror), King, 344n40
Wills, Gary, 296n4
Wycliffe, John, 296n4

Xenophanes, 352n72
Xenophon, 260, 351n68

Yeats, William Butler, 272n7, 349n58
Yorimasa, 300n7

Zeno, 352n72, 354n85